Touring North Carolina's Revolutionary War Sites

ALSO BY DANIEL W. BAREFOOT

General Robert F. Hoke: Lee's Modest Warrior
Touring the Backroads of North Carolina's Upper Coast
Touring the Backroads of North Carolina's Lower Coast

OTHER TITLES IN JOHN F. BLAIR'S *TOURING THE BACKROADS* SERIES

Touring the Backroads of North and South Georgia by Victoria and Frank Logue
Touring the Coastal Georgia Backroads by Nancy Rhyne
Touring the Coastal South Carolina Backroads by Nancy Rhyne
Touring the Middle Tennessee Backroads by Robert Brandt
Touring the East Tennessee Backroads by Carolyn Sakowski
Touring the Western North Carolina Backroads by Carolyn Sakowski
Touring the Carolinas' Civil War Sites by Clint Johnson

Touring North Carolina's Revolutionary War Sites

Daniel W. Barefoot

John F. Blair
Publisher
Winston-Salem,
North Carolina

BOOK DESIGN BY DEBRA LONG HAMPTON
MAPS BY LIZA LANGRALL
PHOTOGRAPHS BY THE AUTHOR, UNLESS OTHERWISE NOTED

*The paper in this book meets the guidelines
for permanence and durability of the
Committee on Production Guidelines for Book Longevity
of the Council on Library Resources.*

Photographs on front cover clockwise from top left—
Edenton waterfront, statue of Lafayette (Fayetteville),
Boggan-Hammond House (Wadesboro), statue of
Nathanael Greene at Guilford Courthouse (Greensboro;
courtesy of NC Travel and Tourism), cannon at
Moores Creek National Military Park, Tryon Palace
(New Bern; courtesy of NC Travel and Tourism)

Library of Congress Cataloging-in-Publication Data
Barefoot, Daniel W., 1951–
Touring North Carolina's Revolutionary War sites / Daniel W. Barefoot.
p.   cm. — (Touring the backroads series)
Includes bibliographical references and index.
ISBN 0-89587-217-X (alk. paper)
1. North Carolina—History—Revolution, 1775–1783—Battlefields—Guidebooks.
2. North Carolina—History—Revolution, 1775–1783—Monuments—Guidebooks.
3. Historic sites—North Carolina—Guidebooks. 4. North Carolina—Tours.
5. United States—History—Revolution, 1775–1783—Monuments—Guidebooks.
I. Title.   II. Series.
E263.NB37   1998
917.5604'43—dc21   98–27003

Once again, to Kay and Kris, with love,
for all the happy trails we've blazed

Table of Contents

Preface

The blood we have shed will be as good seed sown in good
ground, which soon will reap a hundred fold.

> *Regulator marksman James Pugh moments before his*
> *execution at Hillsborough in June 1771*

Forty years have passed since my first visit to a battleground of the Revolutionary War. But I still vividly recall the deep sense of patriotism and pride
I felt when, as a seven-year-old boy, I walked the very slope at Kings Mountain where Americans from the back country of the Carolinas and Virginia
dealt Patrick Ferguson and the British a staggering defeat in October 1780.
Little could I have imagined as I stood atop the historic peak that I would
one day live on the very street where, less than four months before Kings
Mountain, Patriots won the Battle of Ramsour's Mill in the city and county
named for the man selected by George Washington to accept the British
sword of surrender at Yorktown.

Few periods in the history of the United States continue to spark more
interest than the Revolution. The story of how thirteen diverse colonies

were able to band together to defeat an invading army of the best soldiers in the world serves to inspire people around the globe more than two hundred years later. That the same thirteen free and independent states were able to unite in the wake of the grim, bloody, and often internally divisive struggle to craft a republic that has become the marvel of the ages was no less a miracle.

No colony played a greater role in performing the miracles of the Revolution than did North Carolina. Such a bold claim may come as a surprise to some. North Carolinians have often described their state as "a vale of humility nestled between two mountains of conceit." Both Virginia and South Carolina have long boasted of their role in the Revolution—their sterling patriotic achievements, their eminent statesmen and soldiers, their battlegrounds and historic shrines. On the other hand, North Carolina has modestly rested on its peerless record of sacrifice, gallantry, and devotion to duty.

But North Carolina can boast a long litany of firsts and superlatives from the Revolution.

At Brunswick Town on February 21, 1766, Cape Fear Patriots offered the first armed, open resistance to Royal authority in the American colonies.

In Alamance County on May 16, 1771, farmers from the back country—Regulators, they were called—clashed with the Royal governor and his troops in what some have called the first battle of the Revolution.

At New Bern on August 25, 1774, North Carolinians called the First Provincial Congress, the first legislative body convened in the colonies in defiance of Royal decree.

At Edenton on October 25, 1774, more than fifty patriotic ladies assembled for the Edenton Tea Party, the first organized political activity by women in the colonies.

At Charlotte on May 20, 1775, leading citizens convened an assembly that crafted what some historians have called the first declaration of independence in the colonies.

At Moores Creek Bridge on February 20, 1776, Patriot forces from North Carolina won the first battle of the war in the South.

At Halifax on April 12, 1776, the Fourth Provincial Congress enacted the Halifax Resolves, thus making North Carolina the first colony to instruct its delegates at the Continental Congress in Philadelphia to vote for independence.

At Ramsour's Mill on June 20, 1780, and at Kings Mountain on October 7, 1780, militiamen and soldiers from the North Carolina back country won the battles that turned the tide of the war in favor of the colonies.

At Charlotte on December 2, 1780, Major General Nathanael Greene assumed command of the American army in the South.

And finally, at Guilford Courthouse on March 15, 1781, Greene's Americans so badly bloodied Cornwallis's vaunted army that it could never recover.

This book was written to tell the story of North Carolina in the American Revolution at the places where famous (and infamous) events occurred—at the homes of the participants, on the ground where Americans fought other Americans and the British to earn the right of self-determination, at the graves of men and women who sacrificed all they had for a cause they believed was right.

The fourteen tours in the book are arranged geographically rather than chronologically, since most areas of the state were the scene of events throughout the war. For example, the Cape Fear region was the site of early Stamp Act protests in 1766 and was also the place from which the last British soldiers sailed from the state fifteen years later.

From northeastern North Carolina, the tours make their way down the historic coast, then turn inland on a route through the Sandhills, the southern Piedmont, the foothills, and the upper Piedmont before ending in Raleigh, the "unalterable capital" of North Carolina. Because of the large number of sites, you should plan to spend several days to complete and fully enjoy each tour. Or you might organize a day trip to visit specific sites on a tour.

More than 215 years have elapsed since the Revolutionary War ended, and it is logical to assume that few of the sites from that ancient conflict survive because of the passage of time and the lack of historic preservation in days gone by. Sadly, fire, storms, neglect, development, and vandalism have all robbed North Carolina of Revolutionary War landmarks. But the state still holds a treasure trove of historic structures, monuments, and geographic features that bring to life the exciting drama of the fight for independence.

Whether you travel by automobile or armchair, please realize that as exhaustive as this study is, I could not include every existing site. However, by the time you complete the final tour, you will have traveled virtually the length and the breadth of the state and experienced the site of every important battle and event of the war in North Carolina.

As I traveled the state while working on this project, I looked with great sadness at sites that have suffered desecration by vandals or are threatened as a result of development. Immediate and concerted preservation efforts are needed if these priceless pieces of history are to be salvaged for future generations to enjoy.

While I have taken great care to make the information presented herein as accurate as possible, be aware that road numbers change, roads and bridges are rerouted, and historic buildings, landmarks, and markers vanish almost overnight. And please note that unless a site is on a public road or public property, you should not attempt to gain access without first obtaining permission from the property owner.

As you pause at the tour stops, remember that you are visiting the places and standing on the very ground where poignant stories of heroism and sacrifice were played out so many years ago—at a time when North Carolina was fighting to be a free state rather than a subservient colony of the British Empire. Indeed, the historic byways traveled in this book are the paths blazed by the men and women who gallantly made North Carolina "first for freedom."

Acknowledgments

Producing a comprehensive book about the sites related to the Revolutionary War in North Carolina has required the assistance of countless individuals in all parts of our state. While space does not allow me to list each person who provided me information and directions, I offer my gratitude to all and hope that this book will bring them some pleasure.

Research was an essential component of this book, and I found support at libraries all over North Carolina. The staffs at the North Carolina Collection at the University of North Carolina at Chapel Hill, the Scottish Heritage Center at St. Andrews Presbyterian College, and numerous public libraries from the coast to the mountains were helpful in my quest to locate sites.

There are some individuals who deserve special recognition for their contributions to this project. Betty McCain, North Carolina's secretary of cultural resources, offered encouragement from the outset. Michael Hill, the administrator of the state's highway historical marker program, answered questions and provided information about several sites. Richard Clark, the site manager of Historic Halifax, gave me a personal tour of the entire complex and walked in the rain to locate the remains of the home of Willie

Jones. Mike Loveless, the late superintendent of Kings Mountain National Military Park, spent an entire day with me and took me to places in the park that most visitors never see.

As I traveled from site to site, strangers became friends. Some opened their historic homes and churches to me. Mr. and Mrs. Jim Hines of Turkey welcomed my family into their Revolutionary War–era home and told us the heartwarming story of their Patriot ancestor. At Enfield, Mr. and Mrs. James Kovac were only too happy to show me the bedroom at "The Cellar" where Lafayette slept. It was my good fortune to meet Mrs. Locke Neale on a visit to Thyatira Presbyterian Church in Rowan County. She graciously opened the Church Heritage Room and proudly showed me the remarkable portrait of King George III that bears the autograph of General Nathanael Greene. Near the Lower Little River, Tom and Rachel Brooks welcomed my family to their home and escorted us to the nearly inaccessible grave of "Jennie Bahn" McNeill.

In my hometown, two friends went beyond the call of duty to aid me in my work. Judson Crowe, an expert in the war in the foothills and the Battle of Cowan's Ford, spent an entire day showing me sites in western North Carolina. On numerous occasions, he provided me with important information. Darrell Harkey, historical coordinator of Lincoln County, has long been a special friend and a supporter of my every venture. On this project, he accompanied me to many sites both near and far and aided me in innumerable other ways. His loyalty, ceaseless encouragement, and friendship are one of the great joys of my life.

Transforming a manuscript into a quality book requires a publisher dedicated to excellence. For nearly half a century, John F. Blair, Publisher, has produced a long list of outstanding titles. As in all of my past efforts, the folks at Blair have made every effort to make this book a success. Carolyn Sakowski, the company president, saw merit in the project without requiring a single written page, although she knew my propensity to produce mammoth manuscripts. Once again, history repeated itself, but Carolyn patiently aided me in paring the excess material. Steve Kirk edited not only this book but each of my previous titles with great care, skill, professionalism, and patience. He is a genuine friend of this writer. Debbie Hampton, Liza Langrall, Anne Holcomb Waters, Molly Yarbrough, and the rest of the staff at Blair have lent their expertise to the project.

Finally, the Barefoot family remains my source of support and encouragement in my every endeavor.

My parents and my sister are wonderful cheerleaders.

My seventeen-year-old daughter, Kristie, accurately typed every word of the manuscript from my tall stack of handwritten pages filled with erasures, arrows, interlinings, and marked-out lines. During every year of her teens, her father has been busy writing a book. Kristie has borne the many hardships of an author's daughter with patience, maturity, love, and smiles. For that, I shall always be grateful, and of her, I am so very proud.

Finally, my greatest fortune is to have a partner for life in my wife, Kay. This book would not have been possible without her unfailing love and support. She called countless libraries and people for information about and directions to sites; she gave up much of her summer vacation from school to accompany me on grueling, tedious journeys covering thousands of miles to make this book as accurate as possible; and she read every word of the manuscript and gave her suggestions, advice, and constructive criticism. Just when it appeared that we were not going to find an obscure site in an isolated area and I, in a fit of frustration, was ready to give up, Kay would calmly say, "Dan, just go a bit farther." More often than not, the site was around the next bend or just down the road. For almost twenty-seven years, Kay has stood at my side with pride, encouragement, patience, devotion, and love. Because of that, I am the luckiest guy in the world.

Touring North Carolina's Revolutionary War Sites

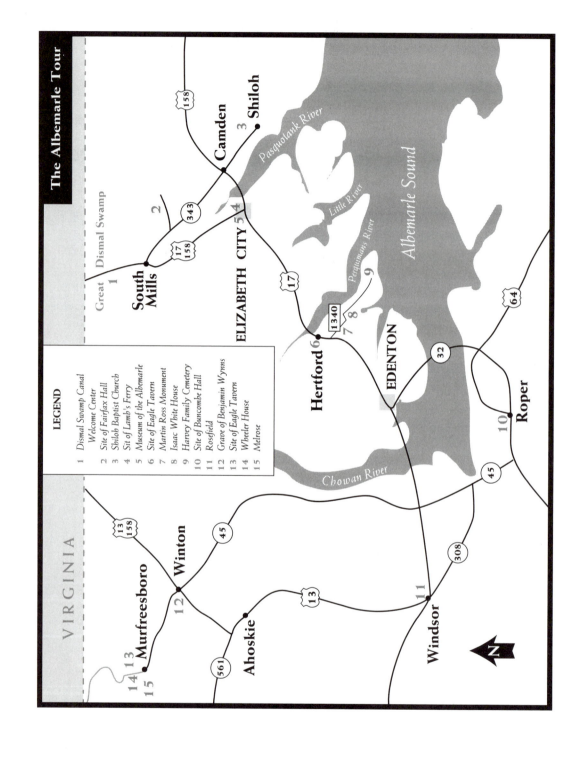

The Albemarle Tour

LEGEND

1. Dismal Swamp Canal Welcome Center
2. Site of Fairfax Hall
3. Shiloh Baptist Church
4. Sit of Lamb's Ferry
5. Museum of the Albemarle
6. Site of Eagle Tavern
7. Martin Ross Monument
8. Isaac White House
9. Harvey Family Cemetery
10. Site of Buncombe Hall
11. Rosfield
12. Grave of Benjamin Wynns
13. Site of Eagle Tavern
14. Wheeler House
15. Melrose

VIRGINIA

Great Dismal Swamp

Murfreesboro
Winton
Ahoskie
Windsor

South Mills
Camden
Shiloh
ELIZABETH CITY
Hertford
EDENTON
Roper

Pasquotank River
Little River
Perquimans River
Chowan River
Albemarle Sound

The Albemarle Tour

This tour begins at the Dismal Swamp Canal Welcome Center in northern Camden County and makes its way through Pasquotank, Perquimans, Chowan, Washington, and Bertie Counties before ending at Murfreesboro in Hertford County. Among the highlights are the Dismal Swamp Canal, the homesite of General Isaac Gregory, historic Hertford, historic Edenton, Rosefield, and historic Murfreesboro.

Total mileage: approximately 199 miles.

This tour traverses the Albemarle, the most ancient of North Carolina's political subdivisions. Established in 1664 by the Lords Proprietors in their new province of Carolina, Albemarle County covered 1,600 square miles in the northeastern part of the colony. Named for George Monck, duke of Albemarle, one of the Lords Proprietors, the massive county was the site of the first permanent white settlement in what is now North Carolina.

The area is rich in sites related to the Revolutionary War. "The Cradle of the Colony," as the region is known, produced many of the leaders who guided North Carolina through the hardships of the war and toward the creation of the new republic. For example, tour stops include the homes of the man known as "the Father of the American Revolution in North Carolina," a signer of the Declaration of Independence, two signers of the Constitution, and a justice on the first United States Supreme Court.

The tour begins at the Dismal Swamp Canal Welcome Center, located on the western side of U.S. 17 approximately 3 miles south of the Virginia line in Camden County, which is in the far northeastern corner of North Carolina.

Named for Sir Charles Pratt, earl of Camden, a distinguished English jurist and statesman who strongly opposed British taxation of the American colonies, Camden County was born of the Revolution in 1777, when it was carved from adjacent Pasquotank County. Camden men fought in large numbers for the American cause. By war's end, the county had provided 416 officers and men, a total greater than any other county in old Albemarle.

The welcome center is located on the fringes of the Great Dismal Swamp. Though this vast wilderness of marshes, peat bogs, lakes, and cypress forests was almost four times as large in Revolutionary War times as it is today, it still covers almost three hundred thousand acres, an area about the size of Rhode Island. Approximately 60 percent of the swamp is located in North Carolina within Camden, Currituck, Pasquotank, Perquimans, and Gates Counties.

On May 25, 1763, a thirty-one-year-old soldier and surveyor from Virginia received his first taste of the Great Dismal. George Washington, the same man who subsequently served as commander in chief of the American armies in the Revolutionary War, made his initial visit to the swamp to inspect the nearly fifty thousand acres granted to a group of land and timber speculators known as "the Adventurers for Draining the Dismal Swamp." Among Washington's associates in the venture were Patrick Henry and Richard Caswell, two statesmen who would play leading roles in the upcoming fight for independence. (For additional information on Caswell, see The Coastal Rivers Tour, pages 56–59.) Washington made five trips to the Great Dismal between 1763 and 1768.

The Dismal Swamp Canal Visitor Center was developed by the state of North Carolina in 1989 to provide travel information for motorists as well as for water traffic on the canal. The docks just west of the parking area are a good place to view the canal and the adjoining swamp wilderness.

One of the earliest legends of the Great Dismal had its origins during the American Revolution. A French warship filled with gold to pay French troops in America sailed to Hampton Roads to avoid a ferocious storm. A British man-of-war sighted the enemy ship, promptly gave chase, and forced the fleeing vessel into the shallow waters of the Elizabeth River. There, the French captain ordered his crew to load the precious cargo onto smaller boats and to burn the ship.

Fearing a British capture of the treasure, the French sailors buried the gold in the river and on its banks, then sought refuge in the Great Dismal. But their attackers hunted them down. In the course of the vicious hand-to-hand combat that followed, all of the French crewmen died without divulging the location of the hidden gold. According to legend, visitors can still hear the voices of the French sailors emanating from the swamp on some nights.

From the parking lot of the visitor center, turn right and proceed south on U.S. 17. This highway, known as George Washington Highway, parallels the Dismal Swamp Canal on the 5-mile drive to the town of South Mills.

Listed on the National Register of Historic Places, the 22-mile canal has been in almost continuous operation since construction began in 1790. Hugh Williamson, one of North Carolina's signers of the Constitution, planted the seed for the canal project in letters to George Washington while the Continental Congress was in session. President Washington ultimately gave his blessing to the waterway in 1785, and the legislatures of Virginia and North Carolina granted their approval in 1787 and 1790, respectively.

Just north of South Mills, turn right on U.S. 17 Business and proceed 1.3 miles to S.R. 1243. Turn right and follow S.R. 1243 for 0.7 mile into the heart of the village. Here, the southern locks of the canal bear testimony to a project initiated in Revolutionary War times. A state highway historical marker for the canal stands nearby.

Return to U.S. 17 Business. Turn right and proceed 0.1 mile to N.C. 343. Follow N.C. 343 south for 12.9 miles to U.S. 158 in Camden. Continue south on U.S. 343 for 2.2 miles, then turn right on S.R. 1132. Near this junction was the estate of Abner Harrison (1745–90). In 1776, the North Carolina Provincial Congress appointed Harrison to serve as a confiscation commissioner, an office unique to the Revolutionary War. Harrison's official duties were "to receive, take care of and make disposition of " the property of Tories and other disloyal persons.

Drive south on S.R. 1132 for 1.1 miles to its terminus near the mouth of Areneuse Creek. This site, now being developed as residential property, was confiscated from Tories during the Revolution. It was granted to Lieutenant Colonel Hardy Murfree as a reward for his distinguished service in the Continental Army. Murfree was the namesake of Murfreesboro, a town visited later in this tour.

Return to the junction with N.C. 343, turn right, and drive 1.6 miles south to S.R. 1121. Turn left and proceed 0.5 mile to the site of Fairfield (Fairfax) Hall, the home of General Isaac Gregory (1737–1800). Until the three-story brick English manor house collapsed into a pile of rubble several decades ago, it stood as a monument to one of the most distinguished Revolutionary War officers of northeastern North Carolina.

General Gregory grew up in the house and inherited it upon his father's death. Before the war, he served as a local judicial official and opposed the Stamp Act. He was a delegate to the Provincial Congresses of 1775 and 1776 and was instrumental in the establishment of Camden County. Gregory began his military service in September 1775, when he was commissioned lieutenant colonel of the militia. On May 12, 1779, the North Carolina General Assembly promoted him to brigadier general.

General Gregory's finest hour came, ironically, in the devastating American defeat at Camden, South Carolina, in 1780. In the course of that fight, the American militia acquitted itself rather poorly. Gregory and his men were an exception. During the intense battle, the general's horse was shot from under him and he was twice wounded by bayonets, the scars of which he bore for the rest of his life. Lord Charles Cornwallis, the commander of British forces in the South, mistakenly listed Gregory among the American fatalities at Camden.

During March and April 1781, Gregory was back in northeastern North Carolina to defend against potential raids from British camps just across the line in Virginia. Before the Redcoats abandoned one of those camps, their commander, Captain Stevenson, penned a fanciful letter wherein he suggested that General Gregory might betray the American forces to the British. Stevenson then affixed Gregory's signature to the letter.

When American soldiers came upon the deserted British camp, they found the letter. They turned it over to military authorities, who promptly charged Gregory with treason and scheduled a court-martial. In the meantime, Captain Stevenson learned of the sensation the letter had caused. With great dispatch, he forwarded a communication that explained the source of the letter. Though Gregory was exonerated, he was greatly puzzled as to how anyone could doubt his loyalty in light of his record of service in the fight for independence.

In a letter to George Washington, Hugh Williamson offered great praise for Gregory: "Gen'l Gregory is recommended as a gentleman where Character as a soldier and Citizen stands high in the universal esteem of his fellow Citizens. He is a man of respectable property; has the full confidence of his Country and is the constant Enemy to public officers suspected of corrupt practices."

After his death in April 1800, Gregory was buried on his plantation. His mansion was located on the left side of the road in what is now a field. On the opposite side of the road is an ancient family burial ground.

From the site of the Gregory plantation, retrace your route to the N.C. 343 junction. Turn left on N.C. 343 and drive 3 miles to Shiloh. The most famous landmark here is Shiloh Baptist Church. Although the existing sanctuary was constructed in 1848, the church was organized in 1727, making it the oldest Baptist church in North Carolina.

During the Revolutionary War era, the pulpit at Shiloh Baptist Church was filled by Reverend Henry Abbott, one of the most learned men in North Carolina. Born in London, Abbott was an ardent Patriot from the onset. A champion of individual liberties, he is recognized as the author of the article in the first state constitution that acknowledges that "all men have natural and inalienable rights to worship almighty God according to the dictates of their own conscience."

Abbott died in 1791 and is believed to have been buried at a site 5 miles northeast of Shiloh.

Among the graves in the historic cemetery at Shiloh Baptist Church is that of Dempsey Burgess (1751–1800). In 1775 and 1776, Burgess served as a youthful member of the Provincial Congresses that met at Hillsborough and Halifax. He rendered distinguished service as a militia officer, rising to the rank of colonel. In the aftermath of the war, he became the first Camden County resident to be elected to the United States House of Representatives, serving from 1795 to 1798 as a member of the Fourth and Fifth Congresses.

From the church, return to Camden via N.C. 343. Just north of Shiloh, the route passes the road leading to Texaco Beach, a small resort on the Pasquotank River. Nearby was the plantation of Captain John Forbes (1737–81). Forbes was killed in action at the Battle of Guilford Courthouse in March 1781.

Turn left off N.C. 343 onto U.S. 158 at Camden and drive west. Near the intersection are state historical markers for Isaac Gregory and Dempsey Burgess. The 3.2-mile drive from Camden to Elizabeth City is via an ancient causeway and the Pasquotank River Bridge.

Nearby is the site of Lamb's Ferry. A river ferry was operated here by the Lamb family from 1779 to 1912. Colonel Gideon Lamb (1740–81), the man to whom the ferry franchise was initially granted, was one of the many unsung North Carolina heroes of the American Revolution.

While serving as a delegate to the Provincial Congress at Halifax in April 1776, Lamb was commissioned a major in the Continental Army. After meritorious service in the South early in the war, he accompanied his troops to reinforce George Washington in the North. An active participant in the important engagements at Trenton, Germantown, and Brandywine, Lamb was court-martialed by General Jethro Sumner for his conduct at the latter battle. A court of inquiry subsequently cleared him, noting that "the Charge is not Supported" and recommending that Lamb "be Acquitted with Honour."

Lamb spent the last three years of his life performing a vital but thankless task. He was charged with recruiting, organizing, and supplying Continental forces in eastern North Carolina. Stricken with "bilious fever," he died at his home, Mount Pleasant, which stood nearby, on November 8, 1781, less than three weeks after his Continental Army had enjoyed the sweet taste of success at Yorktown, Virginia.

Colonel Lamb was the elder member of a rare father-and-son team of commissioned officers. His son Abner was sixteen when the colonies declared their independence in 1776 and only twenty when he sustained a crippling wound at Eutaw Springs, South Carolina, on September 8, 1781, five weeks before Cornwallis's surrender at Yorktown.

Just west of the Lamb's Ferry site, the bridge affords a magnificent view of the 40-mile-long Pasquotank River, which marks the boundary between Camden and Pasquotank Counties. This beautiful river provided local residents vital access to Albemarle Sound during the Revolution.

Once across the bridge, continue on U.S. 158 as it heads west through Elizabeth City and runs conjunctively with Elizabeth Street for six blocks. Turn north on North Road Street. After 0.9 mile, turn left on U.S. 17

(Hughes Boulevard). The Museum of the Albemarle, a branch of the North Carolina Museum of History, is located 3.6 miles ahead.

U.S. 17 crosses into Perquimans County approximately 7 miles west of the museum. After crossing the county line, continue 6.5 miles to where U.S. 17 Business splits off U.S. 17 Bypass. Turn right on U.S. 17 Business and proceed 1.1 miles to Hertford. Just before reaching this quaint, old river town, you will cross the scenic Perquimans River via the only S-shaped bridge in the United States and the largest of its kind in the world.

Once across the bridge, drive three blocks on U.S. 17 (now Church Street) and park in one of the on-street spaces near the courthouse in downtown Hertford.

At the beginning of the American Revolution, Hertford, named for a town in England, was a thriving river village. Many of its street names still proclaim their English heritage: Hyde Park, Covent Garden, Punch Alley.

From the courthouse, follow Church Street to Grubb Street. One of the most famous hostelries in northeastern North Carolina in the last third of the eighteenth century once stood near here. The Eagle Tavern opened in a home in 1762 and quickly grew into a sprawling, two-and-a-half-story, twenty-five-room inn that covered six lots.

According to tradition, George Washington lodged at the Eagle while he was surveying the Great Dismal Swamp. William Hooper, one of North Carolina's three signers of the Declaration of Independence, was among the other notable guests at the tavern in the eighteenth century. In 1915, the old frame structure was razed.

Return to your car and follow Church Street two blocks south to Dobb Street. Two nearby state historical markers pay tribute to a pair of native sons who gained fame during the Revolutionary War era.

One of the markers honors John Skinner (1760–1819). Born into one of the county's earliest families, Skinner served several tours in the Continental Army. When North Carolina officially joined the Union, President Washington appointed him as the state's first federal marshal. He held that post for four years.

The other historical marker honors John Harvey, a man who was instrumental in obtaining the charter for Hertford. Harvey's life is chronicled later in this tour.

Continue on Church Street as it leads out of town. After 1.9 miles, you will reach U.S. 17 Bypass/N.C. 37. Turn right onto U.S. 17 Bypass, proceed 2.5 miles, then turn left on S.R. 1340, which leads south on the river peninsula called Harveys Neck. After 1.6 miles on S.R. 1340, turn right onto S.R. 1341. You will see Bethel Baptist Church on the left just after the turn.

Bethel Baptist Church and the monument to Martin Ross

The handsome two-story sanctuary was built more than a half-century after the war. But the old church cemetery to the rear contains some of the oldest accessible graves in the county. Among the eighteenth-century grave sites here is that of Charles Blount, a Revolutionary War soldier.

A large stone monument on the front lawn of the church pays tribute to another Patriot. Martin Ross (1762–1828) came home to northeastern North Carolina and took up the ministry soon after the war. A Baptist missionary, he founded Bethel and other area churches. The monument proclaims him to be "the Father of the Baptist State Convention of North Carolina."

Return to S.R. 1340 and drive 0.2 mile south to S.R. 1339. Turn left and proceed 2 miles to the Isaac White House. Listed on the National Register of Historic Places, this handsome two-story frame dwelling was constructed around 1760. During the American Revolution, it was owned and occupied by Jonathan Skinner, who served Perquimans County as a wartime delegate in the North Carolina General Assembly.

Continue on S.R. 1339 for 2.3 miles to S.R. 1336. Turn right and drive 6.5 miles south to the southern tip of Harveys Neck on Albemarle Sound. The road ends at the Harvey Point Testing Area, a restricted national defense facility.

Harveys Neck bears the name of one of the most important and influential families in early North Carolina history. Thomas Harvey, the progenitor of this illustrious clan, settled on a 691-acre tract near the current tour stop in the last quarter of the seventeenth century. He began an almost century-long tradition of public service by the Harvey family when he was elected justice of the county court of Albemarle in 1683. Eleven years later, he served as deputy governor of the colony. From 1695 until his death in 1699, he was the chief executive of the colony, since the governor was absent for most of that time.

His son, Thomas Harvey, Jr., built upon the family tradition of public service until his death in 1729 at the age of thirty-six. He was buried beside his father. In 1865, when erosion began to claim the cemetery, his grave and marker were moved to the Harvey family cemetery at Belgrade Plantation. Today, personnel from the nearby military installation maintain the ancient burial ground. Harvey's gravestone, the oldest in the county, can still be seen.

When Thomas Harvey, Jr., died, he left a four-year-old son, John. Seventeen years later, young John Harvey was elected to the colonial assembly. Over the next thirty years, he established himself as one of the most dynamic statesmen and political firebrands in the colony.

In 1766, his unanimous election as speaker of the colonial assembly propelled him to the forefront of the growing crisis with Great Britain. Within two years, he was North Carolina's undisputed leader of the opposition to British colonial policies.

As tensions heightened, Royal Governor Josiah Martin issued a proclamation in 1774 that forbade the defiant Harvey and his political associates from convening a provincial congress. Nevertheless, "Bold John," as Harvey was known, convened the First Provincial Congress at New Bern on August 25, 1774. He was chosen moderator of that assembly, which elected North Carolina's first delegates to the Continental Congress and passed a "no tea" resolution. Members of the First Provincial Congress empowered "Bold John" to convene another assembly at his discretion. Accordingly, the Second Provincial Congress met on April 3, 1775, much to the consternation of Governor Martin.

Tragically, the man who earned the title of "Father of the American Revolution in North Carolina" did not live to see the fruits of his dream for an independent America. His death in May 1775 was the result of a fall from a horse. His large granite tomb at Belgrade now rests in the waters of Albemarle Sound.

Turn around and drive north on S.R. 1336 for approximately 6.5 miles as the road parallels the Perquimans River. The Skinner cemetery is hidden in dense overgrowth near the junction with S.R. 1339. Here, a large marble slab marks the grave of General William Skinner (1728–98), a militia commander who helped save the day for the Americans at Great Bridge, Virginia, in December 1775.

From the cemetery, drive 2.1 miles north on S.R. 1336 to U.S. 17. Turn left on U.S. 17 and proceed 11.7 miles to Edenton; the route crosses into Chowan County after 7 miles.

In Edenton, U.S. 17 runs conjunctively with Broad Street as it winds its way through the heart of this venerable city. The sheer number of state highway markers along Broad Street relating to the Revolutionary War era gives a hint of the importance of Edenton and its residents in the struggle for American independence.

South Broad Street dead-ends at Water Street near the waterfront. Park at or near East Water Street to begin a brief walking tour along the historic waterfront. Begin at the Village Green, which is bounded by East Water Street, Court Street, King Street, and Colonial Avenue. This ancient public area features flowers, walkways, monuments, and a green lawn that slopes gracefully toward the waterfront. It may seem difficult to believe that it once housed stocks, racks, and a pillory and served as the military training site.

A small public park along the water at the foot of the Village Green offers a splendid view of Edenton's picturesque setting on Queen Anne's Creek, a tributary of the Chowan River. In 1712, the colonial assembly authorized a town to be laid out at the forks of the creek. Soon thereafter, Governor Charles Eden, the man for whom the town is named, established his residence nearby on the Chowan. As a result, Edenton served as North Carolina's unofficial capital until 1740. Its economic vitality during the colonial period was enhanced by its designation as the Port of Roanoke, an official port of entry. Edenton remained one of the leading cities in the colony on the eve of the American Revolution. Blessed with a wealth of citizens of rare talents and abilities, it assumed a leading role in the struggle for independence.

Two centuries later, reminders of the revolutionary spirit that pervaded Edenton are evident throughout town. For example, the three Swiss cannon prominently displayed at the park have a fascinating story behind them. Captain William Boritz brought a shipment of twenty-three cannon to Edenton in 1778 aboard his ship, *The Holy Heart of Jesus*. Two Edenton Patriots, Thomas Benbury and Thomas Jones, had, with the aid of Benjamin Franklin, purchased the artillery pieces in France for use in the war effort. When Boritz arrived at Edenton with his important cargo in July 1778, he attempted to levy a transportation charge of 150 pounds of tobacco for every 100 pounds of cannon. But all of the tobacco in the warehouses of Edenton did not total the combined weight of the heavy guns!

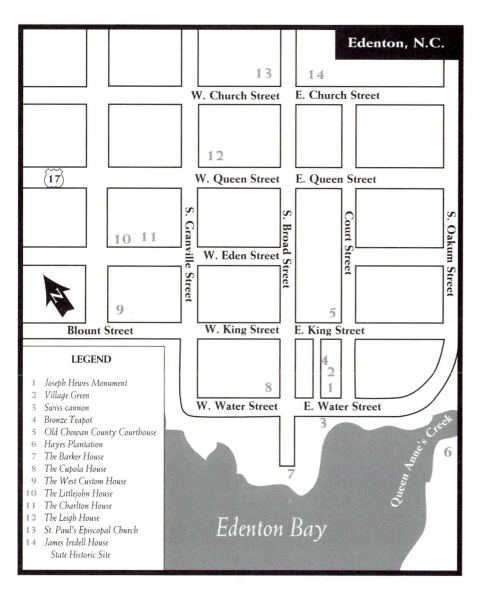

Edenton, N.C.

LEGEND

1 Joseph Hewes Monument
2 Village Green
3 Swiss cannon
4 Bronze Teapot
5 Old Chowan County Courthouse
6 Hayes Plantation
7 The Barker House
8 The Cupola House
9 The West Custom House
10 The Littlejohn House
11 The Charlton House
12 The Leigh House
13 St. Paul's Episcopal Church
14 James Iredell House
State Historic Site

Edenton waterfront with the Revolutionary cannon and the Barker House

Why the cannon were ultimately dumped into the dark waters of Edenton Bay is a subject of dispute. One tradition maintains that they remained on board the anchored ship until British troops threatened the town, at which time patriotic citizens pushed them into the water to prevent their being captured by enemy forces. A more likely story is that the unyielding Boritz ditched the cargo when he realized that his demands were not going to be met.

Although some of the cannon remain in their watery grave, six were rescued for use during the Civil War. Three of the recovered cannon are now mounted on the Edenton waterfront, and others are displayed on Capitol Square in Raleigh.

From the park, walk across Water Street to the Joseph Hewes Monument, located on the southern edge of the Village Green.

During the Revolution, an outside observer remarked that "within the vicinity of Edenton," there were "in proportion to its population a greater number of men eminent for ability, virtue, and erudition than in any other part of America." Foremost in the ranks of Edenton's statesmen in the quest for independence were Joseph Hewes, Samuel Johnston, Hugh Williamson, and James Iredell.

Joseph Hewes earned the respect and admiration of his colleagues as one of the most influential members of the Continental Congress. Some historians consider him the father of the American navy. In effect, his appointment to the Naval Board in 1775 made him the first secretary of the United States Navy. In that position, Hewes procured John Paul Jones's commission in the Continental Navy. By so doing, he provided America with its first naval hero. (For more on Jones's connection to North Carolina, see The First for Freedom Tour, page 44.)

In early 1776, the growing tensions between Great Britain and the colonies led Hewes to remark that "nothing is left but to fight it out." He wrote, "I have furnished myself a good musket and bayonet, and when I can no longer be useful in council, I hope I shall be willing to take the field." Representing North Carolina at the Continental Congress in Philadelphia later that year, he proudly affixed his signature to the Declaration of Independence.

In 1779, as the war wore on, the forty-nine-year-old Hewes was still laboring on the most important and busiest committees of the Continental Congress. Suddenly, his health broke. Unable to travel, he died in Philadelphia on November 10. The stunned members of Congress attended his funeral and burial at Christ Church as a body. In respect to their fallen comrade, they declared a one-month period of mourning. Hewes was immediately recognized as one of the architects of the American nation. One statesman eulogized him thus: "His name is recorded on the Magna Carta of our liberty—his fame will lie until the last vestige of American history shall be blotted from the world."

The Hewes Monument, the only monument to a signer of the Declaration erected by congressional appropriation, was dedicated in Edenton in 1932. Designed by Rogers and Poor, the granite shaft is a fitting tribute to the statesman who, in the spring of 1776, requested instructions from the citizens as to how he should vote on the issue of independence. On April 12, his state answered him. Accordingly, Hewes was the man who made the first utterance for national independence in the Continental Congress when he presented the Halifax Resolves on May 27. (For more information on the Halifax Resolves, see The First for Freedom Tour, pages 33–36.)

Walk north from the Hewes Monument to the bronze teapot monument on the Colonial Street (western) side of the green. This simple marker was crafted in 1910 to honor the patriotic ladies who participated in the so-called Edenton Tea Party on October 25, 1774.

Considered one of the most revolutionary acts in the colonies prior to the Declaration of Independence, the tea party was convened by Mrs. Penelope Barker in the home of Mrs. Elizabeth King. There, fifty-one local ladies executed resolutions in support of the Provincial Congress, which had banned the import and consumption of British tea.

After agreeing to refrain from drinking British tea until it was once again tax free, the defiant women offered a toast with a drink brewed from dried raspberry leaves. Not surprisingly, the town symbol of Edenton is a teapot.

The Edenton Teapot is a reminder of the Edenton Tea Party.

Because this was the earliest known instance of organized political activity on the part of women in the American colonies, the tea party garnered attention outside Edenton. When a copy of the resolutions was published in a London newspaper, it caused quite a commotion. The *London Advisor* subsequently ran a political cartoon of the event.

Gracing the northern end of the Village Green is the old Chowan County Courthouse. Constructed in 1767 to replace its 1719 predecessor, the building is one of the finest examples of Georgian public-building architecture in the United States. Even though Chowan County erected a modern courthouse in 1980, the courtroom in the old courthouse is still used, making the structure the oldest functioning courthouse in the state and perhaps the nation. The two-story brick building features a **T**-shaped roof adorned with a cupola.

Through every day since colonial times, this venerable house of justice, now listed on the National Register of Historic Places, has been used for public affairs. During the American Revolution, local Patriots frequently used it to plot their strategy. When the news reached Edenton that North Carolina had ratified the United States Constitution in 1789, local citizens illuminated the cupola.

Return to your vehicle and proceed a short distance to the end of East Water Street. On the right, a private road leads across a bridge over Queen Anne's Creek to Hayes Plantation, the historic estate of Samuel Johnston (1733–1816).

Johnston was born in Scotland. While still a baby, he was brought to North Carolina by his uncle, Gabriel Johnston, the Royal governor of the colony.

By 1775, Samuel Johnston had become one of the Patriot leaders of North Carolina. He served with distinction in the First and Second Provincial Congresses, then served as president of the Third and Fourth Congresses after the death of John Harvey. When Royal Governor Josiah Martin fled Tryon Palace in New Bern in May 1775, Johnston became the de facto governor—and the first man to act as governor of the colony without Royal authority.

Throughout the Revolution, he served in the Continental Congress. On December 13, 1787, he was elected governor of North Carolina. At both of North Carolina's Constitutional Conventions, Johnston, a staunch Federalist, was elected president. Six days after the state ratified the constitution in Fayetteville in November 1789, the legislators elected North Carolina's first United States senator—Samuel Johnston.

Johnston acquired Hayes Plantation in 1765. He constructed the majestic cupola-topped, two-story mansion with adjoining single-story wings in 1801. Today, the well-maintained home features a two-story portico overlooking Edenton Bay. Johnston's grave is in the family cemetery on the estate. Among the other notable Revolutionary War figures buried there are James Iredell and Penelope Barker.

At the end of East Water Street, turn around and retrace your route to South Broad Street. Near the intersection, take note of The Homestead, located at 101 East Water Street. Constructed in 1771, this two-story frame dwelling has a Revolutionary War history. Built by a business partner of Joseph Hewes, the house was later acquired by Stephen Cabarrus (1754–1808) for use as his town residence.

As news of the hostilities between Great Britain and its American colonies spread throughout Europe, Cabarrus—the son of nobility in Bayonne, France—grew excited about the American cause and set sail for North Carolina. The twenty-two-year-old foreign Patriot settled in Edenton and quickly took his place as a leader.

A Federalist, Cabarrus served as a delegate to both of the state's Constitutional Conventions. In 1789, the North Carolina General Assembly elected him to the first of several terms as its speaker. In that position, he cast the deciding vote to locate the permanent state capital in Raleigh.

Turn left on South Broad Street. On the waterfront at 509 South Broad stands the Barker House, one of the most-photographed houses in a town filled with beautiful historic homes. Erected in 1782 several blocks up the street, the two-and-a-half-story clapboard house was moved to its present location in 1952. Thomas Barker, a successful colonial agent for North Carolina in Great Britain prior to the Revolution, and his wife, Penelope, an instigator of the Edenton Tea Party, were the original owners of the house.

Turn around at the end of South Broad Street and drive north to the Cupola House, located at 408 South Broad. This unique two-and-a-half-story frame structure, named for the large octagonal "lantern" atop its roof, was constructed sometime between 1735 and 1758. The most famous structure in Edenton, it was once owned by Dr. Samuel Dickinson and his wife, Elizabeth. During the Revolution, the physician was a staunch Patriot. His spouse participated in the Edenton Tea Party.

Just north of the Cupola House, turn left on West King Street and proceed west; this block contains a fine assemblage of stately mansions built in the nineteenth century. Continue on West King across South Granville to Blount.

The West Custom House, a large, two-story frame dwelling at 108 Blount Street, was the home of Swiss sea captain William Boritz (of waterfront cannon fame) from 1787 until 1798. The house was built before the Revolution.

Just beyond the West Custom House, turn right on Moseley Street, proceed one block north, and turn right on West Eden Street. Several houses here have a connection with the Revolutionary War.

The two-story frame Littlejohn House, located at 218 West Eden, dates from the early 1790s. William Littlejohn, the commissioner of the Port of Roanoke, and his wife, Sarah, one of the signers of the Tea Party Resolutions, built this home.

Charlton House, located at 206 West Eden near the end of the block, was constructed in the 1760s. Jasper Charlton, an attorney and ardent Patriot, built the handsome gambrel-roofed house. His wife, Abigail, was the first signer of the Tea Party Resolutions.

Turn left off West Eden onto South Granville Street. After one block on South Granville, turn right on West Queen Street. The Leigh House, the gambrel-roofed dwelling at 120 West Queen, was the home of Lydia Bennett, another signer of the Tea Party Resolutions. Gilbert Leigh, the architect of the Chowan County Courthouse, built the house in 1756.

Continue east on West Queen to South Broad Street. Turn left and proceed north on Broad for one block, then turn left onto West Church Street. At the northwestern corner of Broad and Church stands St. Paul's Episcopal Church, one of the nation's most historic religious shrines. Constructed in 1736 and beautifully restored after a terrible fire in 1948, the tall, vine-covered brick edifice is the second-oldest church building in North Carolina. Organized in 1701, the congregation is the oldest in the state.

Many of the colonial and Revolutionary War leaders of the Albemarle worshiped in this church. From the outset of the Revolution, the leaders of St. Paul's supported the American cause. At a meeting on June 19, 1775, members of the local vestry recorded their allegiance to King George III. But with rebellious overtones, they duly noted, "We do solemnly and sincerely promise and engage, under the sanctions of virtue, honor, and the sacred love of liberty and our country, to maintain and support all the acts and resolutions of the said Continental and Provincial Congress to the utmost of our power and ability."

St. Paul's Episcopal Church, Edenton

Adjacent to the church and spilling over into the churchyard is the historic St. Paul's Cemetery. Buried in these hallowed grounds are numerous leaders from the colonial and Revolutionary War periods. Charles Eden, Thomas Pollock, and Henderson Walker—all colonial governors—are buried here. Among the Patriots interred in the cemetery are Stephen Cabarrus and Thomas Benbury, one of the men responsible for bringing the controversial cannon to Edenton.

From St. Paul's, drive west on West Church Street to the end of the block. Turn right on Granville and proceed one block. Located at 108 North Granville near the southeastern corner of Granville and Gale, the Williams-Flury-Burton House (also known as the Booth House) was constructed in 1779. Captain Willis Williams, who built the gambrel-roofed structure as a residence, was commander of the *Caswell*, which helped keep the vital American supply route at Ocracoke Inlet open during the Revolutionary War.

Turn right onto West Gale Street, drive one block to North Broad Street, and turn right. As previously noted, the state historical markers along Broad pay homage to the illustrious sons, places, and events of Edenton during the American Revolution. Of all the markers, one deserves special attention, as there is no other tangible reminder on the Edenton landscape of one of the town's greatest citizens—Hugh Williamson.

Few Americans in the Revolutionary War period were more talented than Williamson (1735–1819), a well-educated Pennsylvanian. Over the course of his long life, Dr. Williamson served as a physician, educator, scientist, scholar, businessman, and statesman.

Even before his arrival in Edenton, Williamson was a fervent Patriot. By 1776, he had witnessed the Boston Tea Party, been a prisoner of war, and carried secret dispatches for the Continental Congress. He settled in Edenton in 1777. Soon thereafter, Governor Richard Caswell named him surgeon general of North Carolina. In that position, Dr. Williamson was a tireless worker on the battlefield, behind enemy lines, and in the laboratory, where his experiments resulted in improved health for the state's fighting men.

Not until the war was over did Williamson embark upon a political career. He served in the Continental Congress and represented North Carolina at the Constitutional Convention at Philadelphia in 1787. Some of the key elements of the Constitution—the procedure for impeaching the president and the six-year term for United States senators—were proposed by Williamson. He was one of three North Carolinians to sign the document.

At the intersection of North Broad and East Church, turn left and proceed to the James Iredell House State Historic Site, located at 105 East Church. Erected in 1773, the white-frame Georgian two-story house was purchased by James Iredell, Sr., in 1776.

A native of England, Iredell (1751–99) was the chief legal officer of North Carolina during much of the Revolutionary War. In his role as the state's attorney from 1779 to 1781, the high-spirited Patriot instituted legal action against Loyalists who interfered with the war effort.

Although he was financially unable to attend the Constitutional Convention in Philadelphia in 1787, Iredell joined with his brother-in-law, Samuel Johnston, to lead North Carolina toward ratification of the Constitution. In 1789, the year North Carolina adopted the Constitution, President George Washington, without Iredell's knowledge, appointed him as an associate justice of the first United States Supreme Court. Iredell served on the nation's highest court for nine years. During his tenure, he wrote the dissenting opinion in the landmark case of *Chisholm v. Georgia*, which later served as the basis for the Eleventh Amendment to the Constitution. In the presidential election of 1796, three electoral votes were cast for Iredell.

Admission to the house and grounds is free. In one of the upstairs bedrooms, James Wilson, Iredell's friend and a fellow associate justice of the Supreme Court, died in 1798. Wilson, a Pennsylvanian, was a signer of the Declaration of Independence.

Continue east on East Church Street as it leads out of town and becomes N.C. 32. Approximately 3 miles southeast of Edenton, N.C. 32 intersects S.R. 1114. Turn right onto S.R. 1114 and follow it for 5.9 miles as it parallels the Chowan River to its confluence with Albemarle Sound.

Turn right at the junction with S.R. 1113. This short road leads to Mulberry Hill. Built on the sound in 1810, this magnificent, four-story, brick Georgian mansion stands on the site of James Blount's plantation. Blount served as a militia colonel in the Revolutionary War, and his wife, Anne, signed the Tea Party Resolution.

Return to S.R. 1114, turn right, proceed 0.8 mile to N.C. 32, and turn right again. The spectacular Albemarle Sound Bridge will come into view almost instantly. Proceed over the 5-mile span, built in 1985 to replace a forty-five-year-old structure. The bridge offers a splendid view of the vast Albemarle Sound, one of the important supply routes for the American cause during the Revolutionary War. Midway across the bridge, Chowan County gives way to Washington County. Established in 1799, the county was named in honor of George Washington.

After crossing the bridge, continue south on N.C. 32 for 1.9 miles to U.S. 64. Turn right and drive 8.9 miles west to the junction with U.S. 64 Business at the old lumber town of Roper. Follow U.S. 64 Business through town.

In the heart of Roper, a state historical marker calls attention to Buncombe Hall, one of the plantations that covered the landscape in and around Roper in the colonial and Revolutionary War periods. Edward Buncombe (1742–79), a native of St. Kitts in the British West Indies, first came to the Albemarle in 1766 after inheriting the 1,025-acre plantation from his uncle. Two years later, he took up permanent residence here in the plantation manor, which he had authorized to be constructed in his absence. The elegant structure, the likes of which had never before been seen in the area, was massive. The two-story, L-shaped mansion boasted fifty-six rooms and three cellars.

Among the guests Buncombe welcomed to his mansion in the months leading up to the Revolution were John Harvey and Samuel Johnston. There, on April 3, 1774, the three men sowed the seeds for the first colonial legislature convened in America in defiance of British orders. (For more information, see The Coastal Rivers Tour, pages 75–76.)

By September 1775, Buncombe was a colonel of the militia. The following April, he was transferred to the Continental Army as commander of the Fifth North Carolina Regiment. He trained and equipped the soldiers under his command at his own expense.

After leading his regiment in the engagement at Brandywine, Pennsylvania, on September 11, 1777, Buncombe fought what was to be his last battle at Germantown three weeks later. Shot down on the same field that cost the life of General Francis Nash and many other North Carolinians, the gallant colonel was left for dead by the American forces as they retreated. It was not until the next day, when a British officer recognized him as an old school chum, that Buncombe received medical care.

He was taken to Philadelphia as a prisoner of war. There, his recovery was hampered by a lack of funds, as Buncombe had depleted his cash resources for the military expenses of his regiment. During a sleepwalking episode, he fell down a flight of steps and reopened his wound. Colonel Edward Buncombe, then thirty-six years old, bled to death.

In the aftermath, his magnificent mansion fell into ruin. The last remnants of the historic dwelling vanished when the Norfolk and Southern Railroad brought its line to Roper.

U.S. 64 Business will return you to U.S. 64 on the western side of Roper. Drive 4 miles to N.C. 45 and turn right. After 3.3 miles, N.C. 45 crosses the Roanoke River into Bertie County. Two miles farther north, turn left on N.C. 308, then proceed west for 11.7 miles to where the road merges with U.S. 13/U.S. 17. Turn right and follow U.S. 13/U.S. 17/N.C. 308 for 1.4 miles as it becomes King Street in Windsor, the county seat of Bertie County.

A state historical marker at the intersection of King and Gray Streets notes that the birthplace of William Blount (1749–1800) stands 0.2 mile southwest. Blount was one of the South's premier statesmen in the late eighteenth century.

To reach the site, turn left on Gray and proceed two blocks to Queen Street. Just after crossing Queen, you'll notice a narrow paved driveway leading up a knoll to Rosefield, the plantation where Blount was born while his mother was visiting his grandfather, John Gray. The original portion of the existing massive frame house was constructed in 1786 and has remained in the Gray family since that time.

William Blount was involved in the pre–Revolutionary War hostilities that engulfed North Carolina. Both he and his father took part in the Battle of Alamance on May 16, 1771. Soon after the war began, Blount enlisted in the Continental Army. He served as paymaster of the Third North Carolina Regiment for the duration of the conflict.

While a member of the Continental Congress in 1787, Blount represented North Carolina at the Constitutional Convention. Though he was one of the thirty-nine men who signed the Constitution, he was not enthusiastic about it. Blount later explained that he affixed his signature only to make the document "the unanimous act of the States in Convention."

In 1790, he moved to the part of western North Carolina that was to become Tennessee. President Washington named Blount governor of "the Territory South of the Ohio River" less than a year later. When Tennessee was admitted to the Union in 1796, its legislature elected Blount the first United States senator from the new state.

Return to the intersection with U.S. 13 in Windsor and proceed north. After 18.1 miles, the route crosses into Hertford County. Continue north on U.S. 13 for 4.8 miles as it passes through Ahoskie. Just north of the town, turn left onto N.C. 561, then drive 2.4 miles to Fraziers Crossroads. Colonel John Frazier, the man for whom the community was named, maintained a home here during the Revolutionary War. He served as a Tory officer.

Turn right onto S.R. 1108 at Fraziers Crossroads and drive north 1.8 miles to N.C. 461. Turn right and proceed 3.8 miles east until the route merges again with U.S. 13. Continue north on U.S. 13 for 2.5 miles to U.S. 158 and N.C. 45. Turn right on N.C. 45 and proceed 0.3 mile to Winton, the seat of Hertford County.

Laid out on the banks of the Chowan River in 1766, Winton was named for Benjamin Wynns (1710–88), a planter and militia officer during the Revolution. As a colonel of the Hertford Regiment of the North Carolina militia, he led his soldiers in the Battle of Great Bridge and the siege at Norfolk that followed. Upon his triumphant return to Hertford County in 1776, Colonel Wynns was rewarded with praise from people all along his route.

At the intersection of N.C. 45 and King Street, turn left on King. Follow it for seven blocks to Cross Street, where you'll note the Hertford-Gates Health Department. Turn left and proceed one block to Taylor Street. Located at the rear of the Health Department building is the Dickinson cemetery, the site of the grave of Eli Foote. Foote was an attorney who remained a Tory during the Revolution but managed to live in accord with his Patriot neighbors after the war. He died in 1792 at the age of forty-four. He was the grandfather of Harriet Beecher Stowe, the author of *Uncle Tom's Cabin*.

The Chowan River is just north of the cemetery. Downriver from Winton at a place called Wyanoke Ferry, a Tory raiding party torched a riverside settlement as Cornwallis marched through northeastern North Carolina toward Yorktown in July 1781.

Retrace your route to the intersection of U.S. 13 and U.S. 158. Proceed west on U.S. 158 for 10.9 miles to Murfreesboro. Turn right onto Second Street and follow it two blocks to Broad Street. Turn right and go one block to East Street. Turn left on East and follow it to Cedar Street and the site of Old Town Cemetery and King's Landing.

Pleasantly situated on the western bank of the Meherrin River, Murfreesboro traces its roots to a settlement that began here in 1707. Named for colonial and Revolutionary War leader William Murfree, the town was known as Murfree's Ferry as early as 1770, when it served as a river port and a "King's Landing," where cargo was inspected by representatives of the Crown. Over the past quarter-century, historic Murfreesboro has benefited from a comprehensive restoration project. Today, its streets are lined with stately old homes and buildings that date from colonial times.

When you are ready to leave King's Landing, retrace your route to U.S. 158, which becomes Main Street as it enters Murfreesboro. A glimpse down the street reveals more than a half-dozen state historical markers, an indication of the historic importance of the town.

Near the intersection of Main and Third Streets stands a marker that honors perhaps the most distinguished visitor ever to call upon Murfreesboro. On the evening of Saturday, February 26, 1825, the Marquis de Lafayette, a Revolutionary War hero, made Murfreesboro and its Eagle Tavern the first stop on his triumphant tour of North Carolina.

To see the site of the Eagle Tavern (later known as the Indian Queen Inn), turn right onto Third and drive two blocks to Broad Street. The tavern stood nearby on the northern side of Broad.

In anticipation of Lafayette's visit, the citizens of Murfreesboro planned a grand ball for their honored guest. But after Lafayette and his entourage crossed the Meherrin River four miles north of town, the muddy roads proved treacherous. As the party neared Murfreesboro, it found the road up the hill to town virtually impassable. Lafayette's carriage sank to its axles, the horses mired up to their knees.

It was nine o'clock that night before the weary sixty-eight-year-old general reached town. Among those traveling with him were his son, George Washington Lafayette, and his personal secretary, August Levasseur. As he entered the town, Lafayette was cheered wildly by every able-bodied resident. A brass band serenaded him.

Levasseur later made notes about the arrival: "We . . . were greatly relieved by the candid hospitality of the inhabitants of Murfreesboro, who neglected nothing to prove to General Lafayette, that the citizens of North Carolina were as sincerely attached to him as those of other states."

Thomas Maney, the only attorney in Murfreesboro at the time, offered the official welcome: "To you, next to dear, great Washington, we are indebted for the triumph of our arms. We salute you as father of our common country, and we hail you also as a benefactor of the human race and gallant champion of the rights of men."

Lafayette delivered a reply. Then, because of the lateness of the hour, he was escorted into the inn's flag-and-bunting-draped dining room, where he enjoyed a meal with forty townspeople. By the time dinner was completed, the clock struck midnight, and the ball was canceled. It was later rescheduled—148 years later, that is. In an effort to raise funds for the restoration

of their town, civic-minded Murfreesboro residents held the Lafayette Ball on Saturday, January 27, 1973.

Turn left on Broad Street and proceed to the northwestern corner of Broad and Fourth. Here stands the Wheeler House, a handsome, two-story dwelling of the Revolutionary War era. The bricks used in its construction came from King's Landing, where they had been brought in as ballast.

John Wheeler, the son of a Revolutionary War surgeon, built the house. Tradition has it that Continental forces used it as a headquarters during the war. Wheeler's son, John Hill Wheeler, an eminent historian of Revolutionary War–era North Carolina, was born in the house in 1806.

Continue west on Broad for one block to Fifth. The Captain Meredith House has stood on the northwestern corner of this intersection since 1775. Colonel Hardy Murfree, whose house is a block away, was honored at a grand ball in the Captain Meredith House in 1781 upon his return from the Revolutionary War.

The Murfree House, better known as Melrose, is one of the most distinctive homes in a city blessed with historic structures. To see it, continue west on Broad; the home is on the northern side of the street midway between Sycamore and Wynn Streets. The original portion of the elegantly restored Georgian-Colonial mansion was constructed in 1757 by William Murfree. Upon his death, he left the house to his son, Hardy.

Hardy Murfree (1758–1809) served with distinction as an officer in the North Carolina Continental Line. He was singled out for his bravery and heroism in the American assault on Stony Point, a British stronghold on the Hudson River. After the war, he successfully petitioned for the incorporation of the town named for his father.

The tour ends at the Murfree House. If you desire a more extensive look at the restored town, you may arrange a tour at the nearby Roberts-Vaughan Village Center, located at 116 East Main Street.

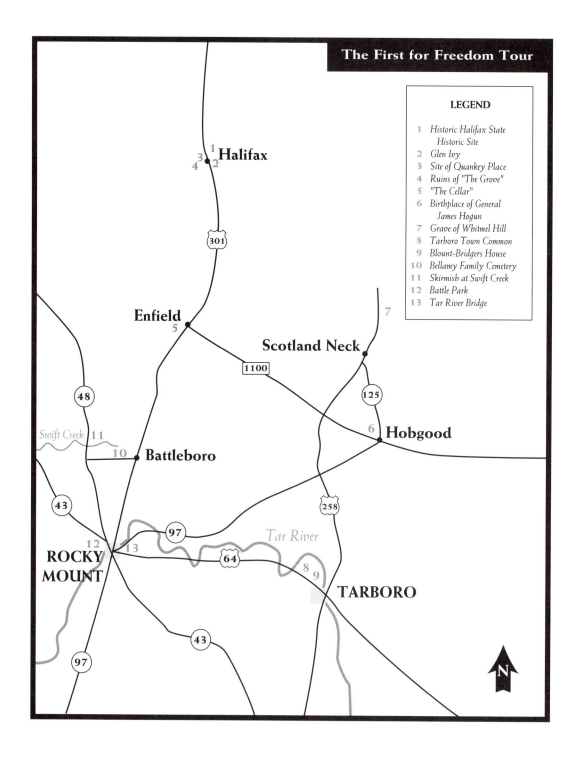

The First for Freedom Tour

3 1 **Halifax**
4 2

301

Enfield
5

Scotland Neck
7

1100

48

125

Swift Creek 11

6 **Hobgood**

10 **Battleboro**

43

258

97

Tar River

12 13

ROCKY
MOUNT

64

8
9

TARBORO

43

97

N

The First for Freedom Tour

This tour begins at Halifax in Halifax County and makes its way through Edgecombe County before ending at Rocky Mount in Nash County. Among the highlights are Historic Halifax State Historic Site, Loretta (the home of William R. Davie), Glen Ivy (White Hall), the ruins of "The Grove," "The Cellar," Tarboro Town Common, the Blount-Bridgers House, the site of the skirmish at Swift Creek, and the place on the Tar River where Tar Heels received their name.

Total mileage: approximately 79 miles.

This tour covers the three-county region in the northeastern part of the state that saw the birth of a free and independent North Carolina in 1776. The area was also the site of the final departure of Lord Cornwallis and the British army from the state five years later. Many of the stirring events that fostered the early spirit of independence took place here: the passage of the Halifax Resolves; the adoption of the first state constitution; and the first public reading of the Declaration of Independence in North Carolina.

The tour begins at the junction of U.S. 301 Bypass and U.S. 301 Business on the western side of Halifax, the seat of the county of the same name. Both town and county were named for George Montague, second earl of Halifax (1716–71). Montague, who served as president of the British Board of Trade and Plantation, is known as "the Father of the Colonies" for his successful efforts in developing American commerce.

Along U.S. 301 Bypass, a half-dozen state historical markers related to the Revolutionary War give a hint of the history written in the nearby village. These markers pay tribute to the Halifax Resolves, the first state constitution, the colonial Masonic lodge, and visits by Cornwallis and George Washington.

Follow U.S. 301 Bypass for 0.2 mile to where it junctions with N.C. 903 and Pittsylvania Street. Turn left onto Pittsylvania. After one block, turn left onto Norman Street. Drive a block, then turn right on St. David's Street. The visitor center for Historic Halifax State Historic Site is just ahead at the corner of St. David's and Dobbs Streets. Park in the lot on Dobbs and walk across the street to the visitor center.

Inside the spacious, modern center, a thirteen-minute slide show orients visitors to the story of the emergence of Halifax as a key town in colonial North Carolina. Attractive exhibits of artifacts from the Revolutionary War era are displayed in the center's museum. A gift shop, an information center, and restrooms are also located in the facility.

There are few sites in all of what was once colonial America that are more historically significant and better preserved than Halifax, located on the banks of the Roanoke River. It was in this town on April 12, 1776, that North Carolina statesmen took the bold initiative that led the other twelve colonies toward a formal declaration of independence from Great Britain.

Founded in 1760, Halifax quickly became an important crossroads town. It was located on the main north-south route of the colonies (a portion of which is traced by King Street today) and the route leading west into the interior of North Carolina. The town was a vital river port and a trading center. Men from the west brought furs and skins to trade for imports stored in the warehouses that once stood along the river. Area planters brought their goods to town for sale or export. Because it was the seat of local government and the headquarters of the militia district, Halifax was the site of many fiery discussions of the revolutionary ideas that began to take hold in colonial America in the mid-1770s. Local taverns provided the setting where early Patriots exchanged opinions and plotted strategy.

Today, while Halifax is not as large or as popular among tourists as Colonial Williamsburg, Virginia, it is an authentic village—restored, not reconstructed. Free guided tours of Historic Halifax and its magnificently restored buildings are available throughout the day and begin at the visitor center. A map for a self-guided tour is also available at the center; however, the interiors of the sites cannot be seen on the self-guided tour.

It is best to take the self-guided tour on foot. To begin, proceed southeast on St. David's Street from the visitor center. You will reach the Eagle Tavern and Tavern Garden at the northwestern corner of St. David's and King

Streets. A state historical marker for the tavern stands nearby. Constructed around 1790, this handsome, two-story, Federal-style structure was enlarged in 1845. It originally stood farther north on King Street at the site now occupied by Andrew Jackson Elementary School. A pre–Revolutionary War tavern preceded the Eagle at the modern school site.

Walk across King Street to the Tap Room. The small, red, gambrel-roofed building was once attached to Pope's Hotel, a larger structure that contained nine chimneys and nineteen fireplaces. Built in 1760, the entire complex served as a tavern where political discussions, dances, and slave auctions took place.

After visiting the Tap Room, walk north along King Street to the site of Market Square. In colonial times, this was the economic center of Halifax. During the American Revolution, the public area here was given over to military activity. A barracks was constructed near the market house, and militia troops paraded and drilled on these grounds.

Behind and to the east of Market Square is the Constitution-Burgess House.

In the late 1800s, the granddaughter of Halifax Patriot Willie (pronounced Wiley) Jones referred to this structure as the "small house in which the constitution [of North Carolina] was framed." While it is certain that North Carolina's first constitution was framed in Halifax in 1776, subsequent historical research has indicated that it was not signed in the Constitution-Burgess House, which was built in the late 1700s at the earliest.

Named for Thomas Burgess, a local attorney who had an office here in 1821, the small Georgian-style house is simply furnished and neatly painted in blue. It was purchased and restored by the Daughters of the American Revolution (D.A.R.) in 1921 and was donated to the state in 1964.

Behind and to the south of the Constitution-Burgess House lies Magazine Springs. Used long before the American Revolution by Indians and then by colonists, this watering hole took its name from a nearby Revolutionary War factory that made ammunition and ironwork for the American cause. A military storehouse was also located here during the war.

Return to the site of Market Square and cross to the other side of King Street, where the town's jail stands. Constructed in 1838, the two-story, brick, fireproof building is on the exact site occupied by two previous wooden jails. The first, built in 1760, was destroyed when escaping prisoners set it

"Redcoats" at the old jail in Halifax

afire. The second, erected in 1764, eventually met a similar fate. But it stood during the Revolutionary War, when it was used to house prisoners of war.

Perhaps the most famous of its wartime captives was Allan MacDonald, a

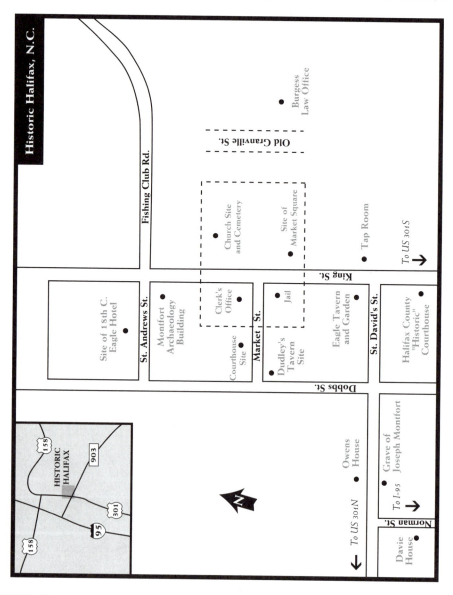

TOURING NORTH CAROLINA'S REVOLUTIONARY WAR SITES

Scottish Highlander taken prisoner at the Battle of Moores Creek Bridge in February 1776. (For more information on this battle, see The Cape Fear Tour, pages 89–90.) Allan was the husband of the famed Flora MacDonald, one of the most noted women of North Carolina during the Revolutionary War period. (For more on Flora MacDonald, see The Scottish Dilemma Tour, pages 114–18.)

Governor Luther Hodges dedicated the restored jail in 1955.

Remain on the same side of King Street as you walk across Market Street to the Clerk's Office. Constructed in 1833, this brick building was designed as a fireproof place to store court and county records. This came in the wake of a holocaust in Raleigh 1831 that destroyed the Capitol and the many irreplaceable documents contained therein.

Walk along Market Street behind the Clerk's Office to the bronze marker at the site where the original Halifax County Courthouse stood. Other than the simple marker, there is nothing on the grassy lawn to proclaim that this is the most historic spot in a town blessed with them. It was in the court-house built here around 1760 that two of the most stirring events of the American Revolution occurred.

On Thursday, April 4, 1776, delegates from throughout North Carolina assembled in Halifax to attend the Fourth Provincial Congress. Halifax seemed the logical place for the assembly at a time when the spirit of inde-pendence was spreading throughout the colonies. In the years leading up to the Revolution, the citizens of Halifax had exhibited a strong distaste for British rule. For example, when Royal Governor William Tryon recruited eastern North Carolina volunteers to suppress the Regulators in 1771, he attracted not a single one from Halifax.

Many of the most distinguished and able statesmen of the colony assembled for the Fourth Provincial Congress: Samuel Johnston, Samuel Spencer, Ri-chard Caswell, Thomas Person, John Ashe, Samuel Ashe, Allen Jones, Thomas Burke, Thomas Harvey, Nathaniel Rochester, Griffith Rutherford, Abner Nash, Cornelius Harnett, and Willie Jones. Virtually every one of them was filled with the revolutionary ardor that characterized Halifax at the time. After his arrival, Samuel Johnston, the presiding officer of the congress, noted that "all our people here are up for independence." Robert Howe, who would soon take the field of battle, concurred: "Independence seems to be the word; I know not one dissenting voice."

The congress was convened to prepare a response to a March 3 request from North Carolina's three delegates to the Continental Congress in Philadelphia. Specifically, William Hooper, John Penn, and Joseph Hewes sought instructions concerning the direction that North Carolina should take in the growing rift between the colonies and Great Britain.

On April 8, the statesmen at Halifax appointed a committee composed of Cornelius Harnett, Allen Jones, Thomas Burke (who would later serve as governor of the new state), Abner Nash (who would likewise later serve as governor), and others "to take into consideration the usurpation and violences attempted and committed by the King and Parliament of Britain against America, and the further measures to be taken for frustrating the same and for the better defense of this Province."

Four days later, the committee delivered a document that would have far-reaching consequences in American history. Harnett, the chairman of the committee, rose to his feet and in his Irish brogue presented to the delegates the bold words that would lead to a national Declaration of Independence less than three months later: "Resolved, That the delegates of this colony in the Continental Congress be empowered to concur with the delegates of the other colonies in declaring independence, and forming foreign alliances, reserving to this colony the sole and exclusive right of forming a constitution and laws for this colony."

Working late into the night on Friday, April 12, the delegates expressed unanimous support for the report, which was known as the Halifax Resolves. Harnett's stirring words and their enactment by the Provincial Congress represented the most revolutionary official act taken by an American colony to that date. North Carolina thus became the first colony to issue an official utterance of independence and a request that its sister colonies follow suit.

Indeed, Hooper, Penn, and Hewes were given an answer in just the terms and the tenor they desired. A copy of the Halifax Resolves was promptly dispatched to Philadelphia for the three men. But only one of their number—John Penn—was there. His two compatriots were in Virginia en route to Halifax, where they planned to take their seats in the Provincial Congress to orchestrate the move toward independence. When Hooper and

Hewes rode into town on Monday, April 15, they were elated to learn of the action taken three days earlier.

The importance of these events cannot be minimized. The two dates that appear on the modern North Carolina state flag both have their roots in the American Revolution. One date (April 12, 1776) commemorates the Halifax Resolves, and the other (May 20, 1775) honors the Mecklenburg Declaration of Independence. (For more information on events in Mecklenburg County, see The Hornets' Nest Tour, pages 189–92.)

The words and spirit of the Halifax Resolves were quickly heard and felt well beyond the boundaries of North Carolina. When the document was read in the Continental Congress, its revolutionary language was well received. In fact, the delegates at Philadelphia sent copies home with the request that their constituents "follow this laudable example." On May 15, Virginia became the first colony to follow North Carolina's lead. Less than two weeks later, the delegates from North Carolina and Virginia presented their instructions to the Continental Congress. On June 7, Richard Henry Lee moved "that these United Colonies are and of right ought to be free and independent states."

The defiant act of the North Carolina statesmen who took a stand in Halifax bore fruit on July 4, when the Continental Congress approved the final draft of the Declaration of Independence. News that independence had been declared reached the Provincial Council (the executive branch of government in North Carolina) at Halifax on July 22. Upon receiving a copy of the Declaration, the council voted that it should be read in public for the first time in North Carolina on August 1.

It was only logical that the place chosen for the momentous event should be the lawn of the courthouse where the first seeds for the Declaration had been sown only months earlier. There was also no question as to the statesman who should offer the state's first public proclamation of the Declaration. Cornelius Harnett, the fearless Cape Fear Patriot who had inspired his colleagues to adopt the Halifax Resolves, was the man accorded the honor.

At high noon on August 1, 1776, the Provincial Council marched to the courthouse amidst an immense gathering of people. Drums reverberated; flags fluttered in the soft summer breeze; and soldiers, dressed in the best uniforms they could find, stood at attention. Suddenly, the crowd roared with delight as a militia detail escorted Harnett to a platform. When the fifty-three-year-old hero mounted the rostrum with the scrolled Declaration clutched in his hand, a hush descended upon the excited multitude. His Irish voice was clear and loud as he began to read the historic words: "When in the Course of human Events . . ." No sooner had he finished the proclamation than an exuberant celebration began. At its height, the jubilant soldiers near Harnett grabbed the staid gentleman, put him on their shoulders, and paraded him through the streets of Halifax as the champion of American independence.

Return to the Clerk's Office, then cross King Street to the colonial cemetery. From 1793 to 1911, this was also the site of the village church. The oldest known grave in the cedar-shaded graveyard dates to 1766. Among the notable persons buried here are two women of the Revolutionary War era.

Justina Davis (1745–71) was laid to rest here at the age of twenty-six. In her short life, she married two men who served as governors of North Carolina. Her first husband was Royal Governor Arthur Dobbs, who married her when he was seventy-eight and she fifteen. (For more information about Dobbs, see The Cape Fear Tour, page 101.) After Dobbs died, his widow married Abner Nash. Nash was elected governor after Justina died.

Also located in the cemetery is the grave of Sarah Jones Davie. Throughout her life, she was surrounded by heroes of the American Revolution. She was the daughter of Allen Jones, the niece of Willie Jones, and the wife of William Richardson Davie.

Adjacent to the cemetery is the Joseph Montfort Amphitheater. This outdoor theater is the venue for the summer drama *First for Freedom*. Written by Maxville Burt Williams, the play has been presented every summer since it premiered in 1976. It dramatizes the events of 1776 that culminated in the Halifax Resolves.

Resume your walk on King Street, continuing about three and a half blocks to the river overlook; the pavement ends en route to the overlook. Vast warehouses and other commercial structures of the eighteenth century once stood at this serene site on the forested banks of the Roanoke River. As Cornwallis was moving his army north toward Virginia in May 1781, he was forced to tarry in Halifax because floodwaters along the river here delayed his crossing. A river ferry operated at Halifax into the twentieth century.

From the river overlook, retrace your route on King Street; follow King to St. Andrews Street. Andrew Jackson Elementary School stands on the northwestern corner of this intersection. In Revolutionary War times, the Eagle Hotel and the Eagle Tavern were located here. It was at this site that North Carolina's first state constitution was drafted and adopted by the Fifth (and final) Provincial Congress, convened in late 1776. On December 19, two days after the constitution was approved, the representatives at Halifax elected Richard Caswell the first governor of the independent state of North Carolina.

Almost five years later, Cornwallis came calling. The British general quartered Colonel Banastre Tarleton and other officers at the Eagle Hotel. A decade later, President George Washington visited Halifax on his famous Southern tour. During his stay on April 16 and 17, 1791, he was feted at a ball at the Eagle Hotel. Halifax was the first North Carolina town visited by Washington after he crossed the Virginia line. "It seems to be in a decline & does not it is said contain a thousand Souls," the president wrote of Halifax.

On February 27, 1825, the Marquis de Lafayette was entertained at the Eagle Tavern during his one-night stay in Halifax. While enjoying his triumphant visit, the aged French general recalled that it was at Halifax where Cornwallis had made his final decision to leave North Carolina for Virginia. Addressing the local citizenry, Lafayette remarked, "It has long been my desire to visit the citizens of Halifax, where the Constitution of the State was framed and the principles of liberty declared." In response to the welcome he received from Major Allen J. Davie, the son of General William R. Davie (who had died five years earlier), Lafayette told the crowd, "The regard and the respect evinced toward me by the citizens are highly gratifying to my feelings, and they are rendered more so by being tendered to me by the son of my old and esteemed friend."

Proceed to the Montfort Archaeology Building, located on King Street near its intersection with St. Andrews. Constructed in 1984, the large, white, two-story structure stands on what was Lot 52 in the original town plan of Halifax. Inside the building are artifacts, exhibits, and the archaeological remains of the town house of Joseph Montfort.

Although Montfort died on March 25, 1776, three weeks before the Halifax Resolves, he exhibited during his life the revolutionary spirit synonymous with his hometown. A regular figure at colonial assemblies until his health began to deteriorate in 1775, Montfort was intensely disliked by Royal Governors Tryon and Martin. In a scathing attack on Montfort, Governor Martin once wrote, "He is well received by all, esteemed by very few, and considered a Problem by everybody."

Two of his daughters married Revolutionary War leaders of North Carolina; Mary Montfort wed Willie Jones, and Elizabeth Montfort married John Baptiste Ashe.

Montfort's greatest claim to fame was his high office in Masonic activities, which will be detailed later in this tour.

Return to the intersection of King and St. Andrews. Turn left and walk west on St. Andrews past the school to Dobbs Street. Turn left on Dobbs and proceed south toward the visitor center.

This quiet, peaceful street gives little hint of the tempestuous events that gripped Halifax more than two centuries ago. Living in and around the village were dozens of lesser-known individuals who had an impact on the struggle for American independence. For example, there were the Pasteurs. Believed to have been brothers, Charles, Thomas, and William Pasteur were descendants of Huguenot immigrants. Thomas served as an officer in the North Carolina Continental Line. William was a surgeon for North Carolina troops and played a vital role in obtaining medicines and supplies for soldiers from his adopted state. Charles, likewise a surgeon and apothecary, furnished state troops with medical supplies.

And then there was Thomas Gilchrist (1735–89), a man best remembered for presenting a future Revolutionary War hero with his first case as an attorney. The young lawyer so engaged was Thomas Jefferson, the author of the Declaration of Independence. During the war, Gilchrist was suspected of treason. His name was subsequently cleared through a petition filed by his wife, Martha, the sister of Willie and Allen Jones.

Stop at the southeastern corner of Dobbs and Market Streets. The tavern of Christopher Dudley stood here on the eve of the Revolution. The mulberry trees growing at its site are more than two hundred years old. They are the remains of an ill-fated attempt to begin a silkworm industry in eighteenth-century Halifax. One significant problem doomed the industry to failure: the trees were of the wrong variety.

Continue south on Dobbs Street. Take notice of the garden at the rear of the visitor center. Its walkways follow the design of a garden shown on the map of the town prepared by C. J. Sauthier in 1769. The plantings here include flora of significance to the colonial and Revolutionary War periods.

At the junction of Dobbs and St. David's Streets, turn right and walk past the visitor center parking lot to the Owens House. A typical eighteenth-century English town house, the handsome gambrel-roofed structure was constructed in 1760 and moved to its present site before 1807. Decorated with furnishings from colonial times and the days of early statehood, the Owens House is the last building open to the public on this tour of Halifax.

Located directly across St. David's Street is the Royal White Hart Masonic Lodge. Constructed in 1769, the two-story white frame building is the oldest Masonic temple built for that purpose that is still in use in the United States.

On the front lawn, enclosed in an iron fence, is the grave of Joseph Montfort. A bronze tablet on the fence gate bears a warning: "This gate swings only by order of the Worshipful Master of Royal White Hart Lodge to admit a Pilgrim Mason."

Inside the fence, an elaborate marble slab pays tribute to Montfort, whose body was originally interred at the colonial cemetery. It notes that he was an orator, statesman, Patriot, and soldier. Montfort served as the first clerk of court of Halifax County, as treasurer of the province of North Carolina, as a colonel of colonial troops, and as a member of the Provincial Congress.

The slab proclaims that Montfort was appointed "Provincial Grand Master of and for America" on January 14, 1771. As such, he stands as the highest Masonic official ever on the continent. In bold letters, the grave marker boasts that Montfort was "**THE FIRST—THE LAST—THE ONLY GRAND MASTER OF AMERICA.**"

Continue on St. David's Street to Norman Street. On the southwestern corner, a state historical marker and a D.A.R. marker pay tribute to William Richardson Davie (1756–1820). His former home, privately owned,

William R. Davie House, Halifax

stands on Norman Street just beyond the markers.

Without question, William Richardson Davie was one of the most remarkable of the many Revolutionary War heroes of North Carolina. Born in England, he moved to America with his Scottish parents in 1764. Davie graduated from the College of New Jersey (later Princeton University) in 1776, just as the war was beginning. He served throughout the conflict as a Patriot officer.

After the war, Davie settled in Halifax to practice law. He married Sarah Jones, the daughter of Allen Jones, and assumed a leading role in the political and social affairs of the area.

Davie was but thirty-three years old when he was elected a delegate to the Constitutional Convention at Philadelphia in 1787. In the heated debates that characterized the convention before the Constitution was presented for consideration, the small, lightly populated states maintained that every state should have the same number of senators, while the larger states contended that the number of representatives in both houses of Congress must be based on population.

When a vote was taken, the result revealed a tie. Confusion was the order of the day. Both sides were intransigent. Gloom prevailed, as it appeared that the convention was about to collapse.

Suddenly, one of North Carolina's five delegates rose to his feet and began to address the assembly of distinguished Americans. In an emotional speech, William Richardson Davie saved the Constitution for the new nation when he proclaimed, "North Carolina is one of the largest states who voted against the plan suggested by the smaller states, but the time has now come when the larger states ought to yield. I am ready, and I believe my colleagues are ready, to vote that each state should have the same number of members in the Senate." Davie's historic oration brought the house down. A new vote was taken, and the North Carolinian's forceful words carried the day.

Back home, Davie worked tirelessly—and successfully—for ratification despite strong opposition from his wife's uncle, Willie Jones.

Elected governor of North Carolina in 1798, Davie was subsequently appointed as a special envoy to France by President John Adams. When he was introduced to Napoleon as "General Davie," the emperor sneered in derision. In an audible aside, Napoleon said, "Oui, General de Melish," the implication being that officers of the militia were of a lesser quality than regular-army officers. But through his intelligence and charm—and his ability to speak French fluently—the North Carolinian soon won the emperor's admiration and respect.

Loretta, Davie's home in Halifax, was constructed in 1787. The tall, well-preserved, two-story frame dwelling retains much of its original interior craftsmanship.

From the junction of St. David's and Norman, turn around and walk east on St. David's to King Street. Turn right and walk one block south on King to the former Halifax County Courthouse. This stately, three-story, tan-brick Neoclassical Revival structure was built in 1909. On its first floor are three items related to the Revolutionary War: a bronze plaque listing the Revolutionary War soldiers from Halifax County; a framed copy of the Halifax Resolves; and a reproduction of an artist's rendition of the signing of the Resolves.

Retrace your route to the parking lot at the visitor center. This ends the walking tour. Return to your car and drive to the junction of St. David's Street and King Street/Main Street. Turn right and follow Main Street (U.S. 301 Business) as it makes its way through modern downtown Halifax; just after the turn, you'll notice the large seal on the former Halifax County Courthouse commemorating the Halifax Resolves.

Approximately 0.5 mile south of the courthouse, as U.S. 301 Business winds gracefully among stately homes, you'll pass a private home on the right known as Glen Ivy (White Hall). This handsome frame dwelling, built in the 1840s, bears the name of the earlier estate of Revolutionary War leader John Baptist Ashe and his wife, Elizabeth, who was the daughter of Joseph Montfort and the sister of Mrs. Willie Jones. The couple are believed to be buried in unmarked graves near here.

While her husband was away fighting for the American cause (see The Cape Fear Tour, page 102), Mrs. Ashe showed herself a heroine, as did the wives of other local Patriot leaders.

When Cornwallis's army headed for Halifax on its march northward in the spring of 1781, only a small band of militiamen was available to defend the town. Colonel Banastre Tarleton led advance units of the British army against the local militia in a skirmish below the town. After routing the hapless Americans, Tarleton altered his route toward Halifax upon the receipt of intelligence that a large force of militia had gathered there. Striking from the west instead of the south, Tarleton's horsemen quickly cleared Halifax of American soldiers by chasing them across the river.

Writing in her diary in 1862 in the house that stands at the current tour stop, Mary Conigland remarked on the conflict from the previous century, noting that "even this spot on which I write has felt the weight of British bullets. The kitchen we now use was made of timbers taken from [the earlier] house in this lot, and in several places [is] perforated with British balls."

For several days while awaiting the arrival of Cornwallis and the main body of the British army, Tarleton's soldiers subjected Mrs. Ashe and the other citizens of Halifax to outrages. They appropriated cows, chickens, pigs, and other animals for food and destroyed what they could not eat. But even the much-feared Tarleton was no match for the defiant Elizabeth Jones Ashe.

During the British occupation, Major General Alexander Leslie made Glen Ivy (White Hall) his headquarters. On one occasion, Tarleton called at the house. In the course of a conversation with some fellow officers, he began to berate his archrival in the American army, Colonel William Washington. Four months earlier, Washington had bested—and personally wounded—Tarleton at the Battle of Cowpens. Tarleton considered Washington a boor, a pest, and a nemesis. In a sarcastic tone, he proclaimed that he "would be happy to see Colonel Washington," because he understood that the American was small and ugly.

Upon overhearing the conversation, Mrs. Ashe remarked, "If you had looked behind you, Colonel Tarleton, at the Battle of Cowpens, you would have enjoyed that pleasure."

The British officer reached to draw his sword just as General Leslie entered the room. The general asked Mrs. Ashe to explain the situation. When she did so, Leslie remarked with a smile, "Say what you please, Mrs. Ashe, Colonel Tarleton knows better than to insult a lady in my presence."

From Glen Ivy (White Hall) continue south on U.S. 301 Business for 0.3 mile to U.S. 301 Bypass. At this intersection, state historical markers calling attention to the Halifax Resolves and Washington's visit to Halifax stand in a parklike plaza. Also located here is a D.A.R. boulder with a bronze plaque memorializing the Halifax Resolves.

Drive across U.S. 301 Bypass onto Quankey Avenue, a short, narrow lane that curves sharply to the south. Park where the pavement ends.

This short street bears the name of the nearby creek where most of Cornwallis's soldiers camped during their stay here. The name also preserved the memory of a plantation that stood in the vicinity during Revolutionary War times. Quankey Place was the plantation of Colonel Nicholas Long (1728–98), who represented Halifax County in the First, Second, and Third Provincial Congresses. After that, Long turned his attention to the military affairs of North Carolina. In May 1776, the Continental Congress appointed him deputy quartermaster under General George Washington.

Leave your vehicle and walk across the railroad tracks, taking care to watch for the speeding Amtrak trains that pass by here on their north-south route. Walk several hundred yards in the field on the western side of the tracks. To the right in a clearing shaded by cedars is a single marked grave in an ancient cemetery. Buried here is Mary Montfort Jones, the three-year-old daughter of Willie and Mary Jones.

Just south of the cemetery in a forested thicket are the remnants of "The Grove," the magnificent plantation house of Willie Jones (1741–1801). Now owned by the state, the three-acre site contains the crumbling chimney and foundation bricks from the two-story house that was once an eastern North Carolina showplace. A cluster of massive oak trees that once surrounded the mansion gave their name to the structure. State officials have given consideration to rebuilding the house, but the cost of such a project has proven prohibitive.

More important than the house itself were the people who lived in it during the American Revolution. Willie Jones was one of the greatest Patriots of his day. Born into an aristocratic family, he was educated at Eton College in England after spending his youth in Northampton County, located on the Virginia border just north of Halifax County. Upon his return to North Carolina, he built "The Grove" with timbers from his family's old home, many of which had been transported from England.

Upon the departure of Royal Governor William Tryon from North Carolina in 1771, Willie Jones's allegiance began to shift to the American cause. He was subsequently elected to all five Provincial Congresses, where he established himself as a champion of democracy and states' rights. When the Fifth Provincial Congress convened in 1776, Jones was appointed to the committee that was to draft the first state constitution. Historians believe he was the chief author of the document.

Throughout the war, Jones served in the general assembly and was one of the leading statesmen in North Carolina. He then went on to serve one term in the Continental Congress. Jones was opposed to the Constitution in its original form because it lacked a bill of rights. He noted his opposition thus: "For my part, I would rather be eighteen years out of the Union than adopt it in its present defective form."

A long-enduring but oft-challenged tradition in North Carolina maintains that America's first naval hero received his last name from Willie Jones. According to the legend, a young Scottish sailor made his way to Halifax in 1775 after a checkered career at sea. Known at the time as John Paul, he made the acquaintance of Willie Jones, who befriended him and opened his home. Greatly impressed with his guest, Willie Jones recommended to Joseph Hewes that the young man be given a commission in the Continental Navy, to which Hewes agreed. When the time came for the young lieutenant to go to sea to fight for American independence, he served under the name John Paul Jones. As the story goes, he selected his new name to express his gratitude to Willie Jones. The newly christened John Paul Jones then proceeded to sail into history. His famous war cry—"I have not yet begun to fight"—remains one of the most famous statements of the Revolutionary War.

An avid sportsman, Willie Jones built a racetrack near his home. The estate acquired a reputation as a social center and a place of hospitality. In addition to the famous naval hero, "The Grove" hosted many other notables, among them George Washington and the Marquis de Lafayette.

Among the less welcome guests were Cornwallis and Tarleton, who were "entertained" at the plantation during their stay in Halifax. Mrs. Willie Jones, the daughter of Joseph Montfort, could not refrain from baiting Tarleton. The feisty cavalry leader, still smarting from a severe slash on his hand inflicted by Colonel William Washington at Cowpens, used the occasion to once again demean his hated adversary. After listening to Tarleton describe Washington as an illiterate fellow who could hardly write his name,

Mrs. Jones retorted, "Colonel, you ought to know better, for you bear on your person proof that he knows very well how to make his mark." Tarleton's response was not recorded.

Return to the junction of Quankey Avenue and U.S. 301 Bypass. If you care to see the state historical markers commemorating several sites and events already covered on this tour (the Masonic lodge, Cornwallis's visit, the creation of the state constitution), turn left and proceed north. Otherwise, turn right, leave Halifax via U.S. 301, and proceed south for 11.9 miles to Enfield.

This venerable town served as the county seat of Edgecombe County from 1745 until 1759, when Halifax County was established. Although few tangible reminders of Enfield's long history survive today, two state historical markers on McDaniel Street (U.S. 301) honor significant sites.

One marker notes that the town was the site of the famous Enfield Riot, which took place on May 14, 1759. Some historians consider this incident the forerunner of the Regulator movement and the spark that ignited the drive for independence. Dissatisfaction among area citizens over illegal fees, corruption, and excessive taxes reached a boiling point that day. When some of the citizens behaved "riotously," Royal Governor Arthur Dobbs had several of their number jailed. Their friends and neighbors, further angered by the imprisonment, broke into the jail and released the protestors.

The second marker, located at the corner of McDaniel and East Franklin Streets, honors John Branch, Jr., a distinguished American statesman. To reach his family's historic home, continue south on U.S. 301 for one block to N.C. 481. Turn right on N.C. 481 and follow it through downtown Enfield, where it becomes Whitfield Street. Continue four blocks on Whitfield.

Located at 404 Whitfield, "The Cellar," as the beautifully restored, two-story home has long been known, was constructed around 1800 by John Branch, Sr., a wealthy landowner, sheriff, and local hero. The elder Branch won celebrity during the Revolutionary War because of his ability to identify and round up Tories. When he died, he left the home to his son Joseph, who had served the American cause as a major of the militia.

When his tour of North Carolina brought him to Enfield in 1825, Lafayette was the guest of Joseph Branch at "The Cellar" and addressed the local citizens from the balcony.

"The Cellar" at Enfield

Retrace your route to the intersection with U.S. 301. Proceed east across the intersection onto S.R. 1003 and follow it for 4.3 miles to S.R. 1100. Turn right, drive 12 miles to N.C. 125, turn right again, and proceed 2.4 miles south to the state historical marker for James Hogun, one of North Carolina's lesser-known Revolutionary War heroes. His home stood sixty yards east of the marker.

When tensions began to heighten between the American colonies and Great Britain, Hogun emerged as a political and military leader. As commander of the Seventh North Carolina Continental Line, he joined General Washington in July 1777 during the campaign in the North. At the Battle of Germantown, Hogun was cited for "distinguished intrepidity."

In December 1778, Hogun and his command were assigned to Philadelphia at the request of Major General Benedict Arnold, the commander of the city. Early the next year, North Carolina was authorized by the Continental Congress to name two brigadier generals. Hogun and Jethro Sumner were selected. (For more information about Sumner, see The Statehood Tour, pages 444–45.) These two men joined Robert Howe, Francis Nash, and James Moore as the only men from North Carolina to serve as generals in the Continental Army.

Soon after his promotion, Hogun succeeded Arnold as commandant of Philadelphia. In November 1779, he was forced to relinquish that post when he was called to reinforce the beleaguered Continental forces at Charleston, South Carolina. When General Benjamin Lincoln surrendered the port city to the British on May 12, 1780, Hogun was incarcerated at Haddrel's Point near Sullivan's Island. (For more information on General Lincoln, see The Tide Turns Tour, page 270.)

During his confinement, Hogun was offered a parole by British authorities, but he refused, choosing instead to remain in prison with his half-starved soldiers. For the remaining six months of his life, the general attempted to lift morale and maintain discipline. While enduring the same hardships as his men, he fell ill. Hogun died on January 4, 1781, and was buried in an unmarked grave.

Turn around near the historical marker and proceed north for 6 miles on N.C. 125 to its merger with U.S. 258. Go north on U.S. 258 as it passes through Scotland Neck. After 2 miles, you'll notice a state historical marker

for Whitmel Hill. To visit the grave of this Revolutionary War leader, park at Old Trinity Episcopal Church, located adjacent to the marker.

Hill (1743–97) was laid to rest in this expansive, gardenlike church cemetery after a life of distinguished service to North Carolina and America. Born into a wealthy family in nearby Bertie County, he received an excellent education, graduating from the University of Pennsylvania.

Devoted to the American cause from the outset of the Revolutionary War, Hill, like many of his compatriots, divided his time between military duties and legislative service. His patriotic activities were a source of great irritation to area Loyalists. As a result, Hill lived under the threat of assassination during the summer of 1777. His timely discovery of a Tory plot to kill the leaders of the Revolution in North Carolina enabled Governor Richard Caswell to foil the plan and arrest the desperate Loyalists.

Hill began a three-year stint in the Continental Congress in 1778. An avid horseman, he was proud of both his skill as a rider and the speedy animals he owned. In an April 1779 letter to Thomas Burke, his fellow

North Carolina congressman and roommate in Philadelphia, Hill boasted that he had made the 350-mile journey home in seven and a half days, "a ride scarcely performed before in so short a time."

From the church, drive south on U.S. 258. After approximately 9 miles, you will enter Edgecombe County. Continue south on U.S. 258 for 10.8 miles to U.S. 64 at Princeville. Turn right and follow U.S. 64 Business/ N.C. 33 for 1.5 miles to Tarboro, the seat of Edgecombe County. Upon reaching the town, U.S. 64 Business/N.C. 33 becomes Main Street.

Among the several historical markers on Main Street related to the Revolution is one that calls attention to the Tarboro Town Common, a sixteen-acre, multiblock public green bounded by Albemarle Avenue, Wilson Street, Park Avenue, and Panola Street. Park nearby and walk to this historic area.

Created by the same legislative act that established Tarboro in 1760, the common covers three tree-shaded blocks. More than two centuries later, the well-maintained grounds lend beauty and a feeling of spaciousness to the town that has grown up around them. Located on Tarboro Town Common is a pin oak brought from George Washington's home at Mount Vernon. It was planted here by the D.A.R. in 1925 as a memorial to the president's visit to Tarboro on April 18, 1791.

A nearby state historical marker commemorates the night Washington spent in town. "This place," the great man recorded in his diary on the subject of Tarboro, "is less than Halifax, but more lively and thriving;—it is situated on Tar River which goes into Pamplico Sound and is crossed at the Town by a means of a bridge a great height from the water. We were recd. at this place by as good a salute as could be given by one piece of artillery."

From the Tarboro Town Common, walk two blocks north on Main Street to Bridgers Street and turn right. Located at 130 Bridgers is the Blount-Bridgers House, also known as "The Grove." Restored to its original elegance in recent years, the two-story frame mansion was constructed in the late eighteenth or early nineteenth century for Thomas Blount.

Blount (1759–1812) was a member of a famous eastern North Carolina family that produced seven sons who distinguished themselves in the Revolutionary War era. His brother William (see The Albemarle Tour, page 23) was one of the North Carolinians who signed the Constitution. Like his brother Reading (see The Coastal Rivers Tour, page 62), Thomas Blount served in the fight for American independence. While a lieutenant in the Fifth North Carolina Regiment, he was captured and imprisoned in England.

"The Grove," Blount-Bridgers House

Following the war, the state appointed him major general of the militia. With the return to peace, Blount resumed his participation in the lucrative family mercantile and shipping enterprise, based in Washington, North Carolina. The Blounts' business, one of the largest in the state, brought Thomas in contact with one of his former comrades in arms, General Jethro Sumner. In 1796, Sumner's daughter, Jackie Mary, became Blount's wife.

Blount gave much of his postwar life to the establishment of the new state and nation. In 1793, he began the first of his six terms in the United States Congress.

Now owned by the town of Tarboro, the Blount-Bridgers House is open to the public. There is no admission charge.

Return to the junction of Bridgers and Main. Turn left and walk seven blocks to St. James Street in downtown Tarboro. A state historical marker here directs visitors to the grave of W. L. Saunders, located four blocks east in the cemetery of historic Calvary Episcopal Church. Turn left on St. James and walk to the cemetery, which covers the yard around the magnificent brick church.

More than a century after his death, William Laurence Saunders (1835–91) remains the most celebrated historian on the subject of colonial North Carolina. A Confederate officer, Saunders served as North Carolina's secretary of state from 1879 until 1892. In 1879, he came across a cache of colonial records in the old arsenal on Capitol Square. This discovery led him on a quest to locate, preserve, and put into book form the colonial records of North Carolina.

Saunders's tireless efforts resulted in the publication of a ten-volume set, *Colonial Records of North Carolina.* Containing 10,982 pages of material and documents covering the period from 1622 to 1776, the massive project was completed in 1890. It has been estimated that Saunders, as editor of the series, has been cited in more footnotes than any other North Carolinian. His tombstone in the Tarboro churchyard reads, in part, "For twenty years he exerted more power in North Carolina than any other man."

Following Saunders's death, another Confederate veteran, Judge Walter

Clark, continued the project by compiling the sixteen-volume *State Records of North Carolina*, which covers the Revolutionary War period through 1790.

Also buried in the churchyard is Mary Sumner Blount, the daughter of General Jethro Sumner and the wife of Lieutenant Thomas Blount.

Return to Main Street. Turn left on Main and go one block to Pitt Street. The commercial building at the southeastern corner of this intersection contains a plaque memorializing George Washington's visit to Tarboro.

Return to your vehicle and proceed north on U.S. 64 Business/N.C. 33. After approximately 7.3 miles, turn right onto S.R. 1252, then drive 4.1 miles north to S.R. 1407. Turn right, proceed 0.8 mile, and turn left on S.R. 1409. Travel north for 1.7 miles to S.R. 1428. Near this junction stood Mount Prospect, a traditional two-story farmhouse that was the home of Exum Lewis, a Revolutionary War soldier. George Washington stopped at Lewis's home in 1791.

Return to the junction with S.R. 1407. Turn right and proceed north for 7.5 miles to Battleboro, located just across the line in Nash County. Established in 1777, the county was named for General Francis Nash, a North Carolina hero killed at the Battle of Germantown. (For more information on Nash, see The Regulator Tour, pages 415–16.)

In Battleboro, S.R. 1407 becomes West Main Street. Follow West Main to U.S. 301 and turn left. After 0.6 mile, you will reach I-95 Business/N.C. 4. Turn right and proceed 0.8 mile to the Bellamy family cemetery, located on the northern side of the highway five hundred feet north of the Bellamy House, which dates from around 1820.

Inside the walled cemetery is the grave of Lieutenant Colonel John Clinch, Jr., an officer in the North Carolina Continental Line. Near the end of the war, Clinch married a daughter of Duncan Lamon, whose bridge is the focus of a stop later in this tour. Clinch's gravestone bears a bronze marker provided by the Sons of the American Revolution.

Continue west on I-95 Business/N.C. 4 for 1.8 miles to N.C. 48. Turn right on N.C. 48 and proceed north for 0.7 mile to the state historical marker for the skirmish at Swift Creek.

At a site several miles west of the marker, Patriot militiamen made a feeble attempt to battle Cornwallis's troops on May 7, 1781, as the British army continued its march north. Untrained and poorly armed, the American forces were no match for Tarleton's dragoons. After suffering a rout at Swift Creek, the Patriots fell back 5 miles north to Fishing Creek, where once again they were swept aside by the experienced British horse soldiers. As Tarleton noted in his journal, "The Americans at Swift creek, and afterwards at Fishing creek, attempted to stop the progress of the advanced guard, but their efforts were baffled, and they were dispenced with some loss."

Turn around near the historical marker and drive south on N.C. 48 for 0.9 mile to Halifax Road (S.R. 1527). Turn right and drive south for 3.9 miles through the town of Dortches to the bridge over Stony Creek.

After he crossed the Tar River in southern Nash County, Cornwallis marched his army north along Halifax Road. When he encountered the waters of Stony Creek, the general decided to camp the army near Hunter's Mill. Grain to feed the British soldiers was ground at the mill. A large, round, bowl-shaped rock can still be found in Stony Creek. Local legend holds that the rock, known as "the Cornwallis Horse Trough," is so named because Cornwallis fed his horse from it.

While Cornwallis was camped here, Robert Beard, a local Tory and a deserter from the American army, met with the British commander. Pursuant to a proclamation by Governor Richard Caswell, Beard was considered an outlaw. As a result of his meeting with Cornwallis, Beard was commissioned as a captain and given the authority to recruit a band of Tories for the British army. Cornwallis also promised Beard a reward of ten guineas for each man active in the American cause whom he could capture.

Tar River, Rocky Mount

A bottle of aged brandy proved to be Beard's undoing. Emboldened by Cornwallis's confidence in him, he led a Tory uprising in Nash County, collected a band of twenty followers, and set out for the home of James Drake on Sandy Creek in the northwestern part of the county. The fifty-four-year-old Drake was a strong Patriot who had earlier ordered Beard to stay away from his home and family. Drake's son, Brittain, was a captain of the local Light Horse Company.

Upon Beard's arrival at the Drake home, a gunfight ensued between the small army of twenty Tories and the two Drake men. Two neighbors who had been visiting the Drakes made their escape to get help. The unfortunate Drakes were wounded and taken prisoner.

In the meantime, Mrs. Drake had prepared some food and brought forth a jug of seventeen-year-old brandy. She invited Beard and his men to refresh themselves before leaving with her captive husband and son. It was her fervent hope that this ploy would buy time for Patriot reinforcements to arrive.

Once the brandy gave out, Beard ordered his men to prepare to leave with the prisoners. In the nick of time, seventy soldiers of the Light Horse Company came riding up. Beard was knocked off his horse and arrested. He was subsequently tried and executed as a traitor.

When you are ready to resume the tour, turn around and proceed north on Halifax Road for 0.1 mile to Hunter Hill Road (S.R. 1604). Turn right and drive east toward Rocky Mount. This street is named for Thomas Hunter (1735–84), a local Patriot who served as a militia officer and as a delegate in the First Provincial Congress. Hunter participated in the skirmish at Swift Creek. His home stood nearby.

Follow Hunter Hill Road for 3.7 miles to N.C. 43/N.C. 48. Turn left, drive 0.2 mile to Battle Park, and turn left on Battle Park Lane.

This municipal park provides a splendid view of the scenic Tar River. A state historical marker and a D.A.R. marker for Donaldson's Tavern are located near the river bridge adjacent to the park. During his tour of North Carolina in February 1825, Lafayette stayed overnight at the tavern, which stood near the marker.

From the park, cross the Tar River via N.C. 43/N.C. 48 and drive south for 1.1 miles to U.S. 301 Business. Turn left on U.S. 301 Business (also known as Hardee Boulevard, for the fast-food chain born here) and go 0.6 mile north to the Tar River bridge. For a good view of the bridge and the river, turn into the parking lot of Rocky Mount's animal shelter, located on the right side of the highway. The tour ends here.

According to some, it was at this river crossing that North Carolinians received the nickname "Tar Heels."

For much of the colonial period, North Carolina led the world in the production and export of naval stores. When Nash County residents learned that Cornwallis's army was making its way toward the county in May 1781, they decided that it would be better to destroy all the naval stores on hand rather than allow them to fall into enemy hands. In advance of the invading army, the tar and pitch were brought to the river and dumped into the dark waters.

When the British soldiers reached the crossing, they pulled off their shoes and stockings, rolled up their breeches, and forded the river. In the process, they stepped into the tar, which greatly impeded their progress. Upon their arrival in Virginia several weeks later, the Redcoats were said to still have a healthy coating of tar on their feet. When someone asked about this, the embarrassed soldiers told of their ordeal in North Carolina. They issued a warning that the rivers down there "flowed tar," and that any one who forded one would get tar on his heels. And so the state's residents got their famous name.

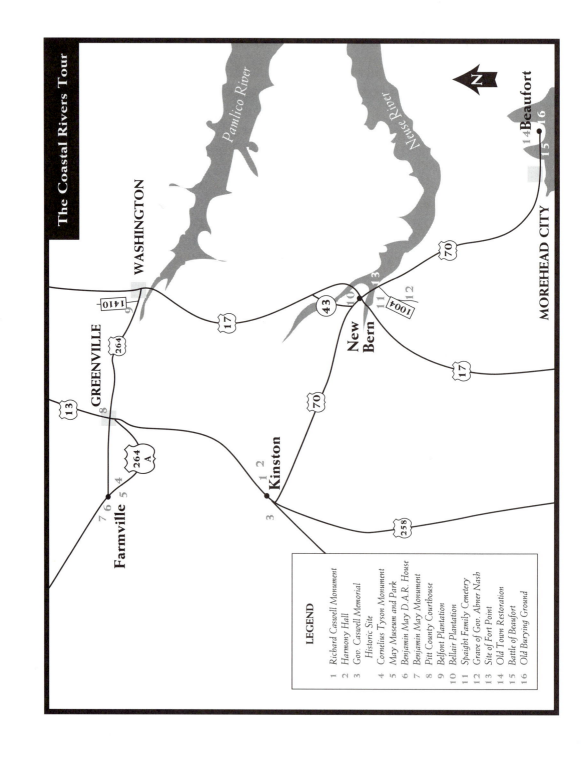

The Coastal Rivers Tour

WASHINGTON

GREENVILLE

Farmville

Kinston

New Bern

MOREHEAD CITY

Beaufort

Pamlico River

Neuse River

N

The Coastal Rivers Tour

This tour begins at Kinston in Lenoir County and makes its way through Pitt, Beaufort, and Craven Counties before ending on the waterfront of Beaufort in Carteret County. Among the highlights are the story of Richard Caswell, Harmony Hall, May Museum and Park, historic Washington, historic New Bern, and historic Beaufort.

Total mileage: approximately 180 miles.

This tour visits a five-county area in the central coastal plain. The area lies around the area's historically significant rivers—the Tar/Pamlico, the Trent, and the Neuse. These scenic rivers were vital transportation and supply arteries during the colonial period, and towns and settlements that subsequently played an important role in the Revolutionary War era are located along their banks.

Among the river communities on the tour are Washington, the original town in the United States named for George Washington; Beaufort, the third-oldest town in North Carolina and the site of what was perhaps the last battle of the American Revolution; and New Bern, the second-oldest town in the state and the capital of North Carolina in Revolutionary War times.

The tour begins at the junction of U.S. 258, U.S. 70 Bypass, and U.S. 70/ U.S. 258 Business on the southern side of Kinston, the seat of Lenoir County.

Formed in 1791 when old Dobbs County was carved up, Lenoir County was named for William Lenoir (1751–1839), a Revolutionary War soldier and statesman whose life is chronicled in The Foothills Tour.

Most of the tour stops in Lenoir County revolve around a Patriot by another name—Richard Caswell. Nathaniel Macon, the foremost public man of North Carolina in the nineteenth century and a young soldier in the

Revolutionary War, called Caswell "one of the most powerful men that ever lived in this or any other country." John Adams of Massachusetts, a leader in the American Revolution and later the second president of the United States, once remarked about Caswell, "He was . . . a model man and true patriot. We always looked to Caswell for North Carolina."

To see the sites related to Caswell, proceed north on U.S. 70/U.S. 258 Business as it crosses the Neuse River into Kinston.

Settled around 1729, the city was incorporated in 1762 under a bill sponsored by Richard Caswell. It was originally called Kingston in honor of King George III. In 1784, with independence firmly secured, area residents dropped the Royal g. Fifty years later, Kinston changed its name to Caswell in honor of its favorite son, but the name was changed back after only a year.

There are lasting legacies of the early Royal influence on the city. As you enter the downtown area, notice that U.S. 70/U.S. 258 Business becomes Queen Street. In the heart of the city, Queen intersects King Street (N.C. 55). Turn right onto King. On the left side of the street near the intersection is the Lenoir County Courthouse. Park nearby and walk to the Caswell Monument on the courthouse grounds. Originally located in the center of a busy downtown street, the tall obelisk suffered extensive damage when it was moved. It was subsequently repaired when it was erected at its present site.

Few men, if any, in North Carolina were more important to the cause of independence than Richard Caswell (1729–89). Born in Maryland, Caswell settled in Kinston as a teenager in 1745. Nine years later, he entered the political life of North Carolina upon his election to the colonial assembly. He served continuously in that body until 1776, when the colony became a state. As a leader in the assembly, Caswell sponsored legislation that promoted trade, colonial defense, and the development of a court system.

During the colonial period, Caswell, a militia officer, honed the military skills that would later prove valuable to the American cause. Royal Governor William Tryon selected him to command the right wing of the army that defeated the Regulators at the Battle of Alamance in May 1771.

In December 1773, as ill feelings against British colonial rule began to grow, John Harvey, the speaker of the colonial assembly, appointed Caswell and eight other men to a committee designed to cooperate with the other colonies in resisting English tyranny. From this august committee came two signers of the Declaration of Independence, three Revolutionary War generals, and three governors.

One of the most respected statesmen in colonial America, Caswell was a leader in all five Provincial Congresses and the first two Continental Congresses. In August 1775, at great risk to his personal safety, he orchestrated the seizure of the provincial treasury by the Provincial Congress, thus choking off the source of revenue for the Royal government in North Carolina.

Six months later, the first Revolutionary War battle in North Carolina took place at Moores Creek Bridge. A brigade commander in the Patriot victory, Caswell emerged as a military hero.

In December 1776, the delegates at the Fifth Provincial Congress elected Caswell the first governor of the independent state of North Carolina. At the same congress, Caswell distinguished himself as one of the authors of the state constitution, which took effect a month later.

He was subsequently reelected to three one-year terms as governor. As North Carolina's chief executive from 1776 to 1779, he successfully defended the state against Indians, Tories, and British regulars, stimulated the state's economy, and helped North Carolina provide more than eighteen thousand officers and men to fight in other states.

Caswell temporarily stepped down as governor in April 1780 due to a term limitation imposed by the constitution he had helped draft. He was promptly elected a major general by the general assembly and given command of the state militia. On August 16, 1780, the North Carolina militia under Caswell suffered humiliation in the disaster that befell the Americans at the Battle of Camden.

After the war, Caswell helped organize the state's finances as comptroller general until he was once again elected governor in 1785. He served until 1787.

From the courthouse, cross King Street to visit Harmony Hall. A nearby state historical marker notes that this two-story frame structure served as the office of James Glasgow, North Carolina's secretary of state, during the Revolutionary War. Because the capital at New Bern was exposed to the threats of British invasion and smallpox, Richard Caswell ordered the state government temporarily transferred to Harmony Hall. All state records were housed in the building until 1781.

Despite its use for governmental affairs, the house was never owned by the state. Caswell owned it until 1782, when he conveyed it to his son Richard, Jr., who had received his baptism under fire as a young soldier at the Battle of Moores Creek Bridge.

Public funding, more than half of it from the North Carolina General Assembly, was used to acquire and restore the structure in the 1980s. Now open to the public, Harmony House is the only extant eighteenth-century building in Kinston. Its interior is attractively furnished with period antiques.

Return to the intersection of King and Queen Streets. Drive nine blocks north on Queen to Vernon Avenue. Turn left and proceed west on Vernon for 2.8 miles to Richard Caswell Grave Road. Turn left to enter the Governor Caswell Memorial State Historic Site. Park in the spacious lot to visit the small brick museum. Dedicated on November 10, 1960, the facility offers a variety of exhibits covering Caswell's storied military and political careers.

Located near the museum is the tree-shaded cemetery containing Caswell's grave.

When he stepped down as the six-term governor of North Carolina, Caswell was suffering from ill health. His postwar administrations had been plagued by personal tragedy—the deaths of two sons, a daughter, his mother, a sister, and two brothers.

Despite the problems that surrounded him in the twilight of his life, North Carolina's elder statesman spent his last two years working for ratification of the United States Constitution. Because of his strong Federalist leanings, he was not a delegate to the 1788 convention at Hillsborough that declined to ratify. While presiding over the state senate at Fayetteville, Caswell suffered a fatal stroke on November 8, 1789. In the same city less than two weeks later, North Carolina voted for ratification.

Caswell's funeral was conducted in Fayetteville. His body was then transported to Kinston, where it was interred at the present site. His son William, the state's adjutant general in the Revolution and an officer in the Continental Army, is also buried here, in an unmarked grave.

Along the highway adjacent to the state historic site and hidden by bushes is a large D.A.R. marker erected in honor of Caswell.

Gravesite of Richard Caswell, Kinston

Return to the intersection of Vernon Avenue and Queen Street. Proceed east across the intersection as Vernon Avenue becomes N.C. 11 and turns north. After 10.7 miles, N.C. 11 enters Pitt County. Continue north for 1.6 miles to the state historical marker located at the junction with S.R. 1103 (Blount Hall Road).

This marker stands ninety yards southeast of the former site of Blount Hall. Built sometime before 1762, the house was part of a six-thousand-acre plantation owned by Jacob Blount (1726–89), the patriarch of one of the most storied families in North Carolina history.

A frequent delegate to the colonial assembly, Blount fought for Royal Governor Tryon and against the Regulators at the Battle of Alamance in 1771. However, as the colony gradually moved toward independence, so did Blount's political philosophy. After serving in the Second, Third, and Fourth Provincial Congresses, he was appointed paymaster of the Second North Carolina Continental Line. Thereafter, he became the paymaster for all state troops.

He was the father of four famous sons: John Gray Blount, William Blount, Thomas Blount, and Reading Blount. Their lives will be detailed at other stops on this tour.

Continue north on N.C. 11. After 3.8 miles, you will reach S.R. 1149, which veers off to the right. Follow S.R. 1149 north as it becomes Lee Street in Ayden. Near the intersection of Lee and N.C. 102 stands a state historical marker commemorating George Washington's visit to Shadrack Allen's inn, which stood 7 miles east of the current tour stop in rural Pitt County. In his diary, Washington complained about the accommodations, noting that he "lodged at one Allan's . . . a very indifferent house without stabling."

From the marker, proceed west on N.C. 102 through Ayden for 1.6 miles to N.C. 11. Turn right on N.C. 11 and drive north for 5.2 miles. On the northern side of the town of Winterville, turn left onto S.R. 1128 (Davenport Farm Road). This road junctions with U.S. 264 Business/U.S. 13 after 3.6 miles. Turn left and drive west for 5.2 miles to U.S. 264A. Turn right on U.S. 264A. After 3.1 miles, you will pass a roadside monument erected by the D.A.R. in honor of local Revolutionary War Patriot Cornelius Tyson, whose farm was located nearby.

Continue on U.S. 264A (which becomes Wilson Street) for 1.3 miles to

Main Street in Farmville. Turn left and proceed two blocks south to the May Museum and Park, located at 213 South Main.

Housed in a frame structure built in 1870 by James Williams May, the museum displays artifacts from five generations of the May family, beginning with heirlooms from the life and times of Major Benjamin May. May (1736–1808), the son-in-law of Cornelius Tyson, was born in Scotland. He settled just west of Farmville in 1750. A militia officer at the time America declared its independence, he served as major of the Pitt County militia during the war. When the Fifth Provincial Congress convened in Halifax in November 1776 to prepare a state constitution, May was on hand as a delegate from Pitt County. He subsequently fought at the Battle of Guilford Courthouse.

Retrace your route to the intersection of Main and Wilson. Turn left and follow Wilson for 0.7 mile to the Benjamin May D.A.R. Chapter House, one of the few such houses in the South. The local D.A.R. chapter erected the two-story, brick, Georgian-style structure in 1938. Located on the left side of the road, the house is marked by an arched metal entrance gate bearing the chapter name.

Continue west for 0.2 mile to see the stone monument for Benjamin May, located on the left near the junction of Wilson and Church Streets. As noted on the marker, May is buried in a nearby family cemetery.

Return to the intersection of Wilson and Main. Turn left on Main and proceed northeast for 0.7 mile to U.S. 264 Bypass. Turn right on the bypass and drive 11 miles east to U.S. 264/U.S. 13 on the western side of Greenville. Go left on U.S. 264/U.S. 13 (Memorial Drive) and head north for 1.6 miles to Fifth Street (N.C. 43). Turn right on Fifth and proceed east for fourteen blocks to Greene Street in the heart of Greenville.

This street calls to mind the namesake of the county seat of Pitt County. Originally called Martinsborough in honor of Josiah Martin, the last Royal governor of North Carolina, the city was incorporated in 1771. Fifteen years later, the name was changed to honor General Nathanael Greene. The town was known at the outset as Greensville; the modern spelling has evolved over time.

Turn left on Greene Street, proceed north for two blocks, then turn right on East Third Street. The Pitt County Courthouse is located two blocks

Benjamin May Monument, Farmville

ahead. Park near the courthouse.

A marker on the courthouse square, erected by the D.A.R. in 1925, commemorates George Washington's visit to Greenville on Tuesday, April 19, 1791. The president's notation in his diary was not flattering to the city: "[I] dined at a trifling place called Greenville."

The cupola-topped courthouse was built around 1911. Inside, a large bronze tablet on the main floor memorializes an important Revolutionary War–era event in North Carolina. Inscribed on the tablet are the text of the so-called Pitt County Resolves and the names of more than seventy-five local Patriots who signed the document on August 23, 1775.

While the signers did not go so far as to declare their independence—to the contrary, the document paid "all due allegiance to his Majesty King George the Third"—their language hinted at the coming conflict with Great Britain: "We do absolutely believe that neither the parliament of Great Britain, nor any member or constituent branch thereof, have a right to impose taxes upon their colonies to regulate the internal policy thereof, and that all attempts, by fraud or force, to establish and exercise such claims and powers are violations of the peace and security of the people, and ought to be resisted to the utmost."

Near the tablet hangs a portrait of the man for whom the county was named, William Pitt, earl of Chatham (1708–78). As Great Britain's secretary of state, Pitt managed the successful war effort against France in the French and Indian War. But during the American Revolution, he was a vocal opponent of the British war against the colonies.

From the courthouse, proceed east for one block on Third Street, turn right onto Cotanche Street, and drive three blocks to where it merges with Charles Boulevard. Follow Charles south for four blocks to U.S. 264 Business (Tenth Street). Turn left and go 1.7 miles to Greenville Boulevard. Drive north on Greenville Boulevard for 1.9 miles to U.S. 264/N.C. 33, turn right, and drive east toward Washington. After 11.1 miles, you will enter Beaufort County. An ancient political subdivision of North Carolina, the county dates from 1705. It was named in honor of Henry Somerset, duke of Beaufort, one of the Lords Proprietors of the colony.

Continue east for 0.8 mile to S.R. 1410. Turn left, drive north for 1.1 miles to S.R. 1411, and turn left again. After 0.3 mile on S.R. 1411, you will see a long driveway on the left side of the road.

Located at the end of the 0.5-mile driveway is the manor house of Belfont Plantation, once the estate of Reading Blount, one of North Carolina's Revolutionary War heroes. Not open to the public, the well-maintained, two-and-a-half-story house was constructed in the late eighteenth century. It is dominated by a chimney nineteen feet in width. The chimney opens into four fireplaces and contains four wardrobes, each with an outside window.

Blount built the house as the centerpiece of his five-thousand-acre plantation on the banks of Tranters Creek, which flows into the Tar River just north of Washington. One of the quartet of Blount brothers who etched their names in North Carolina history, Reading established the plantation upon his return home after serving in the Continental Army for the entire war.

Recognized as the most spirited and daring of the Blount brothers, he was only nineteen when he joined the North Carolina Continental Line as a major on May 12, 1776. Over the next seven years, the Continental Army had few officers who exhibited more gallantry and heroism than Reading Blount. At the Battles of Guilford Courthouse and Eutaw Springs, General Nathanael Greene cited Blount for bravery beyond the call of duty. At the latter battle, Blount teamed with several other North Carolina officers to save the day for Greene. The general later wrote, "I was at a loss which most to admire—the gallantry of the officers or the good conduct of their men."

Blount died at his plantation at the age of fifty and was buried in a cemetery near the mansion.

Retrace your route to the junction of S.R. 1410 and U.S. 264. Turn left onto U.S. 264 and drive 5.9 miles to U.S. 17 in Washington, the seat of Beaufort County. Turn right on U.S. 17 and drive south to Main Street. Turn left on West Main and proceed into downtown Washington. After two blocks, turn right onto Stewart Parkway. Stop at the municipal park that stretches gracefully along the Washington waterfront.

This vantage point offers a spectacular view of the river that has been the very essence of Washington for more than two centuries. To the west looms the modern highway bridge that crosses the river. West of the bridge, the river is known as the Tar; to the east, it is known as the Pamlico.

Established in 1771 by Colonel James Bonner, a friend of George Washington, the town was originally known as Forks of Tar River. Because of its strategic location upriver from Pamlico Sound, the town of Washington quickly emerged as a vital port during the Revolution.

The Washington waterfront is quiet and peaceful today, but in the days of the Revolution, it was cluttered with wharves and warehouses where vital supplies for the American war effort were off-loaded from sailing vessels. From its founding until the Civil War, Washington rivaled Wilmington for status as the chief port of North Carolina.

Stewart Parkway intersects Bonner Street on the waterfront. Turn left on Bonner and proceed one block to Water Street. On the right side of Bonner near the intersection stands a handsome stone monument erected on the two hundredth birthday of this eighteenth-century river town. The attached plaque proudly proclaims that this was the first place in all the nation named for America's most famous hero of the Revolutionary War, General George Washington. Indeed, the little river town was known as Washington as early as 1776, long before the national capital received its name. Since that time, some 422 cities and towns throughout the United States have taken the same name.

When local residents began to refer to their home as "the Original Washington," there came challenges from Washingtons in other states, particularly those in Virginia and Georgia. To authenticate the claim of the town of his birth, United States congressman Herbert C. Bonner (1891–1965) went to the Post Office Department. Records in the postal archives confirmed that Washington, North Carolina, was indeed the rightful owner of the honor. Subsequently, the George Washington Bicentennial Commission agreed that the town in North Carolina is the original.

In one of the ironies of early American history, the first president of the United States toured North Carolina but neglected to visit the first town named in his honor. When he planned his 1791 visit, George Washington had two possible routes from Petersburg, Virginia, to Charleston, South Carolina. The longer of the two—via Edenton and Washington—stretched 504 miles. The president selected the other route—via Halifax, Greenville, and Wilmington—which was 44 miles shorter.

From the junction of Bonner and Water Streets, proceed two blocks north on Bonner to East Main Street. At least three Revolutionary War officers are buried in the cemetery at St. Peter's Episcopal Church, located at the northeastern corner of the intersection. The grave marker of James Bonner, an officer in the Revolutionary War, notes that he was the town's founder. The remains of Nathan Keais, a captain in the Continental Army, and John Bonner, an officer in the Continental Navy, also lie at St. Peter's.

Turn left on East Main and go one block. A state historical marker at the corner of Main and Market Streets commemorates the site where the home of John Gray Blount (1752–1833) once stood.

John Gray Blount's three brothers—William, Thomas, and Reading—all served with distinction as officers in the North Carolina Continental Line during the Revolution. When Washington was in its infancy, John, William, and Thomas were instrumental in developing it as a river port. Their vast mercantile and shipping enterprises included a massive complex of warehouses, riverboats, and sailing vessels that once lined the waterfront just south of the current tour stop.

After the war, the brothers played important political roles in the state and nation. Phenomenally successful in their business enterprises, they were among the largest landowners in American history. Their enormous holdings stretched from the Atlantic Ocean to the Mississippi River.

Turn right on Market Street and proceed to the old Beaufort County Courthouse, located at the corner of Market and East Second.

Constructed in 1786, this square, two-story, brick structure with Georgian and Federal elements is not only one of the oldest buildings in Washington but also one of the oldest public edifices in the nation. Listed on the National Register of Historic Places, the old courthouse has been used as a library and a public assembly hall since the construction of a new courthouse facility.

Atop the old courthouse is a famous clock with roots in the American Revolution. During the war, the seat of Beaufort County was the town of Bath, located 11 miles to the east. The clock was purchased for the courthouse to be built in Bath, but when the general assembly voted in 1785 to move the county seat to Washington, the four-sided timepiece was shipped to the current tour stop. Two centuries later, it ticks on.

Turn left onto East Second Street, follow it for five blocks to U.S. 17,

Former Beaufort County Courthouse with its Revolutionary-era clock

and turn left again, heading south out of Washington. After 13.2 miles, you will enter Craven County, another ancient political subdivision. Created in 1705, the county took its name seven years later from William, earl of Craven, one of the Lords Proprietors.

Continue south on U.S. 17 for 11.1 miles to N.C. 43. Turn right onto N.C. 43 and proceed 7 miles to Bellair, a spectacular, three-story, eighteenth-century plantation house located on the left.

Open to the public on a limited basis, the stately mansion, built around 1790, is one of the few brick houses of its day still surviving in North Carolina. It stands on a plantation once owned by Richard Dobbs Spaight, one of the state's signers of the Constitution. More information on Spaight is offered later in this tour.

Continue east on N.C. 43 for 2 miles to N.C. 55/U.S. 70. Turn left and follow N.C. 55/U.S. 70 for 4.5 miles into historic New Bern, where the road becomes Neuse Boulevard, then Broad Street. At the intersection of Broad and Front Streets, turn right, then go two blocks to the entrance of Union Point Park, located on the left. Turn into the shaded, serene waterfront park, which affords a magnificent view of the confluence of the Neuse and Trent Rivers.

These two great rivers were the reason why, in 1710, New Bern was settled as North Carolina's second town. As the colony grew over the next sixty-five years, so did New Bern's political stature and economic importance. When colonial days gave way to revolutionary fervor, the town was at the center of the transition. In 1775, while it served as North Carolina's colonial capital, it was the site of the first provincial congress convened in America in defiance of the Crown.

Now, more than two centuries later, New Bern survives as one of America's most picturesque cities with an eighteenth-century flavor. Gracing its streets—laid out by John Lawson more than 280 years ago—are well-preserved buildings and homes, prominently marked historic sites, and other reminders of the time when New Bern played a prominent role in North Carolina's evolution from a Royal colony to an independent state.

To enjoy the Revolutionary War history of this magnificently preserved city, turn around at Union Point Park and retrace your route north on Front Street for one block to Pollock Street. Turn left and park in the 300 block of Pollock for a brief walking tour in the heart of downtown New Bern.

Adjacent to New Bern City Hall, located at the northwestern corner of Pollock and Craven, stands a larger-than-life bust of Baron Christophe DeGraffenried. It was DeGraffenried, a land speculator from Bern, Switzerland, who spearheaded the efforts that led to the settlement of New Bern.

Near the DeGraffenried bust is a memorial plaque honoring James Davis (1721–85), one of the many influential figures who called New Bern home during the American Revolution. In 1749, Davis accepted a post as public printer of North Carolina, an office he would hold for thirty-three years. When he set up his print shop on Pollock Street, he became the first printer in the state. He not only produced the first book printed in North Carolina but also published the *North Carolina Gazette*, the colony's first newspaper.

From the beginning of the war, Davis sided with the colonies. He used the *Gazette* to espouse independence until wartime difficulties forced him to cease publication in 1778. An active participant in the political arena, he served as a delegate to the Provincial Congresses, as a member of the Council of Safety and the Council of State, and as a judge of the Admiralty Court. His son was killed in action while fighting for the American cause.

Walk west on Pollock Street to Christ Episcopal Church. Constructed in 1875, this stately Gothic Revival edifice stands on the foundation of the parish's original church, King's Chapel, which dated from 1750.

An incident at the church during the Revolutionary War revealed the divided loyalties of the local citizens. One Sunday, as was his custom, James Reed, the rector at King's Chapel, offered a prayer for King George III. Meanwhile, outside the church, young boys, urged on by their Patriot parents, pounded drums and shouted, "Off with his head!"

President George Washington worshiped at the church when he visited New Bern in 1791.

Open to the public on weekdays, the existing church houses interesting artifacts from the colonial period. A silver communion service was given to the church by King George II in 1752, eight years before his death. Each of the pieces bears the royal arms of Great Britain. The communion service nearly became a casualty of the Revolutionary War when Royal Governor

Josiah Martin unsuccessfully attempted to take it with him upon his flight from New Bern in 1775. A Bible and a *Book of Common Prayer*, both printed in the eighteenth century, were also gifts from King George II.

Some of the city's oldest marked graves are located in the churchyard. A marble slab marks the resting place of the Reverend James Reed. Among the early parishioners believed to be buried here is Isaac Edwards, the private secretary and aide-de-camp of Governor Tryon. Edwards died in New Bern in 1775 after serving in the First Provincial Congress. Amid the graves is a large metal marker that details the history of the church.

Embedded in the sidewalk just outside the iron fence enclosing the churchyard is the cannon from the *Lady Blessington*. A D.A.R. plaque notes that the big gun was captured from the British ship after a ferocious fight during

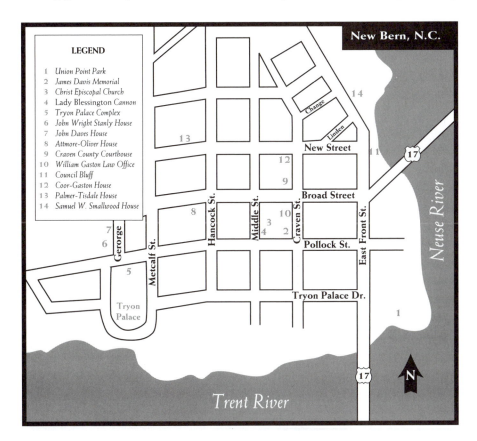

LEGEND

1 Union Point Park
2 James Davis Memorial
3 Christ Episcopal Church
4 Lady Blessington *Cannon*
5 Tryon Palace Complex
6 John Wright Stanly House
7 John Daves House
8 Attmore-Oliver House
9 Craven County Courthouse
10 William Gaston Law Office
11 Council Bluff
12 Coor-Gaston House
13 Palmer-Tisdale House
14 Samuel W. Smallwood House

New Bern, N.C.

the Revolutionary War. The victor was an armed privateer owned by New Bern's John Wright Stanly, whose home is a subsequent stop on this tour. A marble slab in the churchyard honors this remarkable Patriot.

Continue west on Pollock Street for three blocks to George Street. Here, on the southern side of Pollock, stands the magnificent showplace of New Bern—Tryon Palace.

To purchase an admission ticket to the reconstructed palace once described as "the finest house of government in colonial America," enter the visitor center, located on the opposite side of Pollock; an audiovisual orientation program is offered at the center.

Massive iron gates open to an oak-shaded cobblestone walkway leading to the front entrance hall, which has marble floors and a wide staircase of mahogany and pegged walnut. Each room of the ornate structure is filled with period antiques from the time when North Carolina was transformed from a Royal colony to an independent state.

The original palace was a dream realized by William Tryon. Upon his arrival in North Carolina on October 10, 1764, as the colony's newly appointed lieutenant governor, Tryon was in high spirits, the result of assurances that the aged Royal governor, Arthur Dobbs, was set to relinquish his office and retire to his native Ireland. Tryon's optimism turned to dismay when he called upon Governor Dobbs at Brunswick Town and found the seventy-four-year-old living in marital bliss with his new wife, fifteen-year-old Justina Davis.

Tryon was thus forced to bide his time. A year passed before the young lieutenant governor, en route to New Bern from Wilmington, was hailed by a messenger with the news that Dobbs had expired in Justina's arms. A day later, Tryon became the colonial governor. One of his first acts was to dispatch a letter to London with the details of Dobbs's death. In the same communique, Tryon notified the Board of Trade that he had chosen New Bern as the new colonial capital.

On November 8, 1765, the colonial assembly convened in New Bern. The delegates were presented with a request from Tryon for the construction of a public edifice to serve as the house of the colonial government and the governor's residence. Legislators supported the request and appropriated the staggering sum of fifteen thousand pounds sterling for the pur-

Tryon Palace, New Bern

chase of the land and the construction of the government house and related buildings.

Actually, Tryon had laid the groundwork for the palace before he ever set foot in North Carolina. On his voyage from England, the lieutenant governor had brought along John Hawks, one of the most respected and talented architects in Europe.

Tryon's decisions to build a palace and to locate the capital in the eastern part of the colony drew the ire of the people in the North Carolina back country. To fund construction of the palace, the colonial government was forced to borrow money and to impose unpopular taxes. The furor over Tryon's policies fueled the growth of the Regulator movement, which culminated in bloodshed at the Battle of Alamance. (For a more detailed account of the Regulator movement, see The Regulator Tour, pages 403–6.)

Nonetheless, Tryon had his way. By late 1770, his luxurious masterpiece was completed. On December 5, an elaborate gala—complete with blazing artillery, fireworks, and band music—was held to celebrate the opening of the palace. For the first time in the American colonies, a Royal governor lived in and administered the government from the same building.

Tryon and his family were to enjoy their extravagant home for less than a year. Not long after the governor led troops in the bloody clash with the Regulators on May 16, 1771, he received a welcome appointment as the new Royal governor of New York.

His successor in North Carolina, Josiah Martin, received a hero's welcome when he came to New Bern on August 11. His arrival would be the happiest moment of his four-year tenure in the city.

After Martin, his wife, and their six children moved into the palace, the governor spent inordinate amounts of time and money in acquiring lavish furnishings. This came during a period when the colony was rushing headlong toward a formal break with Great Britain. By May 31, 1775, Martin came to understand that he was in an untenable position as a representative of the Crown and fled New Bern with his family.

Following Martin's exodus, the palace suffered from neglect until Richard Caswell, the first governor of the new state, took office on January 15, 1777. Caswell promptly sought and received legislative authority to restore the buildings and grounds to their original grandeur.

In 1780, Abner Nash, a local statesman, succeeded Caswell as governor. The almost constant threat of a British invasion of New Bern made it difficult for Nash to use the palace. During this same period, most of the eight tons of lead used in its construction was removed and melted into musket balls for use in the American war effort.

At the close of the war, the palace faced an uncertain future. After 1781, it no longer served as the state Capitol and the governor's residence, as legislators succumbed to pressure to select a location farther west for the site of the capital.

As North Carolina wrestled with the decision as to whether to join the union of states, the palace was repeatedly violated by vandals. Vagrants and beggars slept where the affairs of colony and state had once been managed. The worst desecration came when a bayonet fight among drunks left one of their number dead on the floor.

However, a few bright moments were yet to come. When President Washington visited town in 1791, he was feted with a grand ball at the palace.

Washington described the structure as a "good brick building now hastening to Ruin." A year after Washington's visit, Richard Dobbs Spaight, another local man elected governor, used the palace as the backdrop for his inauguration. In 1794, the state legislature met in the building for the final time.

Over the next four years, the palace housed New Bern Academy. An accidental fire on the night of February 27, 1798, reduced the main building and its eastern wing to ruins.

For the next 150 years, the surviving western wing bore little resemblance to the dignified palace of old.

In the 1930s, mounting interest in a project to reconstruct the palace led Governor Greg Cherry to establish the Tryon Palace Commission. Aided by a legislative appropriation and the philanthropy of Maude Moore Latham (who had played in the palace ruins as a child), the commission hired noted Boston architect William G. Perry to draw the plans for the ambitious project. Perry benefited immeasurably from original copies of John Hawks's palace drawings.

The $3.5 million reconstruction project began in 1953. Since its completion, more than $5 million in period antiques and furnishings have been added to re-create the atmosphere of the palace when it was the Capitol.

Visitors can see virtually every nook and cranny of the forty-room brick building. A magnificent replica, the reconstructed palace has stood longer than its historic predecessor.

Flanking the main building and connected to it by circular colonnades are the two wings. The eastern wing re-creates the colonial kitchen of the original complex. The western wing, 85 percent of its original brickwork intact, survives as the only remnant of the original palace. It has been meticulously restored as a stable, carriage house, and granary.

Adorning the well-landscaped backyard of the complex are a half-dozen gardens, the most interesting of which is the Maude Moore Latham Garden. This formal garden of clipped dwarf yaupon is said to be similar to the English garden of Governor Tryon's time.

From Tryon Palace, walk north on George Street to the John Wright Stanly House, which is open to the public courtesy of the Tryon Palace Commission. Constructed between 1779 and 1793, the striking, two-story

John Wright Stanly House, New Bern

frame house originally stood at New and Middle Streets. It was moved west on New Street to house the New Bern Library in 1932, then was relocated to the present site when it was acquired by the Tryon Palace Commission in 1966.

This is considered one of the nation's most elegant late Georgian homes. But even more interesting than the fine architectural detail and craftsmanship in the John Wright Stanly House are the people who resided and visited here during the war.

John Wright Stanly (1742–89), the man for whom the house was constructed, was an unsung hero of the American Revolution. Ironically, he traced his lineage to King Edward I. His family coat of arms bore the inscription "Always Loyal."

Born in Virginia, Stanly settled in New Bern quite by accident. The owner of a successful rum, rope, and salt export business in Kingston, Jamaica, he was sailing along the North Carolina coast in 1770 when his ship grounded after encountering a terrible storm in the Graveyard of the Atlantic. Once ashore, Stanly was invited by an acquaintance he had made aboard ship to accompany him to his home in New Bern. That acquaintance was young John Sitgreaves.

Sitgreaves and his family and friends provided the visiting gentleman a warm welcome, even inviting him to attend a ball at Tryon Palace. There, Stanly saw twenty-year-old Ann Cogdell leading a dance with Governor Josiah Martin. Taken by the beauty of the eldest daughter of future Patriot Richard Cogdell, Stanly asked for an introduction. The couple soon fell in love. On June 24, 1773, they were married by the Reverend James Reed.

Stanly settled in New Bern, where he promptly emerged as a leading shipowner and trader with the West Indies. His success led him to open a branch office in Philadelphia. Noted North Carolina jurist William Gaston (whose home is visited later in this tour), once wrote of Stanly, "He was a merchant of the greatest enterprise and most extensive business ever known in this state."

Following the Boston Tea Party and the sanctions imposed by Parliament upon the people of that city, Stanly led North Carolina in the effort to provide "reliefs [for] the distressed Inhabitants." Accordingly, a ship carrying badly needed provisions and money left New Bern bound for Salem, Massachusetts.

As the winds of war blew, Stanly grew more involved in the preparations. Four days before Christmas 1775, he was appointed to the commission charged with equipping "armed vessels for the protection of the Trade of the Province."

The eventful summer of 1776 found Stanly in Philadelphia, where he not only conducted business affairs at his branch office but maintained a home on Seventh Street. While in Philadelphia, Stanly invited an old friend to his home for dinner. The invitee, Thomas Jefferson, happened to be working on the Declaration of Independence at that time. Following dinner, Jefferson requested "a quiet corner" at which to work and was promptly taken to an upstairs room. When the famous Virginian came back downstairs, he supposedly showed Stanly a draft of the Declaration.

A month after the Declaration was signed, Stanly was granted "Letters of Marque," a quasi-legal document that allowed him to operate as a privateer against enemy shipping. Mindful that the American fighting forces had to be fed, clothed, supplied, and armed if their efforts were to stand any chance of success, he was anxious to do all he could. Stanly thus sought to obtain vital war commodities in two ways—through privateering and through direct trade with allies.

Based at New Bern, his vast fleet of privateers plagued British commerce on the high seas and played a pivotal role in keeping the ports at Ocracoke and Cape Lookout open. Moreover, Stanly instituted trade with France, thereby bringing valuable munitions into North Carolina for delivery to the American armies in the North and South.

When the Patriots' fortunes were at their lowest, Stanly rose to the occasion. Alerted to the suffering of General Washington's troops at Valley Forge during the harsh winter of 1777–78, he redoubled his efforts to get supplies there. After General Horatio Gates and the Americans were dealt a costly setback at Camden in 1780, it was Stanly who stepped forward to replace the supplies lost in the defeat. And when Nathanael Greene inherited the remnants of Gates's destitute army in December 1780, Stanly provided him eighty thousand dollars to help in mounting opposition to Cornwallis.

Throughout the war, Stanly suffered heavy personal losses because of his unwavering patriotism. He lost fourteen ships in the service of the colonies. Recognized by the enemy as one of the leading financiers of the American war effort, he was a marked man who lived in constant peril. His life was spared on Sunday, August 20, 1781, only because he was away from New Bern when Tory raiders came looking for him. That same day, Stanly's ships in port, his wharves, and the home he lived in at the time were burned.

Many distinguished men of the American Revolution were guests of John Wright Stanly in New Bern. Major General Nathanael Greene and the Marquis de Lafayette called on him. In May 1786, Samuel Spencer, Samuel Ashe, and John Williams—the first three judges appointed under the state constitution—were Stanly's dinner guests. At the time, they were holding court in New Bern. It was during this session that they heard the case of *Bayard v. Singleton*. Their decision was a landmark in American jurisprudence because it marked the first time that a court by written record ruled that a law was unconstitutional. (For more on Spencer, see The Southern Piedmont Tour, pages 158–59. For more on Ashe, see The Scottish Dilemma Tour, pages 113–14. For more on Williams, see The Statehood Tour, pages 425–456.)

On Wednesday, May 20, 1791, President Washington arrived in New Bern. During his two-day stay, the Stanly mansion served as his headquarters. Rarely one to speak flatteringly of accommodations in North Carolina, the president called the Stanly house "exceedingly good lodgings." Household items used by Washington during his visit are sometimes exhibited at the house today.

John Wright Stanly died tragically at the age of forty-seven, one of the victims of a yellow-fever epidemic that swept through New Bern. His wife succumbed to the disease thirty-two days later.

Their oldest son, also named John, was elected to the United States House of Representatives in 1800 at the age of twenty-six. He succeeded his neighbor, Richard Dobbs Spaight, who had decided to return to the state legislature. Relations between Stanly and Spaight—a veteran of the Revolutionary War, a former governor, and a signer of the Constitution—became strained to the point that Spaight publicly called Stanly "a dirty scoundrel and liar." The result was one of the most famous duels in American history.

On Sunday afternoon, September 5, 1802, Spaight and Stanly faced each other with pistols in the streets of New Bern. On the fourth round of fire, Spaight went down with a wound in the right side. Twenty-three hours later, the youngest of North Carolina's three signers of the Constitution died. (Spaight's grave is visited later in this tour.)

Ironically, descendants of Richard Dobbs Spaight moved into the John Wright Stanly House in the late nineteenth century. During that time, neighbors reported seeing ghosts in and about the mansion.

Located just north of the Stanly mansion at 313 George Street is the Major John Daves House. Erected around 1770, the dwelling is an important example of an eighteenth-century Georgian-style cottage. Daves (1748–1804) came to New Bern when he was two years old. Except for absences while in the service of his country, he spent the rest of his life here.

North Carolina produced few junior officers who were more distinguished or courageous than Daves. His lengthy record in the Continental Army included service on numerous battlefields: Norfolk, Sullivan's Island, Brandywine, Germantown, Valley Forge, Monmouth, Morristown, Stony Point, and Eutaw Springs.

Follow George Street north for one block to Broad Street. Turn right and proceed east on Broad to Metcalf Street. Cross Metcalf. Located at 513 Broad is the Attmore-Oliver House Museum, the home of the New Bern Historical Society. Constructed in 1790 and enlarged in 1834, the magnificent frame house is a veritable treasure trove of artifacts from the long history of this river town.

Just west of the museum, near the intersection of Broad and Hancock Streets, a state historical marker stands near where Congressman Stanly killed Congressman Spaight in their famous duel.

Cross to the northern side of Broad; watch for traffic, as this is one of the busiest thoroughfares in the city. Continue east on Broad for one block to Middle Street, where you'll notice a long row of state historical markers related to the Revolutionary War. These markers lead toward the Craven County Courthouse.

Cross Middle Street and continue on Broad to the courthouse, located at the northwestern corner of Broad and Craven. Along the way, you'll pass the state historical marker for one of the most important events of the American Revolution—North Carolina's First Provincial Congress.

In the aftermath of the Boston Tea Party, a clamor arose throughout the colonies to convene a "continental congress," at which representatives from the colonies from Georgia to New Hampshire could share their concerns about the growing crisis in America. Delegates to the great congress were to be selected by the colonial assemblies. In North Carolina, Royal Governor Josiah Martin decided to delay the opening of the colonial assembly until after the First Continental Congress convened, thereby preventing North Carolina from being represented.

Upon learning of Martin's plan, "Bold" John Harvey, the infuriated speaker of the assembly, set about ensuring that a convention would be held independent of the governor. Invitations to send delegates to the extralegal assembly were dispatched to all parts of North Carolina. In response, thirty counties and four towns elected representatives.

The First Provincial Congress was called to order in New Bern by John Harvey on August 25, 1774, much to the consternation of Josiah Martin. Although the session lasted but three days, it pushed North Carolina into a role as one of the leaders of the revolutionary movement.

Delegates expressed their outrage at the "illegal and oppressive" taxation by Parliament and endorsed an economic boycott of the mother country. They offered enthusiastic support for a continental congress and elected William Hooper, Joseph Hewes, and Richard Caswell as the men who would represent North Carolina in that body. Before the close of the session, delegates authorized Harvey to convene another provincial congress at his pleasure.

The leading statesmen of North Carolina were of one mind as they departed the first legislative session held in the American colonies in defiance of Royal authority. Their colony would continue to resist the harsh policies of Great Britain and would unite with the other colonies in the coming struggle.

Four additional congresses would be convened to ready the state for war and to establish the framework for the government of the free and independent state of North Carolina.

The striking Craven County Courthouse was built around 1883. On its front lawn rests the Governors' Boulder. This D.A.R. marker memorializes the three New Bernians who served as governor of North Carolina. The graves of all three—Abner Nash, Richard Dobbs Spaight, and Richard Dobbs

Spaight, Jr.—are visited later on this tour.

From the courthouse, walk south on Craven Street to the former law office of Judge William Joseph Gaston, located at 307 Craven.

Gaston (1778–1844), one of North Carolina's most renowned jurists, was born in New Bern during the Revolutionary War. His father, Alexander, was an Irish-born surgeon who served as a medical officer in the British navy before settling in New Bern in the 1760s. From the outset of the Revolution, however, the senior Gaston was an ardent Patriot.

He was also a marked man from the time that he and a band of Patriots—including Abner Nash and Richard Cogdell—seized six pieces of artillery at Tryon Palace on June 23, 1775. In August 1781, when a Tory attack on New Bern appeared imminent, Dr. Gaston, fearing for his life, made preparations to leave town. At the very moment he pushed his rowboat from the wharf, a band of Tories rode up. His wife, Margaret, was on the shore. She threw herself before the raiders and tearfully begged for her husband's life. Responding to her pleas, the Tory captain condemned Gaston as a "rebel," grabbed a rifle, and summarily executed him.

That tragic incident became etched in the memory of William Gaston. "The circumstances of his death, I have so often heard from my weeping mother that I can never forget them," he recalled.

Three years old at the time of the murder, William grew up to become one of the most beloved North Carolinians of all time. A dedicated public servant to the young state and nation, he served in Congress and as a justice of the North Carolina Supreme Court. But his most enduring contribution was North Carolina's state song, "The Old North State," which he wrote in 1840.

Continue south on Craven for a short distance to New Bern City Hall and return to your vehicle. Drive north on Craven to Broad. Turn right and proceed east for one block to Front Street on the Neuse River. Turn left on East Front and go north to New Street. A walkway along the riverfront here marks the site of Council Bluff, where Baron Christophe DeGraffenried's settlers landed in 1710.

Turn left on New Street and drive west for two blocks to the Coor-Gaston House, located at the southwestern corner of New and Craven. Constructed in 1770, this stately, two-story Georgian town house was first owned by

James Coor (1737–95), a naval architect and leader in the state legislature during the Revolutionary War. William Gaston purchased the home in 1819. Today, it serves as the eastern office of the governor of North Carolina.

Continue west on New Street for two blocks to Hancock Street. In the next block, at 520 New, stands the two-story, Georgian-style Palmer-Tisdale House, which dates from the late 1760s. In 1771, the house was purchased by Martin Howard, the chief justice of North Carolina. Howard was forced to sell the property in 1776 because of his allegiance to the Crown.

Proceed one block west on New to George Street. Turn right and drive one block to Queen Street. Northeast of the intersection is the sprawling Cedar Grove Cemetery. For two centuries, the most illustrious citizens of New Bern have been laid to rest here.

Established in 1798 by the wardens of Christ Episcopal Church in response to a yellow-fever epidemic that claimed many citizens, the cemetery took its name from a grove of cedar trees that stood when the first burials took place here in the late eighteenth century. It was deeded to the town of New Bern in 1853. The existing three-part arched gateway on Queen Street and the wall—made from coquina and marl—were added a year later.

The cemetery contains numerous reminders of Revolutionary War personages. Beside the impressive monument for Judge William Gaston are the graves of his patriotic parents. The remains of John Hawks, the supervising architect of Tryon Palace, lie here also. An impressive monument honoring John Daves lists the many battles in which he participated; though Daves was originally interred here, his remains were later removed to Guilford Courthouse National Military Park.

At the intersection of George and Queen, turn right on Queen. After one block, turn right on Johnson Street. Proceed east on Johnson for five blocks to Front Street and turn right.

The Samuel W. Smallwood House, located at 520 East Front, was constructed in the Italianate style in 1885. It is best known for the historic tree in its backyard. That cypress tree, estimated to be upwards of a thousand years old, is one of the twenty trees in the Hall of Fame of American Trees. It is said that Major General Nathanael Greene met under the tree with local Patriots and received pledges of substantial financial assistance from John Wright Stanly and Richard Dobbs Spaight. On his visit to the city in

1791, President Washington requested to see the tree where the American war effort received a significant boost.

Located nearby at the southwestern corner of East Front and Change Streets is a marker where the home of Colonel Joseph Leech (1720–1803) once stood. A businessman in colonial New Bern, Leech served as an officer for Royal Governor Tryon at the Battle of Alamance. But his allegiance, like that of many of his fellow soldiers, shifted as the winds of discontent blew across the colony. During the war, Leech was a political leader in the revolutionary government of North Carolina.

When President Washington visited New Bern, he was welcomed with an address read by Leech, who was mayor at the time. Legend maintains that his daughter, Mary "Polly" Leech (later the wife of Richard Dobbs Spaight), had the first dance with Washington at the ball held in his honor at Tryon Palace. After the ball, Washington is said to have attended a small party at Leech's home.

Drive three blocks south on East Front to U.S. 70. Go south on U.S. 70 as it crosses the Trent River near its confluence with the Neuse. It was the historic New Bern waterfront that provided the stage for two significant celebrations related to the American Revolution.

On Saturday, July 4, 1778, the people of New Bern held the first public celebration of Independence Day in the South and the third of its kind in the thirteen states, after only Philadelphia and Boston. In a letter to Governor Richard Caswell penned on the night of the New Bern celebration, Captain Richard Cogdell reported, "In celebration of this day great numbers of guns have been fired at Stanly's wharf, and Mr. Ellis' ship, three different firings from each from early morning, midday, and evening, and liquor given to the populace." James Davis wrote about the celebration in the July 10, 1778, edition of his newspaper. His report of the event is the oldest extant newspaper account of a July 4 celebration in the former colonies.

New Bern was also the first place in America to hold a public celebration of the birthday of George Washington. It was observed at Frilik's Hotel on February 22, 1796, ten months before Washington's death.

On the other side of the Trent River, U.S. 70 reaches a junction with S.R. 1004. Nearby stand state historical markers for Abner Nash and Richard Dobbs Spaight. To see their grave sites, turn right on S.R. 1004.

It is 2.5 miles to the brick-wall-enclosed Spaight family cemetery, located on the right. Richard Dobbs Spaight (1758–1802), the first native-born governor of the state, was the great-great-nephew of Royal Governor Arthur Dobbs and the son of a colonial official. Born in New Bern, Spaight was orphaned at the age of five. Educated in Scotland and Ireland, he returned to New Bern in 1778 and became a militia officer.

Spaight served as an aide to Major General Richard Caswell at the Battle of Camden. After that disastrous setback, Spaight returned to New Bern. Some months later, Major General Nathanael Greene came to town in desperate need of financial assistance to carry on the war in the South. In response to Greene's pleas, Spaight pledged his personal fortune.

During the final years of the war, Spaight represented New Bern in the state legislature. From 1783 to 1785, he served in the Continental Congress. Declining another term, he chose instead to return to the state legislature, where he was elected speaker of the House of Commons. The Constitutional Convention thrust Spaight back into national affairs. After he affixed his signature to the Constitution, he came home and worked tirelessly for its ratification.

Spaight family cemetery, New Bern

Ill health prevented Spaight from accepting a nomination for the United States Senate in 1789. Three years of rest restored his vigor. At Tryon Palace on December 14, 1792, he was inaugurated for the first of three terms as governor of North Carolina. Voters subsequently elected him to the United States House of Representatives for two terms, beginning in 1798.

After he died from the wound he sustained in his duel with John Stanly in 1802, Spaight was laid to rest here. His grave was desecrated by Union troops in 1862. Soldiers removed his skeleton from its resting place and displayed his skull on a gatepost. They then removed the metal coffin of one of the thirty signers of the Constitution and used it for the body of a fallen comrade.

Among the other notables buried in the well-maintained cemetery are Spaight's wife, his parents, his son, Richard, Jr. (elected governor in 1835), and Colonel Joseph Leech.

Nearby on private property along the banks of the Trent is the grave of Governor Abner Nash. The grave is located at Pembroke, the site of the Nash plantation in the eighteenth century. An early-twentieth-century house by the same name stands just west of the grave.

Nash (1740–86) was born in Virginia. In the early 1760s, he settled in Hillsborough with his younger brother, Francis, one of the two North Carolina generals killed in action during the Revolutionary War. In 1771, Abner Nash moved to New Bern and established Pembroke Plantation. He lived here until the place was burned by British soldiers under Major James H. Craig in 1781.

Nash was one of the state's most devoted Patriots. He served in every Provincial Congress. At the fourth such gathering, it was Nash who authored the resolution that proclaimed North Carolina's support of independence.

Elected the state's second governor in 1780, Nash served at a time when the prospects of American victory in the war were bleak. At great sacrifice to both his health and fortune, he guided the state through those dark times. Frustrated with politics and physically debilitated, he refused another term.

A year later, his state called him back to service as a member of the Continental Congress. Nash was at that post in New York City when he died of consumption in 1786. His remains were originally buried at St. Paul's Church in New York but were subsequently moved to the family vault here.

Retrace your route to the junction of S.R. 1004 and U.S. 70. Proceed south on U.S. 70 for 1 mile to S.R. 1167. Turn left and go one block to S.R. 1113. Turn right on S.R. 1113 and drive 0.1 mile to the state historical marker for Fort Point. Built in 1775–76, Fort Point was a river-side fortification designed to protect New Bern. It stood 0.5 mile east.

From the historical marker, retrace your route to U.S. 70. Turn left and go southeast on U.S. 70. After 17.5 miles, you will enter Carteret County. Formed from Craven County in 1722, the county was named for John Carteret (1690–1763), one of the Lords Proprietors.

It is another 13.8 miles to the intersection with Turner Street in Beaufort. Turn right on Turner, which leads into the heart of the old port city. Settled around 1708, Beaufort is one of the best-preserved colonial towns in America.

It is three blocks on Turner to the Old Town Restoration. Operated by the Beaufort Historical Association, the restoration is a complex of houses, shops, and public buildings that give visitors a flavor of Beaufort in colonial and Revolutionary War times. Guided tours of the buildings are offered on a regular basis.

Two buildings in the complex are of particular interest to visitors interested in the Revolutionary War. Considered by many to be the finest home in Beaufort, the red-frame Joseph Bell House was built in 1767; Bell was the county sheriff and a member of the legislature. Nearby is the Carteret County Courthouse of 1796, which survives as the oldest public building in the county. Displayed inside the structure is a rare, original thirteen-star American flag.

Turner Street junctions with Front Street just south of the restoration complex. Turn right on Front, where you'll find a delightful ensemble of historic houses. At least two dozen homes in town date from the American Revolution or earlier. Most have plaques out front that note their name and date of construction.

Located at 229 Front is the handsome, two-and-a-half-story Easton House, built around 1771. This home was the property of Colonel John Easton, a man involved in what historians have called the last land battle of the Revolutionary War, an event covered at the close of this tour.

Continue on Front to where it dead-ends a block west of the Easton House. Located at 105 Front is the Duncan House, which dates from around 1790. The Duncan House boasts an excellent example of the Beaufort gable roof, a unique architectural feature characteristic of many local homes built during the Revolutionary War period. Unlike the palatial estates in coastal cities like Wilmington and Charleston, the Revolutionary War–era homes in Beaufort are relatively small, tidy, white-frame structures. They reflect Beaufort's proud past as a small but important working seaport.

Turn around and go east on Front for four blocks to the public parking lot on the historic waterfront, where this tour ends. If you have time, you might enjoy a stroll on the boardwalk, which offers a panoramic view of scenic Taylors Creek and the nearby islands of the Rachel Carson National Marine Estuarine Sanctuary. No doubt, you'll see luxurious yachts tied up at the waterfront docks, some of the many pleasure craft that make port at Beaufort every year.

Two centuries ago, the fleet that docked here was vastly different.

Throughout the Revolutionary War, Beaufort remained an open port for the American cause. Heavily armed privateers sailed into and out of the harbor. Each of the ships was commanded by a captain who sailed under a

"Letter of Marque," a quasi-legal document authorizing piracy against British ships. Beaufort was a haven for convoys of ships bringing essential supplies for the war effort from the West Indies, France, and Spain. From Beaufort, the vital imports were transported through rivers, creeks, and sounds to Virginia and points north.

The Beaufort waterfront was the site of what may have been the final land battle of the Revolution.

On April 4, 1782, almost six months after Cornwallis surrendered at Yorktown, several British warships sailed into Beaufort. After the ships dropped anchor, several local citizens sailed out to meet them under a flag of truce. Once aboard, they were promptly arrested.

Over the course of the next ten days, British landing parties raided and pillaged the town. Colonel John Easton mustered a group of defenders, and the two factions did battle during the British forays into the town. Both sides suffered casualties and captured prisoners.

Anxious to drive the invaders away, the townspeople set a number of boats and rafts afire and sent them toward the British fleet. However, the wind shifted before the fiery armada reached its destination.

Finally, after two weeks of conflict, the British ships sailed away on April 17, one day short of the seventh anniversary of the first battle of the American Revolution, at Lexington, Massachusetts.

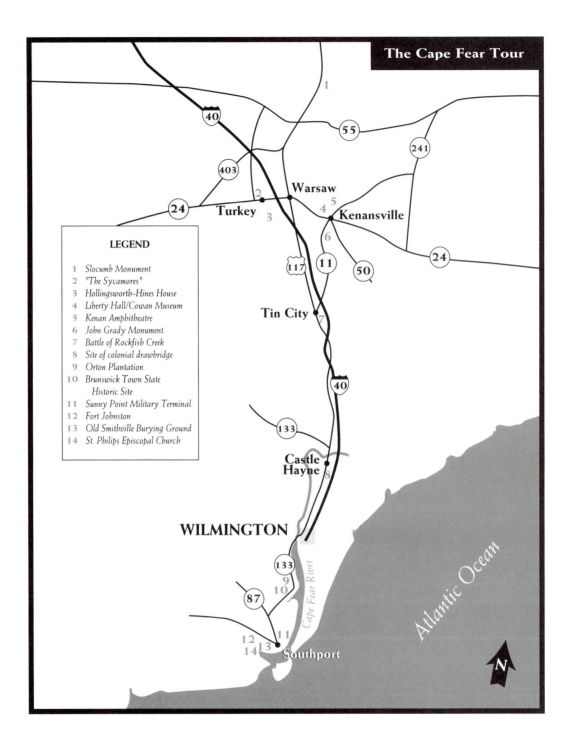

The Cape Fear Tour

LEGEND

1   Slocumb Monument
2   "The Sycamores"
3   Hollingsworth-Hines House
4   Liberty Hall/Cowan Museum
5   Kenan Amphitheatre
6   John Grady Monument
7   Battle of Rockfish Creek
8   Site of colonial drawbridge
9   Orton Plantation
10 Brunswick Town State
      Historic Site
11 Sunny Point Military Terminal
12 Fort Johnston
13 Old Smithville Burying Ground
14 St. Philips Episcopal Church

Warsaw
Turkey
Kenansville
Tin City
Castle Hayne
WILMINGTON
Southport
Cape Fear River
Atlantic Ocean

The Cape Fear Tour

This tour begins near Dudley in southern Wayne County and makes its way through Sampson, Duplin, and New Hanover Counties before ending at Southport in Brunswick County. Among the highlights are the story of Polly Slocumb, the story of Zebulon Hollingsworth, Liberty Hall, the Battle of Rockfish Creek, historic Wilmington, Orton Plantation, Brunswick Town State Historic Site, and historic Southport.

Total mileage: approximately 134 miles.

This tour makes its way through five eastern North Carolina counties that lie along the banks of the mighty Cape Fear River and its tributaries. One of the great rivers of America, it winds its way for 320 miles from the Chatham County–Lee County line in central North Carolina to Cape Fear in Brunswick County.

Because the Cape Fear is the only river in the state that offers a direct deepwater outlet to the Atlantic, the lands along its banks attracted some of the colony's first settlers. Soon after it was chartered in 1739, Wilmington, located 30 miles upriver from the Cape Fear's mouth, became the most important port in North Carolina, a status it enjoyed during the Revolutionary War and that it retains to this day.

Downriver from Wilmington, the ancient port of Brunswick Town served for a time as the colonial capital. As a result, many of North Carolina's leading statesmen were attracted to the area. A number of these men were early leaders of the Revolution. The Cape Fear was thus the stage on which some of the most important acts in the struggle for independence were played out.

At Brunswick Town eight years before the much-heralded Boston Tea Party, Cape Fear Patriots offered the first armed, open resistance to British rule in all of colonial America. And a year before the Declaration of

Independence was signed, North Carolina's last Royal governor, Josiah Martin, boarded a British warship at the mouth of the Cape Fear and fled North Carolina in the wake of mounting tensions.

The tour begins at the junction of U.S. 117 Bypass and U.S. 117 Business in southern Wayne County. Born of the American Revolution, the county was named for Major General "Mad Anthony" Wayne, the energetic officer who captured the heart of the emerging American nation with his brilliant victory at Stony Point, New York, in July 1779.

Follow U.S. 117 Business south for 4.9 miles to the granite marker erected by the D.A.R. on the campus of Southern Wayne High School. It honors the site of the home and former burial site of Ezekial Slocumb and his wife, Polly, whose remains were later interred at Moores Creek National Military Park.

Polly Slocumb had an interesting encounter with the British army at the two-story home that once stood here, an incident that illustrates the defiant spirit of the people of the Cape Fear.

In late April 1781, as the Redcoats marched north from Wilmington toward Virginia, Lieutenant Colonel Banastre Tarleton, accompanied by several aides and a squadron of twenty cavalry troopers, rode up to the Slocumb house. The son of a prominent Liverpool family and a graduate of Oxford University, Tarleton had the charm and grace of a gentleman despite his cocky attitude and short temper. When he saw Polly, he removed his cap, bowed his horse's neck, and addressed her with great courtesy: "Have I the pleasure of seeing the mistress of this house and plantation?"

"It belongs to my husband," Polly responded curtly.

"Is he at home?"

"He is not."

"Is he a rebel?" Tarleton asked.

Without trepidation, Polly replied, "No, sir! He is in the army of his country and fighting against our invaders, therefore not a rebel."

Maintaining his composure, the British officer quipped, "I fear we differ in opinion, madame. A friend to his country will be the friend of the king, our master."

Polly was quick with a comeback: "Slaves only acknowledge a master in this country."

Tarleton had heard enough. Still suffering great pain from the slash wound he had taken from Colonel William Washington at Cowpens and from the two fingers he had lost at Guilford Courthouse, the cavalry chieftain announced that he would occupy the plantation house as his headquarters.

By the time the lady of the house prepared a meal for her unwelcome guest, Tarleton's temper had subsided. Again the gentleman, he made a polite request: "May I be allowed, without offense, madame, to inquire if any part of Washington's army are in this neighborhood?"

In the manner of the patriotic ladies of Halifax, this heroine of the Cape Fear could not forgo the opportunity to vex Tarleton: "I presume that it is known to you, that the Marquis [de Lafayette] and [General Nathanael] Greene are in this state. You would of course not be surprised at a call from [Lieutenant Colonel Henry] Lee, or your friend Colonel [William] Washington, who, although a perfect gentleman, it is said, shook your hand very rudely, when you last met."

Tarleton's response is unknown, but it is said that he sped away soon thereafter, never to return to the Slocumb homestead. The exploits of the legendary Slocumbs are further chronicled in The Scottish Dilemma Tour.

From the Slocumb marker, continue south on U.S. 117 Business for 3.1 miles to N.C. 55. Turn right on N.C. 55 and drive 3 miles west to S.R. 1117, better known as Thunder Swamp Road. Cornwallis's army camped in this area while Tarleton made his visit to the Slocumb plantation. Just east of here, the Northeast Cape Fear River begins its run south to Wilmington, where it enters the Cape Fear.

Continue west on N.C. 55 for 4.2 miles to S.R. 1111 and turn left. It is 0.8 mile south to the Sampson County line. Carved from nearby Duplin County in 1784, the county takes its name from John Sampson, a local planter and colonial official who died the year the county was formed.

From the county line, continue south as the road becomes S.R. 1725. After 7.9 miles, S.R. 1725 intersects N.C. 403 at Hargrove Crossroads. Proceed across the intersection and follow S.R. 1740 for 3.6 miles to S.R. 1904. Turn left on S.R. 1904 and head north for 1.3 miles to S.R. 1909. Turn right and drive 4.2 miles to "The Sycamores," a two-story frame structure on the right. This home was built around 1780 by Thomas Hicks. An officer of the colonial militia before the war, Captain Hicks served as a delegate to the First and Third Provincial Congresses at New Bern and Hillsborough. You'll notice that several of the sycamores from which the house took its name are still growing nearby.

Follow S.R. 1909 for 0.4 mile to N.C. 24 in the village of Turkey. Proceed across the intersection and drive south on S.R. 1004 (Needmore Road) for 3.6 miles to S.R. 1926 (New Hope Church Road). Turn left and head east on S.R. 1926 for 1 mile to the Hines-Hollingsworth House, located on the right.

Built around 1750, this handsome, two-story frame dwelling stands on a farm that has remained in the Hollingsworth family for nine generations. But had it not been for fate, the family would have left the area for Tennessee after the Revolutionary War.

Buried in a grave in a field across the road is Zebulon Hollingsworth, a Revolutionary War soldier who once lived in the house. Hollingsworth served in the North Carolina Continental Line throughout the war and found himself in Massachusetts when the fighting ended. He began the long, arduous trip home on foot. Dressed in his tattered uniform, he endured the cold of winter and the blazing sun of summer; he swam rivers and creeks; and he braved swamps and wilderness areas alone. During the journey, which took more than a year, Hollingsworth often had to stop to find work in order to buy food.

When he finally arrived at the family farm one night, he called at the house, only to find it abandoned. Nearby, his family members were holding a "goodbye dance," for, on the morrow, they planned to start out with their loaded wagons for the Tennessee wilderness. The family had lost all hope for Zebulon months before, but when he appeared from the darkness on the very night before the departure, they tearfully welcomed the young hero home, unpacked their belongings, and resumed their residence here.

Today, the house, which is listed on the National Register of Historic Places, and the farm are owned by James L. Hines and his wife, Esther. James L. Hines is a direct descendant of the Hollingsworth family.

Retrace your route to the intersection with N.C. 24 in Turkey and turn right. It is 1.7 miles to the Duplin County line. Formed in 1750, Duplin County was named in honor of a British colonial official, Thomas Hay, Lord Duplin (1710–87).

Hines-Hollingsworth House, near Turkey

From the county line, continue east on N.C. 24 for 3.7 miles to where it merges with N.C. 50 in Warsaw. Follow N.C. 24/N.C. 50 for 6.5 miles to the Liberty Hall Restoration in the town of Kenansville, the seat of Duplin County.

Here stands the jewel of Duplin County. Open to the public since 1968, the Liberty Hall Restoration features the exquisite two-story, eleven-room Greek Revival house constructed by Thomas Kenan (1771–1843) in the first decade of the nineteenth century. The complex takes its name from the family plantation near Turkey.

On the grounds is the grave of James Kenan (1740–1810), which was moved here from the original Liberty Hall site. James Kenan was one of Duplin's greatest Revolutionary War heroes. As the county sheriff in 1765, he was a leader in the organized protest against the Stamp Act in Wilmington. Elected a militia colonel by the Third Provincial Congress in September 1775, he orchestrated the defense of the Duplin County area throughout the war. He was conspicuous in the campaign that led to the American victory at the Battle of Moores Creek Bridge.

Just weeks after the setback at the hands of Major James Craig at nearby Rockfish Creek on August 2, 1781, Kenan mustered four hundred militiamen and moved on the Tories responsible for the recent reign of terror in the Cape Fear area. According to one of Kenan's men, "[We] marched straight into the neighborhood where the Tories were embodied, surprised them; they fled, our men pursued them, cut many of them to pieces, took several and put them instantly to death. The action struck . . . terror on the Tories in our county."

Adjacent to the Liberty Hall Restoration is the Duplin County–Cowan Museum. Displayed in the facility are artifacts from the colonial and Revolutionary War periods. Restored buildings from the county's historic past are located on the museum grounds.

Continue on N.C. 24/N.C. 50 to N.C. 11. Turn left on N.C. 11 and proceed 0.4 mile northeast to the Kenan Amphitheatre.

One of the finest amphitheaters in the state, this facility is the venue for an outdoor drama that chronicles the story of the Revolution in North Carolina. Written by playwright Randolph Umberger, *The Liberty Cart: A Duplin Story* is a dramatization of events that shaped the area from 1755 to

1865. Among the Revolutionary War characters and events presented in the play are Colonel James Kenan, the Battle of Moores Creek Bridge, and the Battle of Rockfish Creek.

Return to the intersection with N.C.24/N.C. 50 in Kenansville, then continue south on N.C. 11 for 1.4 miles to James Sprunt Community College. The John Grady Monument is located at the flagpole on the front lawn of the campus. Dedicated in October 1976, it is a memorial to a brave Patriot killed at the Battle of Moores Creek Bridge. His story of heroism is recounted later in this tour.

John Grady Monument at James Sprunt Community College

Continue south on N.C. 11 for 16.1 miles to the battlefield park at Rockfish Creek. Turn left at the sign for the water treatment plant. The park is located on the left side of the road within sight of the highway.

Other than a state historical marker and a chipped marble monument, there is nothing here to remind visitors of the spirited battle that took place on the banks of this tributary of the Northeast Cape Fear on August 2, 1781.

Five years after the Declaration of Independence, Cornwallis and his army were long gone from North Carolina, but Major James Craig maintained a base of operations in Wilmington. Strong bands of Loyalist soldiers continued to menace Patriots in the area.

On the day of the battle, Craig and 600 Loyalists appeared on the southern side of the creek in their quest to plunder the counties of eastern North Carolina. To oppose the crossing, Colonel James Kenan placed 150 militiamen behind breastworks lining the creek banks. He was reinforced by 180 men commanded by Richard Caswell.

After an initial attack by the Patriots, Major Craig ordered a counterattack. Craig had one great advantage: artillery. According to Kenan, after a few rounds from the big guns, his men "broak [sic] and it was out of my power and all my Officers to rally them." The result was a rout of the American militia. Once across the creek, Craig marched his army north to New Bern, causing damage all along the way.

From Rockfish Creek, follow N.C. 11 south to U.S. 117. Drive south on U.S. 117 for 20.1 miles to N.C. 133 at the town of Castle Hayne. Continue south for 1.7 miles to the state historical marker near the bridge over the Northeast Cape Fear at the Pender County–New Hanover line. This was the site of one of the few drawbridges in the American colonies. Constructed in 1768, the structure was destroyed by British troops during their occupation of the Wilmington area in 1781.

Formed in 1729 from Craven County, New Hanover County was named in honor of the British Royal family, which was from the house of Hanover. Despite its regal name, the county was anything but loyal to the Crown during the American Revolution. As respected North Carolina historian John H. Wheeler noted, "There is no portion of North Carolina more early and more sincerely devoted to liberty than New Hanover."

One mile south of the Northeast Cape Fear River, U.S. 117 intersects N.C. 132. Take N.C. 132, the left fork, and continue south for 5.3 miles to Market Street (U.S. 17/U.S. 74). Turn right on Market Street and drive west toward downtown Wilmington.

Wilmington National Cemetery, located on the right side of Market Street at its intersection with Twentieth Street, was established in 1867 as a permanent burial ground for Union soldiers who had been killed during the Cape Fear campaign two years earlier. However, there is one grave here that is related to Revolutionary War history. Set amid the long, straight rows of white, government-issue gravestones is the marker for renowned novelist Inglis Fletcher.

Fletcher (1879–1969) penned a widely read, twelve-volume series of historical novels that dramatized the events in the colonial and Revolutionary War periods in North Carolina. Among her most popular titles were *Raleigh's Eden* (1940), *Lusty Wind for Carolina* (1944), *Toil of the Brave* (1946), *Roanoke Hundred* (1948), *Queen's Gift* (1952), and *The Scotswoman* (1955). Her grave, located northwest of the flag circle, lies next to that of her husband, a veteran of the Spanish-American War.

Continue on Market Street to the Cape Fear Museum, located at 814 Market. Home to the museum since 1970, the modified Gothic Revival building was constructed as an armory in the mid-1930s. The growing popularity of the museum has led to numerous modifications of and additions to the structure. Inside, a multilevel exhibition area chronicles the long history of Wilmington and the surrounding area.

On the eve of the American Revolution, Wilmington was the leading city in North Carolina. Its fine harbor, protected from the fierce storms of the Atlantic, was jammed with ships from distant ports. Most came for cargoes of tar, pitch, and turpentine, which were in high demand in Europe. North Carolina was the world leader in the production of naval stores from 1720 to 1870, and Wilmington was the primary port through which they were shipped.

Because of its importance as a port and its location on the King's Highway (see The Scottish Dilemma Tour, page 110), the city became a center for the exchange of political opinions in the years leading up to the Revolution. Wilmington attracted men of great stature, many of them ardent Patriots in the struggle for independence.

Continue west on Market Street. In the middle of Market just east of the intersection with Fourth Street stands the Harnett Obelisk, a monument to one of the most remarkable and talented, yet unsung, heroes of the American Revolution.

Cornelius Harnett (1723–81), a man known as "the Pride of the Cape Fear," was one of the earliest and most ardent leaders in the quest for independence. Born in Chowan County, he spent his formative years at Brunswick Town on the lower Cape Fear River, where he was exposed to the revolutionary ideas being bandied about town.

As a young adult, Harnett moved upriver to Wilmington, where he became active in the political life of the city and colony. An outspoken opponent of British taxation, Harnett provided the leadership that made enforcement of the Stamp Act virtually impossible at Wilmington and Brunswick Town. In February 1766, he served as one of the ringleaders of an armed showdown against Royal authority at Brunswick Town. As a result, Harnett became an overnight hero throughout North Carolina.

In 1770, at a time when most Americans were reluctant to take a public stand against British authority, Harnett openly announced that he was "ready to stand or fall with the other colonies in support of American liberty" and that he "would not tamely submit to the yoke of oppression." These bold statements were made more than four years before the first shots of the war were fired.

Following a meeting with Harnett in March 1773, noted Boston Patriot Josiah Quincey, Jr., spread the fame of the Cape Fear revolutionary throughout the North, calling him "the Samuel Adams of North Carolina."

On May 8, 1775, a horse bearing a special courier galloped into Wilmington with an important dispatch. When it was placed in Harnett's hands, he learned the exciting news that Americans had done battle with British forces in Lexington, Massachusetts. He directed the rider to Brunswick County with a message for fellow Patriots there. Suddenly, the pace of Harnett's quest for independence was quickening.

Fearful of Harnett and other Patriot leaders in the colony, Royal Governor Josiah Martin fled North Carolina in the summer of 1775. Meanwhile, at Hillsborough, the Third Provincial Congress established a thirteen-man Provincial Council. Unanimously selected as president of the council was Cornelius Harnett. In that capacity, Harnett endured great personal risk to serve as chief executive of the colony.

At the Fourth Provincial Congress, held at Halifax in April 1776, Harnett chaired the committee appointed to draft a resolution "to take into consideration the usurpations and violences attempted by the King and Parliament of Britain against America." On April 12, Harnett, the author of the committee report, stepped to the podium and read the Halifax Resolves.

Around this time, Sir Henry Clinton arrived in southeastern North Carolina with a sizable British force. He soon abandoned his plans to invade the colony. But before leaving North Carolina waters, he issued a proclamation from his warship: All subjects who would lay down their arms and pledge allegiance to the Crown would be pardoned by the king, "excepting only from the benefits of such pardon Cornelius Harnett and Robert Howe."

Ten months after he gave the first public reading of the Declaration of Independence in North Carolina, the fearless Harnett was elected—against his wishes—to replace William Hooper in the Continental Congress. During his three terms, the Cape Fear statesman proved one of that body's most prominent and effective members.

Crippled by gout and hardly able to hold a pen, Harnett came home to Wilmington in February 1780. Less than a year later, when Major James Craig began the British occupation of Wilmington, he made it his first order of business to track down the man whose name appeared at the top of the England's "most wanted list."

Having received advance notice of Craig's approach, Harnett fled Wilmington and sought sanctuary with his old friend James Spicer at a plantation in Onslow County 30 miles north of Wilmington. Craig's men quickly closed in on their prey. They found Harnett, pulled him from his bed, and drove him on foot down the road toward Wilmington until fatigue and illness overcame him. When the crippled man fell on his face in the sandy road, his captors grabbed him up, bound his hands and feet, and strapped him across the back of a horse.

Craig was delighted to see his trophy delivered to him. With total lack of regard for his prisoner's frail condition, the British officer ordered Harnett confined in a roofless blockhouse called "the Bullpen." The harsh winter weather soon took its toll, and Harnett grew gravely ill. Only after Whigs and Tories alike implored Craig was Harnett released. But personal freedom came too late. Surrounded by family and friends, Harnett died on April 28, 1781, before his dream of a free and independent America had fully become reality.

Near the thirty-foot obelisk is the cemetery of St. James Episcopal Church, located at the southeastern corner of Market and Fourth Streets. It contains the marked graves of Harnett and several other Revolutionary War figures, among them John "Jack" Walker (1741–1813), an officer who served under George Washington at Germantown, Brandywine, and Valley Forge. As a colonel, Walker acted as aide-de-camp on Washington's staff. Also buried in the cemetery is Thomas Hooper (1746–1821). The younger brother of a signer of the Declaration of Independence, Hooper was a suspected Loyalist during the Revolution.

Continue on Market Street across Third and park nearby to enjoy a short walking tour of downtown Wilmington.

Peter Du Bois, a visitor to Wilmington in 1757, praised the city in this manner: "The Regularity of the Streets are equal to those of Philadelphia and Buildings in General are very good. Many of Brick, two or three stories high with double piazzas which make a good appearance." The town's European-style street grid, laid out in 1739 and modified four years later, has survived virtually intact. Nevertheless, the downtown streets boast few buildings from the Revolutionary War era. Although Wilmington was spared armed conflict, several devastating fires in the nineteenth century destroyed many of the town's eighteenth-century structures.

One of the few pre–Revolutionary War houses still standing and open to the public is the Burgwin-Wright House, located at 224 Market Street, just across Third Street from St. James Episcopal Church. John Burgwin, colonial treasurer under Royal Governor Arthur Dobbs, constructed the magnificent, two-story Georgian mansion in 1770. Its foundation consists of the massive stone walls of a former jail located at the site. Because of his allegiance to the Crown, Burgwin fled Wilmington at the outbreak of war and remained in England until the cessation of hostilities.

For much of the war, Wilmington was free of British troops. But in late January 1781, thirty-three-year-old James Craig sailed up the Cape Fear to take possession of the defenseless city. Major Craig, a soldier since the age of fifteen, immediately commandeered Burgwin's house as his headquarters because it was "the most considerable house in town."

When the battered, demoralized army of Lord Cornwallis limped into Wilmington on April 12, 1781, after its costly "victory" over Nathanael Greene's Americans at Guilford Courthouse, the British commander made

Burgwin-Wright House

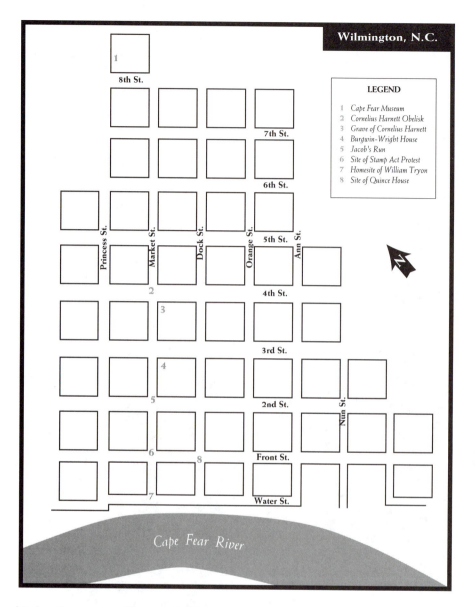

1

8th St.

7th St.

6th St.

LEGEND

1   Cape Fear Museum
2   Cornelius Harnett Obelisk
3   Grave of Cornelius Harnett
4   Burgwin-Wright House
5   Jacob's Run
6   Site of Stamp Act Protest
7   Homesite of William Tryon
8   Site of Quince House

Princess St.

Market St.

Dock St.

Orange St.

Ann St.

5th St.

2

4th St.

3

3rd St.

4

5

2nd St.

Nun St.

6

8

Front St.

7

Water St.

Cape Fear River

his headquarters at Burgwin's House. Consequently, it is sometimes known as "the Cornwallis House."

Cornwallis rested his weary army for almost two weeks in Wilmington while he took on supplies for his march north to Yorktown and destiny.

The floorboards inside the Burgwin-Wright House display marks made by British muskets during Cornwallis's stay.

More than two hundred years after the Redcoats lodged here, another intriguing reminder of the British presence in the house came to light. One particular British soldier under Cornwallis had fallen in love with a beautiful young woman in South Carolina. While he was quartered at Burgwin's house, the soldier etched his sweetheart's name in a windowpane with his diamond ring.

After the war, the soldier returned to South Carolina, married his girlfriend, and took her to live in England. Subsequently, the couple emigrated to the United States and settled in New York. On a visit to Wilmington in 1836, their son was the guest of Dr. Thomas H. Wright, who had inherited the house. In fact, the visitor slept in the same bedroom occupied by his father during the Revolutionary War. He noticed the name etched in the windowpane and immediately recognized it to be his mother's.

John W. Barrow, the grandson of the British officer, came to Wilmington in search of the windowpane forty years later, having been told of it by his father. When he called at the Burgwin-Wright House, the owner informed him that the home had been remodeled. They descended into the cellar, where prisoners had been held during the Revolutionary War. Among the remnants stored there after the renovations was the special pane.

From the Burgwin-Wright House, walk west on Third Street for one block to Princess Street. Located at this intersection is a state historical marker on the site of William Hooper's town house. (For information on Hooper, one of North Carolina's three signers of the Declaration of Independence and one of the foremost Patriots of the American Revolution, see The Regulator Tour, pages 373–423.)

Return to the intersection of Third and Market. Walk south on Market Street past the Burgwin-Wright House in the direction of the waterfront.

Located under the street is Jacob's Run, the most famous of the labyrinthine brick tunnels constructed in Wilmington's distant past. A bricked-over section of the cellar wall of the Burgwin-Wright House was once the opening to a tunnel that runs with the flowing waters of an underground stream to the Cape Fear. Although the original purpose of this tunnel has never been explained, it has been speculated that American prisoners used it to escape from the British jail in the basement of the Burgwin-Wright House.

Continue south on Market Street. On November 17, 1781, famed cavalry officer Henry "Light Horse Harry" Lee, the father of Robert E. Lee, galloped down this street with the glorious news of Cornwallis's surrender at Yorktown.

A marble tablet at the intersection of Market and Front Streets marks the site of the town's courthouse during colonial days. On November 16, 1765, Dr. William Houston, Wilmington's unfortunate stamp master, was escorted here by a hostile crowd. He executed his resignation to the delight of local citizens who had assembled to protest the Stamp Act.

It was also at this courthouse that the members of the local Committee of Safety met on June 19, 1775, and entered into a pledge that contained this bold language: "We do unite ourselves under every tie of religion and honor and associate as a band in her defense against every foe; hereby solemnly engaging that whenever our continental or provincial councils shall decree it necessary we will go forth and be ready to sacrifice our lives and fortunes to secure her freedom and safety."

Continue south on Market Street. Near the junction with Water Street is a granite marker at the site of the home of Royal Governor William Tryon, who maintained a residence here until Tryon Palace was completed.

It was at this residence that the angry mob confronted Dr. Houston, who remembered the showdown this way: "The inhabitants immediately assembled about me and demanded a categorical answer whether I intended to put the Act relating [to] the Stamps in force. The town bell was rung, drums beating, colors flying and a great concourse of people were gathered together."

Walk across Water Street to Riverfront Park, which affords a spectacular view of the Cape Fear. Although the wharves and docks of the Revolutionary War era vanished long ago, the municipal park is located at the site where tall-masted ships once tied up.

If you look north across the river, you'll see a spit of land at the forks of the Cape Fear. Formerly known as Mallette Point in honor of Colonel Peter Mallette, a Revolutionary War hero, it is now called Point Peter. During the war, the area was nothing more than a cypress swamp. But when

Cornwallis called on Wilmington in the spring of 1781, it became a make-shift fort for a small band of Patriots incensed by the arrival of the Redcoats.

The fort was located in the most unlikely of places—the base of a hollow cypress so large that it could have housed a small family. One of the partisans, a skilled gunsmith, crafted a rifle long enough to send a ball from the big tree to the Wilmington waterfront. Soon, unsuspecting British soldiers began dropping like flies about the docks. The small Patriot band continued its reign of terror for more than a week, until a Tory neighbor alerted the Redcoats. When they came ashore on the point, British soldiers found the abandoned cypress outpost.

Walk east along the waterfront to the junction of Water and Dock Streets. Turn left and go one block north to the intersection of Dock and Front.

This is the former site of the Quince House, where President George Washington lodged on Sunday and Monday, April 24 and 25, 1791. While being feted at Dorsey's Tavern, Washington commented about the many swamps he had observed en route to Wilmington and about his concern over the quality of local drinking water. When the president asked the tavern owner about the water, Lawrence A. Dorsey is said to have replied that he could not speak on the subject because he never drank it.

Continue north on Dock Street for two blocks to Third Street, where you'll see a state historical marker commemorating Washington's visit. Turn left on Third and go one block west to Market to return to your vehicle.

Drive east on Third through the downtown area to the intersection with U.S. 17/U.S. 74/U.S. 76. Turn right and proceed west over the river via the magnificent Cape Fear Memorial Bridge. Once across the bridge, you will enter Brunswick County. Created in 1764 from New Hanover County, it was named for the old port town by the same name just downriver.

Continue west approximately 3 miles from the Cape Fear Memorial Bridge to the intersection with N.C. 133 at Belville. Turn onto N.C. 133 and proceed south. The route roughly parallels the Cape Fear River as the mighty waterway makes its way to its mouth at Southport. Just south of the U.S. 17/U.S. 74/U.S. 76 overpass, you'll encounter a long row of state historical markers, including a half-dozen related to the Revolutionary War; the sites described on the markers are included in this tour.

It is 13.2 miles on N.C. 133 to S.R. 1529, where you'll notice historical markers for three important sites of the Revolutionary War era: Orton, Brunswick Town, and St. Philips Church. To see the first of these sites, turn left onto S.R. 1529 and proceed to the entrance of Orton Plantation, marked by massive stone pillars surmounted by eagles with outspread wings.

Once inside the gate, you'll be treated to views of the only surviving colonial mansion on the Cape Fear and its surrounding gardens, considered some of the most beautiful in America. Mansion and gardens are the focus of an estate that once contained ten thousand acres.

Orton was the dream of Roger Moore, a renowned Indian fighter who received an enormous land grant on the banks of the Cape Fear in 1725. Erected by Moore in 1730 and subsequently modified, the mansion is considered one of the finest examples of Greek Revival architecture in the United States. With the exception of the Cape Hatteras Lighthouse, the mansion at Orton is perhaps the most-photographed structure in the state. The house is private, but the adjacent gardens are open to the public for an admission fee.

When "King Roger" died in 1750, the plantation came into the posses-

Wilmington waterfront in 1998, "occupied" by a British warship

sion of his sons, George and William. George (1715–78), the father of twenty-eight children, became caught up in the revolutionary fervor that took hold of the Cape Fear in the mid-1760s. He was a participant in the armed resistance against the Stamp Act at Brunswick Town in 1766. Fifteen years later, the British army retaliated when a landing party of Cornwallis's soldiers looted Orton.

Return to the entrance of Orton on S.R. 1529. Turn left and drive 0.8 mile to S.R. 1533. Turn left and proceed east on S.R. 1533 for 1.1 miles to the ruins of Brunswick Town on the Cape Fear River.

At this state historic site, visitors have an opportunity to take a leisurely stroll along the tree-shaded lanes of a former port town where one of the first events—if not *the* first event—of the American Revolution took place. Tours of the site begin at the visitor center, located adjacent to the parking lot. Inside the center, interpretive displays and artifacts tell the story of the rise and fall of Brunswick Town.

Established in 1726 by the Moore family of nearby Orton, the town was named in honor of King George I of England, the German-born monarch who was duke of Brunswick. The father of Revolutionary War hero Cornelius Harnett purchased the first two lots in the town and moved his family here from Edenton. The town's prosperity appeared to be insured in 1731, when it was named one of the five official ports of entry of the colony.

Brunswick was the seat of New Hanover County from 1729 to 1741, when Wilmington usurped the honor. Upon the formation of Brunswick County in 1764, Brunswick reclaimed its honor as a county seat. Six years earlier, the town had already begun to take on renewed prominence when Royal Governor Arthur Dobbs established his residence at Russellborough, a fifty-five-acre estate on the northern edge of town.

Dobbs (1689–1765), a former member of the Irish Parliament and a promoter of the search for the Northwest Passage, served as Royal governor of North Carolina from 1754 to 1765. Drawn to Brunswick because of its moderate climate, he established the town as the seat of colonial government. From 1758 to 1770, Russellborough was the home of Dobbs and his successor, William Tryon. During the two governors' residency, the general assembly met here.

Governor Tryon was in Brunswick Town on February 19, 1766, when he became embroiled in an armed showdown over Royal authority in the colony. Dissatisfied with Tryon's position on the Stamp Act, a group called the Sons of Liberty—which had several months earlier pledged to prevent enforcement of the legislation—marched from Wilmington to Brunswick Town. Led by Cornelius Harnett, John Ashe, and other Cape Fear Patriots, the angry men surrounded the governor's residence. There, Harnett and George Moore informed the governor that the Patriots were willing to take whatever action was necessary to make the Stamp Act unenforceable.

For a time, Tryon was held under virtual house arrest, as 150 Patriots encircled the house. Several days later, bloodshed was averted when Harnett escorted customs officials and other agents of the Crown into the streets of Brunswick, where, in front of the armed Patriots, they took an oath to refrain from issuing any stamped papers in North Carolina. Soon thereafter, the Patriots returned to their homes. They had taken a firm stand against British colonial rule and won.

In reporting the event, the *Virginia Gazette*, the foremost journal in Virginia at the time, urged its readers to emulate the example set at Brunswick Town: "It is well worthy of observation that few instances can be produced of such a number of men being together so long, and behaving so well, not the least noise or disturbance, nor nay person seen disguised with liquor, during the whole of their stay in Brunswick, neither was there any injury to any person, but the whole affair conducted with the decency and spirit, worth the imitation of all the Sons of Liberty throughout the Continent."

At the time of the showdown, no one could foresee the course the colonies would take toward independence. Since then, the events at Brunswick have been neglected by many historians. But George Davis, the celebrated North Carolina statesman and historian of the nineteenth century, eloquently put them into perspective: "This was more than ten years before the Declaration of Independence and more than nine before the Battle of Lexington, and nearly eight before the Boston Tea Party. The destruction of the tea was done at night by men in disguise. And history blazoned it, and New England boasts of it, and the fame of it is world wide. But this other act, more gallant and more daring done in open day by well-known men, with arms in their hands, and under the King's flag—who remembers it, or who tells of it?"

When Governor Tryon left for his new residence in New Bern in 1770, Brunswick—which had never boasted a population of more than four hundred—began a decline from which it would never recover. In one of the ironies of American history, the town where the sparks of the Revolution first glowed was torched by British attackers in 1776.

A free brochure at the visitor center provides a detailed tour route of the town ruins. Located near the center is the most prominent reminder of colonial Brunswick Town—St. Philips Church.

Authorized by the general assembly in 1759, the Anglican church was completed by Governor Tryon in 1768. Only its massive, thirty-three-inch-thick brick walls stand today. Within these roofless walls are a couple of graves of importance to the Revolutionary War. Royal Governor Dobbs and Alfred Moore are buried here, as is the infant son of Royal Governor Tryon.

Alfred Moore (1755–1810), was the son of Maurice Moore, Jr., a noted jurist in the early days of the Revolution. As a young officer fighting for the American cause, Alfred saw his first action under the command of his uncle, James Moore, at the Battle of Moores Creek Bridge. Near the close of the war, he directed the Cape Fear militia's reprisals against Major Craig's forces at Wilmington.

The ruins of St. Philips Church

Like his father, Moore became a distinguished attorney and jurist. Upon the death of James Iredell in 1799, President John Adams appointed Moore to fill the vacancy on the Supreme Court. Due to ill health, Moore retired five years later. He stands as the last North Carolinian to serve on the nation's highest court.

From the church, visitors can make their way down old Second Street, which veers sharply east toward the river. This quiet, peaceful route passes the ballast-stone foundations of homes and buildings where some of the most important men in colonial North Carolina lived and visited. There are no tangible reminders of the hustle and bustle of the colonial period and the excitement of the early days of the struggle for independence. But legend has it that the specter of the Revolution lingers here. Not surprisingly, a place that became a ghost town two centuries ago counts ghosts as its current residents.

In the days leading up to the Revolution, two Scotsmen fled to America from their native land after a fight against British authorities. They were taken into custody near Wilmington by the infamous Tory David Fanning. (For more information on Fanning, see The Regulator Tour, pages 373–423.) Charged with treason, the two prisoners were held in chains deep in the bowels of a prison ship anchored off Brunswick Town.

Following several unsuccessful escape attempts, the unfortunate men were brought ashore at Brunswick Town. Tried and convicted by a kangaroo court, they were sentenced to death by Fanning himself. They were subsequently killed by a firing squad, but local tradition holds that on stormy nights, they can still be seen in a phantom boat on the river searching for rescuers.

When you are ready to leave Brunswick Town, retrace your route to Orton Plantation and turn left on S.R. 1530. After 0.3 mile, turn left onto N.C. 133, heading south toward Southport, 11 miles distant. En route, you'll pass a sign marking the entrance to the massive Military Ocean Terminal at Sunny Point. This terminal—the nation's largest shipper of weapons, tanks, explosives, and military equipment—covers much of the historic Brunswick riverfront, including one Revolutionary War site. Howes Point, located 1 mile south of Brunswick Town within the confines of Sunny Point, was the site of Job Howe's plantation. His famous Revolutionary War son, Robert Howe, was born here in 1732. (For information on Robert Howe, see The Scottish Dilemma Tour, pages 118–19.) British troops plundered Howes Point on May 12, 1776.

Near the entrance to Sunny Point, N.C. 133 merges into N.C. 87. Continue south on N.C. 87 for 3.7 miles to Southport, where the road becomes Howe Street. Named in honor of Robert Howe, the main thoroughfare into the historic port city is one of a number of local streets that bear the names of Revolutionary War notables. For example, Moore Street honors James Moore, one of the heroes of the Battle of Moores Creek Bridge, and Caswell Street pays homage to Richard Caswell.

Follow Howe Street to its terminus at the picturesque Waterfront Park. Leave your car in the parking lot to enjoy a brief stroll. In the distance looms the mouth of the Cape Fear. Through this inlet, vessels have made their way into the river from the Atlantic for more than four hundred years.

Walk east to the nearby City Pier. Located along the waterfront between the park's picnic area and the pier is an almost unnoticeable wall of crumbling rock now covered with masonry and debris. This wall is the only remnant of the original fortifications of Fort Johnston.

In 1730, Fort Johnston became the first of six military installations authorized by the colonial assembly. Construction did not begin until 1745, and then the project took ten years to complete. Named in honor of Governor Gabriel Johnston (1699–1752), the fort was the last place of refuge in mainland North Carolina for Josiah Martin, the last Royal governor of the colony. A nearby state historical marker commemorates Martin's flight to this spot.

After sending his family north to the relative safety of New York, Martin hastened south from New Bern in the late spring of 1775. Arriving at Fort Johnston on June 2, he holed up temporarily at the installation, which he described as "a contemptible thing, fit neither for a place of arms nor an asylum for the friends of government."

Royal government in North Carolina was now a thing of the past. Nevertheless, Martin formulated plans at the Cape Fear outpost to recover his authority and subjugate the colony to the Crown. But as revolutionary fervor continued to grow, he was forced to flee again. This time, he took refuge on the HMS *Cruizer*, a British warship patrolling the nearby waters. On the morning of July 18, Martin's dreams went up in flames when he scrambled from his berth aboard the *Cruizer* to witness Fort Johnston falling victim to an inferno started by Cornelius Harnett, John Ashe, and a large group of Cape Fear Patriots.

During the war that followed, British troops camped for a time at the ruins of the fort, but there was no fighting at the site.

Just across Bay Street from the City Pier stands the much-altered two-story building that was constructed when the fort was rebuilt around 1800. From its commanding position overlooking the river, this historic structure is the centerpiece of the modern Fort Johnston, which, at eight acres, may be the smallest active military installation in the United States. The old building is used as living quarters for the commander and other officers at the Sunny Point complex. A state historical marker for Fort Johnston stands nearby on Bay Street.

Return to your vehicle and drive one block north on Howe Street to Moore Street. Turn right and proceed east through downtown Southport for four blocks to St. Philips Episcopal Church. Constructed about 1860, the white frame building holds treasures inherited from St. Philips Church at Brunswick Town. Among the fixtures predating the American Revolution are the baptismal font, the altar cloths, and the wooden collection plates.

It is another two blocks on Moore to the Old Smithville Burying Ground, located at the northeastern corner of Moore and Rhett Streets.

Southport celebrated its bicentennial in 1992, but its roots as a seafaring village can be traced to the settlement that grew up around Fort Johnston before the Revolution.

The town was originally named Smithville in honor of Benjamin Smith (1756–1826), one of the greatest soldiers and statesmen of the colony and state. The Old Smithville Burying Ground, consecrated as a cemetery in 1792, holds the remains of Smith, whose life ended in great tragedy and sorrow.

Born in the lap of luxury, Smith was the grandson of "King Roger" Moore. At the age of twenty-one, he served as an aide-de-camp to George Washington in the brilliant American retreat from Long Island in August 1776. Three years later, he was with William Moultrie in South Carolina when the British were driven from Port Royal Island. Following the war, Smith enjoyed a successful political career. He was elected governor of North Carolina in 1810.

At one time, his personal wealth seemed boundless. He owned Belvedere Plantation, Orton Plantation, Smith Island (Bald Head Island), Blue Banks Plantation (located on the Northeast Cape Fear River), a winter residence in Brunswick Town, a summer residence in Smithville, and twenty thousand acres in Tennessee (a gift in recognition of his Revolutionary War service).

It was Smith's generous nature that led to his downfall. After signing as a surety for the debt of a friend, he was forced to sell his vast holdings to pay creditors when the friend defaulted. As a result, he became a virtual pauper.

On the stormy night of January 10, 1826, the penniless hero lay dying in a cold, decrepit house on Bay Street, attended only by his physician friend, Dr. Clitheral, and the physician's wife. Mrs. Clitheral described the pitiful scene this way: "The large street door flew open nor cou'd the strength of one man close; in intervals was heard, the hard breathing and thicken'd ejaculations of the dying.—A quilt had been fastened from the head of his bedside, to supply the place of the door, its flappings, add[ing] to the cold air of the apartment."

At length, Smith gasped, "Doctor, doctor, oh, doctor!" and then a convulsive struggle brought to a close the life of one of the most colorful figures of the Cape Fear.

The tour ends here, at Smith's final resting place.

The Scottish Dilemma Tour

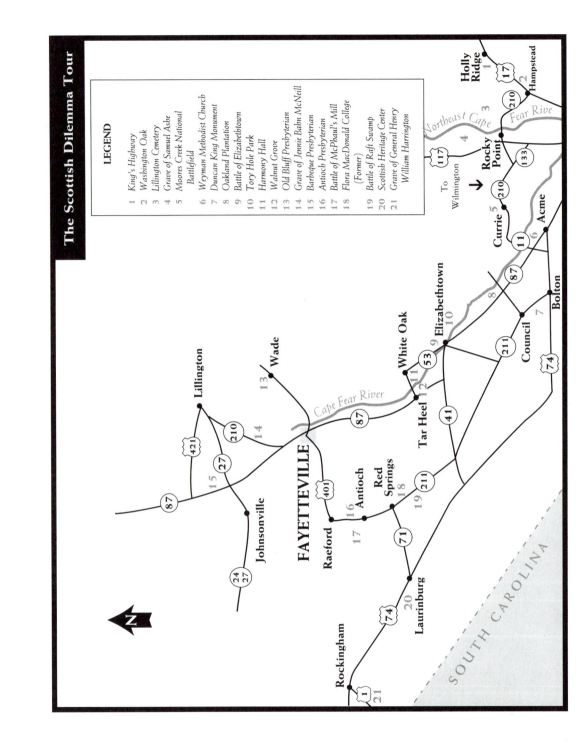

LEGEND

1 King's Highway
2 Washington Oak
3 Lillington Cemetery
4 Grave of Samuel Ashe
5 Moores Creek National Battlefield
6 Weyman Methodist Church
7 Duncan King Monument
8 Oakland Plantation
9 Battle of Elizabethtown
10 Tory Hole Park
11 Harmony Hall
12 Walnut Grove
13 Old Bluff Presbyterian
14 Grave of Jennie Bahn McNeill
15 Barbeque Presbyterian
16 Antioch Presbyterian
17 Battle of McPhaul's Mill
18 Flora MacDonald College (Former)
19 Battle of Raft Swamp
20 Scottish Heritage Center
21 Grave of General Henry William Harrington

The Scottish Dilemma Tour

This tour begins at Holly Ridge in Onslow County and makes its way through Pender, Columbus, Bladen, Cumberland, Harnett, Hoke, Robeson, and Scotland Counties before ending south of Rockingham in Richmond County. Among the highlights are the grave of Alexander Lillington, Moores Creek National Battlefield, the story of Duncan and Lydia King, the Battle of Elizabethtown, Harmony Hall, historic Fayetteville, Old Bluff Presbyterian Church, the story of "Jennie Bahn" McNeill, Barbeque Presbyterian Church, the Battle of McPhaul's Mill, and the Battle of Raft Swamp.

Total mileage: approximately 353 miles.

This tour covers an expansive ten-county area in the southeastern part of the state where thousands of people from the Scottish Highlands settled in the middle of the eighteenth century. Following their bloody defeat by the British at Culloden in 1746, the Highland Scots found their land occupied by English soldiers who made living conditions intolerable. Across the sea, North Carolina offered liberal land grants and the promise of a new life.

Before they were allowed to leave Scotland for the colony, the Scots were required to pledge allegiance to the British Crown and to sign an oath that ended with these harsh, chilling words: "And should I break thee, my solemn oath, may I be cursed in all my undertakings, family and property; may I never see my wife, children, father, mother or other relatives; may I be killed in battle as a coward and lie without Christian burial in a strange land, far from the graves of my forefathers and kindred. May all this come to me if I break my oath."

When the time came for the fight for American independence, the Highlanders who had poured into southeastern North Carolina faced a dilemma: would they honor their oath and support the hated monarchy or fight for the freedom of the colonies? Most of the Scottish Highlanders in North Carolina chose to remain loyal to the Crown. Others fought for American freedom. A few attempted to remain neutral.

A number of eminent Patriots of English and Scots-Irish descent made their homes in this area of Scottish dominance. Neighbors clashed with each other in bloody encounters on numerous occasions during the war. While the fight for American independence raged throughout the colonies, a virtual civil war was fought along the byways covered on this tour.

The tour begins on U.S. 17 at the village of Holly Ridge in southern Onslow County. Along the highway, you'll notice a state historical marker commemorating George Washington's travels through the area. On the night of April 23, 1791, the president lodged at Sage's Inn, which was located two hundred yards east of the marker.

Drive south on U.S. 17, which passes over the route of the first intercolonial roadway through North Carolina. Known as the King's Highway, it went from Virginia into North Carolina at Perquimans County and passed through Edenton, Bath, New Bern, and Wilmington before entering South Carolina. Completed in 1727, the highway stretched 275 miles through North Carolina.

Two miles south of Holly Ridge, U.S. 17 enters Pender County. Continue south as it passes just east of the nearly impenetrable wilderness of the 48,500-acre Holly Shelter Game Land.

When President Washington traveled south through this area along the King's Highway, he was not impressed with the landscape. In his diary, he noted that "the whole Road from New Bern to Wilmington (except in a few places of small extent) passes through the most barren country I ever beheld; especially in the parts nearest to the latter; which is no other than a bed of white sand."

Little did Washington imagine that the ocean strand only a few miles to the east would be packed with expensive resort homes two centuries later.

From the Pender County line, it is 10.5 miles on U.S. 17 to Hampstead, which boasts a landmark from Washington's visit. On the right side of the highway stands the Washington Oak, a massive tree with sweeping limbs under which the president rested in April 1791. The tree has been appropriately marked by the D.A.R.

Just south of Hampstead, U.S. 17 junctions with N.C. 210. Turn right onto N.C. 210 and follow it for 9.6 miles to S.R. 1520 on the eastern side of the Northeast Cape Fear River. Turn right on S.R. 1520, proceed 4.1

miles, and turn right on unpaved Lillington Lane. Drive east for 1.2 miles to the Lillington cemetery, taking care not to veer right where Lillington Lane forks in that direction.

Few areas in North Carolina produced such a group of Revolutionary War leaders as did the banks of the Northeast Cape Fear River. Buried in a well-marked tomb in the ancient cemetery is John Alexander Lillington (c. 1720–86), the first of this eminent group you'll meet on this tour.

Reared in the Cape Fear by his uncle, Edward Moseley, who was perhaps the colony's most important political figure in the first half of the eighteenth century, Lillington participated in Stamp Act protests in 1765 and 1766. But like many of his contemporaries, he served as an officer in Royal Governor Tryon's campaign against the Regulators.

Soon thereafter, he became enmeshed in revolutionary activities in the Cape Fear. Lillington's finest hour came on February 27, 1776, when he and fellow colonel James Moore masterminded the stirring Patriot victory at Moores Creek Bridge. Less than two months later, the Fourth Provincial Congress named Lillington commander of the Sixth Regiment of the North Carolina Continentals, but he declined, citing his advanced age. A militia general for the duration of the war, he rendered effective assistance to Benjamin Lincoln at Charleston and helped defend the Cape Fear area against British and Tory raiders.

Surrounded by a crumbling brick wall, the unkept Lillington cemetery is one of the many isolated shrines of Revolutionary War North Carolina that will soon be lost unless efforts to preserve them are taken. It is located on the grounds where the great plantation house Lillington Hall once stood. Although the manor house was spared the torch during the Revolution by Tories who had great respect for Lillington, it went up in flames at the hands of invading Union troops during the Civil War.

Retrace your route to S.R. 1520. Turn left and proceed 3.4 miles to N.C. 210. Turn right and drive west 1.1 miles to the bridge over the Northeast Cape Fear River.

Several miles down the river from this span were the plantations of Maurice Moore and his son, James. Maurice Moore (1682–1743) was one of the first settlers of the Cape Fear. He was the founder of Brunswick Town, the site of an armed protest against the Stamp Act by Cape Fear residents in 1766.

James Moore (1737–77) led the protest march on Brunswick Town and subsequently became one of the early heroes of the Revolution. An excellent soldier, he served as an officer in the French and Indian War and as the commander of Royal Governor Tryon's artillery at the Battle of Alamance. But four years later, when the news of the Battle of Lexington reached the Cape Fear, Moore made the appeal that led to the First Provincial Congress in New Bern. Thereafter, he assumed a leadership role in the revolutionary movement that took hold in the colony.

At its meeting in Hillsborough in August 1775, the Third Provincial Congress named Moore commander of the First North Carolina Regiment of the Continental Army. Six months later, Colonel Moore executed the brilliant Patriot victory at the Battle of Moores Creek Bridge. Two days after the battle, the Continental Congress promoted him to the rank of brigadier general and gave him command of all Continental troops in North Carolina. In the autumn of 1776, General Moore was elevated to the command of the Southern Department of the Continental Army upon the recall of General Charles Lee to the North.

When orders came in February 1777 for Moore to march the North Carolina regiments north to aid George Washington, he set out from South Carolina to the Cape Fear to prepare for the campaign. En route, he came down with a case of "swamp fever." Moore never recovered. He died at his plantation on the Northeast Cape Fear on April 15.

Military scholars have concluded that George Washington's brilliant victory at Princeton on January 3, 1777, was based on the tactics devised and used by Moore almost a year earlier at Moores Creek.

Local tradition maintains that Moore and his brother, Maurice Jr., a noted colonial jurist and early Patriot who died on the same day as James, are buried in the tangled undergrowth of the old plantation site several miles downriver from the current tour stop.

Continue west on N.C. 210 for 2.8 miles to U.S. 117 at the village of Rocky Point. State historical markers for Maurice Moore, Sr., James Moore, and Alexander Lillington stand here. The Moore plantation was located along the river 3 miles southeast of the markers.

Turn right on N.C. 117 and drive north for 0.7 mile to the state historical marker for General John Ashe.

One of North Carolina's greatest heroes in the early days of the Revolution, Ashe (1705–81) was the son of noted colonial official John Baptista Ashe. Reared in the Cape Fear, John Ashe constructed a magnificent plantation house, Green Hill, when he reached manhood; the home was located east of the current tour stop on the Northeast Cape Fear.

Ashe was a leader in the Stamp Act protests at Wilmington and Brunswick Town in 1765 and 1766 and in the torching of Fort Johnston at Smithville a decade later. As a militia officer, he fought with distinction under the command of his brother-in-law, Colonel James Moore, at the Battle of Moores Creek Bridge. His heroism was rewarded when he was appointed a brigadier general.

A little over two years later, Governor Caswell promoted him to lieutenant general. In early 1779, Caswell dispatched Ashe and a large command of untrained troops to reinforce General Benjamin Lincoln, then the commander of the Continental Army in the South. On February 25 of that year, almost three years from the day he had enjoyed the sweet taste of victory at Moores Creek Bridge, Ashe failed miserably in his attempt to aid Lincoln at Briar Creek, located 45 miles south of Augusta. As a consequence, Georgia fell to the British.

Ashe returned to North Carolina in disgrace. His request for a trial by court-martial was granted. Although he was exonerated of cowardice, he was censured for his lack of foresight.

Forced into hiding when Wilmington came under British occupation, Ashe was betrayed, taken prisoner, and placed in Major Craig's infamous open-air "Bullpen" in the port city. During his long confinement, Ashe contracted smallpox. Seriously ill at the time of his release, he died soon thereafter.

Continue north on U.S. 117 for 2.4 miles to S.R. 1411. At this intersection stands a state historical marker for Samuel Ashe, who, like his brother, John, rendered distinguished service in creating an independent North Carolina. To see his grave, turn right on S.R. 1411 and proceed 3 miles to the family cemetery, located approximately 0.5 mile past the site of Ashe's plantation, "The Neck." His prominent gravestone acclaims him as "a leader in preparing plans for the Revolutionary War and framing the Constitution of North Carolina."

Educated as an attorney, Samuel Ashe (1725–1813) organized groups and committees of like-minded men—men with the revolutionary spirit, that is—in the Cape Fear as early as 1774. In 1776, while his brother was serving as a military leader, Samuel ascended to the presidency of the thirteen-man North Carolina Council of Safety. In that position, he supervised the affairs of state.

In one of his first official acts under the new state constitution that Ashe helped draft, Governor Richard Caswell appointed the Cape Fear Patriot to convene the first court of the state of North Carolina. Ashe thus served as the first state judge. He was also elected the Speaker of the state senate by the first legislature convened under the new constitution.

As the judicial and legislative leader of the state through the Revolution, he remained a fiery Patriot. In 1779, with the outcome of the war very much in doubt, Ashe expressed his undying desire for liberty this way: "The feelings of a few men, for himself and for his country, ready to be enslaved, warmed me into resentment, impelled me into resistance, and determined me to forego my expectations and to risk all things rather than submit to the detested tyranny."

In 1795, Ashe stepped down as presiding judge over the state court after twenty years of service. His retirement from the judiciary was necessitated by his election as governor. He went on to serve three terms as the state's chief executive.

Retrace your route to the junction with U.S. 117, turn left, and go south for 7.5 miles to N.C. 133. Go right on N.C. 133 and drive 4.9 miles to N.C. 210. Turn left and follow the route west for 6.7 miles to Moores Creek National Battlefield.

It was at this site on the bitterly cold February 27, 1776, that North Carolina Patriots won what some historians have called the first decisive American victory of the Revolutionary War. Begin your visit to the eighty-six-acre complex at the visitor center, where an audiovisual program and attractive exhibits and displays tell the story of the events that took place here more than four months before the Declaration of Independence.

On January 10, 1776, Josiah Martin, the exiled Royal governor, appealed to loyal subjects in the colony to unite and quell the rebellion. In response to his call to arms, sixteen hundred Highland Scots and Tories gathered at Cross Creek (modern Fayetteville). Commanded by General Donald

MacDonald, a British army officer and a veteran of the Battles of Culloden and Bunker Hill, these Loyalist troops prepared to march to Wilmington, where they would join a British expeditionary force from Ireland to form an army of sufficient strength to end insurrection in the colony.

Meanwhile, Colonel James Moore, the commander of Patriot forces in southeastern North Carolina, busied himself with plans to thwart MacDonald's forces. No sooner did the Loyalists begin their march from Cross Creek than Moore blocked their path. Consequently, MacDonald altered his course by crossing the Cape Fear en route to Corbetts Ferry on the Black River. There, he planned to avoid Colonel Richard Caswell's militia forces approaching from New Bern. MacDonald would then send his men across the bridge at Moores Creek and on to the rendezvous point at Brunswick Town. (At the time, the swampy creek, which rises in northwestern Pender County and flows into the Black River, was known as Widow Moore's Creek, as it flowed past land owned by Elizabeth Moore, a widow.)

All seemed well for the Loyalists when MacDonald reached Corbetts Ferry. But Moore countered by dispatching Caswell to Moores Creek, where he was reinforced by a Patriot force under Colonel Alexander Lillington.

On the night of February 26, Caswell and his 800 men camped on the western side of the creek and Lillington and his 150 soldiers on the eastern side. Halfway between Moores Creek and Wilmington, James Moore posted another force of Patriots as a roadblock.

Some 1,500 Loyalists were encamped approximately 6 miles from Caswell on the same side of the creek. Aware that Caswell was in a vulnerable position, MacDonald summoned a council of war, at which it was decided—against MacDonald's better judgment—that an attack should be launched. While final preparations were being made for the offensive, MacDonald fell ill, which forced his chief lieutenant, Lieutenant Colonel Donald McLeod, to assume command.

In the early-morning darkness on February 27, McLeod put his troops, armed with broadswords and claymores, on the march through the swampy terrain. After a tedious five-hour trek in frigid temperatures, the Loyalists reached Caswell's camp about an hour before light. To their dismay, it was abandoned. Caswell had pulled his forces to the other side of the creek during the night but had left the campfires burning in a ploy to trick would-be attackers. After his men had crossed the bridge over the creek, Caswell had ordered its planks removed and the girders greased. At their new base on the eastern bank, the Americans had thrown up fortifications and positioned artillery to cover the road and bridge.

The Loyalists regrouped and waited for first light at Caswell's abandoned camp, believing the enemy forces were in retreat. Instead, Caswell and Lillington were waiting just across the dismantled bridge.

As the sun rose, the rallying cry was passed among McLeod's troops. Suddenly, gunfire near the bridge broke the stillness of the swamp. McLeod ordered his forces forward. Three cheers were offered, and then the attackers called in unison, "King George and Broadswords!" Drums rolled and bagpipes played as the soldiers moved forward in battle formation.

Most of McLeod's soldiers were killed as they attempted to cross the creek. Others were wounded, fell into the cold water, and drowned. McLeod, Captain John Campbell, and a small number of their charges were able to make their way over the slippery bridge skeleton. But as soon as they reached the eastern bank, they walked into a hail of bullets. Both McLeod and Campbell were mortally wounded. McLeod fell only a few feet from the Patriot defenses. He attempted in vain to stand once again and spent the last moments of his life shouting encouragement to his soldiers and waving his sword toward the enemy. A post-battle examination revealed that he had taken nine bullets and twenty-four "swan shot."

His bravery was for naught, because the battle was over almost as soon as it began. In three minutes, the Loyalists suffered eighty casualties. The survivors retreated wildly through the swamps to their previous camp, where they reported the debacle to General MacDonald. A short time later, the Loyalists' attempt to escape failed when their relentless pursuers captured MacDonald and his defeated army.

The Battle of Moores Creek Bridge produced effects that reached far beyond the swamps of southeastern North Carolina. Royal authority was forever ended in North Carolina by the short but decisive Patriot victory. Moreover, the Patriots' strong stand here allowed North Carolina to remain free of British troops for most of the Revolutionary War.

In political terms, the victory provided the impetus for North Carolina legislators to be the first in the colonies to instruct their delegates at the

Continental Congress to vote for independence.

It was the foresight of subsequent state legislators that preserved the battle-field site. In 1898, the North Carolina General Assembly purchased the historic grounds for a state park. When Congress created Moores Creek National Military Park on June 2, 1926, the state ceded the site to the federal government.

Several trails lead from the visitor center to where the fighting took place in 1776. Located along the paths are a number of impressive monuments and markers, two of which are of particular interest.

The Mary "Polly" Hook Slocumb Monument towers above the graves of Ezekial Slocumb and his wife, Polly. In 1930, the remains of this legendary couple were moved from their original grave site in Wayne County.

Long regarded as one of North Carolina's greatest Revolutionary War hero-ines, Polly Slocumb, as the legend goes, left her infant son in the care of a servant and made a 50-mile ride through the swamps from her home to Moores Creek after a premonition warned her that Ezekial had been wounded in the battle. Upon her arrival, she found her husband alive and well, and she immediately set about ministering to the wounded Americans. Her di-ary provides a vivid account of this heroic adventure.

In recent years, however, this long-cherished tale has been challenged by historians, who cite records that indicate Ezekial was only fifteen years old at the time of the battle. Indeed, his pension papers reveal that he did not join the armed forces until April 1780, more than four years after Moores Creek. Furthermore, Jess Slocumb, the only son of Ezekial and Polly—the infant left with a servant during the famous ride, presumably—listed his date of birth as 1780 when he was subsequently elected to Congress.

Still, Polly Slocumb has not been knocked off of her pedestal at Moores Creek. Her monument remains one of the most honored places on the battlefield.

The Grady Monument (or Patriot Monument) is the oldest stone monu-ment in the park. It honors the memory and sacrifice of Private John Grady, the only Patriot soldier to lose his life at Moores Creek. In 1857, on the eighty-first anniversary of the battle, his remains were disinterred from his original grave in Wilmington, placed in a small lead box, brought here, and laid in the foundation of the monument. When the monument was relocated

The reconstructed Moores Creek Bridge

in 1974 to restore the battle site to its original condition, an examination of the water-filled lead box revealed bone fragments, teeth, a soggy piece of cloth, and some paper that may have once been a Bible.

Beyond the monuments, a trail leads to the reconstructed bridge. A nearby boardwalk crosses the creek to Richard Caswell's campsite.

When you are ready to leave the battlefield complex, drive west on N.C. 210 for 6.8 miles to N.C. 11 near the Bladen County line. Turn left on N.C. 11 and drive south for 4.8 miles to the bridge over the Cape Fear River. North of the bridge is Lock No. 1 of the mighty river.

Continue south on N.C. 11. On the southern side of the bridge, you will enter Columbus County. One of the largest counties of the state, it was formed in 1808 and named for Christopher Columbus.

After 1.3 miles, N.C. 11 intersects N.C. 87. Turn left on N.C. 87 and proceed southeast for 0.2 mile to Weyman Methodist Church, located on the left.

In the forest near the cemetery of this late-nineteenth-century frame structure is what is purported to be the grave of the highest-ranking Revolutionary War officer from the states south of Virginia. The grave was graced by a D.A.R. marker in 1932.

At the close of the war, Major General Robert Howe ranked seventh in seniority among American generals and enjoyed the respect and admiration of George Washington. But despite his high rank, Howe holds the dubious distinction of being the forgotten man of Washington's inner circle.

Born in 1732 in Brunswick County, Howe was still a young man when he inherited a fortune from his father and his grandmother, the daughter of the governor of South Carolina.

At its meeting in Hillsborough in August 1775, the Third Provincial Congress created two regiments for the newly authorized Continental Army. James Moore and Robert Howe were commissioned as colonels of the First and Second Regiments, respectively. Colonel Howe took his troops onto the battlefield for the first time in Virginia in late November, at which time he won the respect and admiration of his fellow officers. Four months later, he was promoted to brigadier general.

In August 1777, the command of the Southern Department of the Continental Army devolved to Howe. His promotion to major general followed in October. Political problems in Georgia and South Carolina resulted in Howe's reassignment to George Washington's headquarters in September 1778. But before Major General Benjamin Lincoln, Howe's replacement, arrived in the South, Savannah fell to the British. Much of the blame was wrongfully placed on Howe's shoulders.

In the North, Howe proved to be one of Washington's most competent subordinates. At Washington's request, he presided over the court-martial of Benedict Arnold, which resulted in the conviction of the man remembered as America's most infamous traitor. Howe later sat as a member of the military tribunal that condemned Arnold's British conspirator, Major John André.

Following the war, President Washington and Secretary of War Benjamin Lincoln gave Howe little hope that the postwar army would need a major general, and Howe came to the realization that his military career was at an end. Devastated financially by the war, he went to work restoring his Brunswick County plantation, which had been ravaged by the enemy in his absence.

Howe was en route to Fayetteville for a meeting of the general assembly when he died on November 20, 1786, at a site near the current tour stop.

Buried in a well-marked grave in the nearby church cemetery is Elizabeth Hooper Waters, the last surviving child of William Hooper.

Continue south on N.C. 87. It is 1.4 miles to a state historical marker noting the route Cornwallis and his army used on their march from Guilford Courthouse to Wilmington in April 1781.

It is another 1.7 miles on N.C. 87 to U.S. 74. Turn right, drive 10.7 miles to N.C. 211 at the town of Bolton, turn right again, and proceed 3.4 miles to S.R. 1740. Turn left and go 0.1 mile to Shiloh Methodist Church.

In the front yard of this church stands an eight-foot monument honoring Duncan King. His grave and that of his wife, Lydia, are located nearby. Theirs was a storybook tale of fate, love, and romance.

When Captain Duncan King, a young Scottish privateer in the service of the Crown, made port at the mouth of the Cape Fear in 1752, he brought with him a precious cargo—he had rescued a five-year-old French girl, Lydia Fosque, from a Spanish pirate ship. Lydia's parents had been killed when Spanish raiders attacked the merchant ship on which the Fosque family

Monument to Duncan King

was sailing. At Fort Johnston, Duncan placed her in the care of Mrs. Holmes, a French-speaking settler who lived in the area.

Duncan returned to his career at sea and subsequently saw service in the British army during the Battle of Quebec. Meanwhile, in North Carolina, Lydia grew into a teenager of breathtaking beauty.

In 1761, Mrs. Holmes decided that she and fourteen-year-old Lydia should move to Savannah. As the two women waited on the dock at Fort Johnston for the ship that was to take them to Georgia, another vessel made port. Down the gangplank walked Duncan King. After years at sea, he had come to North Carolina to settle.

Smitten by Lydia's beauty, Duncan fell in love with her, and she with him. After they courted briefly, Mrs. Holmes consented to their marriage.

Although Duncan had been rewarded for his military service with sizable land grants in New England, he chose to build a plantation on several thousand acres on the banks of the Cape Fear River at a site still known as Kings Bluff, located near the present tour stop.

During the Revolution, despite pronouncements by the aged Duncan that he intended to remain neutral and wanted no part of the fighting, local Patriots were suspicious of him because of his prior service as a British soldier. On one occasion, as Lydia was returning home from religious services, she was confronted by a group of Patriots who sought information about Duncan's whereabouts. Without replying, she dug her spurs into her mount and raced home to warn her husband. Her fleet horse beat her pursuers by just the amount of time necessary for Duncan to hide. When the angry Patriots arrived, they demanded to know why Lydia had galloped away. Using her charm to calm a volatile situation, she remarked that she had assumed guests would be staying to eat, so she had hurried home to make sure that dinner would be ready.

Duncan and Lydia lived at Kings Bluff the rest of their lives. Duncan died in 1793 and Lydia in 1819. Descendants of this remarkable couple have included Civil War leaders, the founder of Kings Business College, and a vice president of the United States, William Rufus King.

Return to N.C. 211 and proceed north for 0.4 mile to the Bladen County line. An ancient county, Bladen was founded in 1734 and named for Martin Bladen (1680–1746), an English soldier and politician.

Continue north on N.C. 211 for 3.2 miles to S.R. 1730 at the community of Council. Turn right and proceed 4.3 miles to N.C. 87. Here stands a historical marker for Oakland Plantation, a nearby Revolutionary War site. To see it, proceed across the intersection on S.R. 1730 for 1 mile. Oakland stands on the left at the end of a long driveway marked by eagle statuary.

The two-story, brick plantation house is on a bluff overlooking the Cape Fear River. Adorned with double piazzas both front and rear, it is listed on the National Register of Historic Places and is among the best preserved of the few surviving plantations on the river. Not open to the public, this spectacular plantation manor house was built in the late eighteenth century for General Thomas Brown (1744-1811), a local Revolutionary War hero.

Brown took part in the campaign against the Regulators at Alamance, but soon thereafter, his allegiance shifted to the growing independence movement. At the Battle of Moores Creek Bridge, he rendered distinguished service as lieutenant colonel of the Bladen County militia. In recognition of his gallantry, he was promoted to full colonel. Later in 1776, Brown served as a delegate to the Fifth Provincial Congress and assisted in the formation of the state's first constitution.

From 1777 through 1780, Bladen County was free of British troops. During that time Brown, used his militia to suppress Tory activities in the area. A stalwart Patriot, he was known for his vigorous pursuit of Loyalists.

Matters changed after British troops landed in Wilmington in January 1781. Their raiding parties fanned out across southeastern North Carolina and instilled a renewed fighting spirit in the Tories. Brown and his militiamen were forced to take refuge in the area's swamps and wilderness.

His greatest moment came in August 1781, when he helped mastermind a bold raid by a small band of Patriots that culminated in the dramatic American victory at the Battle of Elizabethtown, the site of which is visited later in this tour.

Retrace your route to N.C. 87. Turn right and drive northwest for 16.7 miles to the intersection with N.C. 41 and U.S. 701 in downtown Elizabethtown, the seat of Bladen County. Park on N.C. 87 (Broad Street) near the Bladen County Courthouse and walk to the courthouse grounds, where two small markers pay tribute to the unheralded but significant battle that took place near here in August 1781.

When eyewitness accounts of the Battle of Elizabethtown began to appear in print in the early part of the nineteenth century, no two of them agreed on the details of the event. Nevertheless, some facts of the fascinating story are incontrovertible.

During the summer of 1781, Elizabethtown was in the center of an area under Tory control. To the west, supporters of the notorious Tory leader David Fanning (see The Regulator Tour) held sway. To the north, Cross Creek (Fayetteville) was under Loyalist dominance. To the southeast, Wilmington was occupied by British troops. Four hundred Tory soldiers under Colonel John Slingsby, a native of England, were encamped in Elizabethtown proper. From this base, they carried out raids into the surrounding countryside, ravaging the plantations of local Patriots.

Meanwhile, the local Patriot militia holed up in Duplin County had dwindled to seventy men. Armed with long rifles and equipped with worn-out horses, the small band under the immediate command of Colonel Thomas Robeson, Jr., marched toward Elizabethtown in late August. They vowed to drive the Tories from the town or die in the attempt.

In the early-morning darkness on August 29, the Patriots left their horses with an attendant, undressed, tied their clothing and ammunition on their heads, and made their way across the Cape Fear. Cognizant that they were outnumbered, they realized that they could only prevail through strategy and cunning.

Whether Robeson or Thomas Brown was in overall command of the attack is uncertain. Some accounts indicate that Brown was recovering from wounds and had conferred the command on Robeson. At any rate, it was Robeson who led the predawn assault on the unsuspecting Tory encampment and perpetrated one of the greatest battlefield ruses of the war.

The small army divided into three companies, each detail approaching the enemy from a different direction. At a given signal, the Patriots charged forward yelling, "Washington!" Their initial volley of musket fire spread panic throughout the Tory camp. From the center of the line, Robeson shouted out orders to phantom companies in a loud, clear voice: "On the right! Colonel Dodd's Company! Advance! On the left! Colonel Gillespie's Company!"

Colonel Slingsby and fifteen Tory soldiers fell mortally wounded. Fearing that they were being attacked by Washington's army, the surviving Tories fled helter-skelter toward a deep ravine located just north of the current tour stop. Many of the frightened soldiers plunged headlong into it in an attempt to escape. Since that day, the ravine (now filled) has been known as Tory Hole.

By the time the smoke cleared, seventeen Tories were dead and many others lay wounded. Among the Patriots, no men were killed and only four were wounded. Although the battle was small in terms of the number of soldiers involved, it was important because it brought a sudden and final end to the power of the Tories along the Cape Fear.

One of the markers on the courthouse grounds, a bronze plaque on a granite boulder, gives a brief account of the battle.

The other is a stone marker that pays homage to the battle's heroine. Sallie Salter (1742–1800), a member of a distinguished local family, volunteered to make her way into the Tory camp under the guise of selling eggs. Upon completing her mission of espionage, she hurried to Colonel Robeson with a detailed account of the camp. Aided by this information, Robeson crossed the river 1 mile south of the town and launched his main attack from that direction.

From the courthouse, walk one block west on Broad Street and cross over to the northern side of the street to see the state historical marker for the Revolutionary War battle fought here. Near the marker is a covered walkway known as "Tory Hole Alley."

Return to your vehicle. Turn right off N.C. 87 onto U.S. 701 and proceed 0.2 mile north to the entrance to Tory Hole Park, located on the left along the banks of the Cape Fear. Named for the nearby gully into which the fleeing Tories plunged in 1781, the park offers picnic facilities, hiking trails, and a boat landing in a picturesque, forested setting.

Follow U.S. 701 across the bridge over the Cape Fear. Approximately 1 mile north of the bridge, turn left on N.C. 53. Drive 10.1 miles northwest to S.R. 1318. Located at this junction near a small roadside park is a historical marker for Harmony Hall, which dates from the Revolutionary War era. To reach it, turn left on S.R. 1318, travel southwest for 1.6 miles to S.R. 1351, and turn left. At the end of S.R. 1351 stands Harmony Hall.

Open to the public on a limited basis, this simple, stately, two-story plantation house was constructed prior to 1768 on the twelve-thousand-acre river-side land grant of Colonel James A. Richardson, a native of Stonington, Connecticut, who settled in Bladen County after being shipwrecked off the North Carolina coast at Cape Hatteras.

Richardson was an officer under Nathanael Greene at the time Cornwallis came calling at Harmony Hall in early April 1781. While the British commander was using the house as his headquarters, Colonel Richardson's wife overheard a strategy-planning session between Cornwallis and his staff. Through the plantation overseer, she promptly relayed the intelligence to Greene, who used the information to great advantage in his military campaign in South Carolina.

By the early 1960s, Harmony Hall had fallen into disrepair, and the plantation grounds were an overgrown wilderness. A 1962 effort to restore the house met with little success. It was not until the general assembly appropriated $150,000 in 1986 that serious restoration efforts began. Since that time, the historic structure and a sizable portion of the plantation lands have become a regional showplace.

Retrace your route to S.R. 1318. Turn left, drive 3 miles west to S.R. 1316, and turn left again. It is 0.9 mile to the river bridge, which provides another spectacular vista of the Cape Fear. Once across the bridge, continue on S.R. 1316 for 0.9 mile to N.C. 87 at the village of Tar Heel. One of the several possible origins of the town's name dates from Revolutionary War days, when British troops gave North Carolinians a new nickname upon emerging from a river with tar on their heels (see The First for Freedom Tour, pages 52–53).

Turn left on N.C. 87 and drive 0.5 mile southeast to the state historical marker for Thomas Robeson, Jr., one of the heroes of the Battle of Elizabethtown. The marker stands on the left side of the highway at Robeson's former homesite. Visible from the highway is Walnut Grove, the magnificent plantation mansion constructed by James Robeson in 1855 on the site where his father was born and grew up. The estate is not open to the public.

Thomas Robeson, Jr. (1740–85), served as a delegate at the Fourth Provincial Congress in Halifax in April 1776 and as a member of the first general assembly of the independent state of North Carolina.

Although Tories outnumbered Whigs by five to one in Bladen County, Robeson was an ardent Patriot. He fought as a militia officer at the Battle of Moores Creek Bridge. For the duration of the conflict, he was a Whig leader in the civil war that raged throughout southeastern North Carolina. Using his own personal fortune, he paid the soldiers under his command in order to maintain opposition to local Tories. He never recovered the eighty thousand dollars he spent to further the fight for American independence.

Turn around near Walnut Grove and drive north on N.C. 87. It is 8.3 miles to the Cumberland County line. Formed in 1754 from Bladen County, Cumberland was named for William Augustus, duke of Cumberland (1721–65), the son of King George II and the commander of the victorious English troops at the Battle of Culloden. Ironically, this county, named for a man known as "the Butcher" because of his savagery against his Scottish adversaries, was settled primarily by Scottish Highlanders.

From the county line, it is 7.5 miles north to a state historical marker that calls attention to the site where General James Moore camped from February 15 to February 26, 1776, prior to the Battle of Moores Creek Bridge. Moore and his troops made their temporary home on the banks of Rockfish Creek 1.5 miles north of the marker.

Continue north on N.C. 87 (now alternately known as Elizabethtown Road/Wilmington Highway) for 5.7 miles until the junction with Gillespie Street entering Fayetteville. In the 100 block of Gillespie near the former Cumberland County Courthouse is a state historical marker honoring the man for whom the city was named. During his triumphant visit on March 4 and 5, 1825, the Marquis de Lafayette stayed at the home of Duncan McRae, which stood at the courthouse site.

Lafayette statue, Fayetteville

Lafayette first came to America in 1777 as an inexperienced nineteen-year-old French soldier. Four years later, as a major general in the Continental Army, he pinned down Cornwallis at Yorktown and won the hearts of George Washington and the young American nation. Upon his return to the United States forty-four years later, the aging general toured every American state and became the first foreigner to address both houses of Congress.

Of all the places Lafayette visited on his victory tour, it was perhaps Fayetteville that stirred his proudest feelings. When the city changed its name from Campbellton to Fayetteville in 1788, it became the first in the United States to be named in honor of the most revered foreign soldier of the Revolution. Today, ten Fayettevilles, eleven towns (and fourteen counties) known as Fayette, and one Fayette City are scattered throughout the United States. This North Carolina city is both the oldest and the largest such town.

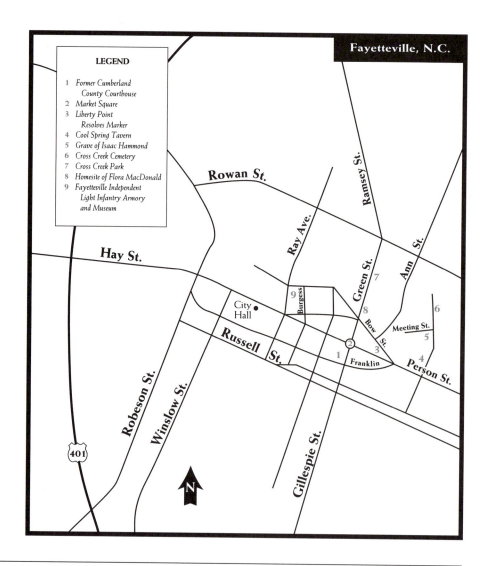

Proceed one block north on Gillespie Street to Market Square, the site of the city's most famous landmark. Market House, erected in the heart of old Fayetteville at the intersection of Green, Gillespie, Person, and Hay Streets, was constructed in 1832 on the foundations of the old State House, which was destroyed by fire in 1831.

At this site on November 16, 1789, Governor Samuel Johnston called the North Carolina Constitutional Convention to order. Its mission was to ratify the United States Constitution. There were 294 delegates on hand, representing fifty-nine counties and six towns.

The state legislature met here on December 11, 1789, and enacted a bill sponsored by General William R. Davie to charter the University of North Carolina, the first state university in the new nation.

Impressive in design, the existing brick structure was inspired by its predecessor. The second-story municipal hall is topped by a cupola with a clock and a bell tower. Plaques attached to the open-air columns of the first floor attest to the important events that took place here after the Revolution.

At Market Square, traffic flows counterclockwise into a circle around Market House. Enter the circle from Gillespie and bear right onto Person Street, named for Revolutionary War hero Thomas Person. (For information about Person, see The Statehood Tour, pages 425–456.)

Proceed one block east to Bow Street. A stone marker at the junction pays tribute to the Liberty Point Resolves (actually entitled the Cumberland Association), a manifesto signed by fifty-five local Patriots on June 20, 1775. Inscribed on the marker are the names of thirty-nine of the daring men who affixed their signatures to the document, which boldly declared, in part,

> We, therefore, the subscribers, of Cumberland County, holding ourselves bound by the most sacred of all obligations, the duty of good citizens toward an injured country, and thoroughly convinced that, under our distressed circumstances, we shall be justified in resisting force by force, do unite ourselves as a band in her defense against every foe, hereby solemnly engaging that whenever our Continental or Provincial Councils shall decree it necessary, we will go forth and be ready to sacrifice our lives and fortunes to secure her freedom and safety.

Cool Spring Tavern, Fayetteville

Unlike the highly controversial Mecklenburg Declaration of Independence, allegedly signed about a month earlier, the original of the Liberty Point Resolves still exists. It was found in the Southern Historical Collection of the University of North Carolina by Fayetteville researcher David Clark in 1975.

The first signature affixed to the document is that of Robert Rowan, who is believed to have been its draftsman. Rowan's language was daring for its time, particularly in a place dominated by people whose allegiance lay with the British Crown.

Continue east on Person Street for 0.2 mile to North Cool Spring Street and turn left. Located at 119 North Cool Spring is Cool Spring Tavern. Built between 1788 and 1789 by Dolphin Davis to house delegates at the North Carolina Constitutional Convention, the massive, two-story frame building with double piazzas is the oldest structure in Fayetteville.

In the same block as Cool Spring Tavern but on the opposite side of the street is a historical marker at the spot where, according to tradition, Flora

MacDonald bade farewell to her husband, Allan, and his band of Scottish Highlanders as they marched off to do battle at Moores Creek Bridge.

Flora MacDonald (1722–90) was the most famous woman in North Carolina during the Revolution. Born in Scotland, she achieved worldwide fame in her native land long before settling in the colony in 1774. When Charles Edward, the Stuart pretender to the British Crown, decided to challenge the Hanover family for the right to hold the monarchy in 1745, he went to Scotland to muster support for his cause. Flora was among his most devoted backers there.

Bloody warfare ensued. In the wake of his crushing victory over the Scots at Culloden, the duke of Cumberland was intent upon capturing "Bonnie Prince Charlie" in order to prevent further resistance from the people of Scotland. At the very moment when it seemed the prince would be taken prisoner on the Scottish island of Skye, Flora masterminded his miraculous escape to France. For her efforts, she became a heroine in Scotland and an outlaw in England.

Arrested for her part in the conspiracy, she was imprisoned first in Scotland and then in the Tower of London. During that time, grateful Scottish citizens lavished gifts upon her. In 1750, three years after her release, she married Allan MacDonald.

When the MacDonalds made port in Wilmington in 1774, they were welcomed as heroes and feted at a grand ball. They stayed but a short time there, choosing instead to come to the town now known as Fayetteville, where they enjoyed another grand reception hosted by Scottish Highlanders, some of whom they had known across the sea. For almost six months, Allan, Flora, and the three children who had accompanied them to America lived in town while they surveyed the surrounding countryside for a place to settle. They subsequently lived at several places in the area, some of which are visited later in this tour.

Flora and her family arrived in North Carolina at a time when tensions were mounting between the colony and the Crown. Although she had been a rebel in her native land, Flora, ever true to the oath she had taken, was a staunch Tory in her new home. She rode throughout the area demanding that her fellow Scots remain loyal to King George III and seeking volunteers to fight against the American rebels. Allan was appointed lieutenant colonel in the Royal Highland Emigrant Regiment, headquartered at Halifax, Nova Scotia. In that role, he was responsible for recruiting Loyalist troops in North Carolina.

In mid-February 1776, Flora stood on the steps leading to Cool Spring, a tributary of Cross Creek, to cheer and inspire the sixteen hundred Highlanders whom Allan had assembled. After the grand send-off, the soldiers, under the overall command of General Donald MacDonald, marched to their devastating defeat at Moores Creek Bridge.

Allan was taken prisoner in the battle. Because of her outspoken loyalty to the Crown, Flora suffered great hardships in the aftermath of Moores Creek Bridge. Not only was she harassed by local citizens sympathetic to the American cause, but her plantation was raided and plundered. Finally, in October 1777, after living in terror for almost twenty months, she fled to Nova Scotia, where she joined Allan, who had been released from prison.

Continue on Cool Spring Street. Just north of the MacDonald marker, you will pass across Cross Creek, the historic waterway that flows from northern Cumberland County through Fayetteville to the Cape Fear River.

The colonial trading center known as Cross Creek emerged along the banks of this creek around 1760. A rival settlement known as Campbellton was established about a mile away by the colonial assembly in 1762. Even though it was the seat of local government, Campbellton could not keep pace with Cross Creek. The two towns were combined by the state legislature just after the Revolution began and were known as Lower and Upper Campbellton until the present name was adopted.

Follow North Cool Spring Street to Meeting Street. In a tranquil, shaded spot at this junction stands a marker over the grave of Isaac Hammond.

Hammond, a free black man, served as a soldier and fifer in the Revolution. After the war, he was a musician in the Fayetteville Independent Light Infantry, which survives today as the second-oldest active militia in the United States. When death came calling, Hammond is said to have begged to be buried here with his fife: "I shall maybe hear the drum and the fife of the company every parade day when the men throng at the spring, and the sound will gladden me in the long, long sleep of the tomb."

Cross Creek Cemetery is located a bit farther north on the opposite side of Cool Spring Street. Established around 1785, this beautiful, shaded cemetery is one of the most historic in eastern North Carolina. A retaining wall of handmade brick on the southern edge of the graveyard is the oldest piece of construction in Fayetteville. James Hogg, a noted Patriot from Orange County, donated the tract for the original part of the burial ground.

Lying in the cemetery are some of the most prominent of the city's early citizens, including a number of men who made their mark during the Revolution. The grave of Robert Rowan was placed here following its removal from nearby Hollybrook Plantation. Rowan's friend and fellow signer of the Liberty Point Resolves, Lewis Barge, was laid to rest here, as was George Fletcher, who along with Rowan and Peter Mallet was named a commissioner of the combined towns. Gabriel Pubeutz, a native of Bordeaux, France, who sailed to America to assist in the fight for independence, stayed in the new nation after witnessing the British surrender at Yorktown; upon his death in Fayetteville, he was buried in these historic grounds. Also laid to rest here was John Lumsden, a Revolutionary War soldier who lived on North Cool Spring Street; Lumsden hosted renowned Methodist minister Francis Asbury on the cleric's early visits to Fayetteville.

Turn left off North Cool Spring onto Grove Street, named for William Barry Grove, a delegate to both North Carolina Constitutional Conventions. The stepson of Robert Rowan, Grove was elected to the First Congress of the United States.

After two blocks on Grove, turn left onto Green Street, then go one block south to Cross Creek Park. Landscaped by New York architects, this municipal greenway offers a scenic walkway along cypress-shaded Cross Creek, where the city was born. A large statue of Lafayette, purchased in 1983 by the Lafayette Society, was erected in the park to commemorate the two hundredth anniversary of the naming of the city.

Continue south on Green Street to Bow Street. Allan and Flora MacDonald lived at the northeastern corner of this junction in 1774. A small marker stands at the site.

Follow Green Street south to the traffic circle at Market Square. Proceed counterclockwise into the circle and exit onto Hay Street. In former days, the Donaldson Hotel stood at the southeastern corner of Hay and Donaldson Streets. It was the site of the grand ball held in Lafayette's honor when he visited in 1825.

Continue one block west on Hay to Burgess Street. Turn right and drive two blocks to the Fayetteville Independent Light Infantry Armory and Museum, located near the junction of Burgess Street and Maiden Avenue.

Included in the museum's collection are documents, uniforms, and artifacts from more than two centuries of service by the military company. Without question, its most prized possession is the carriage Lafayette rode in during his visit to the city.

During his stay, the French general was welcomed by the governor of North Carolina and the most prominent citizens of the area. Toasting his hosts, Lafayette remarked, "Fayetteville—may it receive all the encouragements and obtain all the prosperity which are anticipated by the fond and grateful wishes of its affectionate and respectful namesake."

Of all the local citizens who greeted the aging hero, one had the greatest impact. As a teenager, Isham Blake had served as a fifer and bodyguard for Lafayette in the latter stages of the Revolution. He had last seen his commander during the surrender ceremonies at Yorktown. While Lafayette was in Fayetteville, Blake called at the home of Duncan McRae. Word was promptly sent to Lafayette that one of his old soldiers wanted to see him. Blake and Lafayette embraced warmly as tears flowed from their eyes. As soon as the general regained his composure, he called on his fifer to once again play a tune for him.

Turn east off Burgess onto Maiden Avenue and drive to Green Street. Turn left and follow Green to Grove Street. En route, you'll pass two state historical markers. One pays tribute to Robert Rowan and notes that his grave is in Cross Creek Cemetery. The other commemorates the visit of Cornwallis and his army to Fayetteville. On April 1, 1781, they entered the town on the final leg of their march to Wilmington. Cornwallis stayed in a house that stood nearby, while his soldiers camped here along the creek banks.

Turn right onto Grove Street and proceed east for 0.3 mile to U.S. 301/I-95. Turn left and drive north for 4.8 miles to where I-95 and U.S. 301 divide. Follow U.S. 301 north for 6.4 miles to the village of Wade. One mile north of Wade, U.S. 301 junctions with S.R. 1802. Here stands a state historical marker for Old Bluff Presbyterian Church.

To visit the church, turn left on S.R. 1802 and go 0.6 mile to S.R. 1709.

Turn left again and drive west for 0.5 mile. The venerable church stands at the end of the road near the banks of the Cape Fear River.

Constructed in 1858 by the oldest Presbyterian congregation in Cumberland County, the two-story Greek Revival structure stands on the site where the church was organized in 1758. Among the church's most prized possessions are two inscribed, silver communion cups given by King George III in 1775. In 1908, the membership constructed a new brick sanctuary near Wade. Since that time, the old building has been used only for special occasions.

Graves in the adjacent cemetery date back as far as 1786. Many of the Scottish members of the early congregation are buried here, among them Colonel Alexander McAlister, who represented Cumberland County at the Third and Fourth Provincial Congresses. McAlister subsequently fought for the American cause in the Revolutionary War. A monument stands at his grave.

Another monument memorializes James Campbell (1700–1780), the church's first minister. An ardent Whig during the Revolution, Campbell espoused the American cause from the pulpits of local Presbyterian churches until Tory threats forced him to move to Guilford County. His actual burial site is located in a family cemetery just across the river.

Around 1770, the Reverend John MacLeod was sent to the area to assist Campbell with his duties at Old Bluff and other nearby churches. It was to MacLeod that the cherished communion cups were presented by the British monarch. In sharp contrast to Campbell, MacLeod was an avowed Tory. His sermon rhetoric eventually led to his arrest while in the pulpit at Barbeque Presbyterian Church, which will be visited later on this tour. After a short imprisonment, MacLeod drowned at sea on a trip to his native Scotland.

Retrace your route to Grove Street in Fayetteville; proceed west as Grove becomes Rowan. Follow Rowan to Bragg Boulevard. Turn left on Bragg, drive south to Hay Street, turn right, go west to Bradford Avenue, and turn left. The Museum of the Cape Fear is on the right after one block.

Located in a renovated three-story building that was once a nurse's dormitory for nearby Highsmith-Rainy Hospital, the museum offers exhibits that tell the story of early Scottish residents and the impact of the

Revolutionary War on the area. It is operated as a branch of the North Carolina Museum of History. There is no admission charge.

Return to Hay Street, turn left, and go 0.3 mile. Two blocks east of the U.S. 401 overpass, Hay Street junctions with Fort Bragg Road. Merge onto Fort Bragg and travel 2.1 miles to Bragg Boulevard (N.C. 24). Turn left, follow Bragg Boulevard for 7.3 miles, and turn right on N.C. 210. It is 3.9 miles to the Harnett County line.

Continue north on N.C. 210 for 0.3 mile to S.R. 2051. Turn right and proceed south for 0.4 mile, where the road passes into Cumberland County and becomes S.R. 1798. Follow S.R. 1798 for 0.1 mile to S.R. 1200 (McCormick Bridge Road) and turn left. After 0.1 mile, you will cross the Lower Little River. Continue 0.4 mile to a dirt lane on the left protected by a chain. Some 0.4 mile down this twisting, nearly impassable path is the McNeill family cemetery. Visitors should not attempt to make their way to the cemetery without first obtaining permission from the property owners.

The isolated burial ground is situated on a knoll overlooking the Lower Little River. In it are the graves of British soldiers who died in Cornwallis's retreat from Guilford Courthouse. But of all the markers in the historic cemetery, one towers above the rest. A tall obelisk marks the grave of Janet Smith McNeill (1720–91), one of the most fascinating women in North Carolina during the Revolutionary War.

Born in Scotland, Janet came to the Cumberland County area when her parents moved to America in 1739. Nine years later, she married Archibald McNeill. For the rest of their lives, they lived in the area near the current tour stop.

"Jennie Bahn," as Janet was affectionately known (*bahn* meaning *fair* in Gaelic), was stunningly attractive. Petite in size, she had red hair and a fair complexion. But her size and appearance were deceiving. One observer offered this high praise: "For beauty, sprightliness, and wit, she was regarded as second to none in the Scotch settlements; and for energy of character only to Flora MacDonald."

On the eve of the Revolution, the McNeills were said to be the largest cattle raisers in America. Legend has it that on at least one occasion, the Scottish redhead drove three thousand head to Philadelphia. On one visit to that city, Jennie Bahn met Benjamin Franklin and was greatly impressed

Grave of Janet Smith
"Jennie Bahn" McNeill

by the American statesman. Following Jennie Bahn's visit to the City of Brotherly Love, every succeeding generation of her family boasted of a member named Benjamin Franklin.

She also participated in driving several herds to Petersburg, Virginia. Because she could not take enough feed for the cattle, Jennie Bahn was forced to purchase it along the route. Once, when a Virginia farmer refused to sell her feed, she instructed her trail hands to dismantle his fence and drive the cows into his hayfield.

When the Revolution began, Jennie Bahn declared her neutrality. Throughout the conflict, she sold cattle to both sides. Tradition maintains that she sent three of her sons to each army, so as to protect her property from the ravages of war. In actuality, five of her six sons served with Loyalist forces. Three of them, "Nova Scotia Daniel" (named for his place of removal after the war), "Leather-eye Hector" (so named after losing his eye in a fight with his father-in-law), and "Cunning John" (named for his sly character) were noted Tory leaders.

Even the monument that marks Jennie Bahn's grave has an intriguing story behind it. An immense shaft was crafted in Scotland and shipped to Cumberland County for placement on the grave. When the time came for it to be unloaded from a river steamer, it proved so large and heavy that it could not be lifted onto the bank. It was abandoned in the river for years, until its base was cut into foundation stones for buildings in Fayetteville. Finally, 128 years after delivery, the cap of the original monument was lifted out of the mire and placed at the grave site.

Retrace your route to the junction with N.C. 210 in Harnett County. Formed in 1855 from Cumberland County, Harnett is named for Revolutionary War hero Cornelius Harnett.

Turn right on N.C. 210 and drive 11.3 miles north to S.R. 2056. Turn right and follow S.R. 2056 for 0.3 mile to its terminus at the Lillington American Legion building, located on the banks of the Upper Little River. John McLean's mill, one of the area's two muster grounds for Tory soldiers during the Revolutionary War, stood near here.

Return to N.C. 210, turn right, and drive 2.2 miles to U.S. 401. Continue north on N.C. 210 for 0.4 mile to U.S. 421 in Lillington, the seat of Harnett County. Incorporated in 1859, the town was named for Alexander

Lillington, one of the heroes of the Battle of Moores Creek Bridge. A spirited engagement between Whig forces under Colonel John Hinton and Scottish Highlanders under Captain John McLean took place here in 1781.

Turn right on U.S. 421 and drive west for 10.5 miles to S.R. 1229. Turn left and follow S.R. 1229 for 1.6 miles to S.R. 1280. Lord Cornwallis and his army entered Harnett County near here on April 28, 1781, on their march to Wilmington. They camped at William Buie's plantation, which was located nearby.

To follow Cornwallis's route through Harnett County, turn left on S.R. 1280 and drive 0.2 mile to S.R. 1215. Turn right, proceed south for 5.7 miles to S.R. 1209, turn left, and drive 0.5 mile to Barbeque Presbyterian Church, located near the junction with S.R. 1285.

Although the existing building was constructed in the late nineteenth century, the church was started in 1757 by Scottish Highlanders. One explanation of its unusual name relates to the Revolutionary War. As longstanding tradition has it, General Lafayette and his soldiers stopped at the church to feast on barbecued pigs. However, records as early as 1753 cite the name of the nearby creek as Barbeque.

On April 29, 1781, Cornwallis and his army camped at the church. His cavalry chieftain, Banastre Tarleton, engaged in a bloody encounter with Captain Daniel Buie and a small band of local Patriots. In the aftermath of the skirmish, Buie was left for dead, his head split open by a sword.

A couple of geographical landmarks on the church's eight-acre tract still bear witness to the British presence.

Down the hill from the cemetery is a deep depression called Cornwallis Hole. The British commander is said to have buried his payroll here in order to prevent its capture by American pursuers. As legend goes, one of his own soldiers saw Cornwallis bury the gold. After the war, he returned to recover it. A less-than-tidy individual, the former soldier failed to refill the hole he dug, so it remains today.

Farther into the woods is the Old Spring. Flora MacDonald, who worshiped at Barbeque when she lived nearby, drank from this spring. So did Cornwallis and soldiers from both armies during the war.

Actually, the church was the scene of heated squabbling about the fight for independence long before Cornwallis's arrival. Although Barbeque was organized by Scottish people, many of whom were still members when the war erupted, the church was said to be "an island of Whigs in a sea of Tories." Church members were much at odds with each other. Even the minister was not spared the inflamed passions of parishioners.

Perhaps no story better illustrates the Scottish dilemma in wartime North Carolina than the showdown at Barbeque in late February 1776. The Reverend James Campbell was an outspoken Whig who had one son in the American army and another in the British. During a service at Barbeque on the day before the Battle of Moores Creek Bridge, he invoked the blessings of the Almighty on the efforts of the Patriot forces. Following the service, McAlpin Munn, an aged, respected Tory in the congregation, walked up to Campbell, respectfully removed his hat, and said, "Meenister, yo ha'e been a longer time frae Scotland nor me, an' ye nae ha'ed to take the Blood Oath I ha'ae took. An', noo, if I e'er hear ye pray ay'in as ye did this day, the bullet has been molded and the powder is in my horn to blow it through yer head."

The graves of many church members are in the beautiful, well-kept cemetery adjacent to the brick edifice. One special marker at the edge of the cemetery is inscribed, "Sacred to the Memory of a Stranger—1766." The story behind it explains why Barbeque has long been known as "the Church of the Open Door." It seems that in the church's early days, a wayfaring stranger sought refuge here one bitterly cold night but found the doors locked. His frozen, lifeless body was later discovered on the steps. Members vowed from that day that the church would never again be locked.

Inside the church, the Heritage Room holds a number of artifacts from the Revolutionary War era. Among items related to Flora MacDonald are a portrait of the Scottish heroine and fragments from her home at nearby Cameron Hill.

When you are ready to leave the church, turn right on S.R. 1285 and proceed south for 0.1 mile to N.C. 27. Located at this junction is a state historical marker for Barbeque Presbyterian Church.

Turn right on N.C. 27 and follow it south for 5.2 miles to N.C. 24 at the crossroads community of Johnsonville. Turn left and drive 3.3 miles southeast to where N.C. 24 merges with N.C. 87. En route, you'll notice a state historical marker for the site of Mount Pleasant (also known as Cameron Hill), the home of Annabella MacDonald, Flora's half-sister. Flora lived here during the winter of 1774–75.

Turn right onto N.C. 24/N.C. 87, drive 3.8 miles southeast to S.R. 1117, turn left, and travel 3.6 miles to S.R. 1120. Follow S.R. 1120 for approximately 6.4 miles to the bridge over Anderson Creek.

The amazing Jennie Bahn McNeill lived on this creek during the Revolution. On one occasion, a British foraging party stopped at her plantation and seized her favorite saddle horse. As Jennie rubbed the animal under the guise of bidding it a final farewell, she cunningly slipped off the bridle, slapped the horse with the reins, and screamed, "Git, you beast!" As the riderless horse sped away, Jennie Bahn remarked to her unwelcome guests, "Catch her if you can."

Anderson Creek was also where Colonel Thomas Wade—the gallant American officer for whom Wadesboro was named—and his militiamen camped as they made their way west toward their homes in Anson County in 1781. They had been stationed in the area to protect it until Cornwallis departed from the Cape Fear. While Wade's soldiers were here, one of their number took a coarse piece of cloth that belonged to a Scottish orphan, Marion McDowell. Although the cloth had little value, it was to have been sewn into a dress that the child planned to wear to Barbeque Presbyterian Church. This act of thievery sparked a series of bloody clashes between Whigs and Tories.

Among the Tory leaders who sought to exact revenge for the theft was John McNeill, one of Jennie Bahn's sons. After the war, McNeill was brought to trial for the bloody reprisals he had masterminded. He was acquitted when an alibi witness lied on the stand. Following the trial, McNeill was forever known as "Cunning John."

Continue south from the bridge for 0.3 mile to S.R. 2045 and turn right. After 0.3 mile, turn right onto S.R. 2048. Follow S.R. 2048 west for 3.4 miles to N.C. 210. Turn left, heading south. After 2.1 miles, you will reenter Cumberland County.

Approximately 8.5 miles south of the county line, N.C. 210 merges into N.C. 24 (Bragg Boulevard) within the confines of Fort Bragg Military Reservation. Continue south on N.C. 24 for 5.3 miles to U.S. 401 Bypass. Turn onto the bypass and proceed west. After 9.5 miles, you will reach the Hoke County line.

Continue west for 6 miles to U.S. 401 Business. Turn left on U.S. 401 Business and proceed 3.1 miles to N.C. 211 in downtown Raeford, the seat of Hoke County. En route, you will cross Rockfish Creek, a waterway that rises in southeastern Moore County and flows across Hoke County.

This area was the site of a regrettable incident during the war. Following Cornwallis's march to Wilmington in late March and early April 1781, Colonel Wade deemed the immediate British threat over. Consequently, his Anson County militiamen loaded their wagons and began their march home. In the course of that journey, they set up camp at Piney Bottom, a tributary of Rockfish Creek.

The encampment came to the attention of John McNeill. Seeking retribution for the Patriots' theft of the cloth from the little Scottish girl, he collected area Tories and ordered them to rendezvous to begin pursuing Wade. The next day, about an hour before first light, McNeill and his soldiers launched their attack. The Tories found all of Wade's men asleep save for a lone sentinel. The guard hailed the approaching men but received no answer. He hailed them again, with the same result. He then fired, after which the Tories rushed into the sleeping camp with their guns blazing. Wakened from their slumber, the stunned, disoriented Patriots took flight. Five of their number were gunned down.

During the melee, an orphan boy who had been taken in and cared for by Colonel Wade was roused from sleep. Before he was fully awake, he lifted the flap of the wagon where he had been resting and pleaded for mercy by crying out, "Parole me! Parole me!"

Duncan Ferguson, one of McNeill's soldiers who had long ago deserted the American army, yelled for the boy to come out. The youngster promptly jumped from the wagon and begged for his life. But when Ferguson approached him in a threatening manner, the orphan bolted. Ferguson gave chase and quickly overtook him. Using his broadsword, the Tory split the boy's head "so that one half of it fell on one shoulder and the other half on the other shoulder," according to one account.

Outraged by this act of needless violence, Colonel Wade assembled a large force of dragoons upon reaching his home. They soon returned to the area and launched a series of bloody reprisals for the slaughter of the orphan.

Turn left off U.S. 401 Business onto N.C. 211 and follow it south for 6.8

miles to the village of Antioch.

Here stands Antioch Presbyterian Church. Although the existing building was constructed in 1882, the church is a continuation of Raft Swamp Presbyterian Church, which was organized in 1789. Like so many of the old Presbyterian churches in the area, Antioch has a cemetery filled with the graves of Scottish settlers who participated in the civil warfare that raged in the region during the Revolution.

The church is surrounded by Raft Swamp, a wilderness area that extends from southern Hoke County into central Robeson County. During the Revolution, Raft Swamp was a center of local Tory activity. A state historical marker at Antioch calls attention to the Battle of McPhaul's Mill, one of several fights in the swamp.

To see the battle site, turn right off N.C. 211 onto S.R. 1124 and drive west for 1.7 miles. A large stone with an engraved tablet marks the site of a mill built before the war. On September 1, 1781, Tory partisans under the command of David Fanning and "Sailor" Hector McNeill clashed here with Patriot militia under Colonel Thomas Wade.

In the days preceding the battle, Fanning set out from Wilmington for his base of operations in Chatham County. At McPhaul's Mill, Fanning learned of the recent disaster at Elizabethtown. He also learned that Colonel Wade had crossed over to the eastern side of the Lumber River and was marching his forces to attack McNeill's Tory forces in the Raft Swamp.

Acting quickly, Fanning directed McNeill to move down the swamp to cut off Wade's avenue of retreat. By midday on September 1, Fanning, satisfied that he held the upper hand, launched an attack on Wade's forces. At first fire, Fanning's line lost eighteen horses, but once his soldiers dismounted, they attacked with a vengeance, and Wade's soldiers took flight in utter disarray.

Had McNeill been in position as directed by Fanning, Wade's entire force would have been captured or destroyed. As it was, Fanning gave chase for 7 miles, took 54 prisoners and 250 horses, and killed 19 of Wade's men. For the moment, at least, the Patriot enthusiasm sparked at Elizabethtown was vanquished.

Retrace your route to N.C. 211 in Antioch. Turn right on N.C. 211 and proceed south. After 3.6 miles, you will enter Robeson County.

It is another 1.5 miles to N.C. 71 at Red Springs. A state historical marker at the intersection commemorates the former campus of Flora MacDonald College, located 1 mile east. To see the campus, follow N.C. 71/N.C. 211 (Main Street) for 0.9 mile to Third Avenue. Turn left and proceed two blocks to College Street. Nearby are the buildings of the former college named for the Scottish heroine.

Flora MacDonald College existed from 1896 until 1961, when it became part of nearby St. Andrews College. The site remains the burial ground of two children who some historians claim were born to Flora during the Revolution. Their remains were reinterred here at a special ceremony on April 29, 1937, after they were removed from graves along the Richmond County–Montgomery County line. An impressive shrine marks the burial site. Skeptics argue that the children buried here are not those of Flora MacDonald. The former college campus is now the home of Flora MacDonald Academy.

Return to the intersection of N.C. 211 and N.C. 71 in downtown Red Springs. Go south on N.C. 211 for 2.5 miles to the state historical marker for the site of the Battle of Raft Swamp.

Just four days before Cornwallis surrendered at Yorktown, a portion of a fourteen-hundred-man Patriot force under General Griffith Rutherford came upon Tory forces in the swampy wilderness here. Led by Colonel Thomas Owen and Major Joseph Graham, the Patriots thoroughly routed the Tories, killing sixteen and wounding fifty.

As a result of the Patriot victory at this site on October 15, 1781, the Tory stranglehold on the region was ended and the Loyalist spirit that pervaded many local homes was broken.

Retrace your route to the intersection of N.C. 211 and N.C. 71. Turn left and drive southeast on N.C. 71. It is 8.6 miles to the Scotland County line. Named for the country from which the area's early settlers came, the county was formed in 1899.

Continue 1.1 miles southeast on N.C. 71 to U.S. 74 Bypass. Turn right and go west on the bypass for 8.1 miles to U.S. 15/U.S. 401 in Laurinburg, the seat of Scotland County. Turn south on U.S. 15/U.S. 401, proceed 0.3 mile to Lauchwood Drive, turn left, and go 0.1 mile to Dogwood Lane. Turn right on Dogwood, which leads to the campus of St. Andrews Presbyterian College.

Of special interest here is the Scottish Heritage Center. Founded in 1990, the center is dedicated to the preservation of the area's rich Scottish history and culture. Open to the public during regular school hours, it houses a large collection of antiquarian books and artifacts related to Scottish history. It has been estimated that approximately thirty thousand Scots had settled in this part of North Carolina by the time of the Revolution.

When you are ready to leave the campus, return to the junction of U.S. 15/ U.S. 401 and U.S. 74 Bypass and head west on the bypass. It is 11.1 miles to the Richmond County line. Formed in 1779, the county was named for Charles Lennox, third duke of Richmond (1735–1806), the British secretary of state who openly opposed the policies of his country toward the American colonies.

Continue west on U.S. 74 Bypass for 10.3 miles to U.S. 1 in Rockingham, the seat of Richmond County. Turn left and travel south for 5 miles to S.R. 1104. Turn right and follow S.R. 1104 for 0.7 mile to S.R. 1103 (Old Cheraw Road). You'll notice a gated logging road on the western side of S.R. 1103. Park your car and enjoy a walk of approximately 0.3 mile to the Harrington cemetery.

Located in this old burial ground overlooking the Pee Dee River is the grave of Brigadier General Henry William Harrington (1747–1809). A marble slab engraved with Harrington's achievements marks the site of his interment.

Grave of General Henry William Harrington

Born in London, Harrington was living in South Carolina when the Revolution began. He was active for the American cause there until he moved to Richmond County in 1779. In North Carolina, he was promptly appointed a colonel of the militia.

After serving in the defense of Charleston during the first half of 1780, he came home to take a seat in the North Carolina General Assembly. In June 1780, the thirty-three-year-old Harrington was promoted to the temporary rank of brigadier general. Headquartered near Fayetteville, he was charged with the procurement and protection of supplies.

Harrington was once described as "a very intelligent gentleman, who is well acquainted with this part of the country and with particular circumstances relating to the enemy and to us." Nevertheless, he was replaced as brigadier general by William Lee Davidson in September 1780. (For more information about Davidson, see The Hornet's Nest Tour, pages 172–73.) Although bitterly disappointed, Harrington remarked upon tendering his commission, "So this my country is but faithfully served, it is equal to me whether it be by me or by another." Horatio Gates implored him to remain in military service, but to no avail. Harrington returned home to Richmond County.

During his wartime absence, Harrington had suffered tremendous personal loss. His wife and children had been forced to flee the plantation on two occasions, first to South Carolina and then to Maryland. His baby daughter had died during the latter flight. And Tory raiders had destroyed his personal papers and his extensive library.

After the war, Harrington became the foremost citizen of Richmond County. In addition to his service in the legislature, he served on many local boards and commissions. In honor of his great success as a planter, two important titles were bestowed upon him: "the First Farmer in the State" and "the Father of Export Cotton in North Carolina."

Despite the losses he sustained at the hands of Tories, Harrington showed compassion in the war's aftermath. When he learned that the daughters of Captain John Leggett, the Tory leader who had plundered his plantation, were living in poverty, he conveyed to them the title to their former lands. That property had been awarded to Harrington as compensation for the outrages committed by their father.

When he died at the age of sixty-two, an obituary in a Raleigh newspaper noted about Harrington that "the nicest sense of honor and strictest principles of justice marked every transaction of his life."

The tour ends here, at the resting place of a great Patriot.

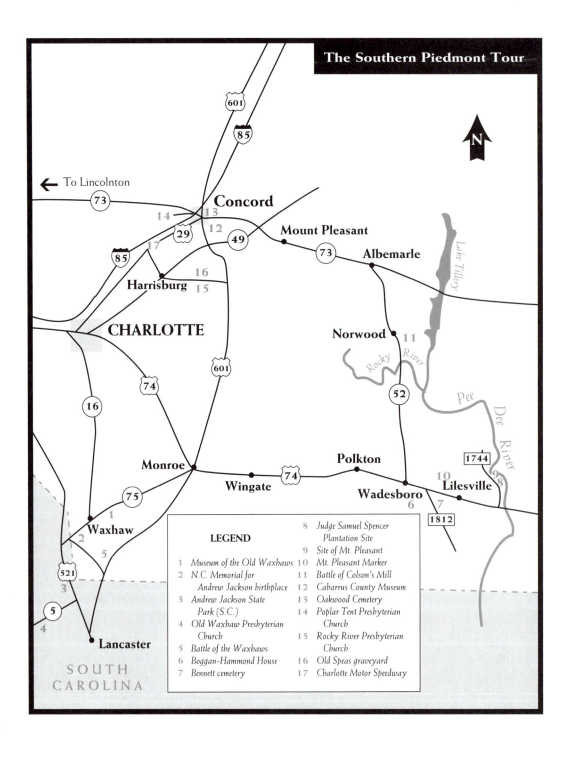

The Southern Piedmont Tour

To Lincolnton

601

85

73

Concord

14 13

29 12

17   49

85

16

15

Harrisburg

CHARLOTTE

Mount Pleasant

73   Albemarle

Norwood   11

52

601

74

16

Lake Tilley

Rocky River

Pee Dee River

Monroe

75

Polkton

Wingate   74

Wadesboro

Lilesville

1744

10

6

7

1812

98

Waxhaw

1

2

521   5

3

5

4

Lancaster

SOUTH
CAROLINA

N

LEGEND

1 Museum of the Old Waxhaws
2 N.C. Memorial for
   Andrew Jackson birthplace
3 Andrew Jackson State
   Park (S.C.)
4 Old Waxhaw Presbyterian
   Church
5 Battle of the Waxhaws
6 Boggan-Hammond House
7 Bennett cemetery

8 Judge Samuel Spencer
   Plantation Site
9 Site of Mt. Pleasant
10 Mt. Pleasant Marker
11 Battle of Colson's Mill
12 Cabarrus County Museum
13 Oakwood Cemetery
14 Poplar Tent Presbyterian
    Church
15 Rocky River Presbyterian
    Church
16 Old Speas graveyard
17 Charlotte Motor Speedway

The Southern Piedmont Tour

This tour begins at Waxhaw in southern Union County and makes its way through Lancaster County, South Carolina, before returning to North Carolina, where it visits Anson and Stanly Counties and ends at Harrisburg in Cabarrus County. Among the highlights are the Andrew Jackson Memorial Museum of the Old Waxhaws, Andrew Jackson State Park, the grave of William Richardson Davie, the site of the Battle of the Waxhaws, the Boggan-Hammond House, the story of Mary Sheffield Dunn, the Judge Samuel Spencer homesite, the story of the Cabarrus Black Boys, Poplar Tent Presbyterian Church, and Rocky River Presbyterian Church.

Total mileage: approximately 168 miles.

This tour winds its way through a four-county area in the Pee Dee River basin along the South Carolina line, where the Sandhills fade into the red clay of the Piedmont. West of the Pee Dee, there is a noticeable rise in elevation and change in soil composition. Likewise, during the Revolutionary War, there was a perceptible difference in the loyalties of the people living east and west of the river.

As in the Sandhills area, many of the Revolutionary War leaders of the southern Piedmont were Presbyterians. But west of the Pee Dee, the Presbyterians were of Scots-Irish descent and were not bound by the Oath of Culloden. Consequently, the sites on this tour tell the story of men and women who were overwhelmingly supportive of the fight for independence.

Symbolic of these Scots-Irish Presbyterians was a native son who was but nine years old when the colonies declared their independence. However, before the Revolution was over, Andrew Jackson would shoulder a musket for the American cause. The exact site of the teenage war hero's birth has never been determined, and the lingering controversy offers a number of interesting tour stops in North and South Carolina.

The tour begins at the intersection of N.C. 16 and N.C. 75 (South Main Street) in the small Union County town of Waxhaw, located near the South Carolina line. Waxhaw and the area lying primarily to the south—still known today as "the Waxhaws"—were named for an Indian tribe that the Scots-Irish settlers encountered when they began pushing into the region from Pennsylvania around 1751.

Andrew Jackson Memorial Museum of the Old Waxhaws

Drive east on N.C. 75 for 0.6 mile to the Andrew Jackson Memorial Museum of the Old Waxhaws. Operated by a publicly supported, nonprofit organization, this new enterprise is located in a beautiful, spacious facility. While the museum chronicles the history of the Waxhaws from 1650 to 1900, its focus is on Andrew Jackson and the Revolutionary War events of the area.

A twenty-minute orientation film offers a good overview of the Waxhaws. Special events—including reenactments—related to the Revolutionary War are offered throughout the year. Each June, the life and times of Andrew Jackson come to life in *Listen and Remember*, presented at the museum's amphitheater. Written by Dare Steele, a local history teacher, the play has been presented in Waxhaw for more than thirty summers.

From the museum, return to the junction of N.C. 75 and N.C. 16 in downtown Waxhaw. Many modern visitors know Waxhaw for its multitude of antique shops, but the place is the center of one of the longest-running and most heated disputes between the two Carolinas—a dispute over the birthplace of Andrew Jackson.

Follow N.C. 75 west for 0.3 mile to S.R. 1107 (Rehobeth Road). A state historical marker here calls attention to the nearby birthplace of the seventh president of the United States. Even the state of North Carolina takes the middle ground in the controversy by noting that Jackson was "born a few miles southwest of this spot."

To delve deeper into the controversy, drive south on S.R. 1107 for 5.4 miles. The road weaves back and forth across the state line; on the South Carolina side, it is known as Church Road (S.R. 29-378). Continue south to the junction with S.R. 1105 (Andrew Jackson Road). Turn left and proceed 0.3 mile to the Andrew Jackson Birthplace Memorial, located at the terminus of S.R. 1105 on North Carolina soil.

A large block of granite proclaims, "Here Was Born March 15, 1767 Andrew Jackson Seventh President Of The United States." Erected in 1910 by the North Carolina D.A.R., the memorial is said to have embedded in it the hearthstone and chimney stones from the cabin in which Jackson was allegedly born. According to some historians and many Union County residents, Jackson was born here in the cabin of George and Margaret McCamie (sometimes spelled McAmey). Mrs. McCamie was the sister of Jackson's mother, Elizabeth.

Much of the controversy as to the exact site of Jackson's birth has resulted from the lack of a definite state line in 1767. Until the exact boundary was fixed by survey on May 5, 1813, the line between North and South Carolina in the Waxhaws was unknown.

That Jackson was born in the Waxhaws at or near the current tour stop is not in dispute. On September 21, 1766, his father, Andrew Jackson, Sr., applied for a patent for two hundred acres on nearby Twelve Mile Creek, a tributary of the Catawba River. A poor farmer who had come to America from Ireland, the senior Jackson was busy clearing land in the Waxhaws in 1767 when he sustained an injury that resulted in his death soon thereafter. The future president was born a few days after his father died.

Proponents of the North Carolina site argue that Elizabeth Jackson was visiting Margaret McCamie when she gave birth. Supporters of the South Carolina birth site contend that Mrs. Jackson was visiting the James Crawford cabin (which was located nearby) when Andrew Jr. entered the world. Their argument was bolstered by the seventh president himself, who stated that he believed himself to be a native of South Carolina.

Several sites related to Jackson's birth are just across the line in South Carolina. Return to the junction with S.R. 29-378, turn left, and go south for 2 miles. A small stone marker on the right side of the road points toward the alleged South Carolina birthplace.

Continue south for 0.4 mile to U.S. 521. At this junction stands a state historical marker erected by South Carolina. Unlike its sister state, South Carolina does not straddle the fence. This sign boldly proclaims, "Near this site on South Carolina soil, Andrew Jackson was born on March 15, 1767 at the plantation whereon James Crawford lived and where Jackson himself said he was born."

According to proponents of the South Carolina site, Mrs. Jackson stopped at the home of another of her sisters, Mrs. James Crawford, after her husband's burial at nearby Waxhaw Presbyterian Church. Andy was supposedly born during her stay. To further cloud the issue, records show that James Crawford paid property taxes to North Carolina.

Statue at Andrew Jackson State Park

South Carolina has established Andrew Jackson State Park to mark the Crawford site. Turn right on U.S. 521 and proceed 0.6 mile north to the park entrance.

Acquired by the state from Lancaster County in 1953, this 360-acre historical park honors Jackson and seeks to provide a setting much like the Waxhaws frontier in which he grew up in the 1770s. A museum displays household furnishings and farm implements of that time. A replica of a one-room schoolhouse from Jackson's time is located near the museum. A large granite monument stands near the site of the James Crawford cabin. Inscribed on it are the details of Jackson's birth. Much of the park is given over to the kind of meadows and woodlands where the youthful Jackson honed his skills as an outdoorsman and horseman, skills that would stand him in good stead all the days of his life. Recreational facilities at the park include picnic and camping grounds, a playground, a fishing lake, and a nature trail.

Visitors are immediately drawn to the fine equestrian statue of young Andrew Jackson, crafted by noted sculptor Anna Hyatt Huntington. The statue and the surrounding meadow are an excellent place to reflect upon Jackson's youth and Revolutionary War career.

By the time the war came to the Waxhaws, Jackson, though very poor, was relatively well educated for a Carolina back-country teenager, having attended a field school before going to Liberty Hall in nearby Charlotte. It was in 1780 that he first learned of the horrors of war, when one of his two older brothers, Hugh, died of heat and battle fatigue at the age of seventeen.

The infamous Buford's Massacre occurred nearby on May 29, 1780. Tarleton's troopers slaughtered Colonel Abraham Buford's Virginians after their surrender. Following the massacre, homes and cabins throughout the Waxhaws were converted into makeshift hospitals. Andrew and his surviving older brother, Robert, assisted their mother in nursing wounded and dying Patriots.

The South Carolina upcountry was overrun with Redcoats that year, and the Jackson family was forced to take temporary refuge at Charlotte. During their short stay there, thirteen-year-old Andrew worked with a blacksmith who mended farm tools. One day, while reflecting upon the recent death of his brother and the invasion of his homeland, Andrew took a scythe and began to cut down weeds with great force, calling out, "Oh, if I were a man, how I would sweep down the British with my grass blade!"

The teenager had his chance sooner than he could have imagined, although he did not enlist in the militia or the Continental Army. Rather, Jackson ran away from home and found himself acting as a courier for William R. Davie, a gallant American officer who made a profound impression on the boy. It was at the Battle of Hanging Rock, fought to the south of the current tour stop on August 1, 1780, that Jackson first used a musket for the American cause.

A year later, both Andrew and his brother Robert were engaged in the defense of the Waxhaws when they were captured by British soldiers. Because of his tender age, Andrew was not initially confined with other American prisoners, but was directed to work in the British encampment.

One morning, a British dragoon ordered the youngster to clean the mud from his boots. Unwilling to comply, Jackson responded, "Sir, I am a prisoner of war, and claim to be treated as such."

Incensed by what he took to be disrespect and impudence, the British officer swung his sword at Jackson's head. Andrew threw his hand forward to deflect the blow. In the process, he received serious gashes on his hand and head. He would carry the resulting scars to his grave.

Robert Jackson was then given the same order. Like Andrew, he refused. The officer struck him down with a sabre cut to the forehead.

The American prisoners were later moved 40 miles south to Camden, the entire trip made without benefit of food or water. For months, the Jackson brothers suffered in the British prison, the victims of unsanitary conditions and little food or clothing. Both contracted smallpox. By the time their mother was able to secure their release, they were little more than living skeletons.

The Jackson family was a pathetic sight on the trip home to the Waxhaws. Mrs. Jackson rode one horse. Robert, so weakened by disease and malnutrition that he could not sit in a saddle, was held on a second horse by a neighbor. Andrew, dressed in prison rags, stumbled along behind the horses on foot without shoes. Not long after the family reached home, Robert died. Andrew was disfigured by smallpox for the remainder of his life.

Ever anxious to serve the American cause, Mrs. Jackson soon set out with friends to deliver medicine and food to American soldiers confined aboard prison ships at Charleston. There, she was suddenly stricken with fever and died. Thus, at the age of fourteen, in the waning stages of the war, Andrew Jackson found himself an orphan. But his strength of character enabled him not only to survive but to thrive. His nickname, "Old Hickory," calls to mind that toughness. Bestowed in later years, it was earned in part during the difficult times of the American Revolution.

When you are ready to leave the park, turn left and drive south on U.S. 521 for 2.5 miles to S.R. 29-775. At this junction stands a state historical marker for Old Waxhaw Presbyterian Church, the oldest church in upper South Carolina and the church where Andrew Jackson was likely christened.

To see it, turn right onto S.R. 29-775 and go 1.3 miles to S.R. 29-35. Turn right and drive north for 1.5 miles.

Organized as Waxhaws Meeting House around 1755, the church began as a log structure. It stood throughout the Revolutionary War and served as a hospital for the American soldiers wounded at Buford's Massacre. British troops ultimately burned the building. A stone marker on the front lawn relates the church's history during the Revolutionary War era.

The existing gabled brick edifice is one of a number of buildings that have succeeded the meeting house where Jackson and his family worshiped.

Adjacent to the church is its historic cemetery. Although the oldest legible tombstone is dated 1758, there are undoubtedly older graves. During the days when the church served as a hospital, many Revolutionary War soldiers died and were subsequently buried here.

Interred here after the conflict was Revolutionary War hero and master statesman William Richardson Davie (1756–1820). Davie settled at Tivoli Plantation, which stood nearby, in 1805. In 1927, the graves of Davie, his parents, two brothers, a granddaughter, and an uncle were disinterred from the original family plot at the church cemetery and placed in a large, enclosed plot between the church and the cemetery. When Davie's grave was opened more than 106 years after it had been covered, it revealed a simple silver button, the badge of an officer in the Revolutionary War, and three pieces of wood with copper tacks spelling out the initials *W. R. D.*

Grave of William Richardson Davie

A granite monument stands at the site where Andrew Jackson, Sr., was buried just days before his famous son was born. But the story is not quite that simple. On a cold winter night following his death, his coffin was placed on a sled. Then, in accordance with the custom of Irish wakes, it was dragged from house to house en route to the cemetery. In the course of the journey, the mourners, who consumed whiskey at each stop, did not notice when low-hanging tree limbs knocked the coffin off the sled. Much to their consternation, the coffin was missing when they reached the cemetery. After it was recovered, Jackson's body was interred in the dark of night amidst a row of smoking torches.

A statue honoring the seventh president's mother stands in the cemetery. Graves on either side of the statue mark the burial sites of her two sons who gave their lives during the Revolutionary War.

Continue on S.R. 29-35 for 0.9 mile to S.C. 5. Turn right and drive east for 1.1 miles to the state historical marker commemorating the site of Major Robert Crawford's home. On May 27, 1791, President George Washington spent the night at the dwelling that once stood here. This was his last overnight stop in South Carolina. While he was here, Washington met with a delegation of Catawba Indian leaders to discuss their fears about the loss of their lands in the area.

Continue east on S.C. 5 to the junction with S.C. 75 and U.S. 521. Proceed across U.S. 521 onto S.R. 29-378 and follow it back into North Carolina. It is 5.1 miles to S.R. 1106. Turn right and drive 1.9 miles to the site of the James Wauchope plantation, located on the right side of the road near the junction with S.R. 1194. Until vandals destroyed it in recent years, a large granite marker erected by the D.A.R. in 1941 stood here to commemorate the Battle of the Waxhaws, fought on this site on September 20, 1780.

Following his victory at Camden, South Carolina, in August, Cornwallis commenced his initial invasion of North Carolina a month later. Weakened by illness, his army, halted for a two-week stay in the Waxhaws in early September. At two o'clock in the morning on September 20, Colonel William R. Davie, twenty-four years old and only recently promoted to cavalry commander in North Carolina, discovered the right flank of Cornwallis's army, composed of British regulars and Tories.

The Americans made a surprise attack at daybreak. The battle took place on the plantation of Captain James Wauchope, one of Davie's officers. Approximately 150 American soldiers poured out of a cornfield to surprise and rout an enemy force of 300 to 400 men. As the fighting subsided, Captain Wauchope enjoyed a brief embrace from his wife and children before taking up his pursuit of the enemy. Fleeing the battlefield in utter confusion, Cornwallis's soldiers set fire to the plantation house and outbuildings. They left behind 60 wounded soldiers, 20 of whom would die. Only a single Patriot soldier was wounded.

This American ambush served as a prelude to the rude greeting that Cornwallis was to receive from Colonel Davie just six days later in Charlotte.

The Greek Revival house that stands on the battlefield was constructed in 1869 by a descendant of Captain Wauchope.

Turn left on S.R. 1194, drive 1.4 miles east to S.R. 1113, turn right, and proceed 2.4 miles to N.C. 200. Turn right and head south for 0.4 mile to S.R. 1100. At this junction stands a state historical marker for the Battle of the Waxhaws.

If you care to see a marker noting the general location where Cornwallis began his invasion of North Carolina in September 1780, continue south on N.C. 200 for 1.4 miles to the state line.

Turn around and head north on N.C. 200 for 15.4 miles to the intersection with North Main Street in Monroe, the seat of Union County. The former Union County Courthouse stands at this intersection. A D.A.R. marker on the grounds pays tribute to the Revolutionary War soldiers from Union County.

One block east of the former courthouse, N.C. 200 merges with N.C. 75/N.C. 84. Follow the combined route 1.7 miles north to U.S. 74 and turn right. It is 10.9 miles on U.S. 74 to the Anson County line. Formed in 1750, Anson County was the mother of many North Carolina counties lying to the west. It was named for Lord George Anson (1697–1762), the British naval officer charged with protecting the North Carolina coast from pirates in colonial times.

From the county line, continue east on U.S. 74 for 13.4 miles to Washington Street in Wadesboro, the seat of Anson County. Incorporated at the close of the Revolutionary War, the town was known as New Town until 1787, when it was renamed to honor one of its cofounders, local Patriot hero Thomas Wade.

A state historical marker at the junction directs visitors to the Boggan-Hammond House, built by Wade's brother-in-law and fellow Patriot, Captain Patrick Boggan. To see the house, turn right on Washington Street, proceed two blocks, and turn left on Wade Street. Named for Colonel Wade, this is one of the many streets in town bearing the names of Revolutionary War luminaries. Other such streets are Greene, Rutherford, Morgan, Washington, Martin, and Caswell.

Located at 210 Wade Street, the restored Boggan-Hammond House was dedicated as a museum in 1970. Constructed in the late eighteenth century by Captain Patrick Boggan, it is the oldest home in Wadesboro. Many of the interior furnishings were donated by the captain's descendants.

Patrick Boggan (1725–1817), born into a noble family at Castle Finn, Ireland, settled in the Anson County area in the 1740s. He prospered as a planter on the North Carolina frontier.

By 1768, Boggan stood at the forefront of the Regulator movement. From the beginning of the Revolution, he devoted himself to the Patriot army. Throughout the war, Tories in the Sandhills and other parts of southeastern North Carolina were tormented by Boggan, who served as a company commander under Colonel Wade.

Because of his avowed animosity toward Tories, Boggan was a wanted man. On one occasion when he made a visit home, Loyalist partisans surrounded his residence, stormed in, and demanded that he surrender. Determined not to be captured, Boggan hid his wife's flax knife under his cloak and obediently followed his captors outside. There, the sandy-haired, athletic Irishman attacked the unsuspecting men, killing three and then escaping. So powerful and agile was Boggan that it was said he could jump over a covered wagon.

Once independence was won, Boggan donated seventy acres of land for a new county seat, which was soon thereafter named for his brother-in-law. Not only did he build the home at the current stop as a wedding gift for his daughter, but he bestowed similar presents upon his other eight children.

Boggan-Hammond House, Wadesboro

Tradition has it that Boggan was furious when each of his nine offspring eloped, but that he quickly forgave them and lavished upon them a house, land, and slaves.

After Boggan's wife died, the soldier spent his last years with his daughter Eleanor Hammond in the house at the current tour stop. Despite his advanced age, Boggan was blessed with good health of mind and body. His hatred of former Tories never waned. One Tory in particular drew Boggan's wrath. Whenever Johnny Lindsay of nearby Lilesville made an appearance in Wadesboro, he was invariably chased out of town by the hot-tempered Irishman.

A monument erected by the D.A.R. to honor Boggan is located adjacent to the house.

Proceed two blocks west on Wade Street to South Greene Street. On the southeastern corner of this intersection stands the Anson County Courthouse. A drinking fountain erected by the D.A.R. on the northern side of the spacious courthouse grounds honors "our Fathers, those Heroes of 1776, who made this America Possible."

Turn right on South Greene, follow it to U.S. 74, turn right, and proceed east for 2.3 miles to S.R. 1812. Turn right and drive south for 0.4 mile to the Bennett cemetery, located on the left.

Buried here, near the site of the log house where she lived for much of her 103 years, is Revolutionary War heroine Mary Sheffield Dunn (1759–1862). A massive boulder adorned with a D.A.R. plaque memorializes the life of the remarkable woman known throughout the area as "Grandmother Dunn."

Memorial to Mary Sheffield Dunn

A well-respected nurse and midwife at the outbreak of the war, Mrs. Dunn promptly joined with her husband, Isaac, to aid the American cause. At times, she could be found by Isaac's side while he fought in Colonel Thomas Wade's regiment.

In response to the Dunns' unwavering patriotism, Loyalist scouts often stopped at their residence to harass them and to try to coerce them into pledging allegiance to the Crown. On one occasion, the Tories found the door barred. They opened fire, bolted in, and demanded to know Isaac's whereabouts. Mary, who had hurried her husband to their prearranged hiding place, remained stubbornly silent. Vexed by her lack of cooperation, one of the Tories struck her with his sword. Hickory splints in her bonnet prevented the blade from cutting through her skull, but even so, the sabre slash left a lifelong scar.

The diminutive Mary weighed less than a hundred pounds. A beautiful woman of fair complexion, she was at home in the saddle. She and her husband often had to flee invading Tories on horseback. During one hot chase, Isaac had their infant daughter, Susannah, in the saddle with him. Cognizant that both he and the child would be killed if captured, he threw the baby to Mary as their horses galloped at full speed. Mary caught the child and tucked her safely away. The Dunn family thus made another miraculous escape.

Throughout the war and for the remainder of her long life, Mary was best known as a woman of medicine. In a time when—and at a place where—physicians were extremely rare, she ministered to the sick and wounded over a wide area. Her ability to use herbs to make potions saved countless lives during the war. The bronze plaque on her tombstone attests that her "patriotic services and kindly ministries to the sick and unfortunate during the Revolutionary War merit the homage of countless descendants and deserve the grateful recognition of succeeding generations."

Return to U.S. 74, turn right, and drive east for 5.2 miles to S.R. 1744. Turn left and drive north for 0.4 mile to S.R. 1730. A state historical marker here honors Samuel Spencer, a Revolutionary War hero and a champion of jurisprudence when the state was in its infancy. His former homesite is a later stop on this tour.

Continue north on S.R. 1744. The road roughly parallels the Pee Dee and winds its way north into the Uwharrie Mountains. The isolated, undeveloped area yields little hint that this was the seat of political activity in Anson County in colonial and Revolutionary War times. Because of the events that occurred here in 1768, some historians consider this to be the birthplace of the Regulator movement in North Carolina.

It is approximately 2.5 miles on S.R. 1744 from S.R. 1730 to a logging road on the right; turn onto the logging road. After 0.5 mile, the road forks. Take the left fork, which ends at the Anson County Law Enforcement Clubhouse on the banks of Smith Creek, a tributary of the Pee Dee.

In the surrounding wilderness is a limestone rock with a bronze plaque erected by the D.A.R. in 1928. This is all that marks the site of Mount Pleasant, the original seat of Anson County. The original log courthouse stood approximately fifty yards east of the marker near the mouth of Smith Creek.

Patrick Boggan and an angry mob of ninety-eight Anson County men marched on this courthouse on April 28, 1768. There, they confronted Samuel Spencer, the clerk of court, and demanded redress for their grievances over unjust taxes and other perceived outrages committed in the name of the Crown. The heavily armed mob was noisy and demanding. When the men threatened to storm the courthouse and pull the magistrates off the bench, Spencer decided to hear their appeal.

He later told the story to Governor Tryon this way:

> I went to the door and demanded what they would have. They told me they came to settle some matters to the county for which they wanted use of the Court House. I immediately proceeded to read them a clause of the Act of Parliament of Geo. 1st against riot and unlawful Assemblies, and procured the Proclamation therein prescribed to be made for their dispersing themselves. They seemed great exasperated and lifted their clubs and threatened—then the mob grew laxer and asked to come in and present grievances.

Ultimately, they presented their concerns to Governor Tryon in the Anson Regulators Protest Paper, which was signed by ninety-nine citizens. In that document, they complained about local officials who "tax the people in an unusual manner" and boldly declared "that no people have a right to be taxed without by consent of themselves or their delegates." Indeed, here was the basis for the universal cry against taxation without representation, heard throughout the war for American independence.

Edmund Fanning, a notorious Loyalist from Orange County who served as a colonial official under Governor Tryon, considered Anson County the birthplace of the Regulator movement, which culminated in the Battle of Alamance in 1771. Tryon agreed. In a May 1768 letter to Samuel Spencer, he noted that "this contagion and disaffection has spread from Anson to Orange County."

The bronze plaque at the site of the old courthouse also marks the resting place of Colonel Thomas Wade (1720–86), the most celebrated Revolutionary War soldier from Anson County.

Around 1770, Wade settled at Mount Pleasant, where he operated a tavern. Before the first shot of the Revolution was fired, Wade was an outspoken opponent of the Crown's colonial policies. As early as 1775, he led an effort to raise men and weapons for the cause of the colonies. That same year, he was appointed colonel of the Minutemen of the Salisbury District.

Throughout the war, the Tories in the Sandhills region of southern North Carolina and upper South Carolina had no more relentless pursuer than Thomas Wade. As a consequence of his devotion to the cause of independence, Wade suffered extensive personal losses. In 1780, his home was sequestered by enemy forces, who ravaged his crops and stole twenty thousand dollars in property.

A year later, as the war neared an end, Wade led troops in two significant clashes in North Carolina, at Drowning Creek and Lindley's Mill.

The limestone rock that holds the D.A.R. plaque for Colonel Wade and the courthouse site has an interesting history behind it. Tradition holds that "the Indian Execution Rock," as it is known, was used in the distant past by Indians to behead their fellow tribesmen. As the legend goes, blood still oozes out of the rock on hot, humid days.

Return to where the logging road forks. Take the other fork and proceed east for 0.4 mile to the well-marked Spencer homesite and family cemetery, located on the right.

At this site on August 15, 1973, the Anson County Historical Society dedicated a restored stone well at the former plantation of Judge Samuel Spencer (1734–93). Here lived one of the most talented North Carolinians of the Revolutionary War era. Ironically, this remarkable man may hold the dubious distinction of being the only veteran of the fight for independence who was killed by a turkey.

Born in Connecticut, Spencer was educated at Nassau Hall, the forerunner of Princeton University, and arrived in the Carolina back country soon after his graduation. Although he was closely aligned with Governor Tryon both as clerk of court in Anson County and in the Battle of Alamance, he shifted his allegiance to the American cause as tensions with Great Britain heightened.

It was in the area of legal affairs that Spencer rendered his greatest contribution to the young state and nation. Richard Caswell, the first governor of the independent state of North Carolina, appointed Spencer one of the state's initial three superior court judges. Ten years later, while holding court in New Bern, Spencer and his fellow Superior Court judges, Samuel Ashe and John Williams, rendered a landmark decision in the case of *Bayard v. Singleton*. For the first time in North Carolina or American history, an officially reported court opinion declared the act of a state legislature unconstitutional. This preceded Justice John Marshall's famous Supreme Court decision in *Marbury v. Madison* by more than fifteen years.

Insistent that the United States Constitution contain a guarantee of individual rights and liberties, Spencer voted against ratification at both state constitutional conventions. His passion for individual freedoms led to his appointment to the committee that drafted proposals for the Bill of Rights, which ultimately amended the Constitution.

One of the true champions of American freedom, Judge Spencer retired to his plantation here along the Pee Dee. By 1793, his health began to fail. One fine day, the judge, a bright red cap adorning his bald head, fell asleep while sitting in a chair in his yard. His head nodded as he snoozed. A passing gobbler was so attracted by the bobbing red cloth that it attacked Spencer with great ferocity. Seriously wounded about the face and neck by the turkey's spurs, he later died as a result of the attack.

A Philadelphia newspaper reported the eerie event in verse:

> In this degenerate age
> What host of knaves engage,
> And do all they can to fatten braver men,
> Dreading that they should be free.
> Leagued with scoundrels pack,
> Even turkey cocks attack
> The red cap of liberty.

Retrace your route to the junction of S.R. 1744 and S.R. 1730. Turn right and proceed south on S.R. 1730 (Old U.S. 74) for 3.4 miles through the town of Lilesville to the cemetery at Cedar Creek Meeting House; the burial ground is on the right near the junction with Eighth and Church Streets. Near the road is a D.A.R. marker that details the history of the first county courthouse at Mount Pleasant.

From the cemetery, follow S.R. 1730 for 1.3 miles to U.S. 74. Turn right, drive west for 4.1 miles to U.S. 52, turn right again, and proceed north for 1 mile. Years ago, this area was known as Tory Hill, because Tory-hater Patrick Boggan once pulled an enemy rider off his horse and killed him near here.

Continue north on U.S. 52 for 15 miles. At the Rocky River, Anson County gives way to Stanly County. Formed in 1841, Stanly County was named for John Stanly (1774–1834), a United States congressman and the son of Patriot John Wright Stanly of New Bern.

A state historical marker near the bridge over the Rocky River calls attention to the Battle of Colson's Mill, a significant skirmish on July 21, 1780. The battle was fought several miles southeast of here, near the now-inaccessible junction of the Rocky and Pee Dee Rivers. In Revolutionary War times, the strategically important river junction was the site of a mill, an ordinary, stagecoach relays, and a ferry crossing.

Prior to the battle, Colonel William Lee Davidson learned that a band of Tories under the command of Colonel Samuel Bryan was operating from a farm near Colson's Mill. Anxious to surround Bryan's men, Davidson divided his army when he arrived at the farm. While Davidson was deploying his militiamen in front of and behind the Tories, Bryan's soldiers opened fire. Davidson quickly formed his line and advanced, leading the charge in his blue Continental Army uniform.

Unfortunately, he proved an attractive target for the blazing Tory muskets. Davidson suffered a near-fatal wound when a ball plowed into his stomach and passed through his body near his kidneys. His soldiers continued to fight, for as Lieutenant Joseph Graham put it, "[Davidson] had inspired a confidence nothing could shake."

In a short time, the routed Tories fled the field, leaving behind three dead, five wounded, and ten captives. According to Graham, the Tories were lucky: "Being in their own neighborhood and where they knew the country, most of them escaped. Their number exceeded that of their assailants, which was about two hundred and fifty. On the Whigs no person was injured save Col. Davidson and one other."

Continue north on U.S. 52 for approximately 2.7 miles to the town of Norwood. The route takes you through a peninsula formed by the Rocky River on the west and the Pee Dee on the east. During the fight for American independence, these fertile agricultural lands were known as North Carolina's "Granary of the Revolution." The historic peninsula is known locally as "the Forks."

From Norwood, follow U.S. 52 north for 9 miles to N.C. 73 in Albemarle, the seat of Stanly County. Turn left on N.C. 73. It is 10 miles to the Cabarrus County line. Formed in 1792 from Mecklenburg County, Cabarrus was named for Stephen Cabarrus (1754–1808), a Revolutionary War hero from eastern North Carolina.

From the county line, it is 10.5 miles on N.C. 73 to S.R. 2408. A state historical marker here honors the Reverend Samuel Suther (1722–88), a German Reformed minister who strongly supported the American cause during the Revolution. One of his churches, Coldwater Union Church, stood five hundred yards north of the junction.

In 1768, Suther was selected by Governor Tryon to serve as the chaplain of the Mecklenburg militia. Three years later, his outspoken support of the American colonies caused discord among his Lutheran and Reformed parishioners. As a consequence, the fifty-year-old minister established a new church, Brick Reformed Church, near the site of the Battle of Alamance.

For the duration of the war, Suther remained in the pulpit. His loyalty to the cause of independence never wavered, despite attacks by Tories on his home and farm.

A monument was erected in his honor in 1975 at nearby New Gilead Church of Christ, the successor of the old Coldwater church.

Continue west on N.C. 73 for 2.2 miles to U.S. 601 Bypass on the southern side of Concord, the seat of Cabarrus County. At the junction, the road you're traveling becomes Church Street. Park near the Cabarrus County Courthouse and walk one block west to the former courthouse, located at the intersection of Means and Union Streets.

Now home to the Cabarrus County Museum, the imposing Victorian structure was built in 1876. Inside, visitors are treated to exhibits and displays detailing the rich history of Cabarrus County. No portion of that history was more dramatic than the Revolutionary War era. "Not a Tory was ever born or breathed" in Cabarrus, according to historian John Wheeler.

A fountain erected by the D.A.R. on the museum grounds honors the earliest rebels in this hotbed of patriotic activity. On May 2, 1771, fourteen days before the Battle of Alamance, nine local men—brothers James, John, and William White; another William White, a cousin to the brothers; James Ashmore; Robert Caruthers; Benjamin Cochran; Robert Davis; and Joshua Hadley—etched their names in the Revolutionary War annals of North Carolina with their bold acts just west of Concord. For their exploits that day, the courageous nine were forever branded "the Cabarrus Black Boys."

When the violence of the Regulators in Anson, Orange, and the surrounding counties reached what he judged to be an unacceptable level in the spring of 1771, Governor Tryon summoned the militia to Hillsborough to quell the insurrections. To ensure that his soldiers would have an adequate supply of munitions and equipment, he ordered three wagonloads of gunpowder and other necessities sent from Charleston, South Carolina, to his army in Orange County.

Memorial fountain to the "Black Boys of Cabarrus"

All went well until the ammunition caravan reached Charlotte. Owing to the lack of support for King George III, no wagons could be found to continue the transport to Hillsborough. At length, Colonel Moses Alexander, the Royal magistrate, impressed the needed wagons. When news of this infringement upon the property rights of local citizens reached Rocky River Presbyterian Church in southern Cabarrus County, the nine men convened a meeting in the church's springhouse. There, they developed a scheme to destroy the approaching wagon trains. By oath, they bound themselves to secrecy.

Around twilight on the evening of May 2, the nine blackened their faces and set out in search of the munitions wagons. All were mounted except the White brothers, whose father had taken their horses to a nearby mill. The Whites met up with their father while he was returning with the animals, burdened now with sacks of grain. Thanks to their disguise, the old man didn't even recognize his three sons when they ordered him to dismount and unload the animals.

At Phifer's Hill, located 3 miles west of Concord, the nine raiders came upon the wagon train's encampment. After subduing and capturing the guards, they put their well-developed plan into action. They unloaded all three wagons, emptied the kegs of powder into one large pile, tore blankets into strips,; and poured a trail of powder from the pile. Then James White fired his pistol into the powder trail. A mighty explosion followed. So forceful was the blast that it sent a stave into White's forehead, causing a severe cut.

All of the supplies intended for Hillsborough were thus destroyed. This defiant strike against Royal authority preceded the much more heralded act by men in similar disguise in Boston Harbor by more than two years.

Return to your vehicle and continue north on Church Street through downtown Concord. After 1.3 miles, you will reach Oakwood Cemetery. For more than a century, this has been the most important cemetery in town.

Near the Spring Street entrance to this sprawling burial ground stands a tall obelisk in memory of Martin Phifer and his sons. Born in Switzerland, Martin Phifer (1720–91) settled in the Cabarrus County area in 1763. In time, he owned three plantations and achieved prominence in political and military affairs.

Governor Tryon found a close friend and supporter in Phifer. In the course of his travels throughout the colony occasioned by the Regulator movement and the Cherokee boundary campaign, Tryon used Phifer's plantation in Cabarrus as his headquarters and as an assembly ground for the militia.

Although Phifer's activities during the Revolutionary War were limited to service in the general assembly, his sons—Martin Jr., John, and Caleb—rendered gallant service as soldiers for the American cause.

Turn around near the cemetery and drive 0.2 mile south on Church to Buffalo Avenue. Turn right on Buffalo, proceed west for 0.1 mile to McGill Avenue, turn right again, and drive west for 0.6 mile to U.S. 29. A state historical marker at the junction directs visitors to the site of Red Hill, one of the Phifer family's plantations.

To reach the site, continue west across U.S. 29/U.S. 601 Bypass as the road changes from McGill Avenue to Poplar Tent Road (S.R. 1394). Red Hill was located 1.5 miles west of the intersection.

William Tryon was not the only important man to call at the Phifer home. President George Washington did, too. When Washington visited on

Sunday, May 29, 1791, he was hosted by Martin Jr. Once described as "the best looking of his father's children and the handsomest man in all that part of the country," Martin Jr. (1756–1837) served with distinction as a cavalry officer in the North during the Revolution. At the time of his death at the age of eighty-one, he was the last surviving officer of the North Carolina Continental Line.

John Phifer (1747–78), the oldest of the brothers, called Red Hill his home until his premature death on the plantation at age twenty-nine. A statesman of great promise, he was a delegate to the Mecklenburg Convention in May 1775 and signed the alleged "Meck Dec." Thereafter, voters elected him a representative to the Third, Fourth, and Fifth Provincial Congresses, at which he voted for the Halifax Resolves and assisted in the creation of the first state constitution. In late 1776, he joined Griffith Rutherford's regiment as a lieutenant colonel. An intrepid officer, he participated in the campaigns against the Cherokees in western North Carolina and the Tories in upper South Carolina. Less than two years later, he died of exhaustion and exposure.

Marked by a marble slab, John Phifer's remains lie in the nearby Phifer family cemetery. His grave site was desecrated in 1780 by Cornwallis's soldiers, who built a fire upon his burial spot.

It was near the Phifer plantation that the Cabarrus Black Boys carried out their daring act in May 1771. When news of the destruction of the powder train reached Governor Tryon, he was outraged. Anxious to capture and make an example of the culprits, he offered a pardon to any of the perpetrators who would turn himself in and provide information about his accomplices. Fearful of the consequences if they were captured, half-brothers James Ashmore and Joshua Hadley made their way to the home of Moses Alexander, where they turned traitor. Alexander, indignant about the affair, summarized his feelings this way: "By virtue of the governor's proclamation they were pardoned, but they were the first that ought to be hanged."

Their identities known, the remaining seven men were forced to go into hiding to avoid execution. Though hunted, they managed to remain hidden for weeks. Sympathetic friends and neighbors provided food and protection. Ultimately, they fled to Georgia, where they remained for a time.

On December 7, 1771, Richard Caswell, the speaker of the colonial assembly, recommended that Royal Governor Josiah Martin offer "a General Pardon to all those concerned in the late Insurrection." Martin agreed and submitted the proposal to the Crown. Through his secretary, the earl of Hillsborough, King George III subsequently gave his approval to the pardon.

Nonetheless, some Loyalists continued to harass the Cabarrus Black Boys. It was not until the revolutionary fervor so apparent at the Mecklenburg Convention swept over the Piedmont in 1775 that the notorious seven could move about freely without fear of reprisal. Each man went on to fight for the American cause in the war that followed.

As for the two who broke the oath, their lives were filled with hardship and tragedy. Ashmore fled the county and was said to have lived "a miserable life, and died as wretchedly as he had lived." Hadley remained in the Rocky River community. Prone to intoxication and fits of rage, he frequently abused his family. When they could tolerate his behavior no longer, some of his neighbors descended upon his residence, chased him from his bed, pulled his nightshirt over his head, and severely whipped him. When death came calling, Hadley, it was said, "died without any friendly hand to sustain him or eye to pity his deplorable end."

Continue west on Poplar Tent Road for 0.6 mile to Poplar Tent Presbyterian Church. Built in 1850, the handsome Greek Revival brick sanctuary is the third house of worship for the Poplar Tent congregation, which was organized under a large poplar tree in the early 1750s.

During the Revolutionary War era, the predominantly Scots-Irish congregation strongly supported the American cause. Buried in the church cemetery are many men who fought for independence, most notably the Reverend Hezekiah James Balch (1745–76), the first minister of Poplar Tent.

When he was six years old, Balch and his family moved from Maryland to Mecklenburg County. In 1766, he graduated from Nassau Hall (later Princeton University) with another North Carolinian and future Patriot, Waightstill Avery. Following a year's service as a Presbyterian missionary in North Carolina, Balch was called as minister by the congregations at Poplar Tent and nearby Rocky River.

Like many of his fellow Presbyterian ministers, Balch was an early supporter of a free and independent America. A delegate to the Mecklenburg Convention, he not only signed the alleged Mecklenburg Declaration of

Independence and the Mecklenburg Resolves but also served with Ephraim Brevard and William Kennon as the draftsmen of the documents. Not satisfied to express his patriotism through the pen and the pulpit alone, Balch also took up the sword, serving briefly as a captain in the Maryland Continental Line.

The American cause was robbed of Balch's further service upon his untimely death in the year the colonies officially declared their independence. His grave went unmarked until 1847, when a fund was established to erect the existing monument. Aged Abijah Alexander, who as a youngster had witnessed Balch's burial, pointed to a location in the center of the old graveyard, and it was there that workmen installed the stone.

Another delegate to the Mecklenburg Convention and signer of the documents produced there lies in an unmarked grave nearby. David Reese (1710–87) was a native of Wales who came to America in 1725. A prominent officer and a member of Poplar Tent Presbyterian, he was too old to participate in combat. However, he readily accepted an appointment by the Third Provincial Congress to serve as a procurement officer for the troops from Mecklenburg County.

A D.A.R. marker at the front of the church honors six delegates to the Mecklenburg Convention who had ties to the church: Balch, Reese, Richard Harris, John Phifer, Benjamin Patton, and Zaccheus Wilson.

One Revolutionary War hero of the Poplar Tent community was laid to rest here in 1997, after his original grave site was claimed by commercial development.

Born near the church, Charles Harris (1762–1825) grew up listening to—and was profoundly affected by—the sermons of the Reverend Balch. In 1780, the eighteen-year-old Harris was a student at Liberty Hall in Charlotte when news of Cornwallis's impending invasion of North Carolina reached Mecklenburg County. Harris had suffered the loss of his father, his mother, and the beloved Reverend Balch four years earlier. Ever mindful of their patriotic zeal, he exchanged his gown for a sword, volunteering for service with Colonel William R. Davie. Harris's baptism under fire came quickly, at the Battle of Charlotte. For the remainder of the war, he served as a cavalryman.

Harris attained postwar fame as a well-trained back-country physician.

After studying under Dr. James Hall at Clio's Academy, he completed his education at the University of Pennsylvania. Dr. Harris built his home, called Favoni, several miles west of Poplar Tent Presbyterian Church around 1810; in a separate log structure located nearby, he operated one of the first medical schools in the state.

Over the years, his original log residence was enlarged into a Greek Revival mansion by his son, William Shakespeare Harris. It was the younger Harris who welcomed Lafayette at the Virginia line and escorted him through North Carolina in 1824. Favoni was destroyed by fire in the late 1980s.

Retrace your route to the junction with U.S. 29/U.S. 601 Bypass. Turn right and proceed south for 0.5 mile to where the highways separate. Follow U.S. 601 for 5.1 miles to S.R. 1132 (Flowes Store Road) at the community of Faggarts. Turn right on S.R. 1132 and drive south for 1.3 miles to the bridge over Irish Buffalo Creek.

Buried in an unmarked grave on the banks of this creek is another signer of the alleged Mecklenburg Declaration of Independence and the Mecklenburg Resolves. Benjamin Patton, one of the earliest settlers in Cabarrus County, was a zealous supporter of American independence before the first shots were fired.

To say that Patton was honored by his election to the First Provincial Congress would be an understatement. Despite his advanced age and his inability to procure a horse or other transportation, he walked almost 300 miles from Charlotte to New Bern rather than miss the opportunity to serve with those who shared his passion for the cause of liberty.

Continue south on S.R. 1132 for 5.3 miles to Pine Grove Church Road. Turn right, drive 1.6 miles to S.R. 1136, turn right again, and go 0.6 mile to S.R. 1139 at the historic community of Rocky River.

Located at this junction is Rocky River Presbyterian Church, a magnificent Greco-Italianate building erected in 1860 and 1861. Named for the river located just north of the site, the church was organized around 1751. The existing building is the church's fourth. A monument stands at the site of the original log church, which was located approximately 1.5 miles northwest of the current tour stop.

The Reverend Alexander Craighead, an advocate of revolutionary principles in the decade before the war, served as Rocky River's first minister.

His congregation boasted many members who later joined the fight for independence. A number of these Patriots—among them William White, one of the Cabarrus Black Boys, and Robert Russell, a Revolutionary War soldier on whose property the first courts of Cabarrus were held—are buried in the church cemetery.

From the church, proceed north on S.R. 1139 for 0.2 mile to a dirt road on the right. Turn onto the dirt road, which leads to the Speas graveyard, located several hundred yards off the highway. In the eighteenth century, this isolated cemetery, enclosed by a rock wall, was apparently the graveyard of Rocky Creek Presbyterian Church. Buried here are two Revolutionary War notables: Robert Harris, a signer of the alleged Mecklenburg Declaration of Independence and the Mecklenburg Resolves, and Captain Archibald McCurdy.

Return to the junction of S.R. 1139 and S.R. 1136, then continue south on S.R. 1139 for 0.7 mile to S.R. 1161. Turn right and proceed 2.9 miles west to S.R. 1168 in the community of Harrisburg. Turn right, go north for 0.5 mile to N.C. 49, turn left, and travel west for 0.3 mile to S.R. 1300 (Morehead Road). At this intersection stands a state historical marker that pays homage to Nathaniel Alexander, the Continental Army surgeon who was elected governor of North Carolina in 1805. Alexander was born 3 miles north of the marker.

Turn right and follow S.R. 1300 north for 3.2 miles to U.S. 29, where the tour ends.

Near this junction stands the Charlotte Motor Speedway, the site of the longest stock-car race in the world. Amid the high-banked asphalt track and the expansive grandstands, it is hard to conceive that President George Washington was once entertained here. That event took place at the home of Robert Smith and his wife on May 29, 1791. Colonel Smith served as an officer in the North Carolina Continental Line. His wife, Sarah, had previously been married to Moses Alexander, the Charlotte agent for Governor Tryon who considered the action of the Cabarrus Black Boys a personal affront.

As the racetrack grew in size and popularity in the 1970s and 1980s, the two-story eighteenth-century structure, originally known as Smithfield, was drastically altered and converted into the ticket office for the speedway.

It is ironic that every year on the last Sunday in May, hundreds of thousands of fans congregate for the World 600 on the same site where—on the last Sunday in May many years ago—George Washington stepped from his ivory chariot on a plantation known as one of the most productive in the Piedmont. Back then, the landscape now covered with asphalt, concrete, glass, and steel offered Washington a vista of green fields of grain and the Rocky River beyond.

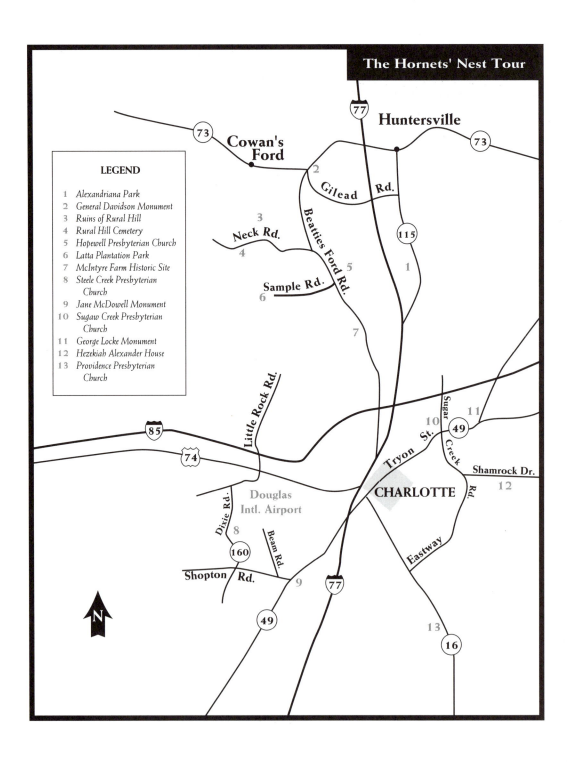

The Hornets' Nest Tour

LEGEND

1 Alexandriana Park
2 General Davidson Monument
3 Ruins of Rural Hill
4 Rural Hill Cemetery
5 Hopewell Presbyterian Church
6 Latta Plantation Park
7 McIntyre Farm Historic Site
8 Steele Creek Presbyterian
  Church
9 Jane McDowell Monument
10 Sugaw Creek Presbyterian
  Church
11 George Locke Monument
12 Hezekiah Alexander House
13 Providence Presbyterian
  Church

The Hornets' Nest Tour

This tour is confined to a single county—Mecklenburg. Included is an ambitious walking tour of downtown Charlotte, which might be best enjoyed on a weekend, when traffic and parking problems in the city are greatly diminished. Among the highlights are Alexandriana Park, the story of General William Lee Davidson, Hopewell Presbyterian Church, the site of the Battle of the Bees, Old Settlers' Cemetery, Independence Square, the story of the Battle of Charlotte, the story of the Mecklenburg Declaration of Independence, Steele Creek Presbyterian Church, the story of Jane Parks McDowell, Sugaw Creek Presbyterian Church, the Hezekiah Alexander House, and Providence Presbyterian Church.

Total mileage: approximately 63 miles.

This tour is confined to a single county, Mecklenburg, the scene of some of the most dramatic events of the Revolution in North Carolina and the home of numerous heroes and heroines of the period.

Charlotte, the county seat of Mecklenburg and the largest city in the Carolinas, was a hotbed of activities during the Revolutionary War. When Lord Cornwallis triumphantly marched his Redcoats into town in the early fall of 1780 in the wake of his overwhelming conquest of the Americans at Camden, South Carolina, he could sense that a total victory in the South was at hand. However, during his three-week stay, the British commander found the city a most inhospitable place. It was literally and figuratively a hornets' nest.

Following the departure of the British army, General Nathanael Greene arrived in the city. One of the defining moments of the entire war took place in Charlotte on December 3, 1780, when Greene assumed command of the American army in the South. Thanks to his skillful maneuvers against the Redcoats over the next four months, the British victory that had seemed so apparent to Cornwallis became total defeat a year later.

But long before these exciting events in 1780, the city was the site of one of the most important events—or nonevents—of the Revolutionary War period: the Mecklenburg Declaration of Independence. Did twenty-seven area Patriots affix their signatures to the first public declaration of independence in the American colonies on May 20, 1775? Despite some compelling evidence that the document was reality rather than legend, the Mecklenburg Declaration remains a source of debate.

Regardless of the controversy surrounding the so-called "Meck Dec," there is no doubt that Mecklenburg County residents were by and large ardent supporters of the cause of independence. Many were Scots-Irish Presbyterians whose graves lie in historic cemeteries in and around Charlotte.

The tour begins in northwestern Mecklenburg County at Alexandriana Park. The park is located on N.C. 115 approximately 11.8 miles south of Davidson.

This is the first of several tour sites related to the Mecklenburg Declaration of Independence. A plaque at the park marks the site of the home of John McKnitt Alexander, the custodian of the original copy of the controversial document. When Alexander's home, Alexandriana, burned in 1800, the best evidence of the Mecklenburg Declaration went up in smoke. Proponents of its authenticity maintain that the document—or at least a portion of it—was drafted here.

From the park, drive north on N.C. 115 for 3.5 miles to Gilead Road (S.R. 2136). Turn left and go west for 0.7 mile to U.S. 21. At this intersection stands a state historical marker for William Lee Davidson, the heroic American general killed at the nearby Battle of Cowan's Ford. (For more information on this battle, see The Tide Turns Tour, pages 283–85.)

Continue west on Gilead Road for 4.1 miles to Beatties Ford Road. Near this junction stands a tall rock monument honoring General William Lee Davidson.

From the General Davidson Monument Area (located at nearby Cowan's Ford) to Hopewell Presbyterian Church (more than 5 miles from the current tour stop), similar monuments and structures erected by later generations of the Davidson family stand as memorials to their Revolutionary War ancestors.

Educated at Sugaw Creek Academy in Charlotte (visited later on this tour), William Lee Davidson was, according to his friend Henry "Lighthorse Harry" Lee, "enamoured of the profession of arms" at an early age. As the pace of events leading to the Revolution quickened in 1775, so did Davidson's patriotism.

In the spring of 1776, when the officers of the Fourth North Carolina Continental Line were selected, Davidson was named major. The Fourth North Carolina moved north in the fall of 1777 to serve under George Washington and took part in the ferocious fighting at Germantown. For his gallantry on the field there, Davidson was promoted to lieutenant colonel of the Fifth North Carolina. During the harsh winter that followed, he endured the hardships of Washington's army at Valley Forge.

Before he returned home in 1778 to recruit men and to care for his wife and children, Davidson formed close personal friendships with Lighthorse Harry Lee and Daniel Morgan. All three men later became significant players in the fighting in Davidson's backyard.

Davidson was at home on furlough when most of the North Carolina Continental Line was captured at the fall of Charleston on May 12, 1780. Suddenly, he was an officer without soldiers. Unwilling to stay inactive when the fortunes of the American colonies were at an ebb, he offered his skills to an old friend, General Griffith Rutherford, the commander of the militia in western North Carolina. Rutherford named Davidson his chief lieutenant.

Weeks later, the militiamen found themselves in a hot fight against Tories at Colson's Mill on the Pee Dee River in Stanly County. There, Davidson, dressed in his blue Continental uniform, proved an attractive target for enemy guns. He sustained a severe stomach wound and was forced to recuperate at home while Rutherford and his men participated in the disaster at Camden in August. Upon Rutherford's capture in South Carolina, Davidson was promoted to brigadier general and assigned to Rutherford's command.

When the British army invaded North Carolina in September 1780, it was Davidson who maintained resistance in the Piedmont. His roving bands of militia constantly sniped at, ambushed, harassed, and raided the Redcoats until Cornwallis left the state and once again entered South Carolina.

Davidson's greatest—and final—moments were soon to come on February 1, 1781, at the Battle of Cowan's Ford.

Turn left onto Beatties Ford Road and proceed 3.5 miles south to Neck

Road. On the right side of the road stands a rock monument honoring Major John Davidson, whose home, Rural Hill, stood nearby.

To see the site and Major Davidson's grave, turn right on Neck Road. After 2.1 miles, a driveway on the right yields a glimpse of a row of columns, the ancient ruins of Rural Hill.

John Davidson (1735–1832) built a palatial mansion here in 1788. A native of Pennsylvania, Davidson migrated to the North Carolina Piedmont with his widowed mother in the 1750s. After his marriage in 1761, he built a substantial log cabin here, on a hilltop about a mile east of Tool's Ford on the Catawba.

Several terms of service in the colonial assembly in the 1770s did nothing to endear Davidson to the government of Great Britain. He took part in—and was the last surviving member of—the convention in Charlotte in May 1775 that allegedly produced the Mecklenburg Declaration of Independence. Davidson was a signer of the document. His testimony as a ninety-four-year-old man did much to lend authenticity to the disputed declaration.

Throughout the Revolution, Davidson rendered conspicuous service as a major in the militia. In preparation for his brilliant stand at Cowan's Ford, General William Lee Davidson spent a night here at Major Davidson's cabin. On that occasion, the general borrowed the major's horse. Indeed, he was riding that horse when he received his fatal wound in battle. According to tradition, General Davidson mounted the borrowed charger under a low-limbed tree. Major Davidson's slaves considered this a bad omen and predicted that tragedy would follow. In the aftermath of the battle on the Catawba, the riderless horse galloped back to the stable at Rural Hill.

Following the war, John Davidson gained wealth and prominence as a pioneer in the area's iron industry. The wealth he amassed allowed him to construct Rural Hill, which has been described as "the first notable house on the Catawba River."

Continue 0.1 mile west on Neck Road. On the left side of the road is the Rural Hill cemetery, the burial site of Major Davidson and many of his descendants. This magnificently landscaped cemetery is surrounded by a stone wall constructed in 1923 of stones from Rural Hill and the nearby Catawba River.

Major Davidson's grave is prominently marked. He was the father of ten children. Two of his daughters, Rebecca and Isabella, married Revolutionary War heroes Alexander Brevard and Joseph Graham, respectively. Both men joined Major Davidson in developing the iron industry that flourished just across the river in Lincoln County in the years following the war. Another daughter married a cousin, William Lee Davidson II, the son of the general. William Lee Davidson II was born just a month before his father's death.

Retrace your route to Beatties Ford Road and turn right. Proceed south for 1.6 miles to Hopewell Presbyterian Church, located on the left.

Although the oldest of the existing buildings here was constructed in the 1830s, Hopewell traces its roots to the decade preceding the Revolution. Pioneering Presbyterian minister Alexander Craighead organized the congregation in 1758.

The adjacent cemetery is of extreme importance to Revolutionary War history.

First and foremost among the Patriots buried here is General William Lee Davidson. A rifle ball plowed through his heart in the first fire at Cowan's Ford. With hordes of Redcoats making their way across the river, the general's retreating soldiers had no opportunity to minister to their fallen commander.

By late afternoon, with Cornwallis's army long gone, Richard Barry, Major David Wilson, and the Reverend Thomas H. McCaule returned to the battlefield to claim Davidson's body. They found his body—stripped bare by British looters—in the water. The three men carefully laid him across Major Wilson's horse and made their way down Beatties Ford Road. After suitable burial clothes were secured, Davidson was laid to rest in the cemetery at Hopewell in a torchlight service on the cold, rainy night of February 1. For many years, his grave was unmarked, but a large stone tablet now makes his final resting place readily identifiable.

Lighthorse Harry Lee observed, "The loss of General Davidson would have always been felt at any stage of the war. It was particularly detrimental in its effect at this period. . . . A promising soldier, was lost to his country, in the meridian of life, and at a moment when his services would have been highly beneficial to her."

Ironically, Davidson's wallet, which was on his person when he died, was found in the British Museum in London 183 years after his death.

Grave of General William Lee Davidson, Hopewell Presbyterian Church

At least four of the signers of the alleged Mecklenburg Declaration of Independence are buried at Hopewell: Richard Barry, John McKnitt Alexander, William Graham, and Matthew McClure.

Richard Barry (1726–1801), one of the many devout Presbyterians said to have signed the declaration, was an elder at Hopewell for many years. When he was fifty-five years old, Barry fought with the American militia at Cowan's Ford and assisted in the recovery and burial of General Davidson's body. His grave is well marked.

John McKnitt Alexander (1733–1817) was not only a signer of the controversial declaration but was also the custodian of the original until it was destroyed in the fire that ravaged Alexandriana. Although he was in his late forties when the British invaded the area, Alexander took an active role in the American defense. After General Davidson fell, he served as a volunteer guide to General Nathanael Greene. His vast experience as a land surveyor enabled him to lead Greene across the Yadkin to the Dan while Cornwallis was giving chase. Alexander's grave is marked by a marble slab along the eastern wall of the cemetery.

William Graham, the third of the signers buried at Hopewell, was an Irishman by birth. As a young man, he settled on a farm about 4 miles southeast of Beatties Ford and promptly emerged as one of the area's earliest advocates for independence. A militia officer, he saw action at Kings Mountain.

Like Graham, Matthew McClure (1725–1808) was born in Ireland and settled in Mecklenburg before the war. He was fifty years old when he signed the "Meck Dec." Even though his age precluded him from military service, McClure offered moral support throughout the conflict. His son, Hugh, fought for the American cause, and his daughter married George Houston, who participated in the Patriot rout of the Redcoats at nearby McIntyre Farm.

Of the many historically significant graves at Hopewell, one other deserves mention. The original gravestone of Francis Bradley (1743–80), recently retrieved from a cemetery far to the west in Old Fort, is now preserved in the Heritage Room at Hopewell Presbyterian. Inscribed on the replacement stone—the one in the graveyard—are the same words as on the original: "Arme Libertatis [Arms of Liberty] In Memory of Francis Bradley, a friend of his country, and privately slain by enemies of his country, November 14, 1780, aged 37 years." Above the words are two drawn swords between two eagles.

Bradley, known in his time as the strongest man in the county, was a terror to the Tories, and then to the Redcoats when they invaded Mecklenburg. From his plantation, located 4 miles to the south, he harassed enemy scouts and foraging parties. He also picked off a number of British sentries with his rifle during Cornwallis's stay in Charlotte. This special weapon had once been the property of Major John Davidson, who could not make it perform to his satisfaction.

One of Bradley's most satisfying wartime exploits occurred on October 3, 1780, at McIntyre Farm, where he and a small band of Patriots chased the British army away. The site of this stirring chapter of Revolutionary War history is visited later on this tour.

Unfortunately for Bradley, his derring-do ultimately led to his demise. On

Grave of Francis Bradley, Hopewell Presbyterian Church

November 14, 1780, four Tories ambushed and killed him at his nearby plantation.

Just across Beatties Ford Road from Hopewell Presbyterian Church is Latta Plantation Park. Operated by the Mecklenburg County Parks and Recreation Department, the 750-acre park offers a glimpse of plantation life in the years following the Revolutionary War. The featured attraction is the restored two-story, Federal-style plantation house constructed by James Latta on the banks of the Catawba in 1799. A number of annual events, including a Revolutionary War encampment, are held on the adjacent grounds.

From Latta Plantation Park, continue south on Beatties Ford Road for 4.3 miles to Hornets' Nest Park. This municipal park takes its name from the memorable events that took place nearby in the fall of 1780.

It is another 0.6 mile on Beatties Ford Road to McIntyre Avenue. Located at the northwestern corner of this junction is the McIntyre Farm Historic Site, owned and maintained by Mecklenburg County. Turn right onto McIntyre Avenue and park in the area provided at the site.

When Lord Charles Cornwallis moved his army into Charlotte on September 26, 1780, he quickly realized he had selected the wrong place to begin his invasion of North Carolina. Few local citizens were sympathetic to the British cause. In a letter to a fellow officer, Cornwallis observed, "Charlotte is an agreeable village, but in a damned rebellious country." Banastre Tarleton, never one to mince words, noted that "it was evident . . . that the counties of Mecklenburg and Rowan were more hostile to England than any other in America."

As he prepared to leave Charlotte on October 12 after a humiliating sixteen-day visit, Cornwallis was heard to remark, "Let's get out of here, this place is a damned hornets' nest." Tarleton agreed, calling the area "a veritable hornets' nest." The phrase used by the two British officers stuck, as Charlotteans considered it a great compliment. In fact, so honored were they that they adopted it permanently. Today, the official seal of Charlotte bears a hornets' nest. Charlotte's police wear uniforms bearing patches emblazoned with a hornets' nest. Local clubs and civic organizations proudly carry the name. The nickname of the city's National Basketball Association franchise is the Hornets.

While the rebellious nature of the entire area provided a figurative basis for the city's famous nickname, it was the skirmish at the current tour stop that made Charlotte a literal hornets' nest. Several monuments along Beatties Ford Road pay tribute to the small band of Patriots who battled the Redcoats here during Cornwallis's stay. Interpretive markers and signs along the nearby trails tell the dramatic story that unfolded here.

McIntyre Farm Historic Site

After a week in Charlotte, Cornwallis discovered that his supplies were all but depleted. To remedy the shortage, he sent out a large foraging party of six hundred regulars under the command of Major Doyle. On the afternoon of October 3, 1780, Doyle's train of sixty wagons rambled up Beatties Ford Road. A local boy plowing in a field observed the approach of the foragers. He notified Captain James Thompson, who hastily assembled a group of thirteen local men to harass Doyle's troops. When a large group of the British soldiers reached McIntyre Farm, Thompson's marksmen were ready and waiting in a nearby forest.

For a brief time, the Americans watched as the marauders plundered the barns and raided the livestock pens. In the course of their activities, the Redcoats also knocked over some beehives. Suddenly, the British soldiers found themselves under attack. For a fleeting moment, even their commander laughed at his men as they attempted to elude the stinging insects.

Thompson's Patriots could wait no longer to join in the bees' work. Using trees and bushes to hide their approach, the Americans made their way to within range of the enemy. Finally, Thompson called out, "Boys, I can't stand this any longer—I'll take the captain—each one of you choose his man, and look out for yourselves."

The guns of Thompson and Francis Bradley blazed simultaneously. Suddenly, the British were under attack by a more deadly adversary. Thompson's aim was true: the English captain who had been enjoying the scene from the doorway of the McIntyre farmhouse keeled over with a mortal wound. Soon, the other sharpshooters showed the same kind of accuracy.

Only Thompson and Bradley were able to reload and fire again before the Redcoats began to scurry. British trumpets blared a recall. Believing that his men were being attacked by a large militia army, Major Doyle ordered a speedy retreat into Charlotte. A Pennsylvania newspaper later reported that when the demoralized soldiers reached Cornwallis's encampment, "many of their horses fell dead in the streets."

Unharmed in the fray, the fourteen Americans had fired but thirty shots, killing at least twenty enemy soldiers and wounding a number of others in what is known as "the Battle of the Bees."

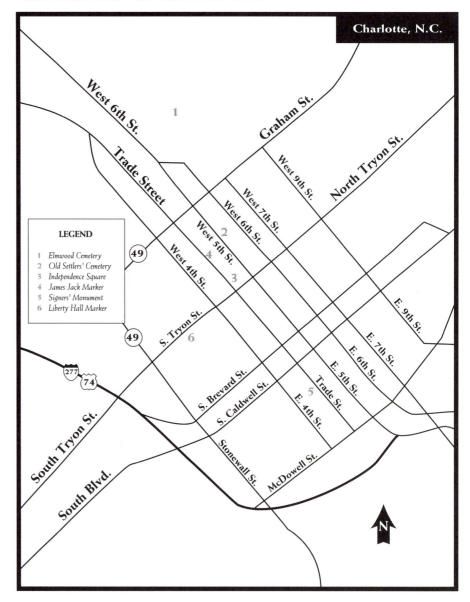

Charlotte, N.C.

LEGEND

1 Elmwood Cemetery
2 Old Settlers' Cemetery
3 Independence Square
4 James Jack Marker
5 Signers' Monument
6 Liberty Hall Marker

The McIntyre farmhouse, its log walls pierced by bullets during the skirmish, stood nearby until the 1960s, when it was razed by a new property owner.

Continue on Beatties Ford Road for 4.6 miles to West Fifth Street in Charlotte.

Ironically, this hornets' nest of rebellion bears names that honor the wife of the British monarch at the time of the Revolution. Mecklenburg County was named for Princess Charlotte Sophia of Mecklenburg-Strelitz (1744–1818), who married King George III. And of course, the city bears the name of Queen Charlotte. Despite the city's rebellious nature during the war, Charlotte's most popular nickname remains "the Queen City."

Turn left onto West Fifth and drive south for 0.7 mile to Cedar Street. Turn left on Cedar and follow it for two blocks to its terminus at Elmwood Cemetery on Cates Street.

Inside the gates of this sprawling municipal cemetery is a monument to Alexander Craighead (1707–66), one of the pioneering Presbyterian ministers of North Carolina. Although Craighead died more than ten years before the Declaration of Independence was signed, he has been called "the Father of Independence in Mecklenburg County." From the time he took the pulpit at Sugaw Creek Presbyterian Church (visited later on this tour) and Rocky River Presbyterian Church in 1758 until his death eight years later, Craighead provided vocal support for his back-country parishioners, who were often at odds with the Royal government in the colony and across the sea.

Ultimately, he served seven area congregations on horseback. Everywhere he spoke, Craighead used inspirational language to urge his listeners to resist the provincial government. In time, many members of the churches where he served emerged as leaders of the local movement for independence.

Return to West Fifth Street, turn left, and proceed southeast for five blocks to Poplar Street in uptown Charlotte. Park nearby to enjoy a brief walking tour.

Sprawling around historic First Presbyterian Church is the Old Settlers' Cemetery. Interred in this ancient cemetery are a number of local citizens who made notable contributions to the fight for independence. The fence, the granite posts, and the gate at the cemetery are all D.A.R. memorials to the numerous Patriots laid to rest here. For example, the historic gate, crafted from native iron by the slaves of Joseph Graham, came from the Revolutionary War hero's plantation in Lincoln County.

Among the graves here is that of Joseph Graham's older brother, George. Like Joseph, George was an unflinching supporter of the American cause. Inscribed on the marble slab covering his grave are the following words: "He lived more than a half century in the vicinity of this place, and was a zealous and active defender of his Country's rights."

More than a year before the Declaration of Independence was signed in Philadelphia, George Graham ran interference for James Jack, the rider who carried the alleged Mecklenburg Declaration of Independence to the Continental Congress in 1775. Graham and several other Patriots rode all night to Salisbury. There, they seized two Tory lawyers, Benjamin B. Boote and John Dunn, who had purportedly planned to detain Jack. Graham subsequently took part in the memorable skirmish at McIntyre's Farm.

Also buried here are Thomas Polk and his wife, Susannah Spratt Polk.

Well educated for his time, Thomas Polk (1732–94) was a prime mover in the creation of Mecklenburg County in 1762. By 1775, he was colonel of the Mecklenburg militia. In that capacity, he sent out the call to his captains to send two delegates each to the convention called to order in Charlotte on May 19, 1775. From that convention came the disputed Mecklenburg Declaration of Independence of May 20 and the undisputed Mecklenburg Resolves of May 31.

Early in the war, Polk was appointed colonel of the newly formed Fourth North Carolina Continental Regiment. After leading the regiment in action in the Cape Fear area, he marched his soldiers to Pennsylvania to reinforce Washington's army. There, they fought at Brandywine and endured the hardships at Valley Forge.

When Polk was passed over for promotion to general in 1778 to replace the fallen Francis Nash, he resigned his commission. Two years later, he answered General Horatio Gates's call to serve as commissary of purchases for the Southern army. Polk remained in that post after Nathanael Greene assumed command of the army in Charlotte. Greene, a great admirer of Polk, sought to have him appointed brigadier general following the death of William Lee Davidson at Cowan's Ford. The resulting commission of "colonel commandant," issued by the general assembly, was refused by Polk.

When President George Washington visited Charlotte in 1791, he was hosted by Polk. An oak tree and a bronze tablet placed by the D.A.R. in honor of Washington's visit are located in the cemetery.

Yet another grave of Revolutionary War importance is in the Old Settlers' Cemetery. Nathaniel Alexander (1756–1808), the only governor of North Carolina born in Charlotte, married a daughter of Thomas Polk. Trained in medicine, Alexander graduated from Princeton in 1776. Two years later, at the age of twenty-two, he was commissioned a surgeon of the North Carolina Continental Line. For the remainder of the war, he labored tirelessly to save the lives of American soldiers despite a constant lack of medical supplies and facilities.

From the cemetery, walk southeast on West Fifth Street for two blocks to Tryon Street. Named for the Royal governor, Tryon is one of the two primary streets in the heart of Charlotte. It is also one of the many streets in the city bearing the names of Revolutionary War personages.

Old Settlers' Cemetery, Charlotte

Nearby arteries are named Graham, Brevard, Davidson, and McDowell.

Turn right on Tryon and proceed one block to the intersection with Trade Street in the very heart of Charlotte. Here is Independence Square—better known to Charlotteans as, simply, "the Square." Now dominated by skyscrapers, this busy intersection is one of the most important Revolutionary War sites in North Carolina. It was this site that noted North Carolina historian John H. Wheeler had in mind when he wrote, "There are some sacred spots which have been specially consecrated in the memorials of all ages of mankind by the holy halo which surrounds the illustrious acts of patriots and martyrs. Of these is Marathon, Bannockburn, and Lexington. History may well add Charlotte."

Thomas Polk built his stately residence and the first Mecklenburg County Courthouse here in 1768. A circular plaque in the center of the intersection marks the site of the building where the Mecklenburg Convention of May 1775 produced the alleged Mecklenburg Declaration of Independence and the Mecklenburg Resolves.

While standing amid the glistening towers of glass, steel, and concrete, it is hard to imagine that one of the most memorable battles of the Revolutionary War was fought here. Following his conquest of South Carolina, Cornwallis broke camp at Camden on September 8, 1780, with one destination in mind. He would march his army to Charlotte, where he would begin the subjugation of North Carolina. Accompanied by former Royal governor Josiah Martin, Cornwallis expected a cordial reception in Charlotte. Neither man could have foreseen that the British army would fight the Battle of Charlotte upon its arrival in the city named for the queen.

It was September 25 when Cornwallis crossed the North Carolina line into Mecklenburg County. Upon receiving the news that the British army had begun its invasion, General William Lee Davidson, camped on McAlpine Creek between Cornwallis and Charlotte, issued a call for militia volunteers and then ordered his four hundred Mecklenburg soldiers to retreat east on the road to Salisbury. His plan was to halt or at least delay Cornwallis at Charlotte.

Davidson stationed a force of 150 Patriots in the heart of the city. Although this small band of Americans was outnumbered by more than 15 to 1, they were commanded by a pair of the most competent soldiers in the state—Colonel William R. Davie and Captain Joseph Graham.

This is how Davie described the current tour stop as it appeared in September 1780, on the eve of the battle: "Charlotte, situated on a rising ground, contains about twenty houses, built on two streets, which cross each other at right angles, at the intersection of which stands the court-house."

He posted Graham and a company of soldiers behind the houses, trees, and fences lining East Trade Street and positioned a second company behind the stone walls of the courthouse at Independence Square.

Silence prevailed on the morning of September 26, as Davie's Americans nervously anticipated the arrival of the Redcoats. Cornwallis entered the city on East Trade Street. Around eleven o'clock, Graham's soldiers observed the approach of Tarleton's cavalry under Major Hangar. Supported by infantry, Hangar promptly formed a line of battle within three hundred yards of the courthouse and gave the order to charge.

Up to this time, the Americans had remained silent. But suddenly, Davie's men rose and offered a galling fire that caused confusion and disorder among the invaders.

An account of the battle published in London in 1794 described the action from the British point of view:

> The legion was ordered to drive them off: but upon receiving a fire from behind the stalls, this corps fell back. Lord Cornwallis rode up in person, and made use of these words: "Legion, remember you have everything to lose, but nothing to gain," alluding, as was supposed, to the former reputation of this corps. Webster's brigade moved on and drove the Americans from behind the court-house; the legion then pursued them; but the whole of the British army was actually kept at bay, for some minutes, by a few mounted Americans, not exceeding twenty in number.

As they were gradually overwhelmed, the Americans withdrew. The fighting spilled out along North Tryon Street to Sugaw Creek Presbyterian, where Graham and his soldiers made another stand.

Banastre Tarleton, never one to overestimate his own casualties, noted that British losses amounted to fifteen killed and wounded, while American losses were twice that number. Whatever the actual casualty rate, Cornwallis's victorious forces had been badly stung by Davie's soldiers. The Redcoats realized that they had run into a hornets' nest.

A brass plaque on the northeastern corner of Tryon and Trade marks the site of Cornwallis's headquarters—Thomas Polk's fine residence—for the duration of his miserable stay in Charlotte. The massive British encampment sprawled outward from Independence Square. During their occupation, the Redcoats did significant damage to the courthouse. Soldiers and horses were quartered at nearby Queen's College.

During his sojourn, the British commander hoped to resupply his army from farms in the surrounding countryside while awaiting good news from Patrick Ferguson, who was operating in the counties to the west. In fact, Josiah Martin, the exiled Royal governor traveling with Cornwallis, issued a proclamation declaring that North Carolina had been restored to Royal authority.

But General William Lee Davidson ensured that the best-laid plans of the British went awry. He and Colonel Davie and their American militiamen galloped about the region to snipe at British foragers and disrupt the line of communication between Cornwallis and Ferguson. As a result of the constant interference, Cornwallis did not receive news of Ferguson's death and the devastating defeat at Kings Mountain until a week after the battle had taken place just 40 miles away.

Tarleton eloquently summarized the problems British forces faced in Charlotte:

> The town and its environs abounded with inveterate enemies. . . .
> The foraging parties were every day harassed by the inhabitants, who
> did not remain at home to receive payment for the product of their
> plantations, but generally fired from covert places to annoy the Brit-
> ish detachments. The vigilance and animosity of these surrounding
> districts checked the exertions of the well-affected, and totally de-
> stroyed all communications between the King's troops and loyalists
> in other parts of the province.

Before leaving the Square, take time to visit Polk Park, located on the northwestern corner of Tryon and Trade. Markers located here detail the history of Charlotte.

From the Square, walk a few paces west on Trade Street. A bronze tablet at 120 West Trade marks the site of Cook's Inn, where George Washington was entertained during his triumphant visit to the city on Saturday, May 28, 1791. In his diary, Washington noted that he "dined with Genl. Polk and a small party invited by him at a Table prepared for the purpose." The president also recorded this less-than-flattering observation about the town: "Charlotte is a trifling place, though the Court of Mecklenburg is held in it."

Continue west to the 200 block of Trade Street. A bronze plaque mounted on a gray stone at 211 West Trade contains a bas-relief likeness of a rider on a horse. This small monument pays homage to James Jack, often called "the Paul Revere of the South." He and his aged father, Patrick Jack, operated a tavern at this site before and during the Revolutionary War.

While Cornwallis occupied Charlotte, Patrick Jack was subjected to numerous indignities by the Redcoats. First, the infirm man was chased from his bed. Then his home was set afire. Citizens were informed that this action was taken because "all of old Jack's sons were in the rebel army."

The most famous of Patrick Jack's four Patriot sons was his eldest, James. Following the Mecklenburg Convention in May 1775, independence-minded citizens collected funds to enable James Jack to deliver the alleged Mecklenburg Declaration of Independence and the Mecklenburg Resolves to the Continental Congress in Philadelphia. In early June, he placed the documents in his saddlebags, mounted his horse, and started out on the long ride to Pennsylvania.

After a stop in Salisbury, Jack turned north to follow the Great Wagon Road—the route many of North Carolina's settlers had traveled on their way to the colony. After an arduous journey, he reached his destination on June 23, the very day George Washington assumed command of the Continental Army. In Philadelphia, Jack immediately sought out the congressional delegation from North Carolina and presented copies of the document to Joseph Hewes, William Hooper, and Richard Caswell. The three delegates cautioned Jack not to show them to—or discuss them with—the Continental Congress as a whole, because that body was in the process of preparing an important address to the king. That address, offered on July 8, declared loyalty to the Crown and expressed no desire for independence.

Jack then began the long ride back to Charlotte without having made the impact he hoped for. But like Paul Revere, he had indeed carried important tidings. The message of independence he bore would come to fruit a year later in a declaration signed by representatives of all thirteen colonies.

Return to Independence Square. Walk east on Trade Street for five blocks to Davidson Street. En route, you'll pass two state historical markers that call attention to this street's importance to the Revolutionary War.

One marker memorializes the Battle of Charlotte, which began on Davidson Street.

The other commemorates Major General Nathanael Greene's assumption of command of the meager, battered remnants of the American army in the South on December 3, 1780. Horatio Gates, who earlier in the war had been rumored to be George Washington's replacement as commander of the Continental Army, relinquished command to Greene in a simple ceremony near the current tour stop.

Though highly embarrassed by his devastating defeat at Camden, the loss of his command, and the charges of incompetence leveled against him, Gates was magnanimous in the transfer of power. His last order as commander of the Southern army went thus: "General Gates returns his sincere and grateful thanks to the Southern Army, for their perseverance, fortitude, and patient endurance of all the hardships and sufferings while under his command. He anxiously hopes their misfortunes will cease therewith, and that victory, and the glorious advantages attending it, may be the future portion of the Southern Army."

At Charlotte, Greene inherited what he called "the shadow of an army," his two thousand soldiers divided almost evenly between Continentals and militiamen. What he saw gave him little hope of future success: "The appearance of the troops was wretched beyond description, and their distress, on account of provisions, was little less than their suffering for want of clothing and other necessities."

Despite the almost insurmountable task facing him, Greene proceeded to mastermind one of the most remarkable transformations in the annals of military history.

Near the intersection of Trade and Davidson stands the former Mecklenburg County Courthouse. Towering above the civic plaza in front of the 1928 structure is an obelisk honoring the signers of the alleged Mecklenburg Declaration of Independence.

Few events in the long history of North Carolina have occasioned more controversy than the "Meck Dec." Ironically, one of the two dates emblazoned on the North Carolina state flag—May 20, 1775—commemorates the signing of that declaration, an event some historians consider a fable. Other historians stand behind the authenticity of the document. If they are correct, the events in Charlotte constituted the first public declaration of independence in the American colonies.

Monument to the signers of the Mecklenburg Declaration of Independence, Charlotte

Proponents of the "Meck Dec" point to a compelling body of evidence to support their claims. There is no dispute that twenty-seven area men—most of them Scots-Irish Presbyterians—assembled at the courthouse on May 19, 1775, as delegates to the Mecklenburg Convention. Their identities are certain. One was a physician, two were attorneys, three were graduates of Princeton, one was a Presbyterian minister, and nine were Presbyterian elders.

That these highly respected men came together in Charlotte to discuss the growing crisis in North Carolina and the other colonies is not subject to dispute. Indeed, the courtroom overflowed, and the excited crowd of onlookers spilled into the streets. While the delegates discussed the need for a local government, their meeting was interrupted by a clamor outside. A courier bearing important news from the North had galloped into town. He delivered the news that British soldiers had fired on Americans a month earlier in Lexington, Massachusetts.

What happened next is open to debate. Proponents claim that even the most cautious among the crowd joined in the cry for a "declaration of independence." In response to the demands of the citizens, and in accordance with the dictates of their own consciences, the delegates appointed three of their number—Dr. Ephraim Brevard, the Reverend Hezekiah Balch, and William Kennon—to draft a document that would declare the citizens of Mecklenburg County free from British control.

In the early-morning hours on May 20, the three men produced a five-part document, to which each of the delegates affixed his signature by candlelight. Around noon, Thomas Polk emerged from the courthouse to read the document to the several thousand people who had gathered at the intersection of Trade and Tryon. The attentive audience heard this, in part: "Resolved, That we, the citizens of Mecklenburg County, do hereby dissolve the political bands which have connected us with the mother country; and absolve ourselves from the British Crown, adjuring all political connection with a nation that has wantonly trampled on our rights and liberties. . . . Resolved, That we do hereby declare ourselves a free and independent people, that we are and of right ought to be a sovereign and self-governing people."

Proponents maintain that the convention adjourned after producing the "Meck Dec" and reconvened later in the month because it had not yet addressed the establishment of a local government. On May 30, the delegates produced the Mecklenburg Resolves, the authenticity of which has never been contested. Milder in language and tone than the document of May 20, the twenty resolves—enacted eleven days later—nonetheless expressed a spirit of independence and specifically declared all British laws and authority null and void.

Soon after the Mecklenburg Convention adjourned, Captain Jack was dispatched to Philadelphia with copies of both documents. News of the action in Mecklenburg County was printed in the only two newspapers in the state—in Wilmington and New Bern. When Royal Governor Josiah Martin read the resolves in the June issue of the *Cape Fear Mercury*, he promptly dispatched a copy of the paper to his superior in London, the earl of Dartmouth, colonial secretary. Martin included a letter that read in part, "The Resolves of the Committee of Mecklenburg which your Lordship will find in the enclosed Newspaper, surpass all of the horrid and reasonable publications that the inflammatory spirits of this Continent have yet produced."

There was little or no challenge to the authenticity of the "Meck Dec" until June 5, 1819, when John Adams read a story about the document in the *Essex Register* of Salem, Massachusetts. The story was a reprint of an article written for the *Raleigh Register* of April 30, 1819, by Joseph McKnitt Alexander, the son of John McKnitt Alexander, the secretary of the Mecklenburg Convention of May 19 and 20, 1775. Adams forwarded the article to Thomas Jefferson, author of the Declaration of Independence of July 4, 1776. Thus began the controversy that continues to the present day.

Jefferson was infuriated that someone would have the audacity to claim that Americans had officially proclaimed independence through a document that preceded his by more than a year. He put forth the opinion that the "Meck Dec" was "spurious" at best.

Since that time, many historians have sided with the third president. They point out that no original copy of the document has ever been produced. Indeed, the best evidence of its authenticity went up in smoke on April 6, 1800, when the records of the convention were destroyed in a fire that consumed the home of John McKnitt Alexander. And the only surviving copy of the June 3, 1775, issue of the *Cape Fear Mercury*—which allegedly contained a copy of the "Meck Dec"—disappeared from the British archives in 1837 at the insistence of Andrew Stevenson, the American ambassador. Proponents claim that the action was taken to protect Thomas Jefferson.

Supporters of the document maintain that John McKnitt Alexander again put the "Meck Dec" into writing after the war, working from memory. Doubters claim that he borrowed the fiery language in his re-creation from Jefferson's famous document.

Some of the best evidence of the authenticity of the "Meck Dec" is the testimony of the men honored at the current tour stop. The twenty-seven whose names are inscribed on the obelisk were men of honor and integrity. None of them ever denied the authenticity of the document.

Moreover, there were other credible witnesses to the happenings of May 20, 1775, who later affirmed that independence was publicly declared in Charlotte that day. One was Dr. Humphrey Hunter, a Revolutionary War hero whose grave site is visited later in this tour. Another was Joseph Graham, a teenager who watched in awe as the events of May 20 unfolded before him. Years later, Graham wrote this concerning the day in question: "After reading a number of papers as usual and much animated discussion the question was taken, and they Resolved to declare themselves Independent."

Perhaps there will never be conclusive proof as to what occurred at the courthouse in Charlotte that day. Be that as it may, no one can deny that the twenty-seven men honored by the monument here took bold steps toward a free, independent America at the Mecklenburg Convention.

Until 1982, Mecklenburg celebrated May 20 as a county holiday. A year later, the state removed the slogan "First in Freedom" from motor-vehicle license plates. Nonetheless, the special day continues to be commemorated every year in Charlotte. And despite repeated attempts to remove it, the date remains on the state flag.

Continue on East Trade Street to McDowell Street. Turn right and walk two blocks to Third Street. Turn right and proceed five blocks to the south-western corner of Third and South Tryon. A small monument here is the only reminder of the first college in North Carolina.

With the blessing of Governor Tryon, the colonial assembly chartered Queen's College in 1771, making it the first college south of Virginia. Under the terms of its charter, the college was authorized to grant bachelor's and master's degrees and was to operate under rules similar "to the Laws & Customs of the Universities of Oxford & Cambridge or those of the Colleges in America." During the years leading up to the Revolution, classes were held in buildings that covered half a block on South Tryon between Second and Third Streets.

As tensions mounted between the colonies and Great Britain, local Patriot leaders met at the school to discuss the issues of the day. The names of many of these men appear on the Signers' Monument. Cognizant of the "disloyal" affairs at the college, King George III disallowed the charter on June 28, 1773.

Not to be outdone, local citizens continued the school, operating it as an academy known as Queen's Museum. Local Presbyterians chose the name as a ruse, hoping Royal officials might get the impression that the facility had been converted into an exhibition hall for antiquities and curiosities. Among the famed Revolutionary War soldiers educated here were George Graham, Joseph Graham, William Lee Davidson, William R. Davie, and Andrew Jackson.

When the war came, the school was given a more appropriate name—Liberty Hall. Upon his arrival in Charlotte, Cornwallis designated the school for use as a hospital. Indeed, a number of his soldiers were buried in the yard. When the site was excavated for the construction of a county courthouse, several skeletons—presumably the remains of Redcoats—were exhumed.

The Liberty Hall site is believed by some historians to be the original burial site of Ephraim Brevard (1744–82), one of the authors of the "Meck Dec." Educated at Princeton and trained as a medical doctor, Brevard served as an assistant surgeon under General Benjamin Lincoln.

Today, a thirty-two-story skyscraper stands at the site. Quite fittingly, Charlotte is home to a four-year school of higher education named Queen's College, supported by the Presbyterian Church. The college is located south of the uptown area.

Turn right onto Tryon Street, walk three blocks, and go left on Fifth to return to your vehicle at Poplar.

To resume the driving tour, proceed south on Fifth, turn right on Church Street, go two blocks, and turn right on Fourth Street. It is four blocks to Cedar Street. Turn left and drive five blocks to Morehead Street. Turn right, go 2.1 miles to U.S. 74 (Andrew Jackson Highway), and turn right again. After 4.1 miles, turn left on Little Rock Road, which becomes Old Dowd Road near the entrance to Charlotte/Douglas International Airport. Continue southwest to Wallace Neal Road. Turn left and drive south on Wallace Neal for 1.5 miles to where the road forks. Take the left fork (Dixie/Steele Creek Road) and drive south for 1.4 miles to Steele Creek Presbyterian Church.

Presbyterians have been worshiping at this site since 1760. The present church, a massive Gothic sanctuary designed to seat a thousand people, was constructed in 1888. It is the fifth building to serve a congregation whose early members were heavily involved in the American Revolution.

Local tradition maintains that upon the creation of Europe, Africa, and Asia, God took a piece of Scotland, smoothed out its highlands, placed it on the eastern shore of the Catawba River, and named it Steele Creek. Since the first Scots-Irish settlers put down stakes here in the decades before the Revolution, Steele Creek Presbyterian has been the focal point of the tightly knit community.

Graves in the adjacent church cemetery date from 1763. Revolutionary War history abounds within the spacious confines of these ancient grounds.

At least one signer of the "Meck Dec" is buried here. Robert Irwin (1740–80) made his way to the Steele Creek community from Pennsylvania in 1763. During the war, Irwin devoted his full attention to military affairs. When Thomas Sumter was forced to flee to Charlotte in July 1780, the South Carolina general found an invaluable friend in Irwin. Upon Sumter's return to South Carolina, he was accompanied by Irwin and his troops. At the ensuing Battle of Hanging Rock, Irwin bolstered the center of the Patriot line.

A marker in the cemetery lists the names of thirteen soldiers of the Revolution interred here. Foremost among them was Dr. Humphrey Hunter (1755–1827). A large tombstone pays tribute to this American hero, truly a man for all times.

Born in Londonderry, Ireland, Hunter came to America with his widowed mother at the age of four and settled on a farm northeast of Charlotte. Six days after his twentieth birthday, Hunter was among the crowd that witnessed the Mecklenburg Convention. When the authenticity of the "Meck Dec" was first challenged, Hunter was one of the surviving eyewitnesses who acknowledged that he had heard the document read on May 20, 1775.

When Griffith Rutherford moved against the Cherokees in the summer of 1776, his army included Hunter. After that campaign, Hunter resumed his studies at Queen's Museum in Charlotte.

Rutherford needed the services of his young officer again in 1780, when he hurried troops to South Carolina to aid in the stand against Cornwallis. In the ferocious fighting at Camden, both Rutherford and Hunter were taken prisoner. Just after that, Hunter witnessed the death of the heroic Baron de Kalb.

He was confined at a British prison in Orangeburg, South Carolina, for three months until he was able to escape. After a harrowing nine-day journey on foot, during which he subsisted on raw corn, the young soldier reached Mecklenburg County. With but a few days rest, Hunter returned to the fight. Serving under Colonel Henry Lee in South Carolina, he displayed exceptional bravery on September 8, 1781, at the Battle of Eutaw Springs, the last major engagement of the war.

Hunter was ordained a Presbyterian minister in 1789. Over the next thirty-eight years, he organized numerous Presbyterian churches in the North Carolina Piedmont. And his services as a physician were in constant demand in the back country in the years after the war.

His son, Cyrus L. Hunter, became a respected North Carolina historian. It was thanks to his efforts that much of the Revolutionary War history of western North Carolina was recorded.

Also buried at Steele Creek are one of the great heroines of the war in North Carolina and her equally noble husband.

Eleanor Wilson was like many other Mecklenburg County women in the fall of 1780. With her husband, Robert, and six of her sons away fighting for the American cause, she labored on the home front under the specter of invasion by the British army.

On October 14, as Cornwallis began his march back to South Carolina after his short stay in Charlotte, he stopped for the night at the Wilson plantation, which was located nearby. Cornwallis and Tarleton used the Wilson home as their headquarters and ordered Mrs. Wilson, their reluctant hostess, to feed them supper.

In the course of the meal preparations, the two British officers were delighted to learn that Mrs. Wilson's husband and one of their sons had been taken prisoner at Camden. Cornwallis then began an eloquent, earnest plea to his hostess: "If you could but induce your husband and sons to leave the rebels, and take up arms for their lawful sovereign, I would almost pledge myself that they shall have rank and consideration in the British army. If you, madam, will pledge yourself to induce them to do so, I will immediately order their discharge."

Politely but firmly, Mrs. Wilson informed Cornwallis that her husband and sons were indeed dear to her and that she was willing to do almost anything for their well-being. Then she offered this pledge:

> I have seven sons who are now, or have been bearing arms—indeed, my seventh son, Zaccheus [named for his uncle, a signer of the alleged "Meck Dec"], who is only fifteen years old, I yesterday assisted to get ready to go and join his brothers in Sumter's army. Now, sooner than see one of my family turn back from the glorious enterprise, I would take these boys [she pointed to three or four small sons who remained at home] and would myself enlist under Sumter's standard, and show my husband and sons how to fight, and, if necessary, to die for their country.

Nearly always short tempered when baited by a woman, Tarleton was quick to remark to Cornwallis, "I think you've got into a hornets' nest. Never mind, when we get to Camden, I [will] take care that old Robert Wilson never comes back."

Cornwallis departed Steele Creek the next morning. Not far into the march, his scouts brought to him young Zaccheus Wilson, who had been captured while sniping at the flank of the British army. Upon recognizing the lad's name, Cornwallis ordered him to guide the British soldiers to a safe ford on the Catawba.

At the place selected by young Wilson, the Redcoats began to move into the river, only to find themselves in deep, treacherous waters. Convinced that the boy had intentionally led the soldiers into danger in order to embarrass their commander, Cornwallis drew his saber and threatened to decapitate him. Much like his mother a day earlier, the youthful Patriot addressed Cornwallis with great courage: "But, sir, don't you think it would be a cowardly act for you to strike an unarmed boy with your sword? If I had but the half of your weapon, it would not be so cowardly, but then you know, it would not be safe."

Moved by Wilson's bravery, Cornwallis regained his composure, complimented the boy, and assured him he would not be harmed. Soon, it was discovered that the river could be forded safely just upstream. Zaccheus Wilson was soon released by Cornwallis on the conditions that he return to Steele Creek to care for his mother and that he instruct her to keep her other sons at home.

Later that year, Robert Wilson and his son John escaped and made their way back to Mecklenburg County.

Robert and Eleanor both died in 1810.

From the cemetery, continue south on Dixie/Steele Creek Road for 1 mile to Shopton Road. Turn left, drive east for 2.6 miles to Beam Road, turn right, and travel south for 0.4 mile to N.C. 49.

Located near the intersection is an impressive monument to Jane Parks McDowell, another Revolutionary War heroine from Mecklenburg County. McDowell lived on a plantation at this site with her small children while her husband, John, was away fighting for the American army. An ardent Patriot, Mrs. McDowell was the granddaughter of Samuel Young of Rowan

County, a member of the Continental Congress. (For more information on Young, see The Yadkin River Tour, pages 307–8.)

In the late summer and early fall of 1780, the war brought hardship to the McDowell family. First, John was seriously wounded and left for dead at the Battle of Camden. Then, in October, when Cornwallis put his army on the march back to South Carolina, the Redcoats paid a visit to the McDowell home.

As the soldiers went about despoiling the plantation, Mrs. McDowell questioned their commander: "Is it soldier-like to plunder a helpless family and leave us nothing?"

The British captain responded rather curtly: "It is the fortune of war, madam. We must have something to eat and these rebels will not bring it."

Hoping to gain some measure of compassion, Mrs. McDowell asked, "Have you no women and children at home?"

Her words and manner moved the Redcoat officer to inquire, "What is you name, madam?"

"McDowell is our name," the lady responded proudly.

"That is my name," the captain said. "Where are you from?"

"Our family came from Scotland, sir."

"Aye, and very likely then you are some kin of mine; I have some here in America," Captain McDowell said. He then snapped orders to his men. The plundering stopped and the property of Mrs. McDowell was restored.

As he put his soldiers on the march, the captain offered a farewell, saying, "And likely you have some of your family among the rebels, but it is the fortunes of war—goodbye!"

No sooner had the Redcoats vanished south into the woods than Mrs. McDowell realized that the small American army encamped at Sugaw Creek Presbyterian Church, located on the northeastern side of Charlotte, must be informed that the British army was leaving North Carolina. There was but one way to deliver the news. She went out into the rainy night to the barn, where she saddled a horse. She then returned to the house, blanketed her two-year-old son, emerged with the child in her arms, climbed onto her black stallion, and galloped off into the darkness.

The eastern sky was beginning to yield its first light as she neared the end of her ride. American sentries were startled by the sight of a rider burdened with a tiny child. As she rode past them, she called out, "The Redcoats are going! The Redcoats are going!"

After relaying the vital information, mother and child made the return trip home. For her heroic deed, Jane Parks McDowell was called "the Female Paul Revere."

In retrospect, her ride may have been even more daring than that of Revere, who galloped through villages under an April moon. McDowell's ride carried her through 10 miles of dense forests on a dark, wet night. And she carried a small child.

John McDowell survived the war. Both he and Jane lie in marked graves at Steele Creek Presbyterian Church.

Turn left onto N.C. 49 (Tryon Street) and drive north for 12.3 miles to Sugar Creek Road. Located on the northwestern corner of this intersection is historic Sugaw Creek Presbyterian Church. On the opposite side of Tryon Street is the oldest section of the historic church cemetery. Another section of the cemetery is on the northeastern corner. Turn left onto Sugar Creek Road and park in the church lot.

Sugaw Creek, the oldest Presbyterian church in Mecklenburg County, takes its name from the Indian word *sugaw*, which means a group of huts. Over the years, the word has been Anglicized to *sugar*. Organized by the Reverend Alexander Craighead, the third Presbyterian minister to work in North Carolina, the congregation built its first log meeting house by 1766. The existing one-story brick edifice dates from 1868. Stones and pillars in the churchyard are remnants of an earlier sanctuary. Near the front of the church stands a brick structure erected by members in 1837 to house Sugaw Creek Academy. It, too, replaced an earlier structure.

It was at Sugaw Creek Presbyterian Church that the Reverend Craighead and his congregation planted the earliest seeds of the Revolution in Mecklenburg County. Several years before the War of Regulation, they took part in the so-called War of Sugaw Creek, during which they voiced strong opposition to the land claims of Governor Arthur Dobbs.

Craighead's influence was still felt among his parishioners after his death in 1766. Three years later, when Parliament enacted legislation that placed restrictions on Presbyterian ministers and levied a tax for the support of the Anglican Church, the members of Sugaw Creek dispatched a petition to the governor containing revolutionary language. The agitated Presbyterians warned that more than a thousand members of the Church of Scotland were "able to bear arms" and were "ready to support that government under which they find the most liberty."

Not surprisingly, nine signers of the alleged "Meck Dec" were elders at Sugaw Creek. Two of them are buried here. The life of one of these men, Hezekiah Alexander, will be detailed later on this tour. The other signer interred here is Abraham Alexander, whose grave is marked by a modest stone near two large trees in the middle of the cemetery on the southern side of Tryon. Alexander was the chairman of the Mecklenburg Convention. He died in 1786 at the age of sixty-eight.

The Reverend Craighead is buried in the northeastern corner of the same cemetery. For years, his grave was marked only by two sassafras trees, one growing at the head and the other at the foot. When a storm destroyed the trees 125 years after the reverend's death, the wood was used to craft the top of the present pulpit at the nearby church Craighead founded. A marker now covers his grave.

Although Craighead didn't live to see the revolution he helped spawn, his daughter, Rachel, married a noted Presbyterian minister, David Caldwell, and both husband and wife went on to become heroes of the war. (For more information, see The Pyrrhic Victory Tour, page 354.) Colonel George Craighead, one of the Reverend Craighead's nephews, became a man of great wealth and an intimate friend of General Washington. The two soldiers, it was said, were often found "dining at the same table and calling each other by the familiar name of George." Still another nephew, the Reverend Adam Boyd, was the editor of the *Cape Fear Mercury*, the newspaper that may have published a portion of the "Meck Dec." And Craighead's congregation provided refuge, comfort, and assistance to the mother of Andrew Jackson when she fled to Charlotte after her young son was captured and confined in a British prison during the war. Indeed, the spirit of the Reverend Craighead lived on.

A monument in the church cemetery on the eastern side of Sugar Creek Road honors the valor of one of the young officers who led the gallant stand against the British army at this very site during the Battle of Charlotte.

As Davie's rear guard was being pushed out of town on the afternoon of September 26, 1780, Captain Joseph Graham continued to offer resistance to the Redcoats. Here at Sugaw Creek, the twenty-year-old officer was engaged in hand-to-hand combat when his horse backed into a tree limb, which caused him to fall. While on the ground, he sustained three bullet wounds in the thigh, one saber thrust in the side, one gash on the neck, and four cuts to the forehead. Concerning his sword wounds, Graham recalled that "from one of these some of [my] brains exuded." Had it not been for a heavy silver buckle he wore at his collar, he would have been decapitated by the saber blow to his neck. The buckle was cut in two.

As the victorious Redcoats retired toward the heart of town, they came upon the badly wounded American. One of their number aimed his pistol at Graham, intending to finish the job, only to be stopped by Major Hangar, who instructed, "Put up your pistol, save your ammunition; he has enough." Graham was thus left to die on the battlefield.

After he regained consciousness, he managed to crawl to a spring near the site of the existing church. Around sunset, Susan Wilson—in later years affectionately called "Aunt Susy" by Graham's children—discovered him while on a visit to the spring for a bucket of water. Noticing that his clothes "were dyed with his blood," the young lady rushed to get her mother.

Monument to Joseph Graham at Sugaw Creek Presbyterian Church

The two struggled to carry Graham to the relative safety of their home. There, they dressed his wounds, placed him in a bed, and tried to hide him from the British. During the night that followed, Graham lay so quietly that they thought he was dead—and even examined him once or twice to see.

A day later, a party of British soldiers stopped in the vicinity. Traveling with the Redcoats was an officer's wife, who came to the house in search of milk. When she discovered the wounded American, she proposed to summon a surgeon from the British encampment. Fearful of capture, Captain Graham induced his friends to help him mount his horse, which had been found after the battle. Miraculously, he made his way to his mother's home, where he began his recovery. In less than five months, Graham was in the saddle once again, trying to stop Cornwallis just miles away at Cowan's Ford.

Susan Wilson Alexander—"Aunt Susy"—the woman who saved Graham's life at Sugaw Creek, is buried in the church cemetery under a large magnolia tree.

Return to the intersection of Sugar Creek Road and Tryon Street. Turn left onto North Tryon (U.S. 29/N.C. 49) and follow it east for 4.8 miles to where U.S. 29 and N.C. 49 split.

Located here is a monument to Lieutenant George Locke, the brother of Colonel Francis Locke, one of the heroes of the Battle of Ramsour's Mill (see The Tide Turns Tour, pages 270–77). As the Battle of Charlotte spilled eastward on September 26, 1780, George Locke was among the small band of Patriots who fought defiantly against the overwhelming British army. He was cut to pieces by Tarleton's dragoons and died near the site of the monument.

Return to the intersection of Tryon and Sugar Creek Road. Turn left and proceed south on Sugar Creek for 1.5 miles to Eastway Drive. Turn right, go 0.3 mile to Shamrock Drive, turn left, and drive 0.5 mile to the entrance for the Hezekiah Alexander House and the Charlotte Museum of History. Turn right to reach the parking lot of this magnificently restored stone house.

Constructed by Hezekiah Alexander in 1774, the handsome two-story structure is the oldest dwelling in Mecklenburg County. Costumed guides lead tours through the house, which is furnished much like it was when Alexander and his family lived here during the war.

Like many other Mecklenburg leaders in the independence movement, Alexander (1728–1801) was born in Pennsylvania. He settled in the North Carolina Piedmont in the 1760s and quickly became one of the most influential men in Mecklenburg County. As an elder at Sugaw Creek Presbyterian Church, he was greatly influenced by the rousing sermons of Alexander Craighead.

Hezekiah Alexander was among the founders of Queen's College. When that school's charter was subsequently revoked by King George III, Alexander was pushed further toward the cause of independence.

He signed the "Meck Dec" and supported the American cause as a soldier and statesman. Elected a delegate to the Fifth Provincial Congress at Halifax in November 1776, Alexander was chosen by his colleagues to serve as a member of the committee charged with drafting the first state constitution and bill of rights. Due in large part to Alexander's influence and leadership, the committee produced a constitution second only to Pennsylvania's in its democratic principles.

Adjacent to the Hezekiah Alexander House stands the Charlotte Museum of History. Designed as a welcome center for the historic house, the museum has since grown in size and scope. Future plans call for the facility to be replaced by a structure three times as large. Numerous artifacts from the colonial and Revolutionary War periods are on display here.

Throughout the year, the complex offers special events related to the Revolutionary War.

Return to the junction of Shamrock and Eastway. Turn left and follow Eastway (which becomes Wendover Road) for 5.3 miles to N.C. 16 (Providence Road). Turn left and drive south for 8.3 miles to Providence Presbyterian Church, located on the right.

This stately Federal-style sanctuary was erected in 1858 as the successor to several less elegant meeting houses that stood nearby. Alexander Craighead began preaching to Presbyterians in this area in 1767.

To see Providence's earliest roots, cross the highway to the church cemetery. A stone outcropping still visible near the graveyard served as the church's first facility, the members worshiping in an open-air setting.

Many of the early members served the American cause in the Revolution and are buried here. Their graves stand within sight of the route Cornwallis used as he made his way to a rather rude reception in Charlotte in 1780.

Three signers of the alleged "Meck Dec" lie in the cemetery.

Not much is known about the Revolutionary War activities of John Flennikin other than that he attended the Mecklenburg Convention. Born in Pennsylvania in 1744, he lived to an old age. Ironically, Flennikin was killed when he was thrown from his horse while on his way to Providence Presbyterian Church.

Likewise, little is known of signer Henry Downs (1728–98).

Neil Morrison (1728–84), the third signer laid to rest at Providence, participated in the campaign against the Indians of western North Carolina in 1776. His son, William, was a student at Princeton when the war began. He hurried home to Mecklenburg, where he joined the American army and served for the duration of the war.

The graves of all three signers are well marked.

The tour ends here, with this last look at three of the men behind the storied "Meck Dec."

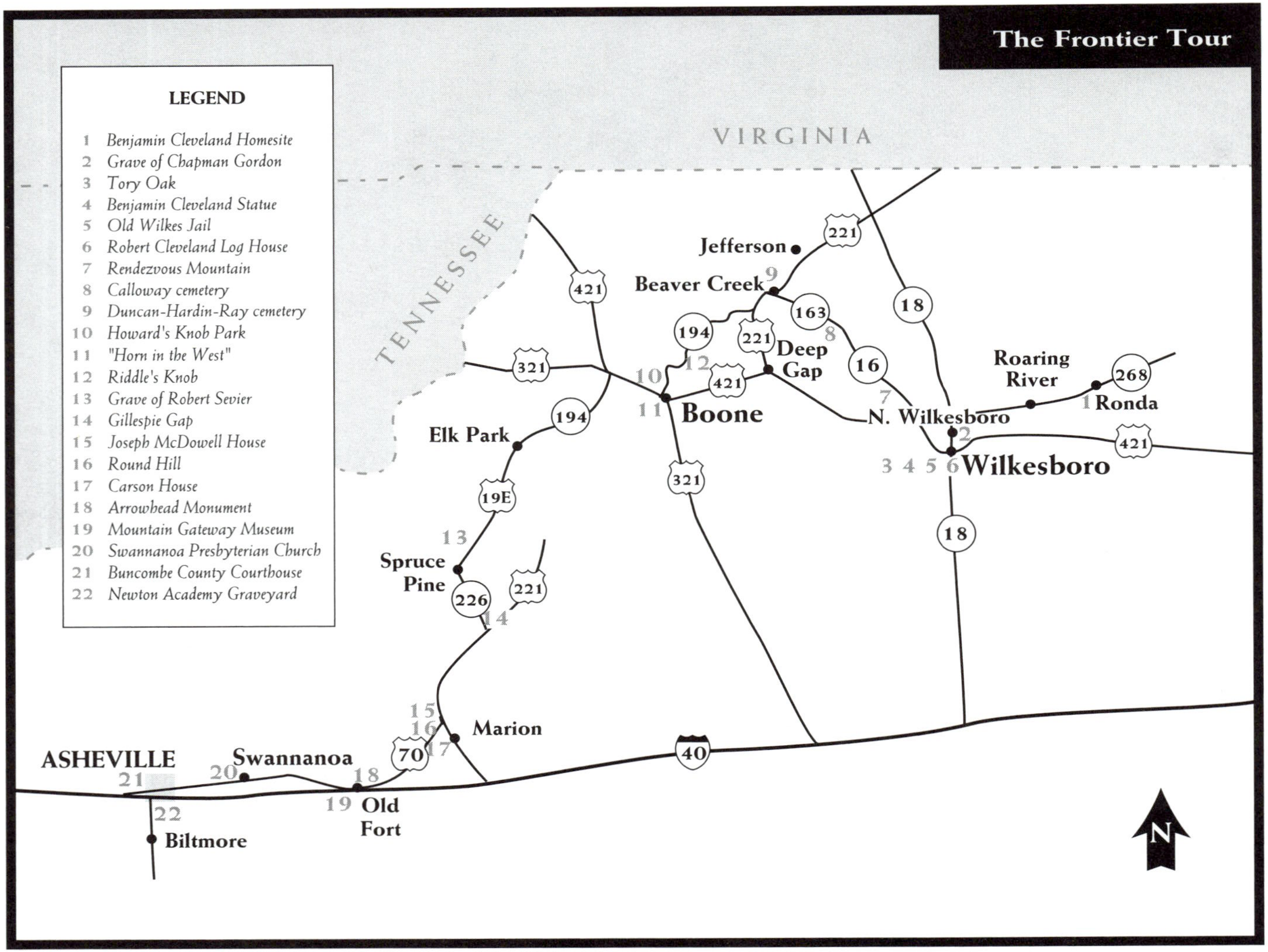

The Frontier Tour

N

VIRGINIA

TENNESSEE

Ronda
268
421

Roaring River

N. Wilkesboro
2
Wilkesboro
3 4 5 6
18

18

221

18

16
7

163
8
Deep Gap

Jefferson
9
221
Beaver Creek
194
12
421
Boone
11
10
321

40

421

321
194

Elk Park
19E
13
221
4
Spruce Pine
226
15
16
Marion
70 17
18
70
19 Old Fort

ASHEVILLE
21
Swannanoa
20
22
Biltmore

LEGEND

1   Benjamin Cleveland Homesite
2   Grave of Chapman Gordon
3   Tory Oak
4   Benjamin Cleveland Statue
5   Old Wilkes Jail
6   Robert Cleveland Log House
7   Rendezvous Mountain
8   Calloway cemetery
9   Duncan-Hardin-Ray cemetery
10 Howard's Knob Park
11 "Horn in the West"
12 Riddle's Knob
13 Grave of Robert Sevier
14 Gillespie Gap
15 Joseph McDowell House
16 Round Hill
17 Carson House
18 Arrowhead Monument
19 Mountain Gateway Museum
20 Swannanoa Presbyterian Church
21 Buncombe County Courthouse
22 Newton Academy Graveyard

The Frontier Tour

This tour begins at Ronda in Wilkes County and makes its way through Ashe, Watauga, Avery, Mitchell, and McDowell Counties before ending at Enka in Buncombe County. Among the highlights are the story of Ben Cleveland, "the Tory Oak," the Robert Cleveland Log House, Rendezvous Mountain, the story of Martin Gambill's ride, Howard's Knob, Wolf's Den, Pleasant Gardens, the Carson House, historic Old Fort, the story of Samuel Davidson, and historic Asheville.

Total mileage: approximately 171 miles.

This tour visits sites in a mountainous seven-county area in western North Carolina stretching from the Virginia line on the north to the Tennessee border on the west.

By the American Revolution, the first white settlers in the region had begun to lay claim to land that until that time had been the exclusive domain of the Cherokee Indians. As North Carolina prepared to join the other American colonies in the fight for independence, it faced an Indian threat on the western frontier occasioned by the clash of the two cultures.

Revolutionary War–era pioneers were independent, hearty individuals, as they had to be to survive the dangers of the Indians and the mountain wilderness. Many of these rugged trailblazers possessed a fiery spirit that led them to march from their homes down the mountain valleys in 1780 to strike a blow for the American cause at Kings Mountain.

The tour begins on N.C. 268 in the Wilkes County village of Ronda. Named for John Wilkes (1727–97), a British statesman who was an outspoken advocate of American rights during the Revolution period, the county was formed in 1778.

A state historical marker on N.C. 268 near the Ronda Town Hall pays homage to Benjamin Cleveland, one of the most colorful military leaders North Carolina produced during the war. His plantation home, "The Round

About," was located in a horseshoe bend of the Yadkin River about a mile southwest of the current tour stop. Cleveland lived there from 1771 until after the war, when he lost his land because of title difficulties.

Born in Virginia in 1738, Cleveland settled on Roaring Creek, a tributary of the Yadkin, in 1769. A neighbor of legendary frontiersman Daniel Boone, he quickly gained a reputation as a fearless Indian fighter in the mountains of western North Carolina. During the organized expedition against the Cherokees in the summer of 1776, Cleveland served as a militia officer and ranger.

When the Revolutionary War began, the good-natured but fiery-tempered frontiersman and other mountain Patriots found themselves threatened not only by Indians but also by the large numbers of Tories living along the banks of the upper Yadkin. North Carolina had no fiercer fighter against both enemies than big Ben Cleveland.

After a short stint as an officer in the North Carolina Continental Line, during which he fought in the Moores Creek campaign, he resigned his commission to serve in the militia, where he believed his skills as a hunter and backwoodsman could best be utilized. Although a speech impediment prevented him from being a skillful orator, it didn't stop him from being a forceful leader. When Wilkes County was created from Surry County in 1778, Cleveland assumed a variety of roles: state legislator, presiding justice of county court, colonel of the county militia, and chairman of the local Committee of Safety.

Clothed with military and judicial authority, Cleveland held the upper hand in the civil war that raged in Wilkes. Determined to avenge the criminal acts of Tories who ravaged the homes and farms of mountain Patriots, he and his soldiers sought out the culprits and brought them to justice. Most often, that justice came in the form of hanging. According to noted North Carolina historian Marshall DeLancey Haywood, "Cleveland . . . probably had a hand in hanging more Tories than any other man in America. Though this may be an unenviable distinction, he had to deal with about as unscrupulous a set of ruffians as ever infested any land—men who murdered peaceable inhabitants, burnt dwellings, stole horses, and committed about every act in the catalogue of crime."

Though a few captured Tories avoided the noose, Cleveland never wasted

Statue of Benjamin Cleveland, Wilkesboro

an opportunity to exact some manner of revenge. In one instance, just after hanging a Tory who had stolen horses, he gave the victim's accomplice, who had witnessed the horrible spectacle, a choice: "Either join your companion on a tree limb, or take this knife, cut off your own ears and leave the country." Choosing to live, the Tory departed with blood pouring down his face after mutilating himself.

Occasionally, Cleveland allowed Tories to take an oath of loyalty and then set them free. One such Tory was a noted enemy leader Cleveland was anxious to execute. He sternly ordered, "Waste no time!—swing him off quick!"

Apparently, the threat of death did not disconcert the prisoner. He calmly remarked to Cleveland, "Well, you needn't be in such a damned big hurry about it."

Taken by the bearing of the condemned man, Cleveland shouted another command, "Boys, let him go!"

So appreciative was the Tory that he enlisted in the American cause and eventually proved one of Cleveland's most faithful and trusted soldiers.

Without question, the brightest moment in Cleveland's military career came during the titanic struggle at Kings Mountain on October 7, 1780. At the height of the battle, Major Patrick Ferguson attempted to push his Loyalist forces through Cleveland's line. In response, the mountaineers poured out rifle fire that fatally wounded the British commander and ensured the American victory.

After Ferguson fell, his splendid white charger was captured by the victorious Americans. By common consent, the magnificent animal was given to Colonel Cleveland, whose mount had been lost in the battle. But there was another reason Ferguson's horse was given to Cleveland—since he weighed more than 300 pounds, the colonel was too heavy to travel afoot.

At the time of his death, Cleveland weighed in excess of 450 pounds. A frequent guest of General Andrew Pickens, Cleveland caused consternation in the Pickens household. One of the general's daughters recalled, "We were always afraid when Colonel Cleveland came to stay over night with us lest the bedstead should prove unequal to his ponderous weight."

After he lost "The Round About," Cleveland moved his family to the Tugaloo River Valley in the South Carolina back country, where he died and was buried.

Proceed west on N.C. 268 for 3.6 miles to the community of Roaring River. En route, you can enjoy views of the northern bank of the Yadkin near the horseshoe where Cleveland's house stood. The two-story structure rested on a promontory, one of the sites from which the colonel sounded his mighty horn to summon his soldiers, men known as "Cleveland's Bull-Dogs" to partisans and "Cleveland's Devils" to Tories.

At Roaring River, a state historical marker pays tribute to Richard Allen, Sr. (1741–1832), a distinguished Revolutionary War officer who served the American cause from 1775 to 1781. Captain Allen was ordered to the scene of four of the most significant engagements in the Carolinas—Moores Creek Bridge, Charleston, Kings Mountain, and Guilford Courthouse. Ironically, because of timing, he took no active part in any of the four.

His marked grave lies 4 miles north.

Continue west on N.C. 268 for 9.6 miles to where it merges with N.C. 18 at North Wilkesboro. Known in Revolutionary War times as Mulberry Fields, North Wilkesboro was where Benjamin Cleveland first lived after he settled in the North Carolina mountains.

Along the way, you'll pass a state historical marker for Montfort Stokes (1762–1842). Like his older brother, John, Montfort Stokes offered his services to the American cause at the outbreak of the Revolution, enlisting in the Continental Navy and serving under Commodore Stephen Decatur. During action off Norfolk in 1776, Stokes's vessel was captured by the British fleet. He suffered great deprivation during his subsequent confinement aboard a prison ship in New York Harbor.

His impressive postwar career as a statesman included service as governor of North Carolina and as a United States senator. Stokes's home, Morne Rouge, stood a mile south of the marker.

Proceed south on N.C. 268/N.C. 18 for 0.8 mile to where it merges with U.S. 421 Business. Continue for 0.3 mile to the junction of Sixth and Main Streets in downtown North Wilkesboro. Drive west on Main for 0.4 mile to Tenth Street, turn right, and go four blocks to D Street. Turn right on D Street and proceed two blocks to Eighth Street. On the northwestern corner of this intersection stands First Presbyterian Church.

A tablet in the basement of the sanctuary serves as the grave marker of Chapman Gordon (1764–1812), one of five Wilkes County brothers—the sons of a member of the Continental Congress—who fought in the Revolution. Although he was only sixteen years old at the time, Chapman Gordon joined his four siblings to fight at the Battle of Kings Mountain.

After the war, he settled in North Wilkesboro. Ironically, he married Charity King, the daughter of Charles King, the man for whom Kings Mountain was named. Their grandson, John B. Gordon, was a Confederate major general and a governor of Georgia.

The Presbyterian church was constructed over Gordon's grave. When a full basement was excavated, his remains were reburied even deeper.

Retrace your route to U.S. 421 Business/N.C. 268/N.C. 18 at the junction of Main and Sixth. Turn right and follow N.C. 268/N.C. 18 for 0.1 mile to Wilkesboro Avenue. Turn left and proceed 0.3 mile to where Wilkesboro again junctions with N.C. 268/N.C. 18. Turn left and follow N.C. 268/N.C. 18 south for 0.2 mile across the Yadkin River to Main Street in Wilkesboro, the county seat.

Turn right and follow N.C. 268/N.C. 18 (East Main Street) for 0.4 mile to the Wilkes County Courthouse, erected in 1903. Bounded by East Main, Broad, North, and Bridge Streets, the white, three-story Neoclassical Revival structure rests on a square that boasts several Revolutionary War landmarks. Park nearby for a short walking tour.

Near the courthouse green, two "fixtures"—one man-made and the other natural—pay homage to Big Ben Cleveland.

One is a large statue of the notorious Tory-hunter sculpted in 1975 as a bicentennial project. It stands just across Bridge Street on the western side of the courthouse.

The other is "the Tory Oak," one of the most historic trees in North Carolina. A tall, stately sprout has survived the demise of the mother tree, which was ravaged by a tornado and other storms in recent years. It is located at the rear of the courthouse near the junction of Broad and North Streets.

Benjamin Cleveland used the once-mighty oak as a gibbet for five Tories during the war. Two of the unfortunate men, named Cowles and Brown, were put to death for stealing horses from the plantation of a Patriot in what is now Catawba County. The other three—William Riddle and his associates, Reeves and Goss—were hanged after a hasty court-martial in

The Tory Oak, Wilkesboro

Wilkesboro, over which Cleveland presided. He was anxious for the trio to die, since Riddle had masterminded a plan that had led to Cleveland's capture earlier in 1780. Riddle had spared Cleveland from the hangman's rope, but after his escape, Cleveland was not as benevolent toward his former captor. (The story of Cleveland's capture by Riddle and his subsequent escape is detailed later in this tour.)

From the rear of the courthouse, walk one block west on North Street and turn right on Bridge Street, where you'll see the Old Wilkes Jail, a museum of Wilkes County history. Inside the two-story, nineteenth-century brick structure are numerous artifacts and exhibits from the long history of Wilkes.

Immediately behind the jail building is the Robert Cleveland Log House. Believed to be the oldest structure in Wilkes County, the house was constructed in the last quarter of the eighteenth century by the brother of Benjamin Cleveland. Moved to this site in recent years from its original location in western Wilkes County, the carefully restored two-story log structure offers visitors a glimpse of the mountaineers' way of life during Revolutionary War times.

Robert Cleveland was instrumental in rescuing his brother from William Riddle. He subsequently marched with Benjamin to Kings Mountain, where he was wounded.

Return to your vehicle. Follow N.C. 268/N.C. 18 west for 1.2 miles to N.C. 16/U.S. 421. Turn right and go west for 2.5 miles to where N.C. 16 and U.S. 421 divide. Turn right, follow N.C. 16 north for 5.2 miles to S.R. 1346, turn left, and proceed 2.2 miles to S.R. 1348. Turn right and follow the winding, twisting road up Rendezvous Mountain.

Towering 2,450 feet above sea level, the mountain offers a breathtaking view of the surrounding countryside. Its name is derived from the Revolutionary War activities of Benjamin Cleveland and his mountain militiamen. From the summit of this lofty peak, Cleveland used his legendary horn to summon his soldiers when they were needed to battle Tories. Three strong blasts from the horn, which could be heard for 30 miles in all directions, brought Patriots from several counties to the mountain. It was here that they trained and drilled and here that they rendezvoused before marching to Kings Mountain.

In 1926, Judge Thomas B. Finley donated 142 acres of the mountain for a state park. Thirty years later, the state decided that the site did not meet the criteria for inclusion in the park system. In 1984, however, the mountain was opened for public use as Rendezvous Mountain Educational State Forest. Its facilities include trails, picnic shelters, restrooms, and an amphitheater. Historical markers erected by the D.A.R. are located near the entrance and at the top of the mountain.

Drive down the mountain to the junction with S.R. 1346. Located just southwest of the intersection are the original site of the Robert Cleveland Log House and the graves of Cleveland and his wife.

Retrace your route to N.C. 16. Proceed northwest on N.C. 16 for 9.9 miles to the Ashe County line. Created from Wilkes County in 1799 and named for Revolutionary War hero Samuel Ashe, the county borders both Virginia and Tennessee.

From the county line, it is 0.3 mile to N.C. 163. Turn left on N.C. 163 and proceed 2.5 miles south to the Calloway cemetery, located on the left side of the road near the community of Obids, which is on the southern fork of the New River.

Perhaps the most unusual grave marker here is a tall, slender rock that resembles a cactus. It marks the final resting place of Captain Thomas Calloway, Sr., an officer in the French and Indian War and Daniel Boone's companion on the famous trailblazer's trips to Kentucky.

Colonel Jesse Ray's grave, Ashe County

Prior to the Revolution, Calloway settled his family on a plantation on the New River north of the cemetery. There, he maintained a garrison for Patriots during the war. His five sons and two sons-in-law were active participants in the fight for independence.

At one time, the unique stone at Calloway's grave was used to mark Daniel Boone's camp at Obids. When Calloway died in February 1800, Boone placed the stone on his friend's grave and chiseled the initials *T. C.* into the rock. A D.A.R. plaque near the grave honors Calloway.

Proceed north on N.C. 163 for 7.1 miles to the junction with U.S. 221 and N.C. 194 near the community of Beaver Creek. Go north on N.C. 194 for 0.1 mile to Beaver Creek School Road, turn left, and drive 1.8 miles to S.R. 1225 (Ray Road). At the junction stands Beaver Creek Christian Church. On the opposite side of the road is the Duncan-Hardin-Ray cemetery.

Because much of western North Carolina was on the frontier at the time of the Revolution, it was not the site of a large number of significant battles. However, the frontier was gradually opened by men who had fought in the conflict. Consequently, many old cemeteries in the North Carolina mountains hold the graves of heroes of the fight for independence. The remains of Colonel Jesse Ray, a Revolutionary War officer who died in Ashe County in 1839, lie here. The unusual stone monument at his grave was designed by an American sculptress in Paris and crafted in Georgia. Bronze plaques on the marker detail Ray's military service.

Retrace your route to the intersection of N.C. 194 and U.S. 221 and go south on U.S. 221. It is 10.8 miles to the Watauga County line. The county takes its name from the Watauga River. An Indian word, Watauga means "beautiful water." It was also the name of the region in what is now Tennessee where pioneers formed a government by 1776. The Watauga settlement was the source of many of the Overmountain Men who played a prominent role in the victory at Kings Mountain.

The highway roughly follows an old Indian trail used by Martin Gambill when he made his patriotic ride in 1780.

Major Patrick Ferguson began his invasion of western North Carolina and South Carolina in the late summer and early fall of 1780, as part of Cornwallis's plan to suppress Patriot activity in the region. In response, Patriots ignited large brush piles atop the loftiest peaks as signal fires calling for militia leaders to assemble. Because the signal fires extended only to Watauga County, it was vital that a horseman spread the alarm to points beyond. Gambill, a resident of Ashe County, volunteered for the important duty.

Gambill rode for twenty-four hours without food or water to alert friends, neighbors, and strangers sympathetic to the cause of independence. In the course of his grueling 100-mile ride, two horses fell dead from exhaustion. His route followed the modern U.S. 221 north into Virginia, ending at the home of Colonel Arthur Campbell at Seven Mile Ford. Campbell promptly put his forces on the march to North Carolina, where they united with other militiamen to form a Patriot army commanded by Campbell's cousin, William. That army subsequently dealt Ferguson his devastating defeat at Kings Mountain.

From the Watauga County line, continue west for 1.2 miles to the community of Deep Gap, where U.S. 221 merges with U.S. 421. Bear right on U.S. 221/U.S. 421 and proceed west for 9.7 miles to Boone, the seat of Watauga County.

Boone was named for the legendary pioneer. Its most prominent landmark is Howard's Knob, a 4,451-foot peak that towers above the town. Howard's Knob Park is an excellent place to explore the beauty and history of the mountain. To reach it, follow U.S. 221/U.S. 421 west through downtown Boone, where it becomes King Street. Just west of the post office, turn right onto Water Street and proceed one block as Water circles into North Street. Turn left off North onto Junaluska Road, proceed up the steep, winding road to the park entrance, and turn right to proceed into the park.

During the Revolution, Benjamin Howard—a noted Tory and the man for whom the mountain was named—fled his Wilkes County home while being relentlessly pursued by Benjamin Cleveland. Howard found safety in a small cave at the base of a low cliff on the mountain. The subterranean passages provide an excellent hiding place, and the mountain peak proved a strategic point from which Howard could watch for Cleveland's approach.

It was thanks to his family that Howard eluded capture. Even a severe switching administered by a group of men could not compel his daughter, Sallie, to reveal the location of his hideout.

In 1778, Howard came forward to take the oath of allegiance. Thereafter, his daughter was a staunch supporter of the American cause.

Retrace your route to the junction of Water and King Streets in downtown Boone. Turn left on King and follow it east to U.S. 321. Turn right on U.S. 321 and follow it south as it skirts the campus of Appalachian State University. After 0.6 mile, you will reach Horn in the West Drive. Turn left and drive east for 0.2 mile to Daniel Boone Native Gardens, one of the two local attractions that honor the North Carolinian who spent most of the Revolutionary War exploring the wilderness and fighting Indians in his quest to further the westward expansion of the new nation.

Adjacent to the gardens is the Daniel Boone Amphitheater, the site of *Horn in the West*, the third-oldest outdoor historic drama in the United States. (The two oldest—*The Lost Colony* and *Unto These Hills*—are also in North Carolina.) Every summer since 1952, *Horn in the West* has brought to life the story of the Revolutionary War in the North Carolina mountains and the efforts of Daniel Boone to win freedom for his people. Among the characters in Kermit Williams's play are Boone, Benjamin Cleveland, Patrick Ferguson, and Banastre Tarleton.

Located on the amphitheater grounds is the Hickory Ridge Homestead Museum, which features a log-cabin village typical of the area during Revolutionary War times.

Return to the junction with U.S. 321. Turn right and proceed to U.S. 221/U.S. 421 at the Daniel Boone Inn. Turn right and go 0.9 mile on U.S. 221/U.S. 421 to N.C. 194 (Jefferson Road). Turn left on N.C. 194, follow it for 4.4 miles to S.R. 1335, then continue north on N.C. 194 for another 1.5 miles to Riddle's Knob.

Nearly five thousand feet tall, this peak provided the backdrop for the only military engagement in Watauga County during the Revolutionary War.

An abandoned farmhouse and barn on the left side of the road marks the site. In the forest behind the old farm is a cavern known as Wolf's Den. It was from this cave that Benjamin Cleveland was rescued by his brother, Robert, and a group of Patriots amid a hail of bullets.

This entertaining piece of Revolutionary War history began six months after Big Ben Cleveland attained immortal fame at Kings Mountain. Captain William Riddle, the noted Tory for whom Riddle's Knob peak was named, sought to rid the area of his archrival, the rotund militia colonel.

At that time, Cleveland owned Old Fields, a considerable tract of land and cattle farm on the southern fork of the New River near the present-day Ashe County–Watauga County line. On April 14, 1781, he arrived at Old Fields after a 35-mile ride from "The Round About." Upon learning of Cleveland's presence, Captain Riddle stole his horse and laid an ambush for him. When Cleveland and fellow Patriot Richard Calloway went searching for the prized animal—the former mount of Major Patrick Ferguson—the following morning, Riddle and his band opened fire. Calloway was unarmed, and Cleveland had but two pistols. Calloway was seriously wounded in the thigh, but Cleveland avoided certain death when he grabbed a local woman, Abigail Walters, and used her as a human shield until Riddle promised he would not be killed if he surrendered. Riddle reasoned that Cleveland would fetch a handsome price from the British if presented alive.

After Cleveland and Calloway were taken prisoner, Riddle and his Tory associates brought their prizes to the current tour stop. Along the way, the ever-resourceful Cleveland broke overhanging twigs to mark the route.

Meanwhile, local Patriot Joseph Calloway learned of the misfortune that had befallen his two comrades. He mounted his horse and galloped to the cabin of Cleveland's younger brother, Robert. Upon receiving the news, Robert assembled a force of twenty to thirty men who had served under Big Ben Cleveland. They immediately took up the chase.

Riddle and his party decided to camp at Wolf's Den. After an uneventful night, the Tories prepared an early breakfast. Cleveland sat on a fallen tree under heavy guard, including one sentinel who held the colonel's pistol to his head. The prisoner was under orders to write out passes to certify that each of his captors was a good Whig. These papers were to be used by the Tories for unfettered passage through the border country. Fearing that he might be considered expendable once he completed his assigned task, Cleveland delaying finishing. As Riddle and his men grew more and more impatient, the prisoner apologized for his lack of progress, blaming it on his poor penmanship.

Cleveland was down to the last pass when his brother and the rescue party attacked with gunfire and loud yells. To avoid the hail of friendly fire, Cleveland rolled off the tree on the side opposite the attackers. Delighted by their presence, Big Ben shouted, "Huzza for brother Bob!—that's right, give 'em hell." One of the Tories was badly wounded in the fray. Riddle and the others escaped, only to meet their fate on the Tory Oak.

Retrace N.C. 194 to its junction with U.S. 421/U.S. 321. Turn right and travel west on N.C. 194/U.S. 421/U.S. 321 for 7.6 miles to where N.C. 194 splits off and turns south. It is 8.9 miles on N.C. 194 to the Avery County line. Established in 1911, the year that North Carolina created the last of its hundred counties, Avery was named for Colonel Waightstill Avery, a Revolutionary War soldier and the first attorney general of the state of North

Carolina. (For more information on Avery, see The Foothills Tour, pages 235–37.)

Continue 9.2 miles west on N.C. 194 to U.S. 19E near Elk Park. Turn left on U.S. 19E and follow it 7.3 miles south to the state historical marker at Roaring Creek Bridge, located southwest of the village of Frank.

The marker calls attention to the site of Yellow Mountain Road, which took its name from Big Yellow Mountain and Little Yellow Mountain, located nearby. In September 1781, Isaac Shelby and John Sevier of Tennessee, William Campbell of Virginia, and the Overmountain Men traveled Yellow Mountain Road on their way to a rendezvous with Carolina militiamen before their battle with Patrick Ferguson at Kings Mountain.

Near the current tour stop, Yellow Mountain Road followed an old Indian trail known as Bright's Trace. Samuel Bright, the lawless individual for whom the path was named, settled in the area prior to the Revolution and remained loyal to the Crown during the war.

Continue south on U.S. 19E for 11.7 miles to the Mitchell County line. Here, the road turns abruptly west. Follow it for 3.3 miles to the bridge over the Toe River. Located on the nearby riverbank is the Bright family cemetery. A ceremony was held here by the D.A.R. on September 9, 1951, to mark the grave of Captain Robert Sevier, a casualty of the fighting at Kings Mountain.

In September 1781, Sevier left his wife and two infant sons in the hills of eastern Tennessee to follow his brother John across the mountains to the showdown at Kings Mountain. Toward the close of the battle, a bullet pierced his kidney. A British surgeon unsuccessfully attempted to extract the bullet. He dressed the wound and told Sevier that if he remained quiet and immobile, the bullet could subsequently be removed. Otherwise, the physician warned, the wound would become inflamed and death would soon follow.

Sevier feared capture by the Tories more than death itself, so he mounted his horse and headed for home with his nephew James Sevier. Nine days later, the two were camped near the current tour stop on land owned by Samuel Bright when Robert fell ill and died. His body was wrapped in a blanket, and he was buried in an unmarked grave under "a lofty oak."

Using descriptions in old court records and research by historians, D.A.R. members concluded that Sevier's grave was most likely located here. On their annual pilgrimage from Tennessee to Kings Mountain, reenactors of the Overmountain Men's march hold a service at Sevier's grave.

Continue on U.S. 19E for 0.7 mile to N.C. 226. The men of Shelby, Sevier, and Campbell camped in this vicinity on September 28, 1780.

Turn south on N.C. 226 and drive 4.8 miles to its intersection with the Blue Ridge Parkway at Gillespie Gap near the McDowell County line. Created in 1842, McDowell County was named for Major Joseph McDowell (1758–95), a young Revolutionary War hero born in the area.

The Overmountain Men poured through Gillespie Gap on Friday, September 29, 1780. Near the site where the North Carolina Mineral Museum stands today, they made the decision to divide their forces for fear that they might march into an ambush. A monument on the museum grounds pays tribute to those long-ago citizen-soldiers.

Approximately 5.4 miles south of Gillespie Gap, N.C. 226 junctions with U.S. 221. Colonel William Campbell and his Virginians camped the night of September 29, 1780, just east of the junction. At the same time, Colonels Sevier and Shelby rested their men near Honeycutt's Creek, located 3.5 miles north. Sevier reportedly spent the night in a house that stood 1.5 miles from the current tour stop in the community that today bears his name.

Near the junction stands a state historical marker for the site of Cathey's Fort. Located a mile to the east, the fort served as a rendezvous point for General Griffith Rutherford and his North Carolina militia in their famous 1776 campaign against the Cherokee Indians. (The campaign against the Cherokees is examined later in this tour; for additional information on Rutherford, see The Yadkin River Tour, pages 296–98.)

Continue south on N.C. 226/U.S. 221; remain on the highway's business route. After 6.8 miles, you will reach U.S. 70 in Marion. Named for Revolutionary War hero Francis Marion, "the Swamp Fox," the city is the seat of McDowell County. The first sites settled in the town were on land granted to Revolutionary War soldiers.

Near this intersection is Pleasant Gardens, the ancestral home of Major Joseph McDowell. A nearby state historical marker calls attention to the site.

In the 1750s, McDowell's father, known as "Hunting John," settled here on a tract he named Pleasant Gardens. Soon thereafter, he built the log cabin in which Joseph McDowell was born in 1758. In recent times, the stately two-story house has been converted into a commercial building. Due to its prime location at a busy intersection, its future existence is in doubt.

A renowned Indian fighter, Joseph McDowell took up arms with his Burke County cousins, Joseph "Quaker Meadows Joe" and Charles McDowell, during the Revolution. (For more on the Burke County McDowells, see The Foothills Tour, pages 237–39.) To distinguish himself from his Burke County cousin of the same name, he usually affixed *P. G.* (for Pleasant Gardens) to his signature.

Pleasant Gardens, home of Major Joseph McDowell

Turn right on U.S. 70 and proceed 0.9 mile west. An unpaved road on the right leads up the mountain to Round Hill, the historic burial ground of the McDowell and Carson families.

Continue west on U.S. 70 for 0.3 mile to the Carson House, located on the left just off the highway.

Open to the public, this three-story clapboard house was constructed of twelve-inch walnut logs by Colonel John Carson in 1780. An Irish immigrant, Carson settled in the Upper Catawba River Valley in 1773. He served as a delegate to the Fayetteville Convention of 1789, at which the state ratified the United States Constitution.

After the death of his first wife, Carson married Mary Moffitt McDowell, the widow of Major Joseph McDowell. Their son, Samuel Price Carson, born in the Carson House in 1798, was elected to the United States House of Representatives in 1825 and went on to serve four terms. After his subsequent relocation to Texas, he became the first secretary of state of the republic of Texas.

Proceed west on U.S. 70 for another 0.2 mile. Just beyond Pleasant Gardens Elementary School is the site of a fort built by local pioneers for protection against Indians.

Continue west for 3.5 miles to S.R. 1214. Nearby stood "The Glades," the home built by Major William Davidson (not to be confused with General William Lee Davidson). Major Davidson and his twin brother were intrepid Indian fighters and pioneer settlers in the region west of the current tour stop. Because William Davidson was a well-known Patriot, Major Patrick Ferguson stopped at "The Glades" in 1780 to try to capture him.

Resume the route westward on U.S. 70. It is 6.2 miles to the town of Old Fort. In the heart of Old Fort stands its trademark, a fifteen-foot-tall arrowhead monument crafted of pink Salisbury granite, erected in 1928 as a memorial to the pioneer settlers of western North Carolina.

It was this place that marked the dividing line between white settlers and the Cherokee Indians prior to the Revolutionary War. Before 1756, by Royal decree, white people were not allowed to settle beyond the crest of the Blue Ridge, which can be seen towering above Old Fort. Thus, when the first settlers began making their way onto Indian land beyond Old Fort on the eve of the Revolution, Cherokee reprisals were frequent events.

Old Fort took its name from a fort constructed here by colonial militia in 1776 for protection against the Cherokees. It has also been known by three other names: Upper Fort (to distinguish it from Cathey's Fort and the fort near Pleasant Gardens), Catawba Fort (for the river or the Indian tribe of the same name), and Davidson's Fort (for Samuel Davidson, twin brother of William, who owned land and a mill here and who became one of the first white settlers west of Old Fort).

Cherokees attacked Old Fort and the surrounding settlements in the spring of 1776, as the first fires of the Revolution were beginning to smoulder. By the time the Declaration of Independence was signed, Old Fort was considered one of the most dangerous spots in North Carolina. Attempts by North Carolina and the other Southern colonies to assure the neutrality of the Cherokees and Creeks were thwarted by the agents under John Stuart, the British superintendent of Indian affairs in the South. Stuart and his men incited the Indians to violence.

Near the arrowhead monument stands a state historical marker describing North Carolina's military response to the Indian uprisings. General Griffith Rutherford used the old log stockade located here as a staging area for his subsequent campaign to quell the Cherokee threat.

From Old Fort on July 14, 1776, Rutherford dispatched a crudely written letter to the Council of Safety wherein he chronicled the desperate situation on the North Carolina frontier:

> I am Under the Nessety of sending you by Express, the Alerming Condition, this Country is in, the Indins is making Grate prograce

in Distroying & Murdering, in the frunteers of this County, 37. I am Informed was Killed Last Wednesday & Thursday, on the Cuttaba River, I am also Informed that Col. McDowel 10 men more & 120 women & Children is Beshaged, in sume kind of fort, & the Indins Round them, no help to them before yesterday. . . . I Expect the Nex account to here they are Distroyed. . . . Pray Gentelman Considere oure Distress, send us Plenty of Powder. . . . This Day I set out with what men I Can Raise for the Relefe of the Distrest.

To put an end to the Indian uprisings, Rutherford assembled an army of twenty-five hundred back-country riflemen. Leaving the bulk of his forces at Old Fort, he moved west with five hundred men on July 29. Over the next several months, he and his soldiers marched deep into the mountains, where they burned thirty-six Cherokee towns, destroyed crops, and drove the Indians into hiding. By the year's end, the Indian threat in western North Carolina was over for the duration of the war, and the militiamen could turn their full attention to the Tory menace.

At the arrowhead monument, turn left onto Catawba Avenue. Proceed two blocks to Water Street and turn left. You'll notice an old stone building. Constructed by the WPA as a community center, it now houses the Mountain Gateway Museum, a branch of the North Carolina Museum of History. The Mountain Gateway Museum offers interesting exhibits and displays that tell the story of Old Fort and the frontier in Revolutionary War times.

Historians believe that Davidson's Fort was located on the bank of Mill Creek on the vacant land next to the museum.

Return to Catawba Avenue and drive south to I-40. Follow I-40 West, which runs conjunctively with U.S. 70 for a time. It is 5.9 miles to the Buncombe County line. Formed in 1791, the county was named in honor of Colonel Edward Buncombe, a Revolutionary War hero from eastern North Carolina.

Located on an access road just west of the county line is a state historical marker that notes the site of nearby Swannanoa Gap. On September 1, 1776, General Griffith Rutherford pushed two thousand soldiers and fourteen hundred packhorses through this passage on a final drive to end the Indian threat in western North Carolina.

Approximately 2 miles west of the county line, U.S. 70 separates from I-40 at the town of Black Mountain. Exit onto U.S. 70 and proceed west for 1.9 miles through the town to the junction with Old U.S. 70. Veer right onto Old U.S. 70 and go 3.9 miles to the town of Swannanoa, situated on the banks of the river of the same name. At the junction of Old U.S. 70 and Bee Tree Road (S.R. 2416), turn right. It is 0.7 mile to Swannanoa Presbyterian Church, organized in 1794. Adjacent to the church is Piney Grove Cemetery.

Interred in a marked grave in this burial ground is Major William Davidson, a devoted Patriot and Indian fighter who was instrumental in the preparations for the Battle of Kings Mountain. Following the war, Davidson left his home, "The Glades," and joined a group of friends and relatives moving across the mountains. They made their homes at the mouth of nearby Bee Tree Creek at what became North Carolina's first white settlement west of the Blue Ridge.

Two of Davidson's brothers were killed by the Cherokees. His other brother, John, was killed near Old Fort in July 1776, and his twin, Samuel, was scalped in 1784. The three brothers were cousins of General William Lee Davidson, the Patriot hero who fell at the Battle of Cowan's Ford. (For more information on General Davidson, see The Tide Turns Tour, pages 282–85, and The Hornet's Nest Tour, pages 172–75.)

Return to Old U.S. 70 and continue west to Riverwood Road (S.R. 2436). Turn left on Riverwood, follow it across the Swannanoa River to U.S. 70, and turn right.

Jones Mountain towers above the right side of the highway after 2.9 miles. Footpaths lead up the mountain to its summit, where a granite gravestone reads, "Here Lies Samuel Davidson. . . . First White Settler In Western North Carolina . . . Killed Here By Cherokees in 1784."

Davidson and his family ventured into the frontier several months prior to his death and established a homestead at the foot of the mountain. It was Davidson's custom to turn his horse out to forage with a cowbell around its neck, so he could keep track of the animal's whereabouts. Cherokee Indians, still smarting from the harsh treatment by Rutherford's troops and angered by Davidson's incursion into their territory, decided to catch the horse and use its bell to lure Davidson into an ambush. Using rifles provided by British agents during the war, they shot the unarmed settler as he reached the trail that ran along the top of Jones Mountain.

At the family's crude cabin, Davidson's wife heard the gunfire. Upon seeing her husband's rifle nearby, she knew what had happened. She grabbed up her baby, and she and a servant girl then made haste to the safety of Old Fort.

Immediately, a band of men set out in the darkness to avenge Davidson's death. They found his lifeless, scalpless body where it had fallen. Lurking nearby were the Indians who had mutilated him. The settlers killed some of them and drove the others away. They buried Davidson at the site.

Though Samuel Davidson's bold venture resulted in his death, it also opened the frontier to his brother and other Revolutionary War soldiers who settled in the mountains in the late eighteenth century.

Continue west for 5.3 miles to downtown Asheville, where U.S. 70 becomes College Street.

Asheville, the seat of Buncombe County, was incorporated in 1797. It was named in honor of Revolutionary War hero Samuel Ashe. Settled around 1792, the city was originally known as Morristown. Although the origin of the name is uncertain, some historians believe that it honored war financier Robert Morris, who owned vast tracts in the area.

Located on the square formed by College, Davidson, Spruce, and Marjorie Streets are the Buncombe County Courthouse and Asheville City Hall. Several monuments and markers related to the Revolution are located on the square. Dedicated by the D.A.R. in 1923, a huge block of granite with an inscribed bronze plaque pays homage to the life and service of Colonel Edward Buncombe, the man for whom the county was named. Other D.A.R. markers on the square honor Patriots Samuel Ashe and David Vance.

Samuel Ashe marker, Asheville

Continue west on College Street for two blocks to Biltmore Avenue. Proceed south on Biltmore for 2.1 miles to Unadalia Avenue, turn left, and go 0.1 mile to Newton Academy Graveyard.

Among the Revolutionary War soldiers interred here is Colonel David Smith. The son-in-law of Major William Davidson, Smith was among the men who went over the mountains to avenge the death of his wife's uncle, Samuel Davidson.

When William Davidson began the settlement at Bee Tree Creek, Smith was there. He subsequently became one of the first two men to settle at the site of Asheville. His gravestone reads, "The soil which inurns his ashes is a part of the heritage wrested by his valor for his children and his country from a ruthless and savage foe."

William Forster, the other early white settler here, is also buried in Newton Academy Graveyard. Born in Ireland, he served in the American army during the Revolution. While suffering from sickness, Forster dreamed he was buried under a particular tree on the land where the cemetery is now located. Although he recovered from that illness, Forster's request that he be interred under the tree of his dreams was honored.

Another marked grave holds the remains of Captain Edmund Sams, an officer in the Revolution and an Indian fighter said to have had "no superior and few equals." Following the war, Sams established the first ferry across the French Broad River.

Return to Biltmore Avenue. Turn left and go south for 0.5 mile to where Biltmore merges with U.S. 25 on the southern bank of the Swannanoa River. Continue south on U.S. 25 for 0.2 mile to Vanderbilt Road. Here stands one of a number of state historical markers in the mountains that identify Rutherford's Trace.

During its expedition against the Cherokees in September 1776, General Griffith Rutherford's army moved along the banks of the Swannanoa River near the present tour stop. On his triumphant return, Rutherford marked his path through the mountains, and the route has been known as Rutherford's Trace ever since. Some later roads in the mountains have been laid out along Rutherford's ancient route.

Continue south on U.S. 25 for 0.8 mile to I-40. Proceed west on I-40 for 7.1 miles to the exit for Smokey Park Highway (U.S. 19/U.S. 23/U.S. 74). Travel southwest on Smokey Park Highway for 1.9 miles to Sand Hill Road (S.R. 3412). Turn left and drive southeast to the state historical marker near the site of the home of Captain William Moore, an officer in the Revolution and the first white man to settle in North Carolina west of the French Broad River.

Moore, an Irish immigrant, lived in Rowan County when the fight for independence began. He first came to the mountains in November 1776, when he commanded a militia company during an expedition against the Cherokees. Setting up camp along nearby Hominy Creek, Moore was so awestruck by the natural beauty of the wilderness that he exclaimed to his immediate commander (who was his father-in-law), "This is Eden's land."

After the North Carolina General Assembly opened the lands west of the Blue Ridge to white settlement in 1783, Moore staked a claim to the area around where the state historical marker stands today. Governor Richard Caswell granted him a 640-acre tract in 1784, upon which Moore constructed a combination cabin and blockhouse. The structure stood until 1930, when it was torn down. Stones from the cabin's foundation were used in the foundation of nearby Oak Forest Presbyterian Church.

Moore is buried in an old family cemetery near the site of his cabin on land owned by American Enka Corporation, which spearheaded the 1981 effort to restore the ancient burial ground. Among the dignitaries who attended the commemorative rites at the newly restored cemetery that October was former North Carolina governor Dan K. Moore, the great-great-grandson of Captain Moore.

The tour ends at Moore's grave site.

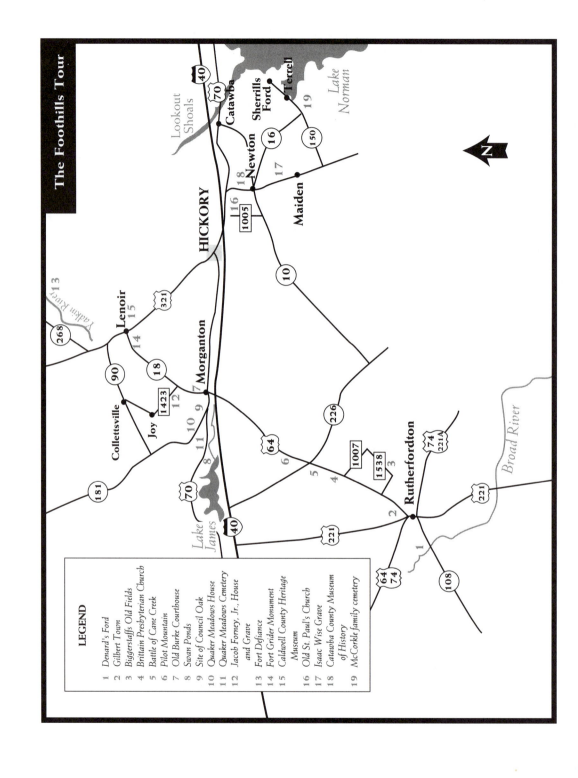

The Foothills Tour

LEGEND

1 Denard's Ford
2 Gilbert Town
3 Biggerstaffs Old Fields
4 Brittain Presbyterian Church
5 Battle of Cane Creek
6 Pilot Mountain
7 Old Burke Courthouse
8 Swan Ponds
9 Site of Council Oak
10 Quaker Meadows House
11 Quaker Meadows Cemetery
12 Jacob Forney, Jr., House and Grave
13 Fort Defiance
14 Fort Grider Monument
15 Caldwell County Heritage Museum
16 Old St. Paul's Church
17 Isaac Wise Grave
18 Catawba County Museum of History
19 McCorkle family cemetery

The Foothills Tour

This tour begins at Forest City in Rutherford County and makes its way through Burke and Caldwell Counties before ending at Lookout Shoals in Catawba County. Among the highlights are Gilbert Town, the site of Biggerstaffs Old Fields, Brittain Presbyterian Church, the Battle of Cane Creek, Quaker Meadows, Fort Defiance, the story of Isaac Wise, the Catawba County Museum of History, the graves of Francis McCorkle and Betsy Brandon McCorkle, and the story of Sam and Charity Brown.

Total mileage: approximately 206 miles.

This tour covers a four-county area lying at the edge of the mountains in southwestern North Carolina. In the two decades preceding the Revolutionary War, white settlers put down stakes here along the fertile banks of the many rivers and creeks that flow down from the mountains. When the fight for independence came, the foothills settlements provided a number of heroes and heroines. While the tour area was for the most part spared as a battleground, it served as a staging ground for action that took place in counties to the east.

The tour begins on U.S. 74 Business/U.S. 221A in the Rutherford County community of Forest City. Follow the highway west for 5.6 miles to N.C. 108. Turn left and drive 3.6 miles to Mountain Creek. Set in the wilderness along the eastern banks of this tributary of the Broad River is the Miller-Twitty graveyard. Buried here are three family members who were staunch Patriots during the Revolution.

William Twitty, a militia captain, was killed in 1775 by Indians while blazing a trail to Kentucky with Daniel Boone. His daughter, Susan Twitty Graham, was born in 1763 in a log cabin located near her final resting place. Susan was only seventeen when she gained enduring fame for her exploits at Graham's Fort in Cleveland County. (For more information, see The Tide Turns Tour, pages 251–53.)

Interred beside the heroine is her first husband, John Miller (1758–1807). A participant in a number of Revolutionary War engagements, Miller later served in the North Carolina General Assembly.

Near the graves of the couple is that of Susan's older brother, William. At nineteen, William was already an experienced soldier when he took part in the Battle of Kings Mountain. During the ferocious fighting there, young Twitty was distressed when one of his best friends was shot down by his side. Noticing powder smoke at a nearby tree and anxious to exact revenge for his fallen comrade, he waited with a loaded musket until a head poked out from the tree. Fire flashed from Twitty's weapon, and the Tory fell dead. When the battle was over, he walked to the tree and found the soldier he had slain. The dead man was one of Twitty's neighbors, a noted Loyalist.

Continue west on N.C. 108 for 1.6 miles to the bridge over the Broad River. Located near this stop was Denard's Ford, the site where Patrick Ferguson and his army camped on October 1, 1780.

Throughout much of September, Ferguson and his force of over a thousand men had operated in the back country of North and South Carolina in a cat-and-mouse hunt for area Patriots, many of whom were in hiding. These mop-up operations were designed to pave the way for the conquest of North Carolina by Cornwallis, who entered Charlotte with his army on September 25.

While camped at Gilbert Town (located 8 miles north of Denard's Ford) on September 30, Ferguson received the alarming news that a sizable frontier army was coming over the mountains in pursuit of him. He had two choices: he could march east to unite with Cornwallis or he could make a stand against the mountaineers and put an end to resistance in the area once and for all. Ferguson chose the latter course. While the bulk of his soldiers made their way to the river at the current tour stop, he dispatched messengers to Cornwallis with pleas for assistance.

In an effort to spread fear before the coming fight, Ferguson issued an inflammatory ultimatum to the people of the foothills while he was encamped at Denard's Ford:

> I say if you want to be pinioned, robbed, and murdered, and see your
> wives and daughters, in four days, abused by the dregs of mankind—

in short, if you wish or deserve to live, and bear the name of men grasp your arms in a moment and run to camp.

The Back Water men have crossed the mountains; McDowell, Hampton, Shelby, and Cleveland are at their head, so that you know what you have to depend upon. If you chose to be pissed upon by a set of mongrels, say so at once, and let your women turn their backs upon you and look out for real men to protect them.

Ferguson's appeal backfired, as he would tragically learn six days later when he made his fateful stand at Kings Mountain.

Turn around at the bridge and retrace N.C. 108, following it to the junction with U.S. 221 (Main Street) in Rutherfordton. Turn left onto U.S. 221 and proceed through the heart of the seat of Rutherford County. Both city and county were named in honor of General Griffith Rutherford, one of North Carolina's greatest Revolutionary War heroes. (For information on Rutherford, see The Yadkin River Tour, pages 296–98.)

After approximately 1.6 miles on U.S. 221, you'll reach a state historical marker calling attention to Gilbert Town, the county seat from 1781 to 1785. In the days leading up to the showdown at Kings Mountain, both Ferguson's army and the Overmountain Men camped here.

The site of Gilbert Town

To see the site of Gilbert Town, continue north on U.S. 221 for 1.2 miles to S.R. 1535 (Broyhill Road). Turn right, go 1.5 miles to S.R. 1520 (Rock Road), turn left, and drive 0.6 mile to a crude wooden sign in a field on the right side of the road.

This sign marks the site of the abandoned county seat. The old, two-story frame house on the opposite side of the road—the McKinney-Twitty House— occasionally flies the colors of the two nations whose soldiers camped here within days of each other in 1780. Other than the homemade sign and the old house, there is nothing in this green, rolling farm country to bear testimony that here was the apogee of Patrick Ferguson's campaign in western North Carolina.

According to tradition, the McKinney-Twitty House contains boards stained with the blood of Ferguson's soldiers. When Ferguson broke camp here in late September, he was forced to leave behind one his most trusted lieutenants, Major James Dunlap. Suffering from a severe wound sustained in the fighting at nearby Cane Creek (a subsequent stop on this tour stop), Dunlap remained behind at the home of William Gilbert, which stood across the road from the existing dwelling.

Although he was confident that the Gilbert family, which was loyal to King George III, would properly care for the injured officer, Ferguson assigned one of his soldiers to wait on Dunlap. Soon after Ferguson departed Gilbert Town, that soldier was murdered when he antagonized one of Gilbert's slaves. According to historian Lyman C. Draper, this incident was an "ill-omen" of another tragedy soon to follow.

Three Patriots hellbent on exacting revenge for recent cruelties perpetrated by Major Dunlap in Spartanburg, South Carolina, appeared at the Gilbert residence upon learning that Dunlap was there. They confronted the wounded officer and shot him. Tradition maintains that Dunlap died and was buried on nearby Ferguson Hill. Draper maintained that he may have survived the wound and recovered to fight another day.

At any rate, boards from the Gilbert home stained with Dunlap's blood

McKinney-Twitty House, Gilbert Town

can be seen in the existing house. Former occupants of the dwelling maintain that the ghost of the officer continues to haunt the place.

Four days after Ferguson and his army departed Gilbert Town, the Overmountain Men, in hot pursuit of the Loyalists, set up camp at almost the same site. While they were here, a letter signed by Benjamin Cleveland, Isaac Shelby, John Sevier, Andrew Hampton, William Campbell, and Joseph Winston was dispatched to Major General Horatio Gates, then the commander of the American army in the South. The officers requested that General William Lee Davidson or General Daniel Morgan be appointed to command the mountain soldiers. Proud of their efforts but anxious for leadership, the militia leaders noted, "We have collected at this place about 1500 good men, drawn from the Counties of Surry, Wilkes, Burke, Washington, and Sullivan Counties in this State, and Washington County in Virginia. . . . As we have at this time called out our Militia . . . with the view of Expelling the Enemy out of this part of the Country, we think such a body of men worthy of your attention."

Time did not allow Gates to act upon the request. At Kings Mountain three days after the letter was dispatched, the Americans struck a defining blow in the fight for independence. Clarence Griffin, eminent historian of western North Carolina, captured the mood of the American encampment at the current tour stop: "Never was the war cry of the ancient Romans more ceaseless and determined that Carthage must be destroyed than that of the mountaineers—to catch and destroy Ferguson."

Turn around at Gilbert Town and follow S.R. 1520 south for 0.7 mile to U.S. 64. Go left on U.S. 64 and proceed north for 3.2 miles to S.R. 1510. Turn right, drive 1.6 miles east to S.R. 1538 (Whiteside Road), turn left, and travel 4.7 miles to a historical marker at the site of Biggerstaffs (or Bickerstaffs) Old Fields. Well into the twentieth century, a storied oak tree long known as "the Gallows Oak" stood near this site.

Less than a week after the Battle of Kings Mountain, the victorious Americans camped here for three days. During their stay, word of the recent hangings of eleven Patriots at the community of Ninety-Six, South Carolina, reached the campsite. That news spelled doom for some of the Tory prisoners captured at Kings Mountain, who were being held by the mountaineers.

In order to retaliate for the South Carolina executions, a group of Patriot

Site of Biggerstaff's Old Fields

officers lodged a complaint with Colonel William Campbell. They informed their commander that a number of the Tory prisoners were guilty of lawless acts including murder and house burning. In accordance with North Carolina law, Campbell ordered a court-martial to inquire into the complaint. Big Ben Cleveland, never one to miss an opportunity to hang a Tory, was one of the presiding justices of the wilderness court. By early evening on October 14, the trials were completed, Cleveland and his fellow magistrates having pronounced the death sentence thirty-two times.

The giant oak was selected for the gallows, and the condemned men were paraded to the site through a forest illuminated only by the flames of hundreds of pine-knot torches held high by the victorious Patriots. The Tories were hanged in groups of three; included in the first trio was Colonel Ambrose Mills. During the initial executions, several prisoners awaiting their trip to the gallows managed to escape. After nine men had died, Colonel Isaac Shelby, sickened by the spectacle, put a stop to the hangings. The other condemned men were pardoned.

Turn around near the historical marker and drive 2 miles south on S.R. 1538 to S.R. 1007. Turn right, follow S.R. 1007 north for 3.5 miles to U.S. 64, and turn left again. After 0.1 mile, you will pass a historical marker for Fort McGaughey, which was erected during the Revolutionary War.

Continue south on U.S. 64 for 0.1 mile to Brittain Presbyterian Church, located on the left. A state historical marker stands alongside the road.

Organized in 1768, Brittain Presbyterian is one of the oldest churches in western North Carolina. It began in a log building that stood at the foot of a hill to the rear of the existing structure. The historic church cemetery grew from a burial ground already here when the church was established.

Because the church site was on land that belonged to Great Britain, it was originally given the name Little Britain. When the Revolution came, that name caused consternation among members who sided with the American cause. Consequently, the Mecklenburg Presbytery granted permission to add a *t* to the spelling to distinguish it from the mother country. Some historians believe that the additional *t* was a compromise between independence-minded members, who wanted to change the name altogether, and Loyalist members, who wanted no change.

The Overmountain Men camped near the church on their march home after the victory at Kings Mountain. They sadly laid to rest the body of Lieutenant Thomas McCollough in the cemetery here. A Virginian who died on October 12 from wounds sustained at Kings Mountain, McCollough is one of seventy-five Revolutionary War soldiers in the ancient burial ground, which was restored during the church's bicentennial celebration in 1968. Many of the graves have D.A.R. markers or identifiable stones.

From the church, proceed south on U.S. 64 for 1.9 miles to the historical marker for Colonel John Walker, located on the left just north of the bridge over the Second Broad River.

Born in Delaware to Irish immigrants, Walker (1728–95) was an intrepid Indian fighter who settled in Lincoln County around 1755. He moved to Rutherford County prior to the Revolution. An ardent Patriot, Walker had six sons, all of whom fought for American independence, five as commissioned officers. Walker's home, located near the current tour stop, was the site of the first court of Rutherford County.

Turn around near the historical marker and proceed north on U.S. 64 for 6.9 miles to S.R. 1700. On October 3, 1780, the Overmountain Men camped beneath Marlin's Knob beside Cane Creek, which parallels U.S. 64 on its route north into McDowell County.

On the day of their encampment here, the American colonels assembled their soldiers, advised them of the task that lay ahead, and offered the opportunity for men to withdraw from the expedition. Colonel Shelby then stood before the assembled Patriots, dressed in their back-country attire, and spoke to them in the plain language to which they were accustomed: "You have all been informed of the offer. You who desire to decline it, well, when the word is given, march three steps to the rear, and stand, prior to which a few more minutes will be granted you for consideration."

In one of the most dramatic moments of the war in North Carolina, the order was then given. Not a man budged. Visibly moved by the determination and loyalty of the soldiers, Shelby told them, "I am heartily glad to see you to a man resolve to meet and fight your country's foes. When we encounter the enemy, don't wait for the word of command. Let each one of you be your own officer, and do the very best you can, taking every care you can of yourselves, and availing yourselves of every advantage that chance may throw your way."

Continue north on U.S. 64. After 1.3 miles, you will cross into the southeastern corner of McDowell County. It is another 1.4 miles to a series of bridges over Cane Creek. A state historical marker notes that the Battle of Cane Creek took place here.

At nearby Cowan's Ford on Cane Creek, Colonel Charles McDowell of Burke County and his American militiamen ambushed Patrick Ferguson's soldiers on September 12, 1780. This skirmish served as a prelude to the pivotal battle at Kings Mountain. Caught off guard by the sudden attack, the Loyalists suffered a number of casualties before they regrouped and chased McDowell's men west into the mountains.

As a result of his modest victory here, Ferguson came to the erroneous conclusion that serious resistance to the Crown in western North Carolina was at an end. He didn't know that McDowell was biding his time until the arrival of the mountaineers he had called to assist him.

In the dense undergrowth on the virtually inaccessible creek banks are fieldstones marking the graves of nine of Ferguson's soldiers who fell here.

Continue north on U.S. 64. It is 2.8 miles to the Burke County line. Formed in 1777, the county takes its name from Dr. Thomas Burke (1747–83), a member of the Continental Congress and the governor of North Carolina during a portion of the Revolutionary War. (For more information on Burke, see The Regulator Tour, pages 408–10.)

Pilot Mountain rises approximately 0.8 mile north of the county line. At the foot of this 2,050-foot prominence stood the early log house of Captain William Moore, the famous Indian fighter of the Revolutionary War era who subsequently became the first white settler west of the French Broad River. (For more information about Moore, see The Frontier Tour, pages 224–25.)

The Overmountain Men camped just south of Pilot Mountain at Bedford's Hill on October 1 and 2, 1780. It was here that they prevailed upon the unpopular Charles McDowell, their senior colonel, to step aside as commander. His reluctant replacement was Colonel William Campbell. According to Lyman C. Draper, the meticulous historian of the campaign of the Overmountain Men, Colonel McDowell "had the good of his country at heart more than any title to command, [and] submitted gracefully to what was done." Anxious to ensure the success of the expedition against Ferguson, McDowell left the encampment en route to a conference with General

Horatio Gates. He hoped to persuade the commander of the American army in the South to provide a general officer for the Overmountain Men. As a result, McDowell was not on hand for the victory at Kings Mountain.

Proceed northeast on U.S. 64 for 12.9 miles to U.S. 70 Business (Union Street) in Morganton.

The seat of Burke County, Morganton was established in 1777 as Morgansborough. It was named to honor General Daniel Morgan (1736–1802), the farmer-turned-soldier who masterminded the Patriot victory at Cowpens, South Carolina, in 1780 and aided Nathanael Greene on his successful retreat through the North Carolina Piedmont. After the war, when Morgan was asked what role he had played in the struggle for independence, he responded simply, "Fought everywhere; surrendered nowhere."

Turn right on U.S. 70 Business and follow it into downtown Morganton to the Old Burke County Courthouse, located at the town square. Built in 1833, the two-story building surmounted by a cupola now houses the Burke County Museum of History. The museum offers artifacts from the long history of Burke, including some from the Revolutionary War era.

It was in the log courthouse that once stood on the site of the present museum that Revolutionary War hero John Sevier was brought to trial in 1788. Sevier was charged with treason for his role in attempting to establish the State of Franklin in western North Carolina. He walked out of the courthouse in the middle of the trial and was never convicted. As a member of the North Carolina General Assembly, he subsequently voted for legislation that pardoned himself. Ultimately, he got his new state, Tennessee, and was elected its first governor.

You will reach a junction with N.C. 181 on the northern side of the Old Burke County Courthouse. Proceed northwest on N.C. 181 for 0.7 mile to N.C. 126. Near the intersection stands a historical marker for Swan Ponds, the plantation of Revolutionary War Patriot and statesman Waightstill Avery.

To see the estate, turn left on N.C. 126, drive west for 2.4 miles, turn left on S.R. 1222, and follow it to its terminus at Swan Ponds. Neither the home nor the plantation grounds is open to the public.

It was during the Revolution that Waightstill Avery (1741–1821) established a thirteen-thousand-acre plantation at this site. A portion of the property has remained in the Avery family ever since that time.

Born in Connecticut and educated at Princeton, Avery came to Edenton, North Carolina, as a young attorney in 1769, There, he became associated with Joseph Hewes and James Iredell. His long career as a legal scholar and jurist began in 1772, when he was appointed by the Crown as attorney general for the colony.

As tensions with Great Britain mounted, Avery was an outspoken advocate for independence. After signing the Mecklenburg Resolves in 1775, he served in the Provincial Congresses that set up the framework for the government of the independent state of North Carolina. In November 1776, he was one of the prime movers in the final Provincial Congress at Halifax, which produced the first North Carolina Constitution. According to Governor David Lowry Swain, Avery's handwriting appeared in the constitution more often than that of any other member of the committee that drafted the document. When the first state legislature met at New Bern in 1777, Avery was selected North Carolina's first attorney general. During the British occupation of Charlotte in 1780, Cornwallis ordered Avery's office burned, a punishment he inflicted only upon "the most foul" Patriots.

Until he was well into his seventies, Avery continued to practice law throughout North Carolina and Tennessee. On one occasion, he engaged in a heated courtroom exchange with a young lawyer who had served in the Revolution as a teenager. Prior to that time, Avery and Andrew Jackson had enjoyed an amicable relationship, indulging in horse racing and cock fighting at Quaker Meadows in Burke County; among their mutual friends was Davy Crockett. But when Jackson, ever the prankster, invaded Avery's saddlebag to substitute a slab of bacon for *Bacon's Abridgement of the Law*, Avery found himself the subject of courtroom jest when he sought to cite a legal precedent from the book-turned-meat. As a result of the humiliating experience, Avery challenged Jackson to a duel.

Both men survived the battle of pistols and parted friends. Avery later recounted that he allowed Jackson to fire first, with no effect. Avery then discharged his pistol into the air, approached Jackson, and lectured the future president "very much in the style a father would use in lecturing a son."

The existing plantation house at Swan Ponds was built in 1830 by Avery's only son, Isaac. Brick from the original home constructed by Waightstill

Avery was incorporated into the dairy house.

Return to the junction of N.C. 126 and N.C. 181, where you'll see a state historical marker for Quaker Meadows, an area on the outskirts of Morganton steeped in Revolutionary War history. It received its name in 1752, when Moravian bishop A. G. Spangenberg passed through the region and was mistaken for a Quaker by the Indians. This grassy area in west-central Burke County was the stage for some of the most dramatic events leading up to the Battle of Kings Mountain.

Drive west on N.C. 181 for 0.4 mile to St. Mary's Church Road. Turn right and go 0.2 mile to the historic house known as Quaker Meadows.

Constructed in 1812, this two-story brick home is the oldest structure in Burke County. It was built by Charles McDowell on the site of the house where his father and uncle, Charles and Joseph, had grown up. Since 1986, the house has been owned by the Historic Burke Foundation, which is in the process of restoring the historic dwelling.

Brothers Charles and Joseph McDowell were militia officers from the beginning to the end of the Revolution. Serving together for much of the war, they participated in Griffith Rutherford's campaign against the Cherokees in 1776 and fought in the Battle of Ramsour's Mill on June 20, 1780. But their signal contribution to the American war effort came following that Lincoln County battle.

To counter the incursions of Patrick Ferguson's Loyalists into western North Carolina during the summer of 1780, the McDowell brothers called for the assistance of the Overmountain Men. In response to their plea, soldiers from all over the mountains assembled at Quaker Meadows on September 30, 1780. Joining the expedition at this site were Benjamin Cleveland, William Lenoir, Joseph Winston, and the men under their commands.

Return to N.C. 181, turn left, and proceed 0.1 mile to Bost Road. Turn left into the parking lot of the restaurant located on the left side of the junction.

Here stands a D.A.R. marker for the Council Oak, a local landmark until it was destroyed by a storm many years after the war. The mighty oak sheltered the council of war among the McDowells and the other commanders. From their deliberations came the plan that resulted in the devastating blow dealt to Ferguson a week later at Kings Mountain.

Return to the junction of N.C. 181 and N.C. 126. To see the McDowell burial ground, known as Quaker Meadows Cemetery, turn right on N.C. 126, drive south for 0.3 mile to Sam Wall Road, turn right, and proceed 0.1 mile to Brandston Drive. Turn right on Brandston and follow it to its terminus at the cemetery.

Located in a majestic setting on a hill overlooking Morganton, Quaker Meadows Cemetery is one of the earliest identified sites associated with white settlement in the western part of the state.

Of the fifty-three marked graves, the oldest is that of David McDowell, the first permanent settler in the area. He died in 1767.

Colonel Charles McDowell is among the other family members interred here. For him, the extraordinary Patriot victory at Kings Mountain was a bittersweet event. It was McDowell who put together the mountaineer army that won the battle, yet he was not on the field to share in the victory. Nonetheless, he has since received his due. As distinguished North Carolina jurist and historian David Schenck noted, "The brothers, Charles and Joseph McDowell of Quaker Meadows, and . . . their no less gallant cousin, Joseph McDowell, of Pleasant Gardens . . . are due more credit and honor for the victory of Kings Mountain than . . . any other leaders who participated in that decisive wonderful battle."

Interred beside Colonel McDowell is his wife, Grace Greenlee Bowman McDowell, one of the most noted wartime heroines of western North Carolina.

Grace's first husband was John Bowman. As the commander of a militia company, Captain Bowman was away from his Burke County home for extended periods during the war. In his absence, Grace proved a thorn in the side of Ferguson's operations in the North Carolina foothills. On one occasion, Loyalist soldiers made off with some of the Bowmans' horses. Grace forthwith made her way alone to Ferguson's camp some miles away, demanded the return of the animals, and promptly rode home with them. On another occasion, a group of Tories raided the Bowman residence while Grace was away. Upon her return, she immediately gave chase, caught up with the culprits, and, at rifle point, forced them to surrender the items they had taken.

When word reached Grace that Captain Bowman had been badly wounded at the Battle of Ramsour's Mill, she climbed upon the family's speediest mount, her child of fifteen months in her arms. She galloped down lonely roads on the 40-mile ride to Lincoln County, reaching her husband's side just before he died on the battlefield, where he was buried.

She married Charles McDowell near the close of the Revolution.

Buried in an unmarked grave beside Charles and Grace is Joseph McDowell. His postwar public career in helping to build the new state and nation was impressive. Like his brother, he was a delegate to both Constitutional Conventions. Unlike Charles, however, Joseph was an adamant anti-Federalist. Nonetheless, after the United States Constitution was ratified by North Carolina, he served two terms in Congress.

Alexander and Sarah Ervin—another married couple of Revolutionary War renown—are buried here.

During the war, Alexander Ervin (1750–1830) served as a captain under Joseph McDowell. Once the hostilities ended, he acted as a military auditor in the North Carolina foothills. His books remain one of the best sources on the Revolutionary War service of the men of western North Carolina.

Ervin's first wife, Sarah, died as a result of a wound sustained during an act of wartime bravery. When a Tory drew his sword to assault a wounded Patriot under her care, Sarah stepped between the two men and received the sword blow meant for the American soldier.

Ervin subsequently married Margaret Crawford Patton, whom he met while delivering the riderless horse and personal effects of her late husband, who had died at the Battle of Ramsour's Mill.

Return to the junction of N.C. 126 and N.C. 181. Turn right and drive east on N.C. 181 to U.S. 70 Business in downtown Morganton. Turn left, go one block north, and turn left on N.C. 18. Drive north for 3 miles to S.R. 1423. Turn left, travel 2.5 miles to S.R. 1440, and turn left again. Cedar Grove Plantation is 0.5 mile ahead.

Not open to the public but visible from the highway, the two-story Federal-style house located here was built by Jacob Forney, Jr. (1754–1840), in 1825. Forney was one of three Lincoln County brothers who fought for the American cause. His father, too old to serve in the Patriot army, attempted to kill Cornwallis when the British commander was quartered at the family's plantation in Lincoln County. (For more information, see The Tide Turns Tour, pages 281–82.)

Jacob Forney, Jr., settled near the current tour stop in 1780. He is buried in a marked grave in the nearby family cemetery.

Return to the junction with S.R. 1423. Turn left and proceed 6.9 miles northwest to S.R. 1405 at the community of Joy. Turn right and follow S.R. 1405 northeast for 3.2 miles to the Caldwell County line. At the county line, the road changes to S.R. 1335. Continue northeast for 1.1 miles to the community of Adako, where S.R. 1335 becomes S.R. 1337. Proceed 1.6 miles on S.R. 1337.

The Johns River is visible on the right side of the road. Martin Davenport, one of Caldwell County's greatest Revolutionary War heroes, lived along this 32-mile watercourse, which flows southward through the western portion of the county.

Because of his distinguished service for the Patriot cause, Davenport was a wanted man among area Loyalists. On one occasion, John McFall led a group of Burke County Tories to Davenport's home. Dismayed to learn from Mrs. Davenport that her husband was away, McFall demanded that she prepare breakfast for the Tories. He also directed the Davenports' ten-year-old son, William (who would later kill the last elk ever seen in North Carolina), to fetch some corn from the barn and feed the Tories' horses.

After McFall finished his meal, he came out of the house and asked William Davenport in a harsh tone why the horses had not been fed. With all the spirit and boldness of his Patriot father, the lad told McFall, "If you want your horses fed, feed them yourself." McFall was outraged. He immediately cut a switch and thrashed the boy.

At the court-martial proceedings at Biggerstaffs Old Fields in Rutherford County following the Battle of Kings Mountain, one of the Tory captives brought before the tribunal was John McFall. When the case against McFall was presented, "Quaker Meadows" Joseph McDowell reasoned that the Tory's conduct was not of such a heinous nature that it merited death. Consequently, he recommended leniency. But Ben Cleveland, one of the judges of the tribunal, thought differently. He snapped, "That man, McFall, went to the house of Martin Davenport, one of my best soldiers, when he was away from home, fighting for his country, insulted his wife, and whipped his child, and no such man ought to be allowed to live."

Cleveland had his way, and McFall paid for the whipping with his life.

He and his eight fellow Tory victims were left suspended from the Gallows Oak after they were executed.

Continue northeast on S.R. 1337 for 1.6 miles to N.C. 90 at Collettsville. Follow N.C. 90 east for 4.1 miles to Mulberry Creek Road at the community of Olivet. Turn left, drive north for 1.1 miles to Roby Martin Road, turn right, and go 3.9 miles to U.S. 321. Turn right, go south for 0.9 mile to N.C. 268, turn left, and drive east for 1 mile to the bridge over the Yadkin River, where a state historical marker notes that Fort Defiance, the home of Revolutionary War luminary William Lenoir, is located nearby.

To visit the site, continue east on N.C. 268 for 4.8 miles to S.R. 1513 and turn right. Fort Defiance, a red, two-story frame dwelling, is on the right just after the turn. The restored home is open to the public for tours on a limited basis.

William Lenoir (1751–1839) began constructing the house in 1788 near a stockade that stood nearby to afford early settlers protection against Indi-

Fort Defiance

ans. A native of Virginia, Lenoir grew up in Edgecombe County, North Carolina. In 1775, on the eve of the Revolution, he moved with his wife and small child from Halifax to Wilkesboro, where he could better use his skills as a surveyor.

Lenoir proved himself an invaluable militia officer during the fight for independence. He first caught the eye of his superiors as a young lieutenant in Rutherford's campaign against the Cherokees. As a captain at the Battle of Kings Mountain, he was wounded in the thick of the fight. Lenoir later described the experience this way: "I received a slight wound in my side, and another in my left arm, and after that, a bullet went through my hair about where it was tied, and my clothes were cut in several places." A year later, at Pyle's Massacre on the Haw River (see The Regulator Tour, pages 400–402), Lenoir escaped injury even though his horse was shot from under him and his sword was broken.

Following the war, he served effectively in the state legislature. However, his numerous attempts at higher offices—United States senator in 1789, governor of North Carolina in 1792 and 1805, and United States representative in 1803 and 1806—proved unsuccessful because Lenoir did not believe in electioneering. He simply refused to campaign for office.

Located at the edge of a field near the house is the family cemetery, where Lenoir is buried. The Masonic symbol on his tombstone convinced Union soldiers to spare Fort Defiance from the torch during the Civil War. The original stockade stood on the site of the cemetery.

When Lenoir's home was acquired by the Caldwell County Historical Society in 1965, a number of important period furnishings and artifacts were included in the purchase. Many of these treasures, including Lenoir's eyeglasses, are on display in the house.

Retrace your route to U.S. 321 and turn left. Proceed south for 6.1 miles to N.C. 18 Business/N.C. 90 at Lenoir, the seat of Caldwell County. The town was named for the builder of Fort Defiance.

Turn right on N.C. 18 Business/N.C. 90 and follow it for 0.5 mile to Main Street in downtown Lenoir. Turn left, proceed 0.2 mile to College Avenue, turn right, then turn left on Vaiden Street. It is 0.1 mile to the Caldwell County Heritage Museum.

Located in the last extant building of Davenport College—a nineteenth-century girls' school named for the family of Martin Davenport—the museum showcases area history from the time prior to the arrival of the first white settlers. Its displays and exhibits provide a wealth of information about the involvement of the area and its residents in the Revolution.

Return to the junction with College Avenue. Turn left, drive 0.2 mile to Willow Street, turn right, and go one block to Harper Avenue.

Fort Grider once stood on the left side of Willow at this junction. An outpost built by Patriots early in the Revolution for protection against Indians, it stood on land owned by Frederick Grider, the man for whom it was named. A monument placed here by the D.A.R. in 1930 marks the site where North Carolina soldiers camped en route to the Battle of Kings Mountain. The large, multistory building now covering the site once housed Lenoir High School.

Turn right on Harper Avenue, drive 0.8 mile to U.S. 321, and turn right again. It is 14.1 miles to the Catawba County line at the Catawba River. From the river, follow U.S. 321 south for 2.9 miles to U.S. 64/U.S. 70 in Hickory. Proceed east on U.S. 64/U.S. 70 for 5.6 miles to St. Pauls Church Road. Turn right, drive 1.8 miles to Old Conover–Startown Road, and turn right again. After 0.1 mile, you'll see Old St. Paul's Church on the right.

Organized in 1759, Old St. Paul's began as a church for people of the Lutheran and Reformed faiths. The tall, two-story sanctuary at the current stop was constructed in 1818 of logs from the original church, which stood nearby. The charter members of Old St. Paul's were the area's earliest settlers. They took up residence along the banks of the nearby South Fork (Catawba) River in the early 1750s.

Two decades later, when the call went out for volunteers to fight for American independence, many of the male members of the church answered. A number of graves of Revolutionary War veterans are located in the ancient burial ground adjacent to the church. Among the soldiers laid to rest here was John Wilfong, Sr. (1762-1838). A teenager during the war, Wilfong holds the distinction of being the only man from what is now Catawba County to serve as a soldier in the Continental Army. But the height of the war in western North Carolina saw Wilfong serving as a militiaman. In 1780, he was involved in some of the fiercest fighting at Kings Mountain, where he was badly wounded in the side.

Continue southwest on Old Conover–Startown Road for 1.9 miles to S.R. 1005 (Startown Road). Turn left, drive 0.9 mile to N.C. 10, turn right, and go west for 0.7 mile to S.R. 1146 (Robinson Road). Turn right on S.R. 1146. After 2.6 miles, slow down and look to the left. The field here was the site of the home of Henry Weidner, the first permanent white settler in Catawba County, and the famous Weidner Oak. The ancient tree died in the 1930s, after standing for centuries.

In colonial times, when area settlers faced a constant threat from the Cherokees to the west, Henry Weidner and his family were forced to flee their home on numerous occasions. The oak was located forty feet from the house. When danger from the Cherokees was imminent, a Catawba chief friendly to Weidner would paint the oak bright red. When all was clear, he would paint it white. Thus, when Weidner slipped back home to check on the state of affairs, he could gauge the Indian threat by the color of the tree.

When the Revolutionary War began, settlers along the banks of the South Fork found themselves at odds with each other over their loyalties. It was under the shade of the mighty oak that Henry Weidner, George Wilfong, Conrad Yoder, John Hahn, and several others met to pledge their support for the American cause. That pledge, known as the South Fork Covenant, exposed the Patriots to great danger from their Tory neighbors.

Weidner and his associates used horns to warn of an attack by Tories or Indians. On one occasion, a band of Tory robbers called at the present tour stop to seize the Weidner family's money. According to contemporary records, the raiders roughed up Henry and "hung him up by the joints." His wife, Catherine, used a mussel shell to sound the alarm, and a band of Patriot neighbors quickly arrived and gave chase to the Tories.

A similar incident took place nearby when Tory robbers arrived at the home of John Hahn. When Hahn refused to reveal the hiding place of his money, he was seized by the Tories, who "drew him up till he turned blue." Unsuccessful in their efforts to gain the desired information, the robbers started for the barn to steal horses when they were confronted by Hahn's two daughters, armed with axes. As soon as the female Patriots told their unwelcome neighbors that they intended to "make sausage" of the first Tory to enter the stable door, the robbers departed as quickly as they had arrived.

In early October 1780, George Wilfong, the father of Continental Army soldier John Wilfong, assembled twenty-five men under the Weidner Oak and then marched them to Kings Mountain, where they suffered heavy casualties as part of "the South Fork Boys."

Retrace your route to N.C. 10. Turn left and drive 4.2 miles east to U.S.321/N.C. 155. Turn right and go 5.7 miles to downtown Maiden.

After his victory over the impetuous Banastre Tarleton at Cowpens on January 17, 1781, General Daniel Morgan began a retreat to escape the wrath of Cornwallis's full army. Morgan's flight took him to Morganton and then to the current tour stop, where he prepared his army to cross the Catawba River and join up with Nathanael Greene's forces.

In Maiden, follow U.S. 321/N.C. 155 (East Main Street) south through town for 1.1 miles to Providence Mill Road. Turn left and proceed south for 0.8 mile to the old Providence Mill, located on the left. Captain Daniel McKissick, a Patriot militiaman who was seriously wounded just miles away at the Battle of Ramsour's Mill, once lived near here. He recovered in time to fight several months later at Kings Mountain.

From the mill, continue north on Providence Mill Road for 0.2 mile to Fred Beard Road. Turn left, drive 0.5 mile to Mays Chapel Road, turn left again, and head west for 1.1 miles to U.S. 321/N.C. 155. Turn right and proceed north for 2 miles to Prison Camp Road. Turn right and drive east for 1 mile. At the edge of a forest across a field on the left side of the highway is the old Haas family cemetery. Buried here is Isaac Wise, who was executed nearby in 1776.

Grave of Isaac Wise

According to Catawba County tradition, seventeen-year-old Isaac Wise ignored the Loyalist leanings of his father, Daniel, and many of his neighbors. At the outbreak of the war, he threw his support to the cause of American independence.

A militant band of local Tories captured Wise near the house of Simon Haas, a pioneer who had settled in the vicinity of the current tour stop. The decision was made to hang the young Rebel, but no rope was readily available. One of the Tory leaders, Martin Shuford, raced away on his steed to secure some. In the process, his horse stumbled and threw him. Shuford broke his nose in the fall, after which he was forever known as "Crooked Nose." (Four years later at the Battle of Ramsour's Mill, Crooked Nose

Shuford gave his life while fighting for the Crown.)

After Wise's hanging, his body was left dangling from the tree. Simon Haas finally cut the body down and removed it to his home, where his wife used her best linen sheet as a burial shroud.

Wise's grave is marked by a bronze plaque erected by the Catawba County Historical Association in 1951. The cemetery is on private property, so ask permission from the owner of the nearby farmhouse if you wish to visit the grave.

Return to the junction with U.S. 321/N.C. 155. Turn right and proceed 3.4 miles north to N.C. 10 in Newton, the seat of Catawba County. Turn right, follow N.C. 10 for 0.4 mile to College Avenue, turn left, and proceed three blocks to the Catawba County Museum of History, located on the old courthouse square.

Housed in the former Catawba County Courthouse, the museum has emerged as one of the most attractive and respected county history museums in the state. Among its holdings related to the Revolutionary War are a British officer's greatcoat (a real redcoat!); a small British ceremonial sword; the worn Bible carried by the Reverend Johann Gottfried Arends, the first Lutheran minister west of the Catawba and a strong supporter of American independence; and the intricately decorated powder horn of Henry Weidner.

On the museum's well-landscaped grounds is a granite monument dedicated to the memory of Matthias Barringer. Barringer was an early settler in the Newton area. His log house, constructed in 1762 approximately 1.5 miles southeast of the museum, served as the first courthouse in Catawba County. After World War II, it was moved to downtown Newton, restored, and used as a public library and museum until it burned in 1952.

When the colonies embarked upon their fight for independence, Barringer cast his lot with the American cause. A militia captain, he used his plantation as a mustering ground for the company of local soldiers he commanded in Griffith Rutherford's expedition against the Cherokees.

He and seven of his men were on a scouting expedition in the Quaker Meadows area of Burke County in early July 1776 when they were massacred by a Cherokee war party armed with British rifles. Barringer was the first to fall. He was subsequently scalped.

Local legend has it that Barringer's wife, back home caring for their two small children, told neighbors on the day of the ambush that she knew her husband had fallen in battle. She said she had heard him groan.

Return to the intersection with N.C. 10. Turn left and drive 1.3 miles to where the highway forks. Take the right fork (N.C. 16) and proceed southeast for 10.1 miles to N.C. 150. Turn left, drive 2.2 miles east to McCorkle Lane, turn right, and follow the short road to the McCorkle family cemetery, located on the shore of Lake Norman. Buried at the most prominent marker in the cemetery are Major Francis McCorkle and his second wife, Betsy Brandon McCorkle.

The son of Scottish immigrants who settled in what is now Iredell County in colonial times, McCorkle lived along nearby Mountain Creek. One contemporary description of him noted that he was a handsome man about six feet tall, with a florid complexion and auburn hair. A staunch advocate of independence, he served as a militia officer throughout the war.

Graves of Major Francis McCorkle and his wife, Betsy McCorkle

Following the Battle of Ramsour's Mill, a local soldier returning home from the fight stopped by the McCorkle residence to report that the major had been killed. McCorkle's family was overjoyed when he subsequently rode up unharmed.

Several days later, McCorkle was awakened at his home by the clatter of hooves. Voices called his name and directed him to get up and come to the door. Fearing he had been surprised by a band of Tories, McCorkle reluctantly complied. In the darkness, he was asked which side he was for. Unwilling to waver from his convictions even as death awaited, he responded boldly, "I will not die with a lie in my mouth—I'm for liberty!"

Suddenly, one of the party of men began laughing, and McCorkle realized the hoax. The would-be Tories were his fellow Patriots, who had come to take him to a celebration over the recent victory at Ramsour's Mill.

McCorkle also served in the crucial battles at Cowpens, Kings Mountain, and Torrence's Tavern.

Betsy Brandon McCorkle was buried beside her husband. She married Major McCorkle around 1795, when she was but a teenager. Her legendary meeting with President Washington is recounted in The Yadkin River Tour.

Return to the junction with N.C. 150. Turn right and proceed east for 3.4 miles to Sherrills Ford Road (S.R. 1848) at the crossroads community of Terrell. Turn left, drive 2.4 miles to Island Point Road at the village of

Sherrills Ford, turn right, and follow the road to its terminus near Lake Norman.

The waters of Lake Norman—that massive "inland sea" created by Duke Power Company in the 1960s—now cover Sherrills Ford, a former river crossing located nearby. During the Revolution, Sherrills Ford served as an important passage over the Catawba River. Named for Adam Sherrill, a pioneer settler west of the Catawba, the ford was one of a number of routes over the river between what are now Catawba and Iredell Counties.

Daniel Morgan arrived at Sherrills Ford with a large portion of his army in late January 1781. Cornwallis and 2,000 Redcoats were in hot pursuit. Morgan's entourage—850 American soldiers, 500 British prisoners, 800 horses, 40 wagons, and two captured cannon—stretched along area roads for more than 2 miles. It was a spectacle few residents ever forgot.

Before Morgan made his river crossing here to link up with Major General Nathanael Greene, he buried two of his finest soldiers from the Maryland Continental Line on Adam Sherrill's farm.

Return to Sherrills Ford Road. Turn right, go 5.3 miles to Lowrance Road, turn right again, and proceed north for 2.9 miles to N.C. 10 in the town of Catawba. Turn right on N.C. 10 and follow it through town for 0.7 mile to U.S. 70. Turn left and drive 0.1 mile to S.R. 1717 (Oxford School Road). Turn right and travel north for 3.6 miles to Lookout Dam Road at the community of Catfish.

This crossroads village received its name during the Revolutionary War when a portion of Daniel Morgan's army caught a large quantity of fish at nearby Lookout Shoals. Morgan's men were in the process of escorting the British prisoners taken at Cowpens to Virginia.

Turn right on Lookout Dam Road and follow it for 1.3 miles to its terminus on the banks of the Catawba River at Lookout Dam. Island Ford, where Morgan's troops made their way across the river with their British captives, was located near this site.

It was also on the nearby river shore that two of the most notorious outlaws of the Revolutionary War had their hideout. The names of Sam Brown and his sister, Charity, were infamous throughout western North Carolina during the war. Members of a family loyal to the Crown, they raided homes and farms in the foothills of North and South Carolina while many of the menfolk were away fighting for independence. Sam Brown was one of the culprits in the attempted robbery of Henry Weidner recounted earlier on this tour.

Known throughout the region as "Plundering Sam" to the Patriots and "Captain Sam" to the Tories, Brown met his demise toward the close of the war when he was shot in the Tyger River region of South Carolina by a Patriot defending his wife from the robber. After Sam's death, Charity fled to the North Carolina mountains.

The Browns' hideout was located on a bluff that once rose three hundred feet near the present tour stop. Their cave stood sixty feet from the base. Although the last plunder the Browns took during their crime spree was supposedly stored in the cave, nothing has ever been found by treasure hunters.

Over the years, the river has covered the cave. Yet the area remains one of mystery and intrigue. Local legend maintains that eerie noises come from the vicinity of the cave whenever someone approaches it. Some locals say that in the distant past, a tree near the cave blown down by a storm yielded twelve sets of pewter ware from its trunk.

The tour ends here, at the Catawba.

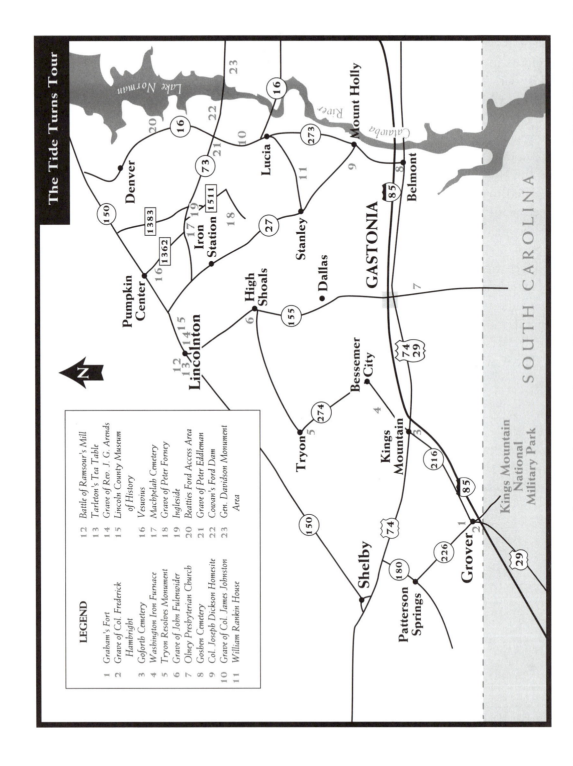

The Tide Turns Tour

LEGEND

1 Graham's Fort
2 Grave of Col. Frederick Hambright
3 Goforth Cemetery
4 Washington Iron Furnace
5 Tryon Resolves Monument
6 Grave of John Fulenwider
7 Olney Presbyterian Church
8 Goshen Cemetery
9 Col. Joseph Dickson Homesite
10 Grave of Col. James Johnston
11 William Rankin House

12 Battle of Ramsour's Mill
13 Tarleton's Tea Table
14 Grave of Rev. J. G. Arends
15 Lincoln County Museum of History
16 Vesuvius
17 Machpelab Cemetery
18 Grave of Peter Forney
19 Ingleside
20 Beatties Ford Access Area
21 Grave of Peter Eddleman
22 Cowan's Ford Dam
23 Gen. Davidson Monument Area

Lake Norman

Denver

Pumpkin Center

Lincolnton

High Shoals

Dallas

Stanley

Iron Station

Lucia

Mount Holly

Catawba River

Belmont

GASTONIA

Bessemer City

Kings Mountain

Tryon

Shelby

Patterson Springs

Grover

Kings Mountain National Military Park

SOUTH CAROLINA

The Tide Turns Tour

This tour begins at Patterson Springs in Cleveland County and makes its way through Gaston County before ending at Cowan's Ford on the Lincoln County–Mecklenburg County line. Among the highlights are the story of Graham's Fort, the grave of Frederick Hambright, the Battle of Kings Mountain, the Henry Howser House, the story of the Tryon Resolves, the grave of John Fulenwider, the Battle of Ramsour's Mill, Machpelah Cemetery, the grave of Peter Forney, the story of Jacob Forney, the grave of Peter Eddleman, and the Battle of Cowan's Ford.

Total mileage: approximately 167 miles.

This tour traverses a three-county area in the southwestern Piedmont of North Carolina and dips into the northern portion of two adjacent South Carolina counties. In a seven-month period from mid-1780 to early 1781, three crucial Revolutionary War battles occurred within this relatively small geographical area.

In this land of gently rolling hills punctuated by a few peaks, the tide of the Revolution began to turn in favor of the American colonies with the Patriot victories at Ramsour's Mill and Kings Mountain in the summer and fall of 1780. Then, in January 1781, Cornwallis moved in with his full army to begin his pursuit of Major General Nathanael Greene, which ultimately brought ruin to the British war effort.

The tour begins at the junction of N.C. 226 and N.C. 180 in the community of Patterson Springs in southern Cleveland County, which takes its name from Revolutionary War hero Benjamin Cleveland.

Follow N.C. 226 south for 6.1 miles to the site of Graham's Fort, located on a knoll on the right side of the road three hundred yards northeast of the state historical marker near Buffalo Creek. The fort stood on a site now occupied by a late-eighteenth-century house incorporated into—and disguised by—a private home that has a modern appearance.

Experienced in building forts for the protection of settlers along the frontier of western North and South Carolina, Colonel William Graham constructed a large log cabin here that became known as Graham's Fort during the Revolutionary War. Graham was an outspoken advocate of American independence. As a delegate to the Fifth Provincial Congress, he took part in the deliberations that produced North Carolina's first state constitution. As a militia officer, he fought courageously in both Carolinas, participating in the important victories at Moores Creek and Ramsour's Mill.

As summer was about to give way to fall in 1780, Graham was a wanted man among local Tories. A band of marauders came calling at Graham's Fort that September. The events that unfolded here that day constitute one of the most dramatic, if unheralded, stories of the American Revolution in western North Carolina.

Congregated inside the fort were many people, most of them young, old, or otherwise unable to take up arms to defend against the twenty-three soldiers in the Tory band. Colonel Graham had only David Dickey and nineteen-year-old William Twitty to help him defend the place.

When the Tories sought to enter the cabin, Graham adamantly refused. To force the issue, they opened fire. After each volley, a demand for capitulation could be heard: "Damn you, won't you surrender now?"

Graham was unyielding, and the attack continued, without much effect. Finally, John Burke, one of the more brazen Tories, decided to take matters into his own hands. He left ranks and raced up to the cabin, where he aimed his musket through a crack at young William Twitty. Just as Burke was about to squeeze the trigger, Twitty's seventeen-year-old sister, Susan, pulled her brother to safety. Burke's musket ball missed its target and penetrated the opposite wall of the cabin.

Susan then observed that Burke was on his knees, reloading in anticipation of firing into the cabin again. She cried out, "Brother William, now's your chance—shoot the rascal!" In an instant, the young Patriot sent a ball that crashed into Burke's head.

As soon as the Tory fell, Susan unbolted the door, ran out into the open, and grabbed Burke's gun and ammunition. Stunned by the teenager's bravery, the Tories momentarily held their fire. But as she headed back toward the door, their guns blazed again. Safely inside, Susan put the captured weapon to use, taking shots at the Tories.

At length, the standoff ended when the attackers left, having suffered four casualties. Fearing another attack, Graham sent his pregnant wife and the others at the fort to a safer location.

Soon thereafter, his fears were realized when Tories plundered the undefended fort.

Less than a month later, Graham was with his command—the South Fork Boys—at the base of Kings Mountain when a courier brought news that his wife was in a "precarious condition" and needed him at once. Torn between his desire to take part in the impending battle and his family responsibilities, Graham chose the latter. He asked Colonel William Campbell for permission to leave.

Reluctant to grant the request, Campbell asked Major William Chronicle, one of Graham's subordinates, "Ought Colonel Graham to have leave of absence?"

Chronicle, who would die leading the men from what are now Lincoln, Gaston, and Cleveland Counties in Graham's stead, responded, "I think so, Colonel, as it is a woman affair, let him go."

There is some dispute as to what happened next, but most accounts indicate that just as Graham headed home, he heard the firing that announced the opening of the battle. Although separated from his command, he could not resist the fight. He returned to the scene, arriving in time to take part in the final charge up the mountain.

The Patriot victory assured, Graham was seen riding away on his black charger waving his sword. He made his way to his wife's side, where, just hours later, she gave birth to his only child, Sarah.

After the war, he returned to the site of Graham's Fort, where he built the house that now stands.

As for Susan Twitty, the young heroine whose quick thinking saved her brother's life, she returned to her home in Rutherford County, where she married John Miller, a Revolutionary War soldier. Years later, after each of their spouses had died, William Graham and Susan Twitty married.

Graham and his first wife are buried in marked graves in an isolated family cemetery several miles from the current tour stop.

Continue south on N.C. 226 for 2.7 miles to U.S. 29 in the town of Grover. Located along the railroad tracks near the junction are two state historical markers marking the sites of important British movements during the campaign in the Carolinas.

One of the markers notes the site of the encampment of Patrick Ferguson and his Loyalist army October 4 and 5, 1780, just before their fateful showdown with the frontier Patriots at Kings Mountain.

The other marker stands at the place where Cornwallis and his British army entered North Carolina on their second invasion, which took place during the third week of January 1781. It was here that Cornwallis began the chase of Nathanael Greene and Daniel Morgan that over the next two months led the British army halfway across the state, then to Virginia, then back into North Carolina.

Despite the costly setback that Banastre Tarleton had just suffered at nearby Cowpens, South Carolina, Cornwallis exuded confidence while encamped at the current tour stop. Reinforced by 1,530 soldiers, the British commander wrote his superior, Sir Henry Clinton, "Be assured, that nothing but the most absolute necessity shall induce me to give up the important object of the Winter's Campaign."

Turn left on U.S. 29, then turn right on S.R. 2278 (Elm Street) and go 0.7 mile to Shiloh AME Zion Church. S.R. 2278 junctions with a short, unnamed, unimproved road almost opposite the church. This treacherous, deeply rutted road terminates at the old cemetery of Shiloh Presbyterian Church. Buried in a well-marked grave in this forested, unkept graveyard is Lieutenant Colonel Frederick Hambright (1727–1817), one of the least-known Patriot heroes at Kings Mountain.

A native of Germany, Hambright settled in North Carolina at a fort near the mouth of the South Fork of the Catawba River around 1760. An Indian fighter in colonial times, he was an early advocate of American independence. In 1777, he was appointed lieutenant colonel of the militia, a position he held for the duration of the war.

When his immediate commander, Colonel William Graham, prepared to start for home just before the Battle of Kings Mountain, the fifty-three-year-old Hambright relinquished command of the South Fork Boys to Major William Chronicle, a much younger soldier. When Major Chronicle fell mortally wounded while leading the soldiers up the steep northeastern side of Kings Mountain, the German-born officer assumed command of the brave band, which included his eldest son, John Harden Hambright.

Frederick Hambright was in the thick of the fight when a rifle ball smashed into his leg. Though blood overflowed his boot, he refused the urgent pleas of his men to care for his wounds. Instead, he said, "Huzza, my brave boys, fight on a few minutes more and the battle will be won." Despite the severity of his wound, Hambright fought on with his men until victory was achieved.

He never fully recovered from the effects of the gunshot and walked with a limp the rest of his life.

Return to the junction of S.R. 2278 and U.S. 29 in Grover. Turn right and drive 1.5 miles northeast to N.C. 216. A state historical marker near the intersection calls attention to the Battle of Kings Mountain and notes that the national military park is located 5 miles southeast.

Turn right on N.C. 216 and drive 1.2 miles south, where the route enters South Carolina and becomes S.C. 216. After another 1.3 miles, you will enter Kings Mountain National Military Park. Follow S.C. 216 as it slices through the forested landscape. Metal signs along the road mark the routes taken by soldiers as they made their way to the showdown on the nearby mountain.

It is approximately 1.9 miles from the park entrance to the visitor center, which is housed in a spacious, modern building of wood and stone. Turn left into the parking area and walk to the center.

Inside, visitors are treated to an excellent audiovisual orientation program and numerous exhibits related to the pivotal fight that occurred here. A self-guided tour of the mountain battleground is also offered. Special events related to the battle and the Revolution are held throughout the year in the amphitheater located nearby. Each year on the anniversary of the battle, reenactors arrive at the park after following the route of the Overmountain Men. Admission to the park is free.

After his overwhelming victory at Camden, South Carolina, on August 16, 1780, Cornwallis began to formulate plans to invade North Carolina, the one state that stood in the path of his total conquest of the South. To pave the way, he dispatched his trusted lieutenant, Major Patrick Ferguson, to northwestern South Carolina and the Piedmont of North Carolina. The thirty-six-year-old career officer from Scotland was to punish insurgents,

Grave of Major Patrick Ferguson

recruit Loyalist soldiers to assist in the invasion, and protect the left flank of the British army as it poured into North Carolina.

Ferguson was fearful of the frontier Patriots of North Carolina, with whom he had skirmished throughout the summer in the South Carolina upcountry. In late September, he was at his encampment at Gilbert Town when he learned that the Overmountain Men had mustered near their homes across the mountains in what is now Tennessee. In a vain attempt to dissuade the frontiersmen from doing battle with him again, Ferguson sent forth a courier with a threat to "the backwater men," as he called them. If they did not "desist from their opposition to the British arms," he would "march his army over the mountains, hang their leaders, and lay their country waste with fire and sword."

On the other side of the mountains, the fiercely independent frontiersmen of Scots-Irish descent did not wait for Ferguson to make good his threat. Instead, they came after him. They poured over the mountains to join ranks with Patriots from the foothills of the Carolinas and Virginia.

When they reached Gilbert Town in early October, the frontiersmen—attired in hunting shirts and leggings—were disappointed that their opponents had fled. Undaunted, they continued south to Cowpens, South Carolina (where just three months later Americans under Daniel Morgan would inflict a severe defeat on Banastre Tarleton).

At Cowpens on Friday, October 6, the Patriots received intelligence that Ferguson and his 1,100-man army were in the vicinity of Kings Mountain, 30 miles distant. There was no time to be lost. A mounted force of 910 soldiers—approximately half the American army—galloped off in pursuit of Ferguson at nine o'clock that evening. The remainder of the men would follow on foot in the dark, rainy night. As Colonel Isaac Shelby put it, "It was determined . . . to pursue him [Ferguson] with as many of our troops as could be well armed and well mounted, leaving the work horses and footmen to follow as fast as they could."

Throughout the miserable night, the men rode and walked in a torrential downpour. When fatigue and exposure threatened both soldiers and horses, Colonels William Campbell, John Sevier, and Benjamin Cleveland conferred with Shelby about the need for rest. Voicing his grim determination, Shelby said, "I will not stop until night if I follow Ferguson into

Cornwallis's lines." His fellow commanders gave no argument, and the march continued.

Meanwhile, Ferguson had positioned his army on a promontory located within walking distance of where the visitor center stands today. The mountain—a rocky, forested spur of the Blue Ridge—has a six-hundred-yard-long plateau that rises sixty feet above the surrounding plains. Ferguson believed himself to be in a defensible position while he waited for reinforcements and an enemy attack.

On October 5, he had written Cornwallis, who was then in Charlotte, that "three or four hundred good soldiers, part dragoons, would finish the business. Something must be done soon. This is their last push in this quarter and they are extremely desolate and [c]owed." Although he was anxious to receive additional manpower, Ferguson exuded confidence: "I . . . have taken a post where I do not think I can be forced by a stronger enemy than that against us."

Now, just prior to the battle, tradition has it that Ferguson restated his assuredness about his army's position with these words: "God Almighty could not drive [us] from it."

By early afternoon on Saturday, October 7, Campbell, Shelby, Sevier, Cleveland, and their soldiers were poised to prove Ferguson wrong. When they were within a mile of the enemy position, the Patriots tied their horses in the mist and proceeded to encircle the mountain. Perhaps a sign that the fortunes of the American war effort were about to turn, the gray skies gave way to bright sunshine in midafternoon. So quiet and secretive was the Patriots' approach—and so ineffective was Ferguson's intelligence—that the Americans were within a quarter-mile of the enemy encampment before the first skirmishers opened fire around three o'clock. The ensuing battle lasted exactly one hour. When it was over, the frontiersmen had achieved one of the most important victories of the Revolutionary War. Patrick Ferguson was dead. His Loyalist army had suffered staggering casualties: 157 killed, 164 wounded, and 698 captured. The Patriots had lost but 38 killed and 64 wounded.

To experience the very landscape where the battle was played out, walk the 1.5-mile battleground trail from the visitor center. This paved path follows a circular route that passes along the forested mountain slopes and onto the plateau of Ferguson's encampment before ending near the visitor center. Numerous monuments, markers, and signs interpret the events that transpired along the route.

The first significant marker is the D.A.R. monument at the site where Major William Chronicle fell during the battle; the marker is on a hillside to the left.

Chronicle and his friend Captain John Mattocks were able to provide invaluable intelligence about the geography of the battleground, for the two men had maintained a deer-hunting camp the previous autumn at the very site of Ferguson's encampment.

In the absence of Colonel William Graham, Major Chronicle assumed command of the South Fork Boys just before the battle began. Sword in hand, the young Lincoln County major spurred his horse up the steep slope to a point near the site of his former camp. There, he spotted the swarming enemy. He turned and exclaimed to his dismounted soldiers, who had put bullets in their mouths for quick loading, "Face to the hill! Come on my boys, never let it be said a Fork boy run!"

No sooner had Chronicle uttered the command than a Loyalist bullet pierced his heart and toppled him from his saddle. But his shouting men rushed onward. Well-directed fire from the ridge took a deadly toll on the Patriots. Soon after Chronicle was mortally wounded, so were his comrades Captain Mattocks, Lieutenant William Rabb, and Lieutenant John Boyd.

Return to the trail. On the right, you'll notice a marker at the common grave of Chronicle, Mattocks, Rabb, and Boyd.

All along the trail, you can observe the treacherous terrain the frontiersmen faced as they stormed up the mountain. As it turned out, the densely wooded slopes worked to the advantage of the attackers. Firing down the mountain, Ferguson's sharpshooters often aimed too high. Moreover, they were forced to shoot at targets who fought from behind trees. As one of the victorious Patriots reported, "[I] took right up the side of the mountain and fought from tree to tree . . . to the summit."

The next significant site is the Hoover Monument, located approximately 0.4 mile from the Chronicle markers. A short side trail on the right leads to the monument, which was erected to commemorate President Herbert Hoover's visit to the battleground on October 7, 1930, during the sesquicentennial commemoration of the Patriot victory. At this site, the president delivered a twenty-two-minute address to an audience of seventy-five thousand—an enormous crowd, considering the isolated location of the battleground and the scarcity of motor vehicles at the time.

Resume the trail as it turns south and begins a steady climb. The Centennial Monument stands near the crest of the hill less than 0.2 mile from the Hoover Monument. Inscribed on this granite memorial are the names of the Patriots killed in the battle.

Soon after the last shots were fired that Saturday afternoon, darkness enveloped the landscape. The victorious frontiersmen, exhausted from their all-night march and the battle itself, had to camp on the ground among the dead and wounded. Injured soldiers suffering from loss of blood screamed out for water. Propped against trees and boulders where they fell, men from both armies expired during the night.

Sunday dawned with a bright sun that cast its rays through the orange, yellow, and red leaves of the dense hardwoods onto a forest floor littered with bodies. One eyewitness described what he saw that day: "The scene became distressing. The wives and children of the poor Tories came in great numbers. Their husbands, fathers, and brothers lay dead in heaps. . . . We proceeded to bury the dead, but it was badly done. They were thrown into convenient piles and covered with old logs, the bark of old trees, and rocks, yet not so as to secure them from becoming a prey to the beasts of the forests, or the vultures of the air. And the wolves became so plenty, that it was dangerous for anyone to be out at night."

Near the Centennial Monument, you can enjoy a spectacular view of the surrounding countryside. This was the vantage point that emboldened Patrick Ferguson to make his fateful boast.

Proceed east on the trail as it makes its way along the plateau to the United States Monument, the most impressive marker in the park. Plaques on the base of the towering obelisk bear the names of the American forces involved in the battle.

Among the prominent officers listed are Colonels William Campbell and Isaac Shelby. These two gallant commanders led their soldiers up the southwestern and northwestern slopes in the face of galling fire.

When the battle stood in the balance, Shelby shouted his famous words of encouragement: "Now boys, quickly reload your rifles and let's advance upon them and give them another hell of fire. . . . Shoot like hell and fight like demons!"

Colonel Campbell, sensing that triumph was near at hand, charged ahead of his Virginians, exclaiming, "Boys, remember your liberty! Come on! Come on, my brave fellows; another gun—another gun will do it! Damn them, we must have them out of this!"

From the courage of Campbell, Shelby, and all the Indian fighters who had left their frontier homes undefended came the decisive victory at Kings Mountain.

The United States Monument proclaims that the battle here was the turning point of the Revolution.

Thomas Jefferson, the third president of the republic born of the war, described the importance of the events at Kings Mountain: "It was the joyful annunciation of that turn of the tide of success which terminated the Revolutionary War with the seal of our independence."

Sir Henry Clinton, the longest-serving British commander in chief during the war, termed the Battle of Kings Mountain "a fatal catastrophe."

Indeed, when news of the devastating setback reached Charlotte, Cornwallis promptly called off his invasion of North Carolina and scampered back to South Carolina, where he lingered for three months while Nathanael Greene assumed command of and reorganized the American forces in the South.

Just east of the United States Monument is a marker at the site where Patrick Ferguson fell.

Until he was brought down, the fearless officer—who was, ironically, the only British soldier on the field—displayed the same gallantry that had earned him a sterling reputation on countless battlefields during the war.

Even as the Patriots began to close in on his position on the plateau, Ferguson, attired in a checkered vest, rode about his troops and blew his silver whistle to urge them to continue the fight. As soon as his junior officers realized the futility of continuing, they pleaded with Ferguson to surrender rather than to have his men annihilated. Their commander was unyielding. Replying that he would not submit "to such a damned banditti," Ferguson galloped forward with sword in hand in a last desperate charge.

As he slashed his way through the oncoming Patriots, his sword broke, yet he rode on until he encountered the waiting rifles of John Sevier's men. Numerous shots rang out. Six or eight struck their target. One pierced Ferguson's head. The Loyalist commander's body and clothing were riddled by bullets. Both of his arms were broken. When he fell from his mount, one of his feet caught in a stirrup. Four of his soldiers stopped his fleeing animal, laid their commander on a blanket, and bore him out of harm's way.

Turn to the left and walk down the stone steps to a marker at the site where Lieutenant Colonel Frederick Hambright was wounded in the dramatic charge of the South Fork Boys.

When Major Chronicle and his fellow officers fell, Captain Joseph Dickson ordered their surviving comrades to charge. With loud yells, they scrambled up the mountain, only to come face to face with a bayonet charge by the enemy. The Patriots momentarily fell back to a safe position to reload. Then they charged again, this time led by the mounted Frederick Hambright, who continued the fight even after being badly wounded in the thigh.

Return to the stone marker where Ferguson was fatally wounded and continue the trail, which turns sharply south. At the bottom of the hill, you'll notice a large monument and cairn on the left at Ferguson's grave site. The dying officer was carried to this spot, where he was propped up with rocks and blankets.

The son of a Scottish judge and the nephew of a major general in the British army, Ferguson (1744–80) aspired to a military career from an early age. By the time he arrived in New York in 1777, he was a veteran soldier who had seen action in Europe and the West Indies. He had achieved his greatest fame in 1776 with his invention of a breechloading rifle. It was said that the weapon could be fired six times a minute by a marksman while lying on his back in a drizzling rain.

Ferguson was considered the best marksman in the entire British army. While serving in the North in the early stages of the war, he once had within the sight of his deadly accurate rifle an unidentified American officer. Yet he refused to squeeze the trigger because he deemed the officer "an unoffending individual who was acquitting himself very cooly [sic] of his duty." The American officer turned out to be none other than General George Washington.

Tradition maintains that Ferguson had two female companions with him at Kings Mountain. One of them, a woman known as Virginia Sal, was killed early in the battle and laid to rest beside her lover. Her red hair was said to have made her a target for American riflemen. Virginia Paul, the other camp follower, survived the battle. Her coolness impressed her captors, including Colonel William Campbell, who told his victorious soldiers, "She is only a woman, our mothers were women. We must let her go."

From the Ferguson grave site, the trail winds approximately 0.2 mile to the visitor center. Return to your vehicle. To resume the tour, turn left out of the parking lot and drive south for 0.8 mile to the D.A.R. marker on the left side of the highway.

This stone monument, which stands near the southern boundary of the national park, notes that the Battle of Kings Mountain was fought in York County on South Carolina soil. Without question, the site is now just south of the state border. However, when the battle was fought, it may very well have been in North Carolina. Tradition in the Tar Heel State has it that engineers assigned to survey the line in later years detected the aroma of "mountain dew" in the area and strayed from their path to find the source. Thus, the battleground wound up in South Carolina.

At any rate, it was a joint effort by the two states that made the national military park a reality. In 1926, Congressmen A. L. Bulwinkle of North Carolina and W. E. Stevenson of South Carolina introduced the legislation that led to the park's establishment.

Turn around near the marker and proceed north for 1.7 miles to the administration office at the national park. Stop here to obtain permission to visit the Henry Howser House, a prominent early-nineteenth-century landmark acquired by the National Park Service in the 1930s.

To reach the house, go north from the administration office for 1.1 miles to Rock House Road (S.R. 11-86). Turn left and drive 0.9 mile to a fire lane on the left. Park nearby and walk 0.3 mile down the lane to the magnificent rock house constructed in 1803 by Henry Howser.

A Revolutionary War soldier who fought in the North, Howser settled near Kings Mountain after the war. Here, he became a friend and neighbor of Lieutenant Colonel Frederick Hambright.

Howser, a talented mason, built the two-story rock masterpiece with the assistance of his wife, Jane, and their slaves. It is similar in construction to the Hezekiah Alexander House in Charlotte.

After years of neglect, the structure was carefully restored by the park service in 1977. Today, it stands in an excellent state of preservation and is surrounded by the forests of the national park.

Retrace your walk on the fire lane. About midway back, you can find the grave of Henry Howser in an ancient family cemetery in the woods on the left.

Return to your vehicle and proceed to the junction of Rock House Road and S.C. 216. Directly across S.C. 216 is an unimproved lane on the eastern side of the highway. The home of Lieutenant Colonel Frederick Hambright stood a hundred yards down this lane until it burned in 1926.

Before Hambright built the house, he lived in a cabin that stood to the east. Traces of the cabin's foundation are still visible on the forest floor. Following the battle here, Hambright purchased significant acreage in the area. In his later years, the former militia officer could proudly proclaim that he owned the very peak where he had gallantly fought to turn the tide for American independence.

Turn left on S.C. 216 and drive back into North Carolina to where N.C. 216 junctions with U.S. 29. Turn right, and follow N.C. 216 for 4.9 miles to U.S. 74 Business (King Street) in the city of Kings Mountain. You'll notice a state historical marker for the battle.

Turn left on U.S. 74 Business and follow it west for 1.6 miles to Afton Drive. Turn left, go 0.1 mile to a driveway on the left, and park nearby. Walk up the driveway approximately a hundred yards to the Goforth cemetery.

Buried in the small, untended graveyard is Preston Goforth (1739–80), one of four Rutherford County brothers killed in the Battle of Kings Mountain. His grave tells one of the many stories of fratricide written during the war. Preston was the only brother to fight for the Patriots. When he and one of his siblings encountered each other in the heat of battle at Kings Mountain, they promptly fired their weapons. According to Colonel Shelby, "Two brothers, expert riflemen, were seen to present at each other, to fire and fall at the same instant."

Retrace your route to the intersection with N.C. 216. Proceed east on

Washington Iron Furnace

King Street for six blocks to N.C. 161 and turn left. It is 1.6 miles to the Gaston County line. Created from Lincoln County in 1846, Gaston County was named for Judge William Gaston, the noted North Carolina jurist whose Patriot father was murdered on the New Bern waterfront by Tories. (For an account of this incident, see The Coastal Rivers Tour, page 77.)

Continue northeast on N.C. 161 for 1.8 miles to S.R. 1402 (Long Creek Road). Turn left and proceed 0.7 mile to the bridge over Long Creek. On the left side of the road near the bridge are a large picnic shelter and the marked remains of the Washington Iron Furnace, a facility that produced cannonballs during the Revolution.

Benjamin Ormand maintained a farm along the banks of Long Creek, the same waterway Frederick Hambright lived on for many years. When Cornwallis passed through the area in January 1781, Banastre Tarleton's cavalrymen raided the Ormand residence, taking bedding and cooking utensils. As they prepared to depart, they removed the blanket from the cradle in which James Ormand, an infant, was lying. One of their number used it as a saddle blanket. In a final act of desecration, the raiders took the large family Bible belonging to Benjamin Ormand and used it for a saddle.

Return to the junction with N.C. 161. Turn left, drive 1.5 miles to N.C. 274 in Bessemer City, and turn left again. It is 4.6 miles to a state historical marker for Tryon County in the community of Tryon. Created by the colonial assembly in 1769 and named in honor of Royal Governor William Tryon, the massive, short-lived county stretched from the Catawba River on the Mecklenburg County line to the western frontier. Because of its less-than-Patriotic name, Tryon County was abolished in 1779, when it gave way to Lincoln and Rutherford Counties.

In 1774, commissioners chose to locate the Tryon County Courthouse at the site of the current tour stop, halfway between what are now Bessemer City and Cherryville. In July 1775, the Tryon County Committee of Safety was organized here. Several weeks later, when the committee convened again, its members joined other county freeholders to form "An Association."

On August 14, the forty-nine members of the "Association" adopted a set of resolutions that were the result of the growing unrest in the colonies. Even though the document did not go so far as to declare independence from Great Britain, its fiery language left no doubt that the signers were displeased with the policies of the mother country.

Resolving to unite "under the most sacred ties of religion, honor, and love of country" in defense of their "natural freedom and constitutional rights against all invasions," the signers pledged to "take up arms and risk" their lives and fortunes in order to maintain "the freedom of their country." While the members of the "Association" agreed to "profess all loyalty and attachment" to King George III as long as he would secure them "those rights and liberties which the principles of our Constitution require," they foresaw the bloodshed that was soon to come. Consequently, the men of Tryon County resolved to obtain a supply of gunpowder, lead, and flints from the Patriots of Charleston.

Despite its irregularities in spelling and grammar, the Tryon Resolves served as strong testimony of the defiant spirit that characterized the North Carolina frontier in 1775. In 1780, some signers of the resolves (including Frederick Hambright) and their families took part in the important battles at Ramsour's Mill and Kings Mountain.

Near the Tryon County marker, a bronze tablet on a granite boulder erected by the D.A.R. commemorates the resolves drafted and adopted at this site. The names of the signers are listed on the tablet.

Tryon Resolves Marker

At Tryon, turn right onto S.R. 1440 (Tryon School Road). Proceed 2.2 miles to N.C. 279, turn right, drive east for 2.9 miles to S.R. 1448, turn left, and head north for 1.2 miles to Pasour Mountain, located on the left.

This 4-mile-long ridge reaches a maximum altitude of eleven hundred feet. It was once known as LaBoone Mountain, for a Tory couple by that name who lived in a cave on the mountainside during part of the Revolution. Area Patriots ultimately pressured the LaBoones to leave their cave. The mountain assumed its present name in honor of a local family whose allegiance was with the cause of independence.

Continue 1.6 miles north on S.R. 1448 to S.R. 1703 (Ike Lynch Road). Turn right, proceed 0.9 mile to N.C. 155, turn left, and go 1.8 miles to the town of High Shoals, located on the banks of the South Fork River. A state historical marker for John Fulenwider stands on the left side of N.C. 155 just north of the small, white High Shoals United Methodist Church.

Fulenwider (1756–1826) came from Switzerland to North Carolina with his family when he was a boy. As a member of the Rowan County militia, he fought with the Patriots in the victories at Ramsour's Mill and Kings Mountain. At the close of the war, he settled in Lincoln County, where, like many of his fellow veterans, he engaged in the lucrative iron-manufacturing business. Through his skill, hard work, and business acumen, Fulenwider accumulated a twenty-thousand-acre estate. He is buried in the rock-walled cemetery adjacent to the church.

From the Fulenwider grave, follow N.C. 155 south for 7.1 miles to U.S. 321 at Dallas, the former seat of Gaston County. Drive south on U.S. 321 through Gastonia, the modern county seat. After 6.6 miles, turn left on S.R. 2411, then drive 0.2 mile east to Olney Presbyterian Church.

This historic church was established in 1792. Located adjacent to it is its equally historic cemetery. A bronze plaque near the old entry gate lists the names of eighteen Revolutionary War soldiers interred here.

Among the names on the list is that of Isaac Holland. A native of England, Holland arrived in America as a child after a harrowing transatlantic crossing. During the voyage, a leak developed that threatened to fill the ship with water. Just as everyone aboard had all but given up hope, the leak suddenly stopped. It seems that a fish got caught in the hole and thus sealed the leak.

A private throughout the Revolution, Holland fought at Kings Mountain. Despite his exhaustion following that engagement, he walked to his house near what is now Gastonia on the night after the battle.

Return to U.S. 321. Turn right and proceed north for 3.3 miles to U.S. 29/ U.S. 74 (Franklin Boulevard). Turn right, drive east for 8.9 miles to N.C. 7, turn left, and go north for 0.9 mile to Woodlawn Street (S.R. 2021) at Belmont Abbey College. Turn left and drive 0.7 mile to Goshen Presbyterian Church in North Belmont. The church is on the right at the junction of Woodlawn and Roper Streets.

Organized in 1764, this is believed to be the first Presbyterian church west of the Catawba River. The present brick structure is the latest in a series of buildings that began with a small log church that was located adjacent to the nearby cemetery. Many charter members of the church were ardent Patriots who fought in the Revolution; some are buried in the cemetery.

To visit the historic burial ground, proceed north on Woodlawn for 0.2

mile. A bronze plaque on the rock-walled entrance to the oldest portion of the cemetery lists the names of nineteen Revolutionary War soldiers interred here. Among the distinguished Patriots is Captain Samuel Martin, a native of Ireland and a veteran of the Battle of Kings Mountain who died in 1836 at the age of 104. Three years before his death, he was granted a pension for his service in the Revolution.

Continue north on Woodlawn for 0.5 mile to Hickory Grove Road. Turn right, then turn right again almost immediately onto Perfection Avenue (S.R. 2040). Follow Perfection as it winds east for 0.9 mile to West Catawba Avenue; continue 1.8 miles on Perfection to Hawthorne Street in the town of Mount Holly. Turn left on Hawthorne and proceed one block north to West Central Avenue, where you'll notice a number of public-school buildings. The home of Captain Robert Alexander—another of the distinguished Patriots buried in the cemetery at Goshen Presbyterian Church—once stood in the vicinity of the school buildings.

Alexander was a respected statesman in the days leading up to the war, serving at the First and Third Provincial Congresses at New Bern and Hillsborough, respectively. Some historians have concluded that he was the draftsman of the Tryon Resolves. When the war of words became a war of bullets, Alexander turned his attention to military matters. He rendered effective service as a militia captain for the duration of the war.

Alexander was married to Mary Jack, the sister of James Jack, the famous courier of the Mecklenburg Declaration of Independence. Their daughter, Margaret Alexander, was the fiancée of Major William Chronicle. Like Chronicle, Captain Alexander fought at Kings Mountain.

Continue on Hawthorne for 0.2 mile to N.C. 27 (West Charlotte Avenue). Turn right and drive east for 0.5 mile to an unpaved road on the left side of the highway just before the bridge over the Catawba River. Turn left and follow the road to its terminus at a landing. This site provides an excellent view of the Catawba at a point near two important fords used during the Revolution.

As Cornwallis pushed his army east through Lincoln County (which at that time encompassed all of what are now Gaston and Catawba Counties) in pursuit of Nathanael Greene in January 1781, General William Lee Davidson posted small bands of American militiamen at Tuckaseegee Ford (on the south) and Tool's Ford (on the north). Tuckaseegee Ford, located on the road leading from Charlotte to Ramsour's Mill, was defended by two hundred men under the command of Colonel Joseph Wilson of Surry County. Less than half that number were stationed at Tool's Ford under the command of Captain Potts of Mecklenburg.

Return to N.C. 27. Turn right and proceed northwest for 2.9 miles to Westland Farm Road (S.R. 1924). A state historical marker here honors Colonel Joseph Dickson (1745–1825), a remarkable soldier and statesman.

Turn left on Westland Farm Road. After 0.3 mile, you'll notice a large house on the left set back from the road. The brick building in the rear (now used as a swimming-pool house) is what remains of the eighteenth-century home constructed by Colonel Dickson.

Six months before the American colonies declared their independence, Dickson was appointed a captain in the Continental Army. When the war came to western North Carolina in 1780, he rendered effective service as a major of "the Lincoln County Men," a militia unit that was conspicuous at Kings Mountain. His leadership in the stand against Cornwallis during the British invasion of North Carolina in 1781 led to his promotion to colonel.

Upon his election to the United States House of Representatives in 1799, Dickson became a strong supporter of Thomas Jefferson's candidacy for president. When the 1800 election resulted in an electoral tie between Jefferson and Aaron Burr, the contest was thrown into the House. After thirty-five ballots, Dickson rose to the floor and used his influence to gain the deciding votes for Jefferson.

General Griffith Rutherford camped at this site on June 19, 1780, in his futile attempt to reach Ramsour's Mill in time for the battle there.

Turn around near the Dickson home and retrace your route to N.C. 27. Turn right, drive 2.6 miles to N.C. 273 in downtown Mount Holly, turn left, and go north for 5.2 miles to N.C. 16. Turn left and go 0.2 mile north to the state historical marker calling attention to Oak Grove, the home of Colonel James Johnston.

To see the grave of this Revolutionary War luminary, turn right just north of the marker onto S.R. 1916 (Killian Road). Proceed 2 miles east to Pine Valley Drive, turn left, go 0.1 mile, and turn left onto Meadow View. After 0.3 mile, you'll notice a small cemetery enclosed by an iron fence on the left side of the road. Johnston (1742–1805) is buried here.

Johnston's father was one of the early settlers along the banks of the Catawba in Tryon County. As a young man, James Johnston was one of the first local citizens to openly advocate independence. It was he who, on the morning of June 19, 1780, notified Griffith Rutherford at his encampment near Joseph Dickson's plantation that Colonel Francis Locke intended to attack Tory forces at Ramsour's Mill in Lincolnton the following morning. Ironically, Locke had not received an earlier dispatch from Rutherford ordering him to come to Dickson's plantation to confer with Rutherford.

At Kings Mountain, Johnston commanded the reserves, who were called into service soon after the battle began.

His magnificent two-story home stood near the cemetery until well into the twentieth century.

Return to N.C. 16. Turn left, proceed south for 0.2 mile to N.C. 273, turn right, and drive 0.2 mile to Stanley-Lucia Road. Turn right and follow Stanley-Lucia as it winds east for 3.3 miles to Willowside Drive (S.R. 1935). Turn left and go 0.5 mile to the Rankin House—otherwise known as "Willowside"—located on the right at 201 Willowside.

Willowside, home of William Rankin

William Rankin settled with his family along nearby Stanley Creek prior to the Revolution and began construction on the two-story structure in 1778. The war intervened before the dwelling could be completed. Rankin volunteered as a private in the company of Captain Robert Alexander. Over the next two years, he saw action in both Carolinas against British regulars, Tories, and Indians.

According to his great-grandson, who now owns and lives in the dwelling, Rankin was badly wounded and lost a leg at Kings Mountain. Rather than entrust his well-being to the scant medical care available on the battlefield, he hired someone to bring him home, where he recuperated. When Rankin died at the age of ninety-three, he was the last surviving Revolutionary War soldier in Gaston County.

Beneath the existing exterior walls of the home are the logs of the original structure. The interior furnishings include two pieces crafted by Peter Eddleman, a local Revolutionary War soldier covered later in this tour.

Return to Stanley-Lucia Road. Turn left, drive west for 1.9 miles to Old N.C. 27. Merge onto old N.C. 27 and proceed west for 0.8 mile to the town of Stanley, and turn right. It is 3.1 miles north to the Lincoln County line.

Created when Tryon County was abolished in 1779, Lincoln County was named in honor of Major General Benjamin Lincoln. Concerning the county's contribution to the war, noted historian John C. Wheeler wrote, "There are few portions of North Carolina, around which the halo of chivalric deeds and unsullied patriotism clusters more brilliantly than this section." In the closing years of the Revolution, Lincoln County served as the landscape for two of the most important battles fought in North Carolina.

A native of Hingham, Massachusetts, Benjamin Lincoln (1733–1810) was a key player at both the high and low points of the war. As commander of the Southern Department of the Continental Army, he suffered the loss of Charleston in 1780. A year later, General George Washington selected him to accept the British sword of surrender at Yorktown. Soon thereafter, Lincoln was appointed the nation's first secretary of war, a post he held until 1783.

From the county line, continue northwest on N.C. 27 for 7.3 miles to N.C. 150. Follow N.C. 27/N.C. 150 west for 1.7 miles to N.C. 155 on the east side of Lincolnton, the seat of Lincoln County. Like the county, the town was named in honor of Benjamin Lincoln. Chartered in 1785, it is the second-oldest incorporated town west of the Catawba.

Turn right on N.C. 155 and drive 1.1 miles north to Sigmon Road at the Lincolnton Plaza Shopping Center. Turn left, proceed west for 0.2 mile to North Aspen Street, turn left again, and go south for 1.2 miles to the state historical marker for the Battle of Ramsour's Mill; the marker is on the right side of the road at Lincolnton High School.

To reach the battlefield, turn right onto Skip Lawing Drive just south of the marker and proceed west for 0.3 mile to Jeb Seagle Drive. Follow Jeb Seagle Drive as it circles around to Battleground Stadium (on the left) and Lincolnton Middle School (on the right). Turn right into the school's parking lot.

Although much of the battlefield's historical integrity has been lost as a result of the construction of three public schools, there is much to be seen at this place where the struggle for American independence ever so subtly began to turn in favor of the colonies. From the parking lot, walk up the hill between Lincolnton Middle and Battleground Elementary Schools. Stop at the audio station, located in a grove of trees, where a three-minute taped message gives a synopsis of the battle fought on this very spot in the early-morning hours of June 20, 1780.

British military control of South Carolina and Georgia was virtually complete with the surrender of Charleston by Benjamin Lincoln on May 12, 1780. Cornwallis then began to shift his attention to North Carolina, which had been relatively free from British troops up to that time. Though anxious to move north, Cornwallis remained in South Carolina for the summer, so his soldiers might rest and be resupplied.

Two of his American officers—Lieutenant Colonel John Moore and Major Nicholas Welch—wanted to pave the way for the British invasion of North Carolina. In early June, they made their way home to Lincoln County, where they began organizing Tories to aid in the conquest of the state. Their efforts paid off. By June 13, their Tory recruits began to arrive at Ramsour's Mill, which was located on Clarks Creek several hundred yards west of the current tour stop.

Upon learning of the Tory gathering, General Griffith Rutherford, camped 35 miles away in Charlotte, dispatched orders to Colonel Francis Locke of Rowan County and Major David Wilson of Mecklenburg County to raise a force to scatter the Loyalists.

On the night of June 19, Locke put his small army of four hundred poorly trained, ill-equipped militiamen from Rowan, Mecklenburg, and Lincoln Counties on a 15-mile march west from Mountain Creek in what is now Catawba County to Ramsour's Mill. By that time, the contingent of Loyalists camped in the woods atop the hill at the current tour stop had grown to thirteen hundred. As many as one-fourth of their number were unarmed. Others were either too young or too old to fight.

Before first light on June 20, Locke's forces were close to the Tory encampment when the colonel was approached by Adam Reep, a local Patriot who had scouted the Tories' position. After being briefed by Reep about the Loyalists' troop strength and the local terrain, Locke decided to launch a surprise attack.

His cavalry captains out front, Locke sent his men up the eastern slope of the hill at dawn. It was a foggy morning, with visibility limited to fifty feet. Despite being caught off guard, the Tories quickly rallied. For almost two hours, a horrific battle was fought atop the hill. The hand-to-hand action pitted neighbor against neighbor—even brother against brother. None of the combatants had uniforms. The Patriots pinned white paper to their hats for identification, and the Loyalists stuck green twigs in theirs.

Symbolic of the fratricidal feelings at Ramsour's Mill is the story of Reuben and William Simpson, two brothers who married daughters of a local Whig, William Sherrill. Like his father-in-law, William Simpson was a Patriot, but Reuben was an avowed Tory. While the Patriot brother was on a scouting party, he learned that Reuben was fighting for the Tories at Ramsour's Mill. William galloped off toward the battlefield, ran his horse to exhaustion, and ran the rest of the way on foot—all for the purpose of seeking out and killing his brother. Upon his arrival, however, he learned that the battle was over.

Although the Patriots were outnumbered more than three to one, they carried the day. The thoroughly routed Tories retreated down the western side of the hill toward the mill. Once the fog lifted and the smoke from the muskets dissipated, the battlefield displayed a grim scene. More than seventy men were dead, some with skulls broken by gun butts. Another two hundred were badly wounded. Losses were equally divided between the two factions.

You'll notice a small marker near the audio station. In a long trench at this spot, where the Tories made their final stand, the bodies of seventy soldiers were interred in a mass grave the day after the battle.

Much like Kings Mountain, the Battle of Ramsour's Mill involved no British troops. Nevertheless, the decisive Patriot victory was of extreme importance to the outcome of the war. It effectively put an end to Tory support of the British war effort throughout the area. Thus, Cornwallis was robbed of assistance he desperately needed when he subsequently crossed into North Carolina. But of more immediate importance, the battle provided the inspiration for the pivotal Patriot victory 30 miles away at Kings Mountain less than four months later.

From the mass grave site and the audio station, walk up the hill to the Warlick Monument, located at the summit in the middle of Battleground

Elementary School's playground. This large stone memorializes Captain Nicholas Warlick, a Tory officer who died while bravely leading his men on horseback. Also buried here are his brother, Phillip, and another Loyalist, Israel Sain.

Continue walking east to the bus parking lot at the rear of Lincolnton Middle School. A small park on the eastern side of the lot contains several millstones from Ramsour's Mill. Ironically, Cornwallis camped here, several hundred yards from the mill, just seven months after the disastrous defeat at the same site.

On January 24, 1781, Cornwallis's army, which had swollen to twenty-five hundred men after a recent infusion of troops under General Alexander Leslie, poured into Lincoln County. The Redcoats were in hot pursuit of the fleeing Daniel Morgan, whose march was slowed by British prisoners taken at Cowpens. Cornwallis hoped to catch General Morgan and destroy his army before he could cross the Catawba and join forces with Nathanael Greene.

By the time Cornwallis, Tarleton, General Charles O'Hara, and the Redcoat army converged at Ramsour's Mill on January 25, Morgan was already on the eastern bank of the river. For three days, the massive British army camped all about the landscape at the current tour stop. Cornwallis set up his headquarters under a chestnut tree. Camped near him were some of his Hessian troops. Cornwallis sent foragers into the countryside to secure grain, and Ramsour's Mill was kept in continuous operation to produce food for the British soldiers and their animals.

Walk through the parking lot to the southern end of Lincolnton Middle School. Proceed around the corner of the building along the trail that runs on the edge of the athletic field. After several hundred yards, look down the hill to your left. You'll see a large brick tomb between the field and Jeb Seagle Drive. Buried here are six of the Whig captains who fell at Ramsour's Mill. Among their number was Captain Galbraith Falls, who led the initial Patriot charge on horseback. He was the first soldier killed in the battle.

Cross the athletic field to the parking lot in front of Lincolnton Middle School. Walk to the western side of Jeb Seagle Drive near the entrance to Battleground Memorial Stadium. Turn left and walk along the shoulder of the road for 0.2 mile to the second driveway on the right. Turn right at the driveway and go through an opening in the trees to the bottom land along Clarks Creek. After passing through the opening, you'll notice the marked grave of Martin "Crooked Nose" Shuford. This Tory leader acquired his soubriquet after suffering a mishap while preparing to hang Isaac Wise, a teenager. (For more information, see The Foothills Tour, pages 245–46.) Wounded at Ramsour's Mill, Shuford died two days after the battle and was laid to rest.

The cabin of Christian Reinhardt was located just south of the Shuford grave site, and Ramsour's Mill was several hundred yards north of Reinhardt's cabin and outbuildings. During the three-day occupation of this site by the British army in January 1781, Cornwallis's Hessians pilfered the Reinhardt farm. Trouble quickly ensued.

One of the mercenaries, upon smelling soup that Mrs. Reinhardt had cooking in the fireplace, stole into the cabin to help himself to some home cooking. When he heard Mrs. Reinhardt's footsteps, the young German quickly gulped a cupful of boiling soup. He fell dead soon thereafter.

His comrades in arms, convinced that Mrs. Reinhardt had poisoned the dead man, threatened to do her bodily harm. Christian Reinhardt reported the threats to Cornwallis, who promptly placed a guard around the Reinhardt place for the protection of the occupants.

Cornwallis asked Reinhardt to show him the position that Lieutenant Colonel Moore and his Loyalists had held at the beginning of the Battle of Ramsour's Mill. After touring the field, Cornwallis remarked, "Moore had a good position, but he did not know how to defend it. . . . In the first place, he ought to have obeyed orders and fallen back on Colonel Ferguson's command. Often the most sanguine are the most disappointed. But Moore deserves credit for his loyalty."

While camped at Ramsour's Mill, Cornwallis made one of the most fateful decisions of his campaign in the Carolinas. Contrary to standard European military practice, the British commander ordered that all his army's expendable baggage—including large quantities of rum—be burned. Most of his wagons—beginning with his own—were torched. Only those carrying salt, medicine, and ammunition were saved. Cornwallis reasoned that he must lighten his army to hasten the chase of Greene and Morgan.

Even Charles O'Hara, Cornwallis's trusted brigadier general, questioned his commander's judgment: "In the situation, without baggage, necessaries, or provisions of any sort for officer or soldier, in the most barren, inhospitable, unhealthy part of North America, opposed to the most savage, inveterate, perfidious, cruel enemy, with zeal and bayonets only, it was resolved to follow Greene's army to the end of the world."

When Nathanael Greene received intelligence of Cornwallis's decision at Ramsour's Mill, he uttered words that predicted the ultimate outcome of the war: "Then he is ours!"

Before he put his army on the march toward the Catawba on January 28, Cornwallis offered his gratitude to the Reinhardt family for its kindness to him and his soldiers. He paid Christian Reinhardt for the leather and beef his army had used. To Mrs. Reinhardt, he addressed a polite note, to be delivered to her with his personal mahogany tea box. Upon mounting his horse to depart, Cornwallis doffed his hat and said to Christian Reinhardt, "I do hope and think that the time is near when you can be down under your own shades in peace with the British Flag floating over your heads."

He then rode away to take up pursuit of the Americans—a chase that would lead him to the British surrender at Yorktown.

Eight acres of bottom land at the current tour stop are owned by the Lincoln County Historic Properties Commission. A long-range master plan is being formulated for the development of a site with period buildings that will re-create the Reinhardt farm and mill site.

Return to your car. Retrace Jeb Seagle Drive and Skip Lawing Drive to Linwood Drive. Turn right on Linwood and proceed 0.3 mile to North Grove Street. Turn left, go to West Main Street, turn left again, and drive east toward the imposing Lincoln County Courthouse. Built around 1923, the courthouse stands on a square in the heart of the county seat.

Park just west of the courthouse near the Lincoln County Citizens Center, the large auditorium/office building on the right. Walk into the lobby of the Citizens Center to see a wall-size mural depicting the scene at Ramsour's Mill at daybreak on June 20, 1780, just as the battle was about to begin.

From the Citizens Center, walk across the street to the courthouse grounds. Near the end of the northern lawn is a granite rock known as "Tarleton's Tea Table." It is marked by a D.A.R. plaque. Legend has it that the infamous British cavalry commander enjoyed tea upon the rock while camped in Lincolnton in 1781. It was moved to its present site from the Ramsour's Mill battleground.

Walk to the southern end of the courthouse grounds and cross the street to South Aspen. Follow the sidewalk for one block to the junction with Church Street at Emmanuel Lutheran Church. A state historical marker for John Gottfried Arends stands in the next block on the left side of the street, at the entrance to the Old White Church Cemetery.

Just inside the cemetery is the imposing gravestone for Arends (1740–1807), the founder and first president of the North Carolina Synod of the Lutheran Church. Born in Germany (his marker is inscribed in German and English), Arends settled in Rowan County in 1773. There, he served as a schoolteacher. On August 28, 1775, as tensions with Great Britain were mounting, he became the first man to be ordained a Lutheran minister in North Carolina.

Throughout the Revolution, Arends traveled by horseback to preach to congregations in Lincoln, Catawba, Iredell, Cabarrus, Rowan, Davidson, Guilford, and Stokes Counties. From his makeshift pulpits came a message of American independence. As a result of his outspoken support for the cause of the colonies, he was threatened, harassed, and persecuted. Nevertheless, he was unflappable, often riding more than 50 miles a day to preach and teach.

Return to your vehicle. Enter the traffic circle around the courthouse, proceeding counterclockwise. On the eastern side of the courthouse, turn right onto East Main Street. Drive through Lincolnton's central business district for three blocks to the junction with Cedar Street at the post office. The Lincoln County Museum of History, located in the Lincoln Cultural Center at the northeastern corner of the intersection, features exhibits and displays dating from precolonial days. Of special interest is an outstanding diorama of the Battle of Ramsour's Mill.

Continue on East Main Street for 0.7 mile to the junction with N.C. 27/N.C. 150/N.C. 155. Proceed east on N.C. 27/N.C. 150 for 2 miles to where the roads separate. Turn left onto N.C. 150 and drive 5.4 miles to S.R. 1349. Turn right, travel 1.2 miles to S.R. 1362, turn right again, go 1.8 miles to S.R. 1382 (Vesuvius Furnace Road), and turn left. Vesuvius, the oldest house in Lincoln County, is on the left after 1.2 miles.

The eastern end of the imposing, two-story frame mansion was constructed in 1792 by Revolutionary War hero Joseph Graham (1759–1836). He made subsequent additions to the structure in 1810 and 1820.

Born in Pennsylvania, Graham came to Mecklenburg County with his widowed mother and four siblings when he was seven years old. As a teenager, he witnessed the proceedings that produced the disputed Mecklenburg Declaration of Independence on May 20, 1775. Three years later, he enlisted in the Continental Army.

From 1778 to 1781, Graham participated in nineteen engagements and rose from private to major. After serving as quartermaster for Benjamin Lincoln in South Carolina, he returned home. At the Battle of Charlotte on September 26, 1780, he commanded the rear guard of William R. Davie's army. His tactics against Tarleton's cavalry enabled Davie to elude capture by Cornwallis.

After the war, Graham settled in Lincoln County, where he began construction of the home at the current stop. He and other Revolutionary War heroes developed the local iron industry, which gave the county an unusually high standard of living in the late eighteenth and early nineteenth centuries. The state used his Vesuvius Iron Furnace to help construct the bridge that stands near the house.

In 1787, Graham married Isabella Davidson, the daughter of Revolutionary War notable John Davidson. (For information on Davidson, see The Hornets' Nest Tour, pages 174–75.)

Return to S.R. 1362, turn left, and drive 1.3 miles to N.C. 73. Turn left, go east for 1.3 miles to S.R. 1511 (Old Plank Road), turn right, and proceed 0.2 mile to S.R. 1360 (Brevard Place Road). Located at this junction is a state historical marker for Machpelah Cemetery.

To visit the cemetery, turn right on S.R. 1360 and park in the lot of Machpelah Presbyterian Church, located 0.1 mile south of the junction. The burial ground is adjacent to the church, which was built around 1848.

Prominent among the historic graves is that of Joseph Graham.

Also buried here is Alexander Brevard (1755–1829). Born in Iredell County, Brevard was one the eleven children of John Brevard. Alexander's oldest sister, Mary, married General William Lee Davidson, the Patriot martyr at the Battle of Cowan's Ford. Another sister married Ephraim Davidson, who as a young soldier alerted Daniel Morgan of the movement of Cornwallis's army toward the Catawba. Alexander's brothers John Jr. and Adam served in the Continental Army. Adam and another brother, Hugh, both fought at Ramsour's Mill. Ephraim, Alexander's oldest brother, is believed to have been the draftsman of the Mecklenburg Declaration of Independence. (For more information on the "Meck Dec," see The Hornets' Nest Tour, pages 189–92.)

Alexander Brevard was one of the few regular soldiers who participated in the American Revolution from beginning to end. Commissioned a lieutenant in the Continental Army, he showed great promise as a young officer in George Washington's campaign in the North. In 1780, when the war shifted to the South, Brevard served as quartermaster under General Horatio Gates. After the American debacle at Camden, he served under Nathanael Greene until the end of the war. He won accolades for his valor in the ferocious fighting at Eutaw Springs, South Carolina, less than a month before Cornwallis's surrender at Yorktown.

An iron-industry associate of Joseph Graham, Brevard married a daughter of John Davidson, as did Graham. He settled in Lincoln County after the war.

Continue south on S.R. 1360 for 1.6 miles. Mount Tirzah, the magnificent Georgian plantation house constructed by Alexander Brevard around 1800, once stood on the left side of the road here. A fire destroyed the mansion in 1969.

It is another 0.2 mile south on S.R. 1360 to the bridge over Leeper's Creek. The almost unidentifiable remains of Mount Tirzah Forge, one of the iron-manufacturing facilities of Alexander Brevard, are on the creek to the left of the bridge.

Turn around and retrace S.R. 1360 to S.R. 1511. Turn right and drive 0.2 mile southeast to a stone D.A.R. marker on the left side of the road. The Old Dutch Meeting House, a church that served the settlers in the eastern part of Lincoln County during the Revolution, once stood at this site. Buried in unmarked graves in the field near the marker are Jacob Forney, Sr., and his wife, Maria. This daring couple braved the Indians and the wilderness west of the Catawba to settle in the area about 1754.

Born in 1721, Forney was too old to shoulder a musket during the Revolution. Nonetheless, he was an unwavering supporter of the Patriot cause. Three of his sons—Peter, Abram, and Jacob Jr.—returned from the war as heroes. While they were away fighting, their father almost capitalized on an opportunity to kill Cornwallis. His encounter with the British commander is recounted later in this tour.

Continue southeast on S.R. 1511 for 3.2 miles to S.R. 1412. Here stands a state historical marker for Peter Forney (1756–1834), whose grave and homesite are located nearby.

Born soon after his father settled in Lincoln County, Peter grew up on the frontier. Over the course of the fight for independence, he battled Indians, Tories, and British troops. He arrived with General Griffith Rutherford just hours too late to participate in the Patriot victory on his home turf at Ramsour's Mill.

In late January 1781, Captain Forney played a key role in General Davidson's unsuccessful attempt to hold back Cornwallis at Cowan's Ford.

Later in 1781, the company of dragoons commanded by Forney was instrumental in convincing Major James Craig to evacuate British troops from Wilmington. Following the war, the state appointed Forney general of the North Carolina militia. He also served the new republic as a presidential elector and congressman.

To visit his grave, turn right on S.R. 1412 and go 0.5 mile south. Park on the shoulder and walk to the driveway on the left side of the road. Proceed along the edge of the woods in a direction parallel to the driveway for 50 yards, then turn right into the woods and walk 150 feet to the forested site containing the graves of Forney, his wife, and other family members. This isolated cemetery is being restored by its owner, the Lincoln County Historic Properties Commission. The knoll on which it rests lies above the site of Forney's plantation home, Mount Welcome.

Return to your vehicle and continue south on S.R. 1412 for 0.6 mile. Park again on the right shoulder and walk to the steel bridge on the right. Now closed to vehicular traffic, the span is owned by the Lincoln County Historical Association. From the bridge, you can enjoy a magnificent view of Dutchman's Creek, where Peter Forney's Mount Welcome Iron Forge was once located. Until 1791, when he sold his interest, Forney was a partner with fellow Patriots Alexander Brevard, Joseph Graham, and John Davidson in "the Big Ore Bank," as the extensive iron deposits east of Lincolnton were known. Forney's mansion stood on the hill across the road on the northern side of the creek.

Walk back to your vehicle and retrace your route to S.R. 1511. Turn left, drive west for 0.6 mile to S.R. 1383 (Ingleside Farm Road), turn right, and drive north for 1.6 miles to N.C. 73. On the left side of the intersection is Ingleside, one of the finest antebellum mansions in the North Carolina Piedmont. For many years, this magnificent two-story brick structure, built around 1817, was considered the finest dwelling in the western part of the state.

Daniel Forney, who succeeded his father, Peter, in the United States House of Representatives, constructed Ingleside. It is said that while he was in Washington, Daniel persuaded Benjamin Latrobe, the architect of the Capitol, to draw the plans for the Lincoln County mansion.

Forney's elegant mansion stands at the site of the home of his grandfather, Jacob Forney, Sr. A pile of foundation rocks on the western side of the house is all that remains of Jacob's multistory log cabin, which stood during the Revolution. A tall wooden structure with gunports is nearby. It served as a fortress for Forney and his family when Indians attacked.

Although he was an accomplished Indian fighter in colonial times, Jacob Forney was too old to serve as a soldier in the Revolution. Nonetheless, he was an unrepentant supporter of the American cause. In 1775, he was on hand at Tryon to sign the defiant resolves enacted there.

Forney suffered his greatest indignity of the war when Cornwallis used his flourishing plantation as a headquarters in early 1781.

After leaving Ramsour's Mill on January 28, Cornwallis, in his quest to overtake Greene and Morgan, marched his Redcoats east across Lincoln County to the Catawba River at nearby Beatties Ford. Upon finding the river impassible because of heavy rains, he moved his army back 5 miles to the current tour stop.

Ruins of Jacob Forney's cabin, headquarters of Cornwallis

For three days and four nights, the massive British army camped at Jacob Forney's plantation. Stretching for more than a mile, the encampment extended to the plantation of Peter Forney, located northwest of Ingleside at that time. The British commander took up residence on the upper floor of Jacob Forney's cabin, while his reluctant hosts were sequestered in the basement.

During their stay, the British soldiers slaughtered and ate Forney's complete stock of cattle, swine, sheep, geese, and chickens and consumed his grain and brandy. Upon being informed by local Tories that Forney had a large treasure of gold, silver, and jewelry hidden on the premises, the Redcoats scoured the entire estate until they found the aged couple's lifetime savings.

The discovery and plunder of the Forney treasure almost cost Cornwallis his life. Jacob had somehow maintained his composure while the enemy troops killed his animals and ate his food. However, when he learned that he had been robbed, Forney grabbed his gun and rushed up the basement steps to kill Cornwallis. His wife interceded and stopped him before a showdown took place.

At two o'clock in the morning on February 1, Cornwallis put his army on the march toward the Catawba, and Jacob Forney was left with a devastated plantation. Historian Cyrus L. Hunter, himself the son of a Revolutionary War hero, Dr. Humphrey Hunter, noted that "few persons during the war suffered heavier losses than Jacob Forney."

Forney soon learned that his misery had been occasioned by a Tory neighbor, a Mr. Deck, who had directed Cornwallis to the plantation. Deck was promptly warned that he must leave the area or Forney would kill him. Deck did not heed the warning, so Forney hunted him down and captured him. Touched by Deck's pleas for his life, Forney spared him upon his promise that he would leave and never return.

From the bridge at the intersection of S.R. 1383 and N.C. 73, drive north on S.R. 1383 for 0.4 mile. There is a large rock on the northern side of the house to the left of the road. (Note that there are large rocks on either side of this house.) This rock, covered with moss and lichen, is known as "Cornwallis's Tea Table," since the British general enjoyed afternoon tea here. His soldiers used the stone table to slaughter Jacob Forney's animals.

Return to the junction with N.C. 73. Go east on N.C. 73 for 2.4 miles to N.C. 16. Turn left, drive north for 2.4 miles to S.R. 1349, turn right, and drive east for 3.7 miles to Beatties Ford Access Area, located near where the road terminates at the Catawba River. Park in the public lot. This stop provides an outstanding view of the river near one of its most historic fords.

Named for John Beatty, considered the first permanent white settler west of the Catawba, the ford assumed strategic value in the last year of the Revolution. Cornwallis marched his army here on January 28, 1781, only to find the rain-swollen river too treacherous to cross. Four days later, he resolved to cross at Cowan's Ford, located 4 miles south. In preparation for crossing, the British commander dispatched Lieutenant Colonel James Webster and some artillery pieces to feint a major British crossing at Beatties Ford in the predawn hours on February 1.

Webster arrayed his soldiers along the riverbank. For thirty minutes, while the bulk of the British army was beginning to attempt a crossing at Cowan's Ford, the early-morning stillness was broken by Webster's booming cannon.

Opposing Webster on the eastern side of the river at Beatties Ford was a small contingent of General William Lee Davidson's militia. Davidson had been assigned the unenviable task of preventing or at least impeding the crossing, in order to give Greene and Morgan time to escape with the haggard remnants of the American army in the South.

As you gaze across to the eastern bank, you can see the spot where Davidson plotted the defense of the Catawba with Greene, Morgan, Colonel William Washington, Colonel William Polk, and Captain Joseph Graham on the afternoon of January 31. While seated on a log at Beatties Ford, the six men devised the strategy to be used to stop Cornwallis. Within twenty minutes, Greene and Morgan departed to push the American army east, out of harm's way. Left behind were Davidson, Polk, and Graham, who on the morrow would lead eight hundred militiamen against twenty-five hundred British regulars.

From the access area, you can look downriver and see Duke Energy's McGuire Nuclear Plant. That facility is located near Cowan's Ford, where Davidson ultimately battled Cornwallis for control of the Catawba on the morning of February 1.

Retrace S.R. 1349 to N.C. 16. Turn left and proceed south for 3.3 miles to unpaved Ben McLean Lane. Turn right onto Ben McLean Lane and park on the shoulder. Walk into the forest on the southern side of the road, where a rock wall borders the ancient cemetery that once belonged to White Haven Episcopal Church. One prominent grave here, marked by the Sons of the American Revolution, is that of Peter Eddleman.

Born in Pennsylvania in 1762, Eddleman moved with his family to North Carolina when he was a child. He grew up in the vicinity of Machpelah Presbyterian Church. As a teenager, Eddleman took up arms with the Patriot forces in the fight for independence. He participated in the pivotal American victories at Cowpens and Kings Mountain. Among the American troops who proudly stood at attention when General Benjamin Lincoln accepted the sword of surrender from General Charles O'Hara at Yorktown on October 19, 1781, was nineteen-year-old Peter Eddleman.

He returned home after the war and became a renowned furniture maker. He married for the first time in 1830, at the age of sixty-eight. Two sons were born of the marriage.

Return to N.C. 16, turn left, and drive north for 1 mile to N.C. 73. Turn right and proceed east for 2.5 miles to the public parking area on the left side of the road at Cowan's Ford Dam. A state historical marker here chronicles the history of the region.

Constructed in the early 1960s, the immense dam towers above the very site where Cornwallis crossed the Catawba while doing battle with American militia in the frigid early-morning hours of February 1, 1781. At that time, the river was a quarter-mile wide here at Cowan's Ford.

Countless stories of gallantry were played out on that fateful morning. Among the militiamen who had taken a defensive position with Davidson's forces on the far side of the river the night before the battle was Robert Beatty, a crippled man who taught at a school downriver near Tuckaseegee Ford. Upon learning that British soldiers were scouring the area to capture local boys for service as musicians, Beatty had dismissed his pupils, picked up his rifle, and limped away to join the fight.

When the British began to attempt their crossing, bullets flew. Beatty was stationed in a group of thirty Lincoln County volunteers that included sixteen-year-old Robert Henry, already a veteran of the Battle of Kings Mountain. Suddenly, a British bullet struck the lame schoolmaster. As he slumped to the ground mortally wounded, he proclaimed to young Henry, "It's time to run, Bob!"

The Redcoats faced a terrific resistance from Davidson's marksmen. They also had to deal with the swirling waters of the mighty Catawba. Mounted on his spirited charger, General Cornwallis was led into the river by a local Tory guide, Frederick Hager. Cornwallis's horse was badly wounded during the crossing but managed to carry its rider to the eastern riverbank, where it dropped dead. When General O'Hara plunged into the raging waters, his mount rolled over, and horse and rider were swept downriver for forty yards. General Leslie encountered the same difficulty.

British foot soldiers lashed themselves together in an effort to gain stability in the dangerous waters. Even then, they were forced to contend with a river bottom that was rocky and filled with holes. Patriot bullets whizzed by the heads of the first Redcoats to reach the opposite shore.

General Davidson was shot from his horse. He was one of the three Americans killed in the battle. British losses were substantially higher: thirty-one killed (including a colonel) and thirty-five wounded.

After several hours of ferocious fighting, the gallant stand at Cowan's Ford was over. The American militiamen fled as seemingly endless waves of Redcoats poured out of the river. Cornwallis, who was now set to put the heat on Greene, later offered "thanks to the brigade of Guards for their cool and determined bravery in the passage of the Catawba, while rushing through that long and difficult ford under a galling fire."

Among the items lost by the crossing army was an elegant beaver cap. It was found floating in the river 10 miles downstream the day after the battle. Inside the fashionable piece were the words, "Property of Josiah Martin, Governor." The last Royal governor of North Carolina had been among the distinguished personages in the British entourage as it crossed the river. In his correspondence following the Battle of Guilford Courthouse, Cornwallis noted that Martin had accompanied him throughout the North Carolina campaign in an attempt to render assistance to the British cause. He said that Martin bore the hardships of camp and the march with cheer.

Continue east on N.C. 73 across the Catawba into Mecklenburg County. On the right side of the highway 1 mile east of the bridge is the General Davidson Monument Area, where this tour ends.

In 1970, a Duke Power Company bulldozer operator discovered an eight-foot stone monument covered in ivy and honeysuckle while he was clearing land for the McGuire Nuclear Plant. A subsequent examination by company officials revealed a forgotten monument to General William Lee Davidson, the Patriot leader who fell nearby in the fight to give Nathanael Greene the time he needed to elude Cornwallis. (For more information on Davidson, see The Hornets' Nest Tour, pages 172–73.)

The power company and local historians dedicated the park on February 1, 1971. Several monuments and a cannon in the forested area pay tribute to Davidson and the Americans who made the important stand at Cowan's Ford.

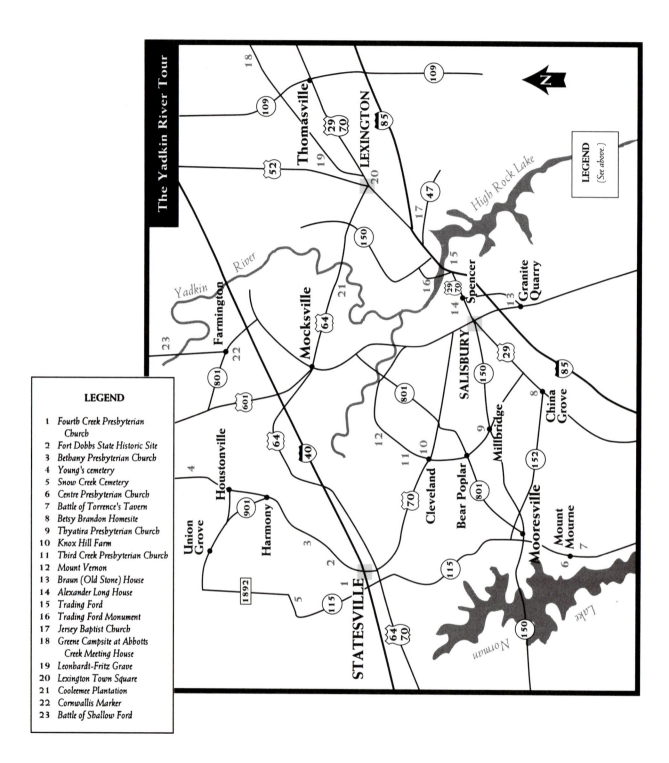

The Yadkin River Tour

LEGEND

1 Fourth Creek Presbyterian Church
2 Fort Dobbs State Historic Site
3 Bethany Presbyterian Church
4 Young's cemetery
5 Snow Creek Cemetery
6 Centre Presbyterian Church
7 Battle of Torrence's Tavern
8 Betsy Brandon Homesite
9 Thyatira Presbyterian Church
10 Knox Hill Farm
11 Third Creek Presbyterian Church
12 Mount Vernon
13 Braun (Old Stone) House
14 Alexander Long House
15 Trading Ford
16 Trading Ford Monument
17 Jersey Baptist Church
18 Greene Campsite at Abbotts Creek Meeting House
19 Leonhardt-Fritz Grave
20 Lexington Town Square
21 Cooleemee Plantation
22 Cornwallis Marker
23 Battle of Shallow Ford

LEGEND
(See above.)

N

The Yadkin River Tour

This tour begins at Statesville in Iredell County and makes its way through Rowan, Davidson, and Davie Counties before ending at Shallow Ford in Yadkin County. Among the highlights are Fourth Creek Presbyterian Church, Fort Dobbs State Historic Site, Bethany Presbyterian Church, Snow Creek Methodist Church, Centre Presbyterian Church, the Battle of Torrence's Tavern, the story of Griffith Rutherford, the story of Betsy Brandon, Thyatira Presbyterian Church, Third Creek Presbyterian Church, historic Salisbury, the Braun House, the Battle of Trading Ford, the story of George Washington's baptism, the story of Valentin Leonhardt and Wooldrich Fritz, and the Battle of Shallow Ford.

Total mileage: approximately 241 miles.

This tour traverses a five-county area in the eastern Piedmont through which flows the lower half of the Yadkin River.

This was the very stage on which some of the highest drama of the Revolution was played out in early 1781. It was here that Nathanael Greene followed up his masterful escape on the Catawba with a miraculous crossing of the Yadkin just ahead of Cornwallis. All along the route of this textbook retreat, stories of heroism and sacrifice were written.

The tour begins at the junction of West End Avenue and Meeting Street in downtown Statesville, the seat of Iredell County. Carved from Rowan County in 1788, Iredell County was named for James Iredell (1751–99), the attorney general of North Carolina during the Revolution and an associate justice on the first United States Supreme Court. Most Iredell residents were strong supporters of the cause of independence.

Fourth Creek Presbyterian Church (now First Presbyterian Church) and its burial ground stand at the junction. A state historical marker alongside the sanctuary acclaims the historic importance of this church. The first Scots-Irish settlers from Pennsylvania who took up residence along nearby Fourth Creek organized the congregation in 1750. The current church building is the successor to the first Presbyterian meeting house west of the Yadkin.

From the church, walk to the triangular plaza located at the junction of the two streets. A large marker set amid flowers and plants memorializes the Reverend James Hall (1744–1826), an early minister at Fourth Creek who took up the sword for the American cause. His grave and homesite are visited later on this tour.

From the plaza, proceed to the cemetery, which covers almost half a block at the northwestern corner of West End and Meeting. Ancient trees tower above the beautifully landscaped grounds dotted with historic graves. At least seven Revolutionary War soldiers are buried at this serene spot in the heart of Statesville.

The most visited of them is that of William "Little Gabriel" Stevenson (1725–1809). A native of Ireland, Stevenson settled on a 369-acre tract granted by the earl of Granville in 1762. Stevenson fought for the American cause during the Revolution, as did two of his seven sons.

But it was through his fourth son, James, and his daughter, Elizabeth, that Little Gabriel achieved his most enduring fame. Elizabeth was an ancestor of Vice President Alben W. Barkley. James was an ancestor of Adlai Stevenson, vice president of the United States; Adlai Stevenson II, governor of Illinois, Democratic nominee for president, and ambassador to the United Nations; and Adlai Stevenson III, United States senator from Illinois. William "Little Gabriel" Stevenson, Revolutionary War veteran from Iredell County, was thus the first American to become an ancestor of two vice presidents. Adlai Stevenson II visited the grave in the 1950s.

Follow West End for one block to N.C. 115. Drive across the intersection onto East Water Street. Follow East Water for two blocks to U.S. 64 (Davie Avenue). Merge onto U.S. 64, follow it for 3.6 miles to U.S. 21, turn left, and go 2.1 miles to S.R. 1930. At the junction, you will see a state historical marker for Fort Dobbs, a frontier outpost that stood nearby in colonial times.

To visit this historic spot, turn left on S.R. 1930 and follow it west for 1.5 miles to Fort Dobbs State Historic Site. The history of this strategic outpost is interpreted inside the log-house visitor center. Although the fortification was destroyed during the Revolution, visitors can trace the outlines of the walls or embankments.

In June 1755, Royal Governor Arthur Dobbs journeyed to the frontier in search of a site for a fort to protect against Indian incursions. His advance team was composed of three companies of soldiers under the command of Captain Hugh Waddell. Born in Ireland, Waddell had settled in North Carolina in 1754 after the appointment of Dobbs (one his father's Irish friends) as governor. Pressed into immediate service as a lieutenant against the French and Indians in Virginia, he proved a soldier of great merit.

Dobbs and Waddell met at the current tour stop in July 1755 and selected it as the site for a fort. Construction began several months later. When completed the following year, the log building contained three floors and measured 24½ feet high, 40 feet wide, and 53 feet long. Waddell was given command of the forty-six-man garrison.

From 1756 until 1762, Fort Dobbs was manned continuously. But little is known of its fate from 1762 until it disappeared during the Revolutionary War.

Tradition has it that the fort was used for storage during a portion of the war. Settlers are said to have taken refuge in the stockade in 1776 when the Cherokees were on the rampage. There is no record of how many settlers found protection at the fort, but it is certain that two children were born in it, Rachel Davidson in 1758 and Margaret Locke in 1776. Fire ultimately ravaged the portion that was not dismantled.

The site of Waddell's fort is the only reminder of North Carolina's participation in the French and Indian War. Prior to the state's acquisition of the historic tract, the Daughters of the American Revolution were instrumental in its preservation. A D.A.R. marker stands near the excavation site today.

Return to the junction with U.S. 21. Turn left and proceed north for 2.1 miles to I-77. Continue north on U.S. 21 for 3 miles to the state historical marker for Dr. James Hall, the fighting Presbyterian minister. He is buried in the cemetery of Bethany Presbyterian Church, which stands within sight of the sign.

Set atop a hill in a grove of oaks, the rectangular, one-story church building was constructed in 1855 for a congregation organized in 1775 as an outgrowth of the church at Fourth Creek. A rock wall encloses the cemetery, located northeast of the church. Buried here are at least fifteen Revolutionary War soldiers. Hall's well-marked grave is located inside the southern gate.

Born in Carlisle, Pennsylvania in 1744, Hall migrated with his Scots-Irish parents to the upper part of Iredell County when he was eight years old. Educated on the North Carolina frontier, he heard the call to the ministry in the decade before the Revolutionary War. Hall graduated from Princeton in 1774, having studied under Dr. John Witherspoon, who two years later would sign the Declaration of Independence.

In the early years of the war, the newly ordained Presbyterian preacher took charge of the congregations at Fourth Creek, Bethany, and Concord in a parish that covered 600 square miles. He remained in the pulpit until 1778, but when full-scale conflict threatened to spread into the Piedmont, he took to the field, first as a chaplain and then as a soldier.

Once Hall reconciled his patriotism with his Christian service, the American cause had no better soldier. Blessed with a tall, muscular body, the minister-turned-soldier was described this way by a contemporary: "An excellent rider, personally almost Herculean, possessed of a very long and durable arm and, taking as he did, daily lessons from a skilled teacher of the art, he became in a short time one of the best swordsmen in the cavalry of the South. . . . As judicious in council as he was formidable in action, he received the sobriquet of the Ulysses of his regiment."

Initially, Hall assisted in raising militia companies. But in 1779, upon hearing reports of massacres and other outrages committed by the British army in South Carolina, the minister was spurred to greater action. He raised a company of soldiers from his congregations, took command as their captain, and led them into battle. During a two-month expedition to the Cherokee country in Georgia, Captain Hall preached the first sermon ever heard in that area.

Hall was in an Iredell County pulpit on the last Sunday in January 1781, at the very time Cornwallis was preparing to cross the Catawba at Cowan's Ford. In the middle of the sermon, a courier from General William Lee Davidson bounded into the sanctuary with a communique for the minister. Given the urgency of the message, the soldier proceeded to the pulpit and handed the paper to Dr. Hall, who stopped his discourse and read it. Moved by its contents, he quickly closed his sermon, descended from the pulpit, read Davidson's appeal for help to the congregation, and urged those listening to put down their Bibles and take up the sword.

A day later, Captain Hall and his followers, fully armed and supplied with five days' rations, assembled at the church. With Hall in the lead, they rode off to take part in Davidson's gallant stand on the Catawba. Such was Hall's fighting skill that he was offered command of the militia after Davidson was mortally wounded. He refused the appointment.

Also interred at Bethany is Dr. Lewis F. Wilson (1754–1802), a medical doctor and minister who succeeded Hall in the pulpit at Fourth Creek Presbyterian Church. During the Revolution, Dr. Wilson served as a surgeon in both the Continental Army and the Continental Navy.

Wilson and Hall had formed a lifelong friendship while students at Princeton. When Wilson settled in the Fourth Creek community, he married Hall's niece, the daughter of Captain Hugh Hall, another Revolutionary War soldier buried at Bethany. So close were Hall and Wilson that Hall requested to be buried beside his friend and fellow minister.

Continue north on U.S. 21 for 1 mile. Turn right onto S.R. 2141 and follow it to its terminus. James Hall's home and his Academy of the Sciences—one of the two noted schools he established in the area—once stood near here.

Return to U.S. 21 and continue north. You will cross the Yadkin after 1.3 miles. It is another 7.2 miles to the crossroads community of Houstonville. Continue north for 1.4 miles to S.R. 1829. Remain on U.S. 21 for 0.4 mile to an unnamed dirt road on the eastern side of the highway just north of a white house. Turn right onto this road and follow it for 0.5 mile to the edge of a forest. This area lies on the banks of Hunting Creek (a tributary of the Yadkin River) and offers a view of the nearby Brushy Mountains. Though nothing remains today, it was once the site of Fort Young.

Thomas Young established a plantation here—in an area infested by Tory partisans—in 1778. Although he was too old for military service, his three sons and three sons-in-law were all actively engaged in the fight for independence.

Young constructed an impressive fortress that served several purposes: it was a home for his family, a fort for the protection of area residents, and a headquarters from which to disseminate information vital to the Patriot war effort. When completed, the log complex consisted of two multistory structures connected by an elevated walkway. Portions of the buildings stood for more than a century.

Young joined with eight neighbors of the Whig persuasion to manufacture gunpowder for use on the home front during the war. Area Tories were outraged by the association. All of Young's confederates were subsequently murdered, and Young only narrowly missed being assassinated himself.

Continue on the unpaved road under a canopy of pines and hardwoods for 0.3 mile to a clearing. On the right side of the road in this secluded spot is the Young cemetery. Thomas Young is interred here with at least four Revolutionary War soldiers.

Two of the graves merit special attention.

Major William Gill, Young's son-in-law, served for much of the Revolution on the staff of George Washington. His bravery and daring at the Battle of Brandywine earned him Washington's personal commendation and was characteristic of his service throughout the war. At the height of the battle, Gill became separated from his command and unwittingly rode through the smoke into enemy lines. His only avenue of escape was to jump his horse over a high fence in the face of artillery fire, which he accomplished to the delight of the commander of the American army.

He was with Washington at Cornwallis's surrender at Yorktown.

Also buried in the isolated graveyard is Captain Andrew Carson, the uncle of noted Indian scout Kit Carson. Captain Carson saw much of his service in the South Carolina upcountry as a courier of vital dispatches. His duties brought him into close contact with Francis Marion, "the Swamp Fox." At the Battle of Camden, Carson was with Baron de Kalb when the noted German general fell. According to at least one account, de Kalb died in Carson's arms.

Retrace your route to Houstonville. At the junction of U.S. 21 and S.R. 1833, turn right. Follow S.R. 1833 for 2 miles to S.R. 1832, turn left, and drive south for 0.3 mile to N.C. 901. Turn right, head west for 4.1 miles to S.R. 1892, turn left, and travel south for 9.1 miles to S.R. 1903. Turn right and follow S.R. 1903 for 2.6 miles to Snow Creek Methodist Church and its burial ground.

The Snow Creek congregation was organized in 1801. The existing church building dates from 1881. Twenty-six soldiers from the Revolutionary War are buried in the adjacent cemetery.

None was more illustrious than William "Lawyer Billy" Sharpe (1742–1818). Born in Maryland, Sharpe settled in upper Iredell County in 1769, a year after he married the daughter of David Reese, a signer of the alleged Mecklenburg Declaration of Independence.

From the outset of the Revolution, there were few more ardent Patriots than Sharpe. He was among the soldiers General Griffith Rutherford took with him on his campaign against the Cherokees in the summer of 1776. Subsequently, Sharpe held Indian hostages at his home to ensure that the Cherokees complied with the treaty they signed in 1777.

On February 4, 1779, Sharpe was elected to the Continental Congress. He was then re-elected for two additional one-year terms. Dissatisfied with the proceedings in Congress, he resigned from what he called "the house of bondage" in late 1781. His tenure in Congress was marked by strong support for the American war effort in the South.

Sharpe then returned home to serve the young state in the general assembly. He was also an unsuccessful candidate for governor. In 1784, his bill for establishing a North Carolina university was rejected. A similar proposal by William R. Davie met with success in 1789, and it was thus Davie, rather than Sharpe, who became known as "the Father of the University."

Ill health prevented Sharpe from attending the laying of the cornerstone in Chapel Hill four years later. Davie was less than magnanimous in saying this about his "ambitious friend": "He was ever eager to serve, but being no Verulam, seems better suited to make a treaty with the savage in the Western Woods than to set afoot a seminary of learning."

Continue west on S.R. 1903 for 2 miles to N.C. 115. A state historical marker at the junction honors William Sharpe.

Turn left on N.C. 115 and drive south for 1.4 miles to S.R. 1905. A state historical marker stands near the site of Clio's Academy, established by Dr. James Hall in 1779. During its ten-year existence, the renowned school educated a number of young men who rose to prominence in the young state and nation.

Continue south on N.C. 115 for 16.5 miles to N.C. 152. Turn left and go east for 0.2 mile to rejoin N.C. 115 in Mooresville. Turn right. It is 3.5 miles to a state historical marker that details the history of Centre Presbyterian Church.

To reach the church, turn right onto S.R. 1246 and proceed west for 0.3 mile to S.R. 1245. Turn right again and go another 0.3 mile. The church is on the right and its cemetery on the left.

Organized in 1765, Centre Presbyterian is housed in a rectangular brick building erected in 1854. In 1788, the Presbyterian Synod of the Carolinas was born here. By that time, Centre Presbyterian had already produced a wealth of men prominent in the military, religious, and political affairs of the state.

During the Revolutionary War, Centre was a hotbed of patriotic activity. A large white marker in the vestibule of the sanctuary memorializes the thirty-four members of the congregation who fought for independence. Among the most prominent were General William Lee Davidson, the Patriot martyr at Cowan's Ford, and Ephraim Brevard, the primary author of the alleged Mecklenburg Declaration of Independence.

The man who pastored the church during the war and who marshaled the patriotic zeal of the parishioners was the Reverend Thomas Harris McCaule. The young McCaule was once described as "scarce of the medium height, of a stout frame, and full body, of dark, piercing eyes, a pleasant countenance, and winning manners, with a fine voice." As did many of his Presbyterian counterparts in the Piedmont, he openly supported the struggle for independence from the pulpit. When the war came to the area, McCaule didn't hesitate to accompany his church members to the battlefield. He was at General Davidson's side when the gallant officer fell at Cowan's Ford.

Many of the soldiers McCaule inspired to action are buried in the church's cemetery. At least thirty-three veterans of the Revolution lie here. The graves of a number of them deserve special attention.

Captain James Houston (1747–1819) led a company of troops at the Battle of Ramsour's Mill. In that engagement, he received a serious thigh wound from which he never recovered. As he fell, he caught sight of the Tory who had wounded him. From the ground, Houston sent a ball that plowed into the back of the Tory and resulted in his death.

After Cornwallis crossed the Catawba at Cowan's Ford, he led his army on a march that took it to the home of Captain Houston, which was located in the Centre neighborhood. Upon advance notice of the enemy's approach, Houston departed, taking the family valuables with him to a nearby swamp known as "Purgatory." Marauding Redcoats verbally abused Mrs. Houston upon their arrival, but she refused to reveal the whereabouts of her husband or their treasures.

Also buried here is John Brevard II (1716–90), who lived several miles east of Centre Presbyterian. A prominent colonial official, Brevard served in the Provincial Congress and was among the early supporters of American independence. Although old age robbed him of the opportunity to serve in the Revolution, all eight of his sons did their duty as soldiers. Four of them—Ephraim, Alexander (of Lincoln County fame), John, and Joseph—were officers in the Continental Line. Brevard's daughter, Mary, married General William Lee Davidson.

After the gallant American stand at Cowan's Ford, where Brevard's son-in-law made the ultimate sacrifice, the British army made haste to the family's plantation. Brevard's reputation as a supporter of the American cause made his home a logical target.

He and his daughters were not at home when the green-coated horsemen of Tarleton's Legion called. One of the British officers summoned Mrs. Brevard from the house, pulled a paper from his pocket, and read aloud from it: "These houses must be burned." His men promptly put the torch to every building on the plantation. The elderly matron struggled to pull some of the furniture from the inferno engulfing her home, but as quickly as she salvaged articles, soldiers threw them back into the flames. When she asked why the soldiers were committing such acts, she was informed it was because she had "eight sons in the rebel army."

Retrace your route to the junction with N.C. 115. Turn right and drive south for 0.6 mile to the state historical marker for the skirmish at Torrence's Tavern.

Torrence's (also known as Tarrant's, according to Tarleton) Tavern was located on the road to Salisbury about 10 miles from Beatties Ford. In conjunction with the defense of the Catawba at nearby Cowan's Ford, the tavern had been chosen as the rendezvous site for American forces on February 1, 1781.

Following his victory on the Catawba, Cornwallis hurried Tarleton and two hundred green-coated troopers ahead to continue pressing their advantage. When the cry "Tarleton is coming!" rang out, retreating militiamen and frightened civilians jammed the road in panic. They were easy prey for the raiding horse soldiers.

The raiders set fire to the homes and plantations of John Brevard and others, then swooped down on the confused mass of men assembled at Torrence's Tavern. With sabers drawn, the British horseman screamed, "Remember the Cowpens"—a reference to Tarleton's terrible defeat in upper South Carolina weeks earlier—as they slashed their victims.

In the aftermath of the bloodshed, Tarleton proudly boasted in his journal that his vaunted legion had killed "near 50 on the spot, wounded many in pursuit, and dispersed near 500 of the enemy." His men had also instilled such "terror among the inhabitants" that "the King's troops passed through the most hostile part of North Carolina without a shot from the militia."

In reality, the American dead totaled about ten, while British losses were seven men and twenty horses.

A D.A.R. marker stands nearby to mark the spot of the tavern and to honor the Revolutionary War soldiers from Centre Presbyterian.

Turn around and retrace the route to the junction with N.C. 152 in Mooresville. Turn right. It is 3.6 miles to the Rowan County line. Formed in 1753 from Anson County, Rowan was named for Matthew Rowan, the governor of the colony when the county was created. In 1780, when Banastre Tarleton described Rowan as one of the two most rebellious counties in all of America, it encompassed a much larger area that included what are now Iredell, Davidson, and Davie Counties.

From the county line, it is 10.3 miles on N.C. 152 to the bridge over Grants Creek. Much Revolutionary War history was written on this waterway, which flows northeast into the Yadkin River.

Macay's Mill, once owned by Judge Spruce Macay, the man who taught Andrew Jackson law in Salisbury, stood on the creek south of the current tour stop until the early twentieth century. During the Revolution, the mill site served as a place to recruit and discharge soldiers.

Grants Creek was also the home of one of North Carolina's greatest Revolutionary War heroes. Griffith Rutherford (1721–1805) settled on a large tract on the southern fork of the creek around 1753. A native of Ireland, Rutherford had arrived in America as an infant after a sea voyage that claimed both his parents. Relatives in Pennsylvania reared the orphan. He came to North Carolina as a young adult, settling in Halifax before coming to Rowan County.

Rutherford's brilliant military career began in 1760 with service as a militia captain under General Hugh Waddell. When Governor Tryon ordered Waddell to move against the Regulators in 1771, Rutherford and his Rowan militia participated in the march.

Rutherford was not as quick as many of his Rowan contemporaries to advocate independence from Great Britain. But when the Third Provincial Congress appointed him colonel of the Rowan Mountaineers, he led his troops in the "Snow Campaign" against Tories in South Carolina in late 1775. He followed that with an expedition against the Tories in the Cape Fear in early 1776, although he and his soldiers arrived too late to take part in the Battle of Moores Creek Bridge.

In recognition of Rutherford's skill as a military officer, the Fourth Provincial Congress named him brigadier general of the militia for the entire western portion of the state.

By the early summer of 1776, the growing unrest of the Cherokees and their bloody attacks on frontier settlers led General Rutherford to gather soldiers at his headquarters on the Catawba in preparation for an expedition into Indian country in the North Carolina mountains. On September 1, his seventeen-hundred-man army—soon to be joined by a smaller force from South Carolina—launched a vicious attack on the Cherokee settlements. In just one month, the invading army laid waste to thirty-six Indian towns, destroyed crops, and virtually neutralized the Cherokees. According to tradition, Rutherford lost only three men during the campaign. He returned home a hero, particularly to the people on the frontier, who had been witnesses to and victims of Indian violence.

As 1778 drew to a close, Governor Richard Caswell dispatched Rutherford to South Carolina and Georgia to help defend the two most southern states. Upon his return to North Carolina in the spring of 1779, Rutherford concentrated his efforts on destroying Loyalist support in the Piedmont. His efforts began to show tangible results at the Battle of Ramsour's Mill, even though the general himself arrived at the battleground just after Colonel Francis Locke, his fellow Rowan County Patriot, had carried the day.

Less than two months later, Rutherford fought gallantly in Horatio Gates's debacle at Camden. After sustaining a serious gunshot wound to the leg and a saber gash to the head, he was captured. Ten months of confinement as a prisoner of war followed, first at Charleston and then aboard a prison ship at St. Augustine. His release in Philadelphia in June 1781 was followed by a sad homecoming. Here on Grants Creek, Rutherford found that his plantation had been stripped by British and Tory raiders during his absence.

Ever bound to duty, the red-headed general immediately took to the battle-field. His brigade marched to the Cape Fear, the last significant British enclave in the state. En route, it crushed a Loyalist force at the Battle of Raft Swamp on October 15, 1781. By the time Rutherford rode proudly into Wilmington, the last British soldier had evacuated the port city in the wake of Cornwallis's surrender.

It is estimated that when Rutherford sold his land on Grants Creek and moved to Tennessee in 1792, he owned upwards to twenty thousand acres west of the mountains. As in North Carolina, he was a hero in Tennessee. Both states honored him by bestowing his name upon a county—North Carolina in 1777 and Tennessee in 1803.

Continue east on N.C. 152 for 0.8 mile to U.S. 29A in China Grove. Turn left and proceed 0.7 mile to U.S. 29. A state historical marker located in the traffic island at the junction notes that General Rutherford's home stood a few miles west.

Proceed north on U.S. 29 for 2.6 miles. You'll note a historical marker on the left side of the highway at the site of the plantation of Squire Richard Brandon. Other than the marker, there is no reminder that one of the most heartwarming stories of the Revolutionary War period took place here.

During President Washington's triumphant tour of the South in the spring of 1791, multitudes of citizens traveled to the cities and towns where he stopped to catch a glimpse of the great hero of the Revolution. Such was the case on May 30, when Washington was scheduled to visit Salisbury, the Rowan County seat.

But gloom pervaded the Brandon house—located at the current tour stop—that sunny morning. Fourteen-year-old Betsy Brandon was minding the plantation. Her parents and the rest of the family had gone to Salisbury, 6 miles north, to be on hand when the first president of the United States arrived. Betsy sat on the porch and pondered her sad lot. Everyone else was about to see the greatest hero of the age while she must endure a long day of loneliness. Never again would she have an opportunity to greet the legendary soldier and statesman.

It was not yet nine o'clock when the morning stillness was broken by the sound of horses galloping up the road from Charlotte. The horsemen stopped at the Brandon residence. Behind them was a great chariot. From the unusual coach emerged a tall, handsome man with blue eyes. He made his way to the porch. Betsy arose from her chair and curtsied.

Without introducing himself, the stranger greeted her: "Good morning, my little maid! I know it is late, but could you not give an old man some breakfast?"

Site where Betsy Brandon prepared breakfast for George Washington

After once again curtsying, the shy, embarrassed teenager replied, "I don't know, sir. All the grown folks have gone to Salisbury to see General Washington and I am the only one left on the place."

The man then said, "Never mind, my pretty maid. If you are alone, I am sure you are quite as brisk as you are pretty. Just give me breakfast, and I will promise that you shall see General Washington before any of your people."

With great dispatch, Betsy prepared the most sumptuous breakfast her family had to offer: a table dressed with her mother's homespun linen and best china and silver, laden with ham, newly laid eggs, fresh milk and butter, and bread.

After relishing a feast fit for a head of state, the gentleman stood up and thanked Betsy for her kindness. Then he stooped, kissed her on the forehead, and said with a smile, "Now, my dear, you may tell your people when they get home that you not only saw George Washington before they did, but that he kissed you."

Continue north on U.S. 29 for 0.5 mile to S.R. 1503. Turn left, travel west for 3.2 miles to S.R. 1509, turn right, and drive 2.5 miles north to N.C. 150. Turn left and proceed 0.1 mile west to S.R. 1728. A state historical marker at this junction honors Revolutionary War hero Francis Locke, whose home stood nearby.

Born in Ireland, Locke (1722–96) came to North Carolina via Pennsylvania in 1752. On the eve of the Revolution, the Provincial Congress named him lieutenant colonel of the Rowan Minutemen. When Griffith Rutherford was elevated to general by the Fourth Provincial Congress, Locke was promoted to colonel of the Rowan militia.

During the first two years of the war, Locke monitored Tory activity in western North Carolina. Then he was assigned to duty in South Carolina and Georgia for much of 1779.

It was upon his return to the North Carolina Piedmont that he became one of the key players in the resistance that proved so crucial to the outcome of the war. On the morning of June 20, 1780, Locke commanded the stunning Patriot victory at Ramsour's Mill in Lincoln County. Then, when Cornwallis initiated his first invasion of North Carolina three months later, it was Locke who stood between the British general and Loyalist forces operating in western North Carolina under Major Patrick Ferguson. At a time when North Carolina Patriots were in desperate need of intelligence, Locke served as the army's eyes and ears. Moreover, he stood ready to strike at Ferguson should the bold Scottish officer decide to unite with Cornwallis at Charlotte.

When Cornwallis embarked upon his second invasion of North Carolina, he encountered an old nemesis—Colonel Francis Locke. Operating on their own turf in February 1781, Locke and his soldiers destroyed the bridge across Grants Creek in advance of Cornwallis's march north from Salisbury. Only after Tarleton's cavalry flanked his force did Locke retire from the field. A month later, as Cornwallis felt the wrath of Nathanael Greene's army at Guilford Courthouse, Locke was poised to strike from the back country in the event that the British army pushed west.

Following his resignation from the army in 1784, Locke returned to Rowan County. His only postwar public service was a stint as attorney for the state. One of his four sons served as an officer during the Revolution, and another was elected to Congress. When Locke died in 1796, he was laid to rest at Thyatira Presbyterian Church, the next stop on this tour.

Continue west on N.C. 150 for 2.8 miles to S.R. 1737. Turn right and proceed 0.1 mile to the majestic brick church. Park in the lot in front of the sanctuary.

Organized as early as 1747, Thyatira is one of the oldest Presbyterian churches in North Carolina. It proudly claims the title, "Mother of Presbyterianism." Constructed in 1860, the Gothic Revival sanctuary is the fourth house of worship for the historic congregation. Among its distinctive architectural features are decorative brickwork and a stately bell tower.

Walk around the right side of the sanctuary to the cemetery, located at the rear of the church. Thyatira Cemetery has been called "the Westminster Abbey of North Carolina" because of the large number of Revolutionary War personages buried here. At least thirty-eight members of Thyatira served as soldiers in the war. Many lie in the beautifully landscaped burial ground, where the oldest identifiable graves date to 1755.

The memorial stone of John Knox and Jean Gracy Knox notes that they were the maternal great-grandparents of President James Knox Polk. Seven of their sons—a number of whom are buried here—served as soldiers for the American cause.

Colonel Francis Locke, the heroic commander at Ramsour's Mill, lies in a grave marked by a simple stone. His brother Matthew (1730–1801) is also buried here.

Francis and Matthew Locke were men of great affluence as a result of their back-country trading business. They thus had much to lose in the gamble for independence. Nonetheless, they both took an early stand for the American cause.

Although he served for a brief time as brigadier general *pro tempore* of the militia of western North Carolina during the absence of Griffith Rutherford, Matthew made his greatest impact as a statesman. A member of the colonial assembly from 1771 to 1775, he participated in the growing movement toward revolution during those turbulent times. Throughout the fight for independence, he helped guide the war effort through his effective leadership in the legislature. And his expertise as a trader enabled him to become an effective source of supplies for American soldiers.

Once independence was gained, Matthew continued his service in the general assembly, sponsoring innovative legislation and supporting social reforms (including universal suffrage) that became popular many years later. On the national level, he served in the last session of the Continental Congress in 1788 and 1789.

Four of his sons served as soldiers in the Revolutionary War. Lieutenant

George Locke was killed in battle near Charlotte.

Other notable figures from the Revolution were laid to rest in the sprawling graveyard as well.

Samuel Eusebius McCorkle (1746–1811) was perhaps North Carolina's most outspoken and relentless proponent of education during the Revolutionary War era. Born in Pennsylvania, he was ten when he came to Rowan County and began worshiping at Thyatira. He was educated by Presbyterian ministers in the North Carolina back country. His love of learning was further nurtured by eminent Presbyterian clergyman John Witherspoon at the College of New Jersey (later Princeton), from which McCorkle graduated in 1772.

In 1776, he accepted the call to become the minister of Thyatira, a post he held until his death thirty-five years later. Throughout the Revolution, he promoted the American cause from the pulpit. Over the years, he became one of the most renowned Presbyterian ministers in the state.

But it was in the field of education that McCorkle left his greatest mark during the state's formative years. Cognizant that North Carolina's first constitution contained provisions for a state university, he worked with William R. Davie (also a former pupil of John Witherspoon) to secure passage of the bill for the establishment of the University of North Carolina. On October 12, 1793, when the cornerstone for Old East—the university's first building—was laid, a group of distinguished men assembled for the ceremony. The man chosen to deliver the principal address was Dr. Samuel E. McCorkle.

In physical appearance, he is said to have borne a great likeness to Thomas Jefferson, who was three years older. Because of this remarkable resemblance, McCorkle was once introduced as the author of the Declaration of Independence.

It was six days before that document was formally adopted in 1776 that McCorkle married Margaret Gillespie of Rowan County. The bride's mother, Elizabeth Maxwell Gillespie Steele (1733–90), was the key player in one of the most patriotic acts of the Revolutionary War. She is buried at Thyatira under an obelisk erected by the D.A.R.

The setting for Mrs. Steele's heroism could not have been more dramatic. On the cold, wet night of February 1, 1781, Major General Nathanael

Greene, the commander of the battered remnants of the American army in the South, was mounted on his horse, all alone, somewhere on the muddy road between Charlotte and Salisbury. The best he could hope was that William Lee Davidson's militia had been able to hold the British army at the Catawba in order to give the Americans enough time to escape.

Greene had sent Daniel Morgan and his forces ahead to Salisbury earlier in the day. He had also dispatched every one of his aides to try to rally his starving, shoeless soldiers, many of whom had received no pay for months.

The fate of the war in the South—and most likely the entire struggle for independence—now hung in the balance. With Cornwallis's massive army on his heels, Greene needed time to reorganize his beleaguered command and resources to restore it to fighting condition. On that dark, bleak night, "the Fighting Quaker" needed nothing short of a miracle.

Suddenly, he heard the sound of splashing hooves. A messenger galloped up with the worst possible tidings: Cornwallis had successfully crossed the Catawba at Cowan's Ford, the American militia had been scattered, and General William Lee Davidson had been slain. This news all but dashed any hope Greene had of eluding Cornwallis and avoiding disaster. With the weight of all thirteen states on his shoulders, he spurred his horse and rode off into the night on the long, solitary journey to Salisbury.

After an exhausting 30-mile ride through heavy rain, the general galloped into town in the wee hours of February 2 and made his way to the inn of Mrs. Elizabeth Maxwell Gillespie Steele, located at the corner of Main and Council Streets.

At the inn's entrance, he was greeted by Dr. Joseph Read, a surgeon in Daniel Morgan's command. Read asked, "How do you find yourself, General?"

In utter dejection, Greene responded, "Wretched beyond measure, fatigued, hungry, alone, penniless, and destitute of a friend."

Mrs. Steele made her way to the door upon hearing the men's voices, arriving in time to catch Greene's comment. Responding to his pessimistic words, the widow addressed him this way: "That I deny, that I most particularly deny, Sir! In me, General, you and the American cause have a devoted friend. Only come in and rest and dry yourself, and in a very short time a hot breakfast shall cheer and refresh you."

Cold, rain-soaked, weary, and dispirited, Greene accepted the invitation, made his way into the inn, and slumped into the nearest chair. Soon, he was wearing dry clothes provided by Mrs. Steele while his cloak and uniform were drying by the fire.

After enjoying the meal promised and prepared by Mrs. Steele, the general was resting at the table with his head in his hands when his hostess entered the room. She closed the kitchen door and looked around to make sure that she and Greene were not being observed. From under her apron, she pulled two bags—one filled with gold coins, the other with silver coins. Handing what represented her entire savings to Greene, Mrs. Steele smiled and said, "Take them, for you will need them, and I can do without them."

Visibly moved by this unexpected act of generosity, the general offered his gratitude: "These two bags now represent the entire treasure chest of the American army in the South. They will put shoes on barefoot soldiers, feed hungry men, and further the cause of liberty."

Encouraged by Mrs. Steele's patriotism and refreshed by several hours of rest, Greene was ready to tackle the awesome task at hand. Just as he prepared to leave the inn in the early-morning darkness on February 2, the portraits of King George III and Queen Charlotte hanging on a nearby wall caught his eye. He rose from the table and walked over to the portraits. After turning the face of the British monarch to the wall, the general used a piece of chalk to scrawl the following message on the back of the portrait: "O George, Hide thy face and mourn!"

Then Greene walked out of the inn, mounted his horse, and rode away into what was literally the new dawn of American history, since he proceeded to mastermind a military miracle in his struggle against Cornwallis over the six weeks that followed.

But there is more to the story of General Greene and Mrs. Steele. From the cemetery, walk to the front of the church. On the left side of the sanctuary stands the magnificent Thyatira Heritage Museum. Open on occasion and by appointment, this treasure trove of artifacts from the long history of the church was dedicated on September 28, 1980, and was the gift of Mr. and Mrs. Locke C. Neal.

Among the most famous of the museum's holdings are the portrait of King George III that Nathanael Greene wrote upon in 1781 and the companion portrait of Queen Charlotte. Although Greene's chalk-written mes-

Portrait of King George III
autographed by Nathanael Greene,
Thyatira Presbyterian Church

sage has faded with age, it can still be faintly seen on the back of the king's portrait.

That the portraits survive is something of a miracle. They remained on the wall of the inn for a number of years after Greene's visit. After Mrs. Steele died, her son, John, inherited them. They then came into the possession of David L. Swain, president of the University of North Carolina and former governor. When Swain's wife's estate was auctioned in 1883, the portraits were purchased for seventeen cents by a young fellow, William J. Andrews. Years later, Andrews moved to California, where the famous portraits remained until 1977.

In that year, Mrs. Locke Neale, the great-great-great-great-granddaughter of Mrs. Steele, learned that the portraits were for sale in an art gallery in Palm Springs. The Neales thus acquired the priceless pieces of history for the museum at Thyatira.

The dramatic meeting of General Greene and Mrs. Steele has been memorialized in a painting by Alonzo Chappel entitled *Female Patriotism— Mrs. Steele and General Greene* and in a poem called "The Dame O' Salisbury Town," published in the *Chicago Journal*.

When you are ready to leave the church, proceed north on S.R. 1737 for 3.1 miles to S.R. 1526, turn left, and go 0.2 mile west to N.C. 801. Follow N.C. 801 South for 3.1 miles to the community of Bear Poplar. Tradition has it that this crossroads village took its name from a poplar tree where Captain Thomas Cowan, a Revolutionary War soldier, treed a bear.

Continue on N.C. 801 for 1.7 miles to S.R. 1752. Turn right, proceed north for 3.2 miles to S.R. 1001, turn right again, and drive east for 0.4 mile to S.R. 1745, where you'll notice a sign for Knox Hill Farm. Turn left and travel 0.9 mile north to the Knox home and farm, located on the right side of the road.

Knox Hill Farm

This farmstead has remained in the Knox family since John Knox (1708–58), a Scots-Irish Presbyterian, settled in Rowan County about 1740. Knox was the great-grandfather of the eleventh president of the United States. Around 1756, his oldest son, William, constructed a log cabin that stood near the two-story nineteenth-century house on the site today. A fire destroyed the cabin in 1943.

William Knox, a militia captain, was killed at the Battle of Ramsour's

Mill. His son, Benjamin, born here in 1760, also served in the Revolutionary War, fighting alongside his father at Ramsour's Mill. A year later, Benjamin took part in the Battle of Cowan's Ford. William's brother, James, also fought for the American cause. He was the grandfather of President James Knox Polk.

Return to the junction with S.R. 1001. Turn left and go 3.6 miles to U.S. 70 at the town of Cleveland. En route, you'll notice Young's Mountain on the horizon. The peak rises several hundred feet above the surrounding landscape and is named for Samuel Young, a Patriot buried at Third Creek Presbyterian Church, the next stop on this tour.

Turn right onto U.S. 70 and proceed east. After 0.2 mile, you will pass a state historical marker for the Knox home. Continue 0.4 mile to School Street in the town of Cleveland. A nearby state historical marker directs visitors to Third Creek Presbyterian Church.

To see the historic church and its cemetery, turn left on School and follow it 0.3 mile to Main Street. Turn right, go 0.3 mile to Maple Street, turn left, and drive 0.1 mile west to S.R. 1957 (Third Creek Church Road). Turn right and head north for 1.8 miles to S.R. 1973; en route, you will cross Third Creek. Turn left onto S.R. 1973. The stately church is located 0.3 mile west on the right side of the road.

No one is certain when Third Creek was organized here, in a colonial settlement that bore the same name. Some records indicate that the church began as early as 1776. The existing two-story brick structure is little altered from its original appearance in 1835.

At least thirteen members of Third Creek fought in the Revolution. Most of these Patriots lie in the large graveyard adjacent to the church.

Of all the Revolutionary War soldiers interred at Third Creek, perhaps the most interesting was Robert McLewrath. A talented gunsmith, he married the granddaughter of the Reverend John Thomson, the first minister at Third Creek. During the war, McLewrath served as the chief armorer for the state of South Carolina.

When American fortunes were at their lowest ebb in the Palmetto State, the Patriot cause there was without a single printing press to disseminate news and war propaganda. Governor John Rutledge was anxious to publish a proclamation of patriotism that was to be characterized by "thoughts that breath[e] and words that burn."

An aide to the governor, cognizant of McLewrath's reputation, suggested to Rutledge that "there is a gunsmith living a few miles away who never failed in a solitary attempt to accomplish anything he put his hands to."

"Well, please send for him," Rutledge responded.

When McLewrath arrived, he was assigned the difficult task by the governor, who said, "My wishes are that you cast forth a set of types with which I might set forth in print my Proclamation."

Materials were promptly requisitioned, and the gunsmith went to work. In a single day, he fabricated a workable press, from which poured copies of the governor's message.

A large memorial stone in the cemetery was unveiled by the Elizabeth Maxwell Steele Chapter of the D.A.R. It pays tribute to one of Rowan County's moving spirits for independence.

According to the inscription on the marker, Samuel Young (1721–93) was born in Scotland and educated at the University of Edinburgh before he came to America and settled on the banks of Third Creek in the 1750s.

When "Bold" John Harvey called on the people of North Carolina to send delegates to the First Provincial Congress in August 1774, the residents of Rowan turned to Samuel Young, their respected magistrate, for leadership.

On August 8, seventeen days before Young and two other Rowan delegates assembled with other distinguished statesmen from throughout the colony at New Bern, the newly formed Rowan Committee of Safety issued a series of resolutions, called the Rowan Resolves. Young served as one of the draftsmen of the paper. While the resolutions affirmed allegiance to the Crown, they also set the tone for the words and actions of North Carolina revolutionaries in the years to come. The pen of Young and his colleagues expressed the principles upon which the fight against Great Britain was based: the rights of free men, freedom from taxation without representation, and the right of the colonies to associate to resist further infringements on the rights of Americans.

Young took a copy of the Rowan Resolves with him to the First Provincial Congress. It was at that gathering that North Carolina ever so subtly began to march down the road to independence. After the assembly in

New Bern adjourned, the Rowan Committee of Safety selected Young to take on the responsibility as its correspondent with both the Provincial and Continental Congresses.

Most visitors to the historic cemetery at Third Creek come to see the grave of a man purported to be a hero of the French Revolution—a man who took his inspiration from the fight for American independence. A large brick mausoleum constructed to prevent vandalism covers the final resting place of Peter Stewart Ney (1769–1846). A bronze plaque on the tomb enclosure characterizes him as "A Native Of France And Soldier Of The French Revolution Under Napoleon Bonaparte."

From the church, proceed east on S.R. 1973 for 0.8 mile to S.R. 1972. Turn left, drive north for 2.8 miles to S.R. 1003, turn right, and proceed 0.6 mile east to S.R. 1986 at Fourth Creek. On the northwestern side of this junction stands Mount Vernon. Built in 1822, this massive, two-story frame house rests in a grove of oak trees where Cornwallis camped as he moved north on February 6, 1781, in his quest to catch Greene. According to tradition, he and his aide slept near the old springhouse on the plantation.

Turn left onto S.R. 1986 and follow it north for 1.7 miles to S.R. 1984. Turn right, proceed east for 4.1 miles to N.C. 801, turn right again, and go 2 miles to S.R. 1948. Turn right, proceed east for 4.8 miles to U.S. 601, turn right, and go south for another 4.8 miles to Salisbury, where the road becomes West Innes Street. Follow West Innes to the intersection with Main Street in the heart of the city; here, West Innes becomes East Innes. Drive one block on East Innes to the Salisbury Visitor Center, located at the corner of East Innes and North Lee.

Nearly from the time it was established as the seat of Rowan County in 1755, Salisbury has been one of the most important towns in western North Carolina. When Royal Governor Arthur Dobbs visited in 1755, he found a settlement with little more than seven or eight cabins, a jail, and a pillory. But over the next fifteen years, Salisbury grew to become the largest town in the western part of the colony.

Few North Carolina towns played a more prominent role in the fight for independence than Salisbury. It served as the military and justice center of the Salisbury District, which was made up of Rowan, Guilford, Anson, Mecklenburg, Tryon, and Surry Counties. During the war, the Rowan District provided twice as many troops (8,792) as any other district in the state.

Turn left off East Innes onto North Lee and go four blocks. Turn left onto West Franklin and drive one block to North Main (U.S. 29/U.S. 70).

General Daniel Morgan's forces marched past this very spot in early February 1781 in their race to escape Cornwallis.

When Colonel Banastre Tarleton called on Salisbury with Cornwallis's army days later, he paid an unwelcome visit to the home of John Lewis Beard, which stood near the corner of Franklin and Main. Beard was away fighting for the Patriot cause when Tarleton arrived and made himself at home. During the British officer's stay, Beard's infant child was subject to fits of loud, continuous crying. Vexed by the noise, Tarleton threatened Mrs. Beard that if she did not silence the child, he would choke it.

Nothing occurred during Tarleton's short stay in Salisbury to alter his opinion that "the Counties of Mecklenburg and Rowan were more hostile to England than any others in America."

Turn right on North Main Street. Daniel Morgan marched his troops along this route when they reached town late in the afternoon on Thursday, February 1, 1781.

Drive five blocks on North Main to East Miller Street. A nearby state historical marker pays tribute to John Steele (1764–1815). To see his home, turn right on East Miller and proceed two blocks to Richard Street. The house is on the left.

Lombardy, as this two-story frame structure is named, dates from 1799. It originally stood on Steele's plantation north of town. It survives today as one of only three eighteenth-century homes in Rowan County.

Born in Salisbury, Steele was the son of Revolutionary War heroine Elizabeth Maxwell Steele, who was widowed when her son was nine years old. John was well educated at a school in Salisbury and then at Clio Academy, run by the Reverend James Hall.

In 1777, when he was only thirteen years old, John Steele enlisted in the Continental Army, much to his mother's dismay. Soon after he departed home, Mrs. Steele, ever the Patriot, sent her son these words of encouragement: "Since you have chosen that manner of life, it would give me the greatest pleasure to hear of your acquitting yourself with honor and faithfulness to your country."

Following the war, Steele was elected to the United States House of Representatives and served in the First and Second Congresses. On July 1, 1796, President George Washington, upon the recommendation of Alexander Hamilton, appointed Steele comptroller of the United States Treasury, a post he held until his resignation in 1802 during the administration of Thomas Jefferson.

Return to North Main. Turn left and proceed to the intersection with West Liberty Street. Park nearby and go to the southwestern corner of North Main and Liberty to begin a brief walking tour of Salisbury.

Proceed south on North Main. A state historical marker in front of the two historic courthouse buildings where you now stand calls attention to George Washington's visit on May 30 and 31, 1791.

After his breakfast with Betsy Brandon west of the city on the morning of Monday, May 30, Washington made his way into Salisbury in the company of a large entourage of leading local citizens, including Congressman John Steele. Washington said this of the surrounding countryside: "The lands between Charlotte and Salisbury are very fine." But when it came to the town itself, the president was not very enthusiastic: "Salisbury is but a small place . . . nor does it appear to be much on the increase."

Washington lodged and was entertained at the home of Captain Edward Yarboro, which stood nearby on Main Street. Throngs of people crowded in the street outside on the afternoon of May 30 in hopes of seeing and hearing the national hero. Washington did indeed emerge for a brief appearance, offering these words: "My friends, you see before you nothing but an old, gray-headed man." That was all the people heard from him that day, for after that single utterance, he stood before them mutely, his handkerchief covering his head from the late-spring sun.

Along this historic block of North Main Street stand the Rowan County Courthouse, built around 1912, and the former courthouse, which dates from around 1855. Courthouse records survive virtually intact from the colonial and Revolutionary War periods. Two metal plaques attached to the front of the former courthouse commemorate Revolutionary War–era events that occurred nearby. One of them, dedicated by the D.A.R. in 1911, honors Elizabeth Maxwell Steele, whose famous inn stood near the site of the two courthouses. The other recalls the visit of President Washington. A

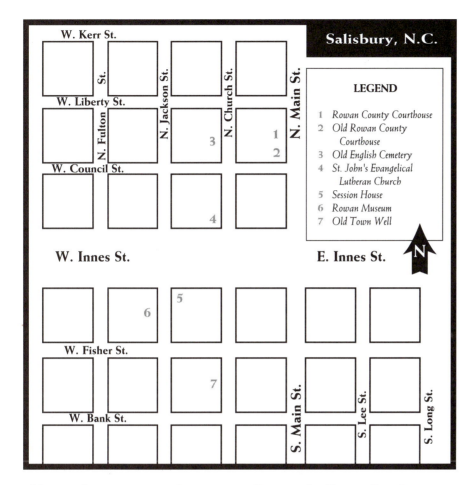

Salisbury, N.C.

W. Kerr St.

St.

N. Jackson St.

N. Church St.

N. Main St.

W. Liberty St.

N. Fulton St.

3

1

2

W. Council St.

4

LEGEND

1 Rowan County Courthouse
2 Old Rowan County
   Courthouse
3 Old English Cemetery
4 St. John's Evangelical
   Lutheran Church
5 Session House
6 Rowan Museum
7 Old Town Well

N

W. Innes St.

E. Innes St.

5

6

W. Fisher St.

7

S. Main St.

S. Lee St.

S. Long St.

W. Bank St.

tablet on the current courthouse pays tribute to the Rowan Resolves.

Turn right off North Main onto West Council, walk one block, then proceed across North Church. In the middle of the block is the Old English Cemetery (also known as Oak Grove Cemetery).

Established on land granted to the city by the British government in 1770, this burial ground is among the oldest in Salisbury. During his several-day stay in early February 1781, Cornwallis camped his army in the vicinity of the cemetery. Several of his soldiers, casualties of the recent fighting with the American militia, were laid to rest in the graveyard. American soldiers of the Revolution are interred here also.

Proceed south on North Church for two blocks to West Innes. At the northwestern corner of this intersection stands St. John's Evangelical Lutheran Church. Originally housed in a log structure, this church was organized sometime after 1747 and is the oldest church in Salisbury.

During Cornwallis's occupation of the town, his commissary was located at the site of the existing Gothic sanctuary. Perhaps he selected the site because the law office of John Dunn was located nearby. Dunn, a native of Ireland, was educated at Oxford before he came to America at the age of twenty. In 1775, he and another leading citizen, Benjamin Boote, were arrested by revolutionary firebrands for allegedly signing a declaration of allegiance to the Crown. Both men were imprisoned without trial in Charleston until Salisbury Patriots interceded and gained their release. Dunn returned to Salisbury, where he lived and practiced law for the duration of the war.

The British commissary was housed in the home of Dunn's daughter, Mrs. Eleanor Faust, which stood just in back of the law office. During the British occupation, commissary officials coveted Mrs. Faust's pet calf, which could often be seen grazing in the yard. When the owner refused to sell the animal for Lord Cornwallis's table, it was "impressed" and slaughtered. A piece of gold was placed before Mrs. Faust in payment, but the outraged woman swept it off the table and stormed out of the room.

Walk one block west on West Innes to South Jackson. At the southeastern corner of this intersection stands the Session House (or Lecture Room) of First Presbyterian Church. Beneath this one-room nineteenth-century brick building are ten graves, including that of Maxwell Chambers. Cornwallis used Chambers's home as his headquarters during his stay in Salisbury.

Turn left on South Jackson and proceed to the Rowan Museum, located at 116 South Jackson in the Utzman-Chambers House, a Federal town house built in 1819. The museum exhibits artifacts from the county's earliest history, which began twenty years before the Revolution. Among the many items of interest are a ball gown worn by a local lady during Washington's visit and a knife box that once belonged to John Steele.

Proceed south to the end of the block. At the intersection with West Fisher, turn left and walk west to South Church. Turn right. The remnants of the old Town Well stand near the driveway for the library. The law office of Spruce Macay, one of western North Carolina's leading jurists in the Revolutionary War period, was located near the well. It was here that the young war veteran Andrew Jackson studied law from 1784 to 1785. William R. Davie also received his legal education in the building.

Go south on South Church for one block to West Bank.

When Cornwallis arrived in Salisbury on Saturday, February 3, 1781, he made his headquarters in a house that stood at the southwestern corner of this intersection. The British army remained in the town until the following Tuesday morning.

From his headquarters here, Cornwallis issued strict orders that prohibited his soldiers from entering private dwellings. However, the threat of military discipline did not deter some of the Redcoats from plundering. Mrs. Elizabeth Maxwell Steele complained that she was stripped of all her livestock.

Follow West Bank one block east to South Main. Turn left and walk one block to West Fisher. At this intersection stands a state historical marker for Andrew Jackson.

Many of Cornwallis's officers were quartered in residences that stood here on Main Street. One such home was that of Dr. Anthony Newman, which stood on the southeastern side of Main. Tarleton and several other officers were enjoying the hospitality of the Whig physician one afternoon while Dr. Newman's two small sons were engrossed in play nearby. Their toys were nothing more than red and white grains of corn.

In recent days, while their home had been occupied by an invading army, the children had listened to much adult talk about the Battle of Cowpens and the fighting between the cavalry forces of Tarleton and Colonel William Washington. Excited by the stories, the boys turned their colored grains into American and British soldiers and proceeded to refight Cowpens. Oblivious to the presence of the fiery British cavalry chief, one of the boys shouted, "Hurrah for Washington! Tarleton is running! Hurrah for Washington!"

Unable to hold back his rage, Tarleton screamed profanities at the children.

A mural of historic Salisbury is painted on buildings in the first block of West Fisher north of the current tour stop. It is a vivid picture of the dramatic events that have taken place in this important city.

From the intersection of South Main and West Fisher, walk one block north on Main to the intersection with Innes. Continue north on Main to where you parked to complete the walking tour.

Drive east on East Innes as it becomes U.S. 52. Follow U.S. 52 out of Salisbury for 3.5 miles to East Lyerly Street in the town of Granite Quarry. A state historical marker for the Braun House (or Old Stone House) stands here.

To see the eighteenth-century structure, which is open to the public, turn left on East Lyerly and proceed north as the road becomes Old Stone House Road (S.R. 2308). Sheltered by ancient cedar and walnut trees, the magnificent two-story house is located approximately 0.5 mile north of U.S. 52. Erected in 1766, it is of enormous historical and architectural importance. It ranks as one of the oldest homes in western North Carolina and is one of the few remaining Pennsylvania Dutch stone houses in the state.

Michael Braun (1722–1807), a native of Germany, arrived in Pennsylvania as a sixteen-year bonded servant in 1737. Some twenty years later, he settled in Rowan County. A skilled craftsman, he subsequently built this house from unhewn native stones.

A legendary frontiersman, Braun was too old for military service when the Revolution began. However, his son acquired the nickname "Continental John" because of his service in the American army. And his house was the scene of high drama in the winter of 1781 as Cornwallis gave chase to the American army.

As the story goes, the main body of the British army passed the house on February 2, 1781, in its futile attempt to catch Greene before he crossed the Yadkin at Trading Ford (visited later on this tour). An American scout happened upon the Redcoats near the house. He turned his horse, and the British dragoons took up pursuit. Thundering down the hill, the Patriot officer spurred his mount through the front door of the Braun House, out the back, and into the wilderness beyond, where he eluded his would-be captors.

Some American soldiers were not so fortunate. For a time, they were held here by the British when the house was used as a temporary prison. The deep sword gashes in the doorposts are said to have resulted from an encounter between an escaping American and an enemy soldier.

Prior to its acquisition by Braun's descendants in 1948 and its subsequent restoration by the Rowan Museum (the current owner), the house was hastening to ruin after years of abandonment and vandalism. For a fee, modern-day visitors can tour the massive dwelling. Its stone walls are two to three feet thick. Much of the interior woodwork is original, and the rooms on both floors are furnished with period antiques. The original function of the four portholes located beside the two chimneys high above the second floor is a matter of dispute. Some people believe they were built for ventilation, while others say they were used by riflemen to ward off Indian attacks.

Members of the Braun family are buried in the cemetery located just across the road. Though his grave is not marked, Michael Braun is believed to be buried there. A monument to his memory was erected in the cemetery in 1981.

Continue north on S.R. 2308 (which becomes Dunns Mountain Church Road) for 1.1 miles to S.R. 1004. At this intersection, you are virtually atop Dunn's Mountain, often called "Rowan's Miniature Mountain." Named for John Dunn, the Salisbury attorney imprisoned during the Revolutionary War, the peak has provided much pink and gray stone for the granite industry long associated with this part of the county. Dunn maintained a country residence and farm nearby. The location of his grave, believed to be at the mountain, is unknown.

Proceed across the intersection onto S.R. 2131 (Earnhardt Road). Follow it north for 1.8 miles to S.R. 1002, turn left, and drive 1.6 miles to the junction with Old Union Church Road and Andrews Street in East Spencer. Turn left and follow Andrews Street north for 1.3 miles to U.S. 29 Business/U.S. 70/N.C. 150 in the railroad town of Spencer. Turn right, proceed 0.9 mile to Sowers Ferry Road, turn left, and go 0.6 mile to where the road terminates.

Here stands the stately Alexander Long House. Erected in 1785 on Grant's Creek, a tributary of the nearby Yadkin, the immense, two-story Georgian mansion is the sole survivor of the many plantation houses that once lined the river. After he left Salisbury on the last day of May 1781, George Washington paused at this house, which is the second-oldest in the county.

Return to the junction with U.S. 29 Business/U.S. 70/N.C. 150. Turn left and drive 2.1 miles east to the state historical marker for Trading Ford, one of the most important sites of the American Revolution.

Now covered by the waters of High Rock Lake, Trading Ford was located approximately 1 mile east of the downriver bridge, near the site of the existing electric power plant. Used by Indians and white settlers of the region, the ford also provided the escape route that saved the American army from virtual annihilation on February 2 and 3, 1781.

Renewed in body and spirit after his meeting with Elizabeth Maxwell Steele in Salisbury, Nathanael Greene rode east toward the Yadkin. There, during the morning and afternoon of February 2, he and General Morgan hurried the exhausted, starving Continentals across the river at Trading Ford. With the relentless Cornwallis in pursuit, Greene realized he had no time to lose.

Battle of Trading Ford Monument

Once the bulk of the Americans were safely across, their commander set up his headquarters in a small cabin on the eastern side of the river. In accordance with his orders, all the boats that had been used to transport men and equipment were secured.

Greene's swift, efficient crossing was a remarkable military feat, but what followed was nothing short of a miracle. The heavens opened up, and torrential rain began to fall. When the first wave of Cornwallis's army, led by General O'Hara and Colonel Tarleton, reached the western bank of the Yadkin around midnight, it was engaged by a small detachment of American marksmen deployed to protect the wagons and property of terrified citizens attempting to flee the British vanguard. After a brief, heated skirmish, the Americans safely escaped into the rainy night.

O'Hara and Tarleton were dismayed that Greene had again made a narrow escape, but there was a greater problem at hand. The heavy rains had gorged the Yadkin, and Trading Ford was no longer passable. As a result, Cornwallis lost almost a week in the chase. He would be forced to cross the Yadkin above its forks, more than 30 miles to the north. For the British, the rain-swollen river represented a nightmare, but for the Americans, it was a godsend. Accordingly, the citizens of Rowan named a local township Providence in gratitude for what they believed was an act of divine intervention in 1781.

Resume the route on U.S. 29 Business/U.S. 70/N.C. 150 as it crosses the Yadkin; during the crossing, you'll enjoy an outstanding view of the site of Trading Ford.

On the opposite side of the bridge, the tour enters Davidson County. Turn left onto Old Salisbury Road (S.R. 1138); a sign at the junction is marked "Yadkin River Trail Access." After approximately 0.2 mile on Old Salisbury Road, turn left onto the dirt road leading down the high banks to a river access area, where you'll have a spectacular view of the river and the terrain that faced the two armies in 1781.

Resume the route on Old Salisbury Road. After approximately 0.7 mile, you'll notice a sizable stone monument on the right side of the road. Erected in 1929 by the North Carolina State Historical Commission, it commemorates Greene's escape at Trading Ford. Situated on a 1.1-acre lot, the marker is eight feet high, six feet wide, and eighteen inches thick.

Two cannonballs, long ago removed by vandals, were once mounted on bases at the foot of the monument. Those cannonballs were graphic reminders of the action that took place at Trading Ford on the morning of February 3.

While the distressing news of Greene's crossing and the swollen river was being relayed to Cornwallis in Salisbury, British artillery was placed on what was known as the Heights of Gowerie, the high banks of the river just below the ford. Using field glasses, British officers could observe the activity on the other side. They trained their guns on the cabin where Greene had established his headquarters. When the order was given, the big guns sent balls that bounded onto the rocks at the rear of the cabin.

Greene was busy inside preparing orders for his army and writing reports to Congress. It wasn't long before the artillerists sharpened their aim and projectiles began to strike the roof, sending clapboards flying. But Greene was undaunted. According to Dr. Joseph Read, an eyewitness, "The General's pen . . . stopped only when a new visitor arrived, or some officer for orders; and then the answer was given with calmness and precision, and Greene resumed his pen."

Years later, when President Washington departed Salisbury during his Southern tour, he crossed the Yadkin at the ford that had played such an important role in his victory over Cornwallis. He breakfasted near the current tour stop while his horses and carriages were being brought across the river. Concerning the area, Washington noted, "The Road between Salisbury & Salem passes over very little good land, and much that is different being a good deal mixed with Pine, but not with sand."

Continue north on Old Salisbury Road for 0.4 mile to N.C. 150. Turn right and drive south for 0.3 mile to I-85. Head north on I-85 for 2.3 miles to the exit for N.C. 47. Turn right on N.C. 47 and follow it for 1.5 miles to Linwood-Southmont Road (S.R. 1396) in the community of Linwood. Turn right, proceed south for 0.6 mile to Jersey Church Road (S.R. 1272), turn left, and drive west for 0.2 mile to Jersey Baptist Church.

Built in 1842, the stately Greek Revival structure is home to a congregation established in 1755, which makes it the oldest in the county. The church stands in the heart of the Jersey settlement, a colonial community of New Jersey immigrants that began to take root here in the 1750s. From the Heights of Gowerie just across the Yadkin, British soldiers had a sweeping view of this riverside community on February 3, 1781, as they looked on in dismay after Greene's miraculous escape. The adjacent cemetery contains the graves of many of the settlers who lived here in colonial and Revolutionary War times.

Two men who were prominent players in the birth and growth of Jersey Baptist Church also made a name for themselves in the Revolution.

One of them was the Reverend John Gano (1727–1804), who arrived in North Carolina as a youthful Baptist missionary in 1754. Two years later, he became the minister of the Jersey congregation. Gano purchased a farm in the area. He owned it for many years thereafter, even though he left North Carolina around 1759 to become minister of First Baptist Church in New York City, a post he held for twenty-eight years.

It was during the Revolution that Gano achieved his greatest fame. One of Washington's chaplains and personal friends, Gano was serving with the general's forces at Valley Forge. He had just completed delivering a discourse on baptism when the general walked up to him and said, "I am thoroughly convinced that baptism is a burial and a resurrection, and I ask baptism at your hands. I do not expect to change my church, my family belongs to the Episcopal Church, and I wish to submit to everything that I am satisfied Christ requires at my hands."

Gano complied with the request, baptizing his commander near Valley Forge in the presence of forty witnesses. Washington urged that the baptism remain private and not be publicized.

Captain Benjamin Merrill was the other member of Jersey Baptist Church who came to prominence during the Revolutionary War era, but for quite different reasons.

In 1771, he and some other members of the church took an active role in the rebellion of the Regulators. The commander of three hundred local men, Merrill drew the ire of Governor Tryon when he was captured in the aftermath of the Battle of Alamance. At Merrill's trial for treason, which began in Hillsborough on May 30, Tryon refused to grant Merrill a pardon after he was convicted. Accordingly, Chief Justice Martin Howard handed down a grisly death warrant: "I must now close my afflicting duty by pronouncing upon you the awful sentence of the law, which is, that you, Benjamin Merrill, be carried to the place from whence you came, that you be drawn from thence to the place of execution, where you are to be hanged by the neck, that your bowels be taken out and burnt before your face; your head be cut off, your body be divided into four quarters, and this be at his Majesty's disposal; and the Lord have mercy on your soul." (For more on the trials of the Regulators, see The Regulator Tour.)

Retrace your route to I-85. Proceed north on I-85 for 10.1 miles to the exit for N.C. 109. Drive north on N.C. 109 for 7.3 miles to the junction with North Old Greensboro Road/Lexington Avenue. Turn right, travel northeast for 2.2 miles to Abbotts Creek Church Road (S.R. 1743), turn left, and go 0.5 mile to the crossing of Abbotts Creek at Willow Creek Country Club.

In its golf-course setting here, the waterway gives little hint of its history and size. Abbotts Creek rises just north of the current tour stop and flows diagonally through Davidson County until it widens dramatically before emptying into the Yadkin several miles south of Trading Ford.

Both Nathanael Greene and Charles Cornwallis visited Abbotts Creek during their passage through the area in the winter of 1781. In a desperate measure designed to lighten his army in its chase of the Americans, Cornwallis ordered a barrel filled with gold and silver coins to be lowered into the creek. Events prevented Cornwallis and his soldiers from returning (see The Pyrrhic Victory Tour). As far as anyone knows, the treasure has never been found. Stories of supernatural phenomena associated with the lost treasure have been popular in this area for years.

Continue north on Abbotts Creek Church Road for 2.3 miles, where you'll see a historic Baptist church on each side of the road. Park at the larger of the two churches, located on the left. A stone marker near the parking lot, erected by the D.A.R., marks a campsite of General Nathanael Greene.

After crossing the Yadkin, Greene rested his fatigued army for several days at Abbotts Creek Meeting House and made his headquarters at the home of a noted local Tory, Colonel Spurgeon, which stood about a mile away. Greene did not find the master of the house, but Mary Spurgeon, as strong a Whig as her husband was a Tory, warmly greeted the Quaker general and offered him hospitality.

During his sojourn along Abbotts Creek, Greene was intent on determining whether Cornwallis was still in Salisbury or was moving upriver in search of a point where his army could cross. He asked his hostess if she knew of a scout who was both loyal to the American cause and knowledgeable of the river. Greene hoped such a person might provide the necessary intelligence.

Without hesitation, Mrs. Spurgeon volunteered her teenage son, John. The boy was put upon the general's own horse and given these instructions: he must ride to Trading Ford, and if the British were not there, he must ride upriver in an attempt to find them.

John Spurgeon followed Greene's orders explicitly and returned to report no sighting of the enemy. His concern growing, Greene ordered the young scout to ride once again, this time as far north as Shallow Ford. After a 30-mile ride to that destination, Spurgeon watched as the British effected their crossing. He dashed back to Greene, who promptly put his army on the march to the site of the nearby city that now bears his name.

Retrace your route to the junction of Old Greensboro Road and N.C. 109. Turn left and proceed 0.1 mile south on N.C. 109. Turn right where the route once again becomes Old Greensboro Road. It is 5.4 miles to Yokley Road. Turn right, proceed west across Tom-A-Lex Lake (a reservoir formed from Abbotts Creek) for 1.9 miles to Ridge Road, turn left, and drive south for 3.1 miles to City Lake Road. Turn right, travel west for 0.3 mile to Pilgrim Church Road (S.R. 1843), turn left, and go 0.4 mile to Pilgrim United Church of Christ.

The modern church complex, erected in 1972, belies the age of this congregation, which was organized in 1757. Weathered gravestones in the adjacent cemetery mark the final resting places of a number of men and women of the Revolutionary War era. Without question, the most fascinating story is told by the large obelisk erected in 1896 by the D.A.R. as a memorial to two of the church's earliest members, who died as martyrs in the final stages of the war.

During the fight for independence, Valentin Leonhardt and Wooldrich Fritz were neighbors in the rolling countryside along Leonard's Creek, just north of what is now Lexington. Leonhardt, a tailor and farmer, owned a substantial tract of land adjacent to the church. He and his friend Fritz were spurred to action by the fiery sermons of the Reverend Samuel Suther, who used his pulpit to espouse the proposition that taxation without representation was wrong. Both men enlisted in the Patriot army, Leonhardt at age fifty-five. All of his sons followed suit.

Fritz and Leonhardt fought side by side in their last battle at nearby Guilford Courthouse on March 15, 1781. Following the bloody combat there, they returned home.

As the war neared its conclusion over the next six months, there remained a large measure of animosity between Tories and Whigs in the area. Many of the two friends' neighbors were Germans who had pledged their allegiance to the Crown. Some of these Tory neighbors were bent on revenge.

On the evening of November 2, 1781, two weeks after Cornwallis had surrendered at Yorktown, Leonhardt was resting peacefully at home after a hard day's work in the fields when a gunshot disturbed the twilight stillness. The bullet, fired from a Tory gun, felled him. His attackers fled, believing he was dead. Though the wound ultimately proved fatal, Leonhardt lingered in misery for eleven days.

Monument at the graves of Valentin Leonhardt and Wooldrich Fritz

That same night, another Loyalist band paid Fritz a similar visit, the only difference being that Fritz died immediately.

When Leonhardt expired, his body was laid to rest beside that of his fallen comrade. The original stones at both graves bear similar messages: "Lo, here doth lifeless Wooldrich lie, Cut off by murder's cruelty" and "Beneath this stone doth now remain, An ancient man by murder slain."

The following words are inscribed on the common monument, erected on July 4, 1896: "The heroes buried in this spot were cruelly assassinated in their own homes by Tories near the close of the Revolutionary War. They were Patriots and bravely fought for American independence."

But even death could not separate the two friends, neighbors, and Patriots. Two of their descendants are now married to each other—Mr. and Mrs. Bob Timberlake. The mingled blood of Valentin Leonhardt and Wooldrich Fritz now flows in the children of the famed North Carolina artist and his wife.

A marker located near the Leonhardt/Fritz obelisk pays homage to the Revolutionary War soldiers buried here in unmarked graves.

Follow Pilgrim Church Road for 0.7 mile to Hill-Everhart Road. Turn left, go 0.9 mile to Clearview Street, turn right, and drive 0.1 mile to U.S. 29/U.S. 70/I-85 Business. Follow U.S. 29/U.S. 70 south for 2.1 miles to the intersection of Main and Center Streets in the heart of Lexington, the seat of Davidson County.

On the southern corner of the town square stands the former Davidson County Courthouse, constructed in 1858. This beautiful building now houses the Davidson County Museum, which offers displays and exhibits on the history of the area.

Just across Center Street from the museum is the portion of the town square devoted to the area's Revolutionary War history. Three markers are located here, one of which commemorates the naming of Lexington. Both city and county have names born of the Revolution.

Lexington earned its name when it was nothing but a small village and fort located on the post road. According to tradition, a lone rider galloped into the settlement in late April 1775 with news of the Battle of Lexington. Citizens decided then and there to name the place Fort Lexington in honor of that early battle in the fight for independence.

The county was so named for General William Lee Davidson when it was formed in 1822. In fact, it was the second county named for the heroic officer. However, the first Davidson County—located in the western part of the state—was lost to Tennessee. It is now the site of Nashville, the Volunteer State's capital.

Benjamin Merrill, the martyr of the Regulators, is memorialized by the second marker on the town square. The third monument is a tablet unveiled on December 1, 1919, in honor of General Nathanael Greene and

Lexington's favorite son, Daniel Boone.

Follow West Center Street for 1.2 miles to U.S. 64 (Mocksville Road). Go west on U.S. 64 for 6.8 miles to the Davie County line at the Yadkin River. Created from Rowan in 1836, Davie County was named for Revolutionary War hero William Richardson Davie (1756–1820).

Continue west for 1.4 miles to S.R. 1812 (Peter Hairston Road). Here stands a state historical marker for Cooleemee Plantation, which is located a mile south of the junction.

Now comprising nineteen hundred acres, this magnificent riverside plantation was once owned by Peter Hairston (pronounced Harston), a veteran of the Revolutionary and Creek Wars. A native of Virginia, Hairston (1752–1832) saw Revolutionary War action in the Cherokee campaign, the first Battle of Shallow Ford, and the Battle of Guilford Courthouse. When Hairston acquired acreage here in 1817, he named it Cooleemee.

In 1997, through the auspices of the Land Trust for Central North Carolina, the Hairston family executed a conservation agreement that will both allow the family to live on and maintain the plantation and give the public access to 2.5 miles of spectacular scenery on the Yadkin.

Continue west on U.S. 64 for 8.1 miles to U.S. 158 at Mocksville, the seat of Davie County. Turn right on U.S. 158 (which becomes Main Street) and proceed 0.2 mile to the county courthouse, located on the right. When the American Revolution began, the small village here was known as Mock's Old Field. It was named for Andrew Mock, who owned a large portion of the land upon which the town was built.

In February 1781, Cornwallis approached from the southwest and marched his army through the village on a route that followed the path of what is now North Main Street.

Andrew Mock was one of 160 area residents hauled into court in 1783 "to show cause why their estates should not be confiscated" as a result of their allegiance to the Crown.

Continue north on U.S. 158 for 2 miles to Elisha Creek. Located nearby on the northern side of this 5-mile-long creek is "the Cornwallis Spring," so named because the British commander paused there to rest.

It is 2.2 miles farther on U.S. 158 to Dutchman Creek. Cornwallis crossed this waterway just east of here on his march north in February 1781.

Approximately 0.5 mile north of Dutchman Creek, U.S. 158 junctions with S.R. 1410. Turn left and drive north on S.R. 1410 for 3.7 miles to where the road crosses Cedar Creek. Two large piles of stones on the creek's northeastern bank are thought to be the graves of a pair of Cornwallis's Hessian soldiers who died during his march.

While passing through this area, Cornwallis called on Jonathan Hunt, an aged Patriot who lived on Cedar Creek. As Hunt's son, Daniel, put it, Cornwallis "killed and destroyed all the property . . . except the dwelling house."

Continue on S.R. 1410 for 0.4 mile. On the left side of the road, you'll notice a tablet honoring Nathaniel Brock and his wife, Sarah. During the Revolution, Nathaniel Brock fought with Patriot forces in Virginia. After the war, the family moved to the Davie County area, where Nathaniel studied theology. He remained until his death in 1818.

It is another 0.5 mile on S.R. 1410 to N.C. 801 in the village of Farmington. On the left side of the intersection is a rock marker with bronze plaques. It commemorates Cornwallis's march through the area in February 1781 en route to his crossing of the Yadkin.

Drive north on S.R. 1410 for 2.1 miles to the Yadkin County line, where the road becomes S.R. 1716. Follow S.R. 1716 north for 2.6 miles to Huntsville. Located just west of the Yadkin, the town was inhabited long before it was chartered in 1792. Many longtime residents know tales of the many artifacts recovered for years after the two Revolutionary War battles at nearby Shallow Ford.

In Huntsville, turn right onto S.R. 1001 and drive 1.1 miles to the Yadkin. Before you reach the bridge, turn right onto the unpaved road leading to the river at the Bob Pate Memorial Access Area. Here, a shaded riverside path affords a spectacular view of the historic waterway. Gaze south. You are looking at Shallow Ford, the site where Cornwallis crossed the Yadkin. Two significant skirmishes were fought here.

On October 14, 1780, Colonel Gideon Wright and 300 Tories attempted to cross the river here on their march west, only to run into 160 North Carolina and Virginia Patriots. In the grim conflict that ensued, the outnumbered Patriots carried the day—and mercilessly clubbed wounded enemy soldiers to death after their comrades had fled.

Among the soldiers fighting for the American cause on that occasion was Colonel Joseph Williams, who lived at Shallow Ford. Williams produced four distinguished sons: Robert served as North Carolina's adjutant general during the Revolution and as a member of Congress from 1797 to 1803; Thomas was the chancellor of Tennessee in the 1850s; his twin brother, Lewis, served continuously in Congress from 1814 until his death in 1842; and John fought heroically under Andrew Jackson against the Creek Indians.

The second fight at Shallow Ford occurred on February 8, 1781, when Cornwallis finally crossed the Yadkin and encountered stiff resistance from a "greeting party" commanded by Joseph Graham.

A British officer killed during the skirmish was buried in Huntsville. A monument was subsequently erected at his grave.

The tour ends here, at the historic Shallow Ford.

The Pyrrhic Victory Tour

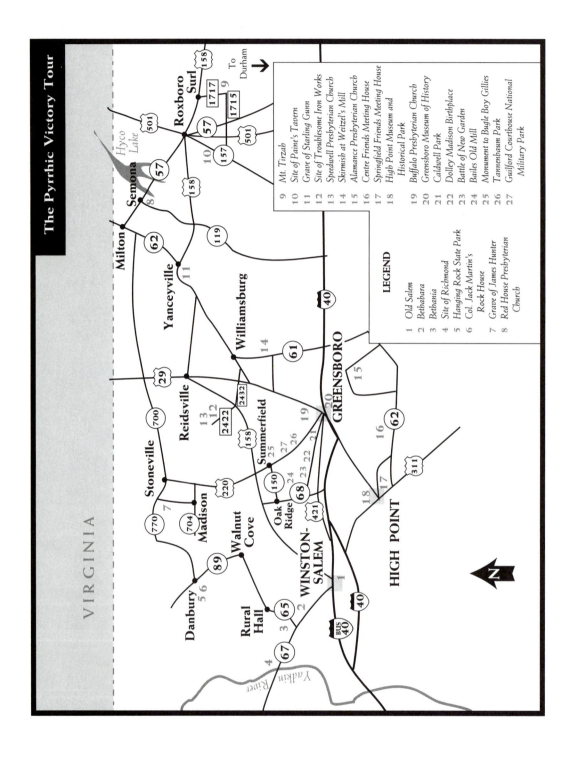

VIRGINIA

Danbury
5 6

Rural
Hall

67
4

Yadkin River

65 3
2
67

WINSTON-
SALEM
1

BUS
40

40

89
Walnut
Cove

704 Madison
770 7
220

Stoneville
700

Reidsville
13 12
2432
2422
158
Summerfield
25 27 26 21
150 24 23 22 19
68
421
Oak
Ridge

HIGH POINT

18 17
311

16 62

GREENSBORO
20

15

61 14

Williamsburg
29
11

Yanceyville

62

Milton

119

158

Semona
57
8

Hyco
Lake

501

57
10
157
501

Roxboro
Surl
158

1717 9
1715
57

To
Durham →

N

LEGEND

1   Old Salem
2   Bethabara
3   Bethania
4   Site of Richmond
5   Hanging Rock State Park
6   Col. Jack Martin's
       Rock House
7   Grave of James Hunter
8   Red House Presbyterian
       Church
9   Mt. Tirzab
10   Site of Paine's Tavern
11   Grave of Starling Gunn
12   Site of Troublesome Iron Works
13   Speedwell Presbyterian Church
14   Skirmish at Weitzel's Mill
15   Alamance Presbyterian Church
16   Centre Friends Meeting House
17   Springfield Friends Meeting House
18   High Point Museum and
       Historical Park
19   Buffalo Presbyterian Church
20   Greensboro Museum of History
21   Caldwell Park
22   Dolley Madison Birthplace
23   Battle of New Garden
24   Bailes Old Mill
25   Monument to Bugle Boy Gillies
26   Tannenbaum Park
27   Guilford Courthouse National
       Military Park

The Pyrrhic Victory Tour

This tour begins at Winston-Salem in Forsyth County and makes its way through Stokes, Rockingham, Caswell, and Person Counties before ending at Greensboro in Guilford County. Among the highlights are Old Salem, Bethabara, Bethania, "Colonel Jack" Martin's Rock House, the grave of Dr. Hugh McAden, the story of the race to the Dan, Troublesome Creek, Speedwell Presbyterian Church, the Battle of Weitzel's Mill, Alamance Presbyterian Church, Springfield Friends Meeting House, Buffalo Presbyterian Church, the Greensboro Museum of History, Caldwell Park, the Battle of New Garden, the story of James Gillies, Tannenbaum Park, and Guilford Courthouse National Military Park.

Total mileage: approximately 418 miles.

This tour traverses a six-county area in the northern Piedmont where the high drama of the Revolutionary War in North Carolina reached its climax in March 1781.

After his failure to catch and destroy the American army at the Catawba and the Yadkin during the first week of February 1781, Cornwallis was determined to overtake Nathanael Greene at the Dan River near the Virginia line. Once again, however, Greene was able to elude his British pursuers.

By mid-February, the Americans had taken up refuge in Virginia. Upon learning that Greene's forces had left North Carolina, Cornwallis decided to temporarily halt his tedious and costly chase.

Over the next month, the two adversaries jockeyed for position.

Greene, unperturbed by the criticism he had received for abandoning North Carolina without a fight, began to lay the groundwork for a showdown with Cornwallis. Unwilling to rashly fling his army into a fight with the British, "the Fighting Quaker" chose to do battle on his own terms. By February 18, the first wave of his American forces made its way back into North Carolina in anticipation of the confrontation.

Meanwhile, Cornwallis chose to rest his fatigued army. But like Greene, he knew that the denouement in North Carolina must come soon. Otherwise, attrition would deplete his army to the point that it would no longer hold the upper hand.

By mid-March, the stage was set: both commanders were ready to fight for control of North Carolina. On the bitterly cold March 15, the two armies clashed at a small village called Guilford Courthouse in one of the most pivotal battles of the war. Though the British won, their victory was costly. In time, it led to their ultimate surrender and defeat. A reflective Cornwallis later conceded, "Our victory at Guilford may have cost us the campaign."

The tour begins at the junction of South Main Street and Old Salem Road in Winston-Salem, the seat of Forsyth County. Follow Old Salem Road for 0.2 mile to the reception center at Old Salem. Information about the pre-Revolutionary War village and about tours of its buildings is available inside the center.

Established in 1766 by the Moravians—European Protestants who came to America in search of religious freedom as early as 1734—Old Salem was a well-established village at the outbreak of the Revolution. From the onset of the fight, its inhabitants found themselves in an awkward and vulnerable position. Although the Moravians had actively participated in the colonial wars against the Indians, they were pacifists and made every attempt to remain neutral during the fight against Great Britain.

In 1775, when patriotic fervor was sweeping the colony, the Moravians of Wachovia (as the 98,985-acre tract owned by the denomination in North Carolina was known) proclaimed that they wished "to remain true to the King" and that they "desired all good for the Province of North Carolina." Over the half-dozen years that followed, their quest for neutrality was almost constantly challenged.

Thanks to an extensive restoration project in the twentieth century, visitors can see much of the village visited by Greene, Cornwallis, Washington, and other notables of the Revolutionary War. Although the once-isolated village was long ago swallowed by the modern city of Winston-Salem, Old Salem retains much of its historic charm and integrity in the shadow of the city's skyscrapers. More than sixty buildings from the eighteenth and early nineteenth centuries have been restored or reconstructed. Thirteen of them are open to the public.

To see the village's Revolutionary War sites, leave your car at the reception center and proceed east on Academy Street for one block to Main Street. Although the ancient streets of Old Salem are open to vehicular traffic, a tour is best enjoyed on foot.

At the southwestern corner of the intersection stands the massive timber-and-brick Single Brothers House, built around 1769. Governor Tryon paid a visit to this house after his expedition against the Regulators in 1771.

Turn right on Main Street and proceed south to West Street. At the northwestern corner stands the store known as T. Bagge: Merchant. Traugott Bagge, the chief spokesman for the Moravians during the Revolutionary War, constructed this store around 1775. Reluctantly, he became a supplier for both armies when they came calling at his place of business. Because the Moravians produced most of their own goods, the store was well stocked during the war. Suspicious Patriots wrongfully suggested that the Moravians got their supplies through trade with the British. Unsuccessful attempts to confiscate the Moravians' lands followed.

Residents of the village suffered other wartime indignities. Following the Battle of Kings Mountain, Patriots used Old Salem as a prison for captured Tories. When Cornwallis began his invasion of North Carolina, American forces used the village as a supply depot and a hospital for ailing Continental soldiers. And in the wake of the passage of Count Casimir Pulaski's legion, forty-three local citizens came down with smallpox.

It was on February 10, 1781, that Cornwallis marched his army to Old Salem. The dragoons reached the village at ten o'clock that morning. By late afternoon, the entire force was on hand. Cornwallis, several officers, and Royal Governor Josiah Martin (who had accompanied the British commander on his second invasion of North Carolina) spent over an hour with Mr. Bagge at the current tour stop.

Cornwallis's departure brought additional misery to the villagers. Some of his undisciplined soldiers and camp followers plundered Old Salem and the other nearby Moravian villages. Food—including eggs pilfered from beneath a sitting goose—stores, and furnishings were hauled away in large quantities.

Continue south to the Salem Tavern (otherwise known as the Tavern Museum), located in the middle of the block between West and Walnut Streets; note that the brick Salem Tavern stands next to the yellow frame Old Salem Tavern (otherwise known as the Tavern Restaurant). The building now housing the Tavern Museum was constructed around 1784 on the foundation of a Revolutionary War–era tavern that was claimed by fire. An upstairs bedroom in the northeastern corner displays a copy of a letter from the most famous man to sleep here. George Washington arrived in Salem on May 31, 1791, intent upon spending one night in the village. Yet when he learned that Governor Alexander Martin, a wartime comrade, was on his way to town, he stayed another day.

From the time of their arrival in America, the Moravians have been meticulous record keepers. Their recorded observations about the Revolutionary War have been invaluable to historians. About Washington's arrival in Salem, the Moravians recorded, "As he descended from the coach, he greeted those who stood around in a friendly manner showing his good will especially to the children who were there. Then he talked on various matters with several Brethren who had accompanied him to the room which had been prepared for him."

In turn, Washington noted this in his diary: "Salem is a small but neat village, & like all the rest of the Moravian settlements, is governed by an excellent police—having within itself all kinds of artisans. The number of Soules does not exceed 200."

The D.A.R. has placed memorial plaques for Washington's visit on the exterior and interior of the old tavern.

Return to the intersection of Main and Academy Streets. Cross to the other side of Main to visit Salem Square.

This square has always been the center of public activity in the village. In fact, some historians contend that the Fourth of July celebration held here in 1783 was the first such commemoration by legislative enactment in the United States.

When the news that Great Britain had officially recognized the independence of the former colonies reached North Carolina on April 19, 1783, the general assembly advocated the observance of the Fourth of July "as a day of Solemn Thanksgiving" and requested that Governor Alexander Martin issue an appropriate proclamation. Martin's edict, issued from his plantation in nearby Rockingham County on June 18, 1783, called on North Carolinians to "set apart the said Day from bodily labour, and employ the same in devout and religious exercises."

It is believed that the Moravians were the only North Carolinians to act upon the proclamation. Their day-long program on July 4, 1783, included music and church services and concluded with a torch-lit procession through the village streets. A plaque on the square proclaims that these activities constituted "the first official 4th of July celebration in the United States."

The longstanding tradition continues today. Religious services, military reenactments, and a torch-lit procession are featured at Old Salem's annual Fourth of July celebration.

Proceed to the Wachovia Museum (otherwise known as the Boys School), located at the northeastern corner of Main and Academy. This expansive, multistory brick building dates from around 1794. Inside is a wide variety of exhibits and artifacts that chronicle the Moravian experience at Wachovia. One room on the first floor is devoted to a display of the unique water system that served the village in the eighteenth century. President Washington is said to have been fascinated by the system of log pipes through which Salem's buildings received fresh water. A special exhibit on the second floor of the museum relates the Moravians' struggles during the Revolutionary War.

Return to your car at the reception center to resume the driving tour. Go six blocks west on Academy to Broad Street. Turn right and proceed north as Broad becomes West End Boulevard after approximately 1.1 miles. Follow West End to its junction with Reynolda Road (N.C 67). Turn left and proceed north for 4.9 miles to Bethabara Park Boulevard. Turn right and drive 1.1 miles to the entrance to Bethabara Park at S.R. 3800. Turn left and park at the visitor center.

The oldest Moravian settlement in North Carolina, Bethabara was established by fifteen Moravians from Pennsylvania on November 17, 1753. Over the next decade, hundreds of other Moravians followed, and buildings sprang up in the town.

During the French and Indian War, the settlement's two forts were protecting residents and serving as supply depots for the Catawba and Cherokee Indian allies of the British. Governor William Tryon visited the village in 1767.

By 1772, the new settlement at Salem was well under way. Many of Bethabara residents moved there by the time the colonies declared their independence. Some buildings were taken down and moved by their owners. Others were allowed to deteriorate.

During the war, American forces held enemy prisoners at Bethabara. Cornwallis passed through in pursuit of Greene in February 1781.

Across the road from the visitor center are the stone foundations and cellars of structures that stood here during the Revolution. Near these ruins is the reconstructed colonial fort. The oldest buildings in the village are the Potter's House (1782) and the Gemeinhaus (1788). Located near the visitor center, God's Acre is the first Moravian cemetery in North Carolina. Its oldest grave is dated 1758.

The park is administered by the city of Winston-Salem. Admission is free. Guided tours of the buildings begin at the visitor center.

Return to the junction of Bethabara Park Boulevard and N.C. 67. Turn right, drive 1.6 miles to Bethania Road (S.R. 1688), turn right again, and proceed 1.3 miles to N.C. 65 (Main Street) in Bethania.

Formerly known as New Town (in contrast to Bethabara, which was called Old Town), Bethania is the second-oldest Moravian settlement in North Carolina. Founded in 1759, it counted ninety residents at the time of the Revolution.

Several structures survive from that era. To see them, turn right on N.C. 65 and drive north for 0.1 mile to Bethania Moravian Church, located on the right. Although the existing brick edifice was constructed in 1809, the church was organized a half-century earlier.

Interred in the graveyard at the rear of the church is Lieutenant George Hauser II, a native of Bethania. A soldier in the American army, Hauser saw action at Kings Mountain and was held prisoner at Bethania when Cornwallis invaded the town in 1781.

Despite the neutral stance taken by the Wachovia settlements during the war, many Moravian men shared the patriotic fervor of Lieutenant Hauser. In 1777, Traugott Bagge recorded that "many in Bethabara and most of those in Bethania embraced the cause of Liberty, and from the latter village many residents, including older Brethren, went to Muster and Drill, though for no better reason than to avoid trouble, and to find out what to do when things became too serious."

Just across N.C. 65 from the church is the two-story Jacob Loesch House, built around 1790. Born in Bethabara, Loesch (1760–1821) moved to Pennsylvania with his family when he was nine years old. In 1781, at the time the Revolutionary War brought both armies to North Carolina's Moravian settlements, Loesch returned to Wachovia. A gunsmith by trade, he was dissuaded by the Brethren from practicing his craft for fear that soldiers would be attracted to Bethania and the other villages.

Located adjacent to the Jacob Loesch House at the junction of Main Street and Jan Hus Lane is the Bethania Historic Preservation Area, a small park dedicated to the history of the village.

Governor William Tryon visited Bethania on two occasions. He toured Wachovia in 1767. Four years later, just after his victory at the Battle of Alamance, Tryon camped his victorious army in an open field on the road between Bethania and Bethabara. That June 6, his troops assembled in battle formation with "musicians leading and playing on the trombones and violins" and proceeded to reenact their recent battle by "firing guns and cannons until everything trembled," according to one contemporary account.

Continue north on N.C. 65 for 0.1 mile to Loesch Lane. On the left side of the road stands the two-story John Loesch House, built around 1775. On the opposite side of the street is the Cornwallis House. Constructed in 1770, the two-story whitewashed dwelling played host to the British commander on the night of February 9, 1781.

Upon his arrival in Bethania, Cornwallis demanded supplies for his troops. To ensure compliance, he seized the Reverend John Jacob Ernst as a hostage. More than sixty head of cattle were slaughtered, and all the available sheep and fowl were taken by the invaders.

In the course of looting the village's houses, one British soldier carried away a pot of vegetables cooking in a fireplace, over the vehement protests of the Moravian housewife. Incensed by the Redcoat's callous behavior, the woman followed the British army from Bethania to Salem, where she demanded an audience with Cornwallis. She informed the general that the soldier was welcome to the food, but that she wanted her pot. The pot was returned and is now part of the collection of the Wachovia Museum at Old Salem.

Retrace your route to N.C. 67. Turn right and proceed northwest for 4.8 miles to the historical marker for the site of Richmond Courthouse.

From 1774 to 1789, Richmond, a former village located a mile northeast of the current tour stop, served as the seat of Surry County. Now part of Forsyth County, the area bears no reminders of its prominent position during the Revolutionary War.

On October 8, 1780, a significant skirmish took place at Richmond. Most local Patriots had hurried toward Charlotte to help resist the British advance into North Carolina. In their absence, Gideon Wright (1726–82), a leading Loyalist on whose land the original Surry County courthouse stood from 1771 to 1774, commanded a force of five hundred men in an attack on Richmond. After a heated fight that produced several fatalities, Wright moved his army to Bethabara. Less than a week later, he commanded the Loyalist forces at the Battle of Shallow Ford.

Twenty-nine-year-old Andrew Jackson was admitted to the bar at Richmond on November 13, 1787.

In 1830, the town earned a dubious distinction: it became the only town in North Carolina history to be completely destroyed by a cyclone.

If you care for a brief, relaxing side trip, continue on N.C. 67 for 0.2 mile to the Yadkin River. On the Yadkin County side of the river, turn right into the Yadkin River Access Area. A shaded picnic area here offers a scenic view of the river on which much Revolutionary War history was written.

Retrace N.C. 67 back toward Bethania. Turn left on N.C. 65 and follow it for 2.1 miles as it passes through the village. At the Cornwallis House, the route veers sharply to the right. Continue north on N.C. 65 for 6.8 miles to the Stokes County line. Formed in 1789 from Surry County, Stokes took its name from Revolutionary War hero and statesman John Stokes (1756–90).

Almost as soon as you enter Stokes County, you will find yourself in the sleepy, historic village of Germanton.

As Nathanael Greene marched his haggard army through this area in February 1781, some of his soldiers were taken by the beauty of the natural surroundings. One such soldier was Ludwig Bitting, a native of Germany who had settled in Germantown, Pennsylvania, before the war. So impressed was Bitting that he decided to settle here after the war, and Germanton was thus born. The town was incorporated in 1790 and served as the seat of Stokes County from 1789 to 1849.

Colonel Joseph Winston (1746–1814) was the man for whom the town of Winston was named; Winston subsequently merged with the Moravian village of Salem to form Winston-Salem. Born in Virginia, Joseph Winston was a first cousin of Patrick Henry. The two spent much of their boyhoods together. As a teenager, Winston served in the French and Indian War. He later moved to the Stokes County area and established a 1,362-acre plantation near Germanton.

He put his military experience to good use at the Battle of Moores Creek in February 1776, serving as major of the Surry County Militia. Over the next four years, Winston occasionally maintained headquarters at Salem. To the chagrin of the Moravians, he often appropriated their goods for the American cause. Nonetheless, his relationship with the Moravians was amicable, as he did all he could to protect the Wachovia settlements from raiding forces from both sides.

Winston participated in the Battle of Kings Mountain. Less than six months later, he proved one of the American heroes at the Battle of Guilford Courthouse. His Surry County militiamen remained in the fight after Greene's Continentals had retired. Indeed, Winston's men were among the last Americans to leave the field.

The father of twelve children, Winston was once asked why he settled near Germanton. He replied, "It's a squirrel jump from heaven." He died at his plantation there.

Continue on N.C. 65 for 5.1 miles to U.S. 311 at Walnut Cove, where you'll note a state historical marker for Joseph Winston.

Turn left onto U.S. 311, proceed 1.7 miles to N.C. 89, turn left, and drive 1.9 miles northwest to N.C. 8. Continue the route on N.C. 89/N.C. 8 for 3.3 miles to Danbury, the seat of Stokes County. Continue west on N.C. 89 for another 2.2 miles to S.R. 1001, turn left, and proceed 1.5 miles to S.R. 2015 at the entrance to Hanging Rock State Park. Turn left and follow the park road to the visitor center. The parking lot and the observation deck at the center provide panoramic views of Hanging Rock and Moore's Knob.

This mountainous region knew its share of bloodshed during the Revolution. Throughout the war, Tories operating out of the caves and wilderness of what is now the state park raided nearby settlers and farmers.

Ambitious hikers and climbers may follow trails to several caves used by the Loyalists. Of particular interest is Tory's Den and Falls. Located almost 4 miles from the visitor center, the cave is twelve feet high, ten feet wide, and twenty-five feet deep. Information about the trails is available at the visitor center.

Retrace your route to S.R. 1001. Turn left and go west for 2.6 miles to S.R. 1484. Turn right, drive north for 2.1 miles to N.C. 268, turn left, and proceed 5.4 miles to S.R. 1187 (Rock House Road). Turn left, drive south for 0.6 mile to S.R. 1186, and turn right. You'll see one of the most fascinating relics of the Revolutionary War era almost immediately after the turn.

The massive structure known as the Rock House was gutted by fire in 1890. Nonetheless, the rock walls of this eighteenth-century dwelling stand as a monument to the Patriot who lived here.

John Martin (1756–1822), or "Colonel Jack," as he was known, moved to Surry (now Stokes) County from his native Virginia prior to the Revolution. His distinguished Norman ancestry included William the Conqueror's admiral.

In the 1770s, Martin began building a great rock house on an eight-thousand-acre grant from the Crown. The four-story home was constructed of native stone. Its three-foot-thick outer walls were plastered with white stucco. The flagstone floors were set in cement.

Colonel Jack Martin's Rock House

Martin used the house as a fortress against marauding Indians and vindictive Tories. On numerous occasions, neighbors made their way here for safety. During the war, the basement and the first floor were used as living quarters, while the upper floors served as a fortress.

Following the war, Colonel Jack married Nancy Shipp. The newlyweds promptly set about finishing and furnishing the immense structure. Mrs. Martin was known as a gracious hostess, and the parties held at the Rock House were lavish occasions. The fireplace in the basement kitchen was of such size that an entire ox could be roasted at one time. Mrs. Martin is said to have had the finest sets of china and silverware in the state.

Legend has it that quarrelsome Tories kidnapped the Martins' daughter years after the war. Using his spyglass from a window of the Rock House, Colonel Jack spotted a speck of color at Tory's Den. It was his daughter, who had been clever enough to wave her petticoat to attract attention. Her father promptly formed a posse and effected her rescue.

Following the devastating fire, the Rock House suffered additional damage from storms in 1897 and 1924. Those storms claimed the roof and one of the exterior walls. By the time the nation was preparing for its bicentennial celebration, the remnants of the Rock House were covered in vines and hastening to ruin. In 1975, the Stokes County Historical Society acquired the 5.5-acres upon which the structure is located. Since that time, the site has been cleaned and the tall walls stabilized through the efforts of students from Wake Forest University and others.

A D.A.R. marker at the site proclaims its importance to the Revolutionary War period.

Follow S.R. 1186 as it circles around to junction again with S.R. 1187. On the eastern side of S.R. 1187 is the grave of Colonel Jack Martin.

Martin was an avowed Patriot from the beginning of the war. As a twenty-year-old, he served as a lieutenant during the expedition against the Cherokees in 1776. For much of the war, he was busy skirmishing with area Tories. A wound he sustained during a scouting expedition prevented him from taking part in the Battle of Kings Mountain, but he recovered in time to participate in the fight at Guilford Courthouse.

Following the war, Martin served Stokes County in the state legislature.

On June 2, 1822, he and Mrs. Martin were taking a walk to survey a portion of their estate. Colonel Jack sat down in a field to rest while his wife proceeded farther. When she returned, her husband was dead.

Retrace your route into Danbury. On the eastern side of town, turn left off N.C. 89 onto S.R. 1652, then go 3.5 miles to S.R. 1674. Turn right and drive north for 6.1 miles to N.C. 770. En route, you will cross Snow Creek.

During the Revolutionary War, James Martin (1742–1834), a militia officer and brother of North Carolina governor Alexander Martin, acquired vast acreage in Stokes County. Much of his land was located here on Snow Creek, a tributary of the Dan River. Following the war, Martin emerged as a pioneer industrialist in North Carolina when he established an ironworks on the creek.

When he was ninety years old, Martin mounted a horse and rode to Germanton, which was then the seat of Stokes County, to apply for his Revolutionary War pension.

Turn right onto N.C. 770 and proceed east. After 4.4 miles, you will enter Rockingham County. Created from Guilford County in 1784, Rockingham was named for Charles Watson-Wentworth (1730–82), the second marquis of Rockingham, who was a strong supporter of American independence. Watson-Wentworth was prime minister when the Stamp Act was repealed.

It is another 0.5 mile to S.R. 1321 (Park Road). Turn right, drive south for 2.9 miles to S.R. 1325 (Beaver Creek Road), and turn left. After 0.6 mile, you will see a cemetery on an embankment on the left side of the road.

Buried in a marked grave at this isolated site is James Hunter (1740–1821). A cousin of Governor Alexander Martin, Hunter moved to North Carolina from Virginia before the war and settled on a tract along Beaver Creek near the current tour stop.

From 1778 to 1782, Hunter represented Guilford County in the general assembly. At the same time, he was a major in the county militia. As the confrontation between Greene and Cornwallis loomed in 1781, Hunter's cousin James Martin summoned the Guilford militiamen to action. Major Hunter played an active role in the subsequent clash at Guilford Courthouse. Tradition maintains that he was the soldier selected to carry the news of the battle to George Washington.

Retrace your route to N.C. 770. Turn right, drive 2.2 miles east to S.R. 1300, turn right again, and go 4.7 miles to N.C. 704 at Madison. Turn left and follow N.C. 704 through downtown for 1.2 miles to the bridge over the Dan River. Continue east for 0.7 mile. On the left side of the road near the intersection with U.S. 220 Bypass is a state historical marker for James Hunter, whose grave you visited earlier. This marker incorrectly identifies Hunter as the leader of the Regulators. Although the commander of the Regulators at the Battle of Alamance was named James Hunter, he was a different person from the soldier buried on Beaver Creek in northwestern Rockingham County.

Continue east on N.C. 704 for 3.2 miles to the state historical marker for Alexander Martin.

Born in New Jersey in 1738, Martin was educated at Princeton. He settled in North Carolina in 1761. Twelve years later, he built his home, Danbury, on a 436-acre grant along the Dan River near the current tour stop.

From the beginning of the Revolution, Martin was an ardent Patriot. When the war of words turned to a war of bullets, the Third Provincial Congress appointed him second lieutenant of the Second North Carolina Regiment. A promotion to colonel soon followed.

During the summer of 1776, Martin marched his troops to South Carolina to aid in the defense of Charleston. Less than a year later, they moved north to assist George Washington.

At the Battle of Germantown, thick fog caused the Continentals to mistake fellow soldiers for enemy troops. In the aftermath of the battle, Martin was charged with cowardice and brought before a court-martial. Although exonerated, he lost his commission.

When the war in the South took a decided turn against the colonies in the spring of 1780, the state legislature created a five-man Board of War. As its president, Martin spearheaded efforts to keep the state's war effort alive.

In 1780, he was elected to the first of three terms in the state senate. In that capacity, he became acting governor when Governor Thomas Burke was captured by Tories in September 1781. (For more information on this incident, see The Regulator Tour, page 410.)

The experience benefited Martin. He was elected governor on April 20, 1782, as the war was winding down. He went on to serve several additional terms, during which he exhibited a conciliatory attitude toward most ex-Tories. It was during Martin's administrations that the permanent state capital was located at Raleigh and the University of North Carolina was chartered.

When he died at Danbury in 1807, his body was laid to rest in a vault on his plantation near the mouth of Jacobs Creek. Less than fifty years later, his grave was claimed by the Dan River.

Return to the intersection of N.C. 704 and U.S. 220 Bypass. South of Madison, U.S. 220 was constructed along Baggage Road, a route cut by Greene's forces for the passage of the American supply train prior to Guilford Courthouse.

Proceed north on U.S. 220; follow the business route when it veers from the bypass. After 7.2 miles, U.S. 220 junctions with N.C. 770 at Stoneville. Turn right, go east for 10.2 miles to N.C. 700, and turn right. It is 14.3 miles to the Caswell County line. Named for Revolutionary War great

Richard Caswell, the county was formed in 1777 from Orange County.

Continue east on N.C. 700 for 3.3 miles to S.R. 1353. Turn right, drive 0.6 mile to S.R. 1360, turn left, head east for 4.9 miles to N.C. 86, and turn right. After 0.2 mile, turn left on N.C. 1503. Proceed east for 2.9 miles to the bridge over a tributary of the Dan. Walter's Mill stood in this vicinity in Revolutionary War times. When President Washington visited Caswell County on June 3, 1791, he spent the night at the home of Whit Gatewood, which stood near the mill.

Continue on S.R. 1503 for 1.7 miles to S.R. 1511. Turn left, drive east for 3.1 miles to S.R. 1523, turn left again, and proceed east for 5.1 miles to N.C. 62. Turn left and go 4.9 miles to N.C. 57 at the town of Milton, located on the banks of the Dan less than 0.5 mile from the Virginia line. By the time the colonies embarked upon the struggle for independence, Milton was an old town, having been settled in 1728. Many of the town's early records were destroyed when Cornwallis and his army passed through in their quest to catch Greene in 1781.

Turn right on N.C. 57 and proceed through the village for 5 miles to N.C. 119. At this intersection stands a state historical marker for Red House Presbyterian Church.

To see the historic church and its cemetery, turn right on N.C. 119 and drive 0.9 mile.

Red House Presbyterian was organized in 1753. Its first regular minister was Dr. Hugh McAden (1720–81), the first Presbyterian missionary in North Carolina. McAden's grave is at the rear of the church. A sizable monument erected in 1913 marks the site.

Born in Pennsylvania and educated at Princeton, McAden arrived in North Carolina in 1755. For the remainder of his life, he served Presbyterian churches in the colony and state. Although he abhorred the Regulator movement, McAden openly supported the cause of independence, as did most other Presbyterian ministers in North Carolina. His death on January 20, 1781, prevented him from seeing the realization of the Patriots' dream.

Two weeks after McAden's body was interred in the churchyard, Cornwallis and his army set up camp at Red House Presbyterian. Tradition maintains that the British commander used the church building as his headquarters. The Redcoats harbored ill feelings toward the Presbyterian clergy because of their encouragement of parishioners in the fight against Great Britain. Frustration from their recent inability to catch Greene only served to fuel the fire. The British torched the library and papers of Dr. McAden at his home near Milton. Not satisfied with this token measure of vengeance, some soldiers chose to desecrate the minister's newly made grave. Disbelieving reports of McAden's death, they opened the grave, removed the corpse, and mutilated the body.

The existing church building, constructed of red brick and granite, is a spectacular sight amid tall hardwoods. Erected in 1913, it is the fourth building on the site. A plaque on the front of the church memorializes Dr. McAden.

Return to the intersection of N.C. 119 and N.C. 57 and turn right. It is 0.3 mile to the Person County line. Formed from Caswell County in 1791, Person took its name from Revolutionary War hero General Thomas Person (1733–1800). (For information on Person, see The Statehood Tour, pages 427–28.)

From the county line, follow N.C. 57 for 6.2 miles over the expansive Hyco Lake Reservoir. Turn left onto S.R. 1340 and drive east for 1.3 miles to the junction with S.R. 1334 and S.R. 1336. Turn left on S.R. 1336, head north for 4.3 miles to S.R. 1322, turn right, and travel east for 7.2 miles to U.S. 501. Turn left and proceed 3.5 miles to the state historical markers for Greene and Cornwallis near the Virginia line.

The Greene marker notes that the American general forded the Dan and entered Virginia northeast of this spot during his retreat from Cornwallis. It was one of the great success stories of the war.

On February 8, Greene's tired army reached Guilford Courthouse, the very place where he would do battle with Cornwallis five weeks later. Greene hoped to confuse the ever-pressing British army by crossing the Dan at the lower fords of the river 10 miles north of the present tour stop, rather than at the upper ferries, as Cornwallis's intelligence supposed. To aid Greene's escape, boats were to be waiting at Boyd's Ferry and Irwin's Ferry.

Greene could spare only a small force to shield his main army from the advancing Redcoats as the Americans marched from the encampment to the river crossing. Colonel Otho Holland Williams, Lieutenant Colonel Lighthorse Harry Lee, and seven hundred elite troops were assigned the awesome responsibility.

About that same time, Cornwallis crossed the Yadkin and quickened his pace in pursuit of Greene. At times during the race to the Dan, the British vanguard was within a musket shot of Williams and Lee.

The forced march to the Dan by the struggling American army was rendered even more difficult by the February cold and the incessant rain and mud. Poorly clothed officers and men had little to protect them from the elements. Many were without shoes, and the blood from their feet literally marked the route of their march, which covered as much as 30 miles per day.

At one point during the retreat, General Greene and John Rutledge, the exiled South Carolina governor, found shelter in an abandoned shack. In desperate need of sleep, they jumped into a dilapidated bed and soon fell asleep. Their slumber was rudely ended when a hog crawled into their bed in search of warmth.

By the night of February 13, the weary Americans longed to pause for rest, but Cornwallis was relentless. As Lieutenant Colonel Lee put it, "The British general was so eager to fall on Greene whom he believed within his grasp, that pursuit was not intermitted."

At seven o'clock the following morning, Colonel Williams had all but lost hope that he could stay ahead of the lead elements of Cornwallis's army. In desperation, he sent a message ahead to Greene that it might be necessary for the rear guard to stand and fight. But before that rash action was taken, Lieutenant Colonel Lee reported that the British pursuit had halted temporarily.

By midnight, the race was on again.

Early in the afternoon on February 14, an American courier delivered a dispatch from Greene bearing heartening news for Williams. In it, General Greene informed his rear-guard commander, "The greater part of our wagons are over and the troops are crossing." At five-thirty, Greene sent even better news from Irwin's Ferry: "All our troops are over and the stage is clear. . . . I am ready to receive you and give you a hearty welcome."

With the main body of the Americans over the Dan, Greene had completed one of the greatest retreats in military history. All the available boats were now on the northern shore of the raging river, and the British were forced to end the chase. Greene could now rest his warriors and devise a grand strategy to destroy or at least badly damage the British army.

The other state historical marker notes Cornwallis's position several miles to the west.

When Colonel Williams received Greene's late-afternoon dispatch on February 14, the American rear guard offered up a lusty cheer. The sounds of the celebration were heard by General Charles O'Hara and the lead elements of Cornwallis's army. To them, the triumphant shouts of the Patriots were a baleful noise, for they realized that the Americans had once again escaped.

Turn around and follow U.S. 501 south for 11.9 miles to U.S. 158 in Roxboro, the seat of Person County. Turn left, drive east for 5.8 miles to S.R. 1717 at the crossroads community of Surf, turn right, and proceed south for 4.3 miles to Mount Tirzah, a home built by Colonel Stephen Moore around 1778. The two-story frame dwelling is on a hill on the left side of the road.

From about 1765 to the time he moved to North Carolina, Moore lived at "Moore's Folly," a 1,795-acre farm on the Hudson River that he had inherited from his father. Disenchantment with the Loyalist sentiment exhibited by many New Yorkers in the early stages of the war led Moore to North Carolina.

After living in Granville County for eighteen months, he chose to settle at the current tour stop because it was a place of natural beauty where "axe had never been laid to tree." Mount Tirzah became the centerpiece of a three-thousand-acre estate.

Moore's previous military experience during the French and Indian War led to his appointment as lieutenant colonel of the militia. In the disaster at Camden, South Carolina, in August 1780, he was among the many Americans taken prisoner by the victorious British forces.

Following the war, Moore pressed claims for the war damages sustained by his New York property. "Moore's Folly" had proven one of the most strategic sites of the entire war. George Washington had established his headquarters there in 1779. In fact, Moore's home had provided shelter for Alexander Hamilton and Benedict Arnold as well.

A congressional appropriation in 1780 made it possible for Moore to recoup a portion of his losses. But inaction on his second claim led him to propose the sale of the 1,795-acre tract to the federal government. At the direction of Congress, Secretary of the Treasury Alexander Hamilton completed the purchase in 1790. A dozen years later, "Moore's Folly"—or "West Point on the Hudson," as it was better known—became the site of the United States Military Academy.

Stephen Moore died on December 29, 1799, at Mount Tirzah and is buried in the family cemetery here.

Continue south for 0.3 mile to S.R. 1715. Turn right, drive west for 2.7 miles to N.C. 57, turn right again, and go north for 0.6 mile to S.R. 1131. Turn left, travel west for 4 miles to N.C. 157, turn right, and go 2.3 miles to S.R. 1142 at the community of Payne's Tavern. A historical marker on the left side of the road proclaims that the first courthouse in Person County stood nearby.

At an undetermined date in the eighteenth century, Dr. James Paine, later a major in the American army, built a brick house here large enough to take in visitors. It soon became known as Paine's Tavern or Paine's Ordinary. In February 1781, Cornwallis spent a night at the hostelry.

But local tradition maintains that the tavern had an even greater claim to fame. Some Person County residents claim that Dolley Payne Madison, North Carolina's famous first lady, was born in the tavern in 1768 while her parents were en route from Philadelphia to Mrs. Payne's home in Guilford County, where she had planned to have her baby. Tradition aside, the best evidence indicates that the birth occurred in Greensboro at a stop visited later on this tour.

Proceed north on N.C. 157 for 4.1 miles to U.S. 158 in Roxboro. Turn left. It is 8.1 miles to the Caswell County line. Continue west on U.S. 158 for 12.4 miles to N.C. 62 at Yanceyville, the seat of Caswell County. Proceed west on N.C. 62 for 0.5 mile to West Main Street at the former Caswell County Courthouse. Drive 0.4 mile on West Main to Cemetery Street. Turn left and proceed 0.2 mile to the cemetery at the end of the road.

Interred here in a well-marked grave is Starling Gunn (1764–1852), a native of Nottoway County, Virginia, who settled in Caswell County after the war. According to an inscription on his tombstone, Gunn, a seventeen-year-old private in the American army, "fired the first cannon at York and was an eyewitness to the surrender of Cornwallis." When Gunn died, an

Grave of Starling Gunn, Yanceyville

obituary noted that he "assisted in placing and firing the first gun upon the British at Yorktown."

His grave was originally located in a family cemetery outside Yanceyville. It was moved to the present location in 1950. About the same time, a box of earth from Gunn's grave was dispatched to Yorktown by the D.A.R. in response to a request that each of the original thirteen states send a piece of ground from some point of Revolutionary War history. The soil collected from each of the states was used in the planting of a tree brought from George Washington's grave at Mount Vernon.

Retrace your route to U.S. 158 and follow it west for 8.3 miles to N.C. 150. Turn left. It is 5.4 miles to the Rockingham County line. Continue west on N.C. 150 for 4.8 miles to S.R. 2619 at the village of Williamsburg. Turn left, proceed southeast for 2.1 miles to S.R. 2614, turn right, and go 1.1 miles to where the road merges with S.R. 2620. Follow S.R. 2620 for 0.3 mile to the state historical marker for High Rock Ford at the bridge over the Haw River.

Following his miraculous crossing of the Dan, Nathanael Greene spent fewer than ten days in Virginia. By February 24, 1781, his entire army was back in North Carolina. Two days later, the Americans crossed the Haw at High Rock Ford, located a hundred feet west of the present tour stop. High Rock Ford was the site of Greene's headquarters from February 28 to March 12, just three days before the pivotal battle at Guilford Courthouse.

Retrace your route to N.C. 150 and turn left. It is 1.8 miles to S.R. 2627. Turn right and go 3.2 miles to U.S. 29 Business. Proceed north on U.S. 29 Business for 0.6 mile to S.R. 2432, turn left, drive west for 4.9 miles to U.S. 158, and turn right. Travel west for 0.1 mile to S.R. 2422. A state historical marker here calls attention to the Troublesome Iron Works, which stood nearby during the Revolutionary War.

To reach the site, turn right on S.R. 2422 and drive north for 1.3 miles to the bridge over Troublesome Creek, so named because it was subject to sudden flooding and difficult to ford.

This creek was the site of an eighteenth-century iron mill and a nineteenth-century gristmill. A few ruins near the creek are the only reminders of the enterprises once carried on here. A plaque on an old millstone cited the mill's importance to the Revolution, but even it has been stripped by vandals.

Constructed by William Patrick in 1770, Troublesome Iron Works (also known as Speedwell Furnace) was visited by both armies during the hectic days before and after the Battle of Guilford Courthouse.

While chasing the Americans toward the Dan, Tarleton's green-coated cavalrymen camped briefly here.

After Greene's return to North Carolina in the last week of February 1781, the American commander established a base at Troublesome Iron Works as he prepared for the clash with Cornwallis.

Following Guilford Courthouse, Greene moved his "defeated" army to Troublesome Creek. His warriors recuperated here while engineers set about designing earthworks on the high ground north of the creek in anticipation of another attack by Cornwallis. According to Lighthorse Harry Lee, "General Greene, after reaching Troublesome Creek, arrayed himself again for battle; so persuaded was he that the British general would follow up his blow."

Had the Americans been assaulted here, the breastworks would have offered their marksmen a good field of fire when the enemy attempted to cross the road over the dam above the mill. High bluffs on the left and a millpond on the right offered protection for Greene's flanks.

En route to the residence of Governor Alexander Martin during his Southern tour in 1791, President Washington asked to stop at Troublesome Creek so he might inspect the site that had been so important in Greene's strategy against Cornwallis.

Near the bridge, S.R. 2422 becomes S.R. 2423. Continue north on S.R. 2423 for 0.2 mile to S.R. 2406. Turn left and proceed 0.7 mile to S.R. 2409. Speedwell Presbyterian Church stands nearby.

Organized in 1769, Speedwell is the oldest church in Rockingham County. The original church building, long vanished, hosted both Cornwallis and Greene as they played cat and mouse in February and March 1781. During Cornwallis's visit, some of his officers were quartered at the Polly Scott Inn, a hostelry that stood near the Troublesome Iron Works. Greene used the church as his headquarters during his encampments in the area.

The adjacent church cemetery is one of the oldest—if not *the* oldest—in the county. The British soldiers interred here are believed to have been badly wounded at the Battle of Guilford Courthouse. They died after being attended by Greene's medical staff.

Continue on N.C. 2406 for 2.6 miles to U.S. 29 Business. Proceed south on U.S. 29 Business for 5.5 miles to U.S. 29 Bypass. Go south on the bypass. It is 1.4 miles to the Guilford County line. Formed in 1771 from Rowan and Orange Counties, Guilford took its name from Francis North, first earl of Guilford (1704–90), a member of Parliament and a close friend of King George III.

From the county line, it is approximately 7 miles to a state historical marker for Weitzel's Mill; the marker is on the left side of the highway 0.5 mile south of S.R. 2565 (Hicone-Skylark Road). At the mill site, located 6 miles east, British and American forces clashed less than ten days before the Battle of Guilford Courthouse.

To visit the area where the skirmish took place, turn around and proceed north on U.S. 29 Bypass to S.R. 2565. Turn right, drive east for 3.1 miles to S.R. 2819, turn right again, and go 2.1 miles to S.R. 2770. Turn left, drive north for 6.7 miles to N.C. 61, turn left again, and go 1.3 miles to the bridge over Reedy Fork Creek. Weitzel's Mill stood on this creek.

From the time the Americans recrossed the Dan into North Carolina until the Battle of Guilford Courthouse, the two armies were never more than 20 miles apart. In the estimation of British general Charles O'Hara, the Americans were "constantly avoiding a general action and we industriously seeking it."

While camped north of the Haw River in Rockingham County during the first week of March 1781, Greene learned that Cornwallis was somewhere south of the American position. Once again, he interposed the light troops of Colonel Otho Williams and Lighthorse Harry Lee as a buffer between the two armies. Joining Williams and Lee in this defensive measure was General Andrew Pickens, the South Carolina hero who had joined Greene in the retreat across North Carolina.

Cornwallis grew more and more desperate to draw Greene into a general action in which he could destroy or soundly defeat the American army. Early on March 6, he decided to press the issue. At five-thirty that morning, the British army, headed by Tarleton's men and the brigade of Lieutenant Colonel James Webster, set out on a rapid march toward the Haw River. By the time Otho Williams received news that the enemy was on the march,

Tarleton and Webster were within 2 miles of the American shield and were closing fast.

As Williams saw it, his only chance was to put Reedy Fork Creek between his troops and their pursuers. With Lee and a rear guard of marksmen providing cover, Williams sent the main body of his troops on a 10-mile race to the ford near Weitzel's Mill. Yet again, the Americans reached the destination first. Williams deployed some companies for battle and sent other soldiers across the creek at the ford within sight of the mill.

Major Joseph Graham, the young hero of the Battle of Charlotte, participated in the skirmish at Weitzel's Mill. He described the scene when the fighting commenced: "The day was still cloudy, a light rain falling at times; the air was calm and dense. The riflemen kept up a severe fire, retreating from tree to tree to the flanks of our second line. When the enemy approached this, a brisk fire commenced on both sides. . . . The ford was crowded, many passing the watercourse at other places. Some, it was said, were drowned."

Williams's Continentals offered a withering fire that was, according to Graham, "equal to anything that had been seen in the war."

One American militiaman called the engagement "a smart skirmish, in which a great many Tories were sent to the lower region."

Nevertheless, inspired by James Webster's leadership, a number of British soldiers surged across the creek. A mile-long pursuit followed. But the results were the same. The Americans escaped to fight another day. That day was soon to come.

Turn around and follow N.C. 61 south for 16.5 miles to N.C. 62. Turn right and proceed 1.7 miles to the bridge over Stinking Quarter Creek.

Ten years before the maneuvers of Greene and Cornwallis in Guilford County, Governor William Tryon camped near the current tour stop on the western bank of Stinking Quarter Creek following the Battle of Alamance. It was at his encampment here that Tryon is said to have accepted the surrender of the Regulators.

Continue southwest on N.C. 62 for 0.2 mile to S.R. 1005. Turn right, proceed 9.1 miles to S.R. 3330 (Presbyterian Road), turn right again, and drive 0.4 mile to Alamance Presbyterian Church.

The existing sanctuary, constructed in 1955, belies the age of a congregation organized in 1762. A monument in the churchyard notes that the Presbyterian Synod of North Carolina was organized here.

Inside the church, a historical room displays artifacts from the church's storied history, some of them related to the Revolutionary War. Records of Dr. Eli Washington Caruthers, minister of the church from 1821 to 1861, are preserved here.

Caruthers (1793–1865), a native of Rowan County, is recognized as one of the most important early historians of the American Revolution in North Carolina. While serving as pastor at Alamance Presbyterian, he perceived that many facts related to the state's participation in the war would be lost forever if they were not recorded. Caruthers took up the task and produced several invaluable works. Caruthers and a number of church members who fought in the Revolution are buried in the adjacent cemetery.

Among the most noted Patriots laid to rest here was Captain Arthur Forbis (1746–81). An elder at Alamance Presbyterian, Forbis was eager to join in the fight for independence. As the commander of the local militia, he often led his men on expeditions known as "Tory hunting."

Forbis was in the thick of the fight at the Battle of Guilford Courthouse when he was felled by a British bullet. Left for dead on the battlefield, the badly wounded officer suffered excruciating pain alone in the cold and rain for thirty hours until he was discovered by a Tory who happened upon the scene. Sympathetic to the plight of the fallen soldier, the man filled his hat in a nearby stream and gave Forbis water. After he departed, another Tory, drawn to the scene by Forbis's pleas for water, thrust his bayonet into the body of the wounded soldier.

Grave of Arthur Forbis, Alamance Presbyterian Church

Finally, on the night of March 16, Forbis was rescued by his sister, who had been looking for her missing brother. After somehow managing to lift him onto her horse, she started toward home, which was located in the vicinity of the church.

En route, they encountered Elizabeth Wiley Forbis, who was desperately seeking news of her husband. Pallid from the heavy loss of blood but still conscious, Forbis was distressed that he was not immediately recognized by his wife. He asked weakly, "Betty, don't you know me?" Shocked by her husband's condition and overcome by emotion, Mrs. Forbis fainted.

Dr. David Caldwell, a noted Presbyterian minister and a surgeon for the

American army, soon arrived. He began using his skills in a gallant but futile attempt to save Forbis's life. Caldwell advised that Forbis's wounded leg be amputated, but the patient flatly refused. He died several days later.

Even in the face of great personal tragedy, Mrs. Forbis displayed the kind of resolve shared by many of the wives of soldiers fighting for American independence.

Some days after Guilford Courthouse, a neighbor of hers, Thomas Morgan, discovered two horses with bobbed tails wandering on his property. He realized that the horses were runaways from British or Tory soldiers, because the horses of American soldiers had long tails. Cognizant of Mrs. Forbis's recent misfortune and her desperate need for a horse, Morgan delivered one of the animals to the widow, who gratefully accepted it.

Because it was time to start a crop, the horse was immediately hitched to a plow. A day later, two men—most likely Tories searching for horses for the retreating British army—appeared at the farm and demanded the return of the horse. At the time, Mrs. Forbis's teenage son was guiding the plow and his mother was behind covering corn seed with a hoe. When their demand was refused by the resolute woman, the men ordered young Forbis to take the horse from the plow. His mother forbade him to obey the command. One of the men then stepped forward to claim the horse, only to be confronted by the hoe-wielding widow, who informed him that if he touched the horse, she would split open his head.

The two men departed without the animal.

Return to S.R. 1005 and proceed north for 1.3 miles to S.R. 3314 (Wiley-Lewis Road). Turn left, go 3.6 miles to S.R. 3505 (Pleasant Garden Road), and turn left again. Proceed south on Pleasant Garden Road (which becomes S.R. 3402) for 7.3 miles to N.C. 62. Turn right and drive 2.2 miles west to Centre Friends Meeting House, located on the right.

By the time the Revolution began, the Guilford County area had attracted a sizable Quaker population. In contrast to their Presbyterian neighbors, who took up arms to fight for independence as if it were a holy war, the Quakers were pacifists. As a result, they often found themselves in the middle as fighting engulfed the county.

Organized in 1757, Centre Friends Meeting House is one of the oldest Quaker meeting houses in the area. The existing church building is the fourth structure to stand on the site. In the adjacent cemetery are the graves of Quaker settlers who were eyewitnesses to the mayhem brought to the area by the Revolutionary War.

Matthew Osborn, an early Quaker settler in Guilford County, lived adjacent to Centre Friends Meeting House. A talented gunsmith, he was in great demand during the war. He is said to have repurchased all the guns he had made and destroyed them after the Battle of Guilford Courthouse.

Two divergent tales explain his conduct. According to one report, Osborn visited the battlefield at Guilford Courthouse the day after the fighting. Appalled by the death and destruction his weapons had wrought, he decided to reclaim the guns he had made. The other tale maintains that a neighbor borrowed a deer rifle from Osborn and proceeded to use it at Guilford Courthouse. Upon returning the gun to its owner, the neighbor related its use in the battle. In disgust, Osborn smashed the rifle against a stump and then went about acquiring all his other guns used in the battle.

Continue west on N.C. 62 for 8.5 miles to N.C. 610. Turn right, drive west for 1.8 miles to Brentwood Street, turn right again, and go north for 0.4 mile to Glenmore Avenue in the city of High Point. Turn left and proceed west for 0.2 mile to the junction with Elva Place and East Springfield Road.

Located here is Springfield Friends Meeting House. Although the present brick sanctuary, the fourth to stand on the site, was constructed in 1926, the meeting was organized way back in 1773. A colonnade connects the Colonial Revival structure to the third house of worship, a Greek Revival building completed in 1858. Inside the third sanctuary is a museum of Quaker life. Among the items displayed are artifacts from the Revolutionary War.

Several graves of interest are located in the well-landscaped cemetery set on a sloping hill nearby.

According to tradition, the first man interred here was John Brazelton. Young Brazelton was the son of an anomaly—a militant Quaker. Because of his family's support for the cause of independence, John Brazelton was disliked by area Tories. His unfortunate end came when he was fleeing from a group of Tories and sought refuge in a barn, where he hid in a haystack. His pursuers picked up pitchforks and proceeded to jab them into the hay until Brazelton emerged. He was then promptly hanged by the Loyalists.

Enos Blair, another Quaker who took up arms for the American cause, is also buried here. At his side lies his wife, Hannah Millikan Blair (1756–1852), one of the area's great heroines of the war. The mother of thirteen children, she is said to have given birth to a new baby every year during the Revolution. Meanwhile, she still managed to render effective assistance to nearby Patriots without violating the dictates of her religion. From her home on the nearby Deep River, Hannah delivered food, clothing, and medical supplies to Patriots forced to hide in the forests to avoid Tory avengers. On a number of occasions, she hid soldiers in her home and protected them from Tory raiders, including the infamous David Fanning.

When Fanning came calling one day, Hannah hastily ripped the corner of a feather tick bed and pushed a soldier inside. As the Tory entered the room, she pulled back the bedcover so he could see the bed, then sat down and began mending the torn corner. In a most innocent voice, she said, "Thee may search as thee pleases."

On another occasion, two soldiers were placed in the corncrib when Tories arrived at the Blair farm. Hannah proceeded to shuck corn while the invaders searched the premises in vain.

She also exposed herself to great danger as a bearer of messages and dispatches. After she took supplies to soldiers in hiding in 1779, Tory scouts apprehended her on her return trip and demanded information. She told them she had taken food to a sick neighbor, and her captors released her.

Ultimately, however, the Tories grew wise to her ways and torched the Blair house and farm. Hannah and her children were made to stand and watch as flames consumed everything they owned.

In recognition of the heroism and sacrifices of Hannah Millikan Blair, the grateful nation bestowed certificates of appreciation and a small pension upon her after the war.

Proceed west on East Springfield Road for 0.4 mile to U.S. 311. Turn right, go north for 1.2 miles to Centennial Street, turn right again, and drive 2.5 miles to Lexington Avenue. Turn right and travel 0.6 mile east to the High Point Museum and Historical Park, located at 1859 East Lexington.

The facility offers museum artifacts and buildings that interpret the area's Quaker heritage. The Hoggart House (1754) and the Haley House (1786) stand in the park surrounding the museum. The park serves as a "base camp" for the Guilford Militia Living Historians. Frequent Revolutionary War re-enactments and demonstrations are held here.

Continue east on Lexington Avenue as it becomes Greensboro–High Point Road. After 2.6 miles, turn left onto Park View Trail at the entrance to City Lake Park. Named for the nearby lake, which is a wide portion of the Deep River, the park contains a D.A.R. marker bearing the inscription, "Cornwallis with 2400 British soldiers forded Deep River at this point and camped on its left bank one mile west prior to the Battle of Guilford Court-house March 15, 1781."

An incident from Cornwallis's stay here is indicative of the compassion the British general displayed during the war. On the eve of the Battle of Guilford Courthouse, Cornwallis learned that a child had become seriously ill in the nearby Quaker village of Jamestown. Without hesitation, he promptly dispatched one of his badly needed surgeons to treat the young girl.

It was at his camp here on March 14 that the British commander re-ceived confirmation of the rumors that Greene had moved his army to Guilford Courthouse. Cornwallis found the news refreshing. He was finally in a position to strike the elusive American army.

On the evening of March 14, the British baggage train, escorted by sev-eral hundred soldiers, was sent south to Bell's Mill. At five-thirty the fol-lowing morning, the remaining two thousand troops set out on a march along New Garden Road that put them on a collision course with the American army.

Return to Greensboro-High Point Road and continue east. After 13.2 miles, the route junctions with N.C. 6 (Lee Street) in Greensboro. Proceed east on N.C. 6 for 3.2 miles to O. Henry Boulevard. Drive north on O. Henry for 1.3 miles to where it merges with U.S. 29. Continue north on U.S. 29 for 0.9 mile to Sixteenth Street, turn left, and drive 0.9 mile to Church Street. On the right side of the road is Buffalo Presbyterian Church.

This church was organized in 1757. The present church building—the third on the site—dates from 1827. Named for nearby Buffalo Creek, the church counted numerous Patriots among its members during the Revolu-tion. Many are buried in the historic cemetery at the rear of the church.

Foremost among the Revolutionary War heroes interred here is Dr. David

Caldwell, an incomparable physician, scholar, and minister who served the congregations at the Buffalo and Alamance churches. His story is told later on this tour at the park dedicated to his memory.

Buried beside Dr. Caldwell is his wife, Rachel Craighead Caldwell (1742–1845), one of the many women from Buffalo Presbyterian who exhibited great patriotism, ingenuity, and bravery during the war.

A native of Pennsylvania, Rachel was the daughter of the Reverend Alexander Craighead, the Presbyterian firebrand who set the tone for the Revolution in Mecklenburg County. Rachel married David at her father's church, Sugaw Creek Presbyterian, in 1766. The newlyweds settled on a 550-acre farm near what is now Greensboro.

Dr. Caldwell was a proponent of independence. Because her husband was frequently away from home treating wounded soldiers during the war, Rachel and their eight young children often found themselves alone.

During the latter part of 1780, a courier bearing an important communiqué from George Washington to Nathanael Greene stopped overnight at the Caldwell residence. He reasoned that he and his classified information would be safe in the home of a minister. But Rachel was quick to point out that her house was the object of sporadic Tory raids and urged her visitor to maintain a watch while she prepared a meal for him. No sooner had the messenger taken his seat to dine than a band of Tories rode into the yard.

In an instant, Rachel hurried the courier out the back door, where he hid in a large locust tree while the Loyalists plundered the home. When the first opportunity presented itself, he left the tree and made his escape.

Mrs. Rachel Denny was another dynamic Patriot from Buffalo Presbyterian. One day when her elderly Scots-Irish husband, Walter, was away from home, British foragers raided the Denny home. Mrs. Denny watched helplessly as they plundered the entire house.

When an officer asked the whereabouts of her husband, she told him she didn't know. When he asked her if she would tell if she knew, she responded, "No, and no gentlemen of honorable feelings would ever ask or expect such a thing."

Subsequent inquiries brought more embittered responses from Mrs. Denny. At length, the Redcoat cursed her and exclaimed that "the women in [this] part of the country are as damned rebels as the men, and that one-half of them, at least, ought to be shot or hung."

Drive east on Sixteenth Street for 0.3 mile to Yanceyville Street. Turn right, proceed south for 2.8 miles to Lindsay Street in downtown Greensboro, turn right again, and drive west for 0.6 mile to the Greensboro Museum of History, located at the junction of Lindsay, Summit Avenue, and Church Street. Free parking for museum visitors is at the rear of the expansive brick building, which once housed First Presbyterian Church of Greensboro.

Recognized as one of the most outstanding municipal museums in North Carolina, the Greensboro Museum of History has two levels of attractive galleries that detail the history of the city named for Nathanael Greene. After all, it was here that the American general literally lost the battle but won the war.

Located on the main level, the military history gallery exhibits an impressive collection of Revolutionary War artifacts, including uniforms, weapons, and flags. The museum holds several items of Nathanael Greene memorabilia. The general obtained a shiny silver cup with an *N. G.* monogram from Boston merchants in 1779. That cup made its second trip to Guilford County in 1987, when a Greensboro couple gave it to the museum after rescuing it from a Charleston antique shop. The museum owns several letters by Greene, one of which is on display.

Every item in the Revolutionary War exhibit—even the old, two-pronged pitchfork—has an interesting story behind it.

During the war, the John Alexander family lived in a log cabin near what is now Greensboro. Like other supporters of the cause of independence, Alexander was the subject of Tory attacks.

On one occasion, John's fourteen-year-old daughter, Jean, was busy spinning by the cabin window when she heard a shout. She called for her mother, and the two of them lifted the heavy bars from the cabin door. A breathless John Alexander rushed in, after which the family quickly closed and barred the door again.

Seconds later, they heard the clatter of horses and then the pounding of fists on the door. Then came a blood-curdling threat: "Come out you Whig, traitor to the Majesty, the King. We'll hang you yet."

Young Jean listened nervously as the men began knocking the chinking from the cabin logs. She then heard more talk from outside: "Make a hole big enough for the end of a gun and a peephole for me."

Chinking fell on the cabin floor as the holes grew wider. In desperation, the teenager scanned the room for a weapon. All she could find was a little pitchfork. Suddenly, the holes revealed a man. In a flash, Jean took hold of the pitchfork and thrust it into the man's abdomen. Screams of pain and confused voices followed. Soon, the horses sped away.

Several days later, a neighbor stopped by to report the presence of Tories in the area. John Alexander pretended to have no knowledge of the incursion. The neighbor said, "Well anyway, them Tories were in an all fired hurry to leave this neighborhood. Oh, I see you've got a spot of new chinking in your wall, what happened?"

Standing beside her father, Jean listened as her father, with a glint in his eye, remarked rather wryly, "Must have been something wrong with the mortar used when the cabin was built, some chinking fell out."

One of the most prominent collections at the museum is related to Guilford's favorite daughter, Dolley Payne Madison. Her parents, devout Quakers, moved from Virginia to the New Garden settlement (visited later on this tour) in 1765. According to the meticulous records maintained by the Quakers there, "Dolley their daughter was born ye 20 of ye 5 mo 1768." Dolley spent her first eleven years in Guilford County and experienced much of the Revolutionary War here. Later, as the wife of President James Madison, she became a heroine of the War of 1812.

In back of the museum near the parking area are several historically significant structures in a parklike setting.

A log cabin from the eighteenth century is dedicated to the memory of Dolley Madison. It is thought to be similar to the structure in which she was born.

Nearby stands the two-story McNairy House. This clapboard-covered log house was originally located on Horsepen Creek, 2 miles to the north. Because of its size and its location near the battlefield, Nathanael Greene selected it for use as a hospital following the Battle of Guilford Courthouse.

Among the procedures Greene's surgeons performed in the home of Francis McNairy was that most radical of treatments—amputation. Because no anesthesia was available, surgeons had to intoxicate each patient with brandy before the procedure. Then attendants held the injured men down while the damaged limb was sawed off. To seal the stump, they plunged it into hot tar. As surgeons labored to save lives after the battle, limbs were tossed from the windows, piled onto a cart, and hauled away for burial.

John B. McNairy (1762–1837), Francis's son, was born and grew up on the plantation at Horsepen Creek, which, according to Dr. Caruthers, was reddened with blood from the battle. Family tradition maintains that Mrs. McNairy and her children watched smoke from the battle from the doorway of the house.

From the museum, continue west on Lindsay Street for two blocks to North Greene Street (named for the general). Turn left, drive six blocks south to Martin Luther King, Jr., Boulevard, turn left again, go two blocks, and turn left onto Davie (named for the Patriot officer and statesman). Drive four blocks north to East Friendly Avenue, turn left, and go 3.2 miles to Hobbs Road. Turn right and drive north for 0.3 mile to Caldwell Park. Turn left into the parking area at the park headquarters. Developed to honor the memory of Dr. David D. Caldwell and his wife, Rachel, the park is located at the site of their home and Dr. Caldwell's famous log college.

From the parking lot, follow the trail north through a forested area to the markers for the Caldwells and the foundation of their home.

Known as Guilford County's "First First Citizen," Dr. Caldwell (1725–1824) was a native of Pennsylvania. Educated at Princeton, he came to North Carolina as a fifty-year-old Presbyterian missionary. For the remainder of his ninety-nine-year life, North Carolina was his home.

He established Dr. David Caldwell's Log College here in 1767. Until the infirmities of old age forced him to close the doors many years later, the classical and theological institution enjoyed a reputation as one of the finest schools of its kind in the South. As many as sixty students studied here every year. Among the graduates were outstanding doctors, lawyers, teachers, ministers, soldiers, and statesmen. Dr. Caldwell educated five state governors. Meanwhile, he also served as pastor for the Buffalo and Alamance congregations.

Caldwell was deeply involved in the American Revolution from the days of the Regulators. He was among the many distinguished delegates at the Fifth Provincial Congress at Halifax, which produced North Carolina's first state constitution. During the long fight that followed, Caldwell urged his congregations to take up arms against Great Britain. So persuasive were his pleas that every adult member at Buffalo and Alamance fought with Greene's army when Cornwallis invaded the area in 1781.

Caldwell's zealous support of the American cause and the great influence he held over his parishioners drew the ire of Cornwallis, who offered a reward of two hundred pounds for his capture. To elude would-be captors, Caldwell built a small, rustic hut in the swampy wilderness along North Buffalo Creek about 2 miles from the family home.

Days before the Battle of Guilford Courthouse, a large body of British soldiers called at the Caldwell house while the doctor was in hiding. They sequestered the house for their use and forced Mrs. Caldwell, her eight children, and an elderly woman into the nearby smokehouse. They remained there through two cold March days and nights, their only food a few dried peaches that Mrs. Caldwell happened to have in her pockets.

In an attempt to add to her misery, a young officer came out to taunt the Patriot matron. "You are rebels and cowards and dare not fight his Majesty's army," the soldier boasted.

Mrs. Caldwell replied with confidence, "Wait and see what the Lord will do for us."

At length, a British officer interceded to stop the harassment and obtain food and necessities for the family.

When the invaders were ready to leave, they laid waste to the home and farm. The British soldiers brought out all of Dr. Caldwell's sermons, papers, and books—including the cherished family Bible—and set them afire. All the livestock save one old goose was slaughtered or carried away. The family's early garden was destroyed, and the provisions not consumed were poisoned. According to Dr. Caldwell's biographer, Eli Caruthers, "Every panel of fence on the premises was consumed or carried away; every living thing was destroyed."

In the wake of the raid, Rachel and the children took refuge with a neighbor. Once again, the enemy appeared. This time, a group of six soldiers came disguised as Americans. One of their number asked, "Where is your husband, Mrs. Caldwell?"

"I suppose he is in General Greene's camp," she responded.

"That can't be, for we have come directly from there," noted the visitors.

A perplexed Rachel replied, "When I saw him last he said he thought he'd go to join General Greene."

After reiterating that Caldwell was not with Greene, one of the soldiers remarked, "General Greene has many sick men in his camp, and having heard that your husband is a good doctor, he sent us to ask him to come and help in the care of the sick."

Anxious to aid the cause, Rachel said, "I am very sorry that he is not here, but you might find him in a certain thicket in North Buffalo Creek." She then offered detailed directions.

The men bowed, expressed their gratitude, and galloped away.

Before they were out of sight, Mrs. Caldwell understood that she had been taken in by a ruse. Throughout the night, she could not sleep for fear of her husband's capture by the enemy. She prayed incessantly for his safety.

While Rachel prayed, David slept at his hideaway. A dream warned him that he was in danger. In fact, before his sleep was over, the dream recurred twice. At first light, he set out for Greene's camp just as his would-be captors began looking for his hiding spot.

After the Battle of Guilford Courthouse, Dr. Caldwell labored at the side of a British surgeon to minister to the wounded and bury the dead. Once the job was completed, he returned home to find his farm in ruins.

When peace came, the Caldwells restored their farm and reopened the log college. Dr. Caldwell continued to serve as minister at his two churches and to play an active role in shaping the new state and nation.

Noted North Carolina historian Stephen B. Weeks eloquently described Caldwell this way: "None did a nobler or more enduring work toward the greatness of the state than the Rev. David Caldwell, D.D., preacher, teacher, and physician, counsellor and guide for his friends and neighbors, servant of the people in many ways, state builder and protagonist of learning in the wilderness of North Carolina."

Return to your vehicle and retrace your route to West Friendly Avenue. Turn right and drive west for 2.3 miles to the After Hours Veterinary Emergency Clinic, located on the left at 5505 West Friendly. A small but dignified monument at the front of the building marks the spot where Dolley Payne Madison was born.

Continue on West Friendly for 0.3 mile to New Garden Road. Located on the northern side of this intersection are two venerable Quaker institutions: Guilford College and New Garden Friends Meeting. Turn right onto New Garden and park near the church.

The existing brick facility belies the age of the church. Quakers began settling in this neighborhood in 1750. The church was organized a year later.

Walk to the historic cemetery at the rear of the church. Located among well-landscaped, tree-shaded graves is a monument for the Revolutionary Oak, which stood nearby when the Battle of New Garden was fought here.

In one of the great ironies of the Revolutionary War, the first shots of the largest battle in North Carolina were fired in the heart of a community of pacifists. Long neglected by historians, the Battle of New Garden was far more than a minor skirmish on the road to Guilford Courthouse.

When the 617 American soldiers commanded by twenty-five-year-old Lighthorse Harry Lee met the 842-man legion of twenty-six-year-old Banastre "Bloody" Tarleton here in the early hours of March 15, 1781, the ensuing battle included three separate encounters that lasted most of the morning. There were numerous casualties on both sides. In contrast, the Battle of Guilford Courthouse, which began about one o'clock that same day, lasted but two hours.

The two "boy colonels" who squared off at New Garden were bitter enemies. The fires of personal dislike had been kindled four years earlier near Valley Forge, when Tarleton had emerged from an encounter with Lee with his hat shot away, three bullet holes in his vest, and a dead horse.

But Tarleton did not take his revenge during the bloody morning fight in the Quaker community. When the two factions disengaged to join their respective armies for the afternoon battle, Tarleton rode away with his arm in a sling. A musket ball had ripped away two fingers on his right hand. As a result, he could not use a weapon at the Battle of Guilford Courthouse.

More important, the Battle of New Garden was a strategic victory for the Americans. Lee was able to delay the British advance toward Guilford Courthouse for three hours, which provided Greene the time he needed to make the final preparations for his showdown with Cornwallis.

Another marker in the cemetery memorializes the many nameless American and British soldiers buried here after they fell at New Garden and

Guilford Courthouse. The Quakers of New Garden witnessed the blood-shed from their residences and interred the soldiers in mass graves. It has been estimated that at least 112 men were laid to rest here.

When he departed the battleground at Guilford Courthouse, Greene was forced to leave behind 250 of his most severely wounded men. He called upon the Quakers at New Garden to minister to those soldiers. A week later, he made another entreaty by letter.

Members of the church responded thus:

> Friend Greene: We received thine, being dated March 20, 1781. Agreeable to thy request we shall do all that lies in our power, although this may inform you that from our present situation we are ill able to assist as much as we would be glad to do, as the Americans have lain much upon us, and of late the British have plundered and entirely broken up many among us, which renders it hard, and there is at our meeting-house at New Garden upward of one hundred now living, that have no means of provision, except what hospitality the neighborhood affords them. . . . But not withstanding all this, we are determined, by the assistance of Providence, while we have anything among us, that the distressed both at the court house and here shall have part with us.

Throughout the war, the faith and abhorrence of violence of the congregation at New Garden were sternly tested. Some of its male members were disowned for "appearing in a warlike manner."

Nevertheless, William Armfield—whose grave can be found in the cemetery—actually fought with the Americans at Guilford Courthouse. Incensed by the recent plundering of his farm by the British army, Armfield grabbed his squirrel gun under the guise of a hunting trip and proceeded to join Greene for the battle. When he returned home, his family questioned him about the lack of game. Armfield responded, "It wasn't worth bringing home."

On the southern side of the cemetery stands a state historical marker for New Garden Friends Meeting, which is considered the most prominent Quaker meeting house in the state.

On the opposite side of New Garden Road is the campus of Guilford College. Established by the Quakers as the New Garden Boarding School in 1837, the college is a repository of much Quaker history.

Return to the intersection of New Garden Road and West Friendly. Cross Friendly and proceed to West Market Street (U.S. 421). Turn right, go west for 4.3 miles to N.C. 68, turn right again, and proceed north for 4.8 miles to S.R. 2132. Located on the right side of N.C. 68 is Bailes Old Mill. For more than 250 years, a water-powered mill has operated along Beaver Creek at this site.

When the Revolutionary War began, the mill was owned by Daniel Dillon, Sr. Because of Dillon's alleged sympathy to the British cause, the mill was confiscated. Court action subsequently returned it to him.

A plaque on a rock in front of the still-functioning mill notes that Cornwallis's troops captured the facility after shooting the miller in the foot. They then set about grinding grain for the British army.

Continue north on N.C. 68 for 3.5 miles to N.C. 150 at Oak Ridge. Turn right, drive east for 5.5 miles to Summerfield Road, turn right again, and proceed 0.5 mile to Summerfield Elementary School, located on the right. In the schoolyard stands an impressive monument to Patriots Charles Bruce and James Gillies. Both men played a role in one of the most heartbreaking stories of the war.

In Revolutionary War times, the community now known as Summerfield was called Bruce's Cross Roads, so named for Charles Bruce, whose house was located 0.5 mile south of the crossroads.

Shortly after the American council of war at Guilford Courthouse ended on February 10, 1781, Lighthorse Harry Lee went about his assigned task of staying between the two armies. Badly in need of rest and nourishment, he stopped at the home of Charles Bruce at midday on February 12.

While food was being prepared for the cavalry officer, Isaac Wright, one of Bruce's neighbors, brought news that British dragoons were no more than 3 miles away. To ascertain the validity of the report, Lee ordered Wright to accompany one of his most trusted officers, Captain Armstrong, on a scouting expedition. Wright was given permission to exchange his small pony for the fleet horse of Lee's teenage bugler, James Gillies. Fearful that his steed would not be returned, Gillies joined the expedition on Wright's pony.

In the course of their mission, Gillies and several of his comrades happened upon the enemy. The Americans began a retreat, but the unarmed teenager and his slow-footed mount could not escape the speedy British horsemen. Gillies was knocked from the pony. He pleaded quarter but was hacked to pieces by Tarleton's green-coated men.

As the butchery was taking place, Captain Armstrong arrived with reinforcements, who promptly slew seven British soldiers. The din of the encounter led Tarleton to bring his full legion forward. Once again, the Americans retreated toward the crossroads, where Lee was ready and waiting.

The lead element of the British cavalry, commanded by Captain Miller, rode into the ambush, which resulted in a general rout and a loss of thirteen more of Tarleton's soldiers. Miller attempted to escape, but Lee's men chased him down. Lee held the British captain personally responsible for the death of his beloved bugler and ordered that Miller be hanged on the spot. But before the execution could be carried out, the main body of Tarleton's troops appeared. Consequently, the British captive was sent to Greene as a prisoner of war.

When Cornwallis passed the site of the skirmish later that day, he ordered the British dead to be interred alongside the road where they had fallen. Bruce's plantation served as the campground for the British army that same night.

Lee's only casualty was young James Gillies, who was laid to rest in the Bruce family cemetery, located on the opposite side of the road from the monument. Charles Bruce was subsequently buried near the slain soldier. A roadside historical marker stands near the burial site.

Continue south on Summerfield Road for 1.5 miles to U.S. 220. Turn right and drive 4.3 miles to New Garden Road, where a state historical marker notes that you have arrived at Guilford Courthouse—the site where Greene and Cornwallis finally clashed on March 15, 1781.

Turn left onto New Garden, then turn into Tannenbaum Park, located on the right. Operated by the city of Greensboro, this facility is located adjacent to Guilford Courthouse National Military Park and is an excellent accompaniment to it.

Park at the North Carolina Heritage Center. Inside, visitors are treated to outstanding exhibits related to life during the colonial period. Among the artwork displayed at the center are several original oil paintings by renowned military artist Dale Gallon.

Foremost among the restored and reconstructed buildings on the spacious grounds surrounding the center is the Hoskins House. Constructed around 1778 by Joseph Hoskins, a newcomer from Pennsylvania, the log cabin stood here during the Battle of Guilford Courthouse. It was used as a headquarters by the British and as a field hospital by both armies.

After your visit to Tannenbaum Park, continue on New Garden Road to the entrance to Guilford Courthouse National Military Park. Follow the signs to the parking lot at the visitor center. Begin your tour at the visitor center, where an audiovisual program and a museum provide an excellent orientation to the place where Nathanael Greene chose to make a stand against Cornwallis.

After being chased halfway across North Carolina in the cold, rain, and snow over countless rivers and creeks, Greene selected the ground near the isolated courthouse at Guilford to face some of the best soldiers that the Crown could field.

Buoyed by the arrival of reinforcements that included the likes of William Campbell—one of the heroes of Kings Mountain—Greene fielded an army of forty-four hundred regulars and militia. For once, he had a numerical superiority over Cornwallis. Though the British commander commanded some of the most battle-tested warriors in the world, the chase through North Carolina had proven very costly. Attrition had reduced his fighting machine to approximately two thousand men.

About noon on March 15, Lieutenant Colonel Lee returned from his adventure at New Garden. He found Greene's army in battle formation. To instill confidence in the nervous American riflemen, Lee rode along the front line shouting encouragement and urging the men to stand tall against the British. As he put it, he had "whipped them three times that morning and could do it again."

The waiting ended around one-thirty. From the woods along Salisbury Road emerged the first wave of Cornwallis's troops, their once-resplendent red uniforms showing the wear and tear of the North Carolina campaign. American field pieces offered the first fire, and the British artillerists countered. Then the infantry took the field. For two hours thereafter, a horrific battle raged. When his artillery was captured and the British threatened to flank his forces, Greene ordered a retreat.

Cornwallis had earned a tactical victory. Greene blamed the defeat on the North Carolina militia, which broke and ran late in the battle. He complained to Governor Abner Nash, "We ought to have had victory and had your militia stood by their officers it was certain."

In retrospect, it seems that Greene's criticism of the militia may have been overly harsh, for the North Carolinians on the first line performed quite admirably, in the estimation of British officers who took part in the battle.

Whatever the case, Cornwallis's victory at Guilford Courthouse was hollow. His losses were staggering: 93 killed, 413 wounded, and 26 missing. His 532 casualties depleted his army by 27 percent. Nearly 30 percent of his officer corps was down. Among the badly wounded were General Charles O'Hara and Lieutenant Colonel James Webster, who subsequently died of his wounds at Elizabethtown. Cornwallis realized that his army was no longer strong enough to fight Greene.

The "defeated" American army suffered far fewer casualties: 79 killed and 185 wounded.

Nathanael Greene Monument, Guilford Courthouse National Military Park

The battlefield and its many monuments and statues can be toured by foot, bike, or vehicle. Because of the sheer size of the park, a driving tour is advised.

Before beginning, note the several monuments and markers on the northern side of the visitor center.

The monuments for Nathaniel Macon and Jethro Sumner do not relate directly to the battle fought here; sites related to Macon (a soldier and statesman) and Sumner (a general in the Continental Army) are included in The Statehood Tour. Sumner's grave was moved to the current tour stop in 1891.

Nearby stands a monument dedicated to Kerenhappuch Norman Turner. Erected in 1902, the life-size figure of a nurse was one of the first tributes of its kind to a woman of the Revolution.

The biblical Kerenhappuch was the third daughter of Job. Kerenhappuch Turner was living in Maryland when news of the Battle of Guilford Courthouse reached her. Upon learning that her son had been badly wounded while fighting under Greene, she felt compelled to hurry to the scene to render assistance. According to local tradition, she grabbed her newborn child, mounted her horse, and started for North Carolina. En route, the infant died. Upon her arrival at the battlefield, Mrs. Turner found her wounded son and had him transported to a nearby cabin, where she nursed him back to health.

Mrs. Turner was the great-grandmother of North Carolina governor John Motley Morehead. She died in North Carolina at the age of 115.

Adjacent to the Turner statue is a monument honoring James Gillies, the teenage bugler slaughtered by British dragoons at nearby Summerfield.

East of the monument to Gillies stands an impressive marker for Martha McFarland McGee Bell, a Revolutionary War heroine whose exploits are examined in The Regulator Tour.

Located north of the Bell marker is a monument commemorating President George Washington's visit to the battlefield on June 2, 1791. He stopped here on the last leg of his famous eighty-three-day Southern tour. At the time of his visit, the place was named Martinville in honor of Governor Alexander Martin, Washington's gracious host in Guilford County. A land speculator, Martin owned much of the property in the county seat, which

Monument to James Gillies

had been chartered in his honor in 1785. The great city he envisioned never materialized. It faded into oblivion after Greensboro replaced it as the county seat in 1808.

Washington reached the battlefield before noon. After enjoying a meal, he and Governor Martin drove over the ground where Greene's forces had inflicted irreparable damage to the British army.

In his diary entry, the president may have been overly critical of the Americans in the battle that put Cornwallis on the road to Yorktown, the site of Washington's greatest victory: "Had the troops done their duty properly the British must have been severely galded [sic] in ye advance, if not defeated."

From the parking area, follow the road marked by tour signs. After 0.1 mile, you'll see a small marker for Arthur Forbis, the American soldier whose grave site was an earlier stop on this tour.

After another 0.2 mile, you'll reach a turnout marking the spot where Greene's first line was located.

Continue 0.3 mile to the turnout at the location of Greene's second line.

Proceed 0.2 mile to a cluster of three markers. The tall statue honors Joseph Winston, the commander of the "Surry County Boys" at Guilford Courthouse. Attached to Lighthorse Harry Lee's command, Winston and his sharpshooters were among the last Americans to retire from the field.

Among the men who joined Winston's militia unit for the battle were Richard Taliaferro and Jesse Franklin (later elected governor of North Carolina). As Winston sounded the retreat, both men ran for their horses, which were tied nearby. Franklin reached his horse and escaped, but Taliaferro was shot down by British dragoons. He is thought to have been the last American killed in the battle.

The current tour stop is the place where the last shots were fired by American riflemen. Franklin and Winston are buried nearby in well-marked graves.

Drive 0.2 mile to the Cavalry Monument (also known as the Francisco Monument). One tablet on the tall obelisk is dedicated to the cavalry of Lieutenant Colonel William Washington, a cousin of George Washington. A tablet on the other side pays tribute to Peter Francisco, perhaps the most unusual soldier to take the field at Guilford Courthouse.

Born in the Portuguese Azores in 1760, Francisco was abandoned on the

Cavalry (Francisco) Monument

docks at City Point, Virginia, at the age of five. Judge Anthony Winston rescued him from a poorhouse and reared him at his home in Buckingham County, Virginia. In 1775, Francisco accompanied Judge Winston to Richmond, where they were on hand to hear Patrick Henry's famous oration, "Give me liberty or give me death!"

So inspired was Francisco that he enlisted to fight for the American cause. Known as a giant with superhuman strength, he stood six foot six and weighed 260 pounds when he joined the Continental Army at the age of sixteen. In comparison, the average American soldier was a foot shorter and a hundred pounds lighter.

Throughout the war, the youthful giant performed extraordinary feats of strength. At Camden, for example, he moved an eleven-hundred-pound cannon without assistance. He then removed a British soldier from his horse and presented the mount to Colonel William Mayo, whose life he had just saved.

But it was at the Battle of Guilford Courthouse that Francisco earned enduring fame. In one brief encounter, he slew eleven soldiers with his terrible broadsword. Later, a Redcoat used his bayonet to pin Francisco's leg to his horse. Francisco helped his adversary extricate the bayonet, then retaliated with a sword blow that was said to have "cleft the enemy's head in twain" as he fled. In a subsequent charge, Francisco sustained another leg wound stretching from hip to knee. He was left for dead, but a Quaker woman rescued him. Following a quick recovery, the giant made his way on foot to rejoin his command in Virginia.

Francisco was the subject of one of the most famous engravings of the Revolution, in which he was pictured doing battle with nine enemy soldiers in Amelia, Virginia.

Tales of his strength spread far and wide. A Kentucky man named Pamphlett, who boasted that he was the strongest man in America, took issue with the reports. He made his way to Francisco and challenged him to a contest to determine who was the stronger.

Francisco allowed Pamphlett to go first. The Kentuckian twice lifted the Virginia soldier from the ground. Then came Francisco's turn. He picked up Pamphlett two times. Then he picked him up again and threw him across a fence. The stunned challenger asked the giant if he would kindly hand him his horse. Francisco obliged him.

In 1975, the United States Postal Service issued a commemorative stamp honoring Francisco. It was entitled "Fighter Extraordinary." One of his immense shoes is on display in the park's visitor center.

Follow the tour route another 0.3 mile to a turnout on the right, where a trail leads to the site of Guilford Courthouse.

Continue the drive for 0.6 mile to a turnout near the site of Greene's third line. Trails lead to five monuments located nearby. Two of the monuments honor troops from Delaware and Maryland. These soldiers were among the best in Greene's army. West of the monument to the Delaware soldiers stands an impressive monument to Dr. David Caldwell, considered by many to be the most revered man in the history of Guilford County.

Follow the tour route for 0.5 mile to the last group of monuments, where this tour ends.

On the side of the road opposite the parking area is a monument to David Schenck (1835–1902). Born in Lincolnton, Schenck spent his boyhood playing on the battlefield at Ramsour's Mill and reliving the Revolutionary War glory of his ancestors. He later became a distinguished attorney and judge. He and his wife (the sister of Confederate general Stephen Dodson Ramseur) lived in Greensboro. Concerned that the integrity of the battle site at Guilford Courthouse was about to be lost forever, he set about leading the Guilford Battle Ground Company in acquiring land and constructing monuments. Had it not been for Judge Schenck's foresight and persistence, Guilford Courthouse would not have become the first Revolutionary War battlefield to be established as a national park.

From the Schenck Monument, walk back across the road, then across the green to the major monument area.

On the right is the Hooper-Penn Monument and Grave. One of David Schenck's greatest desires was to have the remains of North Carolina's Revolutionary War notables reinterred at the battleground. Amid great controversy, the graves of William Hooper and John Penn, two of the state's three signers of the Declaration of Independence, were relocated here in 1894. The grave of the third signer, Joseph Hewes, could not be located in Philadelphia.

Near the signers' monument and grave is the park's centerpiece—a massive equestrian statue of Major General Nathanael Greene. The masterpiece was crafted by renowned sculptor Francis H. Packer after a thirty-thousand-dollar congressional appropriation in 1911. It was dedicated on July 3, 1914.

Perhaps no soldier of the American Revolution is more deserving of a spectacular monument than the Rhode Island Quaker who fought his greatest battle in the Quaker country of North Carolina. Deeply respected by friend and foe alike, Greene won the war in the South without personally defeating Cornwallis in a single battle. Nevertheless, the base of the monument bears this opinion from Cornwallis: "Greene is as dangerous as Washington. I never feel secure when encamped in his neighborhood." Concerning the performance of Greene's men at Guilford Courthouse, Cornwallis noted, "I never saw such fighting since God made me. The fighting was furious."

The breathtaking statue of Greene marks the site of the beginning of the end for the British cause. As the American general himself put it, the enemy was "little short of being ruined." Greene's masterful campaign through North Carolina, which culminated in the bloodbath here at Guilford Courthouse, remains one of the most dramatic and important chapters in American history.

After his showdown with Cornwallis, Greene remained in the Carolinas and defended the two states for the duration of the war. Unfortunately, he did not enjoy his country's hard-earned independence long, dying of sunstroke on his Georgia plantation on June 19, 1786, at the age of forty-three.

Yet the greatness of the man and his North Carolina campaign lives on in the words of his contemporaries.

George Washington once wrote Greene, "It is with a pleasure which friendship alone is susceptible of that I congratulate you on the glorious end you have put to hostilities in the southern states." Washington considered Greene his best subordinate. He designated Greene as his successor in the event the American commander was killed or incapacitated.

Banastre Tarleton, the cavalry commander who shared Cornwallis's frustration in trying to corner Greene, acknowledged that "every movement of the Americans [under Greene] was judiciously designed and vigorously executed."

In London, a vexed Lord Tremain complained that "the rebels conducted their enterprises in Carolina with more spirit and skill than they have shown in any other part of America."

But Charles James Fox, a member of Parliament, said it best when he delivered the news of Cornwallis's "victory" at Guilford Courthouse to the House of Commons: "Another such victory would ruin the British army."

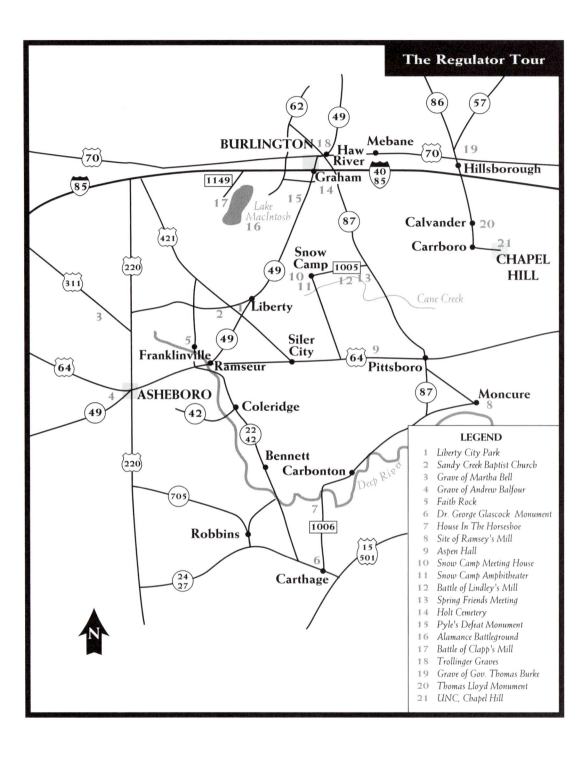

The Regulator Tour

LEGEND
1 Liberty City Park
2 Sandy Creek Baptist Church
3 Grave of Martha Bell
4 Grave of Andrew Balfour
5 Faith Rock
6 Dr. George Glascock Monument
7 House In The Horseshoe
8 Site of Ramsey's Mill
9 Aspen Hall
10 Snow Camp Meeting House
11 Snow Camp Amphitheater
12 Battle of Lindley's Mill
13 Spring Friends Meeting
14 Holt Cemetery
15 Pyle's Defeat Monument
16 Alamance Battleground
17 Battle of Clapp's Mill
18 Trollinger Graves
19 Grave of Gov. Thomas Burke
20 Thomas Lloyd Monument
21 UNC, Chapel Hill

The Regulator Tour

This tour begins at Liberty in Randolph County and makes its way through Chatham, Moore, and Alamance Counties before ending at Chapel Hill in Orange County. Among the highlights are Sandy Creek Baptist Church and the story of the Regulators, the grave of Martha Bell, the grave of Colonel Andrew Balfour, Faith Rock, the story of David Fanning, House in the Horseshoe State Historic Site, the story of Ramsey's Mill, Cane Creek Meeting House, Snow Camp, the Battle of Lindley's Mill, Spring Friends Meeting, the story of "Pyle's Defeat," Alamance Battleground State Historical Site, the Battle of Clapp's Mill, the grave of Governor Thomas Burke, historic Hillsborough, and the Davie Poplar.

Total mileage: approximately 284 miles.

This tour covers a five-county area in central North Carolina where a wide variety of significant events took place during the Revolutionary War period. In many ways, the happenings here from 1771 to 1789 make the region a microcosm of the entire state at that time.

It was here that the Regulator movement—the resistance by settlers in the North Carolina back country to the policies of the colonial government—lived and died. On May 16, 1771, militiamen personally commanded by Governor William Tryon routed an army of Regulators at the Battle of Alamance. The Regulator movement was crushed, but some historians consider the famous clash between Loyalists and Regulators the first battle of the American Revolution.

Hillsborough, located northeast of the Alamance battlefield, was known in colonial times as "the Capital of the Back Country." Throughout the war, it served as host to the governor, the legislature, and numerous military leaders. The town could count as its own some of the state's most famous military and political leaders, including Governor Thomas Burke and General Francis Nash.

Following his unsuccessful race to the Dan against Nathanael Greene, Cornwallis camped in the area covered by this tour. In the aftermath of

Guilford Courthouse, he marched his badly damaged army through here on its retreat to Wilmington.

During a six-month period in 1781, three important battles took place along the tour route. Patriots fought the third—and most significant—of them on September 13, 1781, in an unsuccessful attempt to rescue Governor Burke, who had been captured by Tories led by the infamous David Fanning. In the latter stages of the war, Fanning waged a cruel and bloody civil war throughout this region. So devastating was the conflict between Americans here that Nathanael Greene remarked, "If this carnage between Whig and Tory is continued, this country must be depopulated."

Once independence was secured, the area was the scene of two of the most important events in the fledgling state's early history. In 1788, a great fight over the ratification of the United States Constitution took place at Hillsborough, where a majority of the delegates demanded a bill of rights. Five years later, an august group of men, many of them Revolutionary War heroes, assembled in Chapel Hill to lay the cornerstone of the first state-supported university in the new nation.

The tour begins at the intersection of Swannanoa Avenue and Old U.S. 421 (S.R. 1006) in the town of Liberty in northeastern Randolph County. Established in 1779, Randolph County was named to honor Peyton Randolph (1721–75), a Virginian who served as an early president of the Continental Congress. As for Liberty, one story goes that it was so named because Cornwallis released some Patriot soldiers here. Located near the intersection is Liberty City Park, where a sign notes that Revolutionary War soldiers were liberated on the park grounds.

Proceed one block east on Swannanoa to N.C. 49. Turn right and go south for 3.5 miles to S.R. 2459 (Sandy Creek Church Road). Turn right and proceed west for 4.5 miles to S.R. 2442.

Here stands Sandy Creek Baptist Church. Established in 1755, Sandy Creek has been called "the Mother of Southern Baptist Churches."

In the cemetery adjacent to the historic church is the grave of the Reverend Shubael Stearns, Jr. (1706–71), a Boston native who founded Separate Baptist Church in 1751. A militant evangelist, he settled in North Carolina in late 1755 and promptly organized the original eighteen members of Sandy Creek Baptist Church.

Over the next fifteen years, Stearns's evangelism inspired the church's phenomenal growth and the development of the Sandy Creek Association, a group of associated Baptist churches in North Carolina and Virginia.

The Regulator movement caused the church's decline. Although the Sandy Creek Association sympathized with the plight of the Regulators, it abhorred violence and resolved that "if any of our members shall take up arms against the local authority or aid or abet them that do, he shall be excommunicated."

When the dispute between the Regulators and the colonial government culminated in bloodshed on May 16, 1771, most members of Sandy Creek joined with people from other area Baptist churches in a mass exodus from the region.

A tall obelisk in the cemetery marks the site of the original church and details Sandy Creek's importance in the early history of the Baptist denomination. Several Revolutionary War soldiers are buried here in well-marked graves.

Turn right onto S.R. 2442. After 0.1 mile, you will cross Sandy Creek, the waterway for which the historic Baptist church was named. It was along this creek in 1766 that one of the first attempts—perhaps *the* first attempt—to organize the Regulators was made.

Herman Husband (1724–95), a former land agent who made his home along Sandy Creek, was one of the leaders of the back-country protestors. Inspired by the resistance of coastal residents to the Stamp Act, Husband and other local farmers formed an association to seek redress for the abuses, excesses, and corruption rampant in the local and colonial governments. Their petition, written by Husband, was delivered to the Inferior Court of Orange County (of which this area was then a part) on October 10, 1766. It received no action from local officials.

A group of local citizens then assembled at Sandy Creek on March 22, 1767. They agreed "to form ourselves into an association, to assemble ourselves for conference for regulating public governors and abuse of power." The Regulators, as they called themselves, made several significant pledges: to "pay no more taxes until we are satisfied that they are agreeable to law"; "to pay no officer any more fees than the law allows"; and "to stand true and faithful to this cause, till we bring things in a true regulation."

There were subsequent meetings on Sandy Creek and elsewhere as the movement gained momentum. Ultimately, the Regulators became such a threat to Governor Tryon that he destroyed the movement on a bloody battlefield just 15 miles from the creek where it had been born.

Continue north on S.R. 2442 for 1.6 miles to S.R. 2261 at the community of Melancton; a state historical marker here calls attention to Sandy Creek Baptist Church.

Turn left on S.R. 2261, follow it west for 2.1 miles to S.R. 2245, turn right, and drive 2.3 miles to N.C. 22. Turn right, travel north for 1 mile to S.R. 2113 (Providence Church Road), turn left, and proceed east for 6.1 miles to U.S. 220 Business. Turn right and drive north for 0.8 mile to Branson Road. Turn left, proceed 0.9 mile to U.S. 220 Bypass, and follow the bypass south for 3.1 miles to the Martha Bell Bridge over the Deep River. This twin span was named in honor of Martha McFarlane McGee Bell (1735–1820), one of the North Carolina's most legendary Revolutionary War heroines.

In 1759, Bell, a native of Orange County, married Colonel John McGee, a commissioned British officer who had settled in North Carolina six years earlier. The couple made a home on Sandy Creek, where McGee built a prosperous gristmill and ordinary. His association with the British army brought him under the scrutiny of the area's many Regulators, but he refrained from taking sides in the controversy.

When McGee met an untimely death in 1773, Martha found herself the richest widow in the western half of the colony. Many suitors asked for her hand, but William Bell was her choice. Like Martha, Bell was a mill owner and an ardent supporter of the American cause. His mill was located northwest of the current tour stop on Muddy Creek, a tributary of the Deep River. North Carolina had no truer or fiercer Patriots than the Bells, as will be detailed at later stops on this tour.

Follow U.S. 220 Bypass for 2.6 miles to U.S. 311. Exit onto U.S. 311 and follow it north for 3.3 miles to S.R. 1944 (Branson-Davis Road). Turn right and proceed 1.2 miles to the junction with S.R. 1943 (Earl Johnson Road) and S.R. 1941 (Wall Brothers Road). Turn right on S.R. 1943 and drive east for 0.4 mile to where it merges with Walker Mill Road. Go left onto Walker Mill Road and drive north for 0.4 mile to the bridge over Muddy Creek.

William Bell's mill stood just downstream from the bridge near the creek's confluence with the Deep River. Strategically located on the public road that ran from Guilford Courthouse to Fayetteville, the mill and the Bells' nearby home served as an important gathering spot for Whigs during the war.

Eminently popular with area residents, William Bell was elected the first sheriff of Randolph County on December 13, 1779. However, Tories were anxious to capture him because of his unabashed support for independence. Several raids on the Bell residence by David Fanning forced the sheriff to go into hiding or to travel with Patriot forces for extended periods. As a result, Martha faced the difficult tasks of managing and defending both mill and home during the final years of the war.

Concerning Martha's devotion to the American cause, respected historian Dr. Eli Caruthers noted, "From the very commencement of the contest with England, she espoused the cause of independence with her whole soul. And she was so decided in her opinions and so ardent in her zeal, that she could hardly bear the sight, or even the name of a Tory."

One contemporary account said Martha was a "woman of strong mind, ardent temperament and remarkable resolution, but was not known for her personal beauty." Just as popular with local citizens as her husband, she was known as an angel of mercy who never refused to ride long distances in the cold and dark to minister to the sick and to women in childbirth.

Her lonely rides often carried her along routes frequented by rogues and Tories. Armed with a knife and a pistol hidden in her waist belt, she was equal to any challenge. She also had numerous encounters with marauders. Once, they struck by night, torching the Bells' barn and wounding one of Martha's sons. But that was a rare occasion, for Tories were usually vanquished by Martha Bell.

On one occasion, a deserter blocked the road, took hold of her horse, and ordered her to dismount. In response, Martha drew her pistol, took the man prisoner, and marched him down the road.

Another time, Tory attackers arrived at her home and threatened her elderly father with drawn swords. Martha drew a broadax over her head and shouted, "If one of you touches him, I'll split you down with this ax. Touch him if you dare!" None of the men dared. Instead, they left without harming the old man.

On yet another raid, the Tories were accompanied by one of their leaders, David Fanning. Intent upon burning the Bell house, Fanning was dismayed to hear a woman's voice inside the dwelling shout an order that the windows be raised and that everyone have a Tory in his sights before firing. Fearful that the house was filled with well-armed Patriots, Fanning ordered a quick retreat. Manning the guns for Mrs. Bell were a few farm hands.

A similar ruse once saved Martha's husband from certain capture or death. Upon learning that William Bell had returned home in the fall of 1781, area Tories swarmed the plantation in hopes of hanging the avowed Patriot. Bell attempted to fire upon the attackers from a window but was rendered unconscious by a Tory blow. Martha awakened her sleeping sons and ordered them to shoot from the upstairs window. And in a loud voice, she directed a servant to make haste to their neighbors and return with "light horse, for the Tories are here." Unwilling to chance a battle with local Patriots, the invaders sped away.

Turn around near the bridge and retrace Walker Mill Road for approximately 1.5 miles to the junction of S.R. 1943, S.R. 1944, and S.R. 1941. Turn left on S.R. 1941 and proceed 0.1 mile south to a farm lane on the left side of the road. Follow the farm lane for 0.1 mile to its terminus at the Bell-Welborne cemetery. In this isolated burial ground are the remains of William and Martha Bell, marked by modest gravestones.

It has been written about Mrs. Bell that "she seemed to fear nothing on earth except her maker." By all accounts, she did not fear the British. Following their showdown with the Americans at Guilford Courthouse, the Redcoats marched through the area en route to the Cape Fear. As the chief British miller rode up to the Bell plantation with the advance elements of the English forces, he tossed his hat into the air and exclaimed, "Hurrah for King George!" Without comment, Martha Bell fired on him.

Before long, Lord Cornwallis rode up and promptly made an inquiry of Martha as to the whereabouts of her husband.

She responded rather indignantly, "He's in General Greene's camp."

"Is he a soldier or an officer in the army?" Cornwallis asked.

"He is not," Martha responded curtly. "But he thought it better to go to his friends than to stay and fall into the hands of his enemies."

Then came the pronouncement Martha had expected: "Madame, I must

Martha Bell's grave,
Bell-Welborne Cemetery

make your home my headquarters and have the use of your mill to grind corn for my men for the few days that I stay here."

She calmly replied, "You possess the power, and, of course, you will do as you please without my consent. But after using our mill, do you intend to burn it before leaving?"

"Madame, why do you ask that?" Cornwallis said.

Refusing to yield, Martha said sternly, "Sir, answer my question first, and then I will answer yours, in short time."

Cornwallis proceeded to assure her that the plantation would not be destroyed.

Next came something the general did not expect. Standing eyeball to eyeball with the Redcoat leader, Martha announced, "Had your lordship intended to burn our mill, I had intended to save you the trouble by burning it myself before you derived any benefit from it."

In the course of their conversation, Cornwallis boasted that he had virtually destroyed Greene's army at Guilford Courthouse. While they talked, the general ordered that the front door of the Bell house be kept open, even though the March weather was rainy and cold. Martha finally closed the door, only to have Cornwallis open it again. "General Greene might be coming down the road," he explained.

Martha quipped, "I thought you told me you had annihilated his army, and he could do you no more harm."

"Well, madame," the general admitted, "to tell you the truth, I never saw such fighting since God made me, and another such victory would annihilate me."

Cornwallis was true to his word, and the plantation was not burned. However, before their departure, British troops plundered home, mill, and farm. When one particularly revolting Redcoat rode by her, Martha announced her wish that his horse would throw him and break his neck. Moments later, the horse indeed bolted, throwing its rider down an embankment, where he suffered a fractured skull.

At various times during the war, Martha used her expert knowledge of the area to provide intelligence for the Patriot army. Her most famous act of espionage came after Cornwallis departed her plantation, when American cavalry officers Lighthorse Harry Lee and William Washington arrived in desperate need of information about enemy troop strength and location.

Martha was only too happy to obtain the needed intelligence. Dressed in her husband's uniform, she rode to each neighboring farm to ascertain the route of the Redcoats. Then she galloped boldly into Cornwallis's encampment and was escorted to the general's tent. There, she lodged complaints about the depredations she had suffered at the hands of the Redcoats, which she claimed had been discovered "only after they'd left." All the while, Martha watched and listened to the camp activities.

After her audience with the general, she made haste to Lee and Washington with her findings. They used the intelligence to launch a small but significant counterattack against the retreating British.

In 1997, local historical groups dedicated a long-overdue monument to Martha Bell at the current tour stop.

Retrace your route to the junction with U.S. 311. Turn left and proceed 3.3 miles to U.S. 220. Drive south on U.S. 220 for 7.4 miles to the intersection with N.C. 49/U.S. 64 in Asheboro, the seat of Randolph County. Incorporated in 1796, the city was named in honor of Samuel Ashe, the noted North Carolina statesman and jurist of Revolutionary War times.

Turn right onto N.C. 49, follow it 2.8 miles west to S.R. 1163 (Tot Hill Farm Road), turn left, drive 2.3 miles to S.R. 1199 (Doul Mountain Road), and turn right. Almost immediately, you will cross a tributary of Bettie McGee's Creek. Tradition has it that the creek was named for Martha McGee Bell.

Go 0.3 mile north on S.R. 1199. On the right side of the road, you'll notice a copse of trees in the middle of a field on private property. Beneath the trees is the Balfour cemetery. This isolated graveyard is within sight of the runways of Asheboro Municipal Airport. It is the final resting place of Colonel Andrew Balfour (1737–82), whose story is one of the most tragic of the Revolution.

Born in Scotland to an aristocratic family, Balfour came to the colonies in 1772 in hopes of building a new life for his wife and his infant daughter, Isabel (otherwise known as "Tibbie"), both of whom remained behind. A year later, his wife died. Balfour subsequently married Elizabeth Dayton of Newport, Rhode Island.

A lack of business success in New England and Charleston brought Balfour to North Carolina in the early years of the war. He acquired a sizable plantation on Bettie McGee's Creek and constructed a house here. Balfour brought Tibbie and his sister, Margaret, to live on the nineteen-hundred-acre plantation and also made plans for his wife and his other two children, Andrew Jr. and Margaret, to leave Rhode Island and join him. In anticipation of a reunion, Mrs. Balfour wrote her husband, "It is impossible for me to express the joy I feel at hearing that you are well. . . . After an absence of more than two years and a half, to meet will be a pleasure beyond the power of words to express."

Unfortunately, a war was raging.

Described as "a man of superior intelligence, high moral character, and unflinching courage," Balfour was of "kindred spirit with those who resolved to be free or die." An intimate friend of George Washington, he took up arms as a Patriot and fought with valor as a militia officer in the South.

When Randolph County was formed during the war, voters elected the popular Balfour as one of its first justices of the peace and as a representative in the general assembly. Despite these civic responsibilities, Balfour continued his participation in the military. At one point, he was captured by the enemy but managed to escape.

Cornwallis's capitulation at Yorktown in October 1781 did little to quell the animosity between Whigs and Tories in North Carolina. David Fanning, the most notorious Tory in the South, was aware of Balfour's declaration that there should be no resting place for a Tory's foot on American soil. As a result, Balfour was at the top of Fanning's most wanted list.

On Sunday, March 10, 1782, Balfour was enjoying a brief leave at his plantation with his sister and ten-year-old Tibbie when the morning stillness was broken by the sound of hoofbeats. Balfour hurried to the door, where he found a neighbor, Stephen Cole. Breathlessly, Cole called out, "Run, Colonel! Run, Fanning is upon you!"

The warning came too late. Fanning and a band of twenty-five Tories rode up just as the alarm was being sounded. Absalom Autry, one of the raiders, fired a shot that broke Balfour's arm. Badly wounded, the Patriot made his way back into the house to protect his sister and daughter. They clung to Balfour as Fanning and his troopers poured into the house. He was promptly pulled away from his loved ones, who were pinned to the floor by the invaders and forced to watch as Balfour's body was riddled with bullets. Then Fanning stepped forward and applied the *coup de grâce* by firing his pistol into his helpless victim's head.

Following the execution, the Tories turned their attention to Margaret and Tibbie. The terrified females were kicked, beaten, and hacked with swords before they finally fled to the home of a neighbor. In their absence, the Balfour house was ransacked.

Fanning received no punishment for the murder, but one of his accomplices, Frederick Smith, was hunted down and hanged.

In December 1784, Balfour's widow and his other two children came to North Carolina. They settled in Salisbury, where they lived in a distressed financial state. Greatly disturbed that the family of a slain American hero should have to live in poverty, friends brought the matter to the attention of President Washington. In response, on March 31, 1796, he appointed Elizabeth Balfour as Salisbury's postmistress. She thus became the first woman in the United States to be appointed to such a position.

After twenty-six years of service, Mrs. Balfour retired to the family plantation here. Upon her death, she was laid to rest beside her husband at the current tour stop.

Retrace your route to the intersection of N.C. 49/U.S. 64 and U.S. 220 in Asheboro. Proceed east on U.S. 64 for 7.3 miles to S.R. 2235 (Andrew Hunter Road). Turn left and drive north for 1.6 miles to the Andrew Hunter Bridge, which spans the Deep River. Several hundred yards downriver is the legendary Faith Rock, the site of a Patriot's miraculous escape from Tories in 1781. The historic boulder juts out of the steep riverbank and extends sixty feet into the water.

Andrew Hunter Bridge over the Deep River near Faith Rock

To reach a safer place for viewing that scene of high adventure, continue on S.R. 2235 for 0.3 mile. Just as you pass an old factory on the right, turn right into a parking area near the Andrew Hunter Pedestrian Bridge. A nearby D.A.R. marker pays tribute to the heroism of Andrew Hunter.

Walk onto the bridge, which affords a panoramic view of the Deep River.

Andrew Hunter, a Randolph County Patriot, was an outspoken critic of David Fanning and the violence he spread throughout the region. When Hunter's denunciations reached Fanning, he swore revenge against the Patriot.

Fanning's men captured Hunter several times, but with the help of fellow Patriots, he escaped each time. Frustrated, Fanning pledged to execute him once he was captured again.

Finally, that opportunity came. Upon learning that Hunter was at a mill in Montgomery County, Fanning dispatched his Tories there, and Hunter was once again taken prisoner. "Say your prayers, you damned rebel, for I'm going to swing you from the nearest tree," Fanning told him.

The Tories departed the mill in search of a place to conduct the hanging. En route, they became hungry and found food in Hunter's wagon. Fanning agreed to postpone the execution so his men might take lunch.

While the Tories' attention was on their meal, Hunter looked for an avenue of escape. He spotted Fanning's prize horse, called Red Doe or Bay Doe, tied nearby. After approaching slowly, he jumped atop the animal and sped away before Fanning's soldiers could stop him. Indignant about the escape but fearful of losing his treasured steed, Fanning directed his men to "kill the rascal but spare the mare." One well-directed shot lodged in Hunter's shoulder, rendering his arm useless.

A chase ensued. As Hunter neared the Deep River, he realized there were but two places to cross. He encountered a group of Fanning's men at the first crossing, so he galloped upstream toward the second ford. Upon discovering that it, too, was guarded by Tories, he scanned the riverbank for a way to avoid capture and certain death. He spied a giant rock that sloped into the river at an angle of sixty degrees. With a quick wave to the Tories, Hunter spurred Fanning's horse, and down the steep rock he went. Horse and rider plunged into the water and floated to safety down the swiftly flowing river.

So amazed were the Tories with the courageous escape that they refrained from firing. One of Fanning's men is said to have remarked, "If he has faith enough to try to escape that way we will not shoot again."

The rock has carried its famous name ever since that day.

In the days following the escape, Fanning was more incensed than ever. He had lost his cherished horse, his pistols, and the valuable papers he carried in his saddlebags. A subsequent attempt to recover his property by holding Hunter's pregnant wife hostage failed, and the woman was released unharmed.

Faith Rock survives as a natural monument to one of the most daring and skillful exhibitions of horsemanship of the Revolution. Legend holds that if you make a close inspection of the sloping boulder, you can see the imprint of Baby Doe's hooves.

Continue on S.R. 2235 to its junction with N.C. 22 in the heart of Franklinville. Follow N.C. 22 south for 2.2 miles to U.S. 64, turn left, and drive east on N.C. 22/U.S. 64 for 0.2 mile to where N.C. 22 veers south to run conjunctively with Main Street in the town of Ramseur. Follow N.C. 22 for 1.4 miles to Liberty Street. A state historical marker here calls attention to Cox's Mill, which was located north of the confluence of Mill Creek and the Deep River 4.5 miles southeast of the current tour stop. David Fanning (1755–1825) used the mill as his base of operations in 1781 and 1782.

Follow N.C. 22 for another 2.2 miles to S.R. 2642, turn left, and go 1.7 miles to S.R. 2626 at Parks Crossroads. En route, you will cross Mill Creek. Turn left and drive north on S.R. 2626 for 0.5 mile, where the highway once again crosses Mill Creek.

Fanning had his headquarters in this vicinity during the latter stages of the Revolution. The schemes and raids planned here etched the name of David Fanning on North Carolina's roll of infamy.

That said, Fanning was one of the most dynamic North Carolinians of the Revolutionary War era. According to eminent historian Samuel A. Ashe, "It must be said . . . that he [Fanning] was one of the boldest men, most fertile in expedients, and quick in execution, that ever lived in North Carolina. Had he been on the Whig side, his fame would have been more enduring than that of any other partisan officer whose memory is now so dear to all patriots." The descendant of illustrious Patriots himself, Ashe called Fanning "one of the most extraordinary men evolved by the Revolutionary War."

The infamous Tory was only in his twenties when he wrote his name in the state's history. It was a bit ironic that he chose the Deep River area as his staging ground. His father had drowned in the river just before David's birth. His mother then died during his youth, leaving the orphan to grow up in what is now Wake County under the care of guardians.

From 1775 to 1780, Fanning's military service for the Crown led to his frequent imprisonment, a bounty being placed on his head, several attempts on his life, and a trial for treason.

It was after the Patriot victory at Kings Mountain in October 1780 that Fanning settled near the Deep River, where he immediately laid plans to raise an army of Tories to aid Cornwallis in the upcoming British invasion of North Carolina. During the campaign that culminated at the Battle at Guilford Courthouse, Fanning and his followers served Cornwallis as scouts.

Cornwallis's so-called victory over Greene in March 1781 emboldened Fanning to try to raise an even larger force of Loyalists. Over the next year, from their base at Cox's Mill, he and his soldiers waged a vicious civil war in central North Carolina the likes of which the state has never experienced since. Death and destruction were the order of the day when Fanning's raiders called.

Fanning was once described as "a man of fine physique, small in stature, but very muscular and very athletic." As a warrior, he possessed "the astuteness of the Indian and the fleetness of an Arab, with a constitution capable of bearing almost any amount of toil and with a patience of hunger and fatigue worthy of any cause, he might be said to be always on horseback and always in motion."

His reign of terror, deeply entrenched in the history of the Deep River area, included thirty-six skirmishes and battles and countless raids. The Patriots' numerous efforts to capture him failed.

After the British army abandoned North Carolina in November 1781, Fanning found himself facing an overwhelming opponent. He fled to the relative safety of South Carolina in April 1782 and never returned to the Tar Heel State. In 1783, the state legislature pardoned all Tories in North Carolina with the exception of three. "His crimes and butcheries" deemed "beyond forgiveness," David Fanning was among the trio.

Turn around near Mill Creek and retrace your route to where S.R. 2626 junctions with S.R. 2642 and S.R. 2628 at Parks Crossroads. Turn right on S.R. 2628 and drive south for 2.7 miles to the bridge over the Deep River. This span provides a spectacular view of historic Buffalo Ford, located just to the north.

In late June or early July 1781, General Johann de Kalb, a gallant German officer in the service of the Continental Army, reached this ford with two Maryland brigades, a Delaware regiment, and the First Continental

Artillery. During his two-week encampment along the river, de Kalb learned that his command had been given to General Horatio Gates.

Return to the junction with N.C. 22. Turn right and proceed 2.5 miles to N.C. 42 at the town of Coleridge. Turn right, drive 0.8 mile to S.R. 2873, turn left, and travel south for 6 miles to S.R. 2887. Turn left and go 0.9 mile to where S.R. 2887 terminates near the Deep River.

From his campsite at Buffalo Ford, General de Kalb moved his army to Spinks's Farm, which was located at the current tour stop. Some historians have concluded that General Gates arrived here on July 25 to assume command of de Kalb's forces.

From this point, the Continentals began their march to Camden, South Carolina, where Cornwallis soundly whipped Gates on August 16. General de Kalb laid down his life in the battle.

Retrace your route to S.R. 2873. Turn left, drive south for 0.5 mile to S.R. 1002, and turn left again. It is 3.4 miles to the Chatham County line. Chatham County was carved from Orange county in 1771. It was named in honor of William Pitt, earl of Chatham (1708–78), who urged Britain to recognize the independence of the American colonies in 1777.

Continue east for 0.3 mile to N.C. 22 near the town of Bennett. Anson Road, a route frequently used by Fanning's Tories, once passed near the current tour stop.

Turn right on N.C. 22. It is 3.5 miles to the Moore County line. Named in honor of Alfred Moore, a Revolutionary War officer and United States Supreme Court justice, the county was created in 1784.

Follow N.C. 22 for 2.5 miles to S.R. 1470. Turn right and drive south for 5.5 miles to N.C. 705 in the town of Robbins. Nearby stands a state historical marker for Mechanics Hill, the site of gunsmithing operations in the eighteenth century. The Kennedy family produced long rifles here.

Turn left on N.C. 705, drive south for 2.8 miles to N.C. 22/N.C. 24/N.C. 27, turn left, and go 1 mile to S.R. 1490, where you'll see a state historical marker for John Bethune (1751–1815).

Born in Scotland, Bethune came to North Carolina around 1773. A Presbyterian minister, he was appointed chaplain of the First Battalion of the Royal High Emigrants. In February 1776, he accompanied his Scottish brethren to Moores Creek, where he was captured by Patriot forces. Bethune lived 4 miles south of the historical marker.

Continue east on N.C. 22/N.C. 24/N.C. 27 for 0.2 mile to S.R. 1210. Turn right and proceed south for 4.2 miles to S.R. 1261; en route, you will pass near the site where Bethune lived.

Turn left on S.R. 1261, drive east for 0.8 mile to S.R. 1263 (Scotch Cemetery Road), turn right, and go 0.2 mile to the Old Scottish Graveyard, located in a forested area on the left side of the dead-end road.

There are sixty-five marked graves in this isolated, ancient cemetery. Most of the people interred here were among the second wave of Scottish settlers in southeastern North Carolina. According to tradition, the three-acre burial ground was laid out by Captain John Martin, a Scottish Tory leader. His wife's grave is perhaps the oldest in the cemetery. Captain Martin was to have been buried beside his wife, but he fled to Canada after the Revolution and was interred there.

Return to S.R. 1261 and proceed east for 2 miles to S.R. 1262. The home of John MacRae, a renowned Gaelic poet who emigrated to North Carolina from Scotland in 1774, once stood in this vicinity.

A staunch Loyalist, MacRae fought at the Battle of Moores Creek Bridge. His son, Murdock, was killed there. Thereafter, MacRae was persecuted for his political beliefs and his devotion to the Crown. Tradition maintains that he was executed because of the support for King George III he expressed in his poetry.

Turn left on S.R. 1262 and drive north for 2.4 miles to N.C. 22/N.C. 24/ N.C. 27, where a state historical marker honors John MacRae.

Turn right and proceed east for 4.7 miles to S.R. 1261. En route, you will pass a state historical marker noting the site of Alexander Morrison's home, where John Bethune, John MacRae, and other Scottish Loyalists gathered for the march to Moores Creek Bridge.

An abandoned service station stands at the junction of N.C. 22/N.C 24/ N.C. 27 and S.R. 1261. Located in the forest several hundred feet off the northern side of N.C. 22/N.C. 24/N.C. 27 is an old cemetery that contains the grave of an important Revolutionary War personage.

Dr. George Glascock (1729–87) was a surgeon who served the American cause at the Battle of Guilford Courthouse. His mother was Patty Ball, the maternal aunt of George Washington.

A dispute between Dr. Glascock and Phillip Alston, the controversial man who owned the House in the Horseshoe (visited later on this tour), led to the surgeon's murder. Evidence indicated that Alston had ordered his slave, Dave, to commit the crime. At the time Glascock was gunned down, Alston was staging a lavish party at his plantation. Both owner and slave were implicated in the murder, but neither was ever tried.

Follow N.C. 24/27 east for 2.3 miles through Carthage, the seat of Moore County, to the junction with S.R. 1006 and U.S. 15/U.S. 501. The home of Colonel Alexander McLeod, the commander of Loyalist forces at the Battle of Moores Creek Bridge, once stood several miles south of here. A state historical marker for the site is located on U.S. 15/U.S. 501 south of the current tour stop.

The two state historical markers that stand in a traffic island at the present stop will direct your attention to the grave of Benjamin Williams and the House in the Horseshoe. To see both sites, turn left on S.R. 1006 and drive north for 6.9 miles to S.R. 1621. Bear right onto S.R. 1621, continue north for 2.6 miles to S.R. 1624, turn left, and proceed 0.4 mile west to the House in the Horseshoe State Historic Site.

The site's centerpiece is a splendidly restored, two-story frame house. Called the House in the Horseshoe because of its location atop a hill in a horseshoe bend of the Deep River, the home was constructed in 1772. At that time, it was one of the finest structures of its kind in the back country.

By all accounts, the builder and first occupant of the house was a Patriot who did little to bring honor to the American cause. Labeled a "miscreant" and an "unprincipled scoundrel," Phillip Alston (1745–91) was apparently plagued by character flaws from an early age. Born at Halifax into a wealthy and politically prominent family, Alston inherited only some slaves from his clan's hundred-thousand-acre estate. Fortunately for him, his wife, Temperance Smith, the daughter of a wealthy Halifax County planter, received a nice inheritance.

For unexplained reasons, Alston moved his family to a four-thousand-acre tract here in 1772. Rumors in Halifax at that time hinted that Alston was involved in counterfeiting.

Three years later, he took up the cause of independence and was appointed a major of the militia. In 1776, he was promoted to lieutenant colonel and

House in the Horseshoe

appointed justice of the county court.

Power only served to corrupt him. His friends were few and his enemies many. Robert Rowan, a distinguished Patriot from Cumberland County, once complained to Richard Caswell that "two or three years ago no gentlemen with the least regard for his [Alston's] character would have kept this hectoring, domineering person company. . . . A greater tyrant is not upon the face of the earth." An avowed atheist, Alston refused to worship God and ordered his family to refrain from doing so.

In his role as justice of the county court, he scoured the countryside in an attempt to force Scottish settlers to sign an oath of allegiance to the United States. If they refused, he confiscated their land. If they agreed to take the oath, he promptly turned around and denied them the opportunity—if he liked their land. It was perhaps no coincidence that his estate mushroomed to seven thousand acres by 1777.

Alston's military career did little to improve his reputation. His promotion to colonel of the militia in 1778 was mired in controversy.

In March 1779, it was reported by General John Ashe that Alston had been taken prisoner in the fighting at Briar Creek, Georgia. Following his release, he returned to Moore County. For the remainder of the war, he matched wits with local Tories, including David Fanning. Alston's mistreatment of Scottish settlers drew Fanning's ire.

During the summer of 1781, Alston and his men were chasing Fanning in an attempt to rescue some Patriot prisoners. They happened upon Kenneth Black, a follower of Fanning, near what is now Southern Pines. Black was leading Fanning's favorite bay horse, which was lame. He mounted the crippled animal in an attempt to escape, but one of Alston's men shot him off it. Once Alston reached the wounded man, he used his gun butt to smash Black's head and then left the Tory for dead.

After delivering his prisoners to Wilmington, Fanning learned of the attack on his soldier. In fact, Black spent his dying breath telling Fanning that Alston was responsible. Thus, the stage was set for a showdown between North Carolina's two most notorious Revolutionary War partisans.

At dawn on Sunday, August 5, 1781, Fanning and his Loyalists rode toward the House in the Horseshoe intent upon exacting revenge for Black's death. Alston was quartered inside the home, while a force of twenty-five soldiers slept outside. As he approached, Fanning divided his army into three parties. His men captured a sleeping sentry and then dismounted and took cover.

Accompanying Fanning on the expedition was a British officer who promptly voiced his disapproval of the ground-hugging tactics. The Redcoat maintained that if he had command, he could take the house in a few minutes. Fanning granted his wish.

Sword drawn, the young officer implored the Tories to follow him. Just as he stepped forward to climb a fence, a musket ball fired from the house plowed into his heart.

Guns blazed over the next several hours. Every window in the house was shattered, and the walls were pockmarked by bullets. Both sides suffered casualties, but neither could gain the upper hand.

As the fight wore on, Fanning grew apprehensive that a Patriot force might come to Alston's aid. To end the stalemate, he ordered his men to load a nearby cart with hay. Using the loaded cart as a shield, the soldiers pushed it toward the house, where they were to set it afire.

From his position inside the house, Alston could see what was happening. Realizing he was about to be burned out, he called a council of war. Surrender seemed to be the only alternative, but Alston feared that he and his men would be shot down if they walked out to surrender.

During the skirmish, Mrs. Alston and her two children sought refuge in a bedroom, where the two youngsters were placed in a chimney. Aware of the dilemma facing her husband, Mrs. Alston entered the room where he and the others were and offered to tender the surrender. She reasoned that even the callous Fanning would not fire upon a woman. The Patriots—and particularly Colonel Alston—were not so sure.

When Mrs. Alston emerged from the house with a white cloth, all gunfire ceased. From his position behind the barn, Fanning ordered her to meet him halfway. When the two came face to face, Mrs. Alston announced, "We will surrender, sir, on condition that no one shall be injured; otherwise we will make the best defense we can; and, if need be, sell our lives as dearly as possible."

Moved by her courage, Fanning agreed. Colonel Alston and the surviving Patriots signed a parole agreement penned by Fanning, whose men then plundered the house but refrained from burning it, in deference to their leader's pledge to Mrs. Alston.

A D.A.R. marker in the yard memorializes the skirmish. The bodies of the Tory casualties—estimated to have been between eight and sixteen—are believed to be buried on the hill beyond the house.

His political career in ruins, Alston sold the house and plantation in 1790 and left the state. Records indicate that he subsequently took up residence in Georgia. On October 28, 1791, someone murdered Alston while he slept in his house. Ironically, his slayer is thought to have been Dave, the same man Alston had used to kill Dr. Glascock.

In 1798, Benjamin Williams (1752–1814) acquired the House in the Horseshoe and twenty-five hundred acres surrounding it. He subsequently enlarged the home and renamed it Retreat. Aided by the invention of the cotton gin, he turned the surrounding countryside into one of the state's first large cotton plantations.

Born in Craven County, Williams descended from a distinguished family that included a settler at the original Jamestown colony. Like many of his Revolutionary War compatriots, he served a dual role as politician and soldier during much of the war. Afterwards, he enjoyed a phenomenally successful political career that included four terms as governor of North Carolina. He was buried in a family cemetery on Governor's Creek, located 1.5 miles from the house. In 1970, his grave and that of his wife, Eliza Jones, (the half-sister of Willie and Allen Jones), were moved to the side yard of the historic dwelling.

Each summer, the historic site hosts a reenactment of the dramatic events that occurred here in the summer of 1781. The house still bears bullet holes from the encounter. Its interior is open to the public.

Return to S.R. 1621, turn left, and proceed north for 2.1 miles to the Chatham County line, where the road number changes to S.R. 2307. Follow S.R. 2307 through the town of Carbonton. After 2.4 miles, the road junctions with S.R. 2140. Turn right, follow S.R. 2140 east for 2.7 miles to U.S. 421, turn right again, and go 1.7 miles to S.R. 2145. Turn left, proceed east for 4.8 miles to S.R. 2217, turn left again, and go 1.8 miles to the junction with N.C. 87/U.S. 15/U.S. 501. Turn left and travel north on N.C. 87/U.S. 15/U.S. 501 for 2.9 miles to S.R. 1955. Turn right, drive east for 3.5 miles to S.R. 1012, turn right, and head south for 3.1 miles to S.R. 1011 near the town of Moncure. A state historical marker just west of the junction calls attention to Ramsey's Mill, which stood three hundred yards northwest on the Deep River.

To see the site, turn right and drive 0.3 mile west to an unnamed dirt road on the far side of the bridge over the Deep River. Turn right and follow the road as it makes its way to the riverbank under the span, where you'll have a panoramic view of the river and the site of Ramsey's Mill on the opposite shore. Had it not been for circumstances, Cornwallis's final surrender might have taken place here in March 1781, rather than six months later at Yorktown.

As he retreated south from Guilford Courthouse, Cornwallis stopped on March 22 at the mill and tavern on the steep clay bluffs overlooking the Deep River. Both mill and tavern were owned by Ambrose Ramsey, a militia colonel and a representative in the state legislature.

Cornwallis remained for two days while his engineers and soldiers constructed a bridge across the river at this site, which is less than 3 miles north of the confluence of the Deep and the Cape Fear. Meanwhile, Thomas Riddle and his small band of Patriot snipers stationed themselves in a house on the side of the river where you now stand. Directing their fire at the British soldiers as they labored on the bridge and watered their horses along the shore, they inflicted numerous casualties.

Nathanael Greene had delayed his chase of the British commander after Guilford Courthouse in order to regroup his army and replenish his supplies and munitions. While Cornwallis's soldiers paused here, Greene began his pursuit. Lieutenant Colonel Willie Jones expressed the optimism that prevailed among Greene's officer corps: "We expect to come up with them in a day or two and to take a part if not the whole British army."

Not until the Americans were within 10 miles of Ramsey's Mill did Cornwallis learn of their approach. So hastily did he break camp that he abandoned his badly wounded soldiers and neglected to burn the bridge.

Historians have speculated that had Greene overtaken Cornwallis here, the British army would have been annihilated and George Washington would have made his way to the scene to accept a general surrender.

Ambrose Ramsey's tavern was renamed the Cornwallis Hotel after the

TOURING NORTH CAROLINA'S REVOLUTIONARY WAR SITES

visit by the British commander. Known for its unusual three-cornered chimney, the structure stood until 1929.

A flood in 1901 so badly damaged the mill that it could never be used again. Millstones from the Revolutionary War operations here were subsequently recovered from the river by Carolina Power and Light Company and delivered to the North Carolina Division of Archives and History.

Retrace your route to S.R. 1012. Turn left and proceed 8.5 miles north to the junction with N.C. 87/U.S. 15/U.S. 501. Turn right and drive 0.6 mile to the state historical marker (entitled "Tory Raid") near where the county courthouse stood in Revolutionary War times.

Built soon after Chatham County was organized, the first courthouse was a two-story wooden structure located on the lands of Major Mial Scurlock. Cornwallis camped here just before his stop at Ramsey's Mill. He set up headquarters at the Scurlock home, which stood nearby. Until the dwelling was demolished in the early twentieth century, its hand-hewn boards revealed names and dates inscribed by British soldiers in 1781. Mrs. Scurlock, the widow of a militia officer and the mother of a soldier in the Continental Army, was treated respectfully by Cornwallis, despite her outspoken views about the war.

In the wake of Cornwallis's departure, the old courthouse was the site of one of David Fanning's most daring exploits. At seven o'clock in the morning on July 16, 1781, Fanning and his men rode into Pittsboro, where area Patriots had scheduled a court-martial of several Loyalists to begin at eight o'clock. What followed next was a classic example of Fanning's guile. In his *Narrative*, he recorded how he "posted pickets on every road, and within the spaces of two hours took 53 prisoners. . . . I immediately marched them to Cox's Mill, and paroled all except 14, who I knew were violent against the government."

In a single stroke, Fanning thus captured virtually every important citizen in Chatham County. His catch included Colonel Ambrose Ramsey and the rest of the local delegation in the state legislature; the colonel and the major of the county militia, as well as all the other local officers except for two who were absent; and a captain in the Continental Army.

From the marker, proceed 0.6 mile north to the Chatham County Courthouse, located at the intersection of N.C. 87/U.S. 15/U.S. 501 and

U.S. 64 in the heart of Pittsboro, the seat of Chatham County. Incorporated in 1778, the town was named in honor of William Pitt, earl of Chatham, a champion of American rights in the British Parliament.

Turn left onto U.S. 64 and drive west for 5 miles to Aspen Hall, located on the right. A white wooden fence marks the driveway leading to the mansion, which is screened from the road by trees.

Built in three stages, each in a different style, the house was begun in the second half of the seventeenth century by "Chatham Jack" Alston, the brother of the infamous Phillip Alston of Moore County. Also known as "40-Mile Jack" because of the forty thousand acres he owned, Alston wielded great power in the area during Revolutionary War times.

The Alston brothers are said to have been uncles of Joseph Alston, the governor of South Carolina and husband of the legendary Theodosia Burr.

Continue west on U.S. 64 for 6.2 miles to S.R. 1500. Turn right, drive 3.7 miles north to S.R. 1346, turn left, and go west for 3.8 miles to S.R. 1004. It is 2.4 miles north on S.R. 1004 to the Alamance County line. Alamance was established in 1849. This area was part of Orange County when Governor Tryon did battle with the Regulators in 1771.

From the county line, it is 3.5 miles on S.R. 1004 to a state historical marker that calls attention to Cornwallis's visit to the community of Snow Camp following the Battle of Guilford Courthouse.

Quakers settled in this area along the banks of Cane Creek around the middle of the eighteenth century. Like their counterparts in nearby Guilford County, these peace-loving settlers found themselves thrust into the forefront of the American Revolution as it reached its climax in North Carolina in 1781.

To visit the site where much of the Revolutionary War action in this area took place, continue for 0.2 mile to S.R. 1005, turn left, and proceed 1 mile west to the junction with S.R. 2369 and S.R. 2371. Here stands historic Cane Creek Meeting House.

One of the millstone markers in the adjacent church cemetery honors Simon Dixon (1728–81), a native of Pennsylvania. Dixon and his wife, Rachel, settled on Cane Creek in 1751 on a tract granted by the Lords Proprietors. Two years later, he constructed Dixon's Mill, which attracted the attention of Cornwallis in March 1781.

Despite his Quaker beliefs, Dixon had taken part in the Regulator movement. As a result, he feared reprisals by the British army as it approached after the fight at Guilford Courthouse. According to tradition, Dixon sought refuge at the home of Colonel Robert Mebane in eastern Alamance prior to Cornwallis's arrival. Before he left his mill, he is said to have jammed the mill wheel so it could not be operated by the invaders.

When Cornwallis rode into the community, he commandeered the Dixons' home for his headquarters, and Mrs. Dixon and her children moved into the inoperative mill. Missing her pipe and tobacco, the lady returned to the house, where she encountered two sentries at the door. Cornwallis overheard the argument that ensued and made his way to the door, where he asked, "What is the trouble?" Mrs. Dixon told him what she wanted. Cornwallis escorted her inside, helped her search for the desired items, and then showed her out.

But events at the household turned less hospitable when Simon Dixon returned home while the British were still encamped at Cane Creek. Tradition maintains that the Redcoats tortured Dixon with hot fireplace tongs in an attempt to coerce him into divulging the location of the family treasure. His only response was this: "On the banks of Cane Creek."

Although Dixon survived the torture, he died three weeks after Cornwallis's departure from a disease he had been exposed to during the British encampment. He was buried here in the cemetery at Cane Creek.

A second millstone marker bears a plaque reading, "A memorial to British troops who died in Old Meeting House during Cornwallis encampment here on his retreat from Guilford Courthouse March 1781." Three British casualties who perished from war wounds and disease were buried in the cemetery.

Another grim reminder of the British occupation may be buried here. Legend maintains that Cornwallis had two cannon when he arrived at Snow Camp and only one when he left. Because of the poor condition of his horses, it is believed he abandoned one of the weapons. In order that it not fall into Greene's hands, the decision was made to bury it in the cemetery at Cane Creek.

This historic church was organized in 1751 and is the oldest Quaker meeting in central North Carolina. The existing brick building stands just a few feet from the site of the original church. Until that structure was destroyed by fire in 1879, the benches inside it were stained with the blood from cattle slaughtered by the Redcoats during their stay in 1781.

Turn left on S.R. 2369 and drive 0.4 mile south to the bridge over Cane Creek. Simon Dixon maintained his home and mill in this vicinity. For more than two centuries, stories of Dixon's treasure have abounded. Dixon is said to have buried the family gold and silver in a long stocking along the banks of Cane Creek in advance of the British invasion. His subsequent illness and death prevented him from recovering the valuables.

Over the decades, numerous organized and individual treasure hunts have been conducted, but "the Long Stocking Treasure," as it is known in the Snow Camp community, has never been found. Perhaps erosion washed it away long ago. Or maybe it remains where Dixon hid it in 1781.

Still another tradition from the Revolution explains how Snow Camp received its name. Cornwallis is said to have personally bestowed the name when he halted his army here due to a sudden heavy snowfall.

Just south of the bridge, turn left onto S.R. 2407 (Drama Road) and drive 0.1 mile to the Snow Creek Amphitheater.

Located in a small, reconstructed Quaker village that features a museum, craft shops, and nature trails, the amphitheater is the home of *The Sword of Peace*. Each summer since 1974, the story of the Quakers' struggles in central North Carolina during the Revolutionary War has come to life here. The play was written by William Hardy, a professor at the University of North Carolina. Among the characters in it are Simon Dixon, Charles Cornwallis, Nathanael Greene, and Dr. David Caldwell.

Follow S.R. 2407 to S.R. 2360. Turn left, proceed 0.3 mile east to S.R. 1004, turn left, and drive north for 0.8 mile to S.R. 1005. Turn right, head east for 4.7 miles to S.R. 1003, turn right again, and go 1.4 miles to the bridge over Cane Creek at Lindley's Mill (otherwise known as Sutphin Mill). A mill continues to operate here today.

This was the site of the last significant Revolutionary War battle on North Carolina soil. Dr. Eli Caruthers characterized the Battle of Lindley's Mill, fought on September 13, 1781, as "one of the remarkable feats of the Tories, and one of the most memorable events in North Carolina."

On the day before the battle, Colonel David Fanning led a bold daylight raid on Hillsborough, the temporary capital of North Carolina. His Tories took a number of prisoners, foremost among them Governor Thomas Burke.

Colonel Alexander Mebane watched from a hiding place as the marauders plundered the town. Unable to reach his horse, the Patriot officer ran toward his home, which was located to the southwest. Much in the manner of Paul Revere, he warned area residents as he ran, "The British are coming!"

At length, Mebane reached the Hawfields community and the home of his neighbor, John Butler, a brigadier general of the North Carolina militia. Knowing that Fanning would hurry to Wilmington to deliver his prized captive to the British army there, Butler promptly raised a force of three hundred men in an attempt to rescue Governor Burke.

The Hillsborough and Alamance Roads met at a sixty-acre plateau near Lindley's Mill. Butler selected the site as a perfect place for an ambush. His troops were in place on September 13 when the Tory advance guard rode headlong into the well-laid trap. Patriot marksmen on the brow of a hill on the southern side of Cane Creek offered a galling fire. For a brief moment, it appeared that Butler's men had carried the day. However, the bulk of Fanning's army—which was twice the size of the Patriot force—had not yet come upon the scene.

Alerted by the sounds of Butler's attack, Fanning first took precautions to secure Governor Burke and the other prisoners. Then he launched a vicious counterattack. For four hours, the two armies engaged in a bitter fight.

The heavily outnumbered American militia fought one of its most skillful battles of the war. But just when it appeared that Butler might deal Fanning a devastating defeat, the Patriots began to exhaust their powder supply. Butler ordered a retreat.

Unwilling to leave the field, Colonel Robert Mebane inspired a force of Patriots to fight on. According to Caruthers, "Mebane walked slowly along the line, carrying his hat full of powder, telling every man to take . . . just what he needed."

The battle ended as it had begun, with Governor Burke in captivity. He and the other prisoners were then subjected to a difficult march during which they suffered in the extreme.

Several hundred yards downstream from the mill is the ridge where Butler's men made their stand. It is marked only with a crude, homemade stone marker that reads, "For Justice here was fought the Battle of Lindley's Mill Sept. 14 1781."

The battle here was one of the bloodiest of the entire war. Nearly one-fifth of the participants were killed or wounded. The scene on the field after the battle was horrible. From the plateau to Cane Creek, the dead and dying lay in every direction, some of them in the water. According to one eyewitness, nearby Stafford Branch "ran red with blood." Thirty-four soldiers were buried in a mass grave near the battlefield.

Among the badly wounded survivors was David Fanning. He described his injury this way: "At the conclusion of this action, I received a shot in my left arm, which broke the bone in several pieces, my loss of blood so great, that I was taken off my horse, and led to a secret place in the woods." Fanning's wound was so severe that he was forced to hide in the area for three weeks and was unable to accompany the prisoners to Wilmington.

When you are ready to leave the mill, return to S.R. 1005. Turn right and drive east for 1.4 miles to S.R. 2338. Located here on the right side of S.R. 1005 is Spring Friends Meeting. A state historical marker for the church stands nearby.

This church was organized in 1764 and officially recognized as "Friends of Spring Meeting" in 1773. The existing brick building replaced the original white frame structure, which was destroyed by fire in 1908. Governor Burke and Fanning's other prisoners may have been confined in the original church during the encounter with Butler's militiamen.

Both buildings were erected on a site donated by Thomas Lindley, the owner of the mill where the bloody battle was fought. A monument in the church cemetery memorializes Lindley. A devout Quaker who sided with the Regulators, he provided them with flour from his mill and opened his home to one of their meetings on May 11, 1768. But when it became necessary to choose between the movement and the church, he selected the church.

Ironically, Lindley died at the age of seventy-five on the very day the battle was fought at his mill. Although the true cause of his death is unknown, tradition maintains that the shocking effect of the bloodshed on his estate killed the aged Quaker.

Once the fighting at Lindley's Mill was over, the grim task of caring for the wounded and burying the dead was at hand.

Some family members came to claim their own. One story tells of a lady who walked seventy-five miles to care for her brother, a Tory who died despite her efforts.

But for the most part, the battlefield caregivers came from the neighborhood. One of the first persons to reach the scene was Dr. John Pyle, a Tory who selflessly ministered to Whigs and Tories alike. For that reason, his Patriot neighbors forgave him for his past "transgressions." As the neighborhood around Lindley's Mill was predominantly Quaker, people from the Spring and Cane Creek churches reluctantly assumed a major role in aiding the battle victims. Even the strongest pacifist at the Spring church joined in the effort after hearing a Quaker leader admonish, "Every one of them is a mother's son."

One badly wounded Patriot, Colonel Lutteral, was able to ride to a nearby farmhouse, where he collapsed. The owner carried him to an upstairs bedroom to die. Before he expired, the soldier dipped his finger in his own blood and feebly wrote his name on the wall. The pathetic signature remained visible for many years.

Continue on S.R. 1005 for 1.2 miles to N.C. 87, where a state historical marker commemorates the Battle of Lindley's Mill.

Turn left on N.C. 87, drive north for 12.3 miles to S.R. 2304 (Hanford Brick Road), turn left again, and go 1.8 miles to Tick's Golf Center, located on the right. On the opposite side of the road in a dense thicket of undergrowth on private property is a family cemetery that contains the graves of two Revolutionary War soldiers, Michael Holt, Jr. (1723–99), and his son-in-law John Harden.

Holt, a captain in the king's militia during the Regulator movement, owned substantial acreage along nearby Alamance Creek. When Governor William Tryon came to the area in 1771 to put an end to the trouble occasioned by the Regulators, he chose to do battle with the "insurrectionists" on Holt's farm. Tryon's victory served as a measure of personal revenge for Holt, who had earlier been whipped by the Regulators in Hillsborough. Casualties from Tryon's battle were treated in Holt's home.

When the Revolution began, Holt was an ardent supporter of the Crown. At the request of Governor Josiah Martin, he raised a company of fifty men to combat the Patriots. As he led his recruits toward Fayetteville and a rendezvous with the Highland Tories and other Loyalists, Holt became "fully acquainted with the intention of the Tories," as he put it. His sudden change of heart on the road to Fayetteville led him to return home, where he took up the cause of independence.

Still, as a result of his prior sympathy for the Crown, Patriots arrested him as a Tory and imprisoned him in Philadelphia. A carefully worded petition to the North Carolina Council of Safety resulted in his pardon by the Continental Congress. Holt returned to his home in Alamance, where he lived the rest of his life and acquired a vast estate.

Follow S.R. 2304 west for 0.5 mile to N.C. 49, where a state historical marker calls attention to "Pyle's Defeat," a significant battle fought near here in 1781. Also known as "Pyle's Massacre" and "Pyle's Hacking March," it was one of the most controversial victories earned by the Continental Army in North Carolina.

To see the site, turn south on N.C. 49, proceed 0.1 mile, turn right on S.R. 1148 (Anthony Road), and go 1.3 miles to the stone monument on the left side of the road.

While Nathanael Greene was in Virginia in February 1781, Cornwallis set up headquarters in Hillsborough and dispatched Banastre Tarleton to seek recruits in the area around the current tour stop. American scouts detected the movement and reported it to Greene. The American commander promptly dispatched a portion of his army under the command of Lighthorse Harry Lee and General Andrew Pickens to interfere with Cornwallis's attempt to increase the size of his army.

After crossing the Dan into North Carolina, the Americans made their way to Salisbury Road, located 8 miles west of Hillsborough. That Tarleton had passed through recently was evident: houses had been plundered, farms had been devastated, and all able-bodied males were gone. Hope ran high that Tarleton could be caught. As Pickens noted, "Never was there a more glorious opportunity of cutting off a detachment than this."

On the afternoon of February 25, Lee's green-jacketed dragoons were in the lead when they happened upon two riders from the four-hundred-man contingent of Tories under Colonel John Pyle. The two Tory horsemen were convinced that they had found the British cavalry commander when they saw the coats of the cavalrymen, since Tarleton's men also wore green. Lighthorse Harry Lee was not about to tell them otherwise. As he later noted, "They rejoiced in meeting us."

The two Tories thus unwittingly became informants. Lee learned that Pyle's army was in the road just ahead. But with Tarleton in the area, Pyle's Tories were but a distraction. Therefore, the American cavalry leader decided upon a ploy that would lead him past Pyle's men to an encounter with Tarleton.

First, Lee sent one of the Tory riders in the company of two American dragoons to Pyle with "Colonel Tarleton's compliments." They delivered orders directing that Pyle's column give way in order to allow the "much fatigued troops to pass without delay to their next position."

Next came one of the most famous ruses of the Revolution. Lee divided his forces into three commands. He and Pickens rode out front with a detail of cavalrymen. Captain Joseph Graham, who had recovered from his wounds at the Battle of Charlotte, commanded a second unit that followed Lee and Pickens. Captain Eggleston, another Continental officer, led the American militia—distinguished by the green twigs they wore in their hats—into the woods.

According to Lee, it was his intention to ride up to Pyle, identify himself, and do no harm to the Tories if they agreed to disband or to fight for the American cause.

At first, all went as planned. Pyle's columns peeled off the road as Lee rode by "with a smiling countenance, dropping occasionally expressions complimentary to the good looks and commendable conduct of his loyal friends." A North Carolina Patriot who witnessed the spectacle noted that the Tories "frequently uttered salutations of a friendly kind, believing us to be British."

Known for his flair for military dramatics, Lee rode up to Colonel Pyle and exchanged salutes with the Tory commander. At the very moment Pyle extended his hand to welcome "Tarleton," the grand scheme began to unravel. Firing was heard at the end of the column.

Captains Graham and Eggleston hadn't had the opportunity to confer with Lee since the American commander planned his ruse. Upon reaching Pyle's army, Graham recognized the men as Tories by the red strips of cloth in their hats. When he related that fact to Eggleston, the militia commander rode up to one of the strangers and asked him, "To whom do you belong?"

The man promptly identified himself as "a friend of his Majesty."

Outraged, Eggleston drew his saber and slashed the Tory's head, and the American militiamen went into action.

Colonel Pyle screamed out in horror, "Stop! Stop! You are killing your own men! I am a friend of his Majesty! Hurrah for King George!"

Lee's cavalrymen then went to work slashing their surprised adversaries. Ninety Tories were slaughtered, and most of the remainder were badly wounded. One of the few who escaped was Colonel Pyle. Though severely injured, he made his way to a nearby pond, where he hid underwater with only his nose above the surface. Lee's single casualty was a horse.

But the vengeance-minded Americans were not satisfied. Moses Hall, a young North Carolina militiaman, described what happened as darkness covered the battlefield: "We went to where six [prisoners] were standing together. Some discussion taking place, I heard some of our men cry out, 'Remember Buford' [a reference to Tarleton's merciless slaughter of Americans in South Carolina] and the prisoners were immediately hewed to death with broadswords."

Alerted by the attack on Pyle, Tarleton escaped to Hillsborough. However, the effects of the fight were far reaching. As General Pickens observed, "It has knocked up Toryism altogether in this part." Or as Nathanael Greene put it, "It has had a very happy effect on those disaffected Persons, of which there are too many in this Country."

"Pyle's Defeat" deprived Cornwallis of troops he desperately needed for the looming confrontation with Greene at Guilford Courthouse. As historian Hugh Rankin noted, "Pyle's massacre could possibly have been a factor preventing Cornwallis from gaining a decisive victory at Guilford Courthouse on March 15, 1781."

Proceed west on S.R. 1148 for 2.1 miles to N.C. 62. Turn left and go south for 0.4 mile to the bridge over Alamance Creek. Here, you'll see a state historical marker near the site where Governor William Tryon camped before and after the Battle of Alamance in May 1771.

Continue south on N.C. 62 for 1.4 miles to the state historical marker for the Battle of Clapp's Mill. This encounter between Lee and Tarleton on

March 2, 1781, is covered later in the tour.

It is another 0.6 mile to Alamance Battleground State Historical Site.

To begin your tour of one of the most important sites associated with colonial North Carolina, stop at the visitor center, located on the right side of the highway. Inside the center, exhibits and an audiovisual presentation introduce visitors to the famous battle that occurred here on May 16, 1771.

From the visitor center, drive to the shelter at the far end of the site, from which you'll have an excellent view of the battlefield and its monuments. A large metal map here shows the location of the troops when the drama unfolded.

From its beginnings, the Regulator movement was a source of consternation for Governor William Tryon. Violence was narrowly averted several times. But when judges assigned to hold a term of superior court in Hillsborough in March 1781 refused to do so because of hostile conditions there, Tryon resolved to use force to stop the Regulators. Though Tryon had not addressed the Regulators' legitimate concerns, the back-country men had harmed their own cause by making threats of violence and holding a "rump court" in Hillsborough.

Tryon dispatched General Hugh Waddell to gather all the militia west of Salisbury. He was to bring the soldiers to a designated site just west of Great Alamance Creek, where they would unite with Governor Tryon and his militia army from New Bern.

Tryon arrived at the creek with 1,068 well-trained, well-armed soldiers on May 14. Waddell, it turned out, had mustered only 284 recruits. Approximately 2,000 Regulators were camped 6 miles away.

On May 15, the Regulators entreated Tryon to redress the grievances of the people of the back country. The messenger was none other than Dr. David Caldwell, who had ridden to the Regulator camp in an attempt to avert bloodshed. Tryon promised an answer the following day. Throughout the night, a third of his army stayed on the alert and his cavalrymen kept their mounts saddled.

At first light on May 16, the governor's army began to march toward the Regulators. Soon thereafter, Patrick Mullen rode into camp with the news that Tryon and his militia were on the march. Confusion reigned. The Regulators had not expected a fight. They were not trained as soldiers, they were poorly armed, and they had no military leaders.

Then David Caldwell rode into camp with Tryon's answer. From the grim look on his face, the men knew there would be no compromise. Disgusted by their "outrages" and "open violence," Tryon gave the Regulators one hour to submit to the government and to disassemble.

Herman Husband realized that nothing short of bloodshed would settle the issue and left in despair. But Dr. Caldwell returned to Governor Tryon in one last attempt to bring peace. The bright May sun was directly over the battlefield when he returned and addressed the Regulators: "Those of you who are not too far committed should desist and quietly return to your houses; those who have laid themselves liable should submit without further resistance. I and others promise to obtain for you the best terms possible."

Patrick Mullen, the elderly Scottish Regulator, stepped forward to interrupt Caldwell's speech: "Hold doctor. Ho away yourself or Tryon's men will kill you in three minutes."

Governor Tryon, mounted on a splendid white charger and immaculately dressed in a bright coat and a cocked hat, appeared on the field with his army. The moment of decision had come.

Tryon was within twenty-five yards of the front line of the Regulators when he stopped. His aide-de-camp, Philemon Hawkins, rode ahead. He halted before the anxious frontiersmen, unrolled a proclamation, and read the ultimatum, which ended thus: "By accepting these terms within one hour from the delivery of this dispatch, you will prevent an effusion of blood, as you are at this time in a state of REBELLION against your King, your country, and your laws."

The Regulators huddled as Hawkins returned to his lines. To them, surrender was not an acceptable option, but neither did they relish a bloody confrontation.

They sent one of their number, Robert Thompson, across the field to try to reason with Tryon. Known as an outspoken man, Thompson did little but further antagonize the governor. In a fit of rage, Tryon grabbed a gun from one of his soldiers. He aimed it, pulled the trigger, and sent a ball that plowed into Thompson as he walked back to his lines.

A soldier by training, Tryon knew his anger had led him to commit a grievous error. He hurriedly sent forward a flag of truce, but it was too late.

The flag was ripped away from the bearer by fire from a Regulator marksman.

Realizing the fight he had anticipated was at hand, Tryon rose in his stirrups and shouted, "Fire!" For a few seconds that seemed like minutes, his troops failed to respond. Then their commander issued one of the most famous orders in North Carolina history: "Fire on them—or fire on me!"

From the Regulator line came words of defiance: "Fire and be damned!"

Muskets offered deadly fire from both sides. Although the Regulators outnumbered Tryon's forces by two to one, they had no answer for the governor's artillery. When Captain Montgomery, one of the ablest Regulator officers, was killed by the second cannon blast, many of his comrades fled the field.

Meanwhile, Tryon galloped up and down his lines imploring his militiamen to finish the job. His boldness was tempered after a Regulator bullet tore through the tip of his hat.

A great many Regulators fell back or fled, but some, including James Pugh, held their position and kept up the fight. Pugh, the brother-in-law of Herman Husband, was one of the best Regulator marksmen. Hidden behind a rock ledge (still visible on the battleground), he offered deadly fire as three men loaded muskets and handed them to him. Pugh brought down seventeen of Tryon's soldiers—and ultimately went to the gallows for his exploits on the battlefield.

After two hours of vicious fighting, the Battle of Alamance was over. Tryon's victorious army lost nine killed and sixty-one wounded. The Regulators had a similar number killed but suffered many more wounded than did the militia.

Among the prisoners taken by Tryon was James Few, a poor, demented carpenter who claimed he had been "sent by Heaven to relieve the world from oppression." After a brief interrogation, the governor decided to make an example of the unfortunate man, who was hanged on the nearest tree. Six of Few's fellow Regulators would meet a similar fate a month later in Hillsborough.

From the end of the Revolutionary War to modern times, historians have debated the significance of the Battle of Alamance. Some have gone so far as to claim it was the first battle of the Revolution. Others contend that it was not a fight for independence because the Regulators did not rebel against the Crown. Their movement was crushed and died here.

Whichever the case, the blood spilled on the battleground at Alamance has not been forgotten. The sacrifices of the common man here provided an example for the Americans who rose up against injustice just a few years later.

Two significant monuments are located on the battlefield.

The older of the two, an obelisk mounted on three blocks of granite, was unveiled at a ceremony on May 29, 1880. It bears the following inscription: "Here was fought the Battle of Alamance May 16, 1771 between the British and the Regulators." On the reverse side appears a single word: *Liberty*.

The second major monument, a tall granite shaft topped with the figure of a Regulator, honors James Hunter. When Herman Husband left the field prior to the battle, the Regulators looked to Hunter as their leader. He attempted to refuse command by saying that "everyone must command himself." Nonetheless, he emerged from the battle with the title of "General of the Regulation." The Hunter Monument originally stood on the battlefield at Guilford Courthouse. Despite the protests of his descendants, it was moved to its present site in 1963.

From the state historic site, follow N.C. 62 north for 6.1 miles to I-85. Proceed south on I-85 for 1.7 miles to Exit 141 (Elon College). Exit onto S.R. 1149 (Huffman Mill Road) and go 2.9 miles south to the entrance to Lake MacIntosh Park and Marina, operated by the city of Burlington. Turn left, drive to where the road forks, take the right fork, and proceed to the monument for the Battle of Clapp's Mill.

Located near the shore of Lake MacIntosh are eight bronze plaques on granite slabs encircling a millstone. They tell the story of an encounter between Lee and Tarleton two weeks before the Battle of Guilford Courthouse.

Ever anxious to capture his cavalry rival, Lee laid an ambush on March 2, 1781, at a mill on Beaver Creek near its confluence with Great Alamance Creek. Colonel William Campbell's sharpshooters aided in the surprise attack, but Tarleton's troopers recovered and regrouped. Lee was forced to retreat after losing eight men. The British suffered twenty casualties.

The actual site is now covered by the lake. Nearby picnic facilities and the placid lakeside setting make this modern monument one of the most aesthetically pleasing in the state.

Return to I-85. Follow the interstate north for 6.8 miles to the exit for

N.C. 87. Exit onto N.C. 87 and drive north for 0.8 mile to N.C. 49 (Harden Street) in the heart of Graham, the seat of Alamance County. Turn right and travel north for 2.2 miles to Lang Court near the junction with U.S. 70 in the town of Haw River. Turn left onto Lang Court, follow it 0.1 mile to Church Circle, and turn left again. Park near the Trollinger cemetery, located adjacent to Haw River United Methodist Church.

There is a prominent marker in the cemetery honoring three generations of the Trollinger family. Adam Trollinger, a native of Germany, settled along the Haw River in 1745. His eldest son, Jacob Henry, also born in Germany, constructed the first gristmill on the Haw.

When Cornwallis moved west from Hillsborough toward Guilford Courthouse in March 1781, he camped one night on Jacob Henry Trollinger's farm. When sixty-three-year-old Jacob Henry discovered that the British army had taken grain from his mill, he chastised Cornwallis. His patience worn by the rude greeting he had received throughout the area, the British commander ordered his soldiers to seize the old man and tie him to a tree with a bridle bit in his mouth, so that he could not speak or leave. Trollinger was ultimately rescued by a passing neighbor. The tree to which he was bound stood for many years as an area landmark.

So outraged was the miller that he sent his oldest son, John, to Virginia to make gunpowder for the American army. His other son, Henry, was a Revolutionary War soldier.

Adam, Jacob Henry, and Henry Trollinger are memorialized by the monument.

Return to the junction of N.C. 49 and U.S. 70. Turn left and proceed east on U.S. 70 for 5.4 miles to U.S. 119 in downtown Mebane. A state historical marker located at the junction honors General Alexander Mebane (1744–95), whose home stood in this vicinity.

Born near the town that now bears his name, Mebane was a prominent political figure who served as colonel of the county militia throughout the Revolution. Following the war, he was promoted to brigadier general of the militia. Voters elected the respected statesman to the Third Congress of the United States.

It is another 0.5 mile on U.S. 70 to the Orange County line. Historians believe the county was named for William V of Orange, the grandson of

King George II. It was established in 1752.

Continue east on U.S. 70 for 8.8 miles to N.C. 86 on the northern side of Hillsborough. Turn left and drive 0.4 mile north to N.C. 57. Located at this junction is a state historical marker for Thomas Burke (1744–83), the governor of North Carolina from 1781 to 1782. His grave and the site of his plantation are the next stop on this tour.

Turn right on N.C. 57, drive 0.5 mile north to unpaved S.R. 1551, turn right again, and go 0.8 mile east. A crude wooden sign on the left side of the road directs visitors to Burke's grave, located several hundred yards off the road in a fenced pasture on private property. A sizable granite monolith dedicated in 1944 and a memorial plaque unveiled in 1973 stand at the rock-covered grave of the wartime governor.

Grave of Governor Thomas Burke

Born and raised in Ireland, Burke was a true Renaissance man who was skilled as an attorney, physician, and statesman. In fact, he was once described as the "ablest Advocate and Compleatest Orator our Country Affords." Around 1760, he emigrated to Virginia, where he began to write poetry. One of his earliest works heralded the repeal of the Stamp Act. Many of his poems were published in the newspapers of the day. In the twentieth century, they were collected by Richard Walser and published as *The Poems of Governor Thomas Burke of North Carolina*.

In 1772, Burke settled in North Carolina on a plantation located at the current tour stop. It was named Tyaquin for his family home in County Galway, Ireland.

One of his Irish ancestors, John de Burge—nicknamed "Monoculus" because of the loss of an eye—had accompanied William the Conqueror in his conquest of England. Like his ancestor, Burke had vision in only one eye, the other having been blinded by smallpox. But his handicap did not prevent him from becoming one of the most able and important statesmen in North Carolina during the Revolution.

His political career began in 1775, when voters elected him to the Second Provincial Congress. He then served as a delegate to each succeeding Provincial Congress. At the fifth and final one, held at Halifax in December 1776, delegates selected him to chair the committee that produced North Carolina's first state constitution.

In 1777, North Carolina sent Burke, William Hooper, and Joseph Hewes to Philadelphia to represent the state in the Continental Congress. There, Burke proved farsighted. When the Articles of Confederation came up for debate, he introduced a resolution to guarantee the states all powers not specifically granted to the national government. Fourteen years later, Burke's wisdom proved to be the basis for the Tenth Amendment to the United States Constitution.

An independent thinker, Burke was considered a radical by many of his colleagues. In 1778, at the height of a debate over George Washington's right to exchange prisoners, some congressmen began criticizing Washington and his conduct of the war. When the clock tolled ten o'clock that night, Burke decided he had heard enough. He put on his hat and left the hall, rendering it impossible for Congress to take a vote and conduct further business. A messenger was sent to his room with a demand that he return. Burke refused.

His fellow congressmen subsequently censured him for what they considered "disrespect" and "indecent behavior." Burke made a halfhearted apology that ended with a stern declaration: "I consider the obligation I am under to my constituents superior to any which can be laid on me by Congress."

Back home, the voters maintained great confidence in Burke, reelecting him to another term in the Continental Congress.

Then, in June 1781, they elected him governor after a heated contest with Samuel Johnston.

North Carolina was in great turmoil when Burke took over as its chief executive. In the wake of Cornwallis's destructive movement through the state, the hostilities between Tories and Whigs had evolved into civil war. And economic problems were of an equally serious nature. As Burke lamented, "The public money is unaccounted for, the taxes uncollected and unproductive . . . and the treasury unable to make payment."

In a letter to Burke, Virginia governor Thomas Nelson, Jr., acknowledged the daunting task facing North Carolina's new governor: "The whole system of government in the Southern States is so deranged that the men who can organize and bring them into order will be Magnus Apollo."

Burke went to work to ensure statewide support for the American war effort. But his administration was rudely interrupted when he was abducted by David Fanning in Hillsborough on the morning of September 12, 1781. After Patriots failed to free him at the Battle of Lindley's Mill, the kidnapped governor was hauled away to Charleston. He was paroled a month later. But fearful of Tories in South Carolina—"I considered myself every moment in danger of assassination," he later wrote—Burke broke his parole agreement and fled back to North Carolina. He returned to his duties as governor amid a controversy about breaking his parole.

In 1782, the legislature nominated him for a second term, but he declined to run. In a farewell address to the general assembly, he stated, "My misfortunes during this year have been heavy and complicated and have involved one in debts and in private distress which it would be painful to particularize."

Physically debilitated by his time in captivity, Burke retired to Tyaquin. It was here that North Carolina's thirty-eight-year-old poet-governor died on December 2, 1783.

Retrace your route to the junction of N.C. 86 and U.S. 70 in Hillsborough. Proceed south on N.C. 86 (Churton Street) for 0.9 mile to King Street in the downtown area. Park near the intersection to enjoy a walking tour of this charming, historic town. You'll walk in the very footsteps of the many Revolutionary War heroes who called Hillsborough home and the myriad famous people who visited this place when it was the political center of the state.

Hillsborough residents proudly boast that their town, unlike Colonial Williamsburg, is a restored, not a reconstructed, village. The old buildings here are original and retain much of their eighteenth-century character.

The town was chartered in 1759 as Childsburgh, in honor of Thomas Childs, the attorney general of the colony. Hillsborough took its present name seven years later at the request of Governor Tryon, who had a fondness for the town. The name honors Wills Hill, earl of Hillsborough (1718–93), the secretary of state for the colonies.

Start your walking tour at the Old Orange County Courthouse, located at the southeastern corner of Churton and King. Although this magnificent Greek Revival structure was constructed more than sixty years after the Revolution, the town clock in its octagonal cupola ticks on just as it did when Tryon, Hooper, Burke, Cornwallis, and so many other notables trod the city's streets in the eighteenth century.

Built in Birmingham, England, in 1766, it was a replica of the clock placed in the tower at Independence Hall in Philadelphia and was perhaps shipped to America about the same time as its sister clock. Around 1769, King George III presented the clock to the town of Hillsborough as a Royal gift.

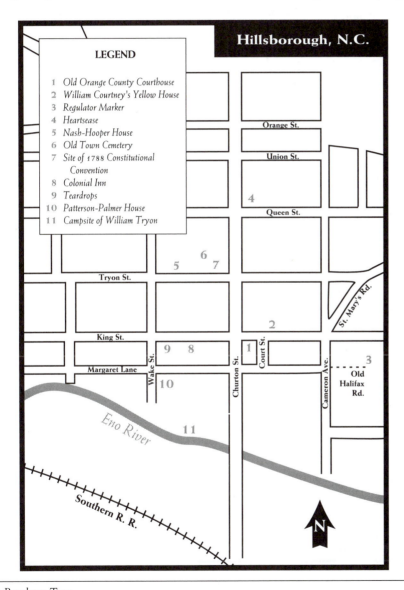

Hillsborough, N.C.

LEGEND

1 Old Orange County Courthouse
2 William Courtney's Yellow House
3 Regulator Marker
4 Heartsease
5 Nash-Hooper House
6 Old Town Cemetery
7 Site of 1788 Constitutional
  Convention
8 Colonial Inn
9 Teardrops
10 Patterson-Palmer House
11 Campsite of William Tryon

Prior to the courthouse's construction in 1844, it was mounted in the tower of the town's original Episcopal church and later in the Market House. Neither of those structures survives.

On the street alongside the old courthouse are several state historical markers. One pays tribute to Thomas Burke. Another notes that the home of Edmund Fanning (1737–1818) stood nearby. Edmund Fanning (no relation to David Fanning) suffered from the wrath of the Regulators perhaps more than any other individual in North Carolina.

A native of New York, he came to Hillsborough in 1760 after graduating with honors from Yale and doing graduate work at Harvard. His subsequent service as a colonial official, his close friendship with William Tryon, and his reputation as a land speculator made him a subject of particular dislike among the Regulators. In 1768, shots were fired through his house. Two years later, the dwelling was cut to pieces by attacking Regulators. In retaliation, Fanning commanded the left wing of Tryon's army at the Battle of Alamance.

Later in 1771, when Tryon moved to New York to serve as its Royal governor, he was accompanied by his new private secretary, Edmund Fanning. Three years later, Fanning was appointed surveyor general of New York.

Throughout the Revolution, he served as an officer for the Crown. Following the war, he was rewarded with a promotion to lieutenant general in the British army and an appointment as lieutenant governor of Nova Scotia.

Yet another state historical marker near the courthouse calls attention to the six Regulators executed in Hillsborough after the Battle of Alamance. The site of the hangings is visited later on this tour.

From the old courthouse, proceed east on King Street to the Yellow House, located at 141 East King. Constructed in 1768 by William Courtney, a Quaker, the stately two-story house is one of the oldest in the city.

In 1780, Methodist bishop Francis Asbury preached to two hundred people at the house. The next year, Courtney was the reluctant host to another visitor, Lord Charles Cornwallis. After failing to catch Greene before he crossed into Virginia, Cornwallis moved his army to Hillsborough, where he hoped to recruit Tories "to take an active part in assisting me to restore order and constitutional government."

Whether by accident or as a deliberate act to antagonize Patriots, Cornwallis planted the "King's Standard" in Hillsborough on February 22, 1781, which happened to be George Washington's birthday. Cornwallis's proclamation to area Tories brought them to the city, but not with the desired result. According to General Charles O'Hara, "The novelty of a camp in the backwoods of America more than any other cause brought several people to stare at us. Their curiosity once satisfied, they returned to their homes."

During his three days in Hillsborough, Cornwallis lived alternately at the Yellow House and at a tavern next door. He broke camp after failing to recruit Tories and feed and supply his troops.

Continue east on King to Cameron Avenue. Proceed across King to the parking lot for the Orange County Board of Education. Walk to the rear of the lot, where you'll find a trail leading to the Regulator Marker.

It was at this site that six Regulators—Benjamin Merrill, Robert Matear, James Pugh, Captain Messer, and two unknown men—were hanged on June 19, 1771, by order of the Court of Oyer and Terminer. They were subsequently buried in a mass grave near the Eno River; the exact location of the grave is unknown.

Captain Messer had narrowly escaped the noose a month earlier. Shortly after the Battle of Alamance, William Tryon had remarked, "This man, Captain Messer, shall hang tomorrow, for he is a leader among them [the Regulators]."

Site where six Regulators were hanged, Hillsborough

When the doleful news was delivered to Messer's wife, she hurried to Tryon's camp near the battlefield, bringing the eldest of her four children, a son ten years old. Wife and child threw themselves in front of Tryon and cried out for mercy.

Unmoved, Tryon ordered the execution to proceed. At the last moment, the boy jumped to his feet, looked at the governor, and bravely exclaimed, "Sir! Hang me and let my father live!"

Tryon inquired, "Who told you to say that?"

"Nobody," said the lad.

"And why do you ask that?" the governor said.

With the sincerity only a child can deliver, the boy responded, "Because if you hang my father, my mother will die and the children will perish."

"My boy, your father shall not hang today," Tryon replied.

The governor was true to his word—quite literally. He marched Messer and the other prisoners from the battlefield to Salisbury and then to Hillsborough. In every settlement along the way, they were displayed as a reminder of the crushing blow dealt to the Regulator movement. Once in Hillsborough, Messer and five of his compatriots were sentenced to death.

The day set aside for the executions dawned clear and bright. As the appointed hour neared, a small crowd assembled in front of the gallows, which stood at the present tour stop. One by one, the condemned men were escorted forward by Tryon's militiamen.

Bareheaded James Pugh, the sharpshooter whose perfect aim had taken a deadly toll on the governor's soldiers on the battlefield, stood silently as the noose was placed around his neck. He was then offered an opportunity to make a last statement. His words were prophetic: "The blood we have shed will be as good seed sown in good ground, which soon will reap a hundred fold."

Return to the junction of King and Cameron. Walk one block north on Cameron to Tryon Street.

En route, you will notice St. Matthew's Episcopal Church on a hill on the right. Built in 1824, the splendid Gothic Revival structure replaced the church that had housed the town clock. That edifice stood at the corner of Tryon and Churton Streets. It burned in 1793.

Tradition has it that while the town clock was housed in the earlier church, Patriots threw portions of it into the Eno River to prevent Tory raiders from melting them into bullets. When the clock was recovered months later, its bell was missing. That bell has never been found.

From the intersection of Cameron and Tryon, continue one block north on Cameron to Queen Street. Turn left and walk to Heartsease, located at 115 East Queen. According to Polly Burke, who owned the house from 1810 to 1837, her father, Governor Thomas Burke, built the central portion. It was supposedly on the steps of this house that Burke was captured by Fanning.

Continue west to Wake Street. By this time, you have probably noticed the historic names of the city's streets. Wake was the maiden name of Governor Tryon's wife.

Turn left and walk one block on Wake to Tryon. Turn left and proceed east to the Nash-Hooper House, located at 118 West Tryon. There is perhaps no home in America that can claim two greater men of Revolutionary War renown as previous owners.

The home's northern wing was constructed in 1768 by Isaac Edwards, Governor Tryon's aide. But the large central block was built in 1772 by Francis Nash (1742–77).

Born to Welsh parents in Virginia, Nash settled in Hillsborough in the 1760s. At the Battle of Alamance, Captain Nash served under Colonel Edmund Fanning. It was in that battle that he began his rise to military stardom.

In the summer of 1775, Nash was appointed lieutenant colonel of the newly raised First North Carolina Continental Regiment. His promotion to colonel came less than a year later, when Colonel James Moore was elevated to general. On February 5, 1777, the Continental Congress promoted Nash to brigadier general. General Moore died about that same time. As a result, when the North Carolina brigade's nine regiments were ordered north to support General Washington, they marched under the command of General Nash.

Throughout the summer, Nash aided in the American effort to thwart the British offensive designed to capture Philadelphia, the national capital. When the two armies engaged at Brandywine on September 11, the North Carolinians under Nash rendered distinguished service. But his greatest moment was yet to come. Tragically, it would also be his last.

After Philadelphia fell to the British on September 26, Washington regrouped and waited for an opportunity to strike back. It came on October 4 at Germantown. Before the tide of the battle turned against the Americans, Nash was wounded while leading his forces down Germantown's main street in pursuit of the retreating Redcoats. A cannonball smashed into his leg, passed through his horse, and killed his aide, Major James Witherspoon. Thrown to the ground by the blast, Nash gallantly tried to hide his wound's severity as he offered words of inspiration to his men: "Rush on, my boys. Rush the enemy. I'll be after you presently."

He was borne from the field and placed in a private home, where he suffered for three days. His wound bled so profusely that two feather beds were soaked. As he drew his last breath on October 7, thirty-five-year-old General Nash uttered these words: "From the first dawn of the revolution I have been ever on the side of liberty and my country."

On October 9, the entire American army—led by its commander in chief, General George Washington—paraded to Nash's funeral. He was laid to rest in the cemetery of the Mennonite church in Kulpsville, 15 miles from Philadelphia. A star in the pavement of a Germantown street marks the spot where he fell.

Nash County, North Carolina, and Nashville, Tennessee, bear his name today. His older brother, Abner, was elected governor of North Carolina in 1780.

On April 10, 1782, William Hooper purchased General Nash's home. He lived here until his death in 1790. The house is the only surviving dwelling once owned by one of North Carolina's three signers of the Declaration of Independence. It remained in the Hooper family until 1853.

Best-selling author Inglis Fletcher used the house as a backdrop for two historical novels set in Revolutionary War North Carolina, *The Wind in the Forest* and *Queen's Gift*.

Continue east on Tryon to the Old Town Cemetery, located adjacent to the Nash-Hooper House and to the rear of the Presbyterian church. Set aside as a burial ground when the town was laid out in 1754, the cemetery includes several family plots that were ultimately incorporated into the larger graveyard.

Two graves in one plot have great significance for the Revolutionary War period.

One of them marks the final resting place of James Hogg (1729–1804). A native of Scotland, Hogg settled on a farm east of Hillsborough in 1775. That same year, he became an official of the Transylvania Company, a land-speculation enterprise headed by Richard Henderson. (For information on Henderson, see The Statehood Tour, pages 437–39.) As an emissary for the company, Hogg presented a request to the Continental Congress that Kentucky be admitted as the fourteenth colony.

A staunch supporter of the American cause, he was taken prisoner by the British at his newly built house in Hillsborough in 1781.

Before he died of a stroke in 1802, Hogg successfully petitioned the state legislature to change his children's last name to Alves, his wife's maiden name, citing as his reason the years of ridicule he had endured over his "swinelike" name. Hogg was buried beside his friend William Hooper.

A sandstone slab commissioned by Hooper's daughter covers the spot where the signer of the Declaration of Independence was originally interred. Amid great controversy, his remains were moved to the military park at Guilford Courthouse during Judge David Schenck's quest to locate the graves of all three signers there.

Of the many distinguished statesmen North Carolina gave the nation in its infancy, none was greater than Hooper (1742–90). Born in Boston, the first child of a Scottish minister, he settled in Wilmington to practice law in 1763, a year after his graduation from Harvard.

On January 25, 1773, Hooper's renowned political career began with his election to the provincial assembly. His service there brought him into contact with men who would serve as the military and political leaders of the Revolutionary War.

In a letter to James Iredell dated April 26, 1774, Hooper penned one of the most prophetic sentences of American history: "They [the colonies] are striding fast to independence, and ere long will build an empire upon the ruins of Great Britain; will adopt its Constitution, purged of its impurities, and from an experience of its defects, will guard against those evils which have wasted its vigor."

Hooper, Richard Caswell, and Joseph Hewes were chosen as North Carolina's three delegates at the First Continental Congress, which convened in Philadelphia in September 1774. Hooper took his seat in Carpenter's Hall among the eminent statesmen and orators of the thirteen colonies. At thirty-two, he was one of the youngest of the fifty delegates, being less than half the age of many.

Hooper attracted the attention of America's forefathers with his brilliant oratory. Among his admirers was John Adams, later to become the second president of the new nation. In his private notes on the great assembly, Adams recorded, "[Richard Henry] Lee, [Patrick] Henry, and [William] Hooper are the orators."

In spite of his strong personal desire to remain loyal to King George III, Hooper expressed the growing sentiment in the colonies when he wrote,

"That the colonies may continue connected as they have been is our second wish. Our first is that America may be free." From Hooper's pen flowed much of the revolutionary rhetoric that solidified the cause of independence.

From 1774 through the end of 1776, Hooper served as a delegate at three Continental Congresses and four Provincial Congresses. Virtually every congressional committee in Philadelphia that required a draftsman for important resolutions or speeches included Hooper either as chairman or as a member. Perhaps his most important assignment was his membership on Thomas Jefferson's committee that composed the Declaration of Independence. In Philadelphia on August 2, 1776, Hooper joined the other congressmen in affixing their signatures to the document that altered the course of human history.

Weakened by the yellow-fever epidemic that swept through Congress in early 1778, Hooper ended his service there and returned to Wilmington, where he resumed the practice of law. The arrival of British forces under Major Craig in January 1781 caused him great consternation, as he knew he would be hunted down. Although Hooper eluded Craig, the British officer expelled his ailing wife and family in April and impounded the Hoopers' property. Mrs. Hooper and the children fled to the home of her brother in Hillsborough. Soon thereafter, the family was reunited and took up permanent residence at the Nash-Hooper House.

Hooper's most heartbreaking setback took place in 1788, when he was not elected a delegate to the state's Constitutional Convention, which met within sight of his house.

Thereafter, Hooper had as his constant companion a bottle of rum. An attack of malaria in May 1790 led to a steady decline in his health. He died at the age of forty-eight on the night of October 18, 1790, the eve of his daughter's wedding.

When you are ready to leave the cemetery, note the small marker with a bronze plaque that stands in the side yard of the Presbyterian church. It notes that the state's Constitutional Convention met at this site in 1788. Delegates to the convention assembled at the Episcopal church that stood here at the time.

Hillsborough's role as host to a gathering of such magnitude was not without precedent. Thirteen years earlier, the town had been the site of the

Third Provincial Congress—also called "the War Congress," since its purpose had been to make preparations for the coming war. From August 20 to September 10, 1775, Samuel Johnston, William Hooper, Joseph Hewes, Thomas Burke, Richard Caswell, and other notable men had labored to raise and equip an army and develop a plan of government to be implemented in the absence of Governor Josiah Martin.

As for the Constitutional Convention in 1788, one delegate reflected on that august body's duty by talking about "the most important single question . . . ever faced, an example never before equalled in the history of the world—the spectacle of a people changing its form of government by a deliberate and authoritative action rather than by bloodshed."

Governor Samuel Johnston, a Federalist, was elected president of the convention. Nonetheless, the Federalists, whose chief spokesman was James Iredell, were outnumbered by Anti-Federalists by 184 to 84.

Leading the opposition to ratification were Willie Jones, Thomas Person, David Caldwell, and Samuel Spencer. Stressing their concerns that the federal constitution, unlike the state constitution, contained no guarantees of personal rights and freedoms, the Anti-Federalists won the day. After all the debating was over, not a single delegate had changed his mind. Ratification failed by a vote of 184 to 84.

The delegates forwarded to Congress and the other states a proposed Bill of Rights and twenty-six amendments. Then, on August 4, 1788, after two weeks' work, they departed Hillsborough. North Carolina would be out of the Union for another year.

Continue on Tryon Street the short distance to Churton Street. Walk south on Churton for one block to King Street. Turn right on King and proceed west to the Colonial Inn, located on the right at 153 West King.

This sprawling, two-story structure stands on a lot once owned by Edmund Fanning. Although no one is certain when it was constructed, tradition holds that it was here before the Revolutionary War. The oldest portion of the building—which continues to serve as an inn and restaurant—encompasses the lobby and the east dining room.

Flagstones cover the building's long front porch. Cornwallis, irritated by Hillsborough's muddy streets, is said to have used similar stones to pave King and Churton Streets. That crude pavement remained until the streets

Colonial Inn, Hillsborough

were hard-surfaced in the 1920s.

Adjacent to the Colonial Inn at 175 West King is Teardrops, a two-and-a-half-story frame house constructed in the 1760s. Among the Revolutionary War luminaries who once owned this house was Thomas Person.

Continue on King to Wake Street. Turn left and walk one block to Margaret Lane (so named for William Tryon's wife). South of Margaret Lane is a meadow along the Eno River where Tryon set up his camp before proceeding to his showdown with the Regulators.

Turn left and walk east to the Patterson-Palmer House, located at 173 West Margaret. Similar in appearance to Williamsburg houses, this dwelling was once owned by General Francis Nash, who operated a mill along the river south of here.

Continue east to Churton Street. Three state historical markers are located on Churton south of the courthouse. One pays tribute to James Hogg. Another notes that the North Carolina Society of the Cincinnati, a fraternity of officers of the Continental Line, was organized in Hillsborough on October 23, 1783. The third stands near the site of a paper mill constructed during the Revolution to alleviate a severe paper shortage. At one point, the problem became so acute that the quartermaster general notified Governor Burke, "I have not at this time one quire of paper nor the means of acquiring it." Little is known about the exact location of the facility.

Return to your vehicle at the junction of Churton and King. Drive south on Churton, which becomes Old N.C. 86 leaving Hillsborough. After approximately 2.5 miles, you will pass under I-40. Continue south on Old N.C. 86 (S.R. 1009) for 6.8 miles to Stony Hill Road and turn left. It is 0.1 mile east to a tall stone memorial for General Thomas Lloyd (1710–92).

Standing at this isolated spot today, it is hard to imagine that twenty-five hundred people assembled here to witness the unveiling of the monument in October 1937. On that occasion, Congressman William B. Umstead dedicated the impressive eight-foot-tall granite shaft to the man who was known as Orange County's most influential citizen prior to the Revolution.

From 1761 to 1770, Thomas Lloyd wielded enormous power as a judicial official, a member of the colonial assembly, a militia officer, and a church administrator. Targeted by Regulators as a member of Hillsborough's "Courthouse Ring," he was forced to flee into the woods surrounding town during the September 1770 insurrection that cost Edmund Fanning his home and property. Lloyd was the only member of "the Courthouse Ring" to remain in the Hillsborough area during the Revolution. His plantation, known as Meadows, was located near the current tour stop.

Old age robbed Lloyd of an opportunity to take an active part in the Revolution. It is believed that he was a stalwart supporter of the Crown.

Return to Old N.C. 86. Turn left and proceed south for 2 miles to where the road forks. Take the left fork (Hillsborough Road) and drive 2.5 miles to Main Street in Carrboro. Merge onto Main Street and drive east for 0.5 mile to the corporate limits of Chapel Hill, where Main Street becomes Franklin Street. Follow Franklin east for 0.9 mile to the state historical marker for the University of North Carolina. Park nearby.

When the delegates to the Fifth Provincial Congress at Halifax crafted the state's first constitution in December 1776, they realized that North Carolina's future depended in large part upon the education of its citizens. Consequently, the document they crafted contained the following provision: "That a school or schools shall be established by the legislature for the convenient instruction of youth, with such salaries to the masters, paid by the public, as may enable them to instruct at low prices; and all useful learning shall be duly encouraged and promoted in one or more universities."

At that time, a state university was little more than a dream, for the Revolutionary War still had to be fought and won. Many of the men who put that dream into writing in the state constitution participated in the fight for independence on the battlefield, in the political arena, or both. Once independence was secured, the survivors among them were not satisfied to rest on their laurels. They went to work to open the first state university in the United States.

To view the fruits of their labor, follow the brick walkway onto McCorkle Place, the shaded mall between Franklin and Cameron Streets. Named for the Reverend Samuel E. McCorkle, it contains several of the campus's most famous landmarks.

McCorkle's voice was instrumental in the decision that the campus be laid out in the quadrangle tradition of Great Britain. Six of the seven men in the university's first graduating class (1798) received their preparatory education from McCorkle.

Had not William R. Davie objected, McCorkle would have probably been the university's first president. Instead, that honor went to Joseph Caldwell (1773–1835), who, like McCorkle, was a Presbyterian minister. Caldwell, his second wife, and his stepson, Dr. William Hooper (the grandson of the signer of the Declaration of Independence), are buried at the eastern base of the Caldwell Monument, a prominent obelisk on the grounds of McCorkle Place.

Just south of the Caldwell Monument stands the venerable Davie Poplar, a towering tree that was standing here when the site selection committee first visited New Hope Chapel Hill in 1792. It was named to honor William R. Davie, the soldier-politician who had introduced the bill to charter the University of North Carolina in 1789. Davie is acclaimed "the Father of the University."

Davie Poplar

Recognized as one of the oldest tulip poplars in the country, the hundred-foot-tall tree has sustained damage from numerous storms over the years and suffers from old age today. Steel cables help to support the stately campus landmark.

A concrete bench at the base of the tree, provided by the D.A.R., honors Davie. A younger, healthier tree nearby is known as "Davie Poplar, Jr."

Just east of the famous tree stands Old East, the oldest public-university building in the United States. When its cornerstone was laid by Davie on October 12, 1793, many Revolutionary War heroes were on hand to listen as the Reverend McCorkle spoke these words: "We hope ere long to see stately walls and spires ascending to [Chapel Hill's] summit. . . . [This university will be] adorned with an elegant village, accommodated with all the necessaries and conveniences of civilized society."

Adjacent to Old East is the campus's most recognizable landmark—the Old Well. It was here that the founding fathers and early students of the university drew their water.

From the Old Well, walk southwest to Person Hall.

Much of the money for the campus's first buildings was given or raised by veterans of the Revolution. Consequently, many of the university's oldest structures are named for these heroes. Such is the case with Person Hall, the nation's second-oldest public-university building. General Thomas Person made significant contributions during a time when money was difficult to come by.

One of the campus's newest monuments is on the southern side of Person. Inscribed on a massive stone shaft (damaged by Hurricane Fran shortly after it was erected) are the names of the university's founders. The homes, graves, and battlefields of many of the men on this long list are visited on the tours in this book. A silhouette of William R. Davie appears above the "honor roll."

Walk south from Person Hall to Cameron Street. Cross the street. Three landmarks stand almost side by side here.

Memorial Hall pays tribute to the sons and daughters of the university. Inside the building are 175 memorial stones, many of them dedicated to the Revolutionary War heroes who founded the institution.

Just east of Memorial Hall is Gerard Hall. Constructed in 1822, this two-story brick building bears the name of Charles Gerard (1750–97), a Beaufort County Patriot who fought under Colonel Edward Buncombe. When he died, Gerard left thirteen thousand acres to the university.

East of Gerard Hall stands the magnificent South Building. Modeled after Nassau Hall at Princeton, it was constructed in 1801 thanks to funds raised through a state lottery. Laurence Baker, a Revolutionary War Patriot from Gates County, was the lucky lottery winner.

The tour ends here, with this look at an educational institution born of the Revolution.

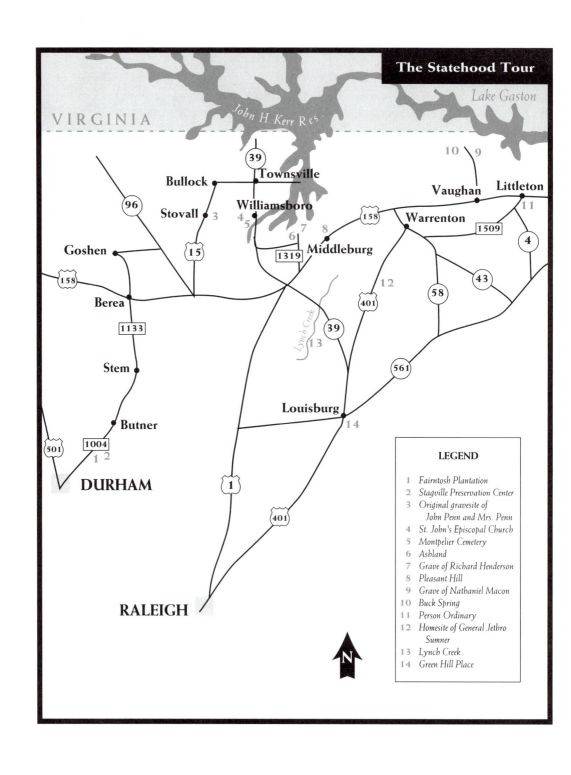

The Statehood Tour

Lake Gaston

John H. Kerr Res.

VIRGINIA

39 Townsville

Bullock

96

Stovall 3

15

Williamsboro
4
5

6 7
8

158 Warrenton

10 9

Vaughan Littleton

11

1509

4

Goshen

158

Berea

1133

1319 Middleburg

6

43

58

12

401

Lynch Creek

39
13

Stem

Butner

561

501 1004
1 2

DURHAM

Louisburg
14

1

401

RALEIGH

N

LEGEND

1 *Fairntosh Plantation*
2 *Stagville Preservation Center*
3 *Original gravesite of*
   John Penn and Mrs. Penn
4 *St. John's Episcopal Church*
5 *Montpelier Cemetery*
6 *Ashland*
7 *Grave of Richard Henderson*
8 *Pleasant Hill*
9 *Grave of Nathaniel Macon*
10 *Buck Spring*
11 *Person Ordinary*
12 *Homesite of General Jethro*
   Sumner
13 *Lynch Creek*
14 *Green Hill Place*

The Statehood Tour

This tour begins north of Durham in Durham County and makes its way through Granville, Vance, Warren, and Franklin Counties before ending at Raleigh in Wake County. Among the highlights are Stagville Preservation Center, the story of Thomas Person, the original grave of John Penn, historic Williamsboro, Ashland, the grave of Richard Henderson, Pleasant Hill, the grave of Nathaniel Macon, Person's Ordinary, the story of General Jethro Sumner, Green Hill Place, and historic Raleigh.

Total mileage: approximately 260 miles.

This tour circles through a five-county area in north-central North Carolina before ending in Wake County at Raleigh.

Following the cessation of hostilities, few events gave the new state of North Carolina more stability and legitimacy than the creation of a permanent capital in 1792.

Many of the tour stops focus on the homes and graves of the leaders who moved North Carolina from being a Royal colony to becoming a sovereign state and then an integral part of the fledgling United States of America. Among the heroes spotlighted are Thomas Person, an important figure in the Regulator movement who emerged as one of the important political and military leaders of Revolutionary War North Carolina; John Penn, one of the state's three signers of the Declaration of Independence; John Williams, one of the first state judges under the Constitution of 1776; James Turner, the early-nineteenth-century governor who fought for Nathanael Greene at Guilford Courthouse at the age of fifteen; Nathaniel Macon, the young Revolutionary War soldier who ultimately became Speaker of the United States House of Representatives; and General Jethro Sumner, who participated in the American Revolution from beginning to end.

The tour begins in northern Durham County at the junction of Roxboro Road and Old Oxford Road (S.R. 1004). Here stands a state historical marker for Stagville, a plantation established by Richard Bennehan in 1776.

To see the site, drive north on Old Oxford Road for 6.5 miles. On the right is Fairntosh Plantation, a private estate located just south of Stagville.

The oldest portion of this spectacular, two-story Georgian-Federal house was constructed in 1802 by Duncan Cameron, a Virginia attorney who settled in North Carolina at the turn of the century. His mother was the niece of General Francis Nash and Governor Abner Nash.

Cameron gained prominence as a superior-court judge. When the heirs of Lord Granville—the only one of the Lords Proprietor who had refused to sell his land to the Crown—sued to recover property confiscated by the state after the Revolutionary War, Duncan Cameron successfully defended the claims of North Carolina landowners.

Considered one of the state's most significant antebellum plantations, Fairntosh was named for the family's ancestral home in Scotland. It was the seat of Cameron's mighty empire, which was reported to be the largest plantation east of the Mississippi. Cameron is buried on the grounds.

Continue north on Old Oxford Road for 0.7 mile to the entrance to Stagville, also located on the right. Open to the public, the old plantation is North Carolina's first state-owned preservation center.

Richard Bennehan, an apprentice merchant who came to North Carolina from Virginia around 1768, built the two-century-old Georgian-style plantation house, which remains the center of Stagville Preservation Center. In 1776, he acquired the first parcel of land in what would become a large plantation.

Like his father-in-law, Bennehan fought for the cause of independence. Following the war, he acquired great wealth and political prominence as a planter. Among the Revolutionary War notables he entertained at Stagville were William R. Davie, Willie Jones, James Iredell, Sr., and Allen Jones. Of one visit here, Iredell noted that Bennehan "attacked us with such hospitality and earnestness we had to stay all day."

Davie, Jones, and Bennehan were leaders in the movement in the early 1790s to locate the state capital at Raleigh.

Bennehan's marble tomb is east of the plantation house.

Continue north on Old Oxford Road. It is 3 miles to the Granville County line. Established in 1746, Granville County was named for John Carteret, earl of Granville (1690–1763), one of the Lords Proprietors. As a result of his refusal to sell his land interests to King George II, Granville's holdings in North Carolina were surveyed and placed in a special district—the Granville District—prior to the Revolutionary War. This 60-mile-wide strip of land held two-thirds of the residents of the colony and an even greater percentage of its wealth. The Granville family's vast North Carolina domain was lost during the American Revolution.

Follow Old Oxford Road north for 8.1 miles to S.R. 1138. Turn left and proceed 7.2 miles on a scenic route through rural Granville County to U.S. 158. Turn left on U.S. 158 and drive 0.7 mile to S.R. 1309. A state historical marker at the junction pays tribute to Thomas Person (1733–1800), one of North Carolina's most outstanding men of the Revolutionary War period. His home, Goshen, stood 6 miles from the marker. Turn right on S.R. 1309 and proceed north for 6.2 miles to the community of Goshen.

Born in Virginia, Thomas Person moved to the Granville District with his parents as a child. Except for the time he was away in service of his colony, state, and nation, he spent the rest of his life here. An astute businessman, Person owned 82,358 acres in North Carolina and Tennessee at his death.

A supporter of the Regulators, Person was one of the men most feared by Governor William Tryon. Although Person did not participate in the Battle of Alamance, Tryon took him prisoner after the engagement and threatened him with execution. When Tryon granted amnesty to the Regulators, he specifically exempted Person from the offer.

One of North Carolina's earliest advocates of independence, Person was appointed a brigadier general more than two months before the Declaration was drafted. It was in the political arena, however, that he made his biggest impact in the early days of the Revolution. Person served in all five Provincial Congresses. As a delegate to the famous assemblage at Halifax in April 1776, he helped draft the resolution that made North Carolina the first colony to instruct its delegates at the Continental Congress to vote for independence. Central to Person's political philosophy was the protection of individual rights and freedoms. He served on the committee at the Fifth Provincial Congress that produced North Carolina's first state constitution and the Bill of Rights contained therein. Person's handiwork served as the model for the first ten amendments to the United States Constitution.

William L. Saunders, the compiler of the *Colonial Records of North Carolina*, observed this about Person: "Wherever devoted, intelligent, efficient patriotism was required, Person was promptly put on duty. . . . And to-day North Carolina bears in her bosom the bones of no purer patriot than those of Thomas Person."

At Goshen, S.R. 1309 junctions with S.R. 1316. Turn right, drive 0.8 mile to S.R. 1317, turn right again, and proceed east for 5 miles to N.C. 96. Turn right and head east for 4.9 miles to U.S. 158. Turn left and follow U.S. 158 Bypass for 4.1 miles as it loops around Oxford, the seat of Granville County. At the eastern limits of Oxford, the bypass junctions with U.S. 158 Business. Turn right and drive 0.5 mile on U.S. 158 Business to the state historical marker for Nathaniel Rochester (1752–1831), the Revolutionary War officer who founded the city in New York that bears his name. His home stood nearby.

Born in Virginia near the birthplace of George Washington, Rochester settled near Oxford with his family when he was eleven years old. He emerged as a political and military leader in Orange County as the colonies teetered on the brink of the fight for independence. As a major of the militia, he commanded a force of three companies (two of infantry and one of cavalry) in pursuit of Tories marching to Wilmington in early 1776. His small army overtook and captured five hundred Loyalist soldiers retreating from the Battle of Moores Creek Bridge.

Though subsequent illnesses robbed Rochester of the bodily strength necessary to display his patriotism on the battlefield, he seized every possible opportunity to serve the American cause. As the head of a commission to build a gun factory in Hillsborough, he led a wagon train north to secure iron for the facility.

Following the war, Rochester moved to the North, where he enjoyed prominence in business and politics. From his holdings on the Genesee River in New York, a town was laid out in 1818.

Return to the junction with U.S. 158 Bypass. Turn left, go 3.1 miles to U.S. 15, turn right, and drive north for 8.3 miles to the state historical marker for John Penn in the village of Stovall. It notes that the home of this signer of the Declaration of Independence stood 3 miles northeast. This marker bears special significance for North Carolina. Erected on January 10, 1936, it was the first of the state's familiar silver-and-black highway signs. On the fiftieth anniversary of the highway-marker program, the original Penn marker was placed in safekeeping and replaced with a replica.

To see Penn's homesite and his original grave, continue north on U.S. 15 for 0.2 mile to S.R. 1430. Turn right, go 2.8 miles to S.R. 1509, turn left, and proceed 2.6 miles on the unpaved road as it gradually bends to the left before ending at a circular turnaround surrounded by forest.

A wide pathway leads into the forest, which was once part of the plantation of John Penn (1740–88); note that this is private property. Two hundred yards down the path is a small cemetery enclosed by a chain-link fence. Buried under the single grave marker is Susannah L. Penn, the wife of the signer. Her husband was originally buried here, but his grave was moved to the site of the Battle of Guilford Courthouse by Judge David Schenck in 1894.

Original grave of John Penn, Stovall

Born into an affluent Virginia family, John Penn moved to Granville County—his wife's native county—and settled on a farm near the current tour stop in 1774. A talented attorney, he was promptly elected to succeed Richard Caswell in the Continental Congress. Unlike North Carolina's other two delegates, Penn was from the back country. But all three members of the North Carolina contingent shared a common goal in 1775—the reconciliation of the differences between the colonies and Great Britain.

Over the course of the next six months, Penn's views on independence began to change. On February 14, 1776, he wrote to Thomas Person, his close friend from Granville County, "Matters are drawing to a crisis. . . . My first wish is that America be free; the second, that we may be restored to peace and harmony with Britain upon just and proper terms."

Penn and William Hooper arrived in Halifax on April 15, 1776, three days after the Fourth Provincial Congress had passed the Halifax Resolves. Upon their return to Philadelphia, they joined with Joseph Hewes to vote for independence on July 2, in accordance with the state's resolution.

Once the die was cast, Penn was a workhorse for the American cause. His service of 1,038 days in the Continental Congress was longer than any other North Carolinian during the Revolutionary War. And he sought to inspire sacrifice and patriotism on the home front. One of his letters to Thomas Person contained an earnest plea: "For God's sake, my Good Sir, encourage our People, animate them to dare even to die for their country."

Despite his personal wealth, Penn never lost touch with the common man. One historian concluded, "The election of Penn to the Continental Congress was the beginning of democratic representation in that body."

Described as "a man of sterling integrity as a private citizen," Penn displayed his strength of character in an incident with Henry Laurens, the South Carolinian who served as president of the Continental Congress. A dispute between the two led the elderly Laurens to challenge Penn to a duel. Because they were boarders at the same inn, they breakfasted together on the appointed day, then set out for the showdown, which was to take place in a vacant lot opposite the Masonic Hall on Chestnut Street in Philadelphia. Upon arriving at Fifth Street, Penn lent his hand to help Laurens across a ditch. At that moment, the two men realized the futility of their proposed course of action and called off the duel.

One year after his retirement from public life, Penn died here on his plantation.

Return to the junction of S.R. 1430 and U.S. 15 in Stovall. Turn right and proceed north on U.S. 15 for 1.5 miles to the state highway marker for Henry Pattillo, located on the left side of the highway opposite the junction with S.R. 1506.

Born in Scotland, Pattillo (1726–1801) was a pioneering Presbyterian minister in colonial North Carolina who proved to be an ardent Patriot during the Revolution.

Pattillo openly denounced the violent tactics used by the Regulators and urged William Tryon to put an end to the insurrection. Tryon appreciated Pattillo's support and asked the cleric to preach to his militiamen.

While serving as a member of, and chaplain to, the Third Provincial Congress, the Presbyterian minister accepted the task of explaining to the Regulators that the oath of loyalty Tryon had coerced from them was not morally binding or an impediment to fighting for independence. Throughout the war, he urged his congregations to support the struggle of the colonies, as did many of his Presbyterian colleagues.

Education was very important to Pattillo. Everywhere he settled, he built schools. Among his students were Revolutionary War notables Nathaniel Rochester and William Blount.

In 1784, Pattillo settled on a three-hundred-acre farm located near the current tour stop.

Continue north on U.S. 15 for 3.9 miles to S.R. 1445 at the community of Bullock. Turn right onto S.R. 1445 and proceed east. After 2.4 miles, the route enters Vance County and becomes S.R. 1342. Continue east on S.R. 1342 for 0.8 mile to S.R. 1348. Turn left and follow S.R. 1348 as it circles north for 5.9 miles to N.C. 39 at Townsville.

Just south of the junction and opposite the local post office stands a state historical marker for the Nutbush Address, a document that led to the birth of the Regulator movement. Its author, George Sims (1728–1808), lived near the present tour stop.

Sims, an ancestor of the Duke family of Durham, grew dissatisfied with local government after he settled in the area in the mid-eighteenth century. He expressed his outrage in a paper drafted on June 6, 1765. Dedicated to Sims's friend Thomas Person, the address reads in part, "Well, Gentlemen, it is not our mode, or form of Government, nor yet the body of our laws, that we are quarreling with, but with the malpractices of the Officers of our County Court, all the abuses which we suffer by those empowered to manage our public affairs." The man who would subsequently lead the Regulator movement thus seized upon Sims's rhetoric.

The paper was widely circulated in the back country. Herman Husband quoted Sims in his pamphlets in support of the Regulators. County officials, alarmed by the inflammatory words, arrested Sims and charged him with libel.

Because of the lengthy legal proceedings that followed and the violence occasioned by the Regulator movement, Sims did not take an active part in the Revolution.

Turn right on N.C. 39 and drive south for 5.1 miles to S.R. 1329 (Old Stagecoach Road) at Williamsboro. Two state highway markers near the intersection give a hint of the historic significance of this old village. One marker gives a brief history of the eighteenth-century town, and the other calls attention to the venerable St. John's Episcopal Church. To see the church and the remains of the town, turn right onto S.R. 1329. After 0.2 mile, you'll reach St. John's, located on the right.

Few North Carolina towns have a more distinguished Revolutionary War

St. John's Episcopal Church,
Williamsboro

history than Williamsboro. Legend has it that the town came within one vote of being the permanent capital of North Carolina. Sadly, much of the old town has been allowed to fall into ruin. However, St. John's stands as a magnificent reminder of a proud past.

When the majestic, two-story, whitewashed church building was constructed in 1757, it stood 0.5 mile from the present site. Throughout the colonial period, the church was commonly known as Nut Bush Church, after a local creek of the same name.

In 1772, the edifice was moved to the current tour stop by Judge John Williams, the son of the man for whom the town was named. It was set upon a foundation of brick imported from England. During the Revolutionary War, soldiers from both armies used the church as a place of refuge from the cold and rain. When Cornwallis passed through Williamsboro in 1781 on his final journey to Virginia, his troops were quartered briefly in the building. A hole still visible in the gallery was allegedly burned by a British soldier.

During the war and the early days of statehood, St. John's membership included some of the most important men of North Carolina. By the middle of the twentieth century, however, the church had no members, and the building sat abandoned in a wilderness of dense undergrowth.

Unwilling to allow the structure to share the fate of many of Williamsboro's eighteenth-century mansions, concerned citizens and church officials embarked upon an extensive restoration project that began in 1951 and culminated in the rededication of the building on Sunday, September 16, 1956.

Although St. John's is now used only for special services, it is of enormous historical and architectural importance to the state. It is the only extant colonial church building outside of the coastal towns, and it is the third-oldest Episcopal church in the state. After making a careful study of the building in preparation for its restoration, the late Thomas T. Waterman, a leading national authority on colonial architecture, reported, "The building . . . is a remarkable survivor of a colonial church of its period. While simple in form, the woodwork, both exterior and interior, is extensive and well-preserved. It constitutes the best example of colonial church woodwork in North Carolina."

A bronze plaque on the exterior of the building tells of its early history. The church cemetery holds the graves of members who worshiped here during Revolutionary War times.

Adjacent to the church is the site of the Sneed Mansion. Several abandoned buildings survive here as reminders of the days when the mansion was the center of a lavish eighteenth-century social life that included dancing, drinking, and gambling. Located in back of the house was a popular racetrack considered the finest in the state.

Continue west on S.R. 1329 for 0.4 mile to S.R. 1330. During the last quarter of the eighteenth century, elegant homes and prosperous businesses stood along this street. Originally known as Lick (supposedly because of the profusion of wild animals that watered in the area), the town achieved early prominence as a result of its location on the colonial road that led from Petersburg, Virginia, to Hillsborough. For much of the colonial period, it was called Nut Bush. Around 1779, it was renamed Williamsboro for John Williams, an early settler here and the ancestor of two Revolutionary War notables from the town.

At the junction with S.R. 1330, you'll notice an old metal sign that bears a single word, *Montpelier*. Other than a historic family cemetery, little remains of this once-grand estate of Judge John Williams, one of the Revolutionary War greats from Williamsboro.

To visit the site, turn left on S.R. 1330 and drive 0.7 mile to the end of the unpaved road. Here stood Montpelier, the home of Judge Williams and his son-in-law, Colonel Robert Burton, both members of the Continental Congress. One of the best-known homes of old Williamsboro, it was destroyed by fire around 1895. A subsequent house known by the same name stood here until it was dismantled around 1995.

In addition to serving as the residence of a pair of heroes of the fight for independence, the original Montpelier had two significant claims to fame during the Revolutionary War period.

During his tenure as the state's wartime governor, Thomas Burke took refuge in Williamsboro and established the town as the temporary state capital. John Williams was a gracious host to Burke during the governor's residence. Numerous communiques issued by Governor Burke in July 1781 were written on letterhead that read, "State of North Carolina, Williamsborough, Granville County." One such letter, dated July 18, was addressed to "Commanding Army Officers," whom it directed to "communicate to me, at Nut Bush, Granville County, all intelligence you can collect, in order that I may take the most effectual measures for counteracting the designs of the Enemy!"

Montpelier was also the site of the first law school in North Carolina. Williams, a distinguished jurist, is said to have opened the school in his home after the war. His personal library of 234 volumes was the largest in a wide area.

The historic graveyard at Montpelier is located 0.2 mile down an overgrown path to the right of the current tour stop; it is on private property. Ironically, the only grave marker for Judge John Williams (1731–99), one of North Carolina's three signers of the Articles of Confederation, is a sixteen-inch upright stone.

Born in Virginia, Williams moved to Granville County (now Vance County) as a child in 1742. Over the next fifteen years, his father donated much of the land upon which Williamsboro was built.

By 1763, Judge Williams and his double first cousin Richard Henderson were engaged in a lucrative law practice that ultimately led to a great land speculation venture—The Transylvania Company—and their close relationship with Daniel Boone. Thus, the famous enterprise that opened Kentucky to settlement began here in Williamsboro.

Williams was deputy attorney general for the Hillsborough District in 1768 when he signed an order that resulted in the imprisonment of two Regulator leaders, William Butler and Herman Husband. Two years later, a riotous crowd intent on revenge attacked Williams with clubs and sticks.

On another occasion, Williams faced a less-than-friendly crowd in Hillsborough. His adversaries put him into a cart, rode him to a pond, and dunked the dignified man. When they finished with their fun, Williams said, "Gentlemen, you rode me down here, I think you should ride me back." They complied.

In 1778, Williams was elected to the Continental Congress, where he joined John Penn and Cornelius Harnett in signing the Articles of Confederation for North Carolina. Several months after his resignation from Congress in February 1779, he was elected to serve as one of the three judges of the first state superior court (the predecessor of the state supreme court). His colleagues were Samuel Spencer and Samuel Ashe. For the next twenty years, Williams rendered distinguished service on the bench. His most important decision was in the case of *Bayard v. Singleton*, wherein the principle of judicial review was established.

Buried nearby in an elaborate brick vault topped with a memorial slab is Colonel Robert Burton (1747–1825), who married Judge Williams's only daughter. Like his father-in-law, Burton was a native of Virginia. He settled in Williamsboro upon his marriage to Agatha Williams in 1775.

An officer in the Continental Army from the beginning of the Revolutionary War, Burton rose from an artillery lieutenant to quartermaster general of North Carolina, where he held the rank of colonel. Following the war, he served numerous terms as a member of the Council of State and two terms in the Continental Congress.

When a commission was selected in 1813 to establish the boundary lines for the Carolinas and Georgia, North Carolina appointed Burton to represent its interests.

His vast landholdings included more than six thousand acres in North Carolina and Tennessee.

In 1789, he donated a bust of John Paul Jones to the state. When the State Capitol burned in 1831, the fire consumed the piece.

Return to the junction with S.R. 1329. Turn left, proceed west for 0.6 mile to S.R. 1335, turn right, and go east for 1 mile to the driveway for Burnside, located on the right.

From the driveway, you'll have an excellent view of the handsome, two-story frame mansion, erected in the eighteenth century. According to tradition, the massive house was once the home of Memucan Hunt (1729–1808), the first treasurer of North Carolina.

Following his service in the colonial assembly as a representative from Granville County, Hunt earned the rare distinction of sitting as a delegate in each of the five Provincial Congresses. Throughout the Revolutionary War, Hunt's skill and foresight as a district treasurer enabled the state to fund its war effort. As a reward for his financial leadership during the struggle for independence, the general assembly appointed him to the new office of state treasurer on January 1, 1785.

Hunt's son, William, served with distinction as an officer in the Revolutionary War.

Return to the junction with S.R. 1329. Turn left and follow S.R. 1329 back through Williamsboro to N.C. 39. As you traverse this ancient road, on which Cornwallis's troops marched in 1781, consider Williamsboro as a case study in "what might have been." One of the favorites for the site of the permanent state capital, the town lost out to Raleigh. When the decision was made about the location for the state university, Williamsboro again finished a close second, this time to Chapel Hill. Ultimately, the once-prosperous town's death blow came when the railroad was constructed 8 miles to the south.

Turn right on N.C. 39 and drive south. After 0.1 mile, you will reach a state historical marker for Governor James Turner (1766–1824). His plantation, Oakland, stood 1 mile east.

In 1781, when he was fourteen years old, Turner left his family's farm in nearby Warren County to enlist in a local volunteer force that joined Nathanael Greene for the grueling North Carolina campaign. It was during his service that Turner formed a lifelong friendship with a neighbor who had also taken up arms for the American cause—Nathaniel Macon.

Much like Macon, Turner was destined for politics. Upon Montfort Stokes's refusal to serve in the United States Senate, the state legislature sent Turner to Washington to assume that seat in 1805. There, he was reunited with Macon, who at the time was Speaker of the House of Representatives.

Continue south on N.C. 39 for 2.2 miles to S.R. 1308. Turn left and drive west for 3.2 miles across Kerr Lake to S.R. 1319 (Satterwhite Point Road). Turn left and proceed north for 1.8 miles to Ashland, the striking colonial mansion that rests atop a hill on the left side of the road.

Ashland

Samuel Henderson brought his family to this area from Virginia in the second quarter of the eighteenth century. He built the oldest portion of the two-story dwelling in 1740. Upon his death, Ashland came into the possession of his oldest son, Richard, the partner and kinsman of Judge John Williams. In 1820, Richard's son, Archibald, added a Greek Revival wing that included a spacious ballroom.

Richard Henderson (1735–85) rose to prominence before the Revolution as a result of his talents as an attorney. In his role as a superior-court judge, he found himself thrust into the middle of the turmoil occasioned by the Regulator movement. During the riots in Hillsborough in September 1770 that resulted in the beating of John Williams, Henderson narrowly escaped the attack by fleeing out a back door. Two months later, his home in Williamsboro was burned by Regulators. The tribunal that subsequently ordered the execution of six Regulators in Hillsborough following the Battle of Alamance included Richard Henderson.

During his travels as a judge throughout the back country of western North Carolina, Henderson nurtured a long-held dream—an expedition beyond the Appalachians. To realize that dream, he organized a three-man land enterprise, Richard Henderson and Company. His associates were Judge John Williams and Thomas Hart, who later became the father-in-law of Henry Clay.

Enthused by the positive reports of his scout, Daniel Boone, Henderson left the bench to devote his time and attention to the venture. He and his partners organized a new company—first called the Louisa Land Company, then the Transylvania Land Company—to acquire property and settle it. Through Boone's assistance, the Transylvania Land Company negotiated one of the largest land transactions in American history when it acquired 20 million acres (constituting most of Kentucky and much of Tennessee) from the Cherokee tribe at Sycamore Shoals on the Watauga River in March 1775. Once the acquisition was completed, Boone was sent back to Kentucky, where he established a permanent settlement called Boonesborough. Others soon followed.

On May 23, 1775, a legislature composed of delegates from the new settlements convened at the behest of Henderson. It enacted the framework for the establishment of Transylvania as the fourteenth American colony.

Later in 1775, James Hogg was dispatched to the Continental Congress to plead the case for the recognition of the "New Independent Government of Transylvania." He found little support from Congress, which questioned the land claims of Henderson and the others and the motives of the free-spirited settlers. John Adams, verbalizing the concerns of his colleagues, noted that "taking under our protection a body of people who have acted in defiance of the King's proclamation will be looked upon as a confirmation of that independent spirit with which we are daily approached."

Without congressional recognition, Henderson's company could not succeed. The late Archer Butler Hulbert, a noted historian of the American West, summarized the company's significance: "The Transylvania Company conferred an inestimable good upon Virginia and North Carolina and the nation when it marked out through the hand of Boone the Wilderness Road to Kentucky. . . . From any standpoint Richard Henderson's brave advance into Kentucky in April 1775, must be considered as one of the most heroic displays of comprehensive aggrandizement of which so much is heard today."

Continue north on S.R. 1319 for 0.7 mile to a gray building on the right at the Kerr Lake Outdoor Educational Area. Leave your car in the parking lot and walk down the gated path on the right for 0.2 mile to the burial site of Richard Henderson. A modern grave marker gives an overview of his career.

Although he is best remembered as the man who opened Kentucky to settlement at the time the colonies began the struggle for independence, Henderson was an active supporter of the American cause during the war. In 1778, he was nominated to serve in the Continental Congress, but he stepped aside when John Williams showed interest in the seat. Henderson held the rank of colonel in the militia and was successful in recruiting troops and obtaining supplies throughout the war.

Retrace your route on S.R. 1319 to the junction with S.R. 1308. Continue south on S.R. 1319 to U.S. 158. Turn left and drive east for 3.5 miles to the state historical marker for Governor William Hawkins, who was born during the Revolutionary War in the nearby home of his Patriot father.

To see the family's home, continue 0.2 mile beyond the sign to S.R. 1371 (Flemington Road). Turn left and proceed 0.7 mile north to Pleasant Hill, located on the right. Constructed sometime in the second half of the eighteenth century, this well-maintained two-and-a-half-story dwelling was the home of a family of Revolutionary War soldiers.

Philemon Hawkins II (1717–1801) settled in the area as a teenager in 1735. Thereafter, he acquired Pleasant Hill Plantation, prospered as a planter, and became the richest man in the county.

When Governor Tryon marched on the Regulators in 1771, he took Philemon with him as his aide-de-camp. It fell to Hawkins's lot to ride to the front of the Regulator line and read Tryon's proclamation only moments before the Battle of Alamance began. Throughout the battle, Hawkins served as the bearer of the governor's commands and exposed himself to great danger. When the fighting ceased, numerous balls were found in his clothing. Tryon praised Hawkins for his bravery during the engagement.

At the onset of the Revolution, Hawkins threw his support to the colonies, despite the concerted effort of Governor Josiah Martin to enlist his aid for the Crown. A member of the Fourth and Fifth Provincial Congresses at Halifax in 1776, Hawkins disdained an appointment as brigadier general of the state militia. Instead, he served for a time as a colonel, as did all four of his sons—John, Joseph, Benjamin, and Philemon III. The elder Hawkins also rendered invaluable service to the young state in the general assembly from 1779 to 1787.

Philemon Hawkins III (1752–1833) was born at Pleasant Hill Plantation and erected the existing house here. As a teenager, he accompanied his father to the fight against the Regulators at the Battle of Alamance. For his bravery on the field, Governor Tryon presented Philemon III with a beautiful rifle.

Four years later, when the news of the events at Lexington and Concord reached North Carolina, a great clamor arose in the colony to assemble troops. One of the first companies in the state was raised by Philemon III.

Like his father, Philemon III was a delegate at the Fifth Provincial Congress in 1776. When he died fifty-seven years later, he was the last living signer of the state's first constitution.

His postwar service included eleven terms in the state legislature.

Philemon III is said to have left 131 children, grandchildren, and great-grandchildren. His oldest son, William Hawkins (1777–1819), the subject of the nearby historical marker, studied law under Judge John Williams before his election as governor. He was the state's chief executive during the War of 1812.

A cemetery at Pleasant Hill holds the graves of some of the members of this historic family.

Return to the junction with U.S. 158 and turn left. It is 2.6 miles east to the Warren County line. Created in 1779 when Bute County was abolished, it was named for General Joseph Warren (1741–75), a soldier-physician who became an early martyr for the American cause when he was killed at Bunker Hill.

From the county line, follow U.S. 158 for 1.6 miles to another state historical marker for Governor James Turner. Bloomsbury, one of the homes of the Revolutionary War soldier, was located 2 miles north.

Continue east on U.S. 158 for 16.8 miles to S.R. 1345 at the community of Vaughan. On the right side of U.S. 158 just east of the junction stands a state historical marker for Nathaniel Macon, whose grave and former homesite are located 4 miles northeast.

Turn left on S.R. 1345 and drive north for 0.7 mile to S.R. 1344. Turn right, proceed 3.4 miles north to S.R. 1348, turn left, and go 0.5 mile to Macon's rock-covered grave, located at a tree-shaded spot on the right. Interred here is the man many historians consider the greatest figure North Carolina has ever produced.

Born on the family plantation on Shocco Creek in Warren County, Nathaniel Macon (1758–1837) enrolled at Princeton as a teenager. While a student there, he volunteered for the New Jersey militia. Soon thereafter, the Revolutionary War forced the college to close, and Macon returned home.

In 1780, his brother raised a full company of soldiers, which Nathaniel joined. He rejected a commission, choosing instead to fight as a private. Nathaniel insisted that he owed his country military service. He accepted no pay as a soldier and later refused to apply for a Revolutionary War pension.

After participating in the American debacle at Camden, the Warren County soldiers were camped on the Yadkin River in 1781 when they received news that twenty-two-year-old Nathaniel Macon had been elected to the North Carolina Senate. Macon responded that he had seen the faces of the British but never their backs, and that he intended to stay in the army until he did. Friends prevailed upon him to accept the seat. Thus, he reluctantly left the battlefield and embarked upon a career in politics that lasted forty-seven years.

After serving five consecutive terms in the state legislature, Macon declined a nomination to the Continental Congress in 1786. Five years later, voters sent him to the United States Congress for the first of twelve consecutive terms. From 1801 to 1807, Macon served as Speaker of the House of Representatives. In 1815, North Carolinians elected him to the United States Senate. He served as president *pro tempore* of that body from 1826 to 1828.

Visitors to this site are often appalled that the grave of North Carolina's foremost statesman is lacking in sophistication, but it is just as Macon wanted it. He deplored vanity and idolatry. In fact, his dislike of pomp led him to oppose federal expenditures for a tomb for George Washington. About his own grave, Macon wrote, "Do not go to the needless expense of marking my grave with a monument; let anyone who cares toss a rock upon my grave."

Grave of Nathaniel Macon

For almost a century, his wishes were honored. Not until 1923 was a large metal tablet erected at the head of the rock pile. The inscription on the plaque begins with a simple phrase—"A soldier of the Revolution"—and ends with the eloquent tribute paid to Macon by his friend and colleague Thomas Jefferson: "The strictest of Our Models of Genuine Republicanism, Nathaniel Macon, Upon Whose Tomb Will Be Written, 'Ultimus Romanorum' [the Last of the Romans]."

Buried beside Macon is his wife, Hannah Plummer Macon. At the conclusion of the Revolutionary War, Nathaniel returned home to ask for

Hannah's hand in marriage. At the time, he had stiff competition from John Randolph. To settle the issue, the two men decided to play a game of cards. Macon promptly lost the game. In agony, he pined, "Hannah, I have lost you fairly, but love is superior to fortune! I cannot give you up, I love you yet!" Touched by the appeal, Hannah warmly embraced Macon, and the two were soon married.

Randolph, who served as executor of the estate of Thomas Jefferson, wrote that Jefferson was "the wisest man I ever knew—except Mr. Macon." Randolph once said to Macon, "With the single exception of General Washington, there is not one of your times who will stand so fair with posterity as yourself."

Before you leave the grave, follow the time-honored tradition of adding a stone to it.

Macon's grave is located at the site of his plantation, Buck Spring. Go across the road to the access road for the 4-H campground. Located here within sight of the grave are Macon's small house and its surrounding outbuildings. The structures were restored during Warren County's commemoration of the bicentennial.

Retrace your route to the junction of S.R. 1345 and U.S. 158. Turn left and drive east. It is 5.2 miles to the Halifax County line. Continue on U.S. 158 for 0.5 mile to N.C. 4 in the historic town of Littleton, located on the Halifax County–Warren County line.

Settled before the Revolution, Littleton bears the name of William Person Little (1765–1829) a horse breeder and early state official. Little served as a delegate to the Constitutional Convention in Hillsborough in 1788. His once-majestic home, Mosby Hill, now lies in ruins on the edge of town.

Turn right on N.C. 4 (Mosby Avenue) and drive south for 0.6 mile. Mosby Avenue was once a track on which Little raced his thoroughbreds.

At the junction of Mosby Avenue and Warren Street is a state historical marker for Person's Ordinary, an important meeting place during the Revolution. Turn left and proceed one block to the one-and-a-half-story tavern, which has been restored by the Littleton Woman's Club. The tavern was constructed around 1774 and is the oldest building in the town. Owned by Thomas Person during the Revolutionary War, it served as a stop on the stagecoach route between Halifax and Hillsborough. William Little, the adopted son and nephew of Thomas Person, was a subsequent owner. The building is open to the public by appointment.

Return to Mosby Avenue and turn left. Drive south for 0.1 mile to S.R. 1509, turn right, and go 14.5 miles to N.C. 58. Turn right and drive west for 2.1 miles to U.S. 158. Continue west on N.C. 58/U.S. 158 for 0.4 mile to U.S. 401 (Main Street) in downtown Warrenton. Like the county itself, the seat of local government was named to honor Revolutionary War hero Dr. Joseph Warren.

Turn right on U.S. 401 and proceed 0.2 mile to Ridgeway Street. Turn left and drive to the handsome two-story house located at 209 Ridgeway. The oldest portion of this Greek Revival dwelling is said to have been constructed by Dr. James Gloster Brehon (1740–1819), a Revolutionary War surgeon.

Born in Ireland, Brehon settled in Warrenton in the early stages of the American Revolution. After volunteering to aid the cause of the colonies, he was appointed a surgeon in the fledgling American navy. After the war, he came home to Warrenton, where he acquired a substantial estate.

Return to U.S. 401, turn right, and drive south through downtown Warrenton. You'll notice a state historical marker for Benjamin Hawkins (1754–1816), whose home was 5.5 miles southwest.

Born at Pleasant Hill, Hawkins was the son of Philemon Hawkins II. Like his father and his three brothers, he served as a colonel during the Revolutionary War. His fluency in French, gained while he was a student at Princeton, drew the admiration of General George Washington, who appointed Hawkins to his personal staff to serve as his interpreter with America's French allies.

In 1789, Samuel Johnston and Benjamin Hawkins became the first United States senators from North Carolina under the newly ratified federal Constitution.

After 7.1 miles on U.S. 401, you'll see a state historical marker at the site of the former Bute County Courthouse. Formed in 1746, Bute County was named for John Stuart, earl of Bute. Stuart served for a time as the first lord of the treasury under King George III. For twenty-five years, all of the area now encompassed by Warren and Franklin Counties was Bute County. But in time, Lord Bute, an advocate of the Stamp Act, proved to be unpopular in the colonies and was burned in effigy.

Because of its name, Bute County became a casualty of the American Revolution. Local residents were among North Carolina's earliest supporters of the cause of independence. High-spirited citizens of Bute County, led by Philemon Hawkins II, assembled at the current tour stop in 1774 to form the Bute County Association. Its secretary recorded the intent of the ninety men who made up that association: "We . . . doe most seriously, Religiously, Join our hearts and hands in embodying ourselves into an Independent Company of Free Men, to be in readyness to defend ourselves against any violence that may be exerted against our persons and properties, to stand by and Support to the utmost of our power the Salvation of America."

By 1775, the war cry "There are no Tories in Bute!" was popular throughout the colony. An initial attempt to dissolve Bute and divide it into two new counties died in the first state legislature in 1777 not from lack of popularity but because the legislators were preoccupied with the war. Two years later, Bute vanished from the map. Its northern half became Warren County and its southern half Franklin County.

Continue south on U.S. 401 for 1.6 miles to the state historical marker for General Jethro Sumner (1733–85), whose home and inn stood nearby.

Sumner began his military career in 1758 at the age of twenty-five, when he reported to Colonel George Washington in western Virginia with a letter of introduction from Governor Dinwiddie. Following several years of service as a junior officer in the French and Indian War, he settled in North Carolina. His wife's sizable inheritance allowed Sumner to purchase a large tract at the current stop, where he lived and operated an inn that was well established by the time of the Revolution. The Bute County Courthouse was located on land owned by Sumner, who served as county sheriff in 1772.

On March 15, 1777, Colonel Sumner was commanding the Third North Carolina Continental Line when it was ordered north to report to George Washington. Exposed to the ferocious fighting at Brandywine, Germantown, and Monmouth and the suffering at Valley Forge, Sumner's command was greatly depleted. A well-deserved promotion to brigadier general came on January 9, 1779.

One of Nathanael Greene's first acts after his assumption of command in the South in December 1780 was a special request to Sumner to recruit soldiers for the Continental Army. Sumner was equal to the difficult task. On June 1, 1781, he reported to Greene in South Carolina with a small brigade of recruits.

On September 8, 1781, Sumner enjoyed what was perhaps his finest hour at the Battle of Eutaw Springs. In some of the bloodiest fighting of the entire war, his men manned the second line, which sustained the brunt of the battle. At the height of the struggle, Sumner ordered a brilliant charge with fixed bayonets.

When he died in 1785, Sumner was buried near the current tour stop, but his grave was subsequently moved to Guilford Courthouse National Military Park. Two years after his death, the state legislature created a new county in his honor; Sumner County is now part of Tennessee.

It is another 3.4 miles on U.S. 401 to the Franklin County line. The county bears the name of yet another hero of the Revolutionary War, that quintessential American Benjamin Franklin.

From the county line, follow U.S. 401 south for 5.2 miles to N.C. 39. Turn right, proceed 0.2 mile north to S.R. 1239, turn left, and drive 4.7 miles east to the bridge over Lynch Creek. Tradition holds that the term *lynch* became part of the English language as a result of an incident that took place here during the Regulator movement.

Sometime in 1768, Governor Tryon dispatched Major Lynch to Bute County to collect taxes. A mob of Regulators seized the unpopular and unfortunate representative of the Crown and brought him before a mock court, which sentenced him to death and summarily executed him by hanging him on a tree along the bank of the creek at the current tour stop.

Since that time, this waterway, which empties into the nearby Tar River, has carried the name of Major Lynch. And so, too, do executions carried out without due process of law.

Turn around near the bridge and retrace your route to N.C. 39. Turn right and drive south for 0.2 mile to where the road merges with U.S. 401. Continue south on N.C. 39/U.S. 401 for 6.6 miles to where the two highways separate in Louisburg, the seat of Franklin County. Authorized to be laid out in 1779, Louisburg was named for Louis XVI, the French monarch with whom Benjamin Franklin negotiated during the Revolutionary War.

Turn left on N.C. 39 and drive 0.4 mile south to S.R. 1760 (Green Hill Road). A state historical marker here will direct you to Green Hill Place—a shrine of the Methodist Church and the home of a Revolutionary War Patriot. Turn right on S.R. 1760 and proceed 0.1 mile to the tidy one-and-a-half-story house, located on the right.

The house takes its name from its builder and first owner, Green Hill (1741–1826). Hill was born in Bute County, but little is known of his early life. In the early 1770s, about the same time he built the house at the current tour stop, he developed a deep interest in a relatively new movement in Protestantism. It was called Methodism.

Before he could act on that interest, the Revolutionary War intervened. A staunch Patriot from the outset, Hill volunteered as a chaplain for the American cause in 1781 and took part in Greene's miraculous retreat across the Yadkin.

Following the war, Hill's service to the state and county continued in the judicial and political arenas. But his interest in Methodism came to the fore. On July 9, 1780, Bishop Francis Asbury drew a crowd of four hundred people when he preached at Hill's home. The site went on to become a popular meeting place for the infant denomination.

On April 20, 1785, history was made here. The events that day constituted not only the first conference of the Methodist Church ever held in North Carolina but the first such meeting in the entire United States as well. At that conference, Hill became the first native North Carolinian to be licensed as a Methodist minister.

Today, the Green Hill House is recognized as one of the ten shrines of American Methodism.

Retrace your route to the junction of N.C. 39 and U.S. 401. Turn left and follow U.S. 401 south. It is 11.2 miles to the Wake County line. Ironically, Wake, the home of the state's permanent capital, born of the American Revolution, bears a name that dates from when North Carolina was part of the British Empire. Carved from Johnston County in 1771, it was named for Margaret Wake (1733–1819), the wife of Royal Governor William Tryon.

Continue south on U.S. 401 for 12.9 miles to its merger with U.S. 1. Proceed south on U.S. 401/U.S. 1 for 0.4 mile to New Hope Church Road.

Turn right on New Hope Church Road and proceed west for 1.8 miles to Wake Forest Road. Turn left and drive south for 0.7 mile to Executive Drive. On the left side of the road in front of Raleigh Community Hospital stands a state historical marker for Isaac Hunter's Tavern, which stood nearby during the Revolutionary War era.

When the Constitutional Convention was called to order in Hillsborough in 1788 to consider ratification of the federal Constitution, it was charged with yet another responsibility: "To fix on the place for holding the future meetings of the General Assembly, and the place of residence for the chief officers of the State; which, when fixed, shall be considered the unalterable seat of government for this State."

Despite their failure to ratify the Constitution, convention delegates came to a decision about the site of the permanent state capital. Many established towns—including Hillsborough, New Bern, Fayetteville, and Tarboro—sought the honor. But on the second ballot at Hillsborough, the majority of the delegates passed an ordinance that located the seat of government at "the said plantation whereon the said Isaac Hunter now resides, or such place as the General Assembly shall fix upon within ten miles of the said plantation." Hunter's hostelry was a well-known inn situated on the primary north-south highway between Virginia and South Carolina. James Iredell, who was soon to become an associate justice of the first United States Supreme Court, led the successful effort for the Wake County location.

The ordinance did not sit well with the powerful towns of the east and the convention minority, which argued against "the establishment of a seat of government in a place unconnected with commerce, and where there is at present no town." It said this would be "a heavy expense to the people." Consequently, the state legislature met for three additional terms in Fayetteville. Finally, both houses of the general assembly met at New Bern on January 5, 1792. In a close vote, they ratified an act to carry out the ordinance of the 1788 convention.

Continue south on Wake Forest Road for 3.4 miles to Blount Street in downtown Raleigh. As you travel about the historic city, you'll notice that many of its streets are named for heroes of the Revolutionary War period. For example, Blount Street honors Thomas Blount (1759–1812), one of

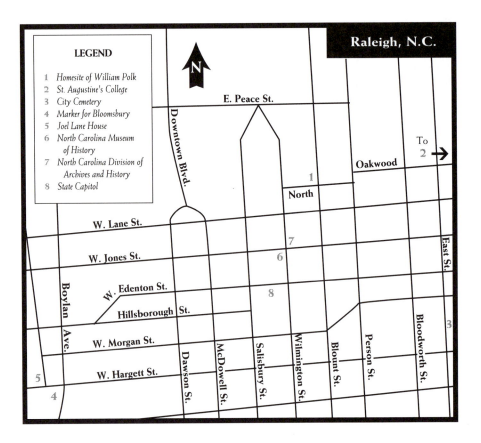

the famous Blount brothers of Washington, North Carolina. A lieutenant in the Fifth North Carolina Regiment, Thomas Blount was taken prisoner during the war and imprisoned in England.

Proceed south on Blount Street for five blocks to North Street. Located on the northeastern corner of the intersection is a state historical marker at the site of the home of William Polk, one of the state's greatest Revolutionary War heroes. As the marker points out, Polk hosted Lafayette in his home during the French hero's visit to Raleigh on March 2, 1825.

Turn left on North Street and drive one block to Person Street (named for Thomas Person). Turn left on Person, then turn immediately onto Oakwood Avenue. Proceed east for 0.6 mile to St. Augustine's College. Buried in an unmarked grave on the 110-acre campus of this historic college for blacks is that incomparable Patriot of the American Revolution,

Willie Jones. His summer home, known as Welcome, was located on the site of the college.

Following the successful conclusion of the war, Jones was a prominent player in the selection of Wake County as the site of the state capital. Thereafter, he served as one of the commissioners who laid out Raleigh. At an uncertain date, he took up residence in the "capital village."

Upon Jones's death on June 18, 1801, the *Raleigh Register* noted, "It may with the greatest truth be said that Carolina has not produced a son of [greater] governmental endowment than Mr. Jones, or one [who] lived more universally and deserved respect or died more affectionately and sincerely regretted."

That Jones was buried in an unmarked grave was of his own choosing. His will specified that if he died in Raleigh, he was to be buried at the side of his young daughter without monument or tombstone. In 1860, a careful search of the area around the current tour stop revealed no trace of the grave.

Retrace your route to the intersection of North and Blount Streets. Turn left on Blount and proceed south for six blocks to East Hargett Street. This street is named for Frederick Hargett (1742–1810), a native of Pitt County who served as a captain of the Eighth North Carolina Regiment during the Revolutionary War.

Turn left on East Hargett and proceed three blocks to East Street. Located at the northwestern corner of the intersection is the historic City Cemetery. Established in 1798, the expansive burial ground is enclosed by an iron fence that surrounded the State Capitol grounds from 1847 to 1898. Most of the graves in the northern half of the cemetery are those of white citizens of Raleigh. Visitors were buried in the southwestern quadrant, while blacks were interred in the southeastern quadrant.

Among the Revolutionary War notables buried here are Joel Lane, Absalom Tatom, and William Polk.

Lane, "the Father of Raleigh," was reinterred here after his original grave site on South Boylan Avenue became a parking lot in 1974. Bagpipes wailed and reenactors from the Second North Carolina Continental Line fired a salute as Lane's new pine coffin, draped with a thirteen-star flag, was lowered into the grave.

Wakefield, the restored Lane home, is visited later on this tour.

Absalom Tatom (1742–1802), a native of Granville County, served the American cause in a variety of military and administrative capacities during the Revolution. On September 1, 1775, he was commissioned a lieutenant in the First North Carolina Continental Line. Six years later, Tory forces took him prisoner at the Battle of Elizabethtown, but he managed to escape after darkness fell.

Few North Carolinians deserved to wear the mantle of Revolutionary War hero more than William Polk (1758–1834). His grave is fittingly marked by a towering obelisk.

As a soldier, Polk had no peer. He was in the forefront of the action in both the North and the South. Samuel A. Ashe praised him thus: "Two generals of North Carolina troops in the army of the Revolution were wounded unto death in battle—Francis Nash at Germantown, Pennsylvania, on the 4th of October, 1777, and William Lee Davidson at Cowan's Ford, North Carolina, on the 1st of February, 1781. Far apart as these battles were, both in time and place, William Polk served with marked bravery in each, being major of the Ninth North Carolina Continentals under Nash and officer of State volunteers under Davidson."

Born in Mecklenburg County, Polk grew up in a hotbed of revolutionary activities. At the age of seventeen, he was on hand to watch as his father, Thomas, and other delegates to the Mecklenburg Convention of May 1775 affixed their names to documents that would later be used as a model throughout the thirteen colonies. Inspired by the fiery patriotism of his family and friends, Polk flung himself into the fight for independence.

Deadly attrition to the officer corps of the Ninth North Carolina Line forced Polk—then an eighteen-year-old major—to assume command of the regiment. Following the action at Brandywine, the young North Carolinian displayed great bravery on the field at Germantown. In the same battle that took General Nash's life, a bullet plowed through Polk's face and tongue. For a time, he was unable to speak.

Three years later, Polk served as aide-de-camp to General Richard Caswell during the horrific defeat at Camden. Things might have been much worse for the Americans after the battle had it not been for Polk, who used his excellent knowledge of the area to enable North Carolina soldiers to escape capture.

Later, Polk fought in his own backyard as he joined General William Lee Davidson in the heroic but futile stand against Cornwallis at Cowan's Ford on February 1, 1781. When Davidson fell in that fight, many of his troops were thrown into confusion. Once again, Polk led the Americans to safety.

Six weeks later, Nathanael Greene enjoyed Polk's able assistance as a volunteer officer at the Battle of Guilford Courthouse.

At the height of the fierce fighting at the Battle of Eutaw Springs on September 8, 1781, Polk's horse was shot from under him. He then witnessed the death of his younger brother, Lieutenant Thomas Polk. According to Samuel Chappelle, a soldier who also watched the tragic event, Colonel Polk gave a sudden outburst of grief "but almost immediately regained self-control and detailed two men to bury the remains." He then rode away to give chase to the enemy.

Polk's postwar career in politics and public service was as illustrious as his military career. Following the death of his first wife in 1799, he moved from Charlotte to Raleigh. Over the last thirty-five years of his life, he became Raleigh's favorite son.

At the intersection of East Hargett and East Streets, turn right onto East. Proceed one block to Martin Street, turn right, and drive seven blocks to Dawson Street. Turn left and travel three blocks to Lenoir Street, named in honor of William Lenoir, the Revolutionary War-era military leader and statesman from western North Carolina.

Turn right onto Lenoir, drive five blocks to Boylan Avenue, turn right again, and go north for five blocks to West Hargett Street.

Located at the southwestern corner of the intersection is a large boulder bearing a bronze plaque that notes that the first courthouse of Wake County stood near here. Known as Bloomsbury in deference to the homestead of Joel Lane, who owned much land in the area, the county seat retained that name until 1792, when it became known as Wake Court-House. The first courthouse, a log building, stood on the hillside near Lane's residence.

Turn left on West Hargett and drive one block to St. Mary's Street. Located on the northwestern corner of the intersection at 728 West Hargett is the Joel Lane House, otherwise known as Wakefield. Constructed by Lane around 1760, the gambrel-roofed frame dwelling is the oldest structure in Wake County. Named in honor of Governor Tryon's wife, Margaret Wake, the house was considered the finest residence within 100 miles when it was built. It originally stood just east of its present location and overlooked the site of the State Capitol.

Because it was located at the junction of two of the colony's primary roadways, Wakefield attracted many visitors. Joel Lane therefore constructed a nearby inn. It was there that the wartime legislature met in 1781. Thomas Burke was elected governor at the inn. For allowing his ordinary to be used as the temporary State Capitol, Lane received two weeks' rent.

Lane, who had introduced the bill that created Wake County in 1771, was a personal friend of a number of the commissioners appointed to select the site of the capital city twenty years later. He invited the commissioners to stay in his home while they deliberated over the seventeen sites under consideration, one of which belonged to Lane himself.

Over a ten-day period, the commissioners pared the seventeen sites to three. When the six officials in attendance cast their votes for their favorite among the three finalists, the results revealed three votes for the tract of Colonel John Hinton (Lane's late father-in-law) in eastern Wake County, two votes for Lane's land, and one vote for a site in what is now Cary. Because the commissioners did not reach a majority, they agreed to recess until the next day.

In the meantime, Lane wined and dined his special guests. When a second vote was then taken, Lane's site received five votes. Just a month later, in April 1792, Lane sold the thousand acres to the state of North Carolina for its permanent state capital.

Unlike most of the state capitals in the United States, Raleigh was designed to be an "unalterable capital." Within five days of the land purchase, surveyor William Christmas completed a plan for the city, which was named for the English explorer whose dreams led to the British colonization of America.

Even if Joel Lane had not provided the land on which Raleigh was built, his name would have been important in the state's Revolutionary War annals. He descended from a family that had made its mark in the earliest history of colonial America. His ancestor Ralph Lane was Sir Walter Raleigh's intrepid explorer of North Carolina. His great-grandfather Richard Lane was a Jamestown colonist.

Joel Lane was born in Halifax County around 1740. He settled in what is now Wake County around 1769 and quickly became one of the wealthiest and most influential citizens in the area. During the war, Lane served on the commission charged with obtaining a supply of salt, an essential commodity.

Cognizant of Wakefield's historical significance, the Wake County Committee of the Colonial Dames purchased the structure in 1927. Subsequent restoration projects have produced an excellent example of North Carolina architecture during the colonial period. The house is open to the public on a limited schedule.

Turn right on St. Mary's Street and proceed one block north to Morgan Street. Turn right, drive one block east to Boylan Avenue, turn left, and drive north for one block to Hillsborough Street. Turn left and go 1.4 miles to Pogue Street. On the left is the campus of North Carolina State University.

D.A.R. marker for the 13 colonies/ states, NCSU campus

A sizable monument erected by the D.A.R. in 1936 adorns the campus here at its Hillsborough Street boundary. Thirteen slabs of Wake County granite, each bearing the name of one of the thirteen colonies, form a tall arch. The slab atop the arch represents North Carolina. A bronze plaque pays tribute to "the Men and Women of the Thirteen Original Colonies Who Achieved Independence and Union for the United States of America."

Turn around near the monument and retrace Hillsborough Street to Boylan Avenue. Continue east on Hillsborough for five blocks to McDowell Street. Turn left, drive two blocks to Jones Street, turn right, and proceed east to Salisbury Street. Continue on Jones across Salisbury and turn right into the underground parking garage at the North Carolina Museum of History. Take the garage elevator to museum's entrance.

Completed in 1993, this massive new facility preserves and exhibits the artifacts of North Carolina's long history. Only a small portion of the collection can be displayed at any given time. Priceless weapons, uniforms, flags, and other relics from the colonial and Revolutionary War periods are almost always on display. Among the original flags held by the museum is a unique banner from Guilford Courthouse with thirteen stars and twelve stripes.

Admission to the facility is free.

After touring the museum, leave through the front entrance and walk

---

south along Bicentennial Mall. Notice the long line of memorial stones honoring all of North Carolina's one hundred counties. Inscribed on each stone is the county's name and date of creation.

From the southern end of Bicentennial Mall, walk across Jones Street to the North Carolina State Archives. Maintained here are countless rare documents, letters, maps, books, newspapers, and other written materials from the eighteenth century. They chronicle North Carolina's evolution from a Royal colony to an independent state. Upon presenting proper identification, visitors may examine many of these papers in the facility's research room.

Statue of Washington in Capitol Square, Raleigh

From the archives, walk east on Jones Street to Wilmington Street. Turn right and proceed south on Wilmington for one block to Edenton Street. Walk across the street to Capitol Square. Here stands the majestic State Capitol, the enduring symbol of the North Carolina established by the sacrifices of its citizens in the eighteenth century. Located on the well-manicured grounds are numerous monuments. Many memorialize people and events related to the Revolution.

On the eastern side of the square stands an impressive monument to the three presidents that North Carolina has given to the United States. The central figure of the sculpture is Andrew Jackson, the teenage soldier of the Revolutionary War.

On the southern side of the square stands a large statue of George Washington. Dedicated in July 1857, it was the first monument placed on the Capitol grounds. Cast in bronze by Virginia artist William Jones Hubard, it is a copy of an original by French sculptor Jean-Antoine Houdon. Several cannon recovered from the Edenton waterfront following the Revolutionary War are displayed near the statue.

Walk to the western side of the square, where you'll find several more of the famous cannon. (For an account of events in Edenton, see The Albemarle Tour, pages 12–14.)

The western side of the stately Capitol Building is its most photographed. Construction of the massive Greek Revival structure commenced on July 4, 1833, and was completed in 1840. It was erected to replace North Carolina's first statehouse after that building (constructed around 1794) was destroyed by an accidental fire in 1831.

Although the present State Capitol was first used seventy-five years after the Declaration of Independence, it contains numerous reminders of the fight for independence.

In the former House chamber hangs Thomas Sully's famous copy of Gilbert Stuart's incomparable portrait of George Washington. The valuable piece of art was one of the few treasures salvaged from the inferno that destroyed the original State Capitol. Commissioned by the state in 1813, the enormous portrait underwent an extensive restoration by the North Carolina Museum of Art in 1981.

The central rotunda of the cross-shaped building is topped by a copper-covered dome and holds numerous Revolutionary War memorials.

Several are D.A.R. tablets. One pays tribute to North Carolina's three signers of the Declaration of Independence, while another memorializes the "Patriots of the Lower Cape Fear Who Resisted British Authority by Preventing Openly with Arms the Enforcement of the Stamp Act 1765–1766."

Without question, *Canova's Washington* is the most interesting Revolutionary War memorial in the State Capitol.

When North Carolina decided to memorialize Washington with a statue, Thomas Jefferson was consulted. Upon his recommendation, Europe's most renowned sculptor, Antonio Canova (1757–1821), was selected for the project.

The marble masterpiece was completed in 1821. It depicted Washington seated, dressed in a toga, and holding a tablet, in the Neoclassical style. One art expert noted, "The statue, first significant sculpture to be imported, was considered everywhere in America the finest work of art in the country."

When the six-foot, five-thousand-pound statue arrived in Raleigh, it was delivered to the State Capitol in an oxcart. William Polk offered the dedicatory address during an elaborate ceremony.

Four years later, when Lafayette began his visit to Raleigh, he was taken to see Canova's likeness of the marquis's former comrade in arms. Lafayette's attention was promptly drawn to the speaker chosen to offer the official welcome—a living comrade in arms, Colonel William Polk. As soon as Polk completed his remarks, the two men, it was reported, "flung their arms about each other in a tender embrace, each deeply affected."

When the State Capitol burned in 1831, concerned citizens attempted in vain to save the statue, but its massive weight made it impossible to move. At length, the dome collapsed and crushed the masterpiece.

Not until 1970 was a replacement secured. Professor Romano Vio of the Academy of Venice was commissioned to craft a replica from the original Canova cast. When completed, it was shipped to the United States from Italy. In Raleigh, the new masterpiece was delivered to the State Capitol by oxcart, fittingly enough. And the speech delivered by Polk in 1821 was read once again.

The final tour ends here, at the likeness of "the Father of Our Country" in the Capitol of the state that was indeed "first for freedom."

Bibliography

Addison, Stephen O. *Profile of a Patriot: Colonel Benjamin Cleveland, Hero of Kings Mountain*. Privately printed, 1993.

Alderman, Pat. *The Overmountain Men*. Johnson City, Tenn.: Overmountain Press, 1986.

———. *One Heroic Hour at King's Mountain: Battle of King's Mountain October 7, 1780*. 2d ed. Johnson City, Tenn.: Overmountain Press, 1990.

Alexander, J. B. *The History of Mecklenburg County (NC) 1740–1900*. Charlotte, N.C.: Observer Printing House, 1902.

Amis, Moses N. *Historical Raleigh with Sketches of Wake County*. Raleigh, N.C.: Commercial Printing Co., 1913.

Anderson, Jean Bradley. *Durham County*. Durham, N.C.: Duke University Press, 1990.

Angley, Wilson. *A History of Fort Johnston on the Lower Cape Fear*. Southport, N.C.: Southport Historical Society, 1996.

Arthur, John Preston. *A History of Watauga County, North Carolina*. Richmond, Va.: Everett Waddey Co., 1915.

———. *Western North Carolina: A History, 1730–1913*. Reprint, Spartanburg, S.C.: Reprint Co., 1973.

Ashe, Samuel A. *History of North Carolina*. 2 vols. Raleigh, N.C.: Edwards and Broughton, 1925.

Ashe, Samuel A., Stephen B. Weeks, and Charles Van Noppen, eds. *Biographical History of North Carolina*. 8 vols. Greensboro, N.C.: Charles L. Van Noppen, 1905–17.

Bailey, J. D. *Commanders at Kings Mountain*. Gaffney, S.C.: Ed H. DeCamp, Publisher, 1926.

Baker, Thomas E. *Another Such Victory*. New York: Eastern Acorn Press, 1992.

———. *The Monuments at Guilford Courthouse National Military Park*.

Barbee, Millie M., ed. *Historic Burke: An Architectural Inventory of Burke County, North Carolina*. Morganton, N.C.: Historic Burke Foundation, 1987.

Barefoot, Daniel W. *Touring the Backroads of North Carolina's Lower Coast*. Winston-Salem, N.C.: John F. Blair, Publisher, 1995.

———. *Touring the Backroads of North Carolina's Upper Coast*. Winston-Salem, N.C.: John F. Blair, Publisher, 1995.

Bennett, Charles E., and Donald R. Lennon. *A Quest for Glory: Major General Robert Howe and the American Revolution*. Chapel Hill, N.C.: University of North Carolina Press, 1991.

Biggs, Walter C., Jr., and James F. Parnell. *State Parks of North Carolina*. Winston Salem, N.C.: John F. Blair, Publisher, 1989.

Bishir, Catherine W., and Michael T. Southern. *A Guide to the Historic Architecture of Eastern North Carolina*. Chapel Hill, N.C.: University of North Carolina Press, 1996.

Blackwelder, Ruth. *Old Charlotte and Old Mecklenburg Today*. Charlotte, N.C.: Mecklenburg Historical Association, 1973.

Blythe, Legette, and Charles R. Brockman. *Hornets' Nest: The Story of Charlotte and Mecklenburg County*. Charlotte, N.C.: McNally of Charlotte, 1961.

Boatner, Mark M., III. *Landmarks of the American Revolution*. New York: Hawthorn Books, 1975.

———. *Encyclopedia of the American Revolution*. Mechanicsburg, Pa.: Stackpole Books, 1994.

Brawley, James H. *The Rowan Story, 1753–1953: A Narrative of Rowan County, North Carolina*. Salisbury, N.C.: Rowan Printing Co., 1953.

Brimeloe, Judith M., ed. *South Carolina Historical Marker Guide*. Columbia, S.C.: South Carolina Department of Archives and History, 1992.

Broadfoot, Mrs. Hal W., et al., eds. *Spirit of Cumberland*. Fayetteville, N.C.: Junior Service League of Fayetteville, 1970.

Brown, Marvin A., and Maurice C. York. *Our Enduring Past*. Lincolnton, N.C.: Lincoln County Historic Properties Commission, 1986.

Brown, Marvin A., Patricia A. Esperson, and Andrew J. Carlson. *Heritage and Homesteads: The History and Architecture of Granville County, North Carolina*. Oxford, N.C.: Granville Historical Society, 1988.

Buchanan, John. *The Road to Guilford Courthouse: The American Revolution in the Carolinas*. New York: John Wiley and Sons, 1997.

Burns, Robert P. *100 Courthouses: A Report on North Carolina Judicial Facilities*. Vol. 2. Raleigh, N.C.: North Carolina State University, 1978.

Butchko, Thomas R. *An Inventory of Historic Architecture: Sampson County, North Carolina*. Clinton, N.C.: City of Clinton, 1981.

———. *Edenton: An Architectural Portrait*. Edenton, N.C.: Edenton Woman's Club, 1992.

Butler, Lindley S. *North Carolina and the Coming of the Revolution, 1763–1776*. Raleigh, N.C.: North Carolina Division of Archives and History, 1976.

Butler, Lindley S., ed. *The Narrative of Colonel David Fanning*. Davidson, N.C.: Briarpatch Press, 1981.

Carpenter, William L. *The Battle of Ramsour's Mill*. Lincolnton, N.C.: Lincoln County Historical Association and Lincoln County Museum of History, 1995.

Carraway, Gertrude S. *The Stanly (Stanley) Family and the Historic John Wright Stanly House*. High Point, N.C.: Hall Printing Co., 1969.

Caruthers, Eli W. *Revolutionary Incidents and Sketches of Character Chiefly in the Old North State*. 2 vols. Philadelphia: Hayes and Zell, 1854, 1856.

Cashman, Diane Cobb. *Cape Fear Adventure: An Illustrated History of Wilmington*. Chatsworth, Calif.: Windsor Publications, 1982.

Clark, Walter, ed. *The State Records of North Carolina*. 16 vols. Winston and Goldsboro, N.C.: State of North Carolina, 1895–1907.

Connor, R. D. W. *Cornelius Harnett: An Essay in North Carolina History*. Raleigh, N.C.: Edwards and Broughton, 1909.

————. *Revolutionary Leaders of North Carolina.* Greensboro, N.C.: North Carolina State Normal and Industrial College, 1916.

————. *Rebuilding an Ancient Commonwealth, 1584–1925.* 4 vols. Chicago: American Historical Society, 1929.

Cope, Robert F., and Manly Wade Wellman. *The County of Gaston: Two Centuries of a North Carolina Region.* Gastonia, N.C.: Gaston County Historical Society, 1977.

Corbitt, David Leroy. *The Formation of the North Carolina Counties, 1663–1943.* Raleigh, N.C.: North Carolina Department of Archives and History, 1950.

Cotton, Elizabeth H. *The John Paul Jones–Willie Jones Tradition: A Defense of the North Carolina Position.* Chapel Hill, N.C.: 1966.

Crabtree, Beth G. *North Carolina Governors, 1585–1958: Brief Sketches.* Raleigh, N.C.: North Carolina Department of Archives and History, 1958.

Crawford, Charlotte, et al. *Centennial, 1893–1993: Bessemer City, North Carolina.* Bessemer City, N.C.: Bessemer City Centennial Committee, 1993.

Creecy, Richard Benbury. *Grandfather's Tales of North Carolina History.* Raleigh, N.C.: Edwards and Broughton, 1901.

Crews, C. Daniel. *Through Fiery Trials: The Revolutionary War and the Moravians.* Winston-Salem, N.C.: Moravian Archives, 1996.

Crews, C. Daniel, ed. *Bethania: A Fresh Look at Its Birth.* Winston-Salem, N.C.: Moravian Archives, 1993.

Crow, Jeffrey J. *A Chronicle of North Carolina during the American Revolution, 1763–1789.* Raleigh, N.C.: North Carolina Division of Archives and History, 1975.

————. *The Black Experience in Revolutionary North Carolina.* Raleigh, N.C.: North Carolina Division of Archives and History, 1977.

Crow, Jeffrey J., ed. *A Guidebook to Revolutionary Sites in North Carolina.* Raleigh, N.C.: North Carolina Division of Archives and History, 1975.

Davidson, Chalmers G. *Piedmont Partisan: The Life and Times of Major General William Lee Davidson.* Davidson, N.C.: Davidson College, 1951.

Davis, Burke. *The Cowpens–Guilford Courthouse Campaign.* Philadelphia: J. B. Lippincott Co., 1962.

Demond, Robert O. *The Loyalists in North Carolina during the Revolution.* Durham, N.C.: Duke University Press, 1940.

Dill, Alonzo T. *Governor Tryon and His Palace*. Chapel Hill, N.C.: University of North Carolina Press, 1955.

Dixon, Kay. *Revolutionary Soldiers and Patriots of Gaston County, North Carolina*. Gastonia, N.C.: William Gaston Chapter, D.A.R., 1955.

Dixon, Max. *The Wataugans*. Johnson City, Tenn.: Overmountain Press, 1989.

Draper, Lyman C. *King's Mountain and Its Heroes: History of the Battle of King's Mountain*. Cincinnati: P. G. Thomason, 1881.

Dula, Lucille Noell. *The Pelican Guide to Hillsborough*. Gretna, La.: Pelican Publishing Co., 1979.

Dykeman, Wilma. *With Fire and Sword: The Battle of Kings Mountain*. Washington, D.C.: U.S. Department of the Interior.

Ellet, Elizabeth F. *The Women of the American Revolution*. 3 vols. New York: Charles Scribner, 1854.

Fair, Victor N. *The Hills of Home*. Lincolnton, N.C.

Ferris, Robert G., ed. *Signers of the Declaration: Historic Places Commemorating the Signing of the Declaration of Independence*. Washington, D.C.: U.S. Department of the Interior, 1973.

Fields, William C., ed. *A Guide to Historic Sites in Fayetteville and Cumberland County, N.C.* Fayetteville, N.C.: Historic Fayetteville Foundation, 1993.

Fleming, John Kerr. *In Freedom's Cause: Samuel Young of Rowan County, N.C.* Salisbury, N.C.: Rowan County, 1958.

———. *History of the Third Creek Presbyterian Church*. Raleigh, N.C.: Presbyterian Synod of North Carolina, 1967.

Flowers, John Braxton, III, and Marguerite Schumann. *Bull Durham and Beyond: A Touring Guide to City and County*. Durham, N.C.: Durham Bicentennial Commission, 1976.

Foote, William Henry. *Sketches of North Carolina, Historical and Biographical, of the Principles of a Portion of Her Early Settlers*. New York: Robert Carter, 1846.

Fossett, Mildred B. *History of McDowell County*. Durham, N.C.: Seaman Printery, 1976.

Fowler, Malcolm. *They Passed This Way: A Personal Narrative of Harnett County History*. Marceline, Mo.: Walsworth Publishing Co., 1955.

Fraser, Walter J., Jr. *Patriots, Pistols and Petticoats*. Columbia, S.C.: R. L. Bryan Co., 1976.

Freeze, Gary R. *The Catawbans: Crafters of a North Carolina County*. Newton, N.C.: Catawba County Historical Association, 1995.

Ganyard, Robert L. *The Emergence of North Carolina's Revolutionary State
Government*. Raleigh, N.C.: North Carolina Division of Archives and
History, 1978.

Gibson, Joyce M. *Scotland County Emerging, 1750–1900*. Marceline, Mo.:
Walsworth Publishing Co., 1995.

Graham, William A. *General Joseph Graham and His Papers on North Carolina*. Raleigh, N.C.: Edwards and Broughton, 1904.

Greene, George Washington. *The Life of Nathanael Greene, Major-General
in the Army of the Revolution*. 3 vols. New York: Hurd and Houghton,
1871.

Griffin, Clarence W. *The History of Old Tryon and Rutherford Counties, North
Carolina, 1730–1936*. Asheville, N.C.: Miller Printing Co., 1937.

Groome, Bailey T., ed. *Mecklenburg in the Revolution*. Charlotte, N.C.:
1931.

Hadley, Wade Hampton, Doris Goerch Hunter, and Nell Craig Stroud.
Chatham County, 1771–1971. Durham, N.C.: Moore Publishing Co., 1971.

Haley, Dru Gatewood, and Raymond A. Winslow. *The Historic Architecture
of Perquimans County, North Carolina*. Hertford, N.C.: Town of Hertford,
1982.

Hall, Louis Philip. *Land of the Golden River*. 3 vols. Wilmington, N.C.:
Wilmington Printing Co., 1975, 1980.

Halma, Sidney, ed. *Catawba County: An Architectural History*. Virginia Beach,
Va.: Donning Co., 1991.

Harkey, W. Hugh, Jr. *Tales from the Hornet's Nest*. Charlotte, N.C.: Hornet's
Nest Publications, 1991.

———. *More Tales from the Hornet's Nest*. Charlotte, N.C.: Hornet's Nest
Publications, 1992.

Hastings, Charlotte Ivey. *Our North Carolina Heritage*. Privately printed, 1956.

Hayes, Johnson J. *The Land of Wilkes*. Wilkesboro, N.C.: Wilkes County
Historical Society, 1962.

Haywood, Marshall DeLancey. *Governor Tryon of North Carolina*. Reprint,
Raleigh, N.C.: Edwards and Broughton, 1958.

———. *Builders of the Old North State*. Raleigh, N.C.: 1968.

Henry, Joseph D. *Historical Guide to Tryon Palace*. Charlotte, N.C.: Americraft, 1960.

Hill, Michael, ed. *Guide to North Carolina Highway Historical Markers*. 5th ed. Raleigh, N.C.: North Carolina Division of Archives and History, 1990.

Historic Murfreesboro Commission. *Murfreesboro, North Carolina*. Murfreesboro, N.C.: 1971.

Honeycutt, James E., and Ida C. Honeycutt. *A History of Richmond County*. Raleigh, N.C.: Edwards and Broughton, 1976.

Hood, Davyd Foard. *The Architecture of Rowan County, North Carolina*. Salisbury, N.C.: Rowan County Historic Properties Commission, 1983.

Houck, Samuel M. *To Receive the Morning Star: Thyatira Presbyterian Church, 1752–1976*. Jacksonville, Fla.: Douglas Printing Co., 1976.

Howell, Andrew J. *The Book of Wilmington*. Wilmington, N.C.: 1930.

Hughes, Fred. *Guilford County: A Map Supplement*. Jamestown, N.C.: Custom House, 1988.

Hunter, C. L. *Sketches of Western North Carolina, Historical and Biographical*. Raleigh, N.C.: 1877.

Iredell County American Bicentennial Commission. *Iredell County Landmarks: A Pictorial History of Iredell County*. Statesville, N.C.: Brady Printing Co., 1976.

James, Hunter. *Old Salem Official Guidebook*. 2d rev. ed. Winston-Salem, N.C.: Old Salem, Inc., 1994.

Johnson, Bob, and Charles S. Norwood, eds. *History of Wayne County, North Carolina*. Goldsboro, N.C.: Wayne County Historical Association, 1979.

Johnson, Lucille Miller. *Hometown Heritage: Fayetteville, North Carolina*. Raleigh, N.C.: Graphic Press, 1978.

Johnson, William. *Sketches of the Life and Correspondence of Nathanael Greene, Major General of the Armies of the United States, in the War of Revolution*. 2 vols. Charleston, S.C.: 1822.

Johnston, Henry P. *The Yorktown Campaign and the Surrender of Cornwallis, 1781*. New York: Harper and Brothers, 1881.

Jordan, Paula S. *Women of Guilford County, North Carolina: A Study of Women's Contributions, 1740–1779*. Greensboro, N.C.: 1979.

Junior League of Wilmington. *Old Wilmington Guidebook*. Wilmington, N.C.: Blake Printing and Graphics, 1978.

Junior Service League of Fayetteville. *Historic Fayetteville and Cumberland County*. Fayetteville, N.C.: Junior Service League, 1975.

Kaplan, Peter R. *The Historic Architecture of Cabarrus County, North Carolina*. Concord, N.C.: Historic Cabarrus, 1981.

Kell, Jean Bruyere. *North Carolina's Coastal Carteret County during the American Revolution, 1765–1785*. Greenville, N.C.: Era Press, 1975.

———. *Historic Beaufort, North Carolina*. Greenville, N.C.: National Printing Co., 1977.

Lawrence, Robert C. *Here in Carolina*. New York: J. J. Little and Ives Co., 1939.

Lee, Richard Henry. *Memoirs of the War in the Southern Department of the United States*. Edited by Robert E. Lee. New York: University Publishing Co., 1869.

Lefler, Hugh T., and Albert R. Newsome. *North Carolina: The History of a Southern State*. 3d ed. Chapel Hill, N.C.: University of North Carolina Press, 1973.

Lefler, Hugh T., and William S. Powell. *Colonial North Carolina: A History*. New York: Charles Scribner's Sons, 1973.

Leonard, Jacob Calvin. *Centennial History of Davidson County, North Carolina*. Raleigh, N.C.: Edwards and Broughton, 1927.

Lewis, Taylor, and Joanne Young. *A Tryon Treasury*. Norfolk, Va.: Taylor Lewis Associates, 1977.

Lingle, Walter L. *Thyatira Presbyterian Church, Rowan County, North Carolina (1753–1948)*. Statesville, N.C.: Brady Printing Co., 1948.

Little, Ann Courtney Ward. *Columbus County, North Carolina: Recollections and Records*. Whiteville, N.C.: Columbus County Commission, 1980.

Little-Stokes, Ruth. *An Inventory of Historic Architecture, Iredell County, North Carolina*. Raleigh, N.C.: North Carolina Department of Cultural Resources, 1978.

Lloyd, Allen Alexander, and Pauline O. Lloyd. *History of the Town of Hillsborough, 1754–1963*.

Lounsbury, Carl. *The Architecture of Southport*. Southport, N.C.: Southport Historical Society, 1979.

Loy, Ursula, and Pauline Worthy. *Washington and the Pamlico*. Washington, N.C.: Washington-Beaufort Bicentennial Commission, 1976.

MacDonald, James A. *Flora MacDonald: A History*. Washington, D.C.: James William Bryan Press, 1916.

MacLean, J. P. *Flora MacDonald in America*. Morgantown, W.Va.: Scotpress, 1984.

Markel, Kimberly I. *The Historic Architecture of Rutherford County*. Forest City, N.C.: Rutherford County Arts Council, 1983.

Mattern, David B. *Benjamin Lincoln and the American Revolution*. Columbia, S.C.: University of South Carolina Press, 1995.

McCorkle, L. A. *Old Time Stories of the Old North State*. Boston: D. C. Heath and Co., Publishers, 1903.

McGeachy, Neil Roderick. *A History of the Sugaw Presbyterian Church, Charlotte, North Carolina*. Rock Hill, S.C.: Record Printing Co., 1954.

McGee, Dorothy Horton. *Famous Signers of the Declaration*. New York: Dodd, Mead and Company, 1957.

Medley, Mary L. *History of Anson County, North Carolina*. Wadesboro, N.C.: Anson County Historical Society, 1976.

Meyer, Duane. *The Highland Scots of North Carolina*. Raleigh, N.C.: Carolina Charter Tercentenary Commission, 1963.

Meyer, Edith Patterson. *Petticoat Patriots of the American Revolution*. New York: Vanguard Press, 1976.

Mitchell, Memory F. *North Carolina's Signers*. Raleigh, N.C.: North Carolina Department of Archives and History, 1964.

Morgan, David T., and William J. Schmidt. *North Carolinians in the Continental Congress*. Winston-Salem, N.C.: John F. Blair, Publisher, 1976.

Morrill, Dan L. *Southern Campaigns of the American Revolution*. Baltimore: Nautical and Aviation Publishing Co. of America.

Moss, Bobby Gilmer. *The Patriots at Kings Mountain*. Blacksburg, S.C.: Scotia-Hibernia Press, 1990.

———. *Roster of the Patriots in the Battle of Moores Creek Bridge*. Blacksburg, S.C.: Scotia-Hibernia Press, 1992.

Murray, Elizabeth Reid. *Wake: Capital County of North Carolina*. Vol. 1. Raleigh, N.C.: Capital County Publishing Co., 1983.

Nelson, Paul David. *William Tryon and the Course of Empire: A Life in British Imperial Service*. Chapel Hill, N.C.: University of North Carolina Press, 1990.

Newlin, Algie I. *The Battle of Lindley's Mill.* Burlington, N.C.: Alamance Historical Association, 1975.

————. *The Battle of New Garden.* Greensboro, N.C.: North Carolina Friends Historical Society, 1977.

North Carolina Daughters of the American Revolution. *Roster of Soldiers from North Carolina in the American Revolution.* Reprint. Baltimore: Genealogical Publishing Co., 1984.

Oates, John A. *The Story of Fayetteville and the Upper Cape Fear.* Fayetteville, N.C.: 1950.

O'Donnell, James H., III. *The Cherokees of North Carolina in the American Revolution.* Raleigh, N.C.: North Carolina Division of Archives and History, 1976.

Pancake, John S. *This Destructive War: The British Campaign in the Carolinas, 1780–1782.* Tuscaloosa, Ala.: University of Alabama Press, 1985.

Parker, Mattie Erma. *Tar Heel Tales.* Raleigh, N.C.: North Carolina Department of Archives and History, 1961.

Peace, Samuel Thomas. *"Zeb's Black Baby": Vance County, North Carolina.* Durham, N.C.: Seaman Printery, 1955.

Perquimans County Historical Society. *Perquimans County Historical Year Book, 1970.* Hertford, N.C.: 1970.

Phifer, Edward William, Jr. *Burke: The History of a North Carolina County, 1777–1920.* Morganton, N.C.: 1977.

Pickens, Suzanne S. *Sweet Union: An Architectural and Historical Survey of Union County, North Carolina.* Monroe, N.C.: Union County Board of Commissioners, 1990.

Powell, William S. *The North Carolina Gazetteer.* Chapel Hill, N.C.: University of North Carolina Press, 1968.

————. *When the Past Refused to Die: A History of Caswell County, North Carolina.* Durham, N.C.: Moore Publishing Co., 1977.

————. *Dictionary of North Carolina Biography.* 6 vols. Chapel Hill, N.C.: University of North Carolina Press, 1979–96.

————. *North Carolina through Four Centuries.* Chapel Hill, N.C.: University of North Carolina Press, 1989.

Power, Scott. *The Historic Architecture of Pitt County, North Carolina.* Greenville, N.C.: Pitt County Historical Society, 1991.

Preservation North Carolina. *The Complete Guide to North Carolina's Historic Sites*. Raleigh, N.C.: Preservation North Carolina, 1994.

Preslar, Charles J., Jr. *A History of Catawba County*. Newton, N.C.: Catawba County Historical Association, 1954.

Puett, Minnie Stowe. *History of Gaston County*. Charlotte, N.C.: Observer Printing House, 1939.

Pugh, Jesse F. *Three Hundred Years along the Pasquotank: A Biographical History of Camden County*. Old Trap, N.C.: 1957.

Purcell, L. Edward. *Who Was Who in the American Revolution*. New York: Facts on File, 1993.

Purcell, L. Edward, and David F. Burg, eds. *The World Almanac of the American Revolution*. New York: Pharos Books, 1992.

Rankin, Hugh F. *North Carolina in the American Revolution*. Raleigh, N.C.: North Carolina Department of Archives and History, 1959.

———. *The North Carolina Continentals*. Chapel Hill, N.C.: University of North Carolina Press, 1971.

———. *The Moores Creek Bridge Campaign, 1776*. Conshohocken, Pa.: Eastern National Park and Monument Association, 1993.

Raynor, George. *Sketches of Old Rowan*. Salisbury, N.C.: 1960.

———. *Patriots and Tories in Piedmont Carolina*. Salisbury, N.C.: Salisbury Printing Co., 1990.

Reeves, Linda, ed. *Historic Halifax Guidebook*. Raleigh, N.C.: North Carolina Division of Archives and History.

Reid, Courtland T. *Guilford Courthouse National Military Park*. Washington, D.C.: U.S. Department of the Interior, 1959.

Richter, Winnie Ingram, et al., eds. *The Heritage of Montgomery County, North Carolina*. Winston-Salem, N.C.: Hunter Publishing Co., 1981.

Robinson, Blackwell P. *William R. Davie*. Chapel Hill, N.C.: University of North Carolina Press, 1957.

———. *The Five Royal Governors of North Carolina, 1729–1775*. Raleigh, N.C.: Carolina Charter Tercentenary Commission, 1963.

Robinson, Blackwell P., ed. *The North Carolina Guide*. Chapel Hill, N.C.: University of North Carolina Press, 1955.

———. *The Revolutionary War Sketches of William R. Davie*. Raleigh, N.C.: North Carolina Division of Archives and History, 1976.

Rockwell, Paul A., ed. *Edward Buncombe and Buncombe County*. Asheville, N.C.: Buncombe County Bicentennial Committee, 1976.

Rogers, Lou. *Tar Heel Women*. Raleigh, N.C.: Warren Publishing Co., 1949.

Romine, Dannye. *Mecklenburg: A Bicentennial Story*. Charlotte, N.C.: Independence Square Associates, 1975.

Rouse, J. K. *Historic Shadows of Cabarrus County, North Carolina*. Kannapolis, N.C.: 1970.

Rumple, Jethro. *A History of Rowan County, North Carolina*. Charlotte, N.C.: Observer Printing House, 1916.

Russell, Anne. *Wilmington: A Pictorial History*. Norfolk, Va.: Donning Co., 1981.

Russell, Phillips. *North Carolina in the Revolutionary War*. Charlotte, N.C.: Heritage Printers, 1965.

Sakowski, Carolyn. *Touring the Western North Carolina Backroads*. Winston-Salem, N.C.: John F. Blair, Publisher, 1990.

Sandbeck, Peter B. *The Historic Architecture of New Bern and Craven County, North Carolina*. New Bern, N.C.: Tryon Palace Commission, 1988.

Saunders, William L., ed. *The Colonial Records of North Carolina*. 10 vols. Raleigh, N.C.: State of North Carolina, 1886–90.

Scheer, George F., and Hugh F. Rankin. *Rebels and Redcoats: The American Revolution through the Eyes of Those Who Fought and Lived It*. Cleveland: World Publishing Co., 1957.

Schenck, David. *North Carolina, 1780–81*. Raleigh, N.C.: Edwards and Broughton, 1889.

Seymour, William. *The Price of Folly: British Blunders in the War of American Independence*. London: Brassey's, 1995.

Sharpe, Bill. *A New Geography of North Carolina*. 4 vols. Raleigh, N.C.: Sharpe Publishing Co., 1954–65.

Sherrill, William L. *The Annals of Lincoln County*. Reprint, Baltimore: Regional Publishing Co., 1972.

Smith, H. McKeldon. *An Inventory of Historic Architecture: High Point, Jamestown, Gibsonville, Guilford County*. Raleigh, N.C.: North Carolina Department of Cultural Resources, 1979.

Snider, Frank W., ed. *First Church, Davidson County: A History of Pilgrim Evangelical and Reformed Church*. Lexington, N.C.: 1957.

Sondley, F. A. *A History of Buncombe County, North Carolina*. Asheville, N.C.: Advocate Print Co., 1930.

Speidel, Frederick G. *North Carolina Masons in the American Revolution*. Oxford, N.C.: Press of Oxford Orphanage, 1975.

Sprunt, James. *Chronicles of the Cape Fear River, 1660–1916*. Reprint, Wilmington, N.C.: Broadfoot Publishing Co., 1992.

Steele, Hall, ed. *Inscriptions on Grave Stones in the Cemetery of Thyatira Church, 1775–1995*. Mill Bridge, N.C.

Stegeman, John F., and Janet A. Stegeman. *Caty: A Biography of Catharine Littlefield Greene*. Athens, Ga.: University of Georgia Press, 1977.

Stevens, Joseph E. *America's National Battlefield Parks: A Guide*. Norman, Okla.: University of Oklahoma Press, 1990.

Stewart, Mrs. W. S., II. *Markers Placed by the North Carolina Daughters of the American Revolution, 1900–1940*. Raleigh, N.C.: Edwards and Broughton, 1940.

Still, William N., Jr. *North Carolina's Revolutionary War Navy*. Raleigh, N.C.: North Carolina Division of Archives and History, 1976.

Stockard, Sallie Walker. *The History of Alamance*. Reprint, Burlington, N.C.: Alamance County Historical Museum, 1986.

Summerville, Charles William. *The History of Hopewell Presbyterian Church*. Charlotte, N.C.: 1939.

Tarleton, Banastre. *Campaigns of 1780–81 in Southern America*. Reprint, Spartanburg, S.C.: Reprint Co., 1967.

Taylor, H. Braugh, ed. *Guide to Historic New Bern, North Carolina*. New Bern, N.C.: Craven County American Revolution Bicentennial Commission, 1974.

Thane, Elswyth. *The Fighting Quaker: Nathanael Greene*. Mattituck, N.Y.: Aeonian Press, 1977.

Thayer, Theodore. *Nathanael Greene: Strategist of the Revolution*. New York: Twayne Publishers, 1960.

Thomas, Maud. *Away Down Home: A History of Robeson County, North Carolina*. Lumberton, N.C.: Historic Robeson, 1982.

Touart, Paul Baker. *Building the Backcountry*. Lexington, N.C.: Davidson County Historical Association, 1987.

Tourism and Promotion Division. *Sheltering Heritage: North Carolina's His-*

toric Buildings. Raleigh, N.C.: North Carolina Department of Conservation and Development.

Treacy, M. F. *Prelude to Yorktown: The Southern Campaign of Nathanael Greene, 1780–1781.* Chapel Hill, N.C.: University of North Carolina Press, 1963.

Troxler, George. *Pyle's Massacre—February 23, 1781.* Burlington, N.C.: Alamance Historical Association, 1973.

U.S. War Department. *The Battle of Kings Mountain and the Battle of Cowpens.* Washington, D.C.: GPO, 1928.

Vining, Elizabeth Gray. *Flora: A Biography.* Philadelphia: J. B. Lippincott Co., 1966.

Wall, James W. *History of Davie County in the Forks of the Yadkin.* Mocksville, N.C.: Davie County Historical Publishing Association, 1969.

Watkins, John Bullock, Jr. *Historic Vance County and Happy, Healthy, Hustling Henderson.* Henderson, N.C.: Henderson Dispatch Co., 1941.

Watson, Alan D. *A History of New Bern and Craven County.* New Bern, N.C.: Tryon Palace Commission, 1987.

———. *Wilmington: Port of North Carolina.* Columbia, S.C.: University of South Carolina Press, 1992.

Watson, Alan D., Dennis R. Lawson, and Donald R. Lennon. *Harnett, Hooper, and Howe: Revolutionary Leaders of the Lower Cape Fear.* Wilmington, N.C.: Lower Cape Fear Historical Society, 1979.

Webster, Mrs. S. F., ed. *Seventy-five Years of Service: History of the National Society, Daughters of the American Revolution of North Carolina.* New Bern, N.C.: Owen G. Dunn, 1975.

Wellman, Manly Wade. *The County of Warren, North Carolina, 1586–1917.* Chapel Hill, N.C.: University of North Carolina Press, 1959.

———. *The Story of Moore County.* Southern Pines, N.C.: Moore County Historical Association, 1974.

Wheeler, John H. *Historical Sketches of North Carolina from 1584 to 1851.* 2 vols. Philadelphia: Lippincott, Grambo, and Co., 1851.

———. *Reminiscences and Memoirs of North Carolina and Eminent North Carolinians.* Reprint, Baltimore: Clearfield Co., 1993.

Whitaker, Walter. *Centennial History of Alamance County, 1848–1949.* Burlington, N.C.: Alamance County Historical Association, 1974.

White, Emmett R. *Revolutionary War Soldiers of Western North Carolina: Burke*

County. Vol. 1. Easley, S.C.: Southern Historical Press, 1984.

White, Katherine Keough. *The Kings Mountain Men*. Reprint, Baltimore: Genealogical Publishing Co., 1966.

Williams, Robert L. *Gaston County: A Pictorial History*. Norfolk, Va.: Donning Co., 1981.

Wood, W. J. *Battles of the Revolutionary War, 1775–1781*. Chapel Hill, N.C.: Algonquin Books, 1990.

Wrenn, Tony P. *Beaufort, North Carolina*. Raleigh, N.C.: North Carolina Division of Archives and History, 1970.

———. *Wilmington, North Carolina: An Architectural and Historical Portrait*. Charlottesville, Va.: University Press of Virginia, 1984.

Wright, Christina, and Dan Morrill. *Charlotte-Mecklenburg Historic Tours: Driving and Walking*. Charlotte, N.C.: Charlotte-Mecklenburg Historic Preservation Fund, 1994.

Index

Hunter, James (Rockingham County), 338

Hunter, Thomas, 52

Huntington, Anna Hyatt, 149

Huntsville, 324, 325

Husband, Herman, 375, 405, 431, 435

Hyco Lake Reservoir, 334

Independence Square, 180, 184, 185, 186, 188

"Indian Execution Rock, the," 158

Ingleside, 280–81

Iredell County, 248, 277, 278, 287–96

Iredell, James, 14, 17, 20–21, 103, 236, 287, 417, 426

Irish Buffalo Creek, 167

Irwin, Robert, 193–94

Irwin's Ferry, 341, 342

Isaac Hunter's Tavern, 447

Isaac White House, 10

Jack, James, 180, 182, 187, 190, 267

Jack, Mary, 267

Jack, Patrick, 187

Jackson, Andrew, 145–51, 236, 296, 313, 325, 334, 454

Jackson, Andrew, Sr., 147, 151

Jackson, Elizabeth, 147, 150, 151

Jackson, Hugh, 149

Jackson, Robert, 149, 150

Jacob's Run, 97

James Iredell State Historic Site, 20–21

Jamestown, 353

Jefferson, Thomas, 38, 73, 191, 260, 268, 302, 418, 442, 455

Jersey Baptist Church, 318, 319

Joel Lane House, 450, 451–53

John Daves House, 75

John Grady Monument, 90, 117

John Wright Stanly House, 71–75

Johns River, 240

Johnsonville, 137

Johnston, Gabriel, 16, 105

Johnston, James, 268–69

Johnston, Samuel, 14, 16–17, 20, 22, 33, 127, 419, 443

Jones, Allen, 33, 36, 391, 426

Jones, Elizabeth Montfort, 38

Jones, John Paul, 15, 44, 436

Jones, Mary Montfort, 38, 43, 44–45

Jones Mountain, 223

Jones, Thomas, 12

Jones, Willie, 31, 33, 36, 38, 43–44, 391–92, 426, 449

Joseph Bell House, 82

Joseph Hewes Monument, 14–15

Joseph Montfort Amphitheater, 36

Joy, 240

Keais, Nathan, 64

Kenan Amphitheatre, 89

Kenan, James, 89, 90

Kenan, Thomas, 89

Kenansville, 89–90

Kennon, William, 189

Kerr Lake Outdoor Educational Area, 438

King, Charles, 208

King, Duncan, 119–20

King, Elizabeth, 16

King, Lydia Fosque, 119–20

King, William Rufus, 120

Kings Bluff, 120

Kings Business College, 120

King's Chapel, 66

King's Highway, 110

King's Landing, 24, 26

Kings Mountain (town), 263

Kings Mountain, Battle of, 255–62

Kings Mountain National Military Park, 255–62

Kingston, 56

Kinston, 55, 56

Knox, Benjamin, 306

Knox Hill Farm, 305–6

Knox, James, 306

Knox, Jean Gracy, 301

Knox, John, 301, 305

Knox, William, 305–6

LaBoone Mountain, 265

Lady Blessington cannon, 67–68

Lafayette, George Washington, 25

Lafayette, Marquis de: reputation in North Carolina, 87; statue of, 125, 131; visits Barbeque Presbyterian Church, 136; visits Enfield, 45; visits Fayetteville, 125, 131–32; visits Halifax, 37, 44; visits Murfreesboro, 25–26; visits New Bern, 74; visits Raleigh, 448, 455; welcomed to North Carolina, 167

Lafayette Society, 131

Lamb, Abner, 8

Lamb's Ferry, 8

Lancaster County, S.C., 148

Lane, Joel, 449–50, 451–53

Lane, Ralph, 452

Latham, Maude Moore, 71

Latta, James, 178

Latta Plantation Park, 178

Laurens, Henry, 430

Lawson, John, 65

Lee, Charles, 112

Lee, Richard Henry "Lighthorse Harry," 341–43, 347, 360, 362–63, 379, 400–402, 406, 417

Lee, Robert E., 98

Leech, Joseph, 79, 80

Leggett, John, 143

Leigh, Gilbert, 18–19

Leigh House, 18

Lenoir, 242–43